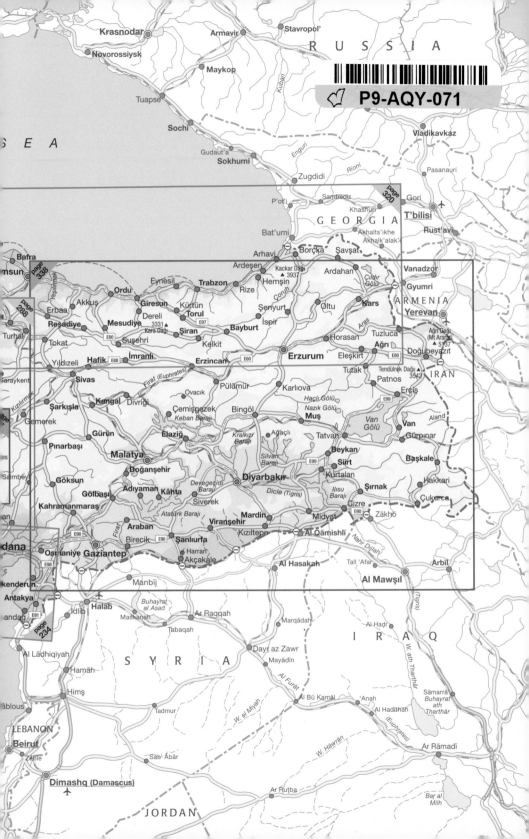

INSIGHT GUIDES
TURKEY

APA PUBLICATIONS L
Part of the Langenscheidt Publishing Group

☀ INSIGHT GUIDE

TURKEY

Editorial

Project Editor
Tom Le Bas
Art Director
Steven Lawrence
Picture Manager
Tom Smyth
Series Manager
Rachel Fox

Distribution

UK & Ireland
GeoCenter International Ltd
Meridian House, Churchill Way West
Basingstoke, Hampshire RG21 6YR
sales@geocenter.co.uk

United States
Ingram Publisher Services
1 Ingram Blvd, PO Box 3006
La Vergne, TN 37086-1986
customer.service@ingrampublisher
services.com

Australia
Universal Publishers
1 Waterloo Road
Macquarie Park, NSW 2113
sales@universalpublishers.com.au

New Zealand
Hema Maps New Zealand Ltd (HNZ)
Unit 2, 10 Cryers Road
East Tamaki, Auckland 2013
sales.hema@clear.net.nz

Worldwide
Apa Publications GmbH & Co.
Verlag KG (Singapore branch)
7030 Ang Mo Kio Avenue 5
08-65 Northstar @ AMK
Singapore 569880
apasin@signet.com.sg

Printing

CTPS - China

©2011 **Apa Publications GmbH & Co.**
Verlag KG (Singapore branch)
All Rights Reserved

First Edition 1988
Sixth Edition 2011

CONTACTING THE EDITORS
We would appreciate it if readers
would alert us to errors or out-
dated information by writing to:
Insight Guides, PO Box 7910,
London SE1 1WE, England.
insight@apaguide.co.uk

ABOUT THIS BOOK

The first Insight Guide pioneered the use of creative full-colour photography in travel guides in 1970. Since then, we have expanded our range to cater for our readers' need not only for reliable information about their chosen destination but also for a real understanding of the culture and workings of that destination. Now, when the internet can supply inexhaustible (but not always reliable) facts, our books marry text and pictures to provide those much more elusive qualities: knowledge and discernment. To achieve this, they rely heavily on the authority and experience of locally based writers and photographers.

This fully updated edition of *Insight Guide: Turkey* is structured to convey an understanding of this fascinating country and its culture, and to guide readers through its major sights and activities:

♦ The **Features** section, indicated by a pink bar at the top of each page, covers the history and culture of Turkey in a series of informative essays.

♦ The main **Places** section, indicated by a blue bar, is a guide to all the sights and areas worth visiting. Places of special interest are coordinated by number with the maps.

♦ The **Travel Tips** listings section, with a yellow bar, provides a handy point of reference for information on travel, hotels, shops, restaurants and more, and also includes a brief language guide. An index to the section is on the back flap of the book.

♦ **Photographs** are chosen not only to illustrate the geography and attractions of the country but as a vivid portrayal of the lives of the Turkish people.

LEFT: a livestock market in eastern Turkey.

on Thrace/Marmara, the north Aegean, İzmir and environs, the South Aegean, Lycia and the Black Sea Coast.

The sections on İstanbul, Central, Southwest and Northwest Anatolia, East of Ankara, and Cappadocia, were fully updated and reworked by **Pat Yale**, a British-born writer who lives with a multitude of cats in a restored cave-house in Göreme. Pat also wrote the photo essay on Turkish Baths. She has written or contributed to numerous guidebooks to Turkey and Iran, and as a columnist and travel writer for the Turkish *Zaman* newspaper. She is the author of *A Handbook for Living in Turkey* (Citllembik), the first comprehensive guide for local expats. She has also written Insight's *Istanbul Select* and *Istanbul Smart* guides. Her latest book is *Istanbul – The Ultimate Guide*, written with Saffet Emre Tonguc.

Turkey specialist, travel writer and resident, **Terry Richardson** first visited the country in 1978. In addition to his writing, Terry also leads tours to various parts of the country and helped mark Turkey's first long distance routes, the Lycian Way and the St Paul Trail.

The book builds upon an original edition project-edited by Turkey specialist **Melissa Shales**. The main photographers for this sixth edition were **Frank Noon** and **Rebecca Erol**. The picture research was undertaken by **Tom Smyth**. The sixth edition was fully indexed by **Helen Peters** and proofread by **Jan McCann**.

The Contributors

A dedicated team in Turkey and London worked hard to update this expanded edition of *Insight Guide: Turkey*. The project was overseen and edited by **Tom Le Bas** at Insight's London office, while three specialist writers brought the book fully up to date.

The main contributor, **Marc Dubin**, first visited Turkey in 1982, and has been involved with the country (and Insight Guides) as a writer since the late 1980s, crisscrossing its length and breadth by every imaginable conveyance (including on foot while researching a trekking guide). For this edition he revised or completely rewrote the history and features sections, the photographic essays on wildlife, festivals and adventure sports, much of the Travel Tips, and the chapters

Map Legend

— · —	International Boundary
— ● —	National Park/Reserve
— — —	Ferry Route
✈ ✈	Airport: International/ Regional
🚌	Bus Station
●	Tram Line and Station
Ⓜ	Metro
🚡	Funicular Railway
❶	Tourist Information
✉	Post Office
✝ ✝ ✝	Church/Ruins
✝	Monastery
☾	Mosque
✡	Synagogue
🏰 🏰	Castle/Ruins
∴	Archaeological Site
∩	Cave
⚊	Statue/Monument
🗼	Lighthouse
★	Place of Interest
⚑	Beach

The main places of interest in the Places section are coordinated by number with a full-colour map (eg ❶), and a symbol at the top of every right-hand page tells you where to find the map.

Contents

LEFT: Temple of Trajan at Pergamon.

Travel Tips

THE BEST OF TURKEY: TOP SIGHTS

The unique attractions of Turkey, from the bright lights of Istanbul to ancient monuments, amazing landscapes and characterful old towns

△ **İstanbul** The capital of two great empires has an unrivalled position on straits separating Europe and Asia, superb Byzantine and Ottoman monuments, and some of the best dining and entertainment opportunities in the country. *See Page 123*

▷ **Colossal heads at Nemrut Dağı** Mountaintop shrine in the middle of nowhere, this monument to the pretensions of an obscure local satrap of the 1st century BC is best viewed at sunrise or sunset. *See Page 345*

△ **Pamukkale** The solidified carbonate-rich "waterfalls" of the pale travertine terraces are a cliché of Turkish tourism, but unmissable nonetheless; the extensive remains of Roman Hierapolis up top are an added bonus. *See Page 217*

▽ **Lycian Rock Tombs** There are literally thousands of them, seemingly no two alike, in the most improbable places along the Turquoise Coast; with their graceful profiles and relief carvings they're irresistibly photogenic. *See Pages 234–45*

△ **Ephesus** The most extensive and best-preserved ancient city in Turkey. *See Page 208*

◁ **Museum of Anatolian Civilisations, Ankara** Outstanding collection of artefacts spanning Anatolia's early history, from the Palaeolithic to the Phrygian eras. *See Page 285*

◁ **Sumela Monastery** An ancient Byzantine monastery hidden away in a spectacular forested canyon. *See Page 327*

△ **Şanlıurfa** Get a feel of the Middle East in this ancient town in the southeast of the country. One of the most atmospheric places in Turkey, replete with overhanging medieval houses and warren-like bazaars. *See Page 349*

▽ **Cappadocian landscapes** Created millions of years ago by two nearby volcanoes, the tuff-pinnacle badlands have been eroded into bizarre shapes to create a dreamlike landscape. *See Page 305*

▷ **Ani ruins** The former capital of Bagratid Armenia, which flourished from the 10th to the 13th centuries, contains several of the finest Armenian churches in this region, amid dramatic scenery. *See Page 362*

THE BEST OF TURKEY: EDITOR'S CHOICE

Magnificent ancient sites, castles, churches and mosques, superb beaches, unique experiences and shopping... here at a glance are our recommendations on what to prioritise

BEST ANCIENT MONUMENTS

● **Trajan Temple, Pergamon**
German archaeologists have re-erected columns and architraves in partial atonement for a compatriot's abduction of the nearby Zeus altar reliefs. *See page 192.*

● **Library of Celsus, Ephesus**
Effectively the logo of the site, this 2nd-century AD endowment with its elaborate façade has been assiduously restored by Austrian excavators.
See page 211.

● **Tetrapylon Gate, Aphrodisias**
An astonishing elaborate structure just to mark the intersection of two Roman streets, this cluster of columns supports finely worked pediments.
See page 217.

● **The Theatre, Aspendos**
Roman imperial structure in almost as good condition as when new – and accordingly a supremely atmospheric festival venue.
See page 256.

● **Zeus temple, Aizanoi**
With standing walls and columns, the most complete of three Zeus temples in Anatolia, a Corinthian affair funded by Emperor Hadrian.
See page 296.

● **Monumental gates, Boğazkale**
Massive gates flanked by relief carvings punctuate the incredible 6km (4 miles) of walls enclosing this capital of the once-mighty Hittite empire.
See page 302.

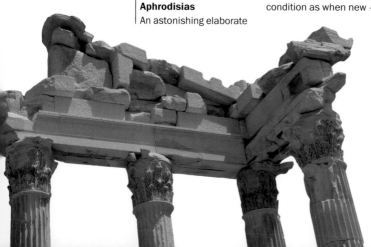

ABOVE: the wonderfully preserved Theatre at Aspendos. **LEFT:** Trajan Temple at Pergamon.

BEST MEDIEVAL CASTLES

● **Bozcaada (Tenedos)**
Huge but now domesticated and fetchingly lit by night; Byzantines, Genoese, Venetians and Turks have successively modified it. *See page 182.*

● **St Peter's, Bodrum**
Once a main stronghold of the crusading Knights of St John, now well restored and home to several worthwhile museums. *See page 221.*

● **Anamur (Mamure Kalesi)**
Among the most romantically sited castles in Turkey, a huge Armenian-built seaside affair with its toes in the sand. *See page 263.*

● **Korykos and Kız Kalesi**
Not-quite-twin castles, built by the Byzantines and local Armenian kings: one on land, the other facing it on an islet. *See page 267.*

● **İşak Paşa Sarayı, Doğubeyazıt**
More fortified pleasure-palace than castle, this engaging pastiche of every conceivable indigenous Anatolian style seems a mirage in this bleak landscape. *See page 363.*

● **Hoşap, Hakkâri**
Fairy-tale castle on a crag, the redoubt of a 17th-century Kurdish chieftain. *See page 369.*

ABOVE: Anamur castle dominates the shoreline.

BEST SOUVENIR PURCHASES

● **İznik tiles**
These quartz-based, intricately glazed products of a revived craft are streets ahead of resort-shop dross, and worth every penny. *See page 171.*

● *Cezeriye*
Forget *lokum* (Turkish delight) with its artificial colours and preservatives; this delectable carrot-and-coconut confection is actually good for you. *See page 409.*

● *Sahlep* mix
Pure *sahlep* – ground orchid root – is banned for export, so buy *sahlep*-rich mixes for this hot drink sovereign against colds. *See page 95.*

● **Leather jackets**
For that slightly retro, elegant-gangster look, nothing beats a black or tan, well-cut item available in almost any significant resort. *See page 408.*

● **Carpets**
Focus of the hard-sell in every resort, but the quintessential Turkish folk art makes a souvenir you'll have decades of enjoyment from. *See pages 108–11, 408.*

● **Nar ekşisi**
Sour pomegranate syrup, a nod to Persian influence in the cuisine, has various uses: in salad dressings, meat marinades, even beer! *See page 91.*

BEST EXPERIENCES

● **"Blue Cruise" along the southwest coast**
Discover secluded, pine-shaded coves and islets between Bodrum and Finike on a traditional *gulet*. *See page 376.*

● **Hot-air ballooning over Cappadocia**
A bird's-eye, early-morning view of the region's volcanic formations. *See page 427.*

● **Mevlevî ceremony, Galata Mevlevîhanesi**
More atmospheric, and genuine, than the tourist events – the whirling dancers here really are practising dervishes. *See page 140.*

● **Taking a Turkish bath**
Indulge yourself with the full treatment in a historic hamam. *See page 148.*

● **Trekking in the Kaçkar mountains**
They may not be Turkey's highest range, but certainly rank among the most beautiful, and user-friendly. *See page 326.*

ABOVE: *gulets* at Bodrum. **RIGHT:** carpet vendor.

BEST BEACHES

● **Kıyıköy, Thrace**
Long, amazingly undeveloped sand beaches fed by lazy rivers flank this old Byzantine stronghold on the Black Sea. *See page 160.*

● **Aydıncık, Gökçeada**
Soft, heaped blonde sand, transparent, flattish waters – and yet a prime windsurfing spot, on this barely developed north Aegean island.
See page 163.

● **Altınkum, Çeşme**
Sand backing to dunes, iridescent water, low-key water sports, and a slightly alternative ethos make this chain of small coves a winner.
See page 195.

● **Mesudiye Ova Bükü, Datça peninsula**
A stretch of gold-brown sand bookended by two headlands framing the island of Tílos, and washed by surprisingly bracing water, make this a popular boat-trip destination.
See page 227.

● **Patara**
The longest (15km/9 miles) continuous beach in Turkey, its thick sand a turtle-nesting ground, with boogie-boarding possible in summer.
See page 239.

● **Çıralı**
Long, sand-and-pebble beach that's another turtle destination, but with a superior inland backdrop to Patara's, and calmer, deeper water.
See page 245.

● **Side**
Plenty of (commercialised) sand here, with every creature comfort to hand, but it offers the novelty of ancient ruins right on the beach. *See page 257.*

ABOVE: Turkey's southern and western coasts are fringed by long sandy beaches and crystal-clear water.

BEST MOSQUES

● **Selimiye Camii, Edirne**
The masterwork of the great Ottoman imperial architect Sinan, its dome and four minarets dominating the town from its hilltop. *See page 156.*

● **Süleymaniye Camii, İstanbul**
Another work of Sinan: some conoisseurs claim it as his best, with its dome soaring 47 metres (154ft) from the floor.
See page 136.

● **Yeşil Cami, Bursa**
Although never quite finished outside, riotous blue and green Tabriz tiles inside, culminating in the sultan's loge, make this exceptional.
See page 169.

● **Ulu Cami, Birgi**
Post-Seljuk, pre-Ottoman oddity that feels almost Andalusian with its interior Roman colonnade, gabled roof and bands of green tile-work. *See page 203.*

● **Eşrefoğlu Camii, Beyşehir**
The apotheosis of all-wood mosques in Turkey, with a veritable forest inside of naturally illuminated carved columns, rafters and galleries. *See page 299.*

● **Mahmud Bey Camii, Kasaba**
This wooden mosque rivals Eşrefoğlu with its polychrome railings, carved entrance and coffered ceiling.
See page 322.

● **Ulu Cami, Diyarbakır**
The first great Seljuk mosque, built in 1091, extensively recycling masonry from earlier pagan and Christian buildings on the site.
See page 365.

LEFT: Friday prayers in Suleymaniye Camii.

BEST TRADITIONAL TOWNS AND VILLAGES

● **Cumalıkızık**
Time-warped village of semi-fortified houses near Bursa. *See page 171.*

● **Adatepe**
Architectural showcase with solid mansions ringed by the same volcanic rocks they're built from. *See page 187.*

● **Şirince**
This hill village of substantial houses is the coolest place to stay near Ephesus. *See page 213.*

● **Muğla**
Sprawling hillside old quarter of tiled houses with beaked chimneys and curious doors. *See page 227.*

● **Safranbolu**
Museum town of elaborate, three-storey, half-timbered mansions that still supports some of the trades that made it prosper. *See page 319.*

● **Amasya**
Ottoman mansions, Selçuk and Mongol monuments and ancient cliff-tombs, all straddling a river. *See page 322.*

● **Mardin**
Tawny-stone, Arab-style medieval dwellings, leavened by churches and mosques in a spectacular blufftop setting. *See page 364.*

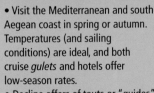

LEFT: passing the time, Amasya.

ABOVE: fresco detail in the Haghia Sophia (Aya Sofya) Monastery in Trabzon.

BEST CHURCHES

● **Kariye Museum (Chora Church), İstanbul**
The finest mosaics and frescoes in Turkey, a late flowering of Byzantine art. *See page 136.*

● **Haghia Sophia, Trabzon**
Vividly expressive and warm-toned frescoes. *See page 327.*

● **Tokalı Kilesi, Cappadocia**
The best-preserved frescoes of the various churches in the Göreme region. *See page 308.*

● **Öşk Vank, Georgian valleys**
Massive interior columns anticipate European Gothic in the grandest of the local monastic churches. *See page 331.*

● **Deyrul Zarafan, Mardin**
Named for its yellowish masonry, this ancient monastery, continuously inhabited since AD 495, was long the seat of the Syrian Orthodox patriarch. *See page 364.*

● **Armenian Church of the Holy Cross, Lake Van**
The most exquisitely set (on an islet) of Anatolian Armenian churches; restored interior frescoes complement exterior reliefs of biblical scenes. *See page 368.*

MONEY-SAVING TIPS

● Visit the Mediterranean and south Aegean coast in spring or autumn. Temperatures (and sailing conditions) are ideal, and both cruise *gulets* and hotels offer low-season rates.

● Decline offers of touts or "guides" in bazaars – their commission will definitely be added to the price of goods bought from merchants they introduce you to.

● Take advantage of no-frills, web-based domestic airlines like Pegasus and Atlasjet. Anatolian distances are enormous, and fares bought in good time can cost little more than a bus journey.

● Buy a local SIM-card with talk-time for your mobile upon arrival. Local roaming charges, not subject to EU caps, are ruinous, and even if your account is blocked (as sometimes happens) after two weeks, you will come out of it in pocket.

WELCOME TO TURKEY

There's something for everyone in Turkey.
The trouble is that, for centuries,
almost everyone has tried to grab a slice

The Romans called it *Asia Minor* – that landmass protruding from Asia into the eastern Mediterranean, defined by the Black Sea on the north, the Aegean to the west and Mesopotamia to the southeast. To the ancient peoples who preceded them, it was simply *Anatolia*; after 1923, under Atatürk, the country became *Türkiye*, the Land of the Turks.

Since prehistory, this sprawling land of mountain ranges, high plateaux and fertile river valleys has divided Orient and Occident. The Persian king Xerxes crossed westwards with his Asian hordes on their way to victory at Thermopylae and defeat at Salamis; Alexander the Great led his Macedonians eastwards to India in pursuit of his great empire, leaving an indelible Hellenistic stamp on Anatolia. The Romans saw in Asia Minor a granary and bulwark against their enemies to the east.

Over the next 1,000 years, Anatolia became the nucleus of the Byzantine Empire, with its capital, Constantinople, undoubtedly the most powerful and magnificent city in the world. It was here that early Christianity first took root, only to be replaced by Islam, first introduced by the 7th-century Arabs, and then imposed by the Seljuk and Ottoman Turks, who pushed the frontiers of the Ottoman Empire from the Persian Gulf to the Atlantic, from Cairo to Budapest.

The collapse of the Ottomans in 1918 was followed by the abrupt and ruthless carve-up of the once-glittering empire. Yet under Kemal Atatürk's leadership, the Turks rapidly regained Anatolia and a new republic emerged to take on a very different role in the 20th century. Today, as Turkey strives for membership of the European Union and struggles to embrace Western notions of statecraft and society within an Islamic framework, it looks to a new future, not as a dividing line or buffer zone between East and West, but as a bridge between them. Meanwhile, a new invasion has begun, more friendly and short-lived, with up to 23 million foreigners arriving annually in search of warm seas, magnificent scenery, echoes of ancient history, fine food and a friendly greeting. *"Hoş geldiniz!"* – Welcome to Turkey. ❑

PRECEDING PAGES: Assos harbour; Nevizade Street, İstanbul; İskele Mosque, İstanbul. **LEFT:** reading in a mosque in Diyarbakır. **ABOVE LEFT:** statues of local heroes guard the entrance to Gazantiep castle. **ABOVE RIGHT:** fisherman at Foca.

GEOGRAPHY

Turkey packs a huge variety of landscapes and climatic
conditions in a correspondingly large area

Some foreigners equate Turkey with camel-populated deserts, a misconception perhaps encouraged by the "Turkish and American blend" tag-line on classic Camel cigarette boxes, and the bazaar and mosque in the desert on the back. In fact, pure sand desert is the one environment you *won't* find in the country, which offers almost everything else from subtropical cloud-forest along the eastern Black Sea coast – conditions also ideal for tea plantations and hazelnut groves – to the olive groves of the balmy Aegean Sea.

A mere three percent of Turkey's 783,560 sq km (302,532 sq mile) area – comprising Thrace and part of İstanbul – falls within Europe, though this is home to 10 percent of the population. The other 97 percent occupies the peninsula of Anatolia (*Anadolu* in Turkish), extending over 1,600km (1,000 miles) from the Aegean on the west to the eastern frontiers (though only about half that distance from the northerly Black Sea to the Mediterranean in the south).

Volcanoes and earthquakes

Geologically, Turkey is a complex jumble produced by the ongoing collision, beginning about 65 million years ago, of the African and Arabian tectonic plates with the Eurasian one. Consequences include volcanoes, numerous hot springs and frequent, destructive seismic activity along the North Anatolian fault, which extends in an arc from the Sea of Marmara to Lake Van. The worst recorded tremor (Richter 8), in December 1939, levelled Erzincan and

killed an estimated 33,000 people, though the August 1999 İzmit earthquake (Richter 7.6), with at least 25,000 fatalities and wide-

> Turkey's principal volcanic cones – Hasan Dağı, Erciyes Dağı, Süphan Dağ and Ağrı Dağ (5,165 metres/17,216ft, the country's highest point) – are all extinct or deeply dormant.

spread damage, figures more in recent memory. Happier results of primordial volcanic eruptions 30 million years ago are the eerie badlands of Cappadocia, consisting of tuff

---

LEFT: wild poppies at Pergamon.
RIGHT: rock formations in the Göreme Valley.

(compressed volcanic ash) very conducive to excellent wine grapes – and bumper crops of tourists.

Anatolia: a natural fortress

The central Anatolian steppes at the heart of Turkey are naturally defended by two mountain systems, which have always isolated the interior from the coast climatically and culturally. The southerly mountain chain, forested with conifers and rising close to the Mediterranean, is the Taurus (*Toros* in Turkish), an extension of a great karst mass beginning in Dalmatia and continuing through Greece to Turkey. The foothills and coastal plain between Fethiye and Adana exhibit plenty of karstic phenomena: caves, sinkholes, deep canyons and suddenly appearing or disappearing rivers and cascades. Further north, the Pontic ranges run parallel – and close – to the Black Sea coast, forming the edge of the Eurasian plate. Partly granitic and, especially in the easterly Kaçkar mountains, heavily glaciated, the slopes are clothed in broadleaf and mixed forest, particularly on the northern edge. Rivers slicing through both ranges – although fewer in the Taurus – are short and sharp as they drain to the Black Sea and the Mediterranean.

To the west, the two Menderes streams and

> Most tourists head for the coast – well over 7,000km (4,300 miles) of it. The Black Sea is generally pebbly; the Mediterranean either side of Antalya is more reliably sandy, while the Aegean has the most deeply indented and variable shoreline, plus many islands.

the Gediz flow more lazily towards the Aegean, watering some of the country's most fertile territory, full of cotton, sultanas, figs or peaches. Yet aside from these areas, the deltas of the Yeşilırmak and Kızılırmak (Turkey's longest river) bracketing tobacco-rich Samsun on the Black Sea, Thrace, and the Çukurova of the Şeyhan (near Adana), made famous by novelist Yaşar Kemal, there's little flat land anywhere in Turkey.

The vast central plateau – with an average elevation of 1,100 metres (3,600ft), divided into discreet *ovas* (uplands) – has always been a breadbasket. The biggest *ova* envelops Konya, but it (like many other agricultural areas) is in deep ecological trouble. Abnormally low rainfall since the millennium, and over-reliance on thirsty crops like sugar beets, have seen water tables drop precipitously as deep fossil reserves are tapped. Hopes are now pinned on the so-called "Blue Tunnel", a costly scheme to divert water from the Göksu River in the Taurus. Before modern irrigation projects and well-drilling technology, *ova* crops were limited to seasonal, rain-dependent wheat, oats and barley.

It's soon evident that, aside from a few clusters of poplars around farms or willows marking a stream bed, much of the interior is treeless – the result of human (or livestock)

TRANSHUMANCE

The ancient practice of transhumance is alive and well in parts of Anatolia, with shepherds migrating with their livestock from winter quarters to highland pastures each summer, just as they always have.

The summertime abode for the herders is the *yayla*, ranging from goat-wool yurts in the Taurus to clusters of wood-and-tin shacks in the Kaçkar. Their inhabitants – various ethnic groups along the Black Sea, Yörüks near the Mediterranean – have an almost mystical bond with their *yayla*.

intervention. Reforestation was one of Atatürk's obsesssions, and most forests still belong to the state; many people have landed in jail for surreptitiously cutting down even one tree.

Driving through inner Anatolia involves covering huge distances of lonely, dun-coloured landscape between towns, akin to transiting Great Basin states like Nevada or Utah, with the main signs of road-side life being the huge rest-stop complexes, modern descendants of the ancient *kervansarays*. The emptiness is not deceptive; the back country has long been depopulating for various reasons, so that Turkey is now 70 percent urbanised.

tezek (cow dung patties). It's a hard-scrabble existence, with the only real rural money-spinners being sugar beets, hay and livestock.

The lower-lying southeast of the country is dominated by the fan-shaped flood plain of the Euphrates and Tigris (Firat and Dicle in Turkish) rivers, Turkey's very own chunk of Mesopotamia. The region is significantly Arab and Kurdish in both culture and terrain, an undulating plateau sloping down to Syria. The colossally ambitious Southeast Anatolia Project (*Güneydoğu Anadolu Projesi* or GAP), begun in 1974, aims to straddle both rivers with no fewer than 22 dams; the largest, Atatürk Barajı on the Firat, has made

The Wild East – and mind the GAP

Close to the Iranian and Armenian borders where the Taurus and Pontic ranges meet in a jumbled topography known formally as the Anti-Taurus, conditions are even harsher. The mean elevation ramps up to nearly 2,000 metres (6,500 ft) and winter snowfall can cut villages off for days; summers are so short that little garden produce matures other than parsley and radishes. Outside of sheltered stream valleys, trees are even scarcer than further west, such that the heating and cooking fuel in many villages is still

cultivation of a variety of crops possible on what was previously wasteland, while 17 of the dams will generate electric power in a country with scant petroleum reserves. But large agribusiness holdings benefit rather than small farmers (the latter often driven out by rising waters), and the scheme has proven otherwise controversial. Relations with Syria have frayed badly as the amount of cross-border water delivered on the Firat has halved, while many major archaeological sites such as Zeugma and Samsat have been submerged before being properly examined. The next victim, amidst ongoing international (and local) uproar, is scheduled to be Hasankeyf on the Tigris, to be flooded by the pending İlisu Dam. ❏

LEFT: view from Tahtali mountain above Antalya.
ABOVE: a village in the Pontic mountains.
FOLLOWING PAGES: stone-carved Medusa at Didyma.

DECISIVE DATES

c.6500–5600 BC
Çatalhöyük, among the oldest agricultural communities, thrives.

c.5600–3000 BC
Fortified towns at Hacılar, Can Hasan and Yumuktepe.

c.3000–2200 BC
Sophisticated Bronze Age metallurgy proven by hoards at Troy and Alacahöyük.

c.2000–1200 BC
Hittites create the first advanced Anatolian civilisation.

c.1230–700 BC
From the Balkans and the Black Sea, the "Sea Peoples" invade; their descendants include the Phrygians.

c.850–590 BC
Urartian kingdom flourishes around Lake Van; Greeks colonise coasts.

546–499 BC
Persian conquest of Anatolia by Cyrus and Darius I.

333 BC
Alexander the Great crushes the Persians at Issos.

281 BC
Pergamon becomes an independent kingdom, allying with Rome in 190 BC.

133 BC
King Attalos III leaves Pergamon to Rome; Anatolia becomes the Roman province of Asia Minor.

AD 45–58
John the Divine and Paul the Apostle evangelise Asia Minor.

AD 325
Council of Nicaea codifies Christian doctrine and condemns heresies.

BYZANTIUM, SELJUKS, CRUSADERS

AD 330
Emperor Constantine establishes capital at Byzantium, henceforth Constantinople, and encourages Christianity.

AD 391–395
Theodosius I prohibits paganism. Upon his death, Constantinople becomes seat of the Eastern, Byzantine empire, with Rome that of the Western, Latin empire.

AD 527–565
Reign of Justinian sees massive building programmes and ephemeral conquests.

637
Arab invasions begin; southeastern Anatolia Islamised. Bulgars, Armenians and Persians soon attack Byzantine borderlands.

726–843
Iconoclasts ban religious images of the human form; many churches are literally defaced.

1071–1243
Seljuk Turks rout Byzantine army at Manzikert; a Turkish-speaking, Islamic kingdom emerges in central Anatolia until defeated by the Mongols. The Byzantines retreat to the Aegean and Black Sea coasts, as well as around İstanbul.

1204
The Fourth Crusade sacks Constantinople, occupying it until 1261.

THE OTTOMANS
1453
The Ottomans, under Mehmet II, conquer Constantinople, and rename it İstanbul.

1512–20
Selim I conquers Mesopotamia and Egypt, and assumes the title of caliph, head of Sunni Islam.

1520–66
Süleyman the Magnificent presides over Ottoman golden age.

1683–1830
Catastrophic European defeats end Ottoman expansion while peace treaties favour the Habsburgs and Russians.

FAR LEFT TOP: the siege of Troy, on a 5th-century BC plate. FAR LEFT MIDDLE: Trojan horse at Çanakkale. LEFT: the adoption of the Nicene Creed in AD 325 at the Council of Nicaea (now İznik). ABOVE: Sultan Mehmet II. RIGHT TOP: Turkish troops at Gallipoli during World War I.

1908
Young Turk revolution results in military-parliamentary rule, with the sultan as figurehead.

1914–18
Turkey defeated in World War I as a Central power, though Mustafa Kemal leads successful Gallipoli resistance.

THE REPUBLIC
1919–22
War of Independence: Nationalists under Kemal expel all foreign armies.

1923
Sultanate abolished; Turkey becomes a republic, with Kemal as president. Treaty of Lausanne recognises Nationalist victory and stipulates exchange of minorities with Greece.

1923–38
Kemal dictates sweeping reforms, including mandatory surnames (his becomes Atatürk).

1939–45
Neutral during most of World War II, Turkey belatedly declares war on Germany, to qualify for UN membership.

1950–52
First free elections; Turkey joins NATO.

1960, 1971, 1980
Military factions lead coups after political-economic crises.

1974
Turkey invades northern Cyprus.

1984
Kurdish separatists (the PKK) begin armed insurrection.

1983–93
Turgut Özal dominates Turkish politics as prime minister and then president.

1996–97
First Islamist party in a short-lived coalition.

1999
Catastrophic Marmara earthquake; Turkey becomes candidate for EU membership.

2002
The religious AK Partisi (Justice and Development Party) decisively elected.

2003
Turkey declines significant cooperation with US in Iraq war; Islamic militants bomb Jewish and British targets in İstanbul.

2007–08
AK re-elected in landslide victory; its candidate, Abdullah Gül, controversially becomes president. Ergenekon military-secularist conspiracy to destabilise country uncovered; trials of suspects commence.

2010
Retired generals arrested as auxiliaries of Ergenekon plot.

THE CRADLE OF CIVILISATION

Straddling Europe and Asia, Anatolia was a natural junction
between cultures, crucial in the development of civilisation

Since the earliest times, Anatolia has figured prominently in the history of civilisation. The upper reaches of the Euphrates
and Tigris rivers, both rising in eastern Anatolia,
form the heart of the so-called Fertile Crescent,
while ancient Mesopotamia now lies partly in
southeastern Turkey. These areas were home to
some of the first human settlements on Earth
(*see panel, page 30*). Somewhat later, the Old Testament refers to local personalities – including
the patriarch Abraham, who came from Edessa
(now Sanlıurfa), and Noah, whose ark supposedly landed on Mount Ararat.

Ancient beginnings

Human presence in the region stretches back
far into the mists of time. Million-year-old
human remains have been discovered in a cave
at Yarımburgaz near İstanbul – the oldest yet
found outside Africa. The first people to have left
any traces other than bones were members of
a hunting colony who built a complex of stone
circles comprising *stelae* intricately carved with
animal figures dated to 9500 BC, at Göbekli Tepe
in Mesopotamia. At about the same time, others executed powerful paintings and carvings on
cave walls at Belbaşı and Beldibi near Antalya.

Within three millennia, the transition from
hunting and gathering to settled communities was mostly complete. Çatalhöyük, south of
Konya, cedes to Jericho the honour of being the
world's first town, but by 6250 BC it had a population of around 5,000, and was the first place
to irrigate crops such as barley, or to domesti-

cate livestock. By 5000 BC, Hacılar (220km/135
miles west of Çatalhöyük) had streets, houses
with doors, and exquisite pottery.

The Bronze Age

With the discovery of copper, the pace of change
accelerated, reflected in the successive levels of
settlement mounds (known as a *höyük* in Turkish) formed by generations of mudbrick houses
crumbling on a single spot. The most famous
mound is at Troy, originally settled in about 3000
BC. Little has survived from its earliest levels, but
this apparently was a sophisticated community
with large houses, while sturdy city walls indicate
well-developed political and military concerns.

LEFT: Antiochus and Hercules at Eski Kâhta.
RIGHT: the Anatolian Mother Goddess, one of the
world's oldest and most potent fertility symbols.

We know the Bronze Age Anatolians largely from their pottery – dark, red, or burnished to a metallic sheen. Unlike in contemporary Egypt and Mesopotamia, there were no written records in the Anatolian patchwork of minor kingdoms and city-states. Nevertheless, archaeological sites show continuous occupation, increasing competence in construction and crafts, and growing trade connections.

The second millennium

Late in the third millennium BC, devastating invasions from the northwest destroyed the prosperous Anatolian civilisation. Once the dust had

settled, we can identify some of the groups living in Anatolia, although their exact origins remain a mystery. Among them were the Hattis (speakers of a native Anatolian language) and newer arrivals, speaking the Indo-European Luwian language in the north and west, and Hurrian in the south and east. Beyond the Euphrates, the Mitanni kingdom was ruled by an Indo-European aristocracy related to the Hurrians.

A chronicle of the second millennium is made partly possible by discoveries of documents written on clay tablets, seals and stone monuments. Hundreds of clay tablets, detailed records of Assyrian traders in metals and tex-

THE FERTILE CRESCENT

The so-called Fertile Crescent, an area corresponding to southeastern Turkey and northern parts of Iraq, is thought to have nurtured the very first human settlements in the period 8000–10000 BC. A unique combination of natural advantages are believed to have encouraged the hunter-gatherers in this region to take up sedentary farming. The initial spark is thought to be linked to the abundance of various forms of wild wheat (emmer, einkhorn and others), easily-gathered and stored, and suitable for cultivation. The other decisive factor was the presence of the wild ancestors of modern sheep and goats, both of which were easily domesticated.

tiles, were discovered early in the 1900s, near Kanesh (modern Kültepe) near Kayseri.

The Hittites

Shortly after 2000 BC, the Indo-European Hittites, probably originating from the eastern Caucasus, conquered Hattuşa (modern Boğazkale), ending the Hatti dynasty centred there and at nearby Alacahöyük. As he left, the last Hatti king cursed the city, decreeing that it should be abandoned for ever. Within two centuries, however, Hittite king Labarnas I made it his capital, seat of a powerful empire stretching from the Aegean coast to Mesopotamia.

When the immense ruins of Hattuşa were first unearthed in the 19th century, they presented a stark puzzle. Memories of the Hittites were limited to the Old Testament reference to "Uriel the Hittite" – and even he came from the much later southern Hittite principalities.

Knowledge of the larger, older Hittite kingdom in the north revived with the discovery of cuneiform and hieroglyphic tablets at Hattuşa. The Sumerian forms could be read at once. It was soon realised that the Hittite language was Indo-European, some words being close to modern English – such as "watar" for water. Hittite culture and religion borrowed heavily from the Hattis, who were assimilated rather than conquered.

From about 1800 to 1200 BC, Hittite rulers presided over a network of client principalities, elaborately administered by a huge caste of scribes. Besides their main cities, Hittite monuments are found at Kemalpaşa and Manisa outside İzmir, at Eflatunpınar west of Konya, and near Adana.

Although their records are lost, rival neighbouring Arzawa, Lukka and Ahhiyawa states seem to have been similar but less powerful, ruled by a warrior class who spoke Luwian, from which the common place name ending *assos* may derive.

The Phrygians

From about 1230 BC onwards, the arrival of the "Sea Peoples" smashed the civilisation of both the Hittites, and the Mycenaeans on the Greek peninsula, so thoroughly that they all but passed out of memory until their rediscovery in modern times. Among the casualties was Troy VII, whose story, eventually told by Homer in the *Iliad* some four centuries later, still stirs the imagination.

The most important of the new peoples were the Phrygians, who appeared around 800 BC and set up a kingdom covering much of west-central Anatolia. Of Thracian origin, they spoke an Indo-European language written in a modified Phoenician alphabet, still seen on monuments at Midas Şehri (Yazılıkaya). They probably also had archives, but excavations at Midas Şehri and Gordion, west of Ankara – have failed to uncover any, perhaps because they no longer used clay tablets. Much of what we know about the Phrygians comes from the Greeks, who had been settled for some time along the Aegean coast of Asia Minor and were significantly influenced by Phrygian religion, art and music.

Two Phrygian kings live on in legend – Gordios (who gave his name to the city, and the riddle of the Gordian knot, broken by Alexander) and his successor, Midas of the golden touch. The massive tomb of another Phrygian ruler, excavated in the 1950s and one of many grave mounds at Gordion, yielded impressive bronze and wooden art but surprisingly no golden objects.

Within a century the Phrygians succumbed to Cimmerian raiders and the semi-indigenous Lydians, who established a powerful kingdom based at Sardis (near İzmir), yet much of central Anatolia continued to speak Phrygian until about AD 300. ❑

FAR LEFT: remains of Bronze Age man found at Karatas. **LEFT:** silver drinking vessel, c.1400–1200 BC. **RIGHT:** throne at Midas Şehri.

THE CLASSICAL YEARS

With the arrival of the Greeks, coastal Turkey
entered a millennium that produced immense
wealth and sophistication

For over a century (*c.*670–546 BC), the Lydians dominated the western half of Anatolia. Famous for their plangent music, love of luxury items and invention of coinage, they remained on friendly terms with their Greek neighbours, whose awe at their wealth has survived in the expression "as rich as Croesus" (560–546 BC), last of the Lydian kings.

Persians versus Greeks

In 546 BC, Lydia was invaded by Persian king Cyrus II, who captured Croesus and burnt him alive. From their capital at Persepolis (now in western Iran), Cyrus' successors Darius I and Xerxes expanded their empire westwards to the Aegean. Lydian Sardis became the seat of one of four Persian satraps (client rulers). The Greek coastal cities of Ionia, which had been intellectual centres – Homer is thought to have been born locally in about 700 BC – hated Persian rule, regarding it as repressive.

> *Persian rule inhibited, though did not entirely stop, the growth of city-states. Throughout coastal Anatolia, thriving towns possessed municipal institutions and sophisticated public amenities, such as theatres and baths.*

The Persians were notoriously vindictive. After quelling a five-year (499–494 BC) revolt, they razed Miletos, one of the most splendid of the Ionian cities, while at Xanthos on the Lycian coast, the inhabitants preferred mass suicide to the Persian yoke. Despite this, a few semi-autonmous dynasties emerged, notably the Hecatomnids at Halikarnassos (now Bodrum).

Inland, the situation may have been better. In Cappadocia, where many Persian nobles settled, their culture remained alive for decades after Alexander's victory (*see below*). Nevertheless, monuments of the period are scarce: the best-known survivals are three stelae from Daskylion in northwest Anatolia, dating from about 400 BC, now displayed in the İstanbul Archaeological Museum.

Alexander the Great and Hellenism

Anatolia between 670 BC and AD 300 is distinguished by the steady advance of classical Graeco-Roman civilisation. The most significant catalyst for change was Alexander the

Great, the youthful king of Macedonia, one of history's meteors (see page 277). Only 11 years separate his first setting foot in Anatolia in 334 BC from his death in 323 BC, yet in that time he managed to set up one of the greatest (if shortest-lived) empires ever known. Motivated by a passionate desire to liberate Anatolia from Persian rule, Alexander spread Greek culture and language everywhere his armies marched, first through the coastal city-states founded centuries before by Ionian traders, then spreading inland and eastwards. Even after his death, the empire remained culturally Greek, with its vast territories carved up amongst four of his generals. For a generation after the death of Alexander the Great and the establishment of rival kingdoms by his successors, the history of Anatolia was marked by constant warfare between would-be kings.

Although these powerful players command attention, the abiding political units of the period were the cities, which ran their own affairs while paying lip service and tribute to overlords. Walls and water, as much as the theatre and *bouleuterion* (city-council hall), comprised Hellenistic and Roman culture in Anatolia. Cities had streets and market squares lined with colonnades, high defensive walls with grandiose gates, temples for the gods, baths and gymnasia for hygiene and health, stadiums, theatres and odeons for entertainment.

It was an age of splendid architecture, erected by slaves; even the smaller municipalities were graced by splendid columns and carved capitals. The most magnificent monument of all was the Zeus altar at Pergamon (whose superb friezes are now in Berlin's Pergamon museum). Equally worthy of respect are some extraordinary engineering projects, notably aqueducts; the end of the ancient world coincides almost exactly with their destruction by Arab raiders during the 7th century.

This period also saw the gradual disappearance of local languages such as Carian, Pamphylian, Lycian and Phrygian, which survive only as monumental inscriptions. There seems to have been no major literature in these languages to rival that of ancient Greece, and the

Anatolian languages faded gradually as first the prosperous classes, and later the peasantry, favoured Greek as a means of communication and for most of their daily purposes. The overall picture is one of slow, voluntary and peaceful assimilation of indigenous peoples.

In southeastern Anatolia, Syria and Palestine, however, Hellenistic culture confronted a written, Semitic language – Aramaic – which it was never fully able to absorb or subdue. Cultural and linguistic tension between the Semitic Middle East and Hellenism bedevilled the Roman (and Byzantine) empires and contributed to the later rise of Islam and Arabic.

The Celts in Turkey

In 279 BC, King Nikomedes I of Bithynia (near present-day Bursa) rashly invited Celtic mercenaries from central Europe into Anatolia for

> The Celts left little mark on Anatolia other than their language – spoken for the next 600 years. According to St Jerome, the Celtic dialect of Ankara could still be understood in northern Gaul late in the 4th century AD.

LEFT: Alexander the Great meets his hostage, the empress of Persia, after the Battle of Issos.
RIGHT: detail of a Greek soldier in full armour, in İstanbul's Archaeology Museum.

assistance in suppressing a rebellious brother, allowing them to settle in eastern Phrygia on the west bank of the Kızılırmak River. These

Celts ("Gauls") were kinsmen of the Gauls who colonised what are now France, Britain and Ireland, and called their new home Galatia. A robust, warrior people, they preyed upon the wealthy Hellenistic city-states. Barbaric but valiant, they were immortalised late in the 3rd century BC by the famous "Dying Gaul" sculpture; the original bronze sculpture is now lost, but a near-contemporary marble copy resides in Rome's Capitoline Museum.

The rise of the Romans

The troublesome Gauls were checked by Attalos I, king of Pergamon, in 230 BC, but a new

and more significant threat was emerging in the shape of the growing political and commercial power of Rome. The turmoil surrounding the rivalry of the Hellenistic Anatolian kingdoms had drawn the Romans to the area. Hard-headed pragmatists, they rarely tried to annexe territory outright unless they had strong economic reasons for it. Anatolia was not only rich with raw materials, but the power vacuum threatened to destabilise existing trade routes. Pergamon, by now one of the wealthiest, largest states in Anatolia, allied itself with the Romans, but the growth of Latin power was generally unpopular, and it came as a shock when, in 133 BC, Attalos III, the last Pergamene king, bequeathed his kingdom to Rome.

Over the next century, local rulers such as Mithridates VI (r. 110–63 BC), king of Pontus on the Black Sea, tried to stem the Roman advance; in 88 BC, uprisings in various Ana-

> Pergamon's water supply began in the mountains 45km (28 miles) north of the town, running through a triple-pipe system with no fewer than 240,000 sections.

tolian cities massacred some 80,000 Roman civilians. Successive Roman military expeditions were organised to defeat Mithridates and consolidate Rome's grip on the province. Mithridates was halted first by Sulla in 84 BC, and much later by Pompey the Great, who forced the cagey old man to flee to the Crimea in 63 BC. Rather than be dragged in chains to Rome, Mithridates tried to poison himself but failed – during his 71 years he had imbibed far too much toxin as an antidote against assassination, and was obliged to have a trusted servant run him through with a sword.

In 47 BC, at the Battle of Zela (modern Zile, near Tokat), Julius Caesar defeated Pharnaces II, son of Mithridates, and uttered the famous boast: "*Veni. Vidi. Vici.*" ("I came. I saw. I conquered.") The remaining semi-independent kingdoms of Anatolia were gradually absorbed by the Romans over the next century, and the eastern frontier was pushed back to Armenia and the Euphrates, though the border often fluctuated thereafter, under continued pressure from the Persians around Lake Van.

The Roman centuries

Roman activity in Anatolia extends from their defeat of the Selucids at the Battle of Magnesia in 190 BC to the division of the empire in AD 395. During these centuries, the Latin Romans, originally pagans and republicans, morphed into Greek-speaking, imperial and Christian Byzantines. Yet they continued to call themselves "*Romaioi*", which is why the Greek Orthodox of Anatolia and Cyprus are still known, in Turkish, as *Rum*.

Roman domination with its *Pax Romana* brought security and prosperity to Anatolian cities, which grew in size and splendour. But it also meant exactions by tax farmers, eager to squeeze all the money they could from the province they had gained at auction; they had no interest in local welfare and inevitably sparked fierce resentment. However, Roman imperial rule also brought many advantages to the less developed interior, where living standards surpassed those of the early 20th century and the population reached about 12 million.

Grave stelae of this period offer a window into its society. Some depict haughty senatorial families; others show simple farming folk. Traces of politics also appear on surviving monuments. Emperors and even certain imperial family members were worshipped as gods, just as earlier the Hellenistic kings had been.

Emperor Valerian was taken prisoner in AD 260 and later executed. The Goths were finally sent packing by Claudius II, who assumed the honorific Gothicus; a column commemorating the victory still stands at Sarayburnu in İstanbul.

Diocletian (r. AD 284–305) reorganised both the army and system of government and attempted to combat inflation. Copies, chiselled in stone, of his famous edict ordering a price-freeze can be seen throughout Anatolia, most notably at Aphrodisias. However, his newly designated regional capital at Nicomedia (İzmit), from where he unleashed a ferocious persecution of Christians, did not last long in that role. ❑

Crises and responses

By the 3rd century AD, the vast Roman empire was increasingly challenged and destabilised by the emerging force of Christianity – consciously opposed to classical civilisation and its values – while its borders were threatened by barbarian raiders. In AD 258, Gothic tribes poured deep into the heart of Anatolia, ransacking many towns and cities, and kidnapping people as slaves. Simultaneously, the Persians renewed their attacks on the eastern borders, and

LEFT: Emperor Constantine I (AD 280–337).
ABOVE: carving at the Genoese fortress behind the village of Anadolu Kavaği, located at the northern mouth of the Bosphorus near İstanbul.

EARLY CHRISTIANS IN ANATOLIA

Christianity took root early and widely in Anatolia, mainly thanks to the tireless evangelising of Paul, a native of Tarsus, in AD 45–58. By AD 100, congregations had formed in most major cities of the Roman world. The powerhouse of early Christian thought was at Antioch (Antakya), the apostle Peter's base before he transferred to Rome. It remained one of the four chief bishoprics of the early Church until taken by the Arabs in AD 637. In AD 110, the governor of Bithynia, Pliny the Younger, wrote to Emperor Trajan requesting advice on how to handle the Christians in his province. This signalled the start of persecutions that lasted for the next 200 years.

BYZANTIUM

The Byzantine Empire, eastern arm of the once-mighty Roman Empire, was a ferment of religious fervour, artistic splendour, palace intrigue and barbarian invasions

The late Roman Empire was marked by the struggle for supremacy between paganism and Christianity. The AD 311 Galerius Edict formally ended the persecution of Christians in the empire; the very next year, at the battle of the Milvian bridge, co-emperor Constantine (r. AD 306–37) defeated his rival Maxentius after having a celestial vision of a luminous cross, and thereafter expressed his preference for Christianity – though for reasons of state he was not baptised until he was on his deathbed.

Over the next decade, Constantine defeated and disposed of the two remaining co-emperors, leaving himself as sole ruler. In 322, he decided to leave the traditional hub of power (and pagan worship) at Rome and establish a new, "clean-slate" capital in Asia Minor, by now the wealthier and more civilised part of the empire. He first chose the site of Troy on the Dardanelles, replete with Homeric associations; the walls were nearly complete when he changed his mind (thanks to another nocturnal heavenly visitation) and selected the small port of Byzantium on the Bosphorus instead.

Dedicated in 330 and extravagantly decorated with plundered treasures from all over the classical world, the new capital was renamed Constantinople (it became İstanbul after 1453). The emperor had been working on the project for six years. Astonished courtiers watched as Constantine marked the bounds of the new city way beyond the edge of old Byzantium.

LEFT: 6th-century Italian (Ravenna) mosaic of the Byzantine Emperor Justinian I (527–65).

RIGHT: a column capital with cross, at the Basilica of St John, Selçuk.

Different strands of Christianity

Constantinople became the seat of Christianity, and the venue for numerous acrimonious disputes over the nature of the True Faith (disputes that had been present right from the new religion's earliest days). This set the tone for hundreds of years: for most of its history, the Byzantine Empire was beset by theological problems which sapped the energy of emperors and scholars, causing sometimes unbridgeable political and social divisions.

Yet these disputes are often virtually impossible to understand today. What was the fuss about? Basically, the young Church was obliged to thrash out agreed versions of its central dogmas – against the rationalisations of philosophers and diverse cultural and linguistic communities with their own vested interests to defend. Once Christianity had ceased to be a matter of private conscience but had become the state religion, discipline and homogeneity of belief were seen as essential. Earlier Roman emperors may have thought themselves divine; by contrast, Byzantine rulers were seen as God's vice-regents on earth, with their courts (and ceremonies) reflecting the unseen heavenly one.

The core issue was whether Jesus Christ was God, man, or (as mainstream Orthodoxy held) both at once. At the two extremes were Mono-physitism and Arianism. Arius, an Alexandrian priest, believed that Christ was not God but more a heroic superman. The Monophysites arose as a reaction, stressing the divinity of Christ. Between the two positions, from the 4th to 8th centuries, lay others of every conceivable variation. The semi-Arians said Christ

> In AD 360, Basil of Kayseri (Cappadocia) wrote a set of monastic rules still used by the Greek Orthodox Church. The Rule of St Benedict is based on them.

was of similar, but not the same, substance as God. He had the mind of God but a human soul (Apolloninarianism) or one will but two natures (Monothelitism), while the Nestorians believed that the Virgin gave birth to Christ, not God. There were numerous other subvariants, and the controversy became so acrimonious that no Anatolian bishop was quite sure of anyone's orthodoxy. Accordingly, Constantine convened the first Ecumenical Council at Nicaea (İznik) in 325, which formalised the system of belief still stated in the Nicene Creed, and condemned the various heresies prevalent up to that time (though more were to emerge, necessitating six further doctrinal councils).

Arianism faded away within a few generations of the first council (but never disappeared: Isaac Newton was an Arian). Monophysitism has survived to the present day amongst Syriac and Armenian Christians. All heretics were persecuted by Constantinople, which greatly weakened the empire over time. There is also evidence to suggest that the doctrinal warfare was used as a pretext to persecute the non-Hellenic peoples of the borderlands.

The advance of the holy men

The first monasteries appeared in Byzantine territory during the 3rd century; throughout the next century, the monks spearheaded a fierce attack on paganism. Temples were closed, trashed or converted, statues were defaced or thrown out and oracles shut down. Emperor Julian the Apostate (361–3), the great-nephew of Constantine, attempted to turn the clock back by espousing Neoplatonism, but died in 363 fighting the Persians. All subsequent emperors were Christians. The final blow came

ICONOCLASM

Byzantium and Islam each influenced the other: in 726, Emperor Leo III banned representations of human beings, provoking a new religious crisis. Iconoclasts – mostly native to eastern provinces and familiar with Islamic practice – battled with advocates of images, mostly from the west. In place of icons or figural frescoes, the Byzantines embossed crosses (or abstract designs) on coins, city walls, Cappadocian rock chapels and urban church apses. The Seventh Ecumenical Council of 787 under Empress Irene reinstated icon worship, a move reversed by Leo V in 813. Only in 843 did the icon-supporters definitively triumph, with iconoclasm condemned as a heresy.

in 392 when Theodosius I definitively prohibited pagan worship throughout the empire and decreed Christianity as the established religion.

The Byzantine ascendance

While the West was wracked by invading Goths, Vandals, Franks and other barbarians culminating in the fall of Rome in 476, the Byzantine Empire thrived, largely unaffected. In Anatolia, the 5th and 6th centuries were periods of tremendous splendour under emperors such as Theodosius I (378–95), Theodosius II (408–50) and Justinian I (527–65). Greek began to replace Latin as the language of the court and administration; the educational system became explicitly Christian. Imperial power grew and municipal traditions waned as senators sought careers as monks or bishops.

Emperor Justinian I has gone down in history as the builder of St Sophia (Aya Sofya) and the codifier of Roman law, but these were only parts of a vast imperial agenda which also aimed to reconquer the western territories lost 60 years earlier to the Germanic chieftains. Justinian's armies secured North Africa and part of Spain relatively easily, but the reconquest of Italy required a long and exhausting war.

To finance all this, Justinian's rapacious minister, John of Cappadocia, squeezed the cities of

> *Justinian's legacy did not endure. His extravagant projects permanently harmed imperial finances, and soon after he rescued Italy from the Goths, it was overrun by the Lombards.*

Anatolia and Greece, weakening what remained of the classical, urban institutions. The contradiction was felt acutely by contemporaries, such as the historian Procopius, who publicly eulogised Justinian for his ambitious campaigns, while privately lambasting him in his *Secret History* as a devil in human form, married to a prostitute, who delighted in humiliating his subjects.

Barbarian invasions

The empire came under renewed threat at the end of the 6th century. The Danube frontier was

---

LEFT: Byzantine icon of the Apostles.
RIGHT: Emperor Theophilos with his bodyguard, from the Skylitzes Chronicle.

attacked by the Avars, a Central Asian people similar to the Huns, and the Slavs, who both flooded south. Emperor Maurice (582–602) struggled to contain the challenge. In the east, the Sassanid Persians – hereditary foes of the empire – crossed the entire length of Anatolia to reach the Sea of Marmara at Chalcedon (Kadiköy) and seized Byzantine provinces as far away as Egypt. It was Persia's greatest local triumph since they had wiped out the Lydian empire.

Settled life was impossible for the next century. Most cities were destroyed, although Constantinople and Thessalonika survived, and the economic and cultural collapse unprecedented

since the long-forgotten invasions which had destroyed the Hittite Empire 2,000 years earlier. In 622, Angyra (Ankara) was sacked and its population massacred or enslaved. Remarkably, Emperor Heraclius (610–41) was able to expel the Persians by 628, but the effort so exhausted both the Persian and Byzantine empires that neither was able to resist the sudden appearance of a new enemy – the Arab armies pouring north and west out of the desert under the banner of Mohammed and Allah.

Islam

The Arab invasions of the 7th century brought Islam to Anatolia – today it is the religion of around 99 percent of the population. To the

Byzantines, the Arabs appeared to be wild, primitive tribesmen, a notion quickly overturned when the Byzantine host was routed by the Muslim horsemen under Khalid ibn al-Walid, the "Sword of Islam", at the August 636 Battle of Yarmuk (in present-day Jordan).

In 647, Arab armies entered central Anatolia, taking Caesarea (Kayseri), the great Byzantine frontier defence station, and other cities. Their first great siege of Constantinople began in 673, lasting four years. It was repulsed by the Byzantine fleet, as was the second siege in 717–18, but the Byzantines lost most of their eastern provinces. Their new frontier stretched from east of Selucia (Silifke) on the south coast, past Caesarea to a point east of Trabzon on the Black Sea. Tarsus, Melitene (Malatya) and Theodosiopolis (Erzurum) became Arab garrison towns from which they raided Byzantine territory.

Islam brought a new civilisation, religion, language and script – a radical departure for an area which had been predominantly Greek-speaking since the days of Alexander. In principle, however, Islam tolerated people of other Bible-based religions, provided they accepted inferior status and paid special taxes. Accordingly, Anatolia remained multiethnic and multireligious until the 20th century.

Byzantine revival

The turning point came in 866, when Byzantium had for a decade been effectively ruled by Caesar Bardas on behalf of his weak nephew Michael III, "the Drunkard". While campaigning against the Arabs, however, Bardas was murdered at the instigation of Emperor Michael's chamberlain, a Thracian peasant called Basil.

Basil, of Armenian descent, had run away from the family farm in Thrace when he was a teenager. He lodged in a Constantinople monastery before getting a job as a stable groom, first in the wealthy household of Theophilitzes, a friend of the emperor, and later, in the palace itself where he doubled as a champion wrestler. He quickly became Michael's favourite (and possibly his part-time lover), found a patron in the wealthy widow Danielis, and was married off to Michael's mistress Eudoxia. After Bardas' assassination, Basil was crowned co-emperor with Michael on 26 May 866.

On 23 September 867, Basil, realising he was falling from favour, murdered Michael III to become the empire's sole ruler. From this sordid beginning emerged Byzantium's most glorious dynasty, the so-called Macedonian. Over the next 200 years, the frontiers were expanded in all directions, with wars fought and won against the Saracens across the Mediterranean, the Egyptian Fatimids, the Abbasids of Baghdad, and the Bulgars to the north.

Basil I was succeeded in 886 by his notional son Leo VI – who may in fact have been the offspring of Michael III and Eudoxia. Less than a century later, the general-emperor Nikeforos Phokas reconquered Crete and Cyprus from the Saracens before being deposed and murdered at the instigation of his empress, Theophano.

EXTREME ASCETICS

Some of the early Byzantine ascetics sought extraordinary ways to demonstrate their faith (and retreat from overly adulant followers). Respected for their extreme self-denial and figurative closeness to heaven, they were the celebrities of their time, and their fulminating pronouncements were heeded even by the emperors. St Simeon Stylites lived on top of a pillar near Antioch for 30 years during the 5th century, while Daniel the Stylite (409–493) spent 33 years on a pillar at Anaplous (Rumelihisar), attracting visitors like the emperors Leo I and Zeno. Other Syrian holy men, called "dendrites", preferred to live in trees, and had far less to do with the public.

Under the plain-spoken, uncouth but very competent Basil II ("Bulgar Slayer", 976–1025), the late Byzantine state reached the apogee of its glory. With the aid of soldiers sent by Vladimir of Kiev (in return for which Basil's sister Anna was given as bride to Vladimir upon his adoption of Christianity), Basil quelled a revolt by two generals before restoring Syria to the empire.

In 1000 he turned to the Balkans to deal with the rebellious Bulgarian tsar, Samuil, who had amassed a large kingdom at Byzantium's expense, comprising much of present-day Greece, Albania, Macedonia (FYROM) and Bulgaria. After 14 years of progressively roll-

to retake Sicily when he died in 1025, an ascetic, unmarried warrior with no heir.

Decline and fall

Although Basil had left the empire's finances sound and the army in good morale, in many ways his death signalled the beginning of the end for Byzantium. The Macedonian dynasty deteriorated through mediocre nonentities – beginning with Basil's brother and successor, Constantine VIII, and continuing with the three hapless husbands of the empress Zoe (r. 1028–50), who spent most effort running her own cosmetics laboratory to keep herself in prime condition,

ing back the Bulgars, Basil crushed the tsar's army at the Battle of Kleidion, taking 14,000 prisoners. They were blinded and sent back to Samuil's court at Ohrid in groups of 100, each led by one man who only had one eye put out. When Samuil beheld this gruesome spectacle, he suffered a stroke and died within two days. By 1018, his lands were annexed to Byzantium.

Basil II also re-extended the frontiers to Crimea and Bagratid Armenian to the northeast, and in the west, restored much of Italy to the Byzantine sphere. He was preparing a campaign

but who – by the time she first married – was too old to produce an heir. Having murdered both her first husband and her adopted son, Zoe was in turn outlived by a third spouse, Constantine IX Monomahos. He more or less finished the dynasty in the same year (1054) which saw the final rupture with the Catholic Church, ostensibly over doctrinal disputes concerning the precedence of the Holy Ghost, but really the result of a turf war over dioceses in southern Italy. This precluded any substantial western aid to isolated Byzantium, while at the same time civilian bureaucrats in the capital feuded with landed generals of the provinces, leaving the frontiers poorly defended by these warlords' personal armies of mercenaries. ❑

LEFT: figures in many frescoes in Cappadocia were targeted by iconoclasts.
ABOVE: Christ with Constantine IX and Zoe, St Sophia.

AN EMPIRE UNDER THREAT

Faced by the onslaught of adversaries from every direction, the Byzantine Empire shrank to a tiny territory around the walls of Constantinople

Byzantium, the final vestige of the Roman Empire, struggled on for another four centuries, at times regaining ground but ultimately doomed to disintegration. The population decreased steadily, invaders breached the frontiers and foreign powers – Seljuks and Crusaders – played an ever greater role in state affairs. The first hint of doom came in 1071 when the Byzantines faced a new enemy, the nomadic Turks from Central Asia.

The Early Turks

Attila the Hun, Genghis Khan and Timur, commanding their hordes (from *ordu* or "army" in Turkish), today evoke images of bloodthirsty horror. However, these figures should be evaluated within the standards of the era – nomads versus settlers, the stirrup versus the plough. In the Central Asian steppes, nomads migrated from one unreliable waterhole to the next, fighting drought and climate extremes. It was only natural that when these poor herdsmen encountered cropland, they pillaged it. From this stock emerged the Turks.

> *"Turks" first appear in 6th-century AD Chinese annals as T'u-chüeh or Dürkö. The 8th-century Orkhon inscriptions of Mongolia, written in runic characters, are the earliest known proto-Turkish texts.*

Language alone sets them apart from Indo-European or Semitic peoples. Besides the western Turkish spoken in modern Turkey, millions of Turkic peoples in central Asia, parts of Iran and the Caucasus speak a form of Turkish or related tongues such as Mongolian or Tatar, members of the Ural-Altaic family of languages along with Estonian, Finnish and Hungarian.

Early Turks, as described in the epic of Dede Korkut, first written during the 14th century, were patriarchal but monogamous. When a couple failed to produce children it was accepted as fate; taking a second wife was not an option. Traditionally, the Turks married outside their tribe to establish alliances, which partially explains the frequent conflation of Mongols and Turks; Temūcin – better known as Genghis Khan – may have been half Mongol and half Turkish.

The Turks, like the Mongols, were renowned horsemen and soldiers. The Abbasid caliphs of Baghdad, once aware of these qualities, recruited (and converted) them as paid warriors or superior slave soldiers. By the early 10th century, most military commanders of the caliphate were Muslim Turks.

The Seljuks

Early in the 11th century, the Turkic Seljuk tribe set up a west Asian state with Persian Nishapur as its capital. Recent, enthusiastic converts to Sunni Islam, they were not content with this but, under Tuğrul Bey, proclaimed themselves the rightful heirs to all lands conquered during and immediately after the time of the Prophet Mohammed, in particular the Levant and Egypt. To secure their rear as they concentrated on these goals, Tuğrul parlayed with the Byzantine emperors of Constantinople.

However, the borderlands between Seljuk and Byzantine territory were hardly peaceful. Armenian and Byzantine aristocrats recruited militias from among Turcoman raiders (a very motley crew with Shi'ite and pagan beliefs) or Byzantine *akritoi* (an equally varied body of regular and mercenary, Greek and exotic, border guards); both engaged in part-time brigandage, leading Seljuks and Byzantines to accuse each other of bad faith.

By 1064, the Seljuks had conquered Byzantine Armenia and were attacking elsewhere. Emperor Romanos IV Diogenes confronted a Seljuk army commanded by Tuğrul Bey's nephew Alp Arslan near Manzikert, north of Lake Van, in 1071. Although vastly outnumbering the Seljuk (and Kurdish) cavalry, the Byzantine troops – who included unreliable mercenaries; one general, Andronikos Doukas, who hated Romanos; and another, Joseph Tarhaniotes, who simply fled with his men – were completely outmanoeuvred. The Turks melted away when charged, lured the main Byzantine force forward, and showered the depleted Byzantine ranks with arrows before closing in on three sides. Although most imperial soldiers (including the treacherous Andronikos) escaped alive, the captives included Romanos himself.

Alp Arslan detained Romanos courteously for a week, releasing him upon payment of a large ransom, the promise of a Byzantine bride, and

LEFT: Attila the Hun, king of the Hun empire from AD 434–453. RIGHT: the Byzantine monastery at Alahan, one of many Christian institutions to thrive under Seljuk rule.

promulgation of a treaty which handed southeastern Anatolia to the Seljuks, though allowing the Byzantines to keep lands to the west. But when Romanos returned to Constantinople, he was deposed by new emperor Michael VII Doukas (Andronikos' kinsman). The treaty was a dead letter, and central Anatolia lay open to resumed Turcoman raids.

The Sultanate of Rum

The reign of Alp Arslan's successor, Malik Shah, marked the zenith of the greater Seljuk empire, now based in Isfahan in the heart of present-day Iran. After Malik's death in 1092,

Seljuk holdings steadily shrank, while shifting west towards Anatolia. The Seljuk Sultanate of Rum, ruled by Kiliç Arslan I from Iconium (Konya), restrained the ungovernable Turcomans, and reached a truce with the Byzantines under Manuel I Komnenos after checking their attempt to retake central Anatolia at the Battle of Myriokephalon in 1176.

With no more Byzantine attacks in the offing, the Sultanate of Rum flourished in the first half of the 13th century, reflected in abundant Seljuk architecture still surviving in modern Turkey. The best examples of such "poetry in stone" can be seen in Erzurum, Divriği, Sivas and Konya. Here the Sufi mystic Jelaleddin Rumi (*Mevlâna*) graced the court of Alâeddin

Keykubad I, and initiated the peculiar whirling dervish ceremony.

Turcoman clans scattered to found Anatolian mini-states even before the final Seljuk decline. Their petty emirs remained obscure except for one of their number, Ertuğrul, a warlord with a patch of land granted him by Sultan Alâeddin Keykubad I *(see page 47)*. His son Osman was destined to found what was to become one of the world's mightiest empires – the Ottoman.

The Mongol hordes

The cultural effervescence of the Sulatnate of Rum suffered an abrupt, unhappy end at the

hands of Genghis Khan's Mongol hordes, who erupted from the depths of Central Asia to devastate much of the known world before returning nearly as quickly whence they came. Just as they had overwhelmed the Byzantines 170 years before, the now-sedentary Seljuks succumbed to this newest wave of nomad arrivals.

On 26 June 1243, despite Frankish mercenary reinforcements and Byzantine auxiliaries sent by the Kingdom of Trabizond, the Seljuk army was routed at Köse Dağ, near Erzurum. The sultanate limped on until 1307, still producing the occasional blue-tiled public monument, but politically subservient to the Ilkhanid Mongol empire, originally shamanic/Buddhist but finally Muslim, which lasted until 1335.

The Armenians

Compared with the *arriviste* Turks and Mongols, the Armenians could claim a long history of set-

> The Armenian alphabet – which is still in use – was devised in AD 404 by the scribe Mesrob Mashtots, and inaugurated a period of literary, scholastic and theological ferment.

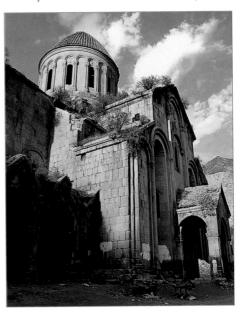

tlement in the region. They were first recorded living beside the Urartians during the mid-6th century BC. Herodotus claimed they came from western Anatolia, though recent theories have the Armenians originating from a short distance east; in either case they spoke an Indo-European language, and gradually colonised an area bounded by modern Sivas, the Çoruh valley, Lake Sevan in the Caucasus, Lake Urmia in Persia and the upper Tigris.

Around 390 BC, local Persian satrap Orontes founded a semi-autonomous Armenian dynasty, replaced by the Artaxiads in 190 BC. Artaxiad King Tigranes II "The Great" (ruled 95–55 BC) assisted father-in-law Mithridates VI of Pontus in his struggle against the Romans, while forging an empire from the Caspian to the Mediterranean. In retaliation the Romans invaded, compelling Tigranes to accept vassal status in 66 BC – though Armenia survived as a buffer state between the Roman and Persian realms until the late 4th century. Christianity was adopted in AD 301 under King Tiridates III, courtesy of St Gregory the Illuminator, making Armenia the earliest Christian nation.

This initial flowering ended with formal partition in AD 387 between Persia and Rome, condemnation by the Byzantines for heresy in AD 451, Arab invasions, and the advent of regional princes. One such clan, the Bagratids of the Çoruh valley, became prominent during the 9th century. The Bagratid kingdom, based first at Kars, then Ani, lasted for almost 200 years; imposing monuments from this period still dot the local landscape.

Despite its relative prosperity, the Bagratid kingdom remained something of a pawn between the Abbasid caliphate of Baghdad and Byzantium; the latter foolishly deposed the last Armenian ruler in 1045, allowing the Seljuks to overrun Armenia. Most Armenians fled, remaining faithful to their language and faith, but some princes converted to Islam to continue opposing the Byzantines with the Seljuks.

By the early 1100s, the Bagratids had re-emerged as a mixed Armenian-Georgian dynasty which controlled northern Armenia (and endowed more splendid churches) until the Mongols arrived in 1236. Meanwhile, Armenian refugees in southerly Cilicia had formed an independent kingdom in 1080, which sided with the Latin Crusaders and even the Mongols against Byzantium. One lasting result of the former alliance was the emergence of an Armenian Catholic Church. After the Cilician kingdom collapsed in 1375, the local Armenian population coexisted, often as a minority, with Turks, Kurds and Arabs.

The Crusades

The final threat to Byzantium came from the European Catholic powers. A plea for help from Emperor Alexios I Komnenos in combating the infidel Seljuks, and the desire to redeem the Holy Land from them, saw the First Crusade proclaimed by Pope Urban II in 1095.

Byzantium, less troubled by theological considerations than by the loss of its lands,

assisted the First Crusade during 1097–8 and the Second Crusade in 1147–8, but both times Crusader passage through Byzantine territory was marked by widespread destruction. The Catholic Crusaders regarded the "heretical" Orthodox state as little better than the Seljuks. They seized Antioch (briefly), Edessa and eventually Jerusalem, establishing autonomous Latin principalities, rather than returning them to Byzantine authority. Matters deteriorated later in the century, with Sicilian Normans occupying Corfu and looting Salonika.

Worse followed in 1204, when the Fourth Crusade, goaded by Greek-hating Venetian

doge Enrico Dandolo, gave up any pretence of fighting Islam, capturing and sacking Constantinople instead. Count Baldwin of Flanders was crowned head of a new Latin Empire around the Sea of Marmara, while various Latin principalities took root in what is now Greece.

The Byzantine nobility set up provisional kingdoms at Trebizond, Arta and Nicaea; their recovery of Constantinople in 1261 under Michael VIII Palaiologos was essentially a twilight action. The once-powerful empire became a tiny rump state, dependent on the toleration of the Venetians, Genoese and Ottoman Turks, whose territory grew to surround Byzantium over the next two centuries. ❑

FAR LEFT: the great Mongol chief, Timur (c.1336–1405). **LEFT:** Georgian Öşk-Vank monastery, near Erzurum. **RIGHT:** engraving of Enrico Dandolo.

THE OTTOMANS

Out of nowhere, the warlike Osmanlı clan supplanted
the Seljuks in challenging the Byzantine Empire,
forming a dynasty that lasted until 1922

As the Mongols first invaded Anatolia in the 1220s, an exhausted band of retreating Seljuks led by Sultan Alâeddin Kaykubad I were cornered by a detachment of the barbarians from the east. Just as all hope seemed lost for these Turks, a wall of horsemen appeared on the crest of a nearby hill, pausing, it seemed, just long enough to determine the victor and claim their share of the spoils. The chieftain of the horsemen signalled his men forward, drawing his scimitar as he charged.

But instead of joining the apparent victors, the horsemen spurred their steeds towards the Mongol flank, and carved their way through to the surprised relief of Alâeddin. Grateful for his life, the Seljuk commander asked the leader of the gallant horsemen his name: Ertuğrul, came the answer.

So legend tells of the advent of Ertuğrul Gazi, the Turcoman warlord *(see page 44)*, and his 444 horsemen, and the subsequent founding of the Ottoman Empire courtesy of Ertuğrul's son Osman (born 1258). Even if the accuracy of the account is questionable, Ertuğrul's intervention did help (temporarily) stem the tide of Mongol incursion, and with Alâeddin's blessing he acquired the small fiefdom of Söğüt, near Eskişehir in western Anatolia. This would become the base from which the Ottoman Empire spread first across Anatolia into Europe, later growing to encompass most of the Middle East.

Beginnings

At the time they settled in Söğüt, Ertuğrul's tribe had not yet converted to Islam. It is also

LEFT: contemporary European oil painting of Süleyman the Magnificent. **RIGHT:** the janissary corps.

DREAMS OF WORLD DOMINATION

While staying at the house of Sheikh Edebali, his spiritual mentor, Osman dreamt that the moon issued from his host's breast before disappearing into his own. Soon a giant tree sprouted from Osman, covering the Caucasus, Atlas, Taurus and Balkan ranges while the Tigris, Euphrates, Danube and Nile watered its roots. In the valleys were towns whose domes and towers were surmounted by the Islamic crescent. The leaves of the tree took the form of swords, and a strong wind sprung up, pointing them all in the direction of Constantinople, which appeared as a fabulous diamond ripe for plucking.

doubtful that they numbered more than 4,000 souls, including women and children – hardly a force to breach the walls of any Byzantine city. But in the chaos resulting from the Mongolian devastation of Anatolia, coupled with internal rifts in the late Byzantine state itself, no dreams were, perhaps, too implausible. As the power vacuum grew, so did the occasion for a new dynasty to impose order, and the Ottoman Turks soon seized this opportunity.

Several factors tilted in their favour. Their fief lay on the march between the Seljuk-Muslim lands of Anatolia and the rump Byzantine state based at Nicaea (İznik). It was a convenient

non-Muslims, while believers paid only a tithe (10 percent). On Christian land, serfs were still bound as feudal labourers to their overlords. Wedged firmly between a rock and a hard place, untold numbers of Byzantine peasants (as well as clergy and soldiery) converted to Islam.

Osman Gazi's forces grew from his father's reputed 444 horsemen to over 4,000 men. In 1301, they came into direct conflict with Constantinople for the first time, near Baphaeon. Although inferior in numbers, the Muslims easily overcame the disorganised forces of Andronikos II Palaeologos.

The defeat of an imperial army by a still-

The gazi *mentality depended on ongoing warfare against the infidel – not least to reward Muslim victors with fresh territory for* timars *or quasi-feudal land grants.*

frontier along which to invite *gazis* (warriors for the faith) to expand the realm of Islam – Dar al-Salam (The Abode of Peace) – at the expense of the infidel's Dar al-Harb (The Abode of War). Local confidence in Christianity was at an all-time low, wrecked by doctrinal schisms which made the road to piety confusing and filled with pitfalls. More to the point, on Ottoman lands, taxes amounted to 50 percent of earnings for

obscure Muslim clan sent shock waves through the recently restored empire. The reverberations (and promise of further booty) brought holy warriors and converts from across Anatolia flocking to join Osman. The next confrontation occurred outside Nicomedia seven years later. Byzantium was routed a second time, and the Ottomans gained effective control of the entire Anatolian hinterland and the remaining Byzantine cities in Asia Minor, chief among which was Bursa.

After a decade-long siege, Bursa's garrison commander finally surrendered in 1326, and he, his forces and most of the city's inhabitants embraced Islam. Osman Gazi had died two years earlier, leaving his son and successor, Orhan, a firm foundation on which to build.

The early Ottoman state

The reign of Osman's second son, Orhan I (1324–59), was marked by reorganisation and expansion. He consolidated the proto-Ottoman state around one religion, Islam; Bursa became one large construction site for mosques and religious schools; and Orhan promoted the *ahis*, brotherhoods analogous to the Christian chivalric orders, whose members were ardent in pursuit of both military success and spiritual exercise.

Next, he reorganised the enthusiastic waves of religiously inspired horsemen into discrete military units ranging from shock troops to a regular cavalry and infantry. Finally, Orhan embarked on a multi-pronged expansion programme. He initially conquered or co-opted minor Turcoman emirates to the south before setting his sights on Christian Thrace, crossing the Dardanelles and Sea of Marmara.

His first entry into Europe came, oddly enough, in 1337 at the invitation of the Byzantine pretender, John Kantakouzenos, who enrolled his daughter, Theodora, into Orhan's harem in exchange for aid during the civil war over the imperial succession. When peace was finally agreed through a co-emperorship, with John VI (as he now was) marrying off another of his daughters to the legitimate Byzantine emperor John V Palaiologos, Orhan's role as king-maker (and relative to kings) in Constantinople was firmly established.

By the end of his reign, Orhan had multiplied his territory several times over, mostly through invitations from his rivals and enemies. Yet with the succession of Orhan's son, Murat, this policy of aggrandisement-by-diplomacy was forgotten; the Ottomans marched on Europe by force of arms and the call of destiny.

Murat I

The second half of the 14th century saw the steady expansion of the Ottoman realm, at the expense of both Constantinople and its would-be heirs in the Balkans. Within 18 months of his accession, Murat I (1359–89) controlled all of Thrace, including Adrianople (renamed Edirne), which was to become the Ottoman's second capital.

Murat I understood the importance of developing new administrative policies to cope with his European conquests. Unlike the Christians of Asia Minor, who had long been exposed to Islam, and were more easily assimilated, the Balkan peoples were tenacious of faith. Neither mass slaughter of these infidels nor forcible conversion were viable options; instead the system of *millets* or subject groups came into existence. Under this system, minority populations – based on religion – were officially recognised, with their leaders held responsible for the communities' taxes, communal and legal affairs.

THE JANISSARIES

Murat I elaborated the practice (begun by Orhan) of drafting the most able-bodied sons of Christian subjects into an elite praetorian guard. Isolated from their origins, they owed absolute, personal loyalty to the sultan. Bereft of everything but their own esprit de corps, these *yeniçeri* (janissaries) would eventually become the scourge not only of Europe, but of the Ottoman Empire itself.

The concept of slavery was different in the medieval Islamic and Christian worlds, and an even greater contrast existed between slaves and the servant-warrior janissaries of the Ottomans, where a royal dynasty eventually arose from such a slave force.

FAR LEFT: 19th-century portrait of Sultan Orhan.
LEFT: young recruit to the janissary corps.
RIGHT: portrait of Yavuz Sultan Selim ("the Grim").

Yet this recognition came only after surrender. During the campaigns, any captured Christian women instantly became the chattel of the Ottoman army – eventually resulting in the extremely heterogeneous bloodline of the modern Turk.

Kosovo and the rise of Beyazit

In 1389, Murat met his end on the battlefield at Kosovo, on the verge of victory over a Serbian-led confederation; he was assassinated by Miloš Obilić, son-in-law of the Serbian leader Stefan Lazar Hrebeljanović, who had accused his relative of treason. Obilić, apparently trying to prove his loyalty with his life, feigned defection

he was forced to supply troops to the Ottoman sultan and allow Muslim settlement in his fief. The repercussions are still being felt today.

Beyazit and the last Crusade

If the Crusades up to 1291 had been inspired by the desire to re-establish the True Faith in

> Until the early 17th century, brothers of each new sultan were strangled with a silken cord – in 1595, Sultan Mehmet III had 19 siblings murdered to safeguard his throne.

and requested an audience with Murat, only to run the 70-year-old ruler through with a dagger as he knelt before him.

Murat's son, Beyazit, was proclaimed sultan immediately upon his father's death. His first act was to have his younger brother, Yakub, strangled in order to ensure his leadership of the state. This grisly practice of fratricide upon enthronement, justified by creative interpretation of the Koran, continued for well over two centuries. Beyazit next avenged the assassination of his father by massacring all the Serbian notables (including Stefan Lazar) captured during the campaign. Finally, he married Lazar's daughter, Despina, allowing her brother to retain a quasi-independent Serbia, although

distant Jerusalem, the last Crusade was a desperate effort to forestall the infidel Turks from knocking down the door to Europe itself. In the summer of 1396, an "international brigade" of nearly 100,000 knights, drawn from across Christian Europe, assembled in Hungary under King Sigismund. The Crusaders initially found little to test their mettle save the women and children of Niš, whom they massacred although they were Orthodox Christian. After marching down the Danube valley, pillaging en route and capturing two minor fortresses, the rampant army made camp around the town of Nicopolis in Bulgaria, hoping to starve the Turkish garrison into submission. At last, Beyazit arrived to relieve the town. While Sigismund urged caution and a thought-out battle plan, certain vainglorious French knights opted for immediate combat. Believing the Ottoman front guard to be their entire formation, they charged on armoured steeds, wreaking havoc on these expendable auxiliaries. They then dismounted and made their way to the crest of the hill, only to find that they had merely dispatched a fraction of an army of over 60,000 highly trained and disciplined archers (including Serbian allies). Some 10,000 knights, hopelessly weighed down and on foot, were slaughtered within hours, with a cowering knot of survivors fording the Danube to safety. Central Europe was left essentially undefended.

Surprisingly, Beyazit did not follow up this victory, returning to Constantinople to resume an intermittent siege of the city, a prize that had eluded his forefathers for over a century. But soon a new and wholly unexpected challenge appeared from the east, in the form of the lame but iron-willed Mongol, Timur, often known as Tamerlane.

Timur the Mongol

Some historians of the Muslim lands refer to a "Big Foot" in Central Asia, which periodically kicks out its nomadic elements, sending them further afield in search of booty, prosperity and power. At the very moment when the Ottomans were relishing their victory over Christian Europe, Timur's mounted Mongol archers came close to extinguishing them altogether.

The build-up to the Battle of Ankara was chiefly due to Ottoman provocation. Inflated by the success of his European victories, Beyazit seized lands belonging to eastern Anatolian vassals of Timur, then threatened to cuckold the Tatar ruler. With personal honour at stake, Timur had no choice but to march against his fellow Muslim, taking Sivas from Beyazit's son Süleyman in 1401.

Beyazit's foolish pride still knew no bounds. In summer 1402, the two armies closed on the plain northeast of the citadel of Ankara, but Beyazit's forces were exhausted after a long march from the Sea of Marmara in torrid conditions. Timur seized the initiative and positioned his army between Beyazit's troops and the citadel, which should have been the Ottomans' last defence. Beyazit's doom was assured when the majority

of his cavalry deserted to Timur. At the end of the day, the once-invincible janissaries and Ottoman foot soldiers lay dead on the field or were in headlong flight, with Beyazit himself taken captive. Bound in chains, Beyazit was used symbolically as Timur's footstool; the Ottoman was also obliged to see his favourite wife, Despina, serve the Tatar overlord naked at dinner, and then raped before his eyes. Beyazit soon went mad, and after eight months of captivity, died.

The Ottoman domains in Asia Minor barely outlived their erstwhile sovereign: Bursa was soon sacked and Timur's hordes ranged as far as Smyrna (modern İzmir) to uproot the last

Christopher Marlowe's drama, Tamburlaine the Great, *contains a scene in which the humiliated Beyazit and Despina are wheeled around Anatolia in a cage, insulted and ridiculed by former subjects.*

colony of Crusaders on the Mediterranean coast, with the skulls of his victims gathered in a pyramid to mark the occasion.

Rising from the ruins

Beyazit was survived by four sons who, as Timur's vassals, were unable to practise fratricide until the old Mongol's return to Samarkand in 1403. Then

LEFT: a bloody version of the battle between the Turks and Crusaders, by Antonio Calza (1653–1725).
RIGHT: Ottoman miniature of acrobatic warriors.

the wars of succession began in earnest; after a decade of chaos, Beyazit's youngest son Mehmet I emerged as the victor. In 1421, his son, Murat II, ascended the throne and oversaw a steady rise in Ottoman fortunes. During his 30-year reign, the Ottomans reoccupied Anatolia, overran most of Greece and turned cannons on the walls of Constantinople for the first time.

But Murat also had a contemplative turn, and in 1444 renounced the throne in favour of his young son Mehmet II, the son of a Serbian princess, in order to retire to his palace at Manisa outside İzmir. After two years, however, he was obliged to return to the throne to deal with

the situation in the Balkans, where Hungarian King Ladislas and his heir, Hunyadi, in concert with the Wallachian prince Vlad III the Impaler (more familiar as Dracula), were gaining ground against the Ottomans. At the second Battle of Kosovo in 1448, Hunyadi and the Wallachians were crushed by Murat's forces. The only persistent threat thereafter was Albanian renegade Gjergj Kastrioti Skanderberg, who from 1443 until his death in 1468 preserved Albanian independence, which was only overcome in 1479.

The fall of Constantinople

In 1453, Constantinople had a population of scarcely 40,000, a shadow of Constantine's metropolis over 1,000 years earlier. The Byzantine

hinterland, which had once stretched from southern Iberia to the Caucasus, had been reduced to a few farms near the city walls. For two centuries the now-minuscule Byzantine "Empire" had been little more than a Turkish dependency, its princesses married into the harems of various sultans in a realpolitik attempt to maintain a fragile, often humiliating, independence. That the city would eventually fall to the Ottomans, especially with distractions like the Mongols now vanished, was a foregone conclusion.

Within months of Murat II's death and the subsequent ascension of his often wayward but talented son, Mehmet, in 1451, the final siege of the imperial city was under way. Mehmet marched his troops within sight of the Byzantine walls before building the castle of Boğaz Kesen ("Throat Cutter"; now known as Rumeli hisarı) on the upper Bosphorus, equipping it with heavy ordnance never seen before in eastern warfare. Pairing it with the earlier castle of Anadoluhisarı on the Asian side of the straits, Mehmet had effectively cut off any aid to the threatened city via the Black Sea.

The Ottoman cannons were cast by Urban, a Hungarian renegade who had first offered his services in 1452 to the Byzantines. So impressed was Mehmet with his work that the young sultan made an order for a new cannon twice the size of that mounted at the Bosphorus castle, which had already sunk a Venetian ship attempting to run the blockade. This new "toy" was so heavy that the bridges between Edirne and Constantinople had to be reinforced before the monstrosity could be transported to within firing range of the city walls.

> *The fall of Constantinople in 1453 is one of the most significant dates in European history, with far-reaching consequences. By disrupting trade and thus information, from the near east, and in encouraging Byzantine scholars to move west, it is likely to have spurred the Renaissance.*

Such fortifications and new armaments contravened existing treaties, but when the last Byzantine emperor, Constantine XI Palaiologos, protested, Mehmet beheaded his envoys. Urban's cannons menaced the walls of Byzantine, and a Turkish fleet – previous attempts to take the city had failed largely through lack of an Ottoman navy – materialised in the Sea of Marmara. The only reinforcements to run the Turkish blockade were 700 Genoese under the command of Giovanni Giustinani, and nine Venetian merchantships (and their crew) at anchor in the Golden Horn, which were transformed into warships. A company of Catalans, some Cretan sailors and numerous Turks under the pretender Orhan also rallied to the emperor's defence.

The siege formally began on 6 April, with Mehmet demanding complete and unconditional surrender. The soon-to-be last Byzantine emperor's reply, in equally formal manner, was that it was Mehmet who had made the decision to break the

waves of attackers and patching up gaping holes in the walls as soon as they were formed.

On 29 May 1453, Mehmet ordered the final assault, promising his men the traditional three days of plunder and rapine to boost their flagging morale. Ranks of Ottoman soldiers, accompanied by the roar of cannons and the crash of

As all hope was lost, the last emperor of Constantinople was seen discarding his royal insignia and plunging into onrushing hordes of janissaries; his body was never found.

peace, and that God would favour the righteous. There was to be neither surrender nor mercy.

As Mehmet's cannons and siege machinery battered away at the city's walls, teams of oxen dragged Ottoman boats over the hill behind Pera and down into the Golden Horn, where this fleet opened up another front against the low harbour walls, stretching the limited number of defenders even further. Still the Christians held on, outnumbered seven to one by the Sultan's army of nearly 90,000. Giustinani and his men performed military miracles by throwing back successive

cymbals, stormed the walls, scenting imminent victory. First the shock troops fought and fell back, then regulars, then line after line of the sultan's well-rested janissaries waded through the human debris in their path to test the ultimate resolve of the city's exhausted defenders. Finally, the Genoese commander, Giustinani, fell mortally wounded, and with him, the whole resistance collapsed. The once-magnificent Byzantine Empire was no more.

Mehmet the Conqueror entered the city in imperial style, wearing a majestic turban and riding on a white stallion. The sultan held prayers at Aya Sofya, which was immediately turned into a mosque. Constantinople was soon renamed İstanbul (an elision of the Greek "Stin Poli"). ❑

LEFT: a magnificent, gilded Ottoman battleaxe, inscribed with the word "Ali". **ABOVE:** medieval painting of Constantinople, now İstanbul.

SÜLEYMAN THE MAGNIFICENT

This influential sultan excelled in many roles: as conqueror, statesman, legislator and patron of the arts. This was the golden age of the Ottomans

ABOVE: twenty-nine painters (half of them Europeans) worked in th Palace Studio, producing many albums of miniature paintings depicting Ottoman military campaigns and court life.

The most famous and powerful of the Ottoman rulers, Süleyman inherited the throne at the age of 26, and reigned for 46 years (1520–66). Painted portraits offer varying pictures of him, but memoirs and historical records are more consistent about his appearance. He was "tall, broad-shouldered", had a "long graceful neck… aquiline nose… dark hazel eyes… fair skin, auburn hair, beetling eyebrows… long arms and hands."

The young sultan immediately proved himself to be a man of many parts – and many titles. The Europeans dubbed him "the Magnificent", even during his reign; he preferred the title "Kanuni" (lawgiver). His ground-breaking *Kanun-i Osmani* (Ottoman legal code) reconciled judgements of the nine preceding sultans with each other, and Islamic law, to establish a comprehensive judicial system with a guarantee of equal justice for all and a measure of leniency in the penal code.

As caliph and ruler of Islam's holiest places, Süleyman consolidated the Sunni Supremacy over the Shia, while his skill as a military strategist more than doubled the size of his empire.

At home, he was a great patron of the arts: architecture, painting, calligraphy, illumination, weaponry, tiles and textiles, woodwork, metalwork and literature all flourished during his reign. He himself was an accomplished goldsmith and a fine poet whose collected works furnished many proverbs.

ABOVE: Süleyman's architect, Sinan, designed some of Turkey's greatest buildings, including the Süleymaniye Mosque.

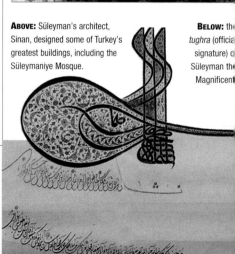

BELOW: th *tughra* (officia signature) o Süleyman th Magnificent

RIGHT: Henry VIII and Elizabeth I of England, Ivan the Terrible of Russia, Francis I of France and Holy Roman Emperor Charles V were all contemporaries of Süleyman.

AN OVERLY UXORIOUS RULER

Until Süleyman, Ottoman sultans traditionally did not marry, enjoying instead large and fruitful harems. But this father of eight sons and one daughter fell in love with and married one of his originally Ukrainian concubines, Roxelana, later known as Hürrem. During their 25-year marriage, it is thought that Süleyman remained monogamous.

Hürrem was clever and ambitious, the first of many generations of harem women to involve themselves in palace politics. Five of Süleyman's sons died in infancy or adolescence, but she was determined to keep the succession path clear for her favourite but useless son, Selim.

She persuaded the sultan to order and then witness the execution first of his capable, well-liked heir-apparent by a previous liaison, Mustafa, and then (after strife between Selim and Beyazıt) her son Beyazıt and Beyazıt's four sons. All were strangled with a silken bow as it was illegal to shed royal blood.

ABOVE AND LEFT: Süleyman's dagger and gold flask with dragon-head spout, rubies and emeralds, in the Topkapı Palace. **BELOW:** even the clothes worn by the royal family were works of art, lavishly embroidered with silk, and gold and silver thread.

ABOVE: Süleyman's naval forces totally dominated the Mediterranean, while his armies swept east, northwest and south across three continents.

THE DECLINE AND FALL OF THE OTTOMANS

After the "golden age" under Süleyman the Magnificent, the next 350 years were downhill all the way

The Ottoman Empire reached its zenith, not only territorially but also in administration and culture during the reign of Sultan Süleyman the Magnificent (r. 1520–66; *see pages 54–5*). But beginning with his successor Selim II, "the Sot", a slow, steady decline set in. Institutions which had once contributed to imperial glory could not adapt successfully. The sultans themselves, with a few exceptions, were mediocre, and the empire's fate depended increasingly on the competence of his Grand Vizier, essentially a prime minister chosen from amongst the top janissaries.

Corrupt janissaries and warlords

Deterioration began with the debasement of the janissary recruitment tradition (*see panel, page 49*) and the system of land tenure. Both the janissary command and palace management had originally been in the hands of the most promising recruits in the annual *devşirme* or levy, rounded up from among Christian village youths. They were sent to İstanbul, converted to Islam, and put through rigorous training which ensured their absolute loyalty to the sultan. Other boys were settled with Turkish families in

> By the 18th century, janissaries had become proverbial for their loucheness and indiscipline – "swears like a drunken janissary" was a favourite late-Ottoman locution.

the provinces, learning a trade and the Muslim way of life before joining the janissary ranks.

The janissary system eventually became corrupted when free Muslims were allowed to join, marry and pursue an independent trade whilst rarely showing up for military duty. Numbers swelled as sons of existing members rushed to sign up to an easy sinecure, and there were frequent mutinies to exact more money both from the sultan and from commoners. The originally subservient slave corps soon in fact became power brokers in the capital, and committed the first regicide to taint Ottoman history.

Osman II (1618–22), unhappy with the listless performance of his troops during his unsuccessful Polish campaign, decided to counter janissary domination by forming an Asian and Egyptian conscript army. Upon learning of the scheme, the janissaries revolted, beheaded the Grand Vizier and forced the young sultan to ride on a broken-down nag amid insults, before raping and then strangling him in the dreaded Yedikule (Seven Towers) prison. When the hapless Selim III (1789–1808) attempted a near-identical reform, he too was deposed and murdered.

Meanwhile, land grants to the *sipahis* (regular cavalry) also became hereditary rather than meritocratic, generating a caste of local warlords known as *derebeys* (lords of the valley). Their revolts and depredations devastated Anatolia, beginning a long-standing pattern of rural depopulation.

"Infidel" supremacy

For centuries, the Ottomans had grown wealthy by controlling vital trade routes to the east – the Silk Road overland from China, and the sea lanes from India through the Red Sea to the eastern Mediterranean, which in many ways had become a Turkish lake. Indeed, one of the motivations of Christopher Columbus in sailing west was to find a way to China and India which avoided Turkish fleets. His success in discovering the New World and Vasco da Gama's later voyage around the Cape of Good Hope to India were unmitigated disasters for the Ottomans. Not only did they lose their grip on trade routes to the Orient, but the shiploads of silver and gold flooding into Europe from the New World effectively debased the Ottoman currency.

Additionally, the Europeans' daring voyages gave new importance to naval, geographical and military science – and better ships, captains, navigation and guns meant "infidel" victories. Inexorably, the Europeans took control first of the Atlantic, then the Indian Ocean and finally the Mediterranean. The Ottoman conquest of Cyprus in 1571 and their successful siege (1648–69) of Candia on Crete said far more about Venetian weakness than Ottoman strength. Within months of the fall of Cyprus, a grand coalition of Spain, the Papal states, Genoa and Venice sunk a Turkish fleet at Lepanto in the Gulf of Corinth, ending notions of Ottoman invincibility.

The Islamic astronomical and mathematical heyday of the 8th to the 11th centuries had become a thing of the past, with fundamentalist Islamic jurisprudence inhibiting further intellectual growth. This contrasted sharply with a

Europe rapidly emerging from the Middle Ages into the Renaissance. Thinkers, freed from religious dogma, were making huge advances in scientific discovery, philosophical speculation and technology. Even the printing press, already used for 250 years in Europe, was only allowed by the Islamic clergy in 1727.

As the once-formidable empire crumbled from within, formerly cowed rivals were eager to nibble away at the edges. The 1606 Peace of Žitava gave Hungary to the Habsburgs, while the second Ottoman siege of Vienna (1683) – a major turning point in East–West relations – failed even more ignominiously than the first

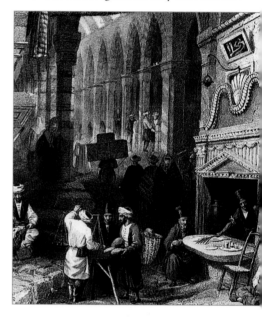

THE KAFES

After Mehmet III (r. 1595–1603) set a grisly record in the macabre power struggles which attended each new succession by killing all 19 of his brothers (some still infants), as well as most of his sisters, the attitude towards fratricide changed. Ahmet I (r. 1603–17) initiated a new system: once the oldest male of the dynasty ascended the throne, other heirs-apparent were kept in luxurious captivity in the so-called Kafes (Cage), accompanied only by eunuchs, women and occasional tutors who reported their every move. Many potential sultans became deranged by this treatment; Ibrahim I "the Mad" (r. 1640–8) drowned 280 harem women in a fit of jealousy.

LEFT: a European idea of a janissary execution. Most Western images of the Turks involved violence or sex. **RIGHT:** Istanbul's Grand Bazaar in Ottoman times.

one. Russia gained the Crimea and parts of the Black Sea northern shore in the Treaty of Küçük Kaynarca (1774); Napoleon invaded Ottoman Egypt in 1789, although nominal Ottoman control of the region was re-established by 1801. Although the Ottomans remained a force to be reckoned with in their core territory, ejecting the Venetians from their last strongholds on the Greek peninsula in 1715, and checking the Aegean naval invasion of Catherine the Great's favourite Count Orloff in 1771, these were brief retrenchments. Moldavia and Wallachia became autonomous principalities (1829), while Greece emerged as an independent kingdom (1832).

Crimea and capitulations

Throughout the 19th century, the empire's balance of trade went haywire as the Industrial Revolution that was transforming Western Europe turned Turkey into a source of cheap raw materials and a market for manufactured European products; domestic commercial concessions granted to the West worsened the situation. Not only were the postal service, urban street cars, electricity generation and railway network managed by foreigners, but legal privileges known as the Capitulations meant that any foreigner who asked for the protection of a foreign consulate could not be tried in an Ottoman court.

ORIENTALIST FANTASY

By the 18th century, Europe had lost its fear of the "Turk", while increased trade and colonial expansion created a market among eager collectors. Images of Turkey began to appear in European music, art and literature: in works such as Mozart's opera *Abduction from the Seraglio*; in paintings such as Jean-Baptiste Vanmour's *A Turkish Hunting Party* (1711), *The Death of Sardanapulus* (1827–28) by Delacroix, Ingres's *The Great Odalisque* (1814) and *The Turkish Bath* (1862); and in romantic literature typified by Byron's *Childe Harold's Pilgrimage* with its pashas and harems, Coleridge's *Kubla Khan* (1816) and Edward Fitzgerald's *The Rubaiyat of Omar Khayyam* (1859).

The Ottoman economy was further disrupted by the Crimean War (1853–56), fought in an alliance with the British and French against Russia. This bloody war, which began with a dispute over the Holy Land (and, more broadly, by Russian expansionism), was characterised by inept strategy, most famously depicted in Lord Tennyson's *The Charge of the Light Brigade*. It is also inspired two English women – Florence Nightingale and Mary Seacole – to establish war hospitals in İstanbul based on modern nursing practice.

Massive borrowing at high interest rates led to state bankruptcy in 1873, and – in a further indication of the way the wind was blowing – the empire came under Western financial supervision with the establishment of the Public Debt Administration in 1881. Despite various attempts at reform during the latter part of the 19th century, territorial losses continued.

> Ottoman railways were notoriously circuitous in their routing – not because the German contractors were paid by the kilometre, as myth asserts, but because of a desire to protect them from naval bombardment.

Reform attempts

Reform of the Ottoman Empire began in earnest with Sultan Mahmut II (1808–39). In 1826, he replaced the decadent janissary corps with a Western-trained, standing army. After obtaining the support of the Muslim clerics, the sultan asked each janissary battalion to spare 150 men for the new planned force; the janissaries refused and overturned their soup kettles in the traditional signal of revolt. But forces loyal to Mahmut opened fire from the Seraglio, and 4,000 janissaries were killed in their barracks. Thousands were slaughtered in the streets of İstanbul and in the provinces as a general purge began.

Next the sultan schooled French-speaking bureaucrats who staffed a formal diplomatic corps and civil service. The Tanzimat edict of 1839 established (in principle) orderly tax collection, fair and regular conscription, and equal treatment in law for non-Muslims.

Yet notions of "equality" held little attraction for many Ottomans, and was resisted fiercely by non-Muslims, who until then had been exempt from military service. As prosperous tradesmen and farmers – often under foreign protection – they were loath to interrupt business for the sake of a lengthy period of national service.

First constitution and the "Young Turks"

In 1876, the Ottoman Empire adopted its first written constitution, just as one of its most controversial sultans, Abdülhamid II (1876–1909), came to the throne. Meanwhile, the growing pan-Slavic movement in the Balkans culminated in a

disastrous 1877–8 war instigated by Russia, which resulted in an autonomous or independent Bulgaria, Romania and Montenegro, while the British annexed Cyprus and the Russians much of northeastern Anatolia. Muslim refugees flooded into western Anatolia as some of the Ottomans' richest hinterland was lost. The crisis prompted Abdülhamid to suspend the new constitution, dissolve parliament and rule autocratically for the next 30 years. The sultan's autocracy (and industrious secret police) inevitably fomented opposition, and a clandestine society, the Committee for Union and Progress (CUP), emerged, intending to restore constitutional rule.

In 1908, in the so-called "Young Turk" Revolution, the CUP-infiltrated army revolted in Salonika, forcing the sultan to schedule elections and reconvene parliament. The following year, after a botched counter-revolution, Abdülhamid II was forced to abdicate in favour of his brother Mehmet V (1909–18). Although at first ostensibly democratic and reformist, the CUP – which had the most deputies in the new parliament – became increasingly militarist and nationalist, almost a foregone conclusion given the traumas of the Italian seizure of Tripolitania and the Dodecanese islands (1911–12) and the Balkan Wars (1912–13), which saw most Ottoman possessions in Europe lost to Bulgaria, Serbia and Greece. Only eastern Thrace was saved.

LEFT: the Sultan Ahmet (Blue) mosque.
RIGHT: Sultan Abdülhamid II – the first Ottoman ruler to be photographed.

All through Abdülhamid's reign, European powers vied to establish influence on the "sick man of Europe", cajoling and threatening by turns. The most successful suitor was Germany, itself a newly formed nation-state. Military delegations, trade and projects like the Berlin-to-

> "I am not ordering you to attack; I am ordering you to die," Mustafa Kemal lectured his troops at Gallipoli. Struck near the heart by shrapnel during the fighting, his life was saved by a pocket watch.

Baghdad and Hejaz railways were used to woo the Ottomans to the imperial German side as Great Power rivalry cranked up in the early years of the new century.

World War I

When war broke out in August 1914, the Ottomans hesitated, while the English promptly seized two warships being built for the Ottoman fleet under public subscription in Turkey. Germany adroitly exploited this by running two warships through an Allied Mediterranean blockade and "donating" them to the Ottomans. With a change of flag but not of crew, the new "Turkish" warships sailed across the Black Sea to launch shells at Russian ports in the Crimea. To the chagrin

of many in İstanbul, Ottoman Turkey officially became a Central Power in November.

Still reeling from humiliating defeats by the Italians and Balkan alliances, Turkey was scarcely prepared for war. The British ousted the last Ottoman khedive of Egypt in 1914, and the former province became a major base for English activities in the Middle East, including the Arab uprising against Ottoman rule, led in part by T.E. Lawrence. Meanwhile, to the northeast, the forces of tsarist Russia pressed inexorably west as far as Erzurum. The only comfort came from the northwest, when Bulgaria entered the war on the Central side in October 1915, which allowed direct rail supply from Austria.

Gallipoli

Aside from defeating the British at Mesopotamian Kut, the only successful Ottoman military action during the war was the 8-month defence of the Dardanelles in 1915, where the combined French, British and Australian–New Zealand (ANZAC) forces had landed at Gallipoli. A certain Colonel Mustafa Kemal (later known as Atatürk, *see page 83*), chief deputy of German commander Liman von Sanders, oversaw a brilliant but brutal defence for the Ottomans, winning a heroic reputation that subsequently served him well when he started building the Republic of Turkey.

Armenian casualties

On all other fronts disaster followed disaster. The situation in the remote eastern provinces, where many Armenian nationalists sided with tsarist Russia or France on the promise of future independence, was especially critical. By now the CUP had become effectively a military triumvirate run by Cemal Paşa, Talat Paşa and Enver Paşa (who had lost an entire army to intense cold and the Russians). Early in the war (and even before) this junta decided that Christian Ottoman subjects constituted a disloyal fifth column and had to be neutralised accordingly. Already in early 1914, nearly half a million Greek Orthodox had been massacred or deported from the Aegean regions in revenge for the ethnic cleansing of Turks during the Balkan wars.

On 24 April 1915, the CUP authorities ordered the deportation of all Armenian civilians, except those in İzmir and İstanbul, and the disarming of all Armenians in the Ottoman army. Over the next ten months, hundreds of thousands were rounded up and marched towards detention camps in Mesopotamia; few made it there, the majority being killed at the outset or falling victim to disease or starvation. The world Armenian community – and many neutral historians – assert that at least a million were killed; Turkish advocates hotly dispute the existence of any deliberate extermination, and admit at most 300,000 casualties under "wartime conditions" – while pointing to nearly half a million Turkish civilian deaths, many of these at the hands of Armenian militias in eastern Anatolia. The Suriyani communities of southeastern Anatolia, similarly accused of throwing in their lot with the British, fared little better.

ent Armenia was soon overrun by Soviet forces and assimilated into the USSR, until it finally achieved independence in 1991.

The end of the empire

When the Ottomans capitulated with the signing of the Mudros Armistice on 30 October 1918, the once-proud empire was but a shadow of its former self. The 1920 Treaty of Sèvres recognised the British occupation of Iraq and Palestine, while Syria (including Lebanon) was ceded to France under the League of Nations' mandate system. Controversially, independent Armenian, Suriyani and Kurdish states were envisioned in the eastern

Whatever the truth of these competing assertions, Anatolia emerged from a decade (1913–23) of war largely bereft of its entrepreneurial Christian population, which early 20th-century censuses had estimated at well over 2 million. Fighting between the Turks and the fledgling Armenian republic (which had emerged in 1918) only ended with the Treaty of Alexandropol in 1920, which spelled the end of the Armenians' dream of their own independent state. Demilitarised, what was left of independ-

provinces. Not even central Anatolia was sacred, thanks to secret wartime agreements made amongst the Allies. Eastern Thrace and much of the Aegean was given to Greece, while Italy and France were assigned "spheres of influence" along the Mediterranean coast. The Dardanelles, Bosphorus and Constantinople were placed under "international control". After almost six centuries the reign of the Ottomans was over.

It took the crushing ignominy of military defeat, invasion by Greece and one man in the right place and time to foster the emergence of a modern Turkish nation-state from the ashes of empire. The place was a Black Sea port, the time May 1919, and the man Mustafa Kemal, hero of Gallipoli. ❑

LEFT: a Pera bar girl before World War I.
ABOVE: the Ottoman army had just two victories in World War I – at Gallipoli in 1915, and against the British at Mesopotamian Kut in 1916.

THE REPUBLICAN ERA

With the end of World War I and the collapse
of the Ottoman Empire, the stage was set
for the rise of Atatürk's republic

Joining the wrong side in World War I cost
the Ottoman Empire millions of lives and
huge chunks of territory. As far as the van-
quished Ottoman empire was concerned, the
victors dispensed with US President Wilson's
Fourteen Points for peace and national self-
determination. The Treaty of Sèvres that the sultan's representatives were forced to sign in May
1920 was merely a redrafting of secret wartime
protocols for the empire's dismemberment.

In late 1918 the British became the main garrison force in İstanbul, still the Ottoman capital,
while the Bosphorus and Dardanelles straits,
sought for centuries by Russia as a gateway to
ice-free seas, were "internationalised" by the terms
of the treaty. The Armenians and the Kurds were
granted their own states in eastern Anatolia, as
were the Pontian Greeks on the eastern Black Sea
coast, but none survived the establishment of the
new Turkish republic just four years later. Having
had their short-lived homeland taken away from
them, the Kurds have continued to fight for their
independence (*see pages 67, 78, 369*).

The French occupied parts of southeast Turkey, while the Mediterranean coast between
Bodrum and Antalya – opposite the Dodecanese
which they had already seized – went to the Italians. Meanwhile, the Greeks, ably represented by
Eleftherios Venizelos at the Versailles peace conference, were after a bigger prize – a state straddling two continents and reuniting the ancient
Ionian colonies with the motherland. Greece
was subsequently given eastern Thrace, and,
more importantly, the principal Aegean port of
Smyrna (İzmir) with its rich hinterland.

This wholesale dismembering of the Ottoman empire left Turkey as a small rump state,
perceived by many as a national humiliation.

The War of Independence

The Greek landing at Smyrna on 15 May 1919
goaded latent Turkish patriotism and resentment into action. Four days later Mustafa
Kemal, the hero of Gallipoli, arrived at Samsun
on the Black Sea coast, ostensibly to supervise
the disbanding of patriotic militias which had
arose in defiance of the Allies. Once safely away
from İstanbul, he renounced his commission
and set about converting these militias into a
proper nationalist army. Two ideological conferences convened in deepest Anatolia promulgated the so-called National Pact – which
demanded an independent Turkey with viable
borders, and abolition of foreign privileges. On
23 April 1920, the nationalists formed the first

Grand National Assembly in Ankara, following the forcible British closure of the last Ottoman parliament.

The beleaguered nationalist army had to fight a multi-front war against the Armenians, the French, the Italians, and most dangerously

> The obligatory adoption of surnames in 1934 elicited patriotic ones often at odds with reputations – as one wag put it, the laziest chose Çalışkan (Industrious) while those with Armenian grandparents opted for Öztürk (True Turk).

the Greeks, whose expeditionary armies had by late 1920 driven deep into Anatolia over French and Italian objections. The only aid came from the new Soviet Union and contributions from Asian Muslims. But in August 1921, the 22-day-long Battle of Sakarya, fought west of Ankara, turned the tide of the war; the Greeks' failure to capture Ankara doomed their occupation. Impressed by Kemal's leadership (and resenting augmented Greek power), the French and Italians soon came to terms with the nationalists and withdrew; only the British still supported the Greek adventure.

The Greeks dug in, but exactly a year later Kemal commanded the decisive counterattack at Dumlupınar, west of Afyon. The bulk of the Greek army was annihilated; its commander-in-chief was taken prisoner; and the ragged remnants were chased back to İzmir, fleeing in waiting boats. The liberation of İzmir on 9 September 1922 was followed within four days by a hugely destructive fire and massacres of Christians. The Greek army, supported by British divisions, remained intact in Thrace, and the threat of further war lingered until the 11 October armistice at Mudanya acknowledged the reality of the Greek defeat.

Establishing the republic

The Allies clumsily sent double invitations to peace talks in Lausanne, Switzerland: one to Sultan Mehmet VI, ruling İstanbul alone, one to the Ankara regime. Infuriated, the latter abolished the monarchy on 1 November 1922. Two

weeks later the last sultan boarded the British HMS *Malaya* under cover of darkness, bound for Malta and exile.

Turkey's sole delegate to the Lausanne conference was Atatürk's trusted confidant and general İsmet Paşa (latter İnönü). By his determined insistence on the National Pact *(see previous page)*, he succeeded in wearing down such eminent diplomatic adversaries as British Foreign Secretary Lord Curzon. The final treaty, signed in July 1923, completely negated Sèvres, endorsed the National Pact – and additionally stipulated the departure of most Muslims from Greece and Orthodox Christians from Anatolia, the first

DRASTIC REFORMS

In early 1924, the caliphate was abolished, religious courts closed, and members of the Ottoman court exiled. In response to the fundamentalist revolt in the east, all dervish orders were proscribed in late 1925 and their *tekkes* (lodges) closed down. In 1926, communal religious law was replaced by a uniform civil code, and the Gregorian calendar introduced. In 1928, Arabic script was supplanted by a Latin alphabet, and Arabic or Persian vocabulary dropped in favour of old-Turkish or French words. The fez and the turban were abolished, though the veiling of women was less easily halted. Women were given the franchise in 1934, and encouraged to compete with men professionally.

LEFT: site of the 1923 Conference of Lausanne.
RIGHT: Greeks escorting Turkish prisoners following the Greek landing at Smyrna, 15 May 1919.

regulated ethnic cleansing of the 20th century.

Kemal and his circle now embarked on the harder task of rebuilding a conflict-ravaged country. On 29 October 1923, the Grand National Assembly proclaimed the Republic of Turkey, with Ankara the capital. Its first president, inevitably, was Mustafa Kemal, and its first prime minister İsmet Paşa, leader of the newly founded Republican People's Party (CHP in Turkish) – for the next 57 years, a nursery for aspiring politicians, a medium for authoritarian government, and a laboratory for paternalistic, top-down social engineering.

Kemal and Co. wanted a radically Western-

ised new state, but existing institutions were unmistakably Eastern. Moreover, Turks historically regarded themselves more as an *ummah* (Muslim community) than a nation, and had shunned involvement in politics, industry or urban commerce, considered "infidel" activities unworthy of Ottoman gentlemen. The new regime faced the daunting tasks of creating a national consciousness, absorbing Western civilisation and reinterpreting Islam.

Social reform by fiat was easy; the Kemalists had more mixed results in the economic sphere. With the departure of the Christian business class, a new bourgeoisie had to be created from scratch. Investment banks were set up as early as 1925, but the 1929 crash and ensuing global

depression discredited capitalism in the eyes of Turkey's elite, who noted the apparent immunity of the Soviet economy from the catastrophe. Newly created state-run enterprises were crucial in an industrialisation modelled on Italian Fascism as well as Communism. Self-sufficiency and import substitution became the order of the day, with heavily subsidised mining, steel, cement, glass, textile and paper works promoted in the first Soviet-style Five-Year Development Plan (1934–9).

An end to isolation

Turkish foreign policy until the 1930s was isolationist and (except for a successful campaign to annexe French-held Hatay) non-interventionist. Though the CHP imitated aspects of authoritarian interwar regimes, it frowned on the aggressiveness and race-baiting of Nazism and Fascism. İsmet İnönü's accession as president upon Atatürk's death in late 1938 produced no major changes.

İnönü's main accomplishment was keeping Turkey out of the world war which erupted in 1939. This required not only skilled tightrope walking above the warring sides – using vaguely worded "treaties of friendship" – but an iron hand domestically. Although officially

> The 1946 visit to İstanbul of the battleship USS *Missouri was so providential for the beleaguered Turks that the authorities ordered the municipally run brothels open for free to the sailors.*

neutral, the country remained on a war footing economically, while supplying chromium ore to both sides, alternately sheltering or expelling Jewish refugees, and crawling with foreign agents of every description. Turkey declared war on Germany only in early 1945, just in time to qualify for UN membership.

Meanwhile, the honeymoon of the 1920s and early 1930s between Turkey and the Soviet Union had reverted to mutual hostility. In 1945, Moscow renewed demands for "international" control of the straits either side of the Sea of Marmara, and for the return of Kars and Ardahan districts on the Armeno-Georgian frontier, ceded in 1920. Given these threats, the offer in 1946 of American protection was eagerly accepted, a mutual courtship spurred by Turkey's sensing the value of a reliable, anti-Communist sponsor and America's delight at finding a malleable and strategic Middle Eastern client state. It led directly to Turkey's involvement in the Korean War (1950), admission to NATO (1952) and its controversial recognition of Israel.

First multi-party politics

Atatürk's rule had been viewed by many as autocratic from the start. In 1924, leading CHP figures defected to form the opposition Progressive Republican Party (PRP). It lasted barely six

Atatürk, formed the opposition Democrat Party (DP). Its platform comprised relaxed regulation of private enterprise, support for the neglected farming sector and more open religious observance, a combination which proved popular with an odd cross section of voters ranging from pious rural peasants to the emerging middle class. By 1950 the DP was in power, with Bayar as president and Menderes as prime minister.

Erratic progress

Copious American economic and military aid under auspices of the Truman Doctrine, in part a reward for apparent democratisation, lent a

months, when the Kurdish-Islamic revolt in the east took months to suppress and gave Atatürk an excellent pretext to ban it in the interests of unity. In 1926, after a plot to assassinate him was uncovered, many former PRP deputies and surviving CUP members were accused of involvement and hanged. Barring another brief experiment with an opposition party in 1930, the CHP monopolised power until 1950.

In 1946, a group of expelled CHP members, including lawyer-landowner Adnan Menderes and Celâl Bayar, a banker and ex-associate of

markedly pro-American tone to DP-era development. In return, Turkey granted the United States extensive military facilities – including

> *Three decades after his hanging, Menderes was rehabilitated by solemn reburial in a mausoleum in İstanbul, and the naming of numerous streets and facilities (including İzmir's airport) after him.*

bases for missiles, later dismantled as part of the negotiations ending the Cuban crisis.

Domestically, populist incentives to free enterprise led to chaotic expansion. More

LEFT: İsmet İnönü, close associate of Atatürk and second president of the Republic. **ABOVE:** Celâl Bayar addresses a Democrat Party election rally.

tractors to farmers boosted production and exports, but massive imports of foreign goods and overly generous rural loans and public spending left the country with a huge trade deficit and national debt leading to repeated currency devaluations. Although re-elected in 1954 and 1957, the DP became increasingly repressive, censoring the press, winding up the CHP and instigating anti-Greek pogroms in İstanbul amidst the first Cyprus crisis. Menderes was finally deposed on 27 May 1960 in a widely popular military coup, then convicted and hung by a military tribunal, along with two of his ministers.

For 16 months, Turkey was run by a National Unity Committee which drafted a new, more liberal constitution. Free elections resumed, the right to strike was confirmed, and Turkey's first socialist party appeared. Members of the now-banned DP enrolled in the newly formed Justice Party (JP), whose chief Süleyman Demirel began a political career spanning 37 years. In 1965 and again in 1969, the JP took power with promises of free-market policies and unimpeded foreign investment.

Descent into chaos

The late 1960s saw an explosion of left-wing activism which continued into the next decade, while political polarisation prompted a low-key 1971 military intervention. The 1973 elections forced Bülent Ecevit's CHP into a coalition with Necmettin Erbakan's National Salvation Party – the first appearance on the national stage for political Islam.

Hoping for a clear parliamentary majority after his Cyprus action *(see panel, below left)*, Ecevit sought early re-election. But far-right forces outflanked him, taking power in April 1975 as a coalition featuring Demirel's Justice Party and Alpaslan Türkeş's neo-Fascist National Action Party (MHP). Thereafter, things degenerated markedly, with the economy hamstrung by shortages, inflation and huge debt, while sectarian and political violence left some 5,000 dead by 1980 and the country on the verge of civil war.

On 12 September, the generals struck again, intent on a more thorough overhaul than in past coups. General Kenan Evren and other military commanders formed the notorious National Security Council, which assumed absolute power. All political parties were shut down and their leaders detained. Tens of thousands of suspected "terrorists" were tried in military courts, with 25 executed for major crimes and massacres, though the radical right and Islamists suffered far less than Marxists, trade unionists, professors and other left-leaning intellectuals. The universities were purged and a new, restrictive constitution promulgated.

From Özal to the crash

General elections were held in November 1983, but with all pre-coup parties and their leaders banned. The surprise, landslide winner among just three parties allowed to campaign was Turgut Özal's ANAP (Motherland Party), a rather

broad group encompassing everyone from economic liberals to Islamists. Özal, a Texas-trained
engineer, charismatic speaker and adherent of
the still-clandestine Nakşibendi dervish order,
embodied its inherent contradictions. There
was a sudden relaxation of trade restrictions, a

> Turgut Özal remains a controversial figure –
> a hero for many as one who opened up the
> country more than anyone since Menderes,
> despised by others for his nepotism and toler-
> ation of sharp practice.

succeeded by Demirel, who handed the DYP
reins to American-trained economics professor
Tansu Çiller. She initially raised hopes as the
first female Turkish prime minister, but her
leadership proved shambolic, dogged by pervasive corruption and coalition infighting.

The immediate beneficiary of this was Necmettin Erbakan's latest Islamicist party, Refah
(Welfare); within a few months he was top dog
in an improbable coalition with Çiller, but in
June 1997 was nudged out of office by discreet
military machinations, having accomplished
little other than closing Turkey's 79 casinos, a
mecca for mafiosi foreign and domestic. Refah

provocative influx of foreign luxury goods, and
encouragement of large, export-orientated enterprises. Enormous sums were spent on developing tourist infrastructure, and foreign investment
was welcomed. Inflation and public budgets
soared, as did corruption, but given overall
economic growth, opportunities existed.

By 1990, four major opposition parties had
emerged – Demirel's DYP, Erdal (son of İsmet)
İnönü's SHP, and the resurgent CHP and DSP –
which soon formed various coalitions to eclipse
ANAP. Özal, now president, died in April 1993,

(and Erbakan) were soon proscribed and, in the
Turkish way, a successor party – Fazilet (Virtue)
– immediately emerged.

The Kurdish question

Denied their own state after 1922, the question of
Kurdish independence has been a long-standing
problem for the Turkish government, particularly with the formation of the PKK militia in the
late 1970s (see pages 78, 369). In November 1998,
Kurdish separatist leader Abdullah Öcalan was
finally captured in Kenya and tried (like Menderes) on a remote island in the Sea of Marmara,
signalling the winding down of the PKK insur-
gency. Many Turks, especially those who had lost
relatives serving as soldiers, supported his death

LEFT: Bülent Ecevit and Süleyman Demirel.
ABOVE: the former prime minister Turgut Özal, who
went on to become president.

sentence, but with the eyes of Europe on Turkey, this was commuted to life imprisonment.

Towards the millennium, earthquakes literal and metaphorical rocked the country. In the small hours of 17 August 1999, a Richter 7.4 shock with İzmit as the epicentre crippled the country's industrial heartland. Aside from an estimated 25,000 dead, and the exposure of massive local corruption permitting erection of shoddy blocks of flats, the quake had less predictable but more positive consequences. The military, which looked after its own barracks first rather than aid rescue operations, had its reputation irretrievably tarnished. Greek

rescuers were among the first foreign teams on the scene, and sympathy led to a *rapprochement* between Turkey and Greece.

In May 2000, President Demirel's attempt to change his permitted term of office from one 7-year to two 5-year spans failed and he was replaced by Turkey's senior judge, Ahmet Necdet Sezer, whose single term was distinguished by his respect for the law and limits to presidential powers.

At the millennium the Turkish economy was in free fall, with numerous spectacular bank failures and implosion of the currency from late 2000 through early 2001. World Bank economist Kemal Derviş was appointed Minister of Economy with extraordinary powers, stabilising the situation – along with an IMF aid package. The harsh winnowing of the banking sector meant that the 2008 financial crisis was less severe in Turkey than in most other countries.

The AK Era

By summer 2002, yet another rickety left-right secularist coalition – headed by Ecevit's DSP – was on the rocks, prior to November elections which the AK (Justice and Development) Party, born out of the ashes of the Refah and Fazilet Parties, won by a landslide, forming the first non-coalition government since 1987 (the only parliamentary opposition was the CHP). Although nominally Islamist, the AK proved to be a competent economic manager, with inflation reduced to single digits and tourism a steady earner despite the Iraq invasion and occasional terror attacks. The AK, which tended to be supported by devout Muslims, threatened to outflank the "White Turks" (mostly of Balkan descent) comprising the army, academia, civil service, big business and much of the media, who had run the country since 1923.

The year 2007 began with the assassination of prominent Turko-Armenian journalist Hrant Dink (*see page 75*) before a political crisis erupted when the AK nominated their foreign minister Abdullah Gül as candidate for president (normally recruited from the secular establishment). The military posted an online warning, the so-called "e-coup", hinting they might act if Gül was chosen by parliament. Millions of secularists took to the streets in orchestrated rallies againt Gül's candidacy and what they saw as creeping Islamisation, yet the AK's gamble of early elections on 22 July paid off with an enhanced majority, and Gül became president.

The biggest issue of the AK's second term has been the Egkenekon conspiracy, whose first defendants were sent to trial in late 2008. A group of high-ranking generals, lawyers, nationalist politicians, journalists, academics and mafiosi stands accused of high-profile *provocateur* assassinations (including Dink's) and bombings of secularist institutions to create the impression of an Islamist threat that would justify a coup.

By 2010 the country was again predictably polarised, with the CHP recapturing most municipalities along the Aegean and Mediterranean coasts, traditional secularist strongholds. ❏

LEFT: commemorating Atatürk's birthday, 19 May.

The EU Debate

The hugely symbolic issue of EU membership has proved divisive; over a decade on, Turkey still waits to be admitted to the club

In December 2000, Turkey became an official candidate for EU membership, with accession negotiations formally underway in October 2005. For local advocates, it would be the culmination of Atatürk's westernization drive, and reorientation away from more obvious regional ties. Many Turkish intellectuals had long regarded membership as a just reward for past services to NATO, one that would grant the country protection against undemocratic rule. European observers, however, pointed out that three EU members – Spain, Portugal and Greece – with a history of unsavoury regimes had disposed of them and much of their legacy well before joining, and that more reform initiatives by Turkey were expected.

These began in earnest during summer 2002, when the moribund coalition passed legislation abolishing the death penalty, increasing (theoretically) media freedom and permitting education or broadcasting in several minority languages. Once the AK took office, the pace of EU-compliant reform accelerated. Objectionable clauses of the 1982, army-drafted constitution were tinkered with, though the nettle of a wholesale redrafting has yet to be grasped. PM Erdoğan, unlike many of his predecessors, seemed to understand just how seriously the Cyprus impasse was affecting Turkey's chances of membership, and accordingly supported the ill-fated UN Annan plan to re-unify the island. But although Turkish Cypriots voted two-to-one in favour, Greek Cypriots rejected it by a three-to-one margin – and still got to join the EU a week later on behalf of all Cyprus.

Yet even if the Cyprus issue gets resolved, and no matter how many remedial measures are implemented to address Turkey's chequered record on corruption, police practice, minority rights and freedom of expression, the main ostacle to membership will remain: much of Europe continues to regard Turkey as an alien, Islamic country inappropriate for a "white, Christian" club. Already Bulgaria and Romania, arguably as corrupt (and far less

wealthy), have "jumped the queue" in 2007, with Croatia set to follow shortly. Turkey would be second only to Germany in terms of population (and perhaps influence), despite its geographically uneven development; accordingly Germany, along with France and Austria, is the most hostile to Turkish membership, threatening binding referenda on the issue. The UK, and surprisingly Greece, are among Turkey's supporters, albeit for self-serving reasons – policing of illegal immigration (currently overwhelming Greece) would be shifted east, and a free-to-emigrate workforce from this demographically very young country would help prop up Europe's collapsing pension systems.

Indefinite deferral of membership or the spectre of outright rejection has prompted resentment within Turkey, where support for membership has dropped from 75 percent to under 50 percent. An "anti" backlash is being orchestrated by a secularist, ad hoc coalition of nationalists with a dim view of increased minority rights, 1960s-style leftists who consider the EU an imperialist plot, and the military brass and "deep-staters" who would no longer be able to run the country as before. It's inescapably ironic that a notionally Islamicist government did more to bring Turkey into line with EU norms than all previous secular coalitions. Reforms – and the accession process – have stalled since 2007, with the AK's declining electoral support a more likely reason than a lack of genuine commitment. ❑

RIGHT: Turkey's Foreign Minister Ahmet Davutogl.

MODERN TURKS: A QUEST FOR IDENTITY

With Turkey modernising rapidly, its people are poised between traditional rural values, liberal Islamicism and global capitalism

Ne *mutlu Türküm diyene!*" (Happy is he who calls himself a Turk!). This famous quotation from a 1927 speech of Atatürk's is still inscribed on monuments country wide. Despite its patriotic sentiment, however, its meaning is ambiguous in a country that has been inhabited for 9,000 years by many tribes and religions, voluntary settlers and refugees, which regards its origins as Asian but aspires to belong to Europe.

Older people steeped in republican ideology will profess vague ethnic kinship to the Turkic nomads who swept into Anatolia early in the last millennium. However, only a few thousand Turks imposed their civilisation and language on a much larger indigenous population. Deeper racial links between modern Turks and Central Asia are more fantastic than factual. Yet the concept lingers stubbornly in the Turkish self-image, a holdover from the time of Atatürk, when the state's founders scrambled to devise a new concept of nationhood which circumvented centuries of Ottoman rule. Only since the 1990s has Turkey acknowledged any value in the kaleidoscope of different ethnicities which have contributed to Anatolian culture.

The republican rewrite

After the collapse of the Ottoman Empire, the republic found it expedient to ignore the recent past and look further back for national heroes. During Atatürk's westernising social revolution, when the hat replaced the fez (itself a

PRECEDING PAGES: Isbank towers and workers in the business district of Levent, İstanbul. **LEFT:** students take a break in İstanbul. **RIGHT:** Atatürk demonstrating the Latin alphabet.

19th-century innovation) and a Latin alphabet supplanted Arabic script (deliberately divorcing contemporary Turks from 800 years of Ottoman history), all things Ottoman were reviled as retrograde; any identification with Muslim, much less Greek, culture was simply inadmissible.

Purported Asiatic ancestors, chosen according to transient intellectual trends (some uncomfortably close to Nazi dogma), included briefly the Sumerians and the Hittites, before the short-lived but glamorous Seljuk Turks were declared suitable national role models. The Huns and Mongols got honourable mentions too, which resulted in many boy-children named Selçuk, Attila and Cengiz (as in Khan): spectacular

PR blunders for a country seemingly oblivious to the last two's bloodcurdling reputation in Europe. At one point the Turkish language was deemed to be the mother-tongue of all others; such crackpot theories remained in school textbooks until the 1970s. All this betrayed a deep-seated insecurity and perhaps doubts that plain old Anatolian Turks – the word had been an Ottoman insult, connoting "rube" or "yokel" – deserved to be in the driver's seat.

Searching for a new outlook

Nearly a century later, Kemalist civic principles still (officially) guide the republic. Turkey's booming cities, new highways, vast dams, extensive tourism infrastructure and increasing involvement in the world economy – it is one of the G20 – can be at least partially credited to Atatürk's reforms. Unfortunately, the cult of personality developed after his death and the force-feeding of Kemalism has led to intellectual complacency that finds it easier to repeat clichés than explore changed realities and pose difficult but essential questions. Ideas designed to motivate 10 million Turks in the traumatic wake of World War I defeat are not necessarily appropriate for today's country of 71 million – and-counting – inhabitants.

PERCEPTIONS OF SELF AND OTHERS

Perceptions of Turkey abroad remain central to Turkish self-esteem. The 19th-century image of the Ottoman Empire as the "Sick Man of Europe" produced a palpable national inferiority complex, while post-World War I humiliation at the hands of the victorious Allies further aggravated sensitivities. Even well-intentioned attempts to voice justifiable criticism of Turkey may be met with extreme defensiveness. There is perpetual exasperation at being prejudicially represented in Western fiction (think *Pascali's Island*) and films (as in *Midnight Express*), while foreign news coverage – especially in the run-up to possible EU membership – is often sensational and poorly informed.

The republic is a diasporic ingathering par excellence, rivalled in this respect only by Israel: the explicit corollary to "Happy is he who calls himself a Turk" has been "A Turk is anyone willing to call themselves a Turk". This has included people from Macedonia, Bulgaria, Romania, the Crimea, Albania, Circassia, Bosnia, Daghestan and other far-flung locales, making a mockery of any theoretical common racial origin espoused by the more fanatical pan-Turkists.

Until the early 1990s, it was hazardous to admit to having (say) Kurdish, Armenian or

ABOVE: a village wedding in southeastern Turkey.
RIGHT: immigrant Armenian children participate in class.

Cretan background; now it's positively trendy among younger people looking to define themselves as pieces in a diverse cultural mosaic. But despite this, a law against "denigrating Turkishness" (a catch-all offence) remains in place, and the late journalist Hrant Dink, before his assassination by ultra-nationalists, attracted prosecution by proclaiming that he was "a Turkish citizen of Armenian descent" – still an unacceptable concept.

A globally aware population

Profound demographic change following both internal and overseas migration (and a certain

Although some conservatives (with little faith in the robustness of Turkish identity) bleakly warn of wholesale westernisation as a result, it's worth remembering that the late Ottoman Empire was adept at assimilating and adapting foreign styles. This continued under the republic in music as *aranjmanlar*, whether this meant tango à la Turca, Elvis Presley imper-

> Seventy percent of Turkey's people live in cities. Of a total population of over 71 million, more than half are aged under 25.

amount of foreign settlement) have helped change Turkey's view of itself in the world. Nearly 4 million Turks now live abroad, about 3 million of these in Europe, with almost 2 million in Germany alone. Foreign tourists continue to pour into Turkey, reaching the country's remotest corners; marriage with locals (something almost unknown before the 1960s) is on the rise. Turks travel and study abroad for short periods in ever-increasing numbers, watch imported (if dubbed) series on over 200 TV channels, speak more languages (especially English) and are positively glued to the internet – even if the authorities frequently block sites (like YouTube) deemed to have breached some lingering repressive law.

sonators, or Anatolian rock. There have recently been genuine, creative attempts at syntheses of foreign and Turkish styles, rather than merely imitation, not just in music but also fashion, art installations and film-making, replacing the derivativeness or ideological prescriptiveness of earlier republican efforts.

Growing pains

Unfortunately, this confident new profile masks deep divisions and disruptive factors within modern Turkey. Recent economic growth rates of 5 percent annually have occurred in one of the most unequal societies on earth. Some industrial magnates are worth billions, but a decent, trained-professional salary is barely 1,000 euros per month. The nationwide minimum monthly wage is supposedly 730TL (about 350 euros) – but, in general, pay scales remain dismal. Unem-

> The long-standing alliance with the US has cooled recently – participation in the second Iraq war was opposed by 90 percent of Turks, with cooperation restricted to allowing US warplanes to overfly Turkish airspace.

ployment is well into double figures, ensuring continued emigration, while unemployment

Education is another battleground, as public education is poor and the often superior Islamic secondary schools have been curtailed. Although tuition for universities and polytechnics – found in every sizeable town – is largely free, competitive entrance exams mean mainly young Turks from rich families attend expensive private cramming academies: thus a university attendance rate of under 10 percent for 18- to 22-year-olds.

Overall, economic development has not produced a genuinely independent civic society. Freedom of expression is still very conditional, with forcible closures of political parties, and

benefits are almost nonexistent. Meanwhile, the cost of many essentials equals that of much of Mediterranean Europe. Accordingly, nightclubs thronged with designer-clad youth and shops bulging with cutting-edge consumer durables can be provocative to some, with petty (and not so petty) crime on the increase.

The class gap remains vast, a chasm of mistrust separating secular urbanites in the west from those still rooted in provincial values even if no longer resident in the provinces. This has meant electoral success for various Islamist parties, the latest – the AK – having governed since 2002 only through pledging to preserve a secular state. The army's watchful eye has precluded any Iran-style fundamentalism.

frequent court cases against writers and intellectuals – including Yaşar Kemal and Orhan Pamuk, the country's best-known novelists, in 1995 and 2005 respectively. Set up, for example, an NGO to promote conscientious objector status as an alternative to mandatory military service and you'll quickly attract prosecution for "defaming the army's honour".

Turkish women

Stereotypes die hard: European art and literature have traditionally depicted oriental, Islamic

ABOVE: Kurdish women dance during a demonstration marking International Women's Day. **ABOVE RIGHT:** the veil is a relatively uncommon sight in modern Turkey.

women as docile creatures, clad in all-enveloping garments when not dancing before their master in transparent silks. As a result, some visitors are surprised to find Turkish women in a bar after a day's work at their chosen profession, be it civil servant, hotel staff, lawyer or doctor. How many wives do Turkish men have? One, legally, in this secular state – the Muslim tradition of four is illegal. Do women still wear head coverings? Some do, but this is often an assertion of national identity in defiance of a too-rapid and rather vulgar westernisation rather than a purely religious observation.

Winds of change: The major social upheavals of World War I and the subsequent War of Independence radically affected the status of Turkish women. Many began working in munitions factories, while wives and daughters of the elite became vocal supporters of the nationalists. Accordingly, female emancipation became one of the cornerstones of the republican reform project. The new civil code adopted in 1926 significantly altered traditional family life. Polygamy and religious marriage were abolished, a minimum age for civil marriage set, while divorce, right to inheritance and child custody became the prerogative of both sexes. Women also gained equality as witnesses in court; previously, under Islamic law, the testimony of two women was equal to a man's. Moreover, female suffrage applied to local elections in 1930, to parliamentary ones in 1934 – years before some European countries.

Theory and practice: But theory is one thing, practice another: the Islamic ethic concerning female submission to male authority still pervades much of modern Turkish society, particularly in rural areas: many urban Turkish women are appalled to see rural wives toiling in the kitchen after a day's labour in the fields while their husbands occupy the local teahouse. Recent changes to the civil code allow married women to keep their maiden name, work without their husband's permission, be the legal head of a household and get an equal split of communal property upon divorce, but alimony can be difficult to claim, given the vast amount of unregistered income in the country. Better-off Turkish women ensure their name appears on family property deeds; uneducated,

HAREM SCARUM

Following their conversion to Islam over 1,000 years ago, the Turks also adopted their practice of secluding women. The area of the house where men entertained guests became the *selamlık*; the part reserved for the women of the household, including daughters and aunts, was the *harem* (forbidden sanctuary). Enough is known about harem life to dismiss as laughable the common stereotype of it as a prison for sex slaves. The harem was, in fact, the domain of the first wife, whose permission was required before a husband could acquire extra wives – something exceptional rather than the rule outside of palace circles, as he would have to support (and

pay attention to) all wives equally. Women in upper-crust harems – notably at Topkapı Palace – were trained in the arts and religion, as well as in household management.

Women born into the upper echelons of society never went out except with a chaperone, and a facial covering; shopping was undertaken by slaves. Only shameless, infidel hussies appeared or performed uncovered in public; most of the great female café singers of late Ottoman times were Greek, Jewish or Armenian. This convention persisted well into republican years – Safiye Ayla, Atatürk's favourite performer, felt obliged to sing from behind a curtain at her 1932 debut.

sometimes illiterate rural women with scant understanding of their rights don't. Thus many remain in abusive marriages – divorce is still a scandal in religious circles, and often a woman's own family will not take her back if she leaves her husband.

There has been a recent upsurge in so-called "honour killings" – the doing away with young, or not so young, women who have supposedly brought shame on their families through extramarital relations, refusal of an arranged marriage or merely flirting with someone disapproved of by Papa. Time was that an underage male relative, thought less likely to serve a

long prison term, was delegated to carry out the murder; lately the offending female is "encouraged" to commit suicide by locking her in a room with weapon or poison until the deed is done. The official tally for such incidents of several hundred annually is an underestimate.

A matter of class: In remoter villages most women wear some kind of head covering, and moving to towns does not imply shedding such garb. Urban feminism tends to be the preserve of educated, well-off women, who disdain their more traditional sisters living nearby in working-to-lower-middle-class neighbourhoods. There, a spectrum of religious "fashion statements", in the main freely chosen, has emerged. At one extreme are wearers of the full, black

"body bag" (*çarşaf*), while the more moderate "raincoat brigade" favours patterned scarves and loose overcoats in pastel colours. Younger "new Islamic" women may wear bright, fashionable clothes covering the wrists and the ankles, but tight enough to show off their figures, with designer headscarves wrapped alluringly around their throats.

ETHNIC MINORITIES IN TURKEY

Since the Stone Age, Anatolia has been home to numerous races, cultures and faiths, many still found here today. Central Asian Turkish blood is a relatively new contribution to the melting pot. The Ottomans did not consider themselves as Turks, and by the 16th century were so intermixed (not least through a harem preference for Circassian or Slavic blonde women) that Asian roots were largely irrelevant. In general, Ottoman society was tolerant of different races and religions, though religion, not ethnicity, was one's mark of identity. But the authorities were not above setting *millets* against each other when it suited them to provoke tensions – for example after Orthodox Patriarch Gregory V was hanged by the sultan in 1821 for failing to quell the Greek revolution, his corpse was given to a group of Jews to desecrate and then thrown into the Bosphorus.

From 1984 onwards, the struggle between the Kurdish PKK insurrectionary militia and the state has loomed large in Turkish politics. The Kurds (*see below*), however, are not the only group whose identity has been suppressed in republican Turkey. Christian minorities such as the Greeks, Armenians and Suriyani often live precariously, quick to be condemned by nationalists as detrimental to the nation's security. The Alevîs, a Shi'ite Muslim sect (not an ethnic group; *see page 84*) who make up almost a quarter of Turkey's population, have also frequently been targeted for physical attack as well as scurrilous calumny. Additionally, the Sunni-dominated Ministry of Religious Affairs gives scant recognition or financial support for Alevî beliefs or social programmes.

The Kurds

Kurdish origins are obscure, but they have certainly inhabited the region between Syria, Iraq, Iran and eastern Turkey since antiquity. Some consider them descendants of the Medes, who dominated the Lake Van area after the collapse of Urartian civilisation. Others maintain they are the Karduchi encountered in 401 BC by the Greek historian-general Xenophon, who described them as a "freedom-loving mountain people".

Kurds identify themselves by clan, within larger tribes headed by powerful *ağas* or chieftains. The Kurdish language, an Indo-European tongue related to Iranian (not Turkish), has four mutually unintelligible dialects, two of which (Kurmanji and Zaza) are spoken in Turkey. They are also divided by faith – Alevî Kurds are concentrated near Erzincan and Tunceli, while in the far southeast Sunni

there are pitched street battles in western Anatolia between Kurdish and local youths. More realistic figures on both sides of the issue

> *There are around 25 million Kurds worldwide, living in six countries. Their only de facto state is in northern Iraq, now being reintegrated after years of effective independence under US-UK protection.*

recognise that an independent Kurdish state is not in the offing, especially if the Turkish state

dervish orders historically had many Kurdish members. There are around 15 million Kurds in Turkey, with war and economic migration meaning that over half have left their original homes in eastern Anatolia.

The PKK conflict has to date left nearly 50,000 dead on all sides, hundreds of thousands of internal Kurdish refugees, and engendered great bitterness amongst Turks. Although the capture of the PKK leader in 1999 saw a pronounced lull in the war, sporadic clashes have resumed in recent years Several times yearly,

allows cultural rights (including teaching and broadcasting in Kurdish), the development of southeast Turkey that truly benefits locals, and a Kurdish-interests party not continually threatened with closure. *See also page 369.*

Ethnic groups of the Caucasus

The Black Sea coast and mountains are home to several Caucasian groups such as the **Laz**, who trace their ancestry to ancient Colchis, where Jason and his Argonauts came to steal the Golden Fleece. Although they converted from Christianity to Islam in the 16th century, they still speak a language related to Mingrelian and Georgian. There are probably not more than 150,000 of them in the eastern Black Sea

LEFT: a Kurdish woman holds a portrait of a woman who died in an "honour killing". **ABOVE:** Kurdish children in the poor section of Alibasha, in Diyarbakir.

region. The Laz are noted for their energetic style and dry sense of humour, as well as their keen business acumen. They are conspicuous in most Turkish cities, especially in the contracting business and the restaurant trade, though traditionally they were farmers and sailors. For many years the repeating of jokes at their expense – akin to Pontian jokes in Greece, or west-country sheep-molesting stereotypes in England – was a favourite pastime; the Laz took it in their stride, retorting that other Turks were merely jealous of their success.

The **Hemşınlis** of the Kaçkar Mountains are an Armenian tribe speaking an archaic dialect of Armenian, who only converted to Islam in the early 1800s. They are famous as pastry cooks across Turkey and somewhat more numerous than the Laz.

There are also perhaps 50,000 **Pontian Greek Muslims** who converted slightly before the Hemşınlis, and were thus allowed to stay in republican Turkey. Their language, *Rumca*, is mutually intelligible with the medieval Greek spoken by the descendants of Orthodox Pontians living in Greece, and there is in fact an annual pastoral festival in the Black Sea mountains where representatives of the two groups meet and socialise.

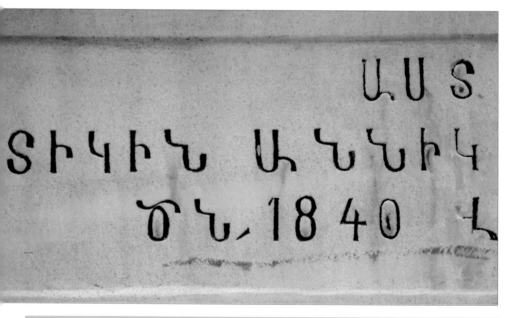

THE ARMENIANS

At its peak, Armenian territory stretched from northeastern Turkey to the Azeri areas of Persia, with an offshoot Cilician kingdom. This once-powerful empire was overrun and dissolved by the Persians and the Ottomans in the 15th century, although many Armenians continued to live locally. The Cilician kingdom gave rise to the Catholic branch of the Armenian nation, while American missionary activity eventually produced a crop of Armenian Protestants.

The late 19th century saw the founding of armed Armenian revolutionary-nationalist organisations, provoking the 1895–6 pogroms which cost 100,000 Armenian lives. Worse came during World War I, when more Armenians saw an opportunity to found an independent state by joining the Russian side. The massacres of 1915–16 remain a source of immense controversy today, hampering efforts to normalise diplomatic relations between Turkey and the ex-Soviet state of Armenia. The promises of independence from the statesmen at the Versailles Peace Treaty came to nothing after the Turks and then, conclusively, the Russians overran the short-lived Democratic Republic of Armenia.

Today about 60,000 Armenians remain in İstanbul, where they are still prominent in the arts and small business; the Armenian Orthodox Patriarchate is at Kumkapı, a district in the oldest part of İstanbul. An indeterminate number of Armenians still live in the east, having nominally converted to Islam; most now fear to identify themselves openly.

The Greeks

Greeks have lived in Asia Minor since the early first millennium BC, and although some hate to admit it, many modern Turks have Greek ancestry, given the degree of intermarriage from the 12th century onwards. Under Ottoman rule, the Greek Orthodox church (*Rum Ortodoks* in Turkish) comprised its own *millet*, and (like the Armenians and Jews) had considerable autonomy in running communal affairs. Until the fall of the Ottoman Empire, Greek Orthodox communities (many speaking Turkish as a first language) were scattered across much of Anatolia, while between a quarter and a third of the population of İstanbul were ethnic Greeks. The seat of the Eastern Orthodox Church has been in İstanbul since the 4th century AD, and the spiritual leader of world Orthodoxy, the ecumenical patriarch, still resides in Fener district.

But in accordance with the 1923 Treaty of Lausanne, Greece and Turkey agreed to exchange religious minorities. Nearly 1.5 million Greek Orthodox were compelled to leave Anatolia (many had already done so), and almost 400,000 Muslims were sent from Greece. The only exemptions were the 110,000 Orthodox of Tenedos and İmroz islands and İstanbul. They who were allowed to stay as a counter to a near-equal number of Muslims (ethnically Turkish, Pomak or Gypsy) left in western Thrace.

The policy may have seemed expedient at the time, but it caused enormous personal suffering and severe economic dislocation for both nations; many now consider it a major error.

> *Returned* Almanyalılar *(German Turks), resented and envied in equal measure, perform approximately the same function in Turkish society as returned Greek-Americans do in Greece, with their cash remittances and perceived vulgarity.*

After anti-Greek riots in 1955, the Cyprus crisis of 1974 and government confiscatory measures or restrictions on education, there was little hope of a continued vital Greek presence

LEFT: Armenian script on a tomb at the Armenian Church of the Virgin Mary in Kumkapı, İstanbul.
RIGHT: girls working in a tobacco field.

in Turkey; the permanently resident İstanbul community now barely exceeds 2,500 (plus a smaller number living in İzmir disguised as "Levantines" with Italian nationality).

The dwindling population of native-born Greek Orthodox pose a major threat to the continued existence of the patriarchate, since by Turkish law every ecumenical patriarch must be a Turkish citizen. The Orthodox theological seminary on Halki (Heybeli) in the Princes' Islands, the major training centre for future clergy, has been closed since 1971. So far international pressure to reopen the school has not had any effect.

Finally, another class of "Greeks" – Muslim in this case – dwells on the Aegean and Mediterranean coasts, with concentrations around Çanakkale, Ayvalık, Bodrum and Side. Most are from Crete or Lesvós, and nostalgically proud of their roots; despite pressure to assimilate, most can still speak island dialects three generations after the transfer from Greece.

The Suriyanis

The Tür Abdin Plateau, east of Midyat and Mardin in southeast Turkey, was an important centre for Syrian Orthodox Christianity from the 6th century onwards, and in medieval times there were 80 monasteries in the region. Only three (Mar Gabriel, seat of the bishop; Mar Yakoub and Deyr-az-Zaferan) still function, along with various churches in Midyat, Mardin and the plateau villages, while just a few hundred Christians still live locally. Nationwide there are now just 5,000 Suriyanis (as they are called), mostly in İstanbul where they have a reputation as superb jewellers. As recently as the 1970s there were 20,000 in the Tür Abdin alone, but Kurdish extortion and general Muslim bigotry resulted in large-scale emigration, in particular to Sweden and the US. Numbers had already been

substantially reduced during World War I, when approximately 250,000 Suriyanis were killed by the Ottomans, allegedly for siding with the British. The church liturgy is conducted in Syriac, a Semitic language essentially identical to biblical Aramaic but written in its own script.

Ethnic Arabs: There are up to 1.4 million ethnic Arabs in the far southeast, in and around Urfa, Harran and the entire Hatay province, historically a part of Syria which was controversially annexed to Turkey in 1939. Although many people speak Arabic as a first language, and Syria long agitated for the return of the Hatay, recent improvement in relations between the two states means that any separatist initiative is off the table.

The Jewish community

There were already indigenous Jews in İstanbul and Bursa before the Ottoman conquest, but most of today's Jewish community trace their ancestry to 1492, when Sultan Beyazit II gave asylum to 150,000 Sephardic Jews escaping death or conversion after the edict of Queen Isabella and King Ferdinand of Spain. Encouraged by the Ottomans, who valued their skills, the Jews established Turkey's first printing press in 1493, and many famous Ottoman court physicians, financiers and diplomats were Sephardic. But the community stagnated educationally and had declined in influence by the 18th century, to be surpassed socially by the Greeks and Armenians.

Neutral Turkey did not officially grant visas to Jews fleeing Nazi-occupied Europe, though individual diplomats saved thousands of refugees. But after a discriminatory wartime tax against religious minorities, and the 1955 anti-Greek riots which also targeted Jews, emigration to Israel accelerated. Today the local Jewish community, mostly in İstanbul and İzmir, numbers a mere 25,000. Yet nearly twenty synagogues still exist in İstanbul, plus a dozen more in İzmir.

The Roma

Turkish-speaking, Muslim Roma live predominantly in Thrace, the Aegean region and around Samsun; as elsewhere in the Balkans, they are generally disadvantaged and scorned by mainstream Turks. The settled Roma of Thrace and the Bergama area are the most well-off. Estimates of their population vary from 500,000 to 1,000,000.

Nomads (Yörüks)

Few true nomads remain in Turkey, but there is still seasonal nomadism (*see panel, page 22*) to *yaylas* (pastoral colonies) in the Toros mountains from northwest of Fethiye to northeast of Adana. Thought to be descendants of the Oğuz Turkic tribe, many have preserved the fair complexion and green eyes of their ancestors; a few are actually Turcoman and Alevî in religion. Mountain trekkers in the Toros will probably encounter inhabited Yörük *yaylas* during the summer. ❑

ABOVE LEFT: patriotic sheepskins on sale at Urfa's bazaar.

Atatürk:
Father of the Nation

The founder of modern Turkey still commands the adulation of his country

Bronze statues or busts of Atatürk occupy the choicest spot in every Turkish town, a canonical repertoire of photos graces hotel lobbies and official foyers, while ridges overhead feature pithy quotes and cut-out silhouettes of the great man pacing about at Gallipoli. His Balkan features and piercing blue eyes bore little resemblance to the purported Central Asian ancestors he identified for Turks; some suggest part-Jewish roots on his father's side, though more scholarly opinion points to a mixed Slavic-Albanian background. Nevertheless, Mustafa Kemal (as he was born) is the focus of one of the most enduring personality cults in modern history, the literal Father (*Ata*) of the Turkish republic.

Born in 1881, the only surviving son of a customs official and a devout peasant mother in the now-Greek northern Aegean port of Salonika, eight-year-old Mustafa chafed at the conventions of the district religious school, the beginning of his distaste for organised Islam.

Kemal enrolled at the local military academy, before transferring to Harbiye War College in İstanbul, where he was caught up in clandestine publication of a seditious newspaper, and punished by a transfer to Damascus as captain – far away from the locus of power. Even so, in 1906 he set up a revolutionary society there which soon merged with the pan-Ottoman Committee for Union and Progress (CUP) headed eventually by the ill-fated triumvirate of Enver, Cemal and Talat. Unlike them, Mustafa Kemal remained a strict legalist, calling for the separation of the military from politics, and evoking the lasting suspicion of the better-known leaders of the time, in particular the jealous Enver.

In 1911, Kemal volunteered for service in Libya against the Italian invasion there; however, the outbreak of the catastrophic Balkan Wars the following year brought him back to Thrace where he helped Enver recapture Edirne, although the latter was given all the credit, and soon contrived to have

RIGHT: a gold bust of Mustafa Kemal Atatürk.

Kemal dispatched to Sofia as a military attaché. Enver went on to drag Turkey into World War I, after which the entire triumvirate met violent ends. Mustafa Kemal, who had emerged as the only undefeated commander at war's end, was well placed to assume leadership of the struggle to save the heartland of the lost empire – the successor state to be known as "*Türkiye*", the Land of the Turks. In the two decades before his death in 1938, he led armies to victory in the War of Independence, replaced the sultanate with a republic (serving as its first president) and introduced sweeping secular reforms.

Today, over 70 years after succumbing to liver cirrhosis, Kemal Atatürk (as he renamed himself

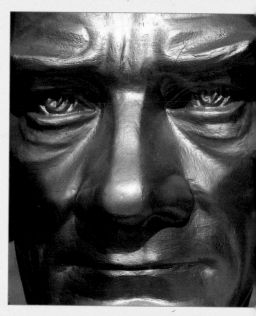

when surnames became obligatory) is still idolised by Turkey, his writings and speeches a source of often contradictory wisdom. His reputation is protected by the 1982 constitution, with severe penalties for infractions. Accordingly, Can Dündar's 2008 biopic *Mustafa*, which attempted to present a more well-rounded portrait of a man who womanised, drank and smoked to excess, was met with howls of outrage and threats of prosecution for insulting his name (and bizarrely, for promoting smoking).

Certainly, the officer corps committed to preserving his heritage have no doubts about former cadet number 1238; every year, when Atatürk's number is called out at the roll call of the graduating class of new military cadets, there is but one uniform response: "He is among us."   ❏

RELIGION IN TURKEY

Sunni Islam in republican Turkey is flourishing,
despite nearly a century of official atheism

Even though 97 percent of Turks are at least notionally Muslim, the republic of Turkey is explicitly secular. Religion is strictly a matter of private conscience, excluded from public life and policy, with all sectarian dress or symbolism banned from state institutions.

Muslims

The *ezan* (call to prayer), issuing from speakers on mosque minarets, exhorts the faithful five times a day: dawn, midday, mid-afternoon, sunset and two hours after dark. Yet the interpretation of Islam in Turkey has traditionally been liberal, bearing little resemblance to the strict codes of practice in Iran and Saudi Arabia. By the 1500s, the Ottomans had adopted the Sunni Hanafite school of jurisprudence, which interpreted the Koran using analogy and opinion.

Alevîs: Most Turks are Sunni, but there are also 20 million Shi'ite Alevîs spread across the

THE SOURCES OF ISLAM

Islam is the newest of the three monotheistic religions, founded in the 7th century AD when divine revelations to the Prophet Muhammad were conveyed orally and memorised by his followers. This was not written down as the Koran until after the Prophet's death, and except for certain recommendations, gave scant direction as to actual practice of the new religion. Accordingly, the *Sunnah* – a collection of anecdotes and sayings *(hadiths)* attributed to Muhammad – became a supplemental basis of much modern Islamic belief and law. The wide disparity in interpretation of the Koran and the *Sunnah* has resulted in today's diversity of Muslim practice.

country, who hold more liberal and even left-wing beliefs. These two distinct sects arose after Mohammed's death, during disputes over the succession of a new caliph. The future Sunnis elected Abu Bakr, who governed consensually; the breakaway Shi'ites believed in a hereditary authority, descending directly from Mohammed through his daughter, Fatima, and her husband, Ali, still greatly revered.

Alevîsm in Turkey dates mainly from the campaigns of Shia Shah Ismail of Persia in the early 16th century; although resoundingly defeated at Çaldıran by Sultan Selim I, stragglers from Ismail's army retreated to isolated areas of Anatolia. Separated from mainstream Shi'ite practice, distinctive Alevî traditions emerged;

itinerant travelling holy elders *(dedes)* replaced the traditional clerical hierarchy, for example, and the Koranic ban on alcohol was relaxed.

Women have equal status with men, praying together in *cemevleri* (meeting houses) rather than mosques, a custom which has led to scurrilous allegations of orgies, and the forcible imposition of "proper" mosques on Alevî villages. Their leftist-secularist inclinations also provoke mistrust among fundamentalist Sunnis, which has occasionally resulted in violence.

Sufis: Other Sunni sects include various Sufi orders *(tariqats)*, whose rituals combine elements of pre- and early Christian practice, Buddhism and Neoplatonism. Dancing, music and repetitive chants have all been used in the central practice of *zikr* (literally, "remembrance of God"). In Ottoman times, the Sufi brotherhoods formed *tekkes* (lodges), similar to Christian monasteries. Orders were led by *şeyhs*, and novices *(murids)* were disciples of a fully fledged dervish; all took vows of poverty, relying on alms.

Atatürk's suppression of the dervish orders (along with the practice of worshipping at the tombs of dervish *şeyhs*) was never entirely effective, and since the 1970s these have discreetly re-emerged. The most famous, and visible, is the sophisticated, urban-based Mevlevî order, which reveres the mystic poet Mevlâna Celaleddin Rumi of 13th-century Konya, but there also were (and still are) the more conservative Halveti-Cerahi, Kadiri, Rifâi and Nakşibendi sects (the late president Özal was an adherent of the latter).

The Mevlevî ceremony, in which dervishes wearing voluminous robes and conical hats whirl to the pulse of drums and strains of mournful music, was revived in recent decades as a "folkloric manifestation" and tourist attraction, especially at the annual (December) Konya festival commemorating the death of Mevlâna. However, more genuine manifestations take place all year at the Galata Mevlevîhane in İstanbul, where participants actually profess to live as Sufis, rather than treating the whirling as merely a fancy-dress exercise.

Bektaşis: The Bektaşi order, followers of Hacı

Bektaş Veli (1209–71), is based at Hacıbektaş, near Kırşehir in central Turkey, where their founder is buried. Like their Alevî affiliates, and indeed all Shi'ite sects, they recognise Ali as the rightful successor to Mohammed; heads of the order are called *babas*. The Bektaşis absorbed numerous non-Muslim practices, including a version of baptism, and also celebrate the Zoroastrian spring-equinox festival, *Nevroz*, as Ali's birthday. Their ethical teachings stress the precedence of inner intent and purity over outward observance, and avoidance of inconsistency or ostentation.

Mainstream Muslims espouse five basic practices: the statement of their creed ("There is no God but Allah and Mohammed is his Prophet"), prayer, giving alms, fasting during Ramadan, and making a pilgrimage to Mecca.

Religion and the Ottomans

Islam, and religion generally, played a crucial role in the Ottoman Empire. Islam helped create solidarity among ethnically diverse elements and, through the *millet* system for Christians and Jews, provided a clear legal structure for subjects of all creeds. The Ottoman sultan became the caliph of the entire

Islamic world following the Turkish conquest of Egypt in the 16th century. Under the Ottomans, a corps of Muslim scholars (the *ulema*) pronounced on all religious matters, taught theology, administered mosques and schools, and controlled the courts.

Early Ottoman theologians were influenced by Al-Ghazali (1058–1111), a Persian scholar who, while vehemently attacking ancient Greek philosophy, encouraged empirical observation and experiment. As a result, many Muslims achieved notable results in astronomy, mathematics and medicine, using (for example) scientific methods to fix the position of the *qibla*

the Ottomans were insufficient to convince a hidebound, arrogant clergy, who saw no need to learn from infidels. It was not until the 19th century that Western innovations were allowed to be widely disseminated within the empire.

Islam under the republic

All this changed with the establishment of the Turkish republic; Atatürk's sweeping reforms *(see page 64)* also meant that the clergy, now effectively paid civil servants, were subordinated to a special Ministry of Religious Affairs. Even the *ezan* in Arabic, the sacred language of Islam, was outlawed in 1932 in favour of a

(prayer niche in mosques), which had to point towards Mecca.

As the empire slowly declined, progress was stifled through a series of reactionary measures. Under pressure from calligraphers whose livelihood was threatened, printing presses were forbidden until the early 18th century. In 1580, Sultan Murat III closed an observatory in İstanbul on the grounds that the astronomers were "insolent enough to try to pry open the secrets of the universe" – secrets known only to Allah. Meanwhile, across much of Europe the Renaissance was in full swing, and the discoveries it fuelled were soon reflected in technological advances. But even the resulting, repeated battlefield successes of Christian states against

> *Repeated attempts to allow female headscarves in public institutions have failed. This effectively bars young women of conservative background from a public career, or even admittance to university.*

Turkish version (until the 1950s Menderes government reinstated it).

The 1980–83 junta, and the Özal government thereafter, encouraged "moderate" religious expression as a bulwark against leftist extremism and Kurdish nationalism. The junta made religious education compulsory in state schools for all primary and secondary pupils, with no parental opt-out allowed as previously. There was a huge increase in the number of *imam hatip okulları* (private religious secondary schools), first set up under Menderes. Godfather of all this was the Ocak (Hearth) movement, which had emerged in the 1970s, advocating a national identity comprised of pre-Islamic Turkism and Islam.

These measures let various genies out of the bottle – and prompted predictable secularist reaction. The military's tolerance of "Islam Lite" did not extend to its own ranks, where radical Islamists were periodically purged from a force seeing itself as the main guardian of the Kemal-

(and their leaders) were successively banned for contravening the constitution, but to no avail; for most Turks, Islam remains a much sounder source of values and spiritual succour than anything imported from the West, and a more indigenous expression of identity than the *de haut en bas* arrogance of the secular elite. Political Islam's current incarnation, the AK party, has its work cut out convincing observers that they really are analogous to the Christian Democratic parties of post-war Germany and Italy, and not (as fearful secularist detractors assert) merely practicing *taqiyya* (dissimulation) prior to the introduction of sharia law. ❑

ist flame. In 1998, obligatory secular primary education was increased from five to eight years, drastically weakening the secondary religious academies by depriving them of influence and tuition money. Many parents were unhappy, as these schools had performed well compared to the woeful state sector and, anyhow, devoted just a few hours weekly to Arabic and Koran study.

The 1990s saw Islamist political parties gain considerable ground, especially in large cities, by addressing issues and providing services apparently beyond secularist capabilities. Such parties

LEFT: Turkish Islamist women rally in support of lifting a ban on headscarves in universities. **ABOVE LEFT:** St Paul souvenirs. **ABOVE RIGHT:** prayers in a mosque.

EXPERIMENTING WITH RELIGION

Long before the advent of Islam, Turkic nomads were practising shamanism, presided over by the sky-god Tengri. Eventually some tribes, such as the Uighurs, adopted Buddhism, while others became Zoroastrians, Nestorians or Monophysites. The Khazar Turkish empire became Jewish from the 8th century until its dissolution some 300 years later. It was not until the 10th century that the encounter between the Arabs and the Turks resulted in most of the latter's conversion to Islam. Today almost 250,000 Christian Turks, the Gagauz, still live in parts of the Balkans, while the Karaim, Jewish Karaylar Turks originally from the Crimea, are found in Russia, Lithuania and Poland.

FIT FOR A SULTAN'S TABLE

Turkey's wide-ranging terrain and climatic diversity produces a variety of foodstuffs. Together with the palette of herbs and spices, it makes for one of the world's great cuisines

For 500 years, the Ottoman Empire ruled much of the medieval world, and at İstanbul's Topkapı Palace great chefs created a sumptuous cuisine which rivalled the epicurean delights of ancient Rome. They were assisted by the sheer variety of fish, fowl, meat, fruit and vegetables produced in Turkey, as well as the numerous cultures that have flourished in Anatolia since ancient times – archaeologists have deciphered a Sumerian tablet that turned out to be a cookbook of sorts, containing almost all the items and spices familiar to present-day Turks.

Today, from the Balkans to the Middle East, from the Caucasus to North Africa, virtually all nations share a taste for the savoury kebabs (*kebaplar*), rice-based pilaus (*pilavlar*), aubergine or chickpea specialities and tangy white sheep, cow or goat cheese (*beyaz peynir*) whose preparation became an art form in the Topkapı kitchens and the province of Bolu, where aspiring cooks started out peeling vegetables in one of the numerous

> *Ottoman court poets used food as metaphor in love verses, the vocabulary still surviving in Turkish romantic discourse today. Prestigious titles were granted to master chefs, and palace recipes were guarded with utmost secrecy.*

culinary schools set up by imperial decree. Even today Bolu remains famous for its chefs.

In early Ottoman times, the riches of the sultan's table owed much to Persian cuisine,

LEFT: Turkey excels in fresh produce. **RIGHT:** traditional *pide* bread is commonly eaten during Ramadan.

notably the Abbasid-dynasty banquets which disappeared after the Mongol destruction of Baghdad. However, the taste for meat charcoal-grilled on a skewer, known as *şiş* (pronounced "shish") kebab, probably originated as "fast food" on the Central Asian steppes or in the shepherds' pastures of Anatolia, while many vegetable- or pulse-based dishes can be found in different versions across the Middle East. Today, Turkish tastes are more notably Mediterranean and Levant-based than Persian-influenced, and visitors may notice an odd conservatism in the native palate.

Accordingly, "Ottoman" food is difficult to find, and not every traveller will be lucky enough to come across the best Turkish cuisine. While on the whole tasty, fresh and nutritious, standard resort fare can get monotonous after a few days, since restaurant owners play safe and pitch the known quantities of *döner* and *şiş kebap* to the wary and unadventurous, steering you away from odd local fish and rich *inegöl köfteleri* (cheese-stuffed meatballs) or, God forbid, *koç yumurtası* (ram's testicles), spit-roasted lamb offal wrapped in gut (*kokoreç*), and *beyin salatası* (raw lamb brains) in favour of pepper steak and hamburgers. To experience the real thing, head for working men's cafeterias or those restaurants which

In the more temperate areas of the country, salad-lovers will find a variety of unusual, spicy greens appearing along with the standard, microchopped tomato-pepper-onion-and-cucumber mix called *çoban salatası* (shepherd's salad). *Roka* (rocket) is an essential garnish for fish, along with lemon and salt; you may also find spiky *tere* (bitter cress, a member of the mustard family), *nane* (fresh mint), or even *kuzukulağı* (sorrel). Cultivated rather than weedy purslane (*semizotu*) is typically served blended with yoghurt; another common *meze* (appetiser) is sharp, crumbly goat's cheese cured in a goatskin (*tulum peyniri*) with chopped walnuts.

have earned a reputation for authentic Ottoman or eastern Turkish cuisine.

Regional specialities

Most native-born urban dwellers in İstanbul and Ankara have an aversion to highly spiced food and garlic, associating them with the Anatolian-peasant culture they disdain. However, as you move south and east, such middle-class prejudices swiftly disappear, and if you know which regional specialities to ask for, there are surprises to match every taste. Freshness and seasonality are essential when ordering meals – a trip to the local *halk pazarı* (street market) should clue you up as to which ingredients are currently available.

The Antalya region is famous for its citrus fruits, notably oranges, at their best in December or January, when it is still sunny. The Turkish word for orange, *portakal*, is derived from Portugal, from where the fruit first came to Anatolia in the 16th century, having originated in China. Further east, towards Alanya, locally grown bananas are smaller and tastier than imported varieties, but are being edged out all the same, while avocados are now fairly well established.

The Aegean region is famous for *çöp şiş*, tiny pieces of lamb threaded onto wooden skewers like satay sticks – a popular truck-stop grub. People buy four or six at a time and dip them in a spicy mixture of cumin, oregano and hot pepper, then roll them up in a *yufka* – akin to a flour tortilla – or a *dürüm* (like a paratha). The Antalya regional speciality, *hibeş*, is a starter made of sesame paste, lemon, hot pepper and garlic. Heading east of Alanya, the bread changes from the European loaf to Middle Eastern unleavened *pide*, similar to Indian nan; *pide*

From Adana eastwards, chillies – often fiery – enliven the most unlikely ingredients (including cows' udders). Sumak, a tart powder made from the ground berries of Rhus coriaria, *is universally dusted on kebabs.*

is also universally served during Ramadan.

Closer to the Syrian borderlands (Şanlıurfa, Gaziantep and Antakya), the food becomes much spicier. Şanlıurfa is known for its onion-laced *şiş* kebabs (as well as the difficulty of ordering a beer: this is a city of pilgrimage for Muslims) and Antakya for hummous – the chickpea paste with garlic now so familiar in the West. *Nar ekşisi* (sour pomegranate syrup) – used in tomato and onion salads, as well as the basis of meat sauces – owes more to Persian heritage than most Turkish food.

The Black Sea is home to the *hamsi* (anchovy, usually crisp-fried in cornmeal), hazelnuts, dairy products, *muhlama* (a sort of fondue made from cheese, butter and corn flour), and cornbread – elsewhere in Turkey corn is considered food fit only for livestock. In central and eastern Anatolia, *saç kavurma* is an elegant meat-and-vegetable medley stir-fried in a shallow wok (usually at your table) which tastes rather like a Hungarian goulash. This dish has clear links with the outdoor cooking of Central Asia.

Through the day

Breakfasts – especially at the simpler kinds of accommodation – are dominated by *beyaz peynir* and various kinds of olives, with butter, honey, jam, tomatoes, cucumbers and boiled egg often making an appearance as well. Alternatively, special bakeries serve a variety of *böreks*, filo pastries with cheese or meat fillings.

The staple of lunch-time *lokantas* (from the

Italian *locanda*) is *sulu yemek* (literally, "juicy food") vegetable- and meat-based stews, or *hazır yemek* (ready food), including more involved oven casseroles. Even simpler are the *çorbacıs* (soup kitchens), open long hours while purveying a range of soups from the innocuous *mercimek* (lentil) to *paça* (trotters) and *işkembe* (tripe), the latter two favourites of clubbers and hardened drinkers in need of a hangover preventative and small-hours restorative. *İşkembe*, similar to Mexican *menudo* but without hominy, is preferentially consumed with crushed garlic from a bowl, red pepper flakes and a lashing of vinegar.

Dining Out

Some of the country's finest restaurants are attached to hotels, many specialising in Ottoman menus. In some upmarket establishments, you might be asked whether you prefer to eat fish or meat – it is not done to mix the two – so that the best seating can be chosen. Ideally, fish – whether ocean-going or freshwater – should be eaten beside the sea or under streamside plane trees, while kebabs and other meat dishes are best enjoyed in a rural scene. Along the south and west coasts, eating al-fresco is the norm – indeed the Ottomans introduced the concept of outdoor dining to Europe. Types of restaurant are described on page 392 of the Travel Tips.

Left: a traditional breakfast of bread, olives and tea.
Right: the *döner* kebab is one of Turkey's most famous exports.

Evening meals usually start with a selection of *mezes* which the waiter brings to the table on an enormous platter. This is particularly convenient for foreigners as written descriptions of the dishes often don't do them justice or are eccentrically translated (eg "cigarette pie" for *sigara böreği*, etc.). Most are *zeytinyağlılar*, cold vegetable-based dishes cooked in olive oil, or salads of pulses or wild greens (extending to such as *deniz börülce*, rock samphire), but you can opt for hot *mezes* like *arnavut ciğer* ("Albanian-style" sautéed lamb's liver with onions), *mücver* (courgette fritata) or *içli köfte* (bulgur wheat, nuts, vegetables and meat in a spicy crust).

It is also well worth keeping an eye out for less common *meze* delicacies, verging on main courses, such as *çerkez tavuğu* (Circassian chicken) – steamed, boned and puréed breast meat smothered in a sauce of walnuts, breadcrumbs, garlic, oil and lemon.

Dolmalar ("stuffed things") are also popular, and can be made with courgettes, aubergines, peppers, grape leaves, cabbage leaves, tomatoes, mussels or artichokes, filled with a mixture of rice, pine nuts, currants, herbs and spices. They are doused in olive oil and lemon juice and served hot with meat, or cold with yoghurt.

Fish is taken very seriously – there are several

AŞURE

Aşure is the Turkish version of a devotional dish found across the Balkans. The name refers to *aşure günü*, the tenth day of Muharrem, when Hasan and Hüseyin, sons of the fourth caliph Alia, were slain at the Battle of Karbala, becoming martyrs for the Shi'ites and their Turkish adherents, the Alevîs and Betaşis. Elders of the latter sect break a 10-day fast at the start of Muharrem with a communal meal of *aşure*. A pudding of pulses, grains, raisins, pomegranate seeds and nuts, it supposedly contains 40 ingredients, after a legend relating how after the first sighting of dry land from the Ark, Noah commanded that a stew be made of the 40 remaining sorts of food on board.

separate names for the bluefish alone, depending on size/age, from *çinakop* (the smallest) to *kanat* (medium) to *lüfer* (adult), never served more than a day old, and at its prime in the autumn. Fish restaurants are likely to feature starters such as fried *kalamar* (squid); *levrek turşu* (marinated sea bass); *balık köftesi* (hot fish rissoles); or salt-cured fish, either the premium *lakerda* (bonito) or *çiroz* (mackerel). Main dishes will encompass grilled or fried fish of the season – though with rare exceptions outside of tourist areas, seafood is as expensive in Turkey as anywhere else in the Mediterranean and you're advised to confirm the per-portion or by-weight price in advance.

Top-drawer fish dishes include *kılıç balığı*, swordfish skewered with peppers and tomatoes;

kalkan, turbot served with lemon wedges; *buğlama*, fish stew often flavoured with dill, made from any of the larger catch of the day; and *karides güveç*, a clay-pot casserole of shrimp, hot peppers, tomatoes and cheese (vegetarians should note that a similar dish made with mushrooms is often available). All the usual Mediterranean breams are found in Turkey; more distinctive (and cheaper) are Black Sea or Marmara species such as *mezgit* (whitebait) and *istavrit* (horse mackerel), or north Aegean favourites like *sardalya* (sardine) and *papalina* (sprat).

Kebab (*kebap* in Turkish) has figured prominently in local cuisine for over 10 centuries, and

ful kebab dishes, often related to their region of origin, include Adana kebab – ground lamb highly seasoned with red pepper, coriander and cumin, wrapped around a skewer and grilled; or İskender (Bursa) kebab, where luscious slices of *döner* meat are spread over *pide* bread, smothered in yoghurt, tomato sauce and hot butter.

If your main course is a meat dish, it might come accompanied by rice, which can be simply cooked with butter and meat broth or, alternatively, richly seasoned with pine nuts, currants, herbs and liver. Alternatively, it may be accompanied by bulgur wheat, or merely a garnish salad and some slices of *pide*.

its meaning has developed to include meats that have been boiled, baked or stewed. Meat is usually cooked with vegetables – for example with *şiş* kebabs, pieces of green pepper, tomato and onion add flavour to the morsels of meat, or in the *güveç* dishes baked in a clay casserole with vegetables. Lamb is the meat par excellence in Turkey and is not only grilled but the basis of various baked dishes like *kuzu tandır* where a whole lamb is baked in a brick oven, still built in the ground in many villages. Other wonder-

FAR LEFT: dining out al-fresco. **LEFT:** fishing on a small scale. **ABOVE:** Turkish cheese for sale in the outdoor markets of Eminönü, İstanbul. **RIGHT:** *simit* are bread rings covered in sesame seeds.

> *Most restaurant owners are mystified by the concept of vegetarianism and may tell you a dish is meatless despite being cooked in stock. In cities and fashionable resorts, however, Western health food has become trendy.*

Dessert

In restaurants, dessert usually means a selection of seasonal fruits. Winter is the time for citrus fruit and bananas; in spring, there may be green almonds and plums, often an acquired taste for foreigners. There are strawberries in May, cherries in June, melons in July and August, and apples, pears, pomegranates and grapes in autumn.

Melon and white cheese are enjoyed when lingering with digestifs after a meal. Fancier restaurants may offer figs stuffed with almonds, apricots bursting with cheese and pistachio paste, or candied pumpkin with clotted cream and walnut chunks.

Another dessert that should definitely be sampled is *muhallebi*, a pudding made from rice flour and rosewater, served cold and maybe dusted with pistachio nuts. Also unmissable, and not cloyingly sweet, are milk-based delicacies like *fırın sütlaç* (rice pudding baked in a clay dish); *keşkül* (vanilla and nut custard); or the incredibly involved *tavukgöğsü*,

chicken breast, semolina and milk taffy. Flour-based sweets include vanilla-laced *kazandibi*, often topped with ice cream, and a kaleidoscope of *helva*, which means any combination of baked flour, butter, sugar and flavoured water. Some or all of these will be available in better restaurants.

Those with a particularly sweet tooth should seek out a traditional *pastane* (patisserie). In earlier days, before fast-food restaurants and cafés provided an alternative, young courting couples or families would make the *pastane* a Sunday ritual. Hence you'll notice, particularly in larger cities, that "traditional" *pastanes* are often romantically decorated in styles from original Art Nouveau to 1950s milk-bar. Even

the names of the desserts themselves – Lady's Navel, Lips of the Beloved and Nightingale's Nests, to name just some – bear witness to the overblown romance loved by Turkish suitors.

At *pastanes*, you'll find all the restaurant-type desserts cited above, as well as *lokum* (Turkish Delight – basically solidified sugar with pectin, flavourings and maybe nuts) and the pan-Middle Eastern confections like *baklava* or *kadayif* made from varying proportions of sugar, flour, nuts and butter. An increasingly popular elaboration of *kadayif* is the artery-cloggingly rich *künefe* – the same sheer filaments poised over soft white cheese and then topped with *dondurma* (traditional Turkish gelato) for good measure. Speaking of which, *dondurma* still (just) holds its own against inroads being made by the rainbow of exotic flavours sold by upmarket standard ice-cream parlours like the Mado chain.

Sweets such as *baklava* or *helva*, rather than alcohol, are the customary gift to take when one goes visiting.

Turkish snacks

Perhaps the most delicious snack – almost a full meal in itself – is *pide* or "Turkish pizza", flat and pointed-oval-shaped like the eponymous soup-bread but stuffed with a range of savoury toppings (typically cheese, mince or *sucuk* – sausage) and then cut into bite-sized pieces before being served. The venue, with its wood-burning oven going from mid-morning until nearly midnight, is a *pide salonu*. *Pide* shouldn't be confused with *lahmacun*, small, round, thin-crust concoctions sold from street-carts, or *simit* – bread rounds topped with sesame seeds. Out in the countryside, stalls (invariably staffed by women) making and selling *gözleme* are ubiquitous. Resembling a stuffed paratha, *gözleme* come in a wide range of sweet or savoury flavours. In İstanbul and İzmir, itinerant peddlers of *midya dolması* (mussels stuffed with rice, pine nuts and allspice) should be treated with caution: never, ever indulge in the summer months.

Dried fruit, seeds or nuts are eaten at any time or during any social occasion, and the little shops that sell them by weight (typically 100gm a shot) are frequently open late at night. Roasted hazelnuts and unshelled black sunflower seeds are the favourites, with powdery dried chickpeas (*leblebi*) not far behind.

Wine, *rakı* and beer

Vineyards are found mostly in the Aegean region, Cappadocia and Thrace, and wine-making has been practised here since the Neolithic era. But despite this long legacy, Turks were never great wine-drinkers, and during Ottoman times wineries were run by the Christian minorities. For decades republican Turkey lagged behind other Mediterranean rivals, given persisting Islamic inhibitions and the negative effect of Tekel, the now-defunct state spirits enterprise. Tension persists today as tourism vies with religious scruples. So the west and south secularist coasts are generally "wet" and most of the devout interior is "dry". Everywhere, alcohol prices are high (except for beer) as excise taxes combine a sense of virtue with fiscal opportunity.

The quality and availability of wine *(şarap)* has improved enormously since the 1990s, as private wineries with foreign-trained oenologists come to the fore. The two largest vintners, Doluca and Kavaklıdere, still dominate the domestic market, but regional brands worth seeking out include Turasan, Narbağ and Peribacası (Cappadocia), Feyzi Kutman (relying on Thracian grapes), Sevilen (Aegean region), Majestik (İzmir) and several on Bozcaada (Tenedos). Red wine is *kırmızı*, white *beyaz*, rose *roze*.

The national aniseed-based aperitif, *rakı*, originated as a dodge to get around the Koran, which only proscribes wine. It's akin to other Mediterranean distilled grape-waste spirits like grappa and ouzo, though a bit stronger at 45–48 percent alcohol. *Rakı* is dubbed "lion's milk" *(aslan sütü)* as it turns cloudy white when it contacts ice or water, and is considered the ideal accompaniment to seafood. Since the state spirits monopoly was wound up, the best of many private distilleries is considered Efe, though Burgaz is much cheaper and nearly as good – with both brands, go for the green label series. Unfortunately, most restaurants and bars offer only the ex-Tekel Yeni Rakı.

The most popular beers are Efes Pilsen, Carlsberg and Tuborg, all at about 5 percent. Efes also makes a Dark label (6.1 percent) and "Xtra" (7.5 percent), and there's even Gusta, a dark, locally brewed wheat beer, possibly a trib-ute to the taste of Turkish workers returned from Germany.

Soft drinks

Uncarbonated bottled water is offered chilled at restaurants; naturally carbonated mineral water *(maden suyu)* is also available. Tap water is best avoided – usually heavily chlorinated and foul-tasting – though some places will filter it and serve it free in jugs. In rural areas, many springs are potable – the popular ones may have queues.

Freshly squeezed juices are also widespread, especially along the coast, where oranges are abundant; a relatively recent craze is for *nar*

suyu (pomegranate juice) and *karadut suyu* (red mulberry juice) – delicious but expensive.

Another excellent summer thirst-quencher (and much the best accompaniment to *pide*) is ice-cold *ayran*, a yoghurt, salt and water frappé. Traditionally the best, frothy *(yayık* or churned) *ayran* was sold by street vendors, though nowadays you're more likely to get it in sealed bottles.

The most popular winter city drinks are cold *boza*, mildly fermented and millet-based, and hot milk with cinnamon and *sahlep*, the latter made from the pulverised tubers of *Orchis mascula*. *Sahlep*, commonly offered on ferries and at street stalls, is considered sovereign against colds and (possibly because of the suggestive shape of the orchid tuber) a mild aphrodisiac. ❏

LEFT: *baklava* consists of filo pastry, honey and pistachio nuts.
RIGHT: *rakı*, the national aniseed-based aperitif.

TURKISH CAFÉS

Encounter the authentic character of a Turkish neighbourhood at one of the numerous tea- or coffee-houses

Turkey is the home of the coffee house. The concept was introduced to Europe by the Ottomans in the 1600s after Western travellers had admired İstanbul's sociable *kahvehanes* – even if Ottoman authorities intermittently banned them as dens of vice and potential sedition, and the *ulema* deemed coffee a stimulant forbidden by the Koran.

These days, Turkish cafés range from traditional *çayhanes* (tea houses) or *kahvehanes* (coffee houses) to contemporary venues indistinguishable from western equivalents. Compared with the more opulent city centre examples, a typical rural café (or a backstreet urban one) can seem desperately unromantic, with spartan decor, dusty windows, a battered woodstove, and an all-male clientele attired in flat caps.

At trendier cafés, *nargiles* (hookahs) – once exclusive to older men – have made a comeback among the young, but these are now threatened (as is all café trade) by stringent 2009 anti-smoking laws. Now one officially can smoke *tömbeki* (compressed tobacco) only outdoors (though violations abound).

As for Turkish coffee itself, this is prepared by combining finely ground, roasted robusta beans with water and sugar in a long-handled, tapering small pot *(cezve)*. (You'll be asked if you want your coffee plain – *sade*; medium sweet – *şekerli*; or cloying – *çok şekerli*). The brew is allowed to rise twice without actually boiling, the esteemed resultant froth decanted first into little cups, then the liquid, and the sediment (never drunk) last.

TOP: also known as a shisha, hookah or waterpipe, the *nargile* filters the flavoured tobacco smoke by passing it through water.
RIGHT: Turkish coffee.

LEFT: a Roma busker playing the accordion streetside restaurant, tea- and coffee house patrons on Sofyali Street, Beyoğlu, İstanbul.

)VE: the best *nargile* cafés in İstanbul can be found at Çorlulu Ali a Medresesi, under the Galata Bridge and at Tophane.

LEFT: cafés and restaurants line the streets of former fishing village Kumkapı, an ideal place to savour Turkey's café-culture.

TEAS

Given the higher cost of coffee, the staple of *çayhanes* is *çay* (tea): served black and sweet (*never* with milk) in small, tulip-shaped glasses. It's prepared in a double boiler, typically aluminium, known as a *çaydanlik* or *demlik* – the tea is steeped in the bottom half, with the resulting brew combined with plain hot water from the top part. You can ask for *açık* (mild) or *demli* (strong) tea – if you say nothing it will probably arrive stewed almost to undrinkability.

Tea is, perhaps surprisingly, a relatively new fashion, promoted during the late 1930s as part of the republican self-sufficiency programme, relying on plantations around Rize in the Black Sea region. Sadly, homegrown tea isn't always of the highest quality, seldom matching the average Indian or Sri Lankan teabag, though patriotic Turks will certainly bridle at this verdict.

There are also several popular herbal teas or tisanes available: *adaçay*, a kind of sage quite common in the Aegean and west Mediterranean areas; *papatya* (chamomile) and *ıhlamur* (linden blossom), the latter two popular for those stricken with colds or flu.

TOP AND LEFT: pouring and serving Turkish tea (*çay*) at the *nargile* café Çorlulu Ali Paşa Medresesi, İstanbul. **ABOVE LEFT:** students hanging out at an Ankara café.

ANATOLIA'S ANCIENT ARTS

Anatolia's historic art is infinitely varied –
from squat Hatti fertility figurines to towering
Roman temples and delicate Ottoman carvings

When most people think of Turkish art and architecture, the first thing that springs to mind is probably the southerly Golden Horn skyline which includes Topkapı Palace, Aya Sofya and the nocturnally illuminated minarets of the Blue Mosque. Here is a fairy-tale vision indeed, but these relics of Byzantine and Ottoman splendour mark only one small segment of Anatolia's dazzling heritage, for the country has been inhabited by many cultures stretching back millennia.

The first city of art

Ongoing excavations at Çatalhöyük (see page 299) south of Konya have astonished even the scholars working there. Some 8,000 years ago, Anatolia's bountiful resources nurtured some of the world's first settled communities, allowing them to develop sophisticated religion, art and architecture as well as indulging in personal vanity, evidenced by finds of obsidian mirrors, lead and copper jewellery, terracotta seals, and pots of what may be body paint. Yet most astonishing relics are the houses, reminiscent of the 2,000-year-old Native American cities in New Mexico and Arizona. These seem to have been used first as domestic dwellings and later as shrines, and yielded some of the earliest wall paintings ever found, as well as fascinating ritual relief sculptures. Some paintings show hunting parties and sexual congress, some a ritual "excarnation" of bodies by vultures, and one a volcanic eruption of nearby Hasan Dağı, known to have been active in the second millennium BC.

Numerous "Venus of Willendorf"-style figurines found in grain bins and graves imply a matriarchal culture, while the famed "horned bench" may have been a slab for laying out the dead. In other Çatalhöyük house-shrines, there are bulls' skulls covered in clay and ranged up the wall, totem-pole fashion, over which a vaguely humanoid form may be perched. The best finds are now displayed in the Museum of Anatolian Civilisations in Ankara (see page 285).

The Bronze Age

Third-millennium BC Bronze Age finds indicate that the development of metallurgy spurred the rise of many central Anatolian civilisations,

---

LEFT: the Sultan's viewing platform in Istanbul's Aya Sofya. **RIGHT:** bronze female figure from ancient Anatolia, a style of figurine known as a bird-goddess.

such as the Hatti, predecessors of the Hittites. Hoards of gold jewellery and lavish ceremonial objects (such as frequently occurring female double-idols) have been found in graves at heavily fortified and densely packed settlements such as Alacahöyük (see page 302).

Both the aboriginal Hatti and later Hittites (c. 2000–1200 BC) knew about astronomy and used the sun disc as a common artistic symbol, together with goddesses, stags, bulls and other animals. Hittite art and architecture is also renowned for its imposing size, epitomised by the fortifications of their capital Hattuşa (see page 301). Here, gigantic rock-cut reliefs of

warrior gods and sphinx-like creatures suggest a powerful, militaristic but also highly organised and humane state without the cruelty depicted in Assyrian reliefs. The late-Hittite summer palace at Karatepe (see page 271) is nearly as impressive, with depictions of royal banqueting scenes, where guests are surrounded by musicians and fanned by servants.

Remains of the Phrygian (c. 800–700 BC) capital at Gordion (see page 289) and elsewhere show superb stone tombs, thrones and fortifications, rock carvings imitating wooden gables with niches for movable cult images, and floors of finely crafted pebble or brick mosaic. Grave goods were generally vessels of cast bronze, while art displays a strong geometric symmetry,

in finds of kilims and gold embroidery as well as crisply designed painted pottery.

The Urartians, who occupied the area around Lake Van from the 9th century BC, were impres-

> Settlements along the coasts during the third millennium BC show that Anatolian metalwork was greatly prized in exchange for semiprecious stones and other luxury items from Greece and Syria.

sive builders and engineers, leaving behind networks of castles and fortresses, together with superbly crafted rock tombs, cisterns and irrigation channels. Their metalwork, especially large bronze sacrificial cauldrons with human or animal heads, was in international demand even in antiquity. These are noted for their similarity to the best Minoan and Etruscan craftsmanship, with high-crowned bearded gods over curling seawave borders under geometric suns.

The Hellenic coast

Ancient Caria was a large region around the Aegean coast, and while its culture underwent many transformations, it can still be characterised as Hellenic. Bodrum (ancient Halikarnassos) was the most prominent Carian city, whose Persian vassal-ruler Mausolos was committed to the Hellenisation of the region. His own pagoda-like mausoleum (whence the word originates) was considered a wonder of the world, but little remains today (see page 223); the tomb became building material in the 14th century for Bodrum Castle. However, a 4th-century BC tomb discovered during construction work in 1989 is thought to be that of his sister, Princess Ada, who oversaw the completion of the mausoleum; she was found with a crown of gold leaves, silk peplos (loose robe) and ornaments intact. The crowned skull was sent to Manchester University's Medical School for facial reconstruction, and the likeness of the result to a bust of Princess Ada discovered at Priene (now in the British Museum) is quite remarkable. Her exquisite jewellery and wine goblet are now displayed in glass cabinets in the Carian Princess Hall, Bodrum Museum.

The Lycians, who occupied the wild, mountainous territory between Fethiye and Antalya, were first documented by the Hittites more than 3,000 years ago as an ungovernable, matriarchal people with an idiosyncratic culture and intense love of freedom; on two occasions, faced with conquest by the Persians and Romans respectively, inhabitants of the largest city of Xanthos preferred to immolate themselves rather than live in vassaldom.

Given the small population of pre-Roman Lycia, its cities probably had no more than 5,000 people, and, as most buildings were made of wood, archaeologists have only been able to identify a few structures. The most enduring Lycian artefacts are their distinctive "Gothic" sarcophagi, many highly decorated and graphically detailing the punishment that awaited vandals. Like other ancient peoples, the Lycians worshipped their ancestors and occasionally sought guidance from the dead through oracles.

There are four basic types of Lycian tomb, the most curious – and no doubt oldest – form being the pillar-tomb, where the burial chamber is perched on top of a column; the best examples are at Xanthos (see page 238). These may indicate that the earliest Lycians continued the tradition of their Neolithic ancestors by offering mortal remains to the birds – much as the Indian Parsis still do today. Temple-tombs, such as those built into the cliffs at Kaunos and Fethiye (see pages 228, 235, are the more sophisticated version of the intriguing "house tombs" like those found at Myra (see page 242) – lovingly rock-cut models of the plain wooden Lycian dwellings, often three storeys high. Finally, there are more conventional sarcophagus-type tombs also used by later cultures.

Xanthos was so intact when the intrepid Sir Charles Fellows (see page 238) got here in 1840 that the majority of the sculptures and inscriptions were filched and now sit in the British Museum. Excavations carried out since the 1950s, however, reveal enough of the city for the imagination to build on. The most curious pillar-tomb is one with plaster-replica reliefs depicting either harpies or sirens carrying away the souls of the dead, and other seated figures receiving gifts or regarding opium poppies.

The classical era

The Graeco-Roman period (950 BC–AD 300) is considered by many to be the zenith of ancient

Anatolian art and architecture, especially in the city-states along the Aegean and Mediterranean coasts. The abundance and richness of these classical sites is a major money-spinner for Turkey. An indispensable read for those interested in Greek and Roman architecture is *The Ten Books on Architecture* by Vitruvius, a Roman architect and engineer of the 1st century BC.

The classic "pediment" or triangular gable structure is an early indicator, typical of Hellenistic, Greek and even Lycian and Lydian rock tombs. Of the three principal column designs, the simple, fluted Doric column is considered the earliest; the Ionic column, typified by the

The most powerful deity in the Hatti-Hittite pantheon, Taru/Tarhun, was the god of sky and storms, who killed the cosmic dragon Illuyanka; his wife, Wurusemu/Arinniti, was the sun goddess.

scroll-shaped capital, may have developed in the Carian region, while the ornate, foliated Corinthian column (which later included a composite with the Ionian style) was not much used until the Roman era.

This period saw the birth of town planning. The Greeks, who preferred to build their cities on slopes, originated the idea of siting the

LEFT: Hittite relief in Karatepe.
RIGHT: the temple-tomb of Amyntas, in Fethiye, is one of the most elaborate of the Lycian rock tombs.

principal temples and treasuries on an acropolis (low hill to one side of town) while the agora below was primarily a marketplace, but also used for political meetings. The Romans renamed this area the forum, and tended to place their civic buildings and temples nearby.

Greek theatres usually occupied natural cavities on hillsides. They often had temples to Dionysos (patron god of actors) nearby; early theatrical performances were religious in nature and only performed during festivals. Jolly Dionysos himself probably originated as an Anatolian god of fertility and wine, possibly related to the Hittite god of agriculture, Telepinu. Indeed, classical culture involved a great deal of mingling with beliefs indigenous to Anatolia.

The Roman era began in 190 BC, concluding in the *Pax Romana* (27 BC–AD 180); under the empire, Ephesus became capital of the province of Asia. Roman town planning was similar to that of their Greek predecessors, but displayed a penchant for colonnaded streets. The Romans were far more interested in blood sports than high drama; the word "arena" actually comes from the Latin word for sand, strewn about to absorb blood and other

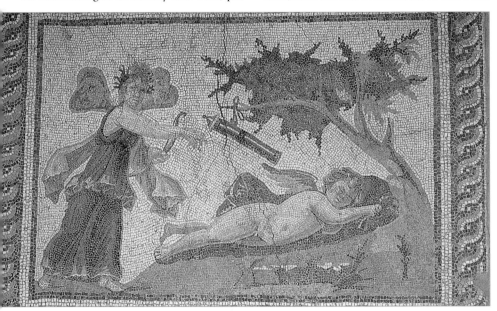

FIRST-CLASS PLUMBING

The homes of the wealthier occupants of Ephesus – the so-called Terrace Houses – offer some of the best-preserved evidence of Roman daily life. The houses were equipped with central heating and hot-water taps, while the walls and floors were adorned with exquisite mosaics and frescoes. However, as is still true in much of the Mediterranean, windows faced an atrium rather than looking out on the town; the life of the rich citizen was considered private and family-oriented. The inward orientation of the courtyard houses emphasised cool dimness and conservation of water; the centre of the roof was open, slanting inwards, and rainwater collected in the *impluvium*, a shallow pool in the atrium, often with a well beneath.

In one house, a grand, two-seater toilet perhaps tells us something about Roman philosophy, though it is open to personal interpretation. The walls are decorated with frescoes of men, perhaps in the agora, near sundials. "Wait for a Convenient Time or Die" is inscribed, cryptically, in Greek on one wall, while on another is emblazoned "Nine to Five".

Especially noteworthy is the way in which tastes have come full-circle since ancient times. Walls were hand-painted with floral motifs, while furniture was of marble-topped wrought iron. The roof, which has been rebuilt to its original design, was made of pine beams with skylights and completely covered in clay tiles.

effluvia from whatever sport took place in the formerly Greek theatres that had been suitably modified for the purpose.

The cult of Artemis

The Greek and Roman religious pantheon is traditionally headed by Zeus/Jupiter and a host of jealous female consorts, although there is evidence that the older mother goddess Kybele had substantial influence in encouraging the worship of the virgin Artemis at Ephesus, and also had a later effect on Christianity in the form of the Virgin Mary.

The original Temple of Ephesian Artemis was built around 700 BC, but the third version – vintage *c.*550 BC – became the largest structure in the Greek world, and the first monument constructed entirely of marble. There were 127 columns, the 36 standing in front covered with reliefs, giving the impression of a forest. It was a suitable setting for a nature goddess – the mistress of animals, like her predecessor Kybele – whose original idol, according to legend, fell from the sky as a meteor. Archaeologists suspect the temple's design was influenced by Egyptian, Assyrian and Hittite architecture, and the Marble Lady who dwelt inside was not very Hellenic either, generally depicted flanked by wild beasts and/or sprouting bulbous protuberances which may represent (scholarly opinion differs) breasts, eggs, the testicles of sacrificed bulls – or those of her priests, who obligatorily castrated themselves and dedicated the result to the goddess. Little remains of the temple, but many examples of Artemis and her antecedents can be found in the nearby Selçuk museum.

Byzantium and the Crusaders

In the 4th century AD, the relocation of the emperor to Constantinople and the state's espousal of Christianity propelled Byzantine architecture away from its Roman origins. Buildings of this era are easily recognisable by square-hewn stonework or two layers of brick-and stone-filled sandwiching rubble that could more readily be curved. Doors and windows are usually constructed as semicircular arches.

Churches have two basic designs. With a nod to the civic architecture of Rome, the early basilica is basically rectangular, twice as long

as it is wide, with two rows of columns dividing it into a central nave and side aisles. By the 6th century, dome construction had been perfected. This required transepts (side arms) to maintain its bulk, and thus the cruciform church emerged. Ingenious curved surfaces –

> The architecture of the Byzantine church was symbolic; the dome represented heaven with Christ at the centre of the firmament, with apostles and saints lower down the walls, reflecting the hierarchy.

pendentives and squinches – are the immediate supports of the dome.

Most Byzantine churches were decorated with frescoes or mosaics representing biblical scenes, usually presented in cartoon-strip fashion accessible to semi-literate or illiterate parishioners. Some of the finest extant paintings are found in the Cappadocian cave-churches (*see page 306*), where they have miraculously escaped the depredations of gravity, Islam and the iconoclasts.

The Crusades (11th–13th centuries) wrought vast damage on whatever native architecture they encountered – "pagan", Jewish, Orthodox or Muslim. Temples were pillaged or burnt for lime and masonry stacked horizontally for hastily built fortifications. Coastal Turkey between

LEFT: Roman mosaic, Antakya. **RIGHT:** 10th-century Byzantine mosaic depicting the Virgin Mary.

the Dardanelles and the Hatay remains dotted with numerous Crusader castles, plus a few Genoese examples built in their capacity as allies of Byzantium.

Islamic art

Seljuk architecture is noted for its delicacy, influenced by Persia, though local Muslims did not baulk at using animal or human reliefs in their stonework. The most characteristic feature of Seljuk mosques is a *mihrab* (prayer niche) over the entrance, looking not unlike an elaborate jelly-mould. The Seljuks also perfected the art of geometric tilework, often formed into Arabic characters or Kufic script, some of the

finest examples of which can be seen in Konya *(see page 298)*.

The Ottomans were great lovers of luxury, and their early arts are distinctly oriental in style, including Chinese dragons and the classic yin-yang symbol. Turkish shadow puppets *(Karagöz)* are clearly related to those of Java, and came to Turkey via Ottoman occupation of Egypt in the 16th century. However, Ottoman culture is primarily noted for its stunning architecture, a unique fusion of Asian, Islamic and Byzantine styles, best exemplified by the works of Mimar Sinan *(see page 157)*. Another art form perfected by the Ottomans was miniature painting and calligraphy, notably the elaborate monogram *(tuğra)* used by each sultan, which was even

engraved on his silverware and is greatly prized by collectors today. Amasya was the centre of calligraphic art in the 15th century; one of its masters, Şeyh Hamdullah, was brought to the capital by Sultan Beyazit II – his work can be seen in the Beyazit mosques of both Istanbul and Amasya.

İznik tilework reached its peak late in the 16th century, and there are outstanding examples of İznik tiles in the mosques of Bursa and in Rüstem Paşa Camii in İstanbul. The craft had essentially vanished by the mid-1700s, and has only recently been revived *(see page 171)*.

The period 1893–1909 produced a flowering of Art Nouveau architecture in Istanbul, most of it the work of resident Italian Raimondo Tommaso d'Aronco. Many fine examples still remain, especially around Beyoğlu, on the Marmara University campus and the Princes' Islands.

Under the republic

It's indisputable that Turkey's artistic and architectural treasures date from pre-republican times. Until the 1970s, painting and sculpture, in accordance with Kemalist ideology, were merely derivative of Western movements – including socialist realism.

The less said about contemporary architecture, the better; the London art critic Brian Sewell's curmudgeonly comment in *South From Ephesus* that "no building built during the republic is worth tuppence" is only slightly over the top. The roots of this baleful profile lie in a toxic cocktail of earthquakes, corruption, the tastes of returned German-Turks, and developer greed. About the best that can be expected in resort areas is faux-Ottoman *rustique*, as at Akyaka near Marmaris.

One of the very few contemporary architects who displayed respect for tradition or the environment was three-time Aga Khan award winner Turgut Cansever (1920–2009), fêted for his Demir Village development and Ertegün mansion in or near Bodrum, and the Turkish Historical Society HQ in Ankara. After three decades battling insensitive urban planners in İstanbul, he too had strong views on the subject, railing against "centralised, technocratic despotism, which clusters human beings in monstrous apartment blocks." ❏

ABOVE: the agora of the ruined city, İzmir.

Vernacular Architecture

Attractive traditional dwellings, in a variety of regional styles, are still much in evidence across Turkey

Despite fires, extensive destruction in the 1919–22 War of Independence, and the inevitable homogenisation brought by cheap concrete, a good deal of vernacular architecture survives in Turkey. By "vernacular" we mean indigenous building styles, disregarding foreign imports like the Russian terraces of Kars, the Levantine gingerbread townhouses of İzmir's Alsancak district, and Greek neoclassical mansions in Ayvalık or Foça.

Ottoman İstanbul was largely built of wood (with interior plastering), from the terraced houses of the common people to the *yalıs* (grand waterside summer mansions of the aristocracy), over 600 of which still line the Bosphorus. The oldest *yalıs* date from 1699, although today many are neglected. Visitors assume that the weathered bare wood was always on view, but in their day both terrace houses and *yalıs* were brightly painted.

Elsewhere in Anatolia, vernacular houses conform to a pattern seen throughout the Balkans, perhaps originally Byzantine. Dwellings are usually two storeyed, the lower floor stone-built, with few or no windows and iron-reinforced double doors. Once through these, there's a stone-paved courtyard *(hayat)*, with rooms around it used for storage and stabling animals. The upper storey is built with light lath-and-plaster *(bağdadi)*, which allows it to overhang the ground floor perched on wooden struts. A rectangular overhang is a *şahnişin*, a rounded bay a *cumba*. The upper living quarters have many

ABOVE: houses in İstanbul's Kumkapı neighbourhood.
RIGHT: the old town in Tarsus.

windows, though these were traditionally fitted with a lattice to protect female virtue (while still allowing ladies of the house to spy on the street). Fireplaces had conical hoods, and wooden ceilings were often elaborately carved; women's and men's quarters were separated as the *haremlik* and *selamlık* respectively.

Cumalıkızık, near Bursa, is probably the most complete surviving vernacular village, although Safranbolu, between Ankara and the Black Sea, is on an even grander scale, many of its mansions attaining three storeys, and employing half-timbering to distribute the extra weight. Mudurnu lies about halfway between them both geographi-

cally and in style, but also has a timber-and-stone mosque. There are several of these dating from the 13th and 14th centuries, the stars being the all-wood Mahmud Bey Camii at Kasaba near Kastamonu and the Eşrefoğlu Camii at Beyşehir near Konya, where forests of wooden columns support the roof.

On the Aegean the main attraction is at Muğla, which lovingly preserves 400 18th-century white-plastered houses with outsized beaked chimneys and wooden doors with a smaller central cutout, the *kuzulu kapı*. The southeast of the country features more Arab-influenced, kasbah architecture, as in Urfa's tawny limestone medieval houses with their corbelled *şahnişins*, and Mardin's mansions, some of which were built by indigenous Christians. ❏

SAZ, JAZZ AND SUFI CHANTS

Turkish music draws on a kaleidoscope of influences
from every corner of the old empire – and lately, the
wider world

Turkey's indigenous music varies from stately Ottoman classical to forms of folk music and devotional or ritual genres such as Mevlevî *(see page 85)* ritual music. *Sanat* (art) singing and gypsy *fasıl* ensembles are both derived from Ottoman classical music, while *özgün* is a progressive outgrowth of "pure" folk.

Turks have also readily assimilated and adapted foreign styles. Jazz has been fashionable among urban intellectuals since the 1950s – after all, the famous Atlantic record label was founded by two Turkish brothers, Ahmet and Nesuhi Ertegün. Today, Turkish record labels are committed to avant-garde projects, while clubbers enjoy hip-hop, electronica and various Western-Turkish fusion genres.

Such a sound spectrum wasn't always a foregone conclusion. The young republic, besotted with all things Western, applied this to music; the rich heritage of Ottoman classical and devotional music was denied official support and banned from the airwaves in favour of sanitised, Soviet-style folk ensembles and Western classical, the two often bizarrely combined, as in Ahmet Adnan Saygun's *Yunus Emre Oratorio.* Not until the 1970s did these strictures relax.

Classical, art and *fasıl* music

The classical music of the Ottoman court was considered to be too heterogeneous to serve as a politically correct basis for a new national music. Many of its composers were Crimean, Azeri, Jewish or Christian, and included several sultans; its modes were (and still are) based partly on the Arabic tradition, partly on ancient Greek treatises. Typical instrumentation includes *ud* (fretless, 11-stringed lute), *ney* (end-blown reed flute), *tanbur* (3-stringed long-

necked lute), *kanun* (finger-plucked zither) and *def* (frame drum).

A direct outgrowth was *sanat* (art) music, which showcased the voice in suites of vocal

Turkish-pressed CDs are considerably cheaper than imports – typically 11–23TL. For recommended music shops, see pages 410–11 in Travel Tips.

improvisations (*şarkı*) interspersed with instrumental interludes; most *şarkı* date from the late 19th century. Standout singers have included Münir Nurettin Selçuk (1901–81), Safiye Ayla

(1907–98), Zeki Müren (1931–96) and Bülent Ersöy (1952–).

Fasıl is an even more commercial descendant of Ottoman classical music, disparaged as "belly-dance music" by the uninformed and played disproportionately by Gypsies in nightclubs. To the classical instrumental mix *fasıl* adds *keman* (violin), *darbuka* (goblet drum), and most significantly the low-pitched G-*klarnet*, which leads the ensemble and defines this irresistibly danceable genre. Şükrü Tunar (1907–62) was considered the first great clarinettist; worthy successors include Mustafa Kandıralı (1930–), Barbaros Erköse and Selim Sesler (1957–).

Sufis and Aşıks

Devotional Mevlevî music consists of *âyin*, complex modal compositions dating back to the 1400s, and the influence of Sufi poet Celaleddin Rumi (Mevlâna). *Küdüm* (small kettle drums), *kanun* and *rebab* (a small lap fiddle) provide accompaniment; however, the *ney* is the principal instrument, its tone considered to symbolise the voice of the soul yearning for union with the divine. The best-known contemporary *ney*-player is Süleyman Erguner.

Aşık means "the ones in love", though Turkish bardic songs concern spiritual or political yearning rather than romantic pursuit. *Aşıks* accompany lyrics by medieval poets such as Yunus Emre and Pir Sultan Abdul on solo *saz* (a simple long-necked wooden lute); most of the bards belong to the Bektaşi and Alevî sects, known for their liberal egalitarianism. Aşık Veysel (1894–1973) was the classic proponent, while Arif Sağ and Feyzullah Çınar keep the flame burning for younger generations.

Rock, *özgün* and new waves

Rock music became popular with students through the 1970s, despite it being frowned on as "corrupting", and politically unsuitable. Guitarist-songwriter Cem Karaca figured in most of the bands of the Anatolian fusion-rock movement which was nearly choked off by the 1980s junta.

Özgün emerged in the late 1970s, combining rural melodies with guitar- or *saz*-based harmonies, other acoustic instruments and mellow vocals; Zülfü Livaneli and group Yeni Türkü were the "founders", followed by Grup Yorum

LEFT: Turkish musicians playing the *darbuka* (goblet drum) and violin. **RIGHT:** whirling dervish.

with its talented female singers Yasemin Göksu and İlkay Akkaya.

Contemporary musicians, especially Birol Topaloğlu and Fuat Saka from the eastern Black Sea coast, continue to reinvent regional folk styles. *Türkü* bars, where young musicians play traditional folk material with rock instrumentation, have multiplied in larger towns.

Jazz fusion projects include those led by percussionist Okay Temiz, Erkan Oğur on fretless electric guitar, and pianist Ayşe Tütüncü drawing on folk themes and other influences.

There is growing interest in the folk and popular music of the upper Balkans and

Greece, spearheaded by accordion player Muammer Ketencioğlu. Nostalgia for the Macedonian homelands of many contemporary Turks' forebears ensured immense popularity for the soundtracks for the 2007–08 television serial *Elveda Rumeli*, filmed in Macedonia, and indeed for any Balkan melodies with Turkish (or Romany, or Slavic) lyrics.

Quality popular music is still dominated by Sezen Aksu, whose career was kick-started by collaboration with Armenian-Turkish jazz musicians Onno and Arto Tunç, and subsequently Goran Bregovic; she has spawned a whole raft of disciples, including Sertab Erener, who won the 2003 Eurovision song contest, and teen idol Tarkan. ❑

HEIRLOOMS OF THE FUTURE

Quality Turkish carpets are among the most beautiful,
intricate and luxurious in the world – but buyers
need to be discriminating

An unforgettable part of a Turkish holiday is being pulled off the street by a multi-lingual carpet dealer and having scores of carpets unrolled before you as you sip tea and listen to the merchant regale you with the origin, meaning and age of each piece.

The Turks claim to have created the knotted-pile carpet, supposedly brought from Central Asia by the Seljuks. When they settled in Anatolia they encountered an already thriving indigenous tradition of flat-weave kilims whose ancestry stretches back to Neolithic times.

Searching for authenticity

Formerly, every village had its own techniques and patterns that made finished carpets as distinctive as fingerprints. These days, however, most weavers use standardised designs and colour schemes tailored to foreign tastes, and the end product often has little bearing on local tradition. This, together with increased population mobility, means that nobody can disentangle the various influences, and many regional styles are in danger of being lost. Some merchants actually beat or intentionally fade their goods to fake "antiquity". Finding a genuinely unique carpet can be hard work.

Quality control and commitment to heritage are two reasons why carpet cooperatives such as the DOBAG Project near Ayvacık have been set up, to reteach women to use traditional designs and vegetable dyes. The quest for authenticity also explains the heightened interest in the vivid kilims and *sofras* (woven mats) produced in the eastern provinces of Hakkâri and Van. These were little valued until the late 1960s, and so escaped direct marketplace influence until then. Today, they are prized for their bold but simple abstract designs, and prices have risen steeply.

Choosing a prize

The quality of a carpet or kilim is generally determined by the density of its weave – if you check the backs of most carpets, it is easy to see which are better made from the clarity of the design. High-quality, pure-wool, knotted-pile carpets are the most expensive, while kilims are much cheaper. *Cicims* have embroidered designs stitched into them, while *sumaks*, flat-weave rugs or saddlebags from Azerbaijan, are heavily overstitched with the pattern visible only on top, and are good for heavily used areas. Pure silk carpets cost nearly three times as much and are generally small, delicately coloured and intricately woven, the very finest containing as many as 900 knots per square centimetre.

Colour is as important as the weave. Kilims and carpets using only traditional, earth-toned vegetable dyes are the most prized by collectors – they have a luminous and subtle quality which chemical colours cannot match, and which are much kinder on the wool, making the carpet last longer. The limited range of very bright colours obtained from natural dyes also serves to curb village weavers' inclinations for garish colours.

It's quite easy to spot chemical dyes, even the subtler "natural-identical" ones which mimic natural hues. Part a section of the pile with your fingers – if the tint at the bottom is different to the top, it's probably a chemical dye – and has

travellers finding that what they receive is not what they paid for. Try, if possible, to carry it home; arranging shipping yourself will almost certainly mean paying more import duty, as you cannot use your traveller's allowance. It is also surprising how much you can knock off the price by refusing the "free" postage.

You are unlikely to encounter genuine antique carpets in any standard bazaar, but remember that Turkey has very strict laws on the export of antiquities. Any carpet or kilim over 100 years old must be cleared by a museum as exportable, and be accompanied by a certificate. ❑

possibly been faded artificially on the surface. Caustic lye or chlorine-bleaching will seriously reduce the carpet's longevity. Moisten a white handerchief and rub the pile; if any pigment comes off, it's again likely to be synthetic; any bleach odour will be evident.

Ultimately, the best way to choose a carpet is personal taste, so shop around before you buy. For more on Turkish carpet types, *see pages 110–11*.

Getting it home

Many shops offer to post your carpet home for you – it's best to demur, as tales abound of

LEFT: a contemporary kilim. **ABOVE:** among the myriad shapes and colours, only one is just right.

BUYER BEWARE

The more pushy carpet dealers are often young men who have invested their savings to buy stock; they rent space in resort areas, then pester the life out of anyone passing, employing touts who work on commission. Owner-occupied carpet shops are usually staffed by more laid-back, older men who know a great deal about their stock. However, all aim to sell carpets at the highest possible price, and most will tell a potential customer anything they want to hear, even extending to so-called certificates of authenticity.

PATTERNS OF LIFE: CARPETS AND KILIMS

Marco Polo, crossing Anatolia in the 13th century, commented on the beauty of Turkey's carpets. Many of today's offerings are equally magnificent

Until the 1900s, most households across the length and breadth of Turkey possessed looms to produce carpets, sacks, saddlebags, cushion covers, baby's slings and various household furnishings. The result of this abundance has been the development of an astonishing range of styles, techniques and designs: the mock-Caucasian thick piles of the Çanakkale area; the sumptuous carnation motifs of Milas; the hard-edged geometric patterns of Cappadocia and Denizli; the stylised figurines of Turkoman rugs near the Persian border; and the wild floral and arabesque designs of Ottoman court carpets, woven at workshops in İstanbul and Bursa. The heirs to this tradition today are the finely woven silk-and-wool carpets of Hereke, home to the 19th-century imperial workshops.

In the past, thread for the domestic looms was handspun from wool, goat hair, cotton or linen; silk was manufactured in the imperial factories in Bursa. Each district had its own specialist dyer. Colours were traditionally obtained from indigenous plants. Madder root produces shades from brick-red to orange, pinks and purple, and was a lucrative export crop as one of the only reliable red dyes until the 1860s. Other important dyes were indigo for blue, saffron for yellow and walnut (also exported) for black and brown.

The earliest known Turkish pile carpets (on display in İstanbul and Konya) are crude but powerful 13th-century Seljuk examples discovered in Konya and Beyşehir; flat-weave kilims have probably been in production locally since the 6th millennium BC.

BELOW: choose from silk Persian rugs, traditional home-woven Anatolian kilims (a woven rather than knotted mat) and prayer ru

BELOW: carpets made at the Ildiz carpet factory in Milas are hand-woven, with the cleaning and spinning of the wool, and the dying of the yarn, all done by hand.

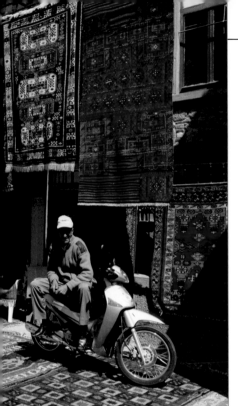

LOUDER THAN WORDS

Turkish carpet and kilim motifs *(nakıh)* are traditionally handed down from mother to daughter. In accordance with Islamic tradition, animal and human motifs are highly stylised. Among Turkish nomads, the *elibelinde* or arms-akimbo motif represents good luck, while flocks of birds may stand for homesickness. The tree of life is a classic spiritual symbol, though the beech tree is thought to relate specifically to Central Asian shamanist beliefs. An eight-pointed star can represent fate or the Wheel of Life.

Prayer rugs *(namazlık)* frequently show a *mihrab* (prayer niche), to be pointed towards Mecca; a mosque lamp hanging from the arch denotes divine light. Funereal carpets, for graveside worship, may contain images of cypress trees, headstones and blue skies above the *mihrab*, representing paradise.

The pattern of two triangles, tips touching, often represents a girl, and may be used in a "dowry" kilim for luck and light work after marriage. Single triangles may represent talismans worn by nomads.

VE: Bergama carpets, made in and around the eponymous town orthwest Turkey, are comprised entirely of wool.

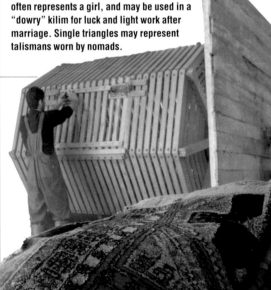

VE: the carpet inside the Blue Mosque (Sultan Ahmet Camii) in nbul. **TOP RIGHT:** bold geometric designs have been an intrinsic of Turkish art since ancient times. **RIGHT:** weaving loom at Ildiz bet factory, where visitors can learn the checks used to test bets' quality and see demonstrations of carpet-weaving techniques.

PLACES

A detailed guide to the entire country,
with principal sites cross-referenced
by number to the maps

Having squeezed Turkey's entire, extraordinary 8,000-year history and modern culture into 100 pages, this book's next task is to take the reader on a tour of Anatolia. The country is simply too huge to treat every sight with the attention it deserves, so we reluctantly concentrate on the more popular and accessible areas. Some parts of Turkey are so remote that reaching them requires your own transport and/or two full days of overland travel. The far southeast is still recovering from the effects of Kurdish-related troubles, and lacks much in the way of tourist infrastructure.

We have divided Turkey into seven regions, each with a short introduction and detailed map. These are then subdivided into manageable geographical bites. In magnificent, stately İstanbul, the old and new cities face each other across the Golden Horn. A separate short chapter describes the Bosphorus and the Princes' Islands. Wrapped around the Sea of Marmara are the small but fascinating regions of Thrace (European Turkey) and Marmara, each in its time hosting the capital of the Ottoman Empire.

The western and southern coasts are lapped by warm, turquoise-blue waters, with limpid sands or shady pines, luring millions of tourists each summer. The Aegean Coast comprises four areas – the north; İzmir and its hinterland; the south coast, beyond Ephesus; and the tourist havens of Bodrum and Marmaris. From here, the beautiful Mediterranean Coast runs east for over 1,500km (1,000 miles), through the ancient realms of Lycia (west), Pamphylia (centre) and Cilicia (east), before turning south into the Hatay.

The Central Anatolia section focuses on the modern capital of Ankara,

around which chapters radiate northwest, southwest, and east to the legendary volcanic landscapes of Cappadocia. To the north loom the little-known Black Sea coast and wild, forested mountains. Eastern Turkey covers nearly half the country's area, but much of it is a harsh, sparsely populated land, whose spectacular beauty remains hidden to all but the most adventurous traveller. ❑

PRECEDING PAGES: dramatic Sümela Monastery near Trabzon; the archaeological site of Assos amid poppies; the Blue Mosque in Istanbul. **LEFT:** skimming over Cappadocia. **TOP:** family transport in Silifke. **ABOVE LEFT:** craftswoman in Assos.

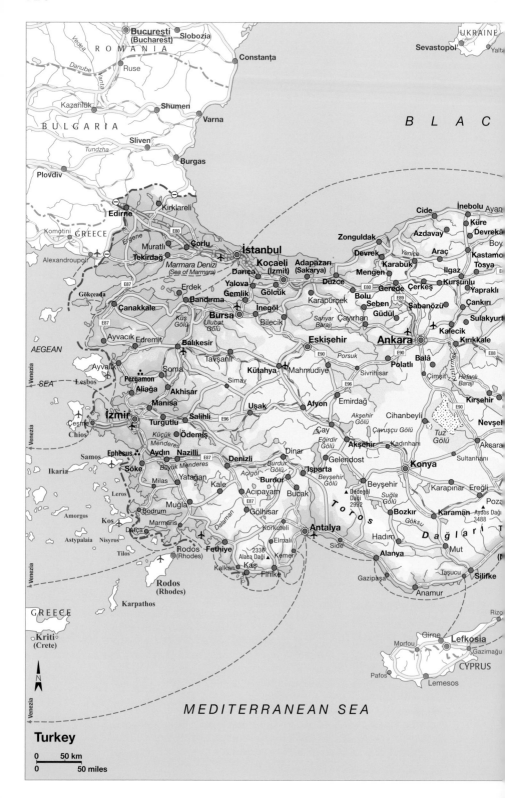

Turkey

0   50 km

0   50 miles

İSTANBUL

Capital in turn to the Roman, Byzantine and
Ottoman empires, modern İstanbul is a busy – but
still romantic – city split in two by the Bosphorus

Maybe it's the magic of its famous trio of names –
Byzantium, Constantinople and İstanbul – but
this is a city which has always brought out the fantasist in visitors. Even today when it is bulging at the seams
with an estimated 16 million residents, İstanbul can still
seem ineffably romantic, not least because you can never
be quite sure what you are going to find around the next
corner. A Byzantine capital reused to make a fountain, an
Ottoman tombstone jutting up unexpectedly in the middle of a busy main road, an early Republican building being given new
life – all such quirks are taken in their stride by a population that has its
eyes far more firmly fixed on the minutiae of day-to-day life.

Most visitors to İstanbul concentrate their attentions on what is called
the Historic Peninsula, the triangle of land at the confluence of the Bosphorus and the Sea of Marmara where first the Greeks and then – much
later – the Ottomans built their cities. Here it's just about possible to
forget about modernity and revel in a dream of ancient splendour.

Just a tram and funicular ride away the modern city
waits to be discovered on frenetic İstiklal Caddesi, where
suddenly the average age of a passer-by slumps to about
25, and virtually every vestige of the ancient past has given
way to shops, clubs, restaurants and bars. Sipping a beer
alongside İstanbul's gilded youth at a pavement café in
trendy Asmalımescit, you could be forgiven for wondering
why a question mark should still hang over Turkey's accession to the European Union.

But even that is to see only two faces of the
modern city. To find the pious İstanbul where
the call to prayer still brings the faithful running five times a day, you need to venture into
Fatih, or further afield to Eyüp – areas of town
still dotted with reminders of the Byzantine
and Ottoman past.   ❏

LEFT: historical tram on İstiklal Caddesi, Taksim, İstanbul. **TOP:** young resident of
the Balat neighbourhood. **ABOVE LEFT:** the Sultan's bath in the Harem section of
the Topkapı Palace. **ABOVE RIGHT:** belly-dancing costumes at the Grand Bazaar.

İSTANBUL: OLD CITY

The heart of Old İstanbul is Sultanahmet,
the area around the Topkapı Palace,
the Aya Sofya and the Blue
Mosque that reeks of past glories

Main attractions
AYA SOFYA
YEREBATAN SARAYI
BLUE MOSQUE
TOPKAPI PALACE
GRAND BAZAAR
SÜLEYMANIYE CAMII
KARIYE MUSEUM

When people speak today of Old İstanbul they are usually thinking mainly of **Sultanahmet**, the extraordinarily beautiful peninsula overlooking the point where the Sea of Marmara meets the Bosphorus and the Golden Horn. This outstanding location became the natural home to Byzantium, the capital first of the Eastern Roman Empire and then of the Byzantine Empire that evolved out of it, and then, after 1453, to the Ottoman Empire that replaced it. Not surprisingly, it's home not just to some of the most splendid monuments of the Ottomans but also to some of the greatest survivors from Byzantium, with the Ottoman Topkapı Palace and Sultanahmet (Blue) Mosque more or less rubbing shoulders with Byzantine Aya Sofya. Even today it's impossible to dig a hole in Sultanahmet without coming upon evocative traces of the romantic Roman, Byzantine and early Ottoman past.

It's Sultanahmet that accounts for a large part of İstanbul's wonderful skyline of soaring minarets, curvaceous domes and pointy chimney stacks that jut up from the wooded surroundings of Topkapı, although in Byzantine times the city actually extended as far as the battered Land Walls that can be seen on the way in from Atatürk airport. These walls, together with the even more battered Sea Walls that defended the Golden Horn, also marked the effective limit of the early Ottoman city – so all the other truly great Ottoman monuments such as the Süleymaniye Mosque are enclosed inside them. It was only in later Ottoman times that foreign traders established a colony in what is now Galata in Beyoğlu, thus beginning the development of New İstanbul. With the exception of Kadıköy and Üsküdar, most of the Bosphorus settlements were not established until the 17th and

LEFT: Carpetmakers Street inside the Grand Bazaar. **RIGHT:** a specialist art: making tops for minarets.

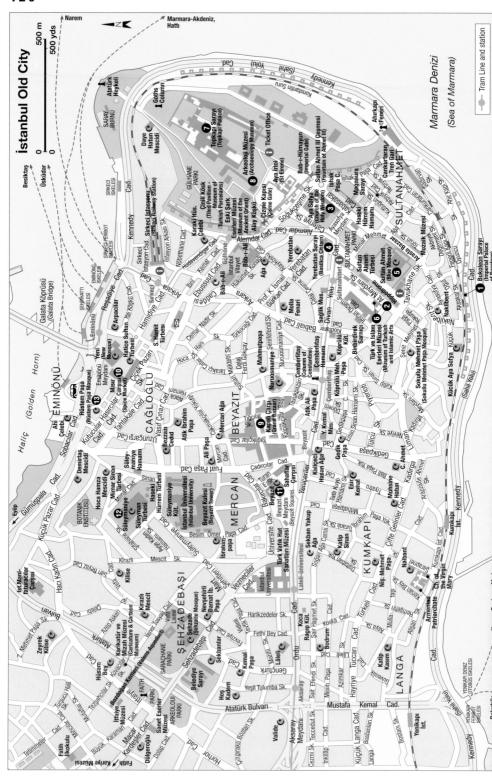

18th centuries. The urban sprawl that has swallowed them all into the maw of modern Greater İstanbul is a product of the latter part of the 20th century.

Origins

According to legend, İstanbul was established by the Megaran leader, Byzas, in the 7th century BC. After consulting the oracle of Delphi in Greece, he was instructed to settle across from the "land of the blind ones". Encountering a community living at Chalcedon on the Asian shore, Byzas concluded that the earlier colonists had, indeed, been deprived of their sight when they overlooked the superb location across the Bosphorus in Europe, and the colony of Byzantium was born on Seraglio Point, where the Sea of Marmara, Bosphorus and Golden Horn meet.

The settlement was largely left in peace until it was captured by Septimius Severus in AD 196 and absorbed into the Roman Empire. Some 130 years later, a heavenly vision inspired Constantine the Great to chose the city as his New Rome (see page 37). Officially founded on 26 November 326, and renamed Constantinople, it was now destined for greatness, and rapidly filled with the treasures of the ancient world.

Constantine and Justinian's city

The name Constantinople soon conjured up images of wealth beyond the dreams of the petty kings and princes of Europe, whose capital cities ranked as villages in comparison. However, it was Justinian the Great who turned it into a truly world-class city in the 6th century, and by the 9th century the population had reached nearly 1 million. Its main streets were not only paved, but covered, and decorated with columns and fountains.

Precious little remains of the glorious Byzantine city, apart from the shattered remnants of the great walls and the occasional sacred structure, most notably the church of Aya Sofya (Haghia Sophia to the Greeks). Other relics lie around the Hippodrome, west of the Blue Mosque. A surprising number of later Byzantine churches, however, are still dotted about the city, most of them converted into mosques.

The **Imperial Palace of Bucoleon** ❶ (Bukoleon Sarayı) dates back to the reign of Justinian and once towered over the private harbour of the Byzantine emperors on the Sea of Marmara. Traces of it can still be seen by walking down Küçük Ayasoya Caddesi and turning left along Kennedy Caddesi, the shore road. When sacked by Crusaders in 1204, the palace was described as containing 500 interconnected halls and 30 chapels decorated with gold mosaic. All that remains now is a single façade connected to the old sea walls, with three enormous marble-framed windows and the corbels of a vast balcony that must have commanded a spectacular view. Gazing over the ruins 200 years later, Mehmet the Conqueror is alleged to have quoted the Persian poet Saadi:

The spider weaves the curtains in the Palace of the Caesars
The owl calls the watches in Afrasiab's towers.

TIP

Camii is the Turkish for mosque; aya means saint (haghia in Greek, the language of Byzantium), so churches that have been converted to mosques can have more than one name.

BELOW: the Aya Sofya, converted from church to mosque in the 15th century.

The Obelisk of Pharaoh Thutmose in the Hippodrome.

Justinian's palace is thought to have stretched inland to encompass the area around Aya Sofya and the Sultanahmet (Blue) Mosque, and to have extended right up to the vast Yerebatan Sarayı underground cistern. The main part of the palace accessible to visitors is the **Mozaik Müzesi** (Mosaic Museum; Wed–Mon 9.30am–5pm; charge), in an alley off the **Arasta Bazaar**, an area of craft and souvenir shops behind the Blue Mosque, which displays a magnificent stretch of the original mosaic floor.

The **Küçük Aya Sofya Camii** (Little Aya Sofya, previously SS Sergius and Bacchus; daily during daylight hours), dating from 527 and the oldest church still extant in the city, stands near the Bucoleon Palace southwest of the Blue Mosque, and contains a beautiful two-storey marble colonnade.

The Hippodrome

The **At Meydanı** ❷ (Hippodrome; beside the Blue Mosque) was originally laid out by the Roman emperor Septimius Severus, but it was Constantine who established the horse-race arena – with a crowd capacity of more than 100,000 – as the public centre of his city. It was here that Justinian's partner, Theodora, the daughter of a bear-trainer, first appeared on the stage of history as a theatrical performer. The Hippodrome was also the site of the notorious Nika riots between the rival Green (lower-class) and Blue (bourgeoisie) chariot-racing factions. Some 30,000 people died in five days of urban warfare; the Aya Sofya (Haghia Sophia; *see below*) was destroyed, and Justinian almost driven from his throne.

There are three monuments left in the Hippodrome. The Dikilitaş (Obelisk of Pharaoh Thutmose) was brought by Constantine from Karnak in Egypt. The Yılanlı Sütun (Serpentine Column), which is formed by three intertwined metal snakes, stood originally in the Temple of Apollo at Delphi. Perhaps the most curious of the three monuments, it represents Constantine's eclectic (and not necessarily Christian) decorative tastes. The Ormetaş (Knitted Column), or Column of Constantine VII Porphyrogenitus, was restored in the early 10th century but is thought to be many centuries older. The bronze plates that originally covered it were carted off to Venice along with the four bronze horses now in St Mark's in Venice after the Crusaders sacked the city in 1204.

Aya Sofya (Haghia Sophia)

At the eastern end of the Hippodrome, across Sultanahmet Park, is the magnificent **Aya Sofya** ❸ (Tue–Sun 9.30am–5pm, June–Oct 9am–7pm; charge), otherwise known by its Greek name, Haghia Sophia or the Church of Holy Wisdom. It's the principal Byzantine building still standing in İstanbul and one of the finest architectural creations in the world, not least because of its stunning and hugely innovative dome. Dedicated in 536 during the reign of Justinian, the church, the third on the site, was the architectural wonder of its day. People have been astounded by its enormous size ever since, even more

overwhelming from the inside than the outside.

The first church, built by Constantine's son, Constantinus, burned to the ground in 404, while the second, built by Theodosius in 415, was torched during the Nika riots of 532. The present structure, whose dome has inspired architectural design for 1,500 years and established the template for other mosques, was the creation of Anthenius of Tralles and Isidorus of Miletus, who laboured for almost six years before the church was consecrated on 26 December 537; it was reconsecrated 26 years later after repairs following an earthquake that ruined the symmetry of the dome. The dome now stands 56 metres (183ft) high and measures 32 metres (105ft) across. The thin marble panels absorbed and reflected the light of thousands of candles, which illuminated the building so well that it was used as a lighthouse.

Tradition maintains that the area around the emperor's throne was the official centre of the world. Enter through a double narthex containing some of the old church's original mosaics and proceed into the vast empty acreage of what was once the nave but which is now dominated by four huge cartouches bearing the Arabic names of the early caliphs that bear witness to its conversion into the prayer hall in 1453. To the left of the entrance is the "sweating column", where Justinian was said to have cured a migraine by resting his head against the stone, leading to the belief that, when rubbed, each of the pillars in the church could cure a specific disease. The touch of centuries of visitors has resulted in a deep dent, now framed in brass and called the "holy hole".

When Justinian built Aya Sofya, he filled it with decorative mosaics. Later emperors added figurative ones, destroyed by the iconoclasts between 729 and 843 (see panel, page 38). Most of the mosaics in the church today postdate that period, and were preserved after the Muslim conquest of the city (when it became a mosque), thanks to a simple coat of whitewash. They were rediscovered during renovations in the 1930s when Atatürk converted Aya Sofya into a national museum.

> *The existence of St Sophia is atmospheric; that of St Peter's [in Rome], overpoweringly, imminently substantial. One is a church to God; the other, a salon for his agents.*
>
> Robert Byron

BELOW: inside Aya Sofya, showing the Sultan's viewing platform.

Detail of the upside-down Medusa head in the Yerebatan Sarayı.

BELOW LEFT: the Yerebatan Sarayı was little more than a ridiculously extravagant water tank. **BELOW RIGHT:** Aya Sofya with a modern tulip sculpture in the foreground.

After walking round the nave you should ascend to the galleries to view the best of the mosaics. The most striking are those on the eastern wall of the south gallery, showing Christ, John the Baptist and the Virgin Mary. In the last bay of the same gallery is an unmissable mosaic of the Empress Zoë and her husband, Constantine IX Monomachus. The latter's head was superimposed over that of Zoë's first husband, Romanus, the stable boy who seduced the 50-year-old spinster before trying to shuffle her off to a nunnery. He failed, and his face – and his life – were removed from all association with the throne for ever. A mosaic depicting Constantine and Justinian giving the city of İstanbul and Aya Sofya to the Virgin and Child can be seen over the exit door.

When you leave Aya Sofya be sure to duck round the corner and pass through the turnstile that leads back into the grounds where you can inspect the newly restored tombs of some of the early Ottoman emperors.

Facing Aya Sofya across the square is the **Haseki Hürrem Hamamı**, built in 1556 for Roxelana, wife of Süleyman the Magnificent. In 2010 it was restored with a view to returning it to use as a Turkish bath.

The Yerebatan Sarayı

Diagonally across from Aya Sofya, near the top of Divan Yolu (Imperial Way), is the **Yerebatan Sarayı** ❹ (Sunken Palace; daily 9am–5pm; charge), otherwise known as the Basilica Cistern. Begun by Constantine but expanded by Justinian in 532 for storing the imperial water supply, it may originally have been accessible from the Imperial Palace complex, but fell into disuse during Ottoman times.

Today, fully restored, its eerily lit underground chamber provides an unusual attraction. The cathedral-like ceiling is supported by 336 columns 9 metres (28ft) high of varying style and origin. The two huge Medusa heads used as pedestals, one upside down and one on its side, were probably poached from pre-Christian ruins. The cistern still contains a metre or so of water, over which bridges have been built to give visitors access. So inspiring is the site that it has been used as a film

set and for audiovisual installations during the İstanbul Arts Biennial.

A few blocks down Divan Yolu, on Klodfarer Cad., the **Binbirdirek Sarnıcı** (Cistern of 1,001 Columns; 8am–midnight; charge refundable if you eat here) is a second, even older, Byzantine cistern, dating back to Constantine's original 4th-century city. Recently restored and opened to the public, this is another extraordinary building, with 264 columns. It was said to hold enough water to support 360,000 people for 10 days. Today, it is home to a restaurant and is also a venue for concerts and folk dancing.

The Blue Mosque

The most famous, if not necessarily the most beautiful, mosque in the old city is the **Blue Mosque** ❺ (Sultan Ahmet Camii; daily, but closed at prayer times – best visited early in the morning; entrance is free, but donations are appreciated), facing Aya Sofya across Sultanahmet Square, and deriving its architectural style from the earlier church. It has blue stained-glass windows, and exquisite İznik tiles decorate its interior. It was built between 1609 and 1616 by the architect Mehmet Ağa, a student of the great architect Sinan, as a means of showing the world that he had outstripped his master – and the architects of Aya Sofya – and as a tribute to the superiority of Islam. It maintains that symbolism for many Muslims. With around 260 windows, and an associated religious school, hospital, caravansaray and soup kitchen (the *külliye* or "complete social centre" in the Islamic sense), the mosque is impressive for its size alone. Its six minarets nearly caused a diplomatic incident as this was as many as the great mosque in Mecca; the sultan had to donate an extra minaret to Mecca to quell the row.

Facing the Blue Mosque across the Hippodrome is the **İbrahim Paşa Sarayı**. This private palace houses the **Museum of Turkish and Islamic Arts** ❻ (Türk ve Islam Eserleri Müzesi; Tue–Sun 9am–5pm; charge), which is considered one of the best museums in Turkey and one of the finest extant Ottoman residential buildings in İstanbul. Built in 1524 for one of Süleyman the Magnificent's grand viziers, its quality and location point to a man of great power, who ruled as second in command for 13 years before Roxelana persuaded Süleyman that the man had become too big for his turban and had him strangled. The museum specialises in religious artefacts and antique carpets, with some fragments dating back to the 13th century. Don't miss the ethnographic exhibition in the basement, which traces the rich history of domestic life and dress and contains fascinating reminders of the lost nomadic lifestyle.

Topkapı Palace

Located to the northeast of Aya Sofya is the **Topkapı Palace** ❼ (Topkapı Sarayı Museum; Wed–Mon 9am–5pm; separate charge for the Harem). The complex is considerably smaller than the original, which used to extend down to the Sea of Marmara and include the area covered today by Sirkeci railway

TIP

Mosques are free and open to visitors except at the five prayer times, but you will be expected to remove your shoes. Shorts and bare arms are forbidden, and women must wear head-coverings. Scarves and guarded shoe racks are usually available at the entrance, and donations towards the mosque's upkeep are encouraged.

BELOW: entering the Blue Mosque.

station and Gülhane Park, but the grounds are still enormous. You need half a day to appreciate it properly.

The Topkapı was the nerve centre of the extensive Ottoman Empire after Mehmet the Conqueror's great-grandson, Süleyman the Magnificent, made the decision to make it the seat of the Ottoman Empire and his royal residence. The vast palace provided the setting for many events, both sublime and sordid, for 400 years until the construction of Dolmabahçe Palace (see page 136) further up the Bosphorus in the mid-19th century.

Though reflecting Mehmet I's original plans, the sprawling, eclectic compound overlooking the confluence of the Bosphorus, the Golden Horn and the Sea of Marmara bears no single particular architectural stamp. Every new sultan elaborated on the building according to need, and four major fires wrote off whatever architectural unity might initially have existed. The only original buildings left from the time of Mehmet I are the Raht Hazinesi (or Treasury building), which was Süleyman's original palace, the inner

and outer walls, and the **Çinili Köşk** (Tiled Pavilion), just below the palace in Gülhane Park.

The Tiled Pavilion is now home to the **Museum of Turkish Porcelains**, which displays early Seljuk and Ottoman ceramics as well as some exquisite İznik tiles from the 17th and 18th centuries. It lies in a separate museum complex that includes the city's excellent **Arkeoloji Müzesi** ❽ (Archaeology Museum), and the recently refurbished **Eski Şark Eserleri Müzesi** (Museum of the Ancient Orient; Tue–Sun 9.30am–5pm; single charge for all three) containing Sumerian, Babylonian and Hittite treasures. The archaeological museum has Greek and Roman antiquities and a magnificent sarcophagus erroneously claimed to belong to Alexander the Great.

The main Topkapı Palace complex consists of several distinct areas including the **Birun** (Outer Palace), **Enderun** (Inner Palace) and the **Harem**, each containing courtyards connected by a maze of passageways. At one time more than 50,000 people lived and worked in the palace, a veritable city within a

BELOW: the Ottoman Empire's coat of arms at the Topkapı Palace.

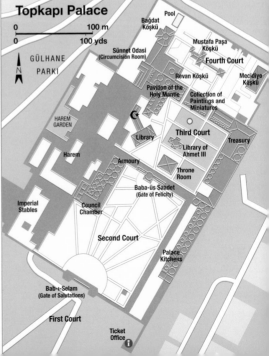

Topkapı Palace

0   100 m
0   100 yds

Pool
Bağdat Köşkü
Mustafa Paşa Köşkü
Sünnet Odası (Circumcision Room)
GÜLHANE PARKI
Fourth Court
N
Revan Köşkü
Mecidiye Köşkü
Pavilion of the Holy Mantle
Collection of Paintings and Miniatures
HAREM GARDEN
Library
Third Court
Treasury
Harem
Library of Ahmet III
Armoury
Throne Room
Baba-üs Saadet (Gate of Felicity)
Imperial Stables
Council Chamber
Second Court
Palace Kitchens
Bab-ı-Selam (Gate of Salutations)
First Court
Ticket Office

city, with dormitories for guards, craftsmen and gardeners, all wearing their own distinctive garb for easy identification. In addition to discreet neighbouring mosques and baths, the palace even had its own zoo, where lions, elephants, bears and other gifts from foreign rulers were kept.

The main entrance, the **Bab-ı-Hümayun** (Imperial Gate), was erected by Mehmet I in 1478. It leads to the First Courtyard where the janissaries, the Praetorian Guards of the Ottomans, were once headquartered. To the left is **Haghia Eirene** (Aya Irini), one of the oldest Byzantine churches in İstanbul. Originally dedicated in 360, it was completely rebuilt in 537, and briefly functioned as the cathedral of Constantinople until the Aya Sofya was completed later the same year. Never converted into a mosque, the breathtaking church served as an armoury and is now used as a venue for visual arts events and concerts.

Near the ticket office and the shop, the second gate, built by Süleyman the Magnificent in 1524, is known as the **Bab-ı-Selam** (Gate of Salutations). This

is the proper entrance to the palace. The courtyard beyond was renowned for its cypress trees, fountains, peacocks and gazelles designed to create an impression of calm and tranquillity. On the right are the domes and chimneys of the palace's huge kitchens, which now house a vast collection of glass, silver and rare Chinese porcelain.

The **Baba-üs Saadet** (Gate of Felicity) leads to the **Throne Room** and the **Treasury**, home to the Ottomans' almost obscene accumulation of jewels and precious metals. Security is tight for the staggering display of opulence, which includes bejewelled daggers, ivory book covers, huge slabs of emerald and the 84-carat Spoonmaker's Diamond, the fifth largest in the world. Also in this courtyard is a collection of early Turkish and Persian miniatures, some holy relics of the Prophet Mohammed and a sumptuous display of imperial robes.

The Harem

Of all the parts of the palace, it is the Harem in the Second Courtyard that most inflames visitors' imaginations,

The Kaşıkçı ("Spoonmaker's") Diamond, star of the film Topkapı.

BELOW: shady grounds of the Topkapı Palace.

BELOW: miniature showing a birth in the Harem.

fuelled by images of odalisques and slaves reclining on divans waiting for the sultan's pleasure. There were over 300 rooms (40 are open today), but half were cramped cubicles for the lesser eunuchs, servants and concubines. Rooms increase in size and opulence as you approach the chambers of the favourite concubines and four legal wives. Thanks to the legacy of Roxelana, chief wife of Süleyman the Magnificent, the Valide Sultan ("mother of the sultan") became effective queen of the domain and could exert great influence – her apartment was second only to the sultan's voluptuously ornate private rooms.

Even in its most decadent days, the Harem was hardly the den of unfettered sex and iniquity conjured up by many – there was too much competition. Sex with the sultan could hardly be a spontaneous affair – according to records left by one legal wife, he simply requested the Chief Black Eunuch to inform the girl he had chosen, after which she was bathed, perfumed, dressed and sent a gift. Unless she was especially favoured, he then presented himself at her chamber, (only a very few ever entered the sultan's rooms), where the date and time were recorded. If she became pregnant, that, too, was recorded; if the birth resulted in a boy, she acquired the elevated status of *Haseki Sultan*. Some sultans were known to be uninterested in and even hostile towards women and a preference for boys was not unknown. Osman II even wore spiked shoes in the Harem so that the grating sound would warn the women to get out of his way.

For the first 150 years of Ottoman rule, the brothers of each new sultan were strangled with a silken cord – in 1595 Sultan Mehmet III had 19 siblings murdered to forestall later power struggles. This could lead to difficulties later if no heir was forthcoming, and later Ottomans rethought the strategy. The Fourth Courtyard contains the **Veliaht Dairesi** (Gilded Cage – actually just another suite of rooms) where, in an effort to cut down on such rampant fratricide, the siblings of the heir apparent were kept safely out of the way in indulged isolation awaiting the possibility of power. Such conditions were not ideally suited to

Life in the Harem

Daily life in the Harem must have been a chaos of wailing babies, competitive mothers and harassed servants. The only men allowed in were the various princes, black eunuchs (colour-coded by job for easy identification) and, in emergencies, the so-called Zülfülü Baltacılar ("Firemen of the Lovelocks"), who wore exaggeratedly high collars to screen their prying eyes. As the empire decayed, the complex became more and more overcrowded; by the mid-1800s, there were over 800 odalisques in the Harem – virtual slaves living in often squalid conditions.

Yet despite its oppressive reputation, real romance could also flourish in the Harem. The 17th-century Sultan Abdülhamid I wrote a love letter to one of his paramours proving that political status is no match for the arrows of passion: "My Rühhah, your Hamid is yours to dispose of. The Lord Creator of the Universe is the Creator of all beings, and would never torment a man for a single fault. I am your bound slave, beat me or kill me if you wish. I surrender myself utterly to you. Please come tonight I beg of you. I swear you will be the cause of my illness, perhaps even of my death. I beg you, wiping the soles of your feet with my face and eyes. I swear to God Almighty, I can no longer control myself."

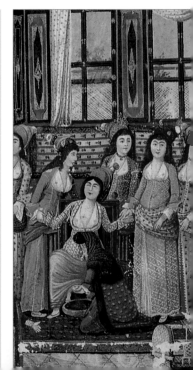

producing great leadership, however, and are often considered to have contributed to the fall of the empire. Deli Ibrahim (Ibrahim the Mad) suffered from extreme paranoia after 22 years in debauched isolation – his reign is primarily remembered for the 280 concubines he ordered to be drowned in the Bosphorus upon hearing rumours of a Harem plot.

The Grand Bazaar

Heading west towards the city walls, **Divan Yolu**, once the avenue of state trodden by viziers and pashas (high officials of the Ottoman Empire), is now lined with tourist shops, travel agencies and uninspired restaurants, while tramlines occupy the street. Several blocks west, Divan Yolu changes its name to Yeniçeriler Çaddesı (Avenue of the Janissaries) and arrives at Beyazit Square and the entrance to the **Kapalı Çarşı** ❾ (Grand Bazaar), a favourite tourist haunt, the size of a city street block, where everything from carpets to leather jackets, antiques, silver, icons and gold is haggled over. The selection is superb. Competition also keeps the prices reasonable,

but shop around before you commit to heavy bargaining. Don't expect to pick up some rare and dusty item for peanuts; the bazaar is a high-rent area, and traders have to be sharp. Some have even written books on their areas of specialisation, and all know the international value of real treasures.

Another popular bazaar, close to the ferry docks at Eminönü, is **Mısır Çarşısı** ❿ (Egyptian Spice Market). There are few things on sale here that you can't get more cheaply elsewhere, but it provides a good range of herbal products, Turkish Delight and cold meats, as well as the eponymous spices. More interesting is the medieval warren of old craftsmen, coppersmiths and woodworkers behind and to the right of the bazaar, home also to the delightful Rüstem Paşa Camii (see page 136).

Just west of the Grand Bazaar is Beyazit Square, which opens onto the main campus of İstanbul University. The **Beyazit Camii** ⓫, clearly inspired by the domes of Byzantine Aya Sofya, was the earliest of the classical Ottoman religious buildings that soon came to dominate the Islamic world,

Traditional figurines for sale in the Grand Bazaar.

BELOW: inside the atmospheric Grand Bazaar.

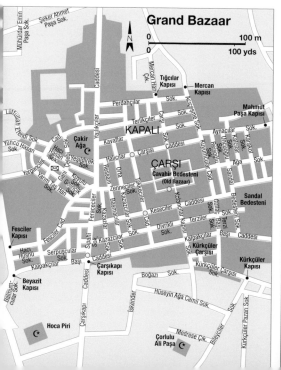

Grand Bazaar

0 — 100 m
0 — 100 yds

İznik tiles in the
Rüstem Paşa Camii.

replacing the traditional open courtyard structures favoured by the Arabs.

The spire at the centre of the University is the **Beyazit Kulesi**. Originally built of wood and used as a fire tower, it burned in one of the periodic infernos that have plagued the city since earliest times, and was replaced by the present stone structure in 1828.

Beyond the university is the towering splendour of the **Süleymaniye Camii** ⑫, or Sülemaniye Mosque, built by Mimar Sinan for the great man himself. It is the second-largest mosque in the city, and one of the finest in the world. Construction began in 1550. Inside, the mosque is almost square, measuring 58 by 57 metres (190 by 186ft); the diameter of the dome is 57 metres (186ft) and its height 47 metres (154ft). Less ornate than most imperial mosques, the structure invites you to find a corner in which to meditate. It was comprehensively restored in 2010.

In the peaceful back garden, through a forest of ornate tombstones including those of two other sultans, are the tombs of Süleyman the Magnificent and Roxelana. Süleyman's tomb is octagonal

and covered with İznik tiles, while his wife's is smaller, with a cylindrical base recessed from the corners of the building. Sadly, they are rarely unlocked.

Other mosques worth seeking out are the **Atık Ali Paşa Camii** (Boğazkesen Cad., Karaköy), one of the oldest in the city, and **Azapkapı** (next to the Atatürk Bridge, Galatasaray), a swansong built by Sinan in 1577. Especially beautiful, however, is the small **Rüstem Paşa Camii** ⑬, on Kutucular Caddesi, Eminönü, not far from Galata Bridge. Yet another Sinan-designed structure, it was commissioned in 1561 by the grand vizier Rüstem Paşa, husband of Süleyman the Magnificent's favourite daughter, Mihrimah, and is notable for its superb İznik tile work.

West to the Fatih district

Away from Sultanahmet the tourists quickly melt away, and Fatih, like most of the rest of the old city, is very much traditional Turkey where women still wear headscarves and men obey the call to prayer.

About 20 minutes' walk or a ten-minute cab ride from the Süleymaniye Mosque is the **Kariye Museum** (Kariye Müzesi; Chora Church; Thur–Tue 9am–5pm; charge). Chora is Greek for "in the country", reflecting the fact that the church was originally built beyond the city walls in the 6th century. In the 12th century it was glorified with extensions and decorations under the patronage of Theodorus Metochitus. In the years between 1453 and 1948 when it served as a mosque, its mosaics and frescoes, – the finest to survive in all Byzantium – were whitewashed over. Today it is a museum, the walls restored to relate the stories of Christianity according to Greek Othodoxy.

Close to the Chora Church is **Edirnekapı**, one of the gates in the Land Walls that date back in part to the 5th century, although they were much patched up and added to in the ensuing centuries until Sultan Mehmed the Conqueror finally crashed through them in 1453 to seize the city for

Islam. It's well worth taking a short stroll along this section of the walls to admire their size and construction.

Also in Fatih is the **Molla Zeyrek Camii** (formerly the Church of the Pantocrator), built around 1120 and the largest Byzantine church in the city after Aya Sofya and the Kariye Müzesi. You may also want to examine the **Aqueduct of Valens**, a huge structure dating back to 375 and straddling busy Atatürk Bulvarı that was once an important in the complex system that brought water into the city from as far away as Thrace.

Eyüp

On the upper reaches of the Golden Horn, **Eyüp** is one of Turkey's most holy sites. In fact, after Mecca, Medina and Jerusalem, **Eyüp Camii** (daily except at prayer times) vies with Damascus and Karbala for the honour of being the fourth most important place of pilgrimage in the Islamic world. "The Süleymaniye is glorious, Sultanahmet is beautiful, but it is the Eyüp Mosque which is holy" so the saying goes, and, indeed, the conservative religious nature of Eyüp will be instantly apparent from the number of women wearing chador-like black robes. Visitors are advised to dress modestly, behave respectfully and refrain from taking photographs, especially of the women. Avoid Eyüp on Fridays, the main day of prayer.

The mosque was built in the 15th century under Mehmet the Conqueror on the spot where Eyüb Al-Ansari, an elderly companion of the Prophet Mohammed, fell during the first Arab siege of Constantinople in 688. His tomb is enshrined here. At weekends, newlyweds arrive after their legal, secular wedding to be blessed by the imam, the bride often wearing a stylish white wedding dress, but with a white satin scarf covering her hair, another of the wonderful ways in which Turkey mixes East and West.

From here, take the cable car or walk up through the cemetery, its old Ottoman tombs topped with stone turbans, to reach the much touted **Pierre Loti Café**, made famous by a Turcophile French author (real name Julien Viaud) in the 1800s. From here there is a fabulous view over the Golden Horn. No alcohol is served, nor is there any food. The setting is all. ❑

TIP

Take the tram that hogs Divan Yolu to reach the Eminönü waterfront, the Galata Bridge, Beyoğlu (New Town) and the Dolmabahçe Palace.

BELOW: the Pierre Loti Café at the top of the Golden Horn in Eyüp.

The Golden Horn

The Golden Horn is a flooded river valley, once the private playground of the sultans and a favourite place to picnic – at least until the 1950s, when the once-pristine waters had deteriorated into a polluted mess in which no living thing could survive. In recent years, however, the water has been cleaned up (to the great delight of the fishermen who haunt the Galata Bridge all year round), and promenades laid along both sides, attracting back the local picnickers who flock here over summer weekends.

There are several stories about how the Golden Horn got its name, which appears to be of Greek origin. Was it because of the golden glow cast on the water by the setting sun? Or because gold coins were tossed into it in 1453 by panicking Byzantines? Or because of its shape? Whatever the truth may be, the Turks call it more prosaically the Haliç, meaning simply "bay".

The southern shore is more inviting, with a pleasantly landscaped waterfront running from beside the Atatürk Bridge and passing close to the **Greek Orthodox Patriarchate**, the **Church of St Stephen of the Bulgars** and the **Ahrida Synagogue**, showing the once-rich religious mix of the city in just a short distance. On the opposite shore at Hasköy, the **Rahmi M Koç Museum** (Hasköy Caddesi; Tue–Fri 10am–5pm, Sat–Sun 10am–7pm; charge), housed in an old iron foundry, is a fascinating private collection of everything involving science, technology and transport – great for kids.

İSTANBUL: THE NEW CITY AND THE BOSPHORUS

"New İstanbul" is a jazzy mix of Ottoman alleys, Art Nouveau mansions and steel-and-glass skyscrapers. To the east, dividing Europe and Asia, the Bosphorus is lined with handsome summer houses and attractive fishing harbours

BELOW: Taksim Square, the heart of modern Istanbul.

I t is perhaps misleading to describe the area loosely termed **Beyoğlu** – the area north of the Golden Horn, which stretches from the 14th-century Galata Tower to the swinging nightclub district of Taksim – as the "new" city (as any Turk would think of it). Most of the genteel architecture is more than a century old, and its history, predominantly one of foreign settlement, dates from the Middle Ages. Most intriguingly, it was the designated European Quarter during early Ottoman times, earning a reputation for both cul-

ture and debauchery, which attracted many curious Muslims and off-duty janissary soldiers. Later, the area was settled by other minorities welcomed by the Ottomans, and the ensuing cultural cosmopolitanism has survived to the present day through the impact of Greek, Jewish, Armenian, Italian, Russian and other settlers, whether merchants, natives or refugees. Today it is still the part of town most popular with expat foreigners, who continue a long-established tradition of making homes here.

The original Greek name for the area was Pera, meaning "beyond" or "across" (from the old city). By the 17th century it had become synonymous with taverns and bawdy licentiousness. According to the Turkish traveller Evliya Çelebi, there were "200 taverns and wine houses where the Infidels divert themselves with music and drinking". Prostitution, both male and female, was (and still more or less is) overlooked by the authorities.

In the 19th and early 20th centuries, the Western powers built their embassies here, imprinting a European stamp on the neighbourhood. Many of these mansions are now used as consulates, although the Americans have long since retreated to a more easily fortified location up the Bosphorus in İstiniye.

Cultural capital

Despite the fact that the city was dethroned in 1923, when Ankara was

declared the capital of the new Republic of Turkey, İstanbul has remained the undisputed commercial and cultural hub of the nation. This is where most major businesses maintain their head offices, where all new trends in art, literature, music and film begin, and where most of the money is made and kept.

All this has caused something of a conflict within the social fabric of the city, as poor rural migrants – frequently from the troubled east – pour into İstanbul looking for employment, only to find themselves treated as second-class citizens. All too often, they fall easy prey to the utopian promises of radical Islam. Today, the Galata area near the bridge is conservatively Islamic, settled primarily by rural migrants, although fashionable restaurants and teahouses have successfully invaded.

In the face of this conservatism, the area's once famous nightlife has simply moved uphill to Tünel where the underground funicular railway deposits visitors in super-trendy **Asmalımescit**, while the area around the Galata Tower has become fairly touristy.

Galata Bridge to Galata Tower

One of the most famous city landmarks is the **Galata Bridge** ❶ (Galata Köprüsü) that connects Eminönü with Karaköy, thus linking the old city to the new. The fifth bridge on the site seems so crucial to getting around today that it's hard to believe there was no permanent crossing point here until the 19th century. Today it is permanent home to a colony of fishermen who pay little heed to the tram rattling to and fro behind their backs. The current model opened in 1994; its predecessor has been re-erected along the Golden Horn to provide a footbridge between Eyüp and Sütlüce.

Karaköy is home to a small, lively fish market, as well as ferries to Kadıköy and Haydarpaşa station. It's also where the cruise ships dock to disgorge thousands of tourists into the old city. Originally a Customs warehouse further east along the pier at Karaköy, **İstanbul Modern** ❷ (Meclisi Mebusan Caddesi Liman Sahası; Tue–Sun 10am–6pm, Thur until 8pm; charge but free on Thur) houses contemporary Turkish paintings,

Fishing bait for sale on Galata Bridge, home to a colony of fishermen.

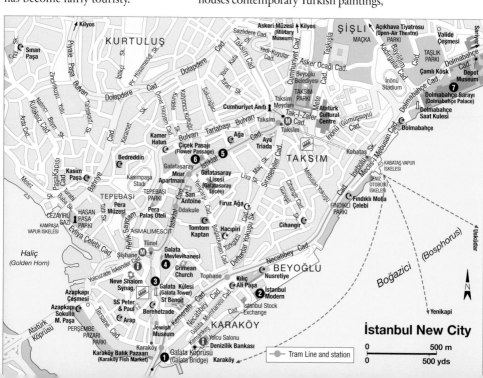

İstanbul New City

0   500 m

0   500 yds

Tram Line and station

Simit *vendors are ubiquitous in İstanbul.*

BELOW: the Galata Tower looks down on a Beyoğlu street.

sculpture, photography, video and sound installations. It also has regular touring exhibitions, an arthouse cinema and a chic café-bar with superb views.

From Karaköy most people ascend to Galata and Tepebaşı using the **Tünel**, a short funicular railway that has been in business since 1875 and that leaves from a street best known to İstanbul residents for its innumerable hardware and lighting shops.

Galata Tower ❸ (Galata Kulesi; off Yüksekkaldırım Cad.; daily 10am–6pm, evening show at 8pm; charge) was built as a watchtower in 1348 by Genoese settlers who had been granted free trade and semi-independent status following the Latin occupation. Take an elevator to the top for a sweeping view of the city. The square at the bottom of the tower is a popular meeting place, occasionally used for outdoor concerts. From here **Galipdede Caddesi** winds uphill past a concentration of music shops interspersed with small cafés, boutiques and hostels to reach the upper end of the Tünel funicular.

Beyoğlu and Galata are also home to several functioning Christian churches, including liberal Anglican, Dutch Reform and Roman Catholic establishments. There are also several synagogues in Galata, including the Neve Shalom, which was the target of a massive Al Qaeda bomb that killed 25 people in November 2003. Most of İstanbul's dwindling Jewish community is Sephardic, having been welcomed into Turkey when they fled the Inquisition in 1492.

Nor are Muslim minorities left out: the public are able to visit the **Galata Mevlevihanesi ❹** (Sun–Mon 9.30am–4.30pm; charge), a particularly open-minded dervish centre that is officially a museum. Although their beliefs are derived from those of the Konya dervishes *(see page 299)*, the Galata dervishes follow a separate Dede (master) and are decidedly New Age, being the first to allow women to participate in the dance ceremony. Performances of their whirling trance-dance form of worship take place every fortnight or so in summer, with dates and times

posted outside the building. They also perform regularly in the run-up to the Mevlevi Festival on 17 December.

Moving uptown

The Tünel funicular from Karaköy deposits you at the western end of İstiklal Caddesi **⑤**, the main street through the New Town, running from Tünel to Taksim Square, which is primarily dedicated to shopping, entertainment and culture. Just over 1.6km (1 mile) long, it is serviced by an atmospheric old tram which trundles along the pedestrianised street. There are more cinemas here than in any other part of the city (films are shown in their original languages with Turkish films tending to rule the roost these days), as well as many small art galleries. Housed in the handsome old Hotel Bristol, the **Pera Museum** (Meşrutiyet Cad. 41; Tue–Sat 10am–7pm, Sun noon–6pm; charge) has first-rate 19th-century Turkish portraits, paintings and porcelain.

Nearby is one of the more famous landmarks of old Beyoğlu. The wonderful, century-old hotel made famous by Agatha Christie, the **Pera Palaş Oteli**

was built to accommodate passengers from the Orient Express, and was completely refurbished between 2009 and 2010. Its lobbies are cluttered with 19th-century furniture and its plush corridors redolent with intrigue.

In recent years the **Asmalımescit** district, a veritable warren of alleyways leading west off İstiklal Caddesi to the north of Tünel, has become particularly fashionable, with all sorts of restaurants and art galleries opening in the narrow pedestrian streets. **Tepebaşı**, the area around the Pera Museum and the Pera Palace Hotel, is similar. Don't expect to get a table at any of the myriad pavement cafés unless you stake out your claim early in the evening.

The nightlife zone continues through the lively *meyhanes* (boozy, cheap restaurants) of **Çiçek Pasajı ⑥** (Flower Passage) and **Nevizade Sokak** to Taksim, where many of the "alternative" (gay, transsexual, rave, techno and new jazz) nightclubs are found. In these often decrepit-looking streets are some of the best (and cheapest) small restaurants in town: on the menus Russian and Armenian specialities rub up against classic

Anchovies for sale at the daily fish market in Karaköy.

BELOW: the restored historic tram runs along İstiklal Caddesi from Taksim to Tünel.

The name Taksim refers to the 18th-century stone reservoir that once stood on the site of Taksim Square, an important part of the city's water system.

Turkish fare and the general sense of internationalism that defines the cultural heart of İstanbul. Nevizade Sokak, which runs off the same fish and vegetable market as the more famous Çiçek Pasajı, and where Gypsy musicians and hawkers still stroll the tables, offers more of the original flavour of the district – though it is somewhat rowdier. Get there early on summer evenings or seats may be hard to find.

Taksim and beyond

At the far end of İstiklal Caddesi, Taksim is the high-rise heartland of modern İstanbul, a bustling, raucous cacophony of plate glass and designer restaurants. In Taksim Square, a major transport hub, is the **Cumhuriyet Anıtı** (Republic Monument), created in 1928 by Italian sculptor Pietro Canonica, depicting Atatürk among the founders of modern Turkey. It is flanked by an enormous Turkish flag.

The area around the Hilton Hotel and Harbiye, just to the north of Taksim, is a centre for business and entertainment, with many of the city's cultural events held in venues such as the **Cemal Reşit**

BELOW: the cafés and bars of Nevizade Street, off İstiklal Caddesi.

Rey Concert Hall, the **Lütfi Kırdar Convention and Exhibition Centre** and the **Açıkhava Tiyatrosu** (Open-Air Theatre).

The **Askeri Müzesi** (Military Museum; Wed–Sun 9am–5pm; charge) has an interesting collection of weaponry, elaborate costumes and some impressive embroidered tents from Ottoman military campaigns. In summer, the Ottoman Mehter Military Band dresses up in janissary finery for concerts between 3pm and 4pm daily.

Harbiye leads to Valikonağı Caddesi in **Nişantaşı**, a glitzy shopping area. Adjoining Teşvikiye and Maçka are also home to some of the city's best small art galleries and boutiques. North of here are the upmarket residential neighbourhoods of **Etiler** and **Levent**, full of the sort of trendy-cum-pricey restaurants and malls favoured by the see-and-be-seen crowd.

The Dolmabahçe Palace

The wonderfully over-the-top **Dolmabahçe Sarayı** ❼ (Dolmabahçe Palace (Tue–Wed and Fri–Sun, Oct–Feb 9am–3pm, Mar–Sept 9am–4pm; guided tours only; charge) was the 19th-century vision of Sultan Abdülmecid, its vainglorious excess fuelled by his desire to upstage his European rivals. It represents everything that is jarring about İstanbul aesthetics, with tons of gold being wasted on overelaborate decoration that bankrupted the state, although there are also some stunning carpets and objets d'art on display. Atatürk died here, his simple room a stark contrast to the general impression of overwhelming kitsch. A janissary band performs here on Tuesday afternoons in summer.

Abdülmecid died shortly after the palace's completion; his successor and brother, Abdülaziz, was apparently so disgusted with the building that he built his own palace, the **Beylerbeyi**, on the opposite shore *(see page 146)*.

THE BOSPHORUS

According to legend, the Bosphorus ("Ford of the Cow") gained its name

when Zeus, playing away from home as usual, had an affair with the beautiful goddess Io. Jealous Hera sent a swarm of gnats to irritate Io who, for some inexplicable reason, turned herself into a heifer to swim the channel and escape.

Since Greek times, the deep, 32km (20-mile) strait linking East and West has been one of the most strategically significant waterways in the world, witnessing the passage of Jason's Argonauts and the arrival of the first Greek settlers of Byzantium. Because of its unique strategic value, the 1936 Montreux Convention declared the Bosphorus an international waterway, and Turkey can only police vessels flying a Turkish flag. In 1936, around 150 ships passed through the straits; today that number is more like 55,000 and growing, mainly due to the huge export demand for Russian, Central Asian and Caucasian oil. Understandably, with the channel sometimes no more than 800 metres (½ mile) across, there are real safety fears, and control of the Bosphorus has become a political hot potato. When you see tiny fishing boats and heavy-laden commuter ferries zipping beneath the bows of the giant tankers, it seems astonishing that so few disasters have occurred.

Summer retreat

In the late Ottoman period, the Bosphorus shore was occupied by villages and summer residences for aristocrats and wealthy citizens attracted by the cool breezes, forests and opportunities to row their brightly painted *caïques* (traditional wooden boats). The pashas built themselves airy stone palaces, while other privileged members of İstanbul society erected beautifully carved wooden mansions called *yalı*. Some are still standing, though many more have fallen victim to fire, storms or errant ships.

These days, the European and Asian shores north of Beşiktaş and Üsküdar are part of the rapidly expanding suburbs, even if the less developed Asian shore still retains its plane trees with Byzantine roots (or so the coastal teahouse owners will tell you). Both shorelines are desirable places to live, dotted with seafood restaurants and expensive modern dwellings. By far the best way to admire them is on a Bosphorus cruise.

Golden tea urn in the Dolmabahçe Palace.

BELOW: no expense was spared in the construction of the ornate Dolmabahçe Palace.

TIP

Make sure to visit Emirgan Park in April when the Tulip Festival is in full swing and the grounds are a fantastic riot of colour.

Cruising the Bosphorus

Relatively inexpensive municipality-run round trips leave from the main ferry dock at Eminönü close to the southern end of the Galata Bridge. There are three sailings daily in summer and one in winter, starting around 10.30am (check times and latest information at www.ido.com.tr), taking two hours each way, with a stop for lunch in Anadolu Kavağı on the Asian side near the Black Sea. A number of private companies also run Bosphorus cruises, such as Plan Tours (tel: 0212-234 7777; www.plantours.com), which offers dinner cruises (*for details on cruises and ferry services, see Travel Tips pages 375–6*).

The circular tour first passes out of the mouth of the Golden Horn, with the Topkapı and Seraglio Point to your right. Midstream is **Kız Kulesi** (Maiden's Tower; *see page 146*), a Greek watchtower rebuilt as a lighthouse in the 12th century and completely remodelled several times since, while the **Dolmabahçe Sarayı**, in all its over-the-top Baroque glory, is on your left (*see page 142*).

Next up along the European waterfront is the **Çirağan Sarayı** ➑, also built by Abdülaziz. Burned to a shell in the 1920s, it has been restored as the luxury Çirağan Hotel Kempinski complex. Behind it, on the slopes leading uphill, is the attractive **Yıldız Park**, once part of the sultan's private estate but now favoured by courting couples and wedding parties. Near the Beşiktaş ferry dock stands the **Deniz Müzesi** or Naval Museum (Fri–Tue 9.30am–5pm; charge), which displays some of the elaborate *caïques* used by the sultans to move between their waterfront palaces.

Beneath the first **Bosphorus Bridge**, built in 1973 and, at 1,074 metres (3,525ft), one of the world's longest single-span suspension bridges, the once modest village of **Ortaköy** ➒ has ceded its waterfront to a succession of trendy galleries, gift shops and ambitious bars and restaurants as well as a pricey Sunday crafts market. On the Asian shore near the bridge is the **Beylerbeyi Sarayı** (*see page 146*).

Arnavutköy (Albanian Village) is known for its wooden mansions in Art

BELOW LEFT: crossing the Bosphorus, from Üsküdar to Beşiktaş. **BELOW RIGHT:** fisherman near Emirgan.

Nouveau style, refurbished and selling at astonishing prices. Further north, wealthy **Bebek**, the former home of distinguished 19th-century Turkish poet Tevfik Fikret, houses the **Aşiyan Museum** (Aşiyan Yokuşu; Tue–Wed and Fri–Sun 9am–5pm; free) and a long strip of waterfront restaurants, bars and cafés.

Asian **Anadolu hisarı** ❿ (Anatolian Castle) and European **Rumeli hisarı** ⓫ (European Castle) mark the gates to the Black Sea. The **castle** (Thur–Tue 9am–5pm; charge) was built in 1452 when Sultan Mehmet used the two fortifications to choke off aid to beleaguered Constantinople during the final siege of the city. The ramparts are still largely intact and are fun to explore, but be warned – some of the upper reaches involve vertiginous ascents along narrow walls, and there are no safety rails. The semi-ruined amphitheatre within the castle is still used for occasional concerts.

Beyond the second Bosphorus bridge, the village of Emirgan is home to the **Sakıp Sabancı Müzesi** (Tue–Sun 10am–6pm, Wed until 10pm; charge) a magnificent private museum displaying fine and decorative art, and calligraphy; several rooms are kept as they were when the Sabancı family lived here. The café has live music during Sunday brunch.

At Sarıyer, two fine old mansions house the **Sadberk Hanım Museum** (Büyükdere Caddesi 27–29; Thur–Tue 9am–5pm; charge), with evocative displays of archaeological finds and 19th-century life.

At the far end of the Bosphorus, Anadolu Kavagi's **Genoese castle** has great views out towards the Black Sea, and the 45-minute walk (round-trip) will give you an appetite to eat at one of the many waterfront fish restaurants.

On the return journey the ferry also stops in **Kanlıca** which is famous for its delicious yoghurt, served with sugar. If you're tiring of the boat by now (or in a hurry), you can easily catch a bus back to Üsküdar from here.

THE ASIAN SIDE

Not everyone wants, or has time, to take a full Bosphorus cruise. However, it's perfectly easy to get a taste of things by hopping on a ferry at Eminönü and heading across to the Asian side of İstanbul at **Kadıköy** ⓬.

Not that Kadıköy, a lively modern suburb, feels particularly Asian. It may not be especially beautiful to look at and lacks any big historic monuments, but it does offer a delightful market area whose narrow cobbled streets are always packed with local shoppers.

This part of the city was originally founded as Chalcedon by Megaran settlers, although there is nothing left to remind visitors of that today. Instead you can admire a few 19th-century churches that recall İstanbul's lost Greek and Armenian populations, or hop on an elderly tram to trundle up to Moda where it's possible to have lunch in what was once a pretty little ferry terminal at the end of a causeway.

Üsküdar

An alternative destination accessible by ferry from Eminönü is **Üsküdar** ⓭,

Colourful bracelets at the Sunday crafts market in Ortaköy.

BELOW: the fortress of Rumeli hisarı.

TIP

Ferries to the Princes' Islands leave from Kabatas, just south of Dolmabahçe Palace. The inexpensive two-hour trip to the car-free island of Büyükada makes a great day out from the city.

a far more conservative Asian suburb which is adorned with many magnificent mosques. As soon as you disembark from the ferry you'll see the first of them, the **İskele Camii** (also called the Mihrimah Sultan Mosque), which originally stood right on the waterfront. Facing it is a fine 18th-century fountain rather like the one in front of the gate leading into Topkapı Palace.

To see more of the old mosques you should walk along the waterfront in the direction of Kadıköy. This route will take you past the **Şemsi Paşa Camii**, dating back to 1580, and then out along a stretch of the shore that has been given a promenade. This is **Salacak**, from where you can catch a ferry for the short hop out to **Kız Kulesi**, the Maiden's Tower, a prominent and much photographed landmark tower that has served all sorts of functions over the years but now is essentially a café-cum-restaurant with views. The "maiden" after whom it was named was a girl whose father had been told she would die from a snakebite. To guard against such a disaster he had her confined to the offshore tower where,

predictably enough, she was sent a basket of fruit that turned out to contain the lethal snake.

If you journey inland from the shore at Salacak you should be able to find the **Rum Mehmet Paşa Camii**, which looks rather like a Byzantine church from the outside, and the imposing 18th-century Ayazma Camii, named after a sacred spring in the grounds. Finally, if you head straight inland and keep walking uphill you should come to the **Atik Valide Sultan Camii**, regarded as one of the architect Sinan's finest works.

Heading north from Üsküdar beyond the first Bosphorus bridge is the 19th-century **Beylerbeyi Sarayı** ⑭ (Tue–Wed and Fri–Sun 9.30am–4pm; charge), built by Sultan Abdülaziz (who ignored the fact that there was no money left in the till) after he had taken an intense dislike to the Dolmabahçe Palace recently built by his father, Abdülmecit. The lavishly furnished summer palace will still strike many visitors as excessive, although its smaller size and relative lack of visitors make it seem more bearable. Abdülaziz

BELOW: travelling by horse-drawn carriage around Büyükada, one of the Princes' Islands.

s thought to have conducted an affair with the Emperor Napoleon's wife Eugenie here.

The Princes' Islands

Wonderful as İstanbul is, at the height of summer when temperatures are soaring and the traffic is oppressive you may feel the need to escape. Of course the locals got there before you and colonised the **Princes' Islands** 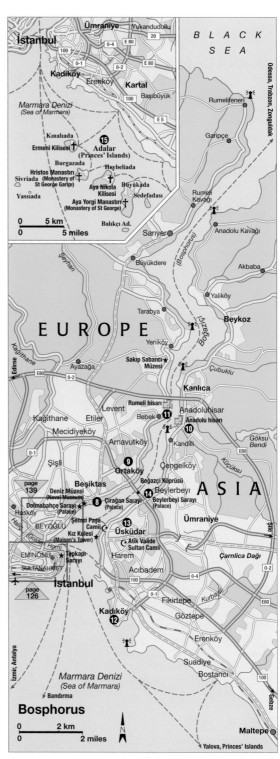 in the Sea of Marmara as the perfect city getaways – far enough away to escape the heat and fumes, but near enough to be accessible readily and cheaply by ferry from the mainland. There are actually nine Princes' Islands but only four of them are regularly inhabited: Kinaliada, Burgazada, Heybeliada and Büyükada.

Ferries to the islands stop at each of them in turn, and in theory you could just about squeeze in a lightning visit to them all in the same day. That would, however, miss out on what makes the islands so special, and that is that they are the perfect places to slow down and relax in. Although there are now quite a few administrative vehicles on Büyükada, for the most part these islands are still blissfully traffic-free; you walk, cycle or get about them in the horse-drawn carriages that can be hired on all except Kinaliada.

Büyükada ("Big Island") is the last stop on the ferry run and by far the most popular destination with visitors if only because it offers the greatest choice of places to eat and drink, as well as the chance to climb uphill to **St George's Monastery**, an atmospheric cluster of chapels with memorable views. It's also well worth taking a stroll along **Çankaya Caddesi** to appreciate the beautiful wooden houses in a multitude of different designs and their colourful gardens.

Heybeliada is dominated by a Naval Academy, as well as being home to the Seminary which once trained all the priests who served in the Greek Orthodox churches here; today it is the predictable subject of endless bouts of bickering. ❑

A Trip to the Turkish Bath

The soapy pleasures of a trip to the hamam are revitalising, and an authentic Turkish experience

As a spectator sport, nothing surpasses a trip to a Turkish bath, or hamam. Be sure to visit one during your stay. Many people are put off the idea because they don't know what to expect (or what to do). Don't worry. The rules are simple, based on those of the old Roman baths or the Scandinavian sauna, and the locals will soon steer you straight. The sexes are usually segregated either in different baths or by different hours. Nudity is not the norm, so wear underpants beneath the tea-towel-like *peştamal* (sarong) that you will be given. In the better baths you will also be given a towel and wooden clogs *(takunya)*, although in more rural areas it's best to bring your own towel.

Change out of your clothes in the reception area *(camekân)*. From there, you move through to a cool side room where you can wash down before entering the central hot steam room *(hararet)*. In the old baths, this is often a spectacular domed space at the centre of which is a large marble slab *(göbektaşı)*. The surrounding walls are lined with basins which you fill with water to the required temperature before scooping it over yourself very carefully so as not to get any soap in the basin *(hurna)*. Then lie down on the slab and receive an energetic face, foot and/or full-body massage, or a scrub down with a camel-hair glove *(kese)*.

Most five-star hotels feature luxurious, modern hamams, but, while rougher, some of the more traditional bathhouses are well worth a visit for the atmosphere.

Above: lavender soaps at the Çemberlitaş Hamam in İstanbul. Oil massages are administered in a different room to the *hararet*.
Above Right: sarongs *(peştamals)* are the traditional attire worn in hamams; they are usually made from cotton and thinly woven to ensure they dry quickly.
Right: you can choose to either wash yourself or opt for a massage.

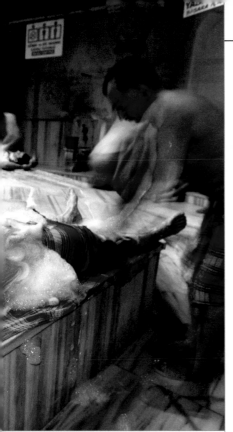

ABOVE: receiving a vigorous full-body massage whilst lying on the central heated marble slab, known as a *göbektaşi*, in the hot steam room. A *kese* is used to exfoliate the skin.

ABOVE: inside İstanbul's Çemberlitaş Hamam, one of the city's most prominent bathhouses and probably the most popular hamam.

THE TRADITIONAL HAMAM

Today Turkish baths are largely places that people visit for fun, but there was a time before modern plumbing reached most houses when a visit to the baths was more of a necessity. In those days the baths played an important role in social life. In them mothers would quite literally size up potential brides for their sons, and before their weddings women would often resort to the baths for a party. Frequently they would come to the hamam for much of the day, bringing with them their children (including pre-pubescent boys) and enough food to keep them going. In the baths women would henna their hair and wax their bodies; men would gather to exchange news and just to enjoy themselves.

Many museums in Turkey preserve relics of the days when wealthy hamam-goers routinely showed up for their bath wearing clogs inlaid with mother-of-pearl and clutching a little metal "bag" in which could be found delicate combs and towels embroidered with silver and gold thread. In comparison with these days of omnipresent plastic, it was a much more elegant time.

ABOVE: hamams remain sociable places. Before home plumbing, baths were a communal activity that could last the entire day as families bathed and talked.
BELOW: *peştamals* ready for use.

THRACE AND MARMARA

Northwestern Turkey is the meeting point of Europe
and Asia, with European Thrace and Asian Marmara
wrapped around the eponymous sea

Thrace and the south Marmara coast attract numerous visitors annually. History fans find a land of ghosts – from the warriors at ancient Troy who clashed for the sake of a pretty face to the many thousands who died in the horrific battles at Gallipoli. Although the area is close to İstanbul, it differs substantially in character from that great city.

Thrace (Trakya) forms the tiny northwestern part of Turkey-in-Europe, occupying about a quarter of the ancient region of Thrace. Rolling, forested hills, tracts of fertile sunflower fields or vineyards, and stream valleys – stretching from the Marmara to the Black seas – are bisected by the D100 and E80, successors to the Roman Via Egnatia, and Turkey's main road links with Europe.

To the southwest, Thrace ends at the Aegean and the Dardanelles, that strategic strait between the Sea of Marmara and the Aegean that featured so prominently during World War I. Its principal city, Edirne, which replaced Bursa as the Ottoman capital, stands near the borders with Greece and Bulgaria. Thracian beaches are few and mostly uninspiring – except for Kıyıköy, Erikli and the glorious ones on Gökçeada (İmroz) island.

The southern Marmara displays great physical variety. Verdant hills around İznik hint little at the great, snowcapped mountain overshadowing Bursa. Despite runaway development, its old quarters and important monuments – and showcase suburb village of Cumalıkızık – never fail to charm. West of Bursa lie two lakes – Uluabat Gölü, where a charming village sits amidst ancient Apollonia, and Küş Gölü, hosting an important bird sanctuary. Back on the coast, offshore islands in the Sea of Marmara are mostly the preserve of the working classes from İstanbul at weekends. Bustling Çanakkale, on the south Dardanelles shore, marks the gateway to the Aegean – and to Troy, the most famous local ancient site, where Schliemann's spirit still broods over the plundered hill. ❏

PRECEDING PAGES: ancient and modern – the view across Bergama from the ruins of Pergamon acropolis. **LEFT:** children in the timeless streets of Bursa. **TOP:** taking a break in front of Selimiye Mosque in Edirne. **ABOVE LEFT:** fishermen at Lake İznik.

THRACE

The last remnant of European Turkey, prosperous Thrace lends a geographical basis to the country's bid to join the EU

ccording to the philosopher Xenophanes (*c.*570–475 BC), the ancient Thracians were a blue-eyed, red-haired people matching the images of their gods. Herodotus reckoned they would have been invincible, if only they could have united, while later Thracians maintained this martial reputation. Before the turbulent 20th century, the population was extremely mixed, with Greek or Bulgarian Orthodox, plus settled Roma, everywhere, and Armenian and Jewish communities in the towns. Under the republic Thrace became home to Slavic Muslim refugees, particularly from Macedonia and Bulgaria, who have brought a more worldly outlook with them.

Despite venerable religious monuments, Thrace is a secularist stronghold, with a higher standard of living than Anatolia's. The main earners here are tobacco, wine, sunflower oil and assorted root crops. Tourism, except at a few beach resorts and the Gallipoli battlefields, is insignificant.

Edirne

Modern **Edirne** ❶ (estimated pop. 140,000) straddles the main land route linking Turkey with southeastern Europe. There has been a settlement at this strategic junction of the Meriç, Arda and Tunca rivers since the ancient Thracian town of Uskudama.

An important Roman garrison which manufactured shields and weapons, it was renamed Hadrianopolis in honour of Emperor Hadrian's visit in AD 125. Under Diocletian (245–305), it became capital of one of the four provinces of Thrace. It was sacked three times by the Bulgars between 814 and 1002, and occupied thrice during the 12th century by Crusaders before falling to the Ottomans in 1361. Now renamed Edirne, the growing city served as the empire's capital from 1413 to 1458. Süleyman the Magnificent (1520–66)

Main attractions
EDIRNE: SELIMIYE CAMII
EDIRNE: KALEIÇI HOUSES
KIYIKÖY
GALLIPOLI CEMETERIES
GÖKÇEADA: HILL VILLAGES
GÖKÇEADA: AYDINCIK BEACH

BELOW: sunflower oil is much more common in Turkish cooking than vegetable oil.

LEFT: worshippers entering the Ottoman Selimiye Camii in Edirne.

was one of several emperors who liked to hunt in the local countryside, returning to Constantinople only when the croaking of the unconquerable marsh frogs made sleep impossible.

By the early 19th century, Edirne had become a provincial backwater, with almost half of its population consisting of Bulgarians, Armenians, Greeks or Jews. However, such multicultural tranquillity did not last. Edirne was occupied briefly by the Russians in 1829 and 1878, and by the Bulgarians in 1913. Recaptured by Turkey the same year, it was taken by the Greeks in 1920 and held by them until 1922; Turkish sovereignty was only confirmed in 1923.

Today, Edirne is a university town with a leading medical school, youthful population and busy cafés, though the pious atmosphere created by numerous venerable mosques means that licensed restaurants are scarce. Thanks to its location near the E80, Turkey's main motorway to Europe, Edirne has also become a major business centre, although conventional tourist facilities are meagre.

The master's masterpiece

The magnificent **Selimiye Camii** Ⓐ dominates Edirne from its hilltop position. Considered by many to represent the pinnacle of Ottoman architecture, it was built between 1569 and 1574 for Sultan Selim II by master architect Sinan, who was 80 years old when he accepted the commission. The enormous *külliye* (mosque complex), comprising the mosque itself, an *arasta* and a *medrese*, looms above the Dilaver Bey Park. The *arasta* (shopping arcade whose rents maintain the mosque), where souvenirs and religious objects are sold, is the work of Sinan's pupil, Davut Ağa.

Sinan's design of the Selimiye comprises 18 small domes, which lead the eye to a great central cupola framed by four slender, 71-metre (232ft) -high minarets. Red Edirne sandstone has been used extensively and effectively for decoration, particularly over the arches in the courtyard. Inside, one is awed by the extraordinary sense of space and light conveyed by the great floating dome (31.28 metres/103ft in diameter and 44 metres/144ft above

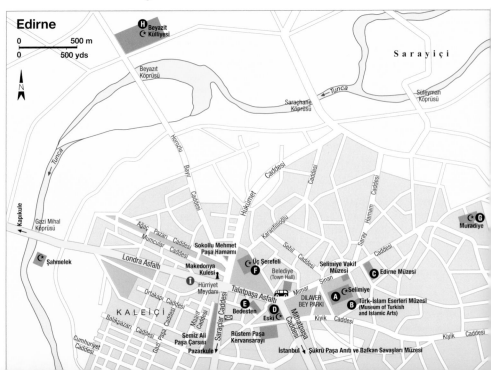

he floor), supported by eight giant,
tately pillars arranged in a circle. The
mosque's rectangular plan is cunningly
masked by the arrangement of the side
galleries – those on the lower floor
open to the outside while the upper
floor opens inwards. The lower part of
he *mihrab* and the sultan's *loge* (balcony) are clad in fine İznik tiles, and
here is a beautifully carved marble
mimber (pulpit).

The courtyarded *medrese* behind
the mosque is now the **Türk-İslam
Eserleri Müzesi** ❸ (Museum of Turkish and Islamic Arts; Tue–Sun 9am–
pm; charge). Its collection includes
n embroidered satin tent used by
Ottoman viziers, embroidery, weapons, glass, photographs and records
f oil-wrestling matches. The nearby
Edirne Müzesi ❹ (Edirne Museum;
Tue–Sun, summer 9am–5pm, winter
until 4.30pm; free) has items, some
of which are labelled in English, from
ancient Aenos at the mouth of the
Meriç, as well as Hadrianopolis. There
is also an ethnographic section with
the emphasis on village carpet-weaving
and colourful bridal costumes.

The city centre

The restored **Eski Cami** ❺ in the city
centre was constructed between 1403
and 1414. Modelled on Bursa's Ulu
Camii, it is a square building divided
into nine domed sections. Its upkeep
was paid for by revenues from the
Bedesten ❻, built in 1418 to store
and sell valuable goods; according
to the 17th-century chronicler Evliya
Çelebi, 60 nightwatchmen guarded
its treasures. Nearby stand two more
of Sinan's buildings, the **Caravansaray** built for Grand Vizier Rüstem
Paşa (now a hotel) and the **Semiz Ali
Paşa Çarşısı** (market). Shop here for
Edirne's novelty soap (*meyve sabunu*),
shaped like fruit and vegetables; other
local specialities, catering for the sweet
of tooth, are *badem ezmesi* (marzipan)
and *deva-i-misk* (a type of *helva*).

Across the road, the **Üç Şerefeli
Camii** ❼ (the Mosque of the Three
Balconied Minarets, built 1438–47)
marked a stylistic innovation in early
Ottoman architecture. For the first
time a massive central dome was
placed over a rectangular floor plan,
a concept that the architect evidently

*Architectural detail
on the portal of the
Eski Camii.*

BELOW: Sinan's
masterpiece, the
Selimiye Camii.

Sinan, Architectural Genius

Mimar Sinan (1489–1588), the greatest Ottoman architect, influenced religious and civic architecture during his lifetime and long
after his death. Born probably to Armenian parents near Kayseri, he was
recruited in 1512 as a janissary under the *devşirme* system and rose
rapidly through the ranks. His ability as a military engineer, along with
the knowledge gained from viewing so many monuments – Christian
and Islamic – on his extensive travels across the empire, eventually
brought him to the attention of Sultan Süleyman the Magnificent, whose
grand vizier appointed him chief imperial architect in 1539 – a position
Sinan retained under two subsequent sultans.

Over five decades Sinan's output was prodigious, amounting to nearly
400 constructions across the Balkans and Middle East. In addition to
minor works like aqueducts and fountains, he was involved in the design
and construction of 35 palaces, 84 mosques, 46 hamams, 22 tombs, 12
kervansarays, 17 *imarets* (soup kitchens) and 57 *medreses*. In his lengthy
memoirs, the *Tezkeret-ül-Bünyan*, he classed pre-1550 commissions like
the Şehzade Camii in the capital as apprentice works, but the Süleymaniye Camii, also in İstanbul, as the fruit of maturity, and the Selimiye
Camii in Edirne as his masterpiece. He was buried in a simple tomb he
had designed for himself in the gardens of the Süleymaniye mosque.

TIP

Edirne's few licensed restaurants and bars cluster at the south end of Saraçlar Caddesi, or between the two bridges over the Tunca and Meriç rivers, in the area known as *Bülbül Adası* – "Nightingale Island".

found difficult to realise – the dome is supported by massive pillars with awkward wedge-shaped areas filled by small, turret-like domes at the sides. Yet although patently experimental, the interior breathes strength and reassurance, while the exterior has beautiful decorative details in the mellow local red sandstone. The courtyard, festooned with arcades of pillars, was the first built for a mosque by the Ottomans, while the three minarets, each decorated in a different stone pattern, were the tallest in Edirne until the construction of the Selimiye Mosque. Each of the balconies is approached by separate staircases within the same minaret, an engineering miracle.

Opposite stands the **Sokollu Mehmet Paşa Hamamı** (daily 7am–10pm, women's section closes 6pm; charge), also built by Sinan and still a functioning traditional bath, with a fine dome and plasterwork. Near the hamam stands the Makedonya Kulesi, the last remaining tower of the **Roman-Byzantine fortifications**. The rest of the walls were pulled down after the Ottomans had expanded deep into

Europe. Today, the partly restored tower overlooks an excavated patch of Roman Hadrianopolis.

Across busy Londra Asfaltı lies the compact, grid-plan **Kaleiçi** quarter. This is the oldest part of town, with many ornate Belle Epoque wooden town houses built by the now-vanished Jewish and Bulgarian communities, as well as some good restaurants and hotels.

Beyond the centre

On a hillock a short distance west of the Edirne Museum is the **Muradiye Camii** ⑤ (only open at prayer times), built by pious sultan Murat II between 1426 and 1435 as a *zaviye* (monastery) for the Mevlevî dervishes. Later the dervishes moved into a *tekke* (lodge) in the garden, and the main building was converted into a mosque. Sadly its once-glorious interior was wrecked when the tiles were stolen in 2002.

A 20-minute walk (or short drive) northwest of town into the countryside, over bridges, dykes and islands of the Tunca, brings you to the **Beyazıt Külliyesi** ⑥. The largest such charitable foundation in the Islamic world

BELOW: the mosque in the Beyazit Külliyesi complex.

it was built in 1484–88 by Beyazit II; it comprises a mosque, insane asylum, hospital, *imaret*, pharmacy, hamam, travellers' hostel, storerooms and kitchens. Here, Lady Mary Wortley Montagu, wife of the British ambassador to the Ottomans, took the bold step in 1716 of having her children inoculated against smallpox, a practice unknown in most of Europe until decades later.

The asylum's hexagonal, white stone treatment room had domed alcoves where patients were soothed by the sound of running water or music. The hospital and asylum, at the southwest corner of the complex, now house the **Sağlık Müzesi** (Museum of Health; daily 9am–6pm; charge), with wax figures of patients being treated, medical instruments and copies of some lurid 15th-century pictures of operations in progress.

You may walk back to the city on paths or lanes running parallel to the complicated system of dykes that protect Edirne from floods, while inspecting the half-dozen graceful Ottoman **bridges** over the Tunca. The Meriç, further south, has only one

bridge, the huge but elegant **Mecidiye**, erected 1842–47 and now essentially the municipal logo.

On the highest hill, southeast of the centre, the **Şükrü Paşa Anıtı ve Balkan Savaşları Müzesi** (Tue–Sun 9am–5pm; free) is a memorial-museum dedicated to the Bulgarian siege of Edirne during the 1912–13 Balkan War, built around the tomb of the Ottoman defence commander Şükrü Paşa.

The rest of Thrace

Uzunköprü ❷, 64km (40 miles) south of Edirne along Highway 550, gets its name from a 1,400-metre (4,600ft) -long bridge, with 174 arches, at the north of the town, built during the reign of Murat II. Like Edirne's smaller Ottoman bridges, it is far too narrow for contemporary traffic; an ugly but necessary modern replacement has been built 2km (1½ miles) east. Beyond Keşan, a quiet side road off the 550 leads to Edirne's designated beach resort on the Aegean, **Erikli ❸**. Its buildings, as so often, are nondescript but the sand – almost 2km (1 mile) of it – is anything but. Nearby, beachless İbrice Limanı

Detail from a 4th-century Roman family tombstone in Edirne.

BELOW: a fishmonger in Erikili.

Onions and root vegetables are a Thracian speciality.

hosts several scuba schools taking advantage of good diving conditions in the gulf.

Due east of Edirne on a relatively minor, bucolic road, **Kırklareli** is, perhaps surprisingly, the current capital of Thrace, rather than larger Edirne. Saránda Ekklisíes (40 Churches) to its former Greek inhabitants, Lozengrad (Vineyard-ville) to its departed Bulgarians, it epitomised the ethnic stew of pre-Republican Thrace. Today its main attraction is a Roma festival held in early May, while beyond beckons an official border crossing to Malko Tărnovo in Bulgaria. In **Lüleburgaz ❹**, the **Sokollu Mehmet Paşa Külliyesi**, built by Sinan in 1549–69, comprises a mosque, hamam, *medrese* (religious school), *türbe* (tomb) and market. Bosnian Sokollu Mehmet, a product of the *devşirme* system (*see page 56*), began funding the project while governor of Rumeli but finished it serving as grand vizier.

Equidistant from both **Kırklareli** and **Lüleburgaz** on the sparsely populated Thracian Black Sea coast lies **Kıyıköy ❺**, the ancient Medea. It is flanked by two rivers which carry sand down to magnificent beaches, among the best in Turkey. The fortified old town has considerable charm, as do surviving half-timbered fishermen's houses, but it's no secret, and can be packed with İstanbullus in season.

Tekirdağ ❻ (formerly Rodosto) is the main bright spot of the Thracian Marmara shore, a major port famous for its *rakı*-distilling industry, eponymous meatballs, ferry services across the Marmara, and the unexpected, well-signposted **Rakoczi Müzesi** (Rákóczi Museum; Tue–Sun 9am–noon, 1–5pm; charge). Since 1932, the museum has been installed in the house where Transylvanian Hungarian Prince Ferenc II Rakoczi (1676–1735) spent his last years. After leading a futile revolt against the Habsburgs during 1703–11, the prince escaped via Poland and France to the Ottoman capital. Here he was granted asylum by Sultan Ahmet III in 1719 provided he accept comfortable house arrest. The building, owned and recently restored by the Hungarian government, rather overshadows the paltry exhibits.

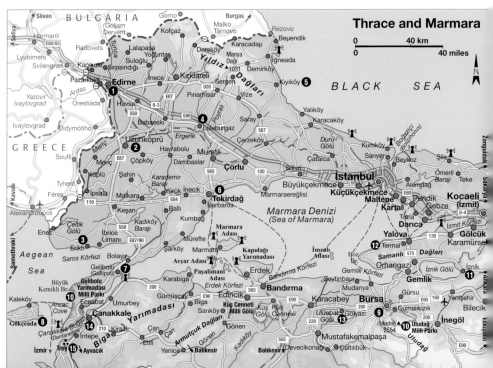

Thrace and Marmara

0   40 km
0   40 miles

Southwest of Tekirdağ extends Thrace's major vineyard and winemaking region, though a potentially scenic coastal road is rough and impossible to find without local navigators. Instead, follow the D110 highway west, then turn off along Highway 555 to Şarköy, typical of the resorts pitched towards locals here.

The Gelibolu (Gallipoli) Peninsula

Bolayır marks the narrowest point of the Gelibolu Peninsula; here one can see both the Saros Gulf and the Dardanelles. Otherwise it's only remarkable for two tombs: one of Süleyman, favourite son of Sultan Orhan I, who died in a hunting accident nearby, and the other of Namık Kemal (1840–88), prominent Ottoman reformer, essayist and poet. There are more sturdy tombs in **Gelibolu** ❼, whose attractive old harbour is flanked by fish restaurants and the lone surviving tower of the Byzantine fortifications. The tower is now a small museum dedicated to 16th-century Turkish admiral and cartographer Piri Reis.

Despite the shared name, the town is not really a practical base for visiting the tragic World War I Gallipoli battlefields, still another 50km (30 miles) distant. Poignantly, this is one of the most beautiful regions of Turkey. Once shell-blasted and treeless, the peninsula now supports fertile farmland or pine forests with rich flora and fauna, making up the **Gallipoli National Historic Park** (Gelibolu Yarımadası Tarihi Milli Parkı). Moderate temperatures even in summer and a lack of heavy traffic makes it uniquely suitable for touring by mountain bike.

Gallipoli battlefields

It takes a full day to visit the major battlefields, cemeteries and memorials, with a packed lunch advisable as restaurants are almost nonexistent. The Allied cemeteries and memorials date from the early 1920s, mostly designed by Scottish architect Sir John Burnet to replaced makeshift graveyards of 1915. A useful introduction – and first stop for standard tours – is the **Kabatepe Information Centre and Museum** (daily 9am–1pm, 2–6pm; charge). Nine km

BELOW: oil wrestlers struggle for a slippery hold.

Oil Wrestling

Turkish Yaglı Güres (oil wrestling) is a traditional summer sport. According to legend, it began as a means to keep Ottoman soldiers trim. Competitions began in 1360, when Süleyman, son of Sultan Orhan I, invited 40 champions to wrestle while returning from a battle. By dawn the next day, the last two had died of exhaustion, but where each hero fell a spring gushed from the ground. To this day the festival is held at Kırkpınar ("40 Springs"), just outside Edirne, and the basics of the sport have remained the same.

Most modern wrestlers are village boys with some regional success, dreaming of fame and riches.

Each year, about 1,000 wrestlers, covered with olive oil and clad only in leather breeches, compete at Kırkpınar in several categories classed by height, not weight, from toddler to full-sized. Betting is brisk, a listless performance booed, and no quarter is given by the *pehlivan* (wrestler). Referees only monitor illegal holds and announce the winner after a wrestler's shoulder is forced to the ground or a contestant collapses. Matches last 30 to 40 minutes on average depending on size category, with 10 to 15 minutes of "overtime" allowed to break draws. After each relay of matches, victorious competitors pair off again until only one – the *başpehlivan* (champion) – remains standing.

Gallipoli was one of the bloodiest and most tragic campaigns of the Great War, characterised by hopelessly heroic uphill charges against trenches defended by machine-guns. After eight months of fierce fighting, in which nearly half a million men had been deployed in total by both sides, casualties – including an estimated 46,000 Allied dead and 86,000 Ottoman dead – exceeded 50 percent.

BELOW: Gallipoli exhibit in Eceabat, the nearest town to the battlefields.

(5½ miles) northwest of Eceabat, it features archival photos, maps, touching letters home, weapons, uniforms, mess-kits and personal effects.

The most famous sites are nearby at the Lone Pine Cemetery and **Anzac Cove**, where Australian and New Zealand troops lie, and **Çonkbayırı**, site of particularly desperate encounters, dramatised in Peter Weir's film *Gallipoli*. Also in this area is the cemetery of the 57th Ottoman regiment, one of many Turkish memorials assiduously marked in recent years, many of whose poorly armed members were ordered to their deaths by Mustafa Kemal to buy time for reinforcements to arrive.

The Anglo-French landings were well south, either side of Cape Helles, the Turkish equivalent of Land's End; here loom the huge British memorial obelisk near the cape, the French monument and cemetery at Morto (Corpse) Bay, and the colossal Abide, or cenotaph, for all the Turkish dead.

A cement monument at Arıburnu Cove bears Atatürk's 1934 message of reconciliation:

There is no difference between the Johnnies and the Mehmets to us,

Where they lie side by side here in this country of ours,

You, the mothers who sent their sons from faraway countries, wipe away your tears;

Your sons are now lying in our bosom and are in peace.

After having lost their lives on this land,

They have become our sons as well.

Every year on 25 April, ANZAC Day, a solemn 5.30am ceremony at adjacent Anzac Cove is attended by dignitaries of the two antipodean nations – and up to 10,000 others. They commemorate the Allied campaign undertaken to knock Ottoman Turkey out of the war by storming İstanbul, after attempts in late 1914 and early 1915 to force the Dardanelles by sea had failed owing to comprehensive Turkish mining. An amphibious assault on several points along the peninsula, commencing at dawn on 25 April 1915, quickly went awry: Anglo-French landings near Cape Helles were almost annihilated and ANZAC forces came ashore at the wrong beach. Under heavy Ottoman fire, they nonetheless advanced inland over two days toward Çonkbayır, where one Mustafa Kemal, later Atatürk, commanded the Turkish lines and miraculously escaped death on several occasions. On 27 April, he launched a silent, pre-dawn bayonet charge which stopped the ANZACs. Thereafter, except for an abortive British landing at Cape Suvla in the north, the battle settled into trench warfare until in November the Allies threw in the towel, and evacuated Gallipoli by January 1916.

Gökçeada

Gökçeada ❽ (formerly İmroz or Imvros), northwest of the entrance to the Dardanelles, is easily reached by car-ferry from Kabatepe, or catamaran from Çanakkale, bound for Kuzu Limanı. Taken by Greece during the

Balkan Wars, the island reverted to Turkish control in 1923, although the 7,000 local Orthodox Greeks were more or less left in peace for 40 years thereafter. However, when the Cyprus conflict flared up in 1964, Turkey turned up the pressure through land expropriation, heavy garrisoning, the closure of all Greek schools, restrictions on grazing and fishing, and Muslim settlement from the mainland. This had the desired effect: today only about 250 ethnic Greeks remain, the rest having long since left for Athens, Istanbul or further afield.

Since the recent thaw in Greco-Turkish relations, this diaspora has returned seasonally to renovate abandoned houses and attend some of the many churches – a point of honour given that Ecumenical Patriarch Vartholomeos (the highest official in the Orthodox Christian Church) was born here in 1940. Still, the older generation remains wary, dependent as they are on governmental good will, and resentful that they can't leave property to their children who don't qualify for Turkish citizenship.

Gökçeada is now awakening to its potential to attract tourists, thanks to rugged volcanic landscapes, characterful villages and excellent south-coast beaches. Summer visitors comprise a few Romanians and Bulgarians, but mostly thousands of returning Greeks and their descendants, plus cosmopolitan Turks who enjoy their company, especially at the 14–16 August Orthodox *panayır* (Festival of the Virgin).

Most facilities are in the northwest, around the functional inland capital of **Merkez** (Panayiá), its fishing port of **Kaleköy** (Kástro), with crumbled castle overhead, and **Eski Bademli** (Glykí). Still very Greek in feel are the remoter villages of **Zeytinli** (Ágii Theodóri), with its many sweetshops, and **Tepeköy** (Agridía), venue for the *panayır*. The largest village and former capital was **Dereköy** (Skhinoúdi) in the west, its 1,900 houses now mostly abandoned. **Aydıncık** in the far southeast is one of the best beaches in the Turkish Aegean, with windsurf schools; **Lazkoyu** (Agía Káli) and **Gizli Liman** further west have few or no amenities but are even more scenic. ❑

Vendor selling varieties of Turkish bread.

BELOW: small Greek Orthodox church in Gökçeada.

MARMARA

This green and fertile region south of the Sea of Marmara features prominently in legends, from Karagöz shadow plays to the siege of Troy

Main attractions
BURSA: MURADIYE COMPLEX
BURSA: YEŞIL COMPLEX
CUMALIKIZIK
İZNIK TILES
YALOVA: TERMAL
TROY

BELOW: studying the Koran in a Bursa mosque.

In classical times the area south of the Sea of Marmara (the ancient Propontis) was divided between Bithynia and Mysia. According to Herodotus, the Bithynians were a fierce, warlike people who originally came from Thrace. After Alexander the Great expelled the Persians from Asia Minor, the Bithynians formed an independent kingdom based at Nicomedia (modern İzmit). According to Homer, the Mysians were allies of the Trojans, but Mysia's location and extent were unclear, and there is no record of a Mysian kingdom. Before the Romans made it part of the Province of Asia in 129 BC, Mysia had been ruled by the Lydian, Persian and Pergamene kings.

Bursa

The historic city of **Bursa** ❾ is dominated by the great bulk of 2,554-metre (8,377ft) **Uludağ**. Until the 1980s Turks spoke of "*Yeşil*" Bursa ("Green" Bursa) because of the city's sylvan setting. Unfortunately, concrete underpasses, overpasses and new high-rise structures now disturb its symmetry and skyline, while new quarters straggle interminably along the E90 through road. Some lament that Yeşil Bursa has become "Çimento Bursa". Fortunately, the historic Ottoman quarters remain.

According to the ancient Greek geographer Strabo, Bursa was founded by the Bithynian King Prusias I Kholos "the Lame" (reigned 228–182 BC), who gave his name – altered to the Hellenistic "Prousa" – to the city. Legend has it that Carthaginian general Hannibal helped him choose the site.

In 74 BC, Bithynia was willed to Rome by its last ruler, the ineffectual Nicomedes IV Philopator. Prousa prospered under Roman and early Byzantine rule, but suffered greatly from the 7th- and 8th-century Arab raids and fell to the Seljuks in 1075. Subsequently it was fought over by the Crusaders, Byzantines and Turks until, in 1326, it was conquered by Gazi Orhan I, whom the 13th-century Arab traveller, Ibn

Battuta, described as "the greatest of the Turkmen kings, and the richest in wealth, lands and military forces."

Bursa was the first true Ottoman capital, and its rulers lavished money and care on it. Orhan issued his first coins here in 1327 and set up a bazaar with a *bedesten* in 1340. Apart from recent development, the present form of the city still follows Ottoman lines, with the central areas surrounding the mosques and religious foundations built by the first six Ottoman sultans. Today, with over 2.5 million inhabtants (many of them from Artvin province or of Balkan Muslim descent), Bursa is the fourth-largest city in Turkey, with the same civic pride felt by its first Turkish citizens in the 14th century. True, its industrial prosperity has produced an unsightly proliferation of warehouses, factories and offices, and here is too much traffic; nevertheless, ts old quarters present an unrivalled display of early Ottoman architecture.

Çekirge

The elegant suburb of **Çekirge Ⓐ**, 4km 2½ miles) west of the city centre, is the best place to stay if you're driving.

The **Eski Kaplıca**, erected on the site of Roman and Byzantine baths, and the **Yeni Kaplıca**, built in 1552 by grand vizier Rüstem Paşa, are two of Bursa's many historic mineral baths. Mineral water, rich in iron, sodium, sulphur, calcium, bicarbonate and magnesium, used to gush in abundance from the mountainside at temperatures ranging from 47–78°C (116–172°F), but in 2009, for reasons either geological or climatic, the flow was sharply curtailed. Nobody knows if or when it will recover, and hotels here are "Termal" in name only for the time being. In tandem with the hydrological crisis, Bursa's oldest luxury hotel, the **Çelik Palas**, closed in 2009 indefinitely for a much-needed overhaul.

You may be able to catch a shadow puppet play at the **Karagöz Evi** (Karagöz Theatre and Museum; museum open Tue–Sat noon–5pm) at Çekirge Caddesi 3. Further information is available from the Karagöz Antique Shop (*see margin, right*). Shadow-puppet plays probably came with the Turks from Central Asia. A

Bursa's traditional shadow puppets are made from camel hide, oiled to become translucent, then painted. Şinasi Çelikkol's Karagöz Antique Shop in the bazaar at Eski Aynalı Çarsı 12 (tel: 0224-222 8727, www.karagozshhop.com) has an interesting range of puppets for sale and organises performances.

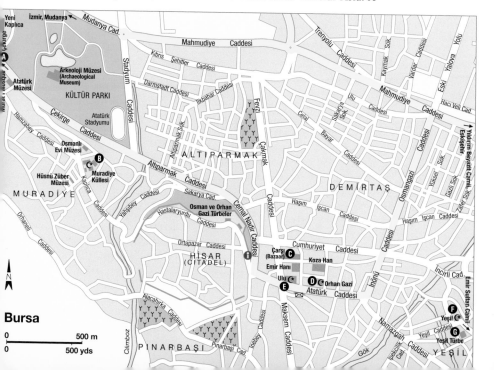

Bursa

There are over 125 mosques in Bursa. Of these the most important, most interesting and most beautiful were those created by the first Ottoman rulers, many of whom are buried here.

popular form of entertainment in Ottoman society, they were often performed in coffee houses. The stories feature Karagöz (Black Eye) and his stooge Hacivat in a series of comic, often rather bawdy, routines. The two characters were originally based on workmen who laboured on the construction of the Orhan Gazi Camii. Their antics so amused the other workers that they held up work on the building of the mosque and, as a result, were executed on the orders of the angry Sultan Orhan.

Tomb and Mosque of Murat I

Also in Çekirge is the **Mosque of Murat I**, built between 1366 and 1386. Murat, known as Hudâvendigâr ("Creator of the World"), spent most of his reign at war (thus the long delay in the mosque's completion). The tomb of the warrior-sultan, murdered in the hour of Ottoman victory at the 1389 Battle of Kosovo, lies across the road in a lovingly tended garden, his sarcophagus resting between eight columns which support the dome.

The mosque is based on the usu inverted T-plan, but has unusual fe tures which are sometimes attribute to its possible design by a Christia architect. On the ground floor was *zaviye* (dervish lodging), upstairs *medrese*. Some suggest that this was f teaching "orthodox" Islam, and that position above the dervish quarte represents some kind of victory ov heterodox mysticism. Today only tl lower floor is open to visitors.

Heading towards the old city, yc reach the **Kültür Parkı** (Çekirge Ca desi; always open; charge), with plea ant gardens, a small boating lake, ar a few expensive restaurants and nigh clubs. Inside the park, the **Arkeolo Müzesi** (Archaeological Museun Tue–Sun 8.30am–12.30pm, 1.30–5pr charge) has an interesting if bad labelled collection, in particular int cately worked metal ornaments fro all over Anatolia.

Muradiye and Hisar

Just south of Çekirge Caddesi, t **Muradiye Külliyesi** ❸ (daily 8.30am 5.30pm in summer, 8am–5pm

BELOW: as well as being nature's strongest natural fibre, silk is highly absorbent, making it easy to dye.

The Story of Silk

The ancient Chinese first realised that the small caterpillars that infested the leaves of the white mulberry tree spun themselves a cocoon, whose single gossamer thread, hundreds of metres long, can be used to produce a fabric of filmy lightness and incredible strength. For about 3,000 years they jealously guarded the secret and monopolised the market.

Byzantine Emperor Justinian I (AD 527–65) persuaded two Persian monks to smuggle silkworms hidden in bamboo canes from China to Constantinople. Silk production became a state monopoly, based in Bursa. The Ottomans encouraged local production and imports from the Far East, producing magnificent fabrics and carpets. Among the 2,500 items on display in the wardrobe section of the Topkapı Palace are many superb silk brocade and velvet garments, made in Bursa.

The silk industry had collapsed by the 1800s, outcompeted by French and Italian enterprises, but state intervention has since revitalised it. Some 300 Bursa companies now make silk, about 70 percent of it used for weaving silk carpets, especially the Hereke type. However, villagers seem increasingly reluctant to raise the troublesome silkworms – which must be kept in temperature-controlled, dark lofts – so merchants are complaining that they cannot buy enough silk, even at the annual cocoon auctions. Whether the home-grown trade will last is questionable.

winter; no charge but you may want to tip the *bekçi* – warden) was built between 1424 and 1426. It comprises a mosque, an *imaret* and a *medrese;* the tombs of Murat II (ruled 1421–51) plus various other members of Ottoman royalty were added incrementally over the next century. Above the portico of the mosque, brick patterns highlighted in azure tiling depict the heavenly spheres, while thunderbolts in blue glazed tiles are set into the marble to the right of the entrance. The T-shaped interior plan, with *eyvans* (alcoves) flanking the main domed space, is typical of early Ottoman mosques, based on Seljuk prototypes.

In the lovely gardens are 12 tombs of various styles, open in rotation. Murat's austere tomb lies under a dome raised on Roman columns. Like all the early Ottoman sultans, Murat was a renowned fighter on the battlefield, but, as recorded by Edward Gibbon, "He seldom engaged in war till he was justified by a previous and adequate provocation. In the observance of treaties his word was inviolate and sacred." Attracted to the mystical

life, he voluntarily abdicated briefly to be a dervish, and eschewing pomp and circumstance, he chose to be buried under the open occulus of the dome, so that the rain and moonlight might bathe his grave.

Deeper in the garden, past beds of flowering shrubs under the cypresses, is the tomb of Cem Sultan, one of Ottoman history's more tragic figures. After the sultan's death in 1481, intrigues prevented Cem, the favourite son of Mehmet II, from reaching Istanbul before his brother Beyazit, who proclaimed himself sultan. The two fought briefly, then Cem fled abroad to seek refuge with various Christian powers, who used him as a pawn to extract protection money from Beyazit II. He died in Naples on 25 February 1495, probably poisoned by Pope Alexander VI at Beyazit's behest. A man of action, culture and poems redolent of the pain of exile, had Cem ascended the throne Ottoman history might have been very different. Now he rests in a tomb full of blue tiles below and extravagant painted calligraphy above. Nearby,

Bursa, western terminus of the Silk Route, is still an excellent place to shop for silk, from scarves to shirts, at bargain-basement prices.

BELOW: the Muradiye complex.

Mescit (*small mosque*) in the courtyard of Koza Han in the old silk market, Bursa.

Süleyman the Magnificent's regrettably murdered first-born son, Şehzade Mustafa, lies in a tomb lined with İznik tiles depicting hyacinths, tulips and blossoming shrubs.

Muradiye is in one of Bursa's older quarters. A couple of streets south from the külliyesi, the **Hüsnü Züber Müzesi** (Tue–Sun 10am–noon, 1–5pm; charge) occupies a well-refurbished Ottoman mansion dating from 1836. The collection comprises various carved wooden implements, some made by the late Hüsnü himself, though the building is the main attraction. Across the park from the külliyesi is the **Ottoman House Museum** (Osmanlı Evi Müzesi; Tue–Sun 10am–noon, 1–5pm; charge), in a restored 17th-century house.

From here, continue along Kaplıca Caddesi, across the Cılımboz Deresi, to the other old residential quarter of **Hisar** (Citadel), still enclosed in fortifications. At the northeast edge, with fine views, stand the **Osman ve Orhan Gazi Türbeler**, tombs of the first Ottoman leaders, indifferently restored in 1868. Below to the northwest, beyond stepped parkland, begins Sakarya

Caddesi, now home to most of the rather tame nightlife in this devout, alcohol-scarce city.

The Bazaar area

The **Çarşı** (Bazaar), founded by Gazi Orhan in the 14th century but substantially extended by subsequent sultans, is still the commercial centre of Bursa, crowded with locals inspecting wares laid out in the narrow alleys lined with small shops. The gleaming modern Zafer Plaza pyramid-mall sits to the west. At the bazaar's northwest corner, the **Bedesten**, built by Sultan Beyazit I but completely restored in 1960 after a fire, still sells precious goods like jewellery and gold brocade, its impregnable doors locked each night. As so often in the Ottoman system, some of its revenues helped support the nearby Orhan Gazi Camii and Ulu Cami.

Just off the bustling market lanes stand several *hans* (shop-halls) built around quiet courtyards often shaded by trees, cooled by fountains and provided with a teahouse. Orhan built the **Emir Han**, the earliest example of the rural *kervanserai* adapted to the

equirements of urban commerce. Much altered since, its rooms could be used as shops, storage areas or dwellings. The rather grand two-storeyed Koza Han has a tiny octagonal *mescit* (small mosque) in the courtyard where the annual summer silk-cocoon auction is now but a shadow of its former self. Dazzlingly coloured silk wares still adorn the counters of the surrounding shops though.

Just uphill stands the much-restored Orhan Gazi Camii **D** (Orhan Gazi Mosque), established in 1339. A massive five-bayed porch adorned with Byzantine columns fronts the T-shaped main building, the first of several such in Bursa. The two main domed chambers are flanked by *eyvans* with smaller cupolas, where apparently *ahis* (members of an apprentice guild and religious brotherhood) stayed and worshipped. Orhan himself ruled for 33 years and, as the son-in-law of Byzantine Emperor John VI Kanatkouzenos, was intricately involved in the civil wars attending the final Byzantine decline.

Bursa's great mosques

The massive bulk of the **Ulu Cami** **E** (Great Mosque), built by Yıldırım Beyazit I (reigned 1389–1403), dominates the bazaar from the southwest. Before battling a Crusader army at Macedonian Nicopolis in 1396 he supposedly promised that, if victorious, he would build 20 mosques – a vow interpreted afterwards as one mosque with 20 domes arranged in five rows and upheld by massive pillars. Beneath the higher, central dome, once open to the sky, is the *şadırvan* (ablutions fountain). The rough-hewn walls of warm-toned, Uludağ limestone from the mountain are pierced at intervals by windows, while doors on three sides are surrounded by carved marble portals. The door on the north side was apocryphally modified by Timur when he occupied Bursa in 1402.

From here, walk east, then southeast, cross one of Bursa's two mountain streams – the Gök Dere – until reaching the **Yeşil Cami** **F** (Green Mosque), begun in 1419 by Çelebi Mehmet I (reigned 1413–21) and still the most spectacular of the city's imperial mosques, despite never being finished and severe 19th-century earthquake damage. Its name comes from the turquoise-green tiles which once covered the roof and the tops of the minarets, and still persists (along with delicate carving) around the windows. Inside, the eye is overwhelmed by the richness of the decoration. Circles, stars and geometric motifs on turquoise, green, white and blue tiles explore all possible permutations in a composition which is both harmonious and complex. By the beautifully decorated *mihrab*, a Persian inscription credits the work to the master craftsmen of Tabriz.

The Yeşil Cami, like others in Bursa, is another *zaviye*-type mosque with a *şadırvan* in the middle of the central hall, flanked by two *eyvans*. Doors also open off the central space to rooms with elaborate stucco shelving and fireplaces, thought to be *tabhanes* (dervish hostels). Immediately to the

Window detail of the Yeşil Camii (Green Mosque) in Bursa.

BELOW: a traditional Bursa house, now used as an antique shop.

Harvesting cherries in Cumalıkızık, an Ottoman village on the outskirts of Bursa.

BELOW: the interior of the Yeşil Türbe (Green Tomb).

right and left of the entrance, narrow stairs lead to the richly decorated sultan's *loge* (balcony), overlooking the prayer hall. You will need the *bekçi's* (warden's) consent to see this.

Across the road, past various view-cafés competing for your custom, Mehmet I's **Yeşil Türbe** (Green Tomb; daily 9am–1pm, 2–6pm) is among the loveliest buildings in Bursa. Walk slowly around the tomb to enjoy the extraordinary turquoise of the plain tiles, now replaced when necessary with new İznik material, and the richness of the patterned tiled lunettes over the seven windows. Apart from the elaborately decorated *mihrab*, the interior features plain Tabriz tiles on which are set lozenges of patterned tiles. The empty sarcophagus of the sultan – the body is actually well below, in accordance with Islamic law – is flanked by those of his family.

Slightly to the right of Yeşil Türbe, set among the cypresses of a large cemetery, is the **Emir Sultan Camii**. Rebuilt after 1804 in the kitsch-Baroque style popular at that time, it was originally erected around 1400 by Emir Sultan,

the Bokharan dervish and counsellor of both Beyazit I and Murat I.

To reach the much-restored **complex of Beyazit I**, walk through a quiet residential neighbourhood, then climb to the outcrop on which the complex stands. Built between 1390 and 1395, it consisted originally of a mosque, *imaret*, two *medreses*, a hospital, palace and Beyazit's *türbe*. Today only the mosque, tomb and one *medrese* remain. Beyazit's body was brought back to Bursa after his unhappy captivity and death at Akşehir, as a prisoner of Timur. Reviled by subsequent sultans for his defeat (Murat IV visited Bursa expressly to kick the tomb), Beyazit rests under a plain sarcophagus.

Around Bursa

Just south of Bursa, at an altitude of 1,900–2,500 metres (6,235–8,200ft), the richly forested **Uludağ Milli Parkı** ❿ ("Big Mountain" National Park) long claimed to be Turkey's premier ski resort, but has now been overtaken by others in central Anatolia. At the 1,800-metre (5,850ft) contour there's a dense cluster of hotels, mostly empty

during the summer months.

In summer, the mountain attracts people more interested in natural history, offering long walks by tumbling brooks and across slopes carpeted with wild flowers to several glacial tarns near the summit, actually outside park boundaries. Meat-grill restaurants abound near the Sarıalan picnic area, terminus of the cable car which leaves regularly (8am–9.30pm in summer; subject to weather conditions) from the city centre. The ascent by road takes about an hour.

Some 17km (11 miles) from the city centre, in the eastern foothills of Uludağ, **Cumalıkızık** is a picture-perfect Ottoman village which entered (inter)national consciousness by serving for five years as a location for a Turkish TV serial. Low-key tourism has not been long in following, with at least two of the delightful old houses restored as inns – reservations at weekends are essential.

İznik (Nikaia)

The small lakeside town of **İznik** ⓫ (formerly Nikaia) lies 80km (50 miles)

northeast of Bursa. It was founded in 316 BC by Antigonos I Monopthalmos (the One-Eyed), one of Alexander's successors. It was seized 15 years later by rival general Lysimakhos and renamed Nikaia after his deceased wife. The city prospered under Roman rule; Pliny the Younger, governor of Bithynia (AD 111–13), lived here and rebuilt the theatre and gymnasium.

The town has played an instrumental role in the history of Christianity. In AD 325, Nikaia was the venue for the First Ecumenical Council, which condemned the Arian heresy and formulated the Nicene Creed still used by most Christian denominations. The Iconoclastic controversy (whether Christians should continue to revere idols) was settled by the Seventh Ecumenical Council, held in the Basilica of St Sophia in 787.

The city was held briefly by the Seljuks after 1081, and was the capital of the Byzantine Laskarid dynasty during the Crusader occupation of Constantinople in the 13th century. Nikaia was taken for the Ottomans by Orhan I in 1331 and renamed İznik. Skilled

Climb Uludağ the easy way – on the 5km (3-mile)-long, 1980s vintage gondola.

BELOW: detail of an İznik tile in the Topkapı Palace in İstanbul.

İznik Tile Manufacture

Since 1993, the İznik Vafkı (İznik Foundation) has led efforts to revive traditional tile-manufacturing techniques; there are now many workshops in town. Innovative designs, beyond Ottoman floral cross sections, include depictions of the region's fruit and olive trees, or ships, all extremely popular motifs. Most kilns work primarily to order for domestic customers, and usually stock only a few specimens of any design – those casually dropping by hoping to decorate an entire kitchen or bathroom may be disappointed.

The toughest, highest-quality (and priciest) tiles are not ceramic-based but made from locally quarried quartz. This is finely ground up, reconstituted to 85 percent purity and formed into "biscuits". These are sanded, underglazed and left to air-dry for a week, then fired at over 900°C (1,652°F) for 17 hours. Next, designs are stencilled on, painstakingly painted in (usually by women) using metal-oxide pigments mimicking semiprecious stone colours, a top glaze applied, and the tile popped back in the kiln for four days. The temperature of final firing determines whether the glaze emerges glossy, half-glossy or matte. Quartz-rich tiles are porous to air, have excellent acoustic qualities (hence their use in mosques), modulate light reflections and make excellent insulators, as they contract slightly in winter and expand in summer.

craftsmen brought here from Tabriz in Iran by Yavuz (the Fierce) Selim I (reigned 1512–20) consolidated an existing ceramic industry which made İznik tiles famous. Those used to adorn the classical Ottoman mosques were all produced here; technique had declined before production moved to Kütahya late in the 17th century.

İznik sights

İznik merits a visit just for its beautiful lakeside situation, though sadly nearby beaches are not first-rate. However, there are plenty of restaurants and hotels overlooking the water.

The city's ancient double walls and two of the seven original gates are intact, while in the **Aya Sofya Müzesi** (Aya Sofya Museum; Tue–Sun 8.30am–noon, 1–5pm; charge), sections of the mosaic pavement of Justinian's original 6th-century church and a faded 7th-century fresco of Christ, John the Baptist and the Virgin can be seen. During Nikaia's 57 years as Laskarid capital, this basilica hosted the coronation of four Byzantine emperors.

The **Hacı Özbek Camii**, built in

1333, is the earliest Ottoman mosque in Turkey which can be dated accurately. Nearby, the **Yeşil Camii** (Green Mosque), built between 1378 and 1392 by Candarlı Kara Halil Paşa, has particularly harmonious proportions. Sadly, the original İznik tiles on the minaret disappeared a long time ago and have been replaced by inferior substitutes from Kütahya.

İznik's **Arkeoloji Müzesi** (Archaeological Museum; Tue–Sun 8am–noon, 1–5pm; charge) is housed in the three-domed Nilüfer Hatun İmareti. Nilüfer Hatun, wife of Orhan I, was a beautiful and distinguished Greek noblewoman (though not the daughter of Emperor John VI Kanatkouzenos as stated in some accounts). Orhan trusted his wife completely, leaving her in charge of affairs of state during his many military campaigns. Exhibits, besides the expected complement of fine İznik tiles, include a sarcophagus in perfect condition and a Roman bronze of a dancing Pan. The museum warden has the keys for the **Yeraltı Mezar**, a vividly frescoed Roman or Byzantine tomb 6km (3½ miles) outside town.

Yalova, Termal, Mudanya and Zeytinbağı

Yalova, Bursa's main port on the southern shore of the Gulf of İzmit, is served by regular car-ferries from İstanbul. More appealing is the spa of **Termal ⑫**, 12km (7 miles) inland in a forested area, popular with Arab and Turkish holidaymakers. There are several good hotels, while the hot pool of the Kurşunlu Banyo (most days 8am–10.30pm, earlier closure Thur and Sun; charge) is a testing 60°C (140°F) at source. The thermal springs were popular with the Romans and Byzantines; interest in them revived during the Belle Epoque.

Mudanya, though much closer to Bursa, is its less busy port (*see margin, left*). The rocky coastline just west is unremarkable except for **Zeytinbağı** (Trilye in Ottoman times), a formerly Greek-inhabited port with a Byzantine

BELOW: the minaret of the Yeşil Camii (Green Mosque) in İznik.

church (now a mosque), old mansions and some seafood restaurants.

The Mysian Lakes

West of Bursa, the two great lakes of ancient Mysia appeal in different ways. **Uluabat Gölü** ⓭ is still often called by its old name Apollyon, after ancient Apollonia, whose masonry has been seamlessly interwoven with the charming village of **Gölyazı**, accessible by local bus from Bursa, 31km (19 miles) away. There's a morning fish auction, storks' nests, a few half-timbered houses and lake fish to eat at the single restaurant. **Küş Gölü**, about 64km (39 miles) further west, hosts the **Küş Cenneti Milli Parkı** (Bird Paradise National Park; daily 7am–5.30pm; charge), one of the largest wildlife sanctuaries in western Anatolia. From the observation tower you can see up to 266 species of birds, both resident and migratory – the best seasons are spring and autumn.

Çanakkale

Because of the location it is likely that there were settlements here before recorded history, as control of the Dar-

danelles brought wealth and power. The Persian King Xerxes I built his bridge of boats across these straits' narrowest part in 480 BC to land 200,000 troops in Thrace, but his planned conquest of Greece ended in defeat at Salamis and Plataea. Ever since, the Dardanelles have remained a crucial control point between the European and Asian continents, as well as between the Aegean and the Sea of Marmara and the Black Sea beyond.

Çanakkale ⓮ is several hours by car or bus from İstanbul, with most long-distance buses using the ferry link with Eceabat – though the local airport receives popular daily flights from İstanbul. The town became an active trading and transit point between Asia and Europe after Sultan Mehmet II built opposing fortresses here in 1452, to tighten his stranglehold on Constantinople. Although the town may not have entirely reclaimed the status it enjoyed in the 19th century, when it was a cosmopolitan mini-Smyrna home to scores of consulates and customs houses, Çanakkale has improved considerably since the 1990s. The compact

With her brother Phrixos, Helle fled on the back of a winged ram from their evil stepmother, Ino, who wished to kill them. Tragically, she fell from the ram's back and drowned in the strait that for the ancients bore her name – the Hellespont.

BELOW: the harbour at Çanakkale.

Relaxing by the harbour.

old quarter with its houses built by the vanished Christian and Jewish communities has been refurbished, and there is an attractive seaside promenade. Visitors to Troy and Gallipoli frequently base themselves here.

Quayside restaurants serve fresh (if pricey) seafood. Enjoy a glass of tea or a beer in one of the cafés while you savour the bustling activity of the port and its never-ending parade of large freighters, fishing boats and car-ferries. For a bird's-eye view of the area, walk to the small promontory near the entrance to the military installation at the north end of town. From there you have a spectacular view of central Çanakkale, its Ottoman fortress (closed to the public), the harbour and, beyond, the broad sweep of the Dardanelles.

The local **Arkeoloji Müzesi** (Archaeology Museum; 1.5km/1 mile south of the town centre on the road to Troy; daily, summer 8am–6.45pm, winter until 5.30pm, closes 1pm Sun/hols; charge) badly needs a makeover for its under-utilised galleries. Most of the collection consists of brass implements, glazed pottery, gold and jewellery, unfired clay lamps and Hellenistic figurines from the nearby Bozcaada and Dardanos tumuli. The star items are two sarcophagi: the late Archaic "Polyxena", in perfect condition with a procession on one side and the sacrifice (in grisly detail) of Priam's daughter on the other, plus the fourth-century BC "Altıkulaç", more battered but with a finely detailed boar hunt and combat scene.

Troy

The name **Troy** ⑮ conjures up visions of the star-crossed lovers Helen and Paris, of Greek and Trojan heroes, of betrayal and revenge, of cunning and deceit, of a huge wooden horse, of the destruction of a great city and of blind Homer who immortalised it all in two epic poems, the *Iliad* and *Odyssey*. Did Helen and Paris, Agamemnon and Klytemnestra, Achilles and Odysseus ever exist? Was there really a siege of Troy? Are Homer's epics at all historical?

Whether you regard Homer as just an early minstrel and itinerant entertainer, or as the source of history's most profound legends, the adventures of his characters have become an integral part of world literary heritage, and their fates have enthralled and moved countless generations.

A little history

In 333 BC, Alexander the Great came to Troy, where he made a propitiatory sacrifice to the spirit of Priam (king of Troy during the Trojan War, according to Greek mythology) and received a gold crown from a citizen of Sigeion (where, it was believed, the Greeks had beached their ships). He also exchanged his weapons and armour for some kept in the Temple of Athena – thought to date from the time of the Trojan War. He then anointed his body with oil and ran naked to the mound where Achilles was supposedly buried. His lover, Hephaestion, did the same at the purported tomb of Achilles' companion, Patroklos.

Troy was destroyed during the Mithridatic War of about 82 BC and rebuilt by Julius Caesar. It received

BELOW: pumpkins and squashes sold at a roadside stall.

pecial honours from several emperors as the birthplace of Aeneas, legendary founder of ancient Rome. When Emperor Julian the Apostate (AD 61–3) visited Ilion, as Troy was then known, he was greeted by the bishop, Pegasios, who offered to show him the sights of the ancient city. Julian was astonished to find a fire smouldering on an altar at the so-called tomb of Hector and the statue of the hero covered in oil. The bishop explained: Is it strange that they [the people of Troy] should show [their] respect... as we show ours for our martyrs?"

Because of the growing importance of nearby Alexandria Troas, the city soon began to decline, something accelerated by the silting of its harbour. Khrisodoulos of Imbros relates how Sultan Mehmet II "inspected the ruins...[was] shown the tombs of Achilles, Hector and Ajax [and said] 'It is to me that Allah has given to avenge this city and its people... Indeed it was the Greeks who before devastated this city, and it is their descendants who after so many years have paid me the debt which their boundless pride had contracted...

towards us, the peoples of Asia.'"

The early 17th-century Scottish traveller William Lithgow was not particularly impressed by Troy: "I wot I saw infinite old sepulchres, but for their particular names and nimonation of them I suspend: neither could I believe my interpreter, sith it is more than three thousand odd years ago that Troy was destroyed!"

In a May 1810 letter to Harold Drury, Lord Byron seemed preoccupied with rather more earthy matters: "The only vestige of Troy, or of her destroyers, are the barrows supposed to contain carcasses of Achilles, Antilochus, Ajax, etc – but Mt Ida is still in high feather, though the Shepherds are nowadays not much like Ganymede."

Schliemann's great discovery

From 1871 to 1873, self-made millionaire and amateur archaeologist Heinrich Schliemann excavated at Troy using the *Iliad* (and preliminary digs by the Briton Frank Calvert) as his guide, while academics laughed at the mad German who was squandering

> She [Aunt Dot]... would have liked to see Troy's walls and towers rising once more against the sky like a Hollywood Troy, and the wooden horse standing beside them, opening mechanically every little while to show that it was full of armed Greeks.
>
> Rose Macaulay, *The Towers of Trebizond*

BELOW: remains of the odeon at Troy.

BELOW: a modern wooden horse captures the imagination of children at Troy.

his wealth so foolishly. But Schliemann found treasure, starting with a necklace, then gold cups, copper daggers, axes, lance-heads and cauldrons, silver vases and two extraordinary golden diadems worn, he judged, by royalty. In fact he had not found Homer's Troy: this collection came from the remains of a prehistoric Bronze Age civilisation a millennium earlier.

Ongoing controversy

Subsequent investigations by other archaeologists revealed more than nine separate levels of occupation at Hisarlık tumulus. Professor Carl Blegen, leader of the 1932–38 University of Cincinnati expedition, believed that Troy VII was Priam's city, and that it was destroyed in about 1260 BC; in the 1950s, Professor Moses Finley countered that there was no evidence of a hostile Mycenaean expedition to Troy. The late archaeologist George Bean also maintained there were no finds from Hisarlık to connect Troy's destruction with a Greek invasion, and that the paltry remains of Troy VII bore little resemblance to the fine

city described by Homer. But then in the 1990s the late Manfred Korfmann discovered traces of distant perimeter fortifications that indicated a town far larger than just the citadel ruins – and just possibly resistance to a siege during the 13th century BC.

In late 2009, Dr Oliver Dickinson elegantly summarised the sceptics' arguments against a historical 10-year campaign: no documented prior interaction between Greeks and Hittites at Wilusa, the latter's name for Troy; striking inaccuracies in the Homeric Catalogue of Ships compared to the real attributes of Greek city-states of the era; pervasive anachronisms in Homeric description of Mycenaean religion, palace architecture and weaponry, making the *Iliad* and *Odyssey* a vintage-700 BC pastiche of Bronze and Iron Age customs.

Another point of controversy is the modern replica of the Trojan horse. Many visitors find it ridiculously out of place; for others it is a pleasantly frivolous attraction at an otherwise visually dull site. Others are reminded of the moment when the stunned defenders realised that they had been duped and that their city was doomed. As in the literary original, the reconstruction is entered from underneath, and you can look out over the ruined city and the Troad plain to see with modern eyes what Homer could only imagine.

The site (daily, summer 8am–7pm winter 8am–5pm; charge) has relatively little to show for its illustrious pedigree, though multiple explanatory panels placed along a circular touring path help make sense of the place. Begin your tour at the massive tower in the great wall of Troy VI. Continue through the east gate, passing the carefully constructed houses of Troy VI, to the more careless constructions of Troy VII. From the summit you look over the plain to Homer's "wine-dark sea" and can see Schliemann's great north-south trench. Northwest of the paved ramp, against the wall of Troy II, he found his hoard of treasure.

Treasure-Seekers

As elsewhere in the region, Western archaeologists have plundered Turkey's priceless heritage

In 1829, a seven-year-old German boy, Heinrich Schliemann, received a Christmas gift, Ludwig Jerrer's *Illustrated History of the World*. It contained a striking engraving of Aeneas fleeing from burning Troy bearing his father Ankhises on his shoulders and leading his son Askanios by the hand. Deeply impressed, the precocious child pestered his father with questions, deciding there and then that one day he would find Homeric Troy.

The well-travelled adult Schliemann amassed a fortune trading in gold, indigo and gunpowder in California and Russia, while learning 13 modern languages. In 1868, finally ready to realise his childhood dream, he visited sites in Greece and Turkey, producing a book, *Ithaca, the Peloponnese and Troy*, which named the mound of Hisarlık as the site of Troy. Classical scholars, who dismissed the *Iliad* and the *Odyssey* as merely poetic myths, ignored him.

In 1871, Schliemann began to dig a huge trench through the 32-metre (105ft)-high mound, convinced that Homeric Troy lay at the lowest level. In 1873 he found the ruins of a fortified city and a cache of gold, copper and silver objects, as well as precious jewellery, which he called "Priam's Treasure". In fact, his discoveries were much older, being the remains of a Bronze Age town from 2400 BC. He made three more excavations at the site before his death in 1890.

Schliemann has been criticised for the cavalier way he treated Hisarlık mound, but there was then no canon of established practice for him to follow. His determined publicising of his finds, both at Troy and Mycenae, helped stir the public imagination,

and he is now regarded as one of the fathers of modern archaeology.

His illegal removal of the treasure is harder to excuse, and indeed the Ottoman government banished him from the site until 1876. His wife briefly wore some of the jewellery before presenting it to the German nation. Since then, the cache has had a chequered history. Stolen from Berlin by the Red Army in 1945, it reappeared in Moscow in 1993 and is now the subject of a dispute involving Turkey, Germany and Russia.

Schliemann is the most famous of them, but other Western "treasure-hunters" also plundered Turkey. Motivated by a desire "to lay bare the wonders of Lycia" – and enrich collections in the West – Sir Charles Fellows rediscovered 13 ancient cities. With the sultan's permission, he shipped 78 cases of Lycian sculpture and architectural fragments to England in 1840, removing a further 27 cases of artefacts from Xanthos two years later. However, every piece was charted, assessed for damage and numbered first. Thomas Newton, who later became Keeper of Antiquities at the British Museum, took a statue of Demeter and a carved lion from Knidos, plus some colossal seated figures from the Sacred Way at Didyma. Fellows' and Newton's spoils now grace the galleries of the British Museum.

All three treasure-hunters must be censured for their arrogant rape of Turkey's patrimony, but Schliemann did have permission to dig, if not remove the finds, and the others were also given permission by the sultan. Their intentions, at least, were honourable. ❏

TOP: Heinrich Schliemann, obsessed by a dream, helped create modern archaeology. **RIGHT:** depiction of the site of ancient Troy excavated by Schliemann.

THE AEGEAN COAST

Turkey's west coast is a heady mix of ancient ruins,
sandy beaches and beautiful scenery

The Aegean coast marks the western edge of Asia Minor,
an alias of the Anatolian peninsula which has figured
so prominently in history. But where ancient armies
once marched and clashed, now only gentle winds off the
azure-hued Aegean caress the ruins of the past. Even seasoned
travellers will be impressed by the alluring oak- or pine-tufted
scenery and culturally significant sites.

Between Troy and İzmir, the main archaeological destination of ancient Pergamon requires almost a full day to see
its scattered attractions, while smaller Assos is just as incomparably situated. Despite a relatively short tourist season
for the north Aegean, beaches – most notably on Bozcaada
(Tenedos) island, at Sarımsaklı near Greek-built Ayvalık, and along the
Çeşme peninsula – are in ample supply. Conveniently, most major sights
are located near the coastal highway,

İzmir is a massive city, uncharacteristic of the Aegean coast
but convenient for journeys inland to Ottoman Manisa
and ancient Sardis. The resort of Kuşadası is a more likely
seaside base, where one can enjoy hedonistic nights while
devoting the day to sightseeing. Priene, Milet (Miletus) and
Didyma are only short trips away, though at least half a day
is needed for Efes (Ephesus), the single most-visited local
site. The nearest towns to Ephesus are monument-studded
Selçuk and the architectural preserve of Şirince. Also inland,
but still in the Aegean region, beckon the commercialised
but unmissable travertine terraces of Pamukkale, and the
comparatively unvisited charms of Aphrodisias.

South of the eerie lake of Bafa, ringed by unsung ancient sites, the
coast becomes more convoluted in bays and peninsulas either side of
Bodrum, the premier southwest Aegean resort. Between here and more
recent upstart Marmaris yawns the little-frequented Gulf of Gökova, one
of many venues for the Mavi Tur (Blue Cruise) out of either port. ❑

PRECEDING PAGES: the magnificent limestone cascades at Pamukkale are
Turkey's most dazzling natural wonder. **LEFT:** the Library of Celsus, Roman
monument extraordinaire. **TOP:** keeping a close eye on fish in harbour shallows.
ABOVE LEFT: flag bearing the image of Atatürk.

THE NORTH AEGEAN COAST

Troy may be more famous, but nearby Assos
and Pergamon are of greater interest,
while the northern Aegean coast itself
is sufficient to charm any visitor

Main attractions
BOZCAADA
ASSOS ACROPOLIS
BEHRAMKALE HARBOUR
ADATEPE
AYVALIK
CUNDA
BERGAMA MUSEUM
PERGAMON ACROPOLIS
ESKI FOÇA
ALTINKUM BEACHES
ALAÇATI

BELOW: the
amphitheatre at
ancient Assos.

Astonishingly, there are still parts
of the north Aegean coast that
have not been overrun by tourists (mostly Turkish hereabouts). Head
only a short distance from the few
resorts and it is still possible to see
many traditional aspects of rural Turkish life, with shepherds and their flocks
blocking the road, farmers working
their fields and a ruggedly beautiful
landscape of mostly volcanic origin.

Bozcaada (Tenedos)

The small island of **Bozcaada ❶**,
barely 7 nautical miles from the main-

land and visible from Troy, is where
– according to Homer who knew it
as **Tenedos** – the Greek fleet moored
while canny Odysseus and his men
hid inside the wooden horse, waiting
to surprise the Trojans. Even more than
neighbouring Gökçeada (İmroz), it has
been "discovered" with a vengeance
since the 1990s, mostly by İstanbul
yuppies, and can be quite overrun in
midsummer. Access is by sea-bus from
Çanakkale – mostly timed to coincide
with flights to and from İstanbul – or
conventional car-ferry from **Geyikli
İskelesi**, about 60km (37 miles) southwest of Çanakkale.

During spring and autumn Tenedos
– the name still used, unofficially – is a
fairly tranquil place, which trades on its
assets of a single, architecturally homogeneous port guarded by a huge castle,
a half-dozen south-coast beaches and
an equal number of wineries. The **castle** (daily 10am–1pm, 2–6pm; charge)
originally Byzantine, has subsequently
been modified by every occupier. The
town, with some exquisite old mansions along its cobbled streets, was
once 80 percent Greek Orthodox but
now, after the same sort of measures
exercised on İmroz, there are fewer
than 20 elderly Greeks remaining
in their old quarter. There is also no
longer a resident priest (though Prime
Minister Erdoğan personally paid to
have the main church belfry repaired
in 2005). In a Homeric echo, there is
still a fishing fleet at anchor, but that'

deceptive – much of the seafood at the quayside restaurants is frozen and unseasonal, and an undemanding clientele means that listless cooking and rip-offs are not uncommon.

In season a few minibuses scoot around the island, or you can rent scooters and mountain bikes to reach the excellent, sandy beaches. The most developed one is **Ayazma**, its name recalling the sacred spring (now run dry) of the disused monastery just inland. **Sullubahçe**, just west, is even sandier but without facilities, while **Habbelle** has a single snack bar. East of Ayazma, **Beylik**, "**Aqvaryum**" Bay and **Tuzburnu** cove all have their partisans, but no amenities.

Assos (Behramkale)

Ancient **Assos** ❷, about 100km (60 miles) south of Çanakkale, commands the straits separating Anatolia from the Greek island of Lésvos. To get there, turn off the main E87/550 highway at the picturesque small town of **Ayvacık**, set in rolling farmland a few kilometres from the coast. In late April, the annual *panayır*, derived from an ancient pagan

festival, is an unusual week-long celebration of food, livestock-trading and music which brings together the area's people, most of them settled nomads. Ayvacık is also the main centre for the DOBAG carpet-weaving project, with guaranteed natural dyes *(see pages 110–11)* – though note that the results are not generally sold locally.

From Ayvacık – an equally good road heads west from Küçükkuyu, along the coast – a narrow road threads over hills covered in olive and oak trees. After crossing a splendid 14th-century Ottoman bridge, with views toward the ancient acropolis, one fork in the route ends at the edge of upper **Behramkale**. The typical basalt-built houses – protected from modern adulterations by law – line increasingly narrow streets hairpinning past small shops and eateries on the way to the acropolis. Just below it, a 14th-century mosque has been converted from a Byzantine church, hence a cross and Greek inscription above the door.

The main road continues sharply downhill, past ancient walls and tumbled sarcophagi of the necropolis, to

Local crafts in Assos' modern village.

BELOW: the picturesque harbour at Assos.

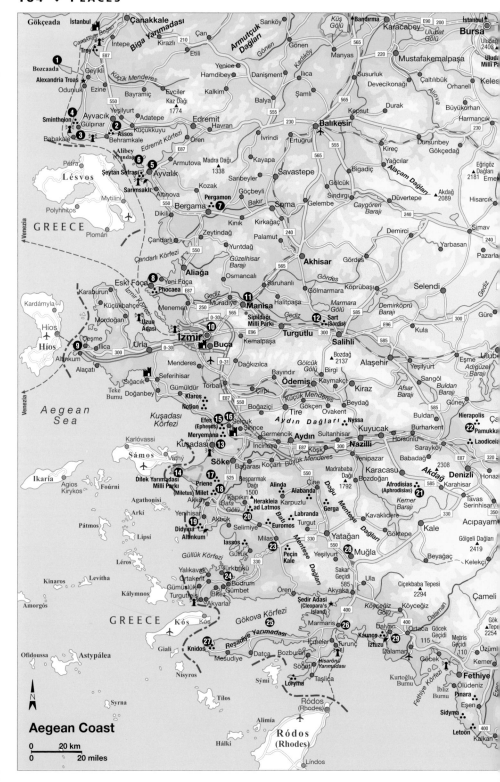

ehramkale's little **harbour**. Like its phill neighbour, it was largely inhab-ed by Greek-Orthodox before 1923. oth became fashionable with Turk-h artists, actors and academics well efore Bozcaada, and the same caveats pply – show up midweek, or during May and September, and you should e able to secure prime accommoda-ion at a reasonable price. You can wim at lower Behramkale's narrow bbon of seashore fringing the stone uildings here (most of them aban-oned acorn warehouses converted to otels), but the closest proper (pebble) each is 4km (2½ miles) east, at less ramped **Kadırga**.

ssos acropolis

he Hellenistic walls of ancient Assos re nearly 3km (2 miles) long, enclos-ng the modern village, and their ntact patches stand to a height of 14 metres (46ft). The Byzantine circuit is ar more compact, enclosing only the emnants of the **Temple of Athena** daily 8.30am–sunset; charge), built n about 530 BC at the top of a near-ertical drop of 240 metres (750ft), and edicated to the goddess of both war nd handicrafts. The temple was first xcavated by the young Francis Bacon f the Antiquarian Society of Boston n 1881, and a few Doric columns e-erected by another American dig lmost a century later. Unfortunately, ement was ill-advisedly used; there is ow a Turkish programme to replace hem with masonry from the origi-al quarry, and beside the road into Behramkale you can see the new col-mn sections being prepared. Yet the etting, not the paltry remains, is the hing: visit near dawn or sunset for he most impressive panorama from he temple platform, taking in the dremit Gulf to the east and Lésvos sland (Midili to the Turks) floating pposite in the Aegean, just 6 nautical niles away.

It was from Lésvos that colonists ame to found Assos in about 950 C. The city reached its zenith dur-ing the 4th century BC when ruled by Hermeias, a eunuch disciple of Plato; Hermeias attempted to devise the ideal city-state as described by Plato in his famous work *The Republic*. From 348 to 345 BC Aristotle – who ended up marrying Hermeias' niece – and Theo-phrastos both lived in Assos as Her-meias' guests, carrying out important early work in the natural sciences. St Paul also passed through en route to Lésvos during his third evangelical journey (*c.*55 AD).

Babakale, Smintheion and Alexandria Troas

West of Behramkale, a good road threads high above the Aegean, still oppposite Lésvos, through more stone-built villages, whose male inhabitants tend to be skilled masons (and involved in the Assos column-replacement project). End of the line, 34km (21 miles) from Assos, is sleepy **Babakale ❸**, at the westernmost point of Asia Minor. A working fishing port with ambitions (currently being realised) to be a major yacht marina, Babakale offers some of the most

Fishing boats in Babakale harbour, which is being transformed into a yacht marina.

BELOW: the last remaining columns of the Temple of Athena, Assos.

The old quarter in Ayvalik, whose maze-like street plan, it is said, was designed to help smugglers escape the authorities.

BELOW: dramatic sunset at Ayvalik.

dramatic sunsets in the Aegean, a well-restored 18th-century castle (among the last such structures the Ottomans built), a medieval mosque and a few carved fountains.

Some 9km (5½ miles) inland stands the shrine of **Apollo Smintheion** ❹, at the edge of **Gülpınar village**. This temple (daily 8am–5pm; charge) – slowly being restored by funds from the Efes beer foundation – honours one of the more bizarre avatars of Apollo, as Destroyer of Mice. The mythical original colonists here, Teukros and Skamandros of Crete, had their weaponry eaten by mice, and remembered an old sage who had advised them to settle where attacked by the "sons of earth". This they assumed to mean the rodents, founding the ancient town of Khryse nearby. This too is being excavated and restored, with a square reservoir, arcaded baths and part of the Sacred Way from nearby Alexandria Troas uncovered thus far.

Khryse is rich in Homeric significance, as the place where Agamemnon abducted Khryseis, the resident priestess of Apollo. Her father Khryses the

priest appealed for help to Apollo, who duly inflicted a plague on the Greeks, lifted only when the girl was returned to her father. Agamemnon then demanded Briseis, the mistress of Achilles, as compensation, leading to a feud between the two warriors that permeates the entire *Iliad*. A one-room museum by the temple contains damaged pediment reliefs showing many of these scenes.

From here, the coast road follows the course of the ancient Sacred Way 34km (21 miles) to **Alexandria Troas**, founded by Antigonos I, a general of Alexander the Great, in 300 BC. For years a half-buried jumble of ancient masonry, it's now being properly excavated by German archaeologists. Revealed so far are 8km (5 miles) of city wall, a shop-lined avenue, an odeion, an unidentified agora temple and some baths. There's no fencing or admission (yet) though the warden may give you a tour (in Turkish only).

The Gulf of Edremit: Adatepe to Ören

The easterly access road for Assos meets

the main highway again at Küçükuyu, a small fishing port and olive-oil pressing centre that's the gateway to **Adatepe**, 4km (2½ miles) northeast in the forested foothills of Kazdağ, the ancient Mt Ida. Like Cumalıkızık near Bursa, it has sprung to fame through appearance in a Turkish TV serial, and its imposing stone mansions, of a piece with the volcanic boulders lying around, are statutorily protected. **Yeşilyurt**, a similar distance northwest of Küçükuyu, has a more free-wheeling building code, to the detriment of its yellow-masonry houses, though it does have a fine, late medieval mosque.

From Küçükuyu to the county town of Edremit, the gulf coast here presents a dreary sequence of holiday villa developments for urban Turks, interspersed with the area's remaining olive groves. The only relief comes beyond Edremit at the more human-scale resort of **Ören**, with its long sandy beach facing west, and ample accommodation.

Ayvalık

A short side road goes southwest from the E87/550 highway, through an undistinguished, modern suburb like most others in Aegean Turkey, before suddenly entering the distinctive older core of **Ayvalık** ❺. With its many small, secluded harbours, the region has been settled since ancient times, but the town visible today dates from the early 18th century, when it was established, as Kydonies, by Ottoman Greeks. As of 1790, the place was conceded many privileges by Grand Vizier Cezayırlı Hasan Paşa, who, while serving as Ottoman admiral, had been rescued in 1771 by the Greeks of Ayvalık after a calamitous defeat by the Russian navy. The numerous Greek-built mansions, olive mills and over a dozen churches all date from this heyday, which made the town the second most elegant and prosperous on the Aegean coast after Smyrna (İzmir). This period ended with the exchange of populations, when local Orthodox Christians were replaced largely by Muslims from

Crete and Lésvos (Midili) island opposite. Their older generations still speak – and understand – Greek.

Ayvalık lives increasingly on tourist revenue and second-home sales rather than olive-based products, though the clientele is largely Turkish, and from İstanbul, owing partly to substantial distance from the nearest international airport. The picturesque south quay, with its fishing and excursion-boat fleet, overlooks an almost completely landlocked bay guarded from the open sea by two dozen wooded islands.

The old quarter just inland has meandering lanes lined by handsome Greek **mansions** and more modest dwellings, many of them becoming progressively, deplorably more dilapidated due to inheritance feuds and impoverished owners unable to fund necessary repairs. The maze-like street plan threading the entire town was supposedly devised to assist smugglers eluding the authorities. Equally apocryphal – or equally true – is the story that many of Ayvalık's better-off families came into their riches without much effort after the population exchanges.

TIP

The sheltered waters around Ayvalık, famous for their coral, submerged archaeological artefacts and sea caves, provide ample opportunities for scuba diving. At least two dive operators run trips from the south quay.

BELOW: fisherman in Ayvalik's south quay.

Ancient capital on display in Bergama Museum.

The departing Greeks, convinced that they would eventually return, hid gold and jewellery in the walls or under the floorboards, where it was discovered by the new occupants.

Almost all of the town's Greek Orthodox **churches** have been converted into mosques, while preserving their original features – thus juxtaposed belfries and minarets are an essential part of the Ayvalık skyline, best enjoyed (along with the spectacle of tiled roofs) from one of the hillier neighbourhoods. The main landmark churches are Ágios Ioánnis, now called the Saatli Cami after its clocktower, and Ágios Geórgios, lately the Çınarlı Cami. Unconverted Taksiyárhis, up the slope, or Faneroméni with its *ayazma* (sacred spring), near the fish market, may some day reopen as museums.

Sarımsaklı and Cunda

The closest proper beach to Ayvalık is at **Sarımsaklı**, 8km (5 miles) south, one of the longest sandy strands along the north Aegean coast, with all the usual water sports offered. The somewhat downmarket resort just inland, with

BELOW: wild flowers grow amongst the Pergamon ruins.

its standard-issue accommodatio eateries and bars, is considerably le inspiring. From the link road betwee Ayvalık and the Sarımsaklı resort stri a narrower road leads up to the hig est point in the Ayvalık area, **Şeyta Sofrasi** (the Devil's Table). This afforc a spectacular view north over Ayval Bay and pine-covered islets, and we towards Lésvos (Midili). It's *the* place be at sunset, but preferably out of pea season. During summer or at *bayra* times evening bus tours converge her and access becomes impossible.

The largest of the area's islets, clear visible opposite Ayvalık, is **Cunda ⊙** known officially as **Alibey Adasi** an to its departed Greeks as Moskhonis Although now connected to the mai land by a causeway (and bus service the half-hourly boat journey fror Ayvalık quayside is more pleasant. Th old town – built to a sloping grid pla unlike labyrinthine Ayvalık – rewarc a wander on foot. Sleepier than i neighbour but restored to a greate extent, Cunda is a favourite target fc well-heeled, vehemently secular cit Turks keen on owning an Aegea

The Pergamene Dynasty

Although Pergamon had existed since the 8th century BC, it became prominent only under Lysimakhos, one of Alexander the Great's successor-generals. His eunuch-steward Philetaeros inherited the town and its treasure after betraying Lysimakhos to the Seleucids in 281 BC. With ready largesse he exercised considerable influence well beyond Pergamon before bequeathing it all in 263 BC to his nephew Eumenes I, first of the Pergamene dynasty.

This dynasty established a kingdom which grew to encompass much of western Anatolia, and it was responsible for erecting the many fine public buildings that made Pergamon such a glittering city. Eumenes' nephew Attalos I saved the region from marauding Gauls, while Eumenes II (ruled 197–159 BC) allied himself with the Romans. He also built the theatre, Zeus temple and most famously the library, which rivalled Alexandria's. Parchment (derived from "pergamene") was invented here after the jealous Egyptians cut off the supply of papyrus.

In 133 BC, the last Pergamene ruler, Attalos III – of a scholarly bent, but unpopular because of his cruelty – left the kingdom to the Romans, who gladly accepted it as a toehold from which to expand into all of Anatolia. Except in 88 BC, when the city's Italian inhabitants were slaughtered during the Mithridatic wars, it prospered under Roman rule.

second home. They can be found thronging the main quay with its cafés and seafood tavernas, the latter featuring fried *papalina* (sprat).

At the heart of the architecturally protected town stands the earthquake-shattered Taksiyárhis cathedral, its interior off limits and supported by scaffolding pending long-deferred restoration. Although Cunda has almost no sandy beaches, there are plenty of secluded swimming bays and two derelict rural monasteries reachable only by sea. Boat tours operate from Cunda's quay. The northern part of Cunda, called Patriça, is in theory a protected nature reserve, but even here modern villas are encroaching.

Modern Bergama, ancient Pergamon

Beyond Ayvalık, the main highway leads southeast through the territory of ancient Aeolia, veering inland away from the minor resort of Dikili past productive farmland – and some geothermal installations near extinct volanic cones. On the quieter side roads, horse carts still trundle along, and

there is a noticeable Roma presence. One of these roads leads, along the valley of the Bakır Çayı (the ancient Kaikos River), past the Maltepe tumulus, to the market town of **Bergama**. The centre is busy and characterful, worth a walk if you have the energy after the ruins. The colourful annual Bergama Festival, usually the third week of June, highlights local crafts, dance, sports, music and food.

Towering 300 metres (1,000ft) above the city, the ruins of **Pergamon** ❼ command an extraordinary 360-degree view. One can understand how this great Hellenistic city dominated the entire region, as a centre of culture, commerce, rhetoric and medicine to rival other centres of Mediterranean Hellenism such as Ephesus, Alexandria and Antioch.

Allow several hours to visit the ruins. There are two main areas – the Asklepion and the Acropolis (open daily 8.30am–5.30pm, until 6.30pm in summer; separate charges) – as well as some minor sites within Bergama town itself. Visitors without their own transport should consider a package tour

TIP

Drivers or cyclists should take the old, direct road from Ayvalık to Bergama, via the Kozak plateau – it's no slower and more enjoyable than the main highway. The magnificent stone-pine forests seen en route are the source of the famous local pine nuts (*çam fıstığı*). Buy these in Ayvalık, not for inflated prices in Bergama.

BELOW: girls parade on Youth Day, also known as the Commemoration of Atatürk Day, in Bergama.

In legend, Asklepios, son of Apollo and the nymph Koronis, was raised by the centaur Khiron, who instructed him in the healing arts. Asklepios was killed by one of Zeus' thunderbolts for resuscitating too many people with the blood of the Gorgon, thus depriving Hades of a steady supply of deceased souls.

BELOW: the colonnaded Sacred Way (Via Tecta), part of the Asklepion ruins.

that includes transport to and from both sites, since they are some 8km (5 miles) apart, with a long, twisty access road up to the Acropolis. Taxi tours from ranks in the town centre tend to be overpriced – bargain strenuously.

The Asklepion and the Museum

The ruins of the **Asklepion** are about 2km (1½ miles) gently uphill from central Bergama and just about feasible to walk to, if the day is not too hot. Initially dedicated to Asklepios, god of healing, this was not your average medical clinic but the first complete health spa in history.

The process went something like this: a tired, overwrought Greek or Roman businessman, politician or military leader would arrive at the Asklepion to be greeted by attendants. He was then led down the colonnaded Sacred Way (a busy bazaar of merchants and advisers) before choosing from a variety of treatments or sensuous experiences designed to eliminate stress. Prospective patients would have their dreams analysed (2,000 years before

Freud), browse through good books in the library, go for a dip in the sacred healing springs, and then round it all off with a visit to the 3,500-capacity theatre, for an exciting production of a play by Sophocles and some socialising with friends. In theory the process could take as little as a few hours, but one usually spent days or even weeks here relaxing and recuperating from the strains of Graeco-Roman life.

The 2nd-century AD **Temple of Asklepios**, easily recognisable due to its circular shape, is worth a closer look, if only to appreciate the fine skill of the stonemasons who created it. It was designed as a miniature of Rome's Pantheon, and archaeologists have since found an underground tunnel that brought in water from a nearby spring. Just southwest of this, downhill, is the circular, rather more intact Temple of Telesphoros, son of Asklepios. As part of the healing ritual patients slept in both temples, perchance to have Asklepios appear to them in a dream with his advice to be analysed later. A fine Ionic colonnade fronts the somewhat over-restored theatre.

Pergamon

0   500 m

0   500 yds

Back in Bergama, stop at the small but satisfying **Pergamon Arkeoloji Müzesi** (Archaeological Museum; daily 8.30am–noon, 1–5.30pm; charge), on the main street near the tourist office. This is one of the earliest museums to collect artefacts from Pergamon and its surroundings; unfortunately the best exhibits are in Berlin, so the museum has to content itself with a model of the impressive Temple of Zeus. Still, there are many vivid statues evincing a pioneering naturalistic technique in depicting anatomy, which later influenced Renaissance sculpture. There's also a large figurine of Aphrodite, found at the Roman spa and asklepion **Allianoi**, 19km (12 miles) to the east. Allianoi had barely been excavated before the Yortanlı irrigation dam was built, threatening it with submersion. Despite protests, it seems the reservoir will be filled in the next few years.

Kızıl Avlu (Red Basilica) and Old Town

Approaching the Bergama Çayı (the ancient Selinos stream), you come upon an imposing structure straddling

the river, the **Kızıl Avlu** (Red Basilica; daily 8.30am–5.30pm, May–Sept until 6.30pm; charge). Dating from the 2nd century AD, it was originally a vast temple to the Egyptian gods Serapis, Harpokrates and Isis. Two underground tunnels carried river water beneath the building's foundations. Pergamon was one of the Seven Churches of the Apocalypse addressed by St John the Divine, who cited it in the Book of Revelation 2:13 as "the throne of Satan", perhaps a reference to the Egyptian cult; later, the Kızıl Avlu was converted into a much smaller basilica by the Byzantines. Originally, the red-brick building was covered in marble, but this has long since vanished and nowadays only the floor paving retains any marble finish.

There are some interesting antique and carpet shops opposite the Red Basilica, but too many coach tours have had their effect on prices of the merchandise, which itself is a mixture of genuine antiques, old pots and pans and the odd fake.

Just uphill is the fascinating old town, its hillside lane-houses part Greek-inhabited before 1923. The **Ulu Cami**

The Turkish baths in Bergama.

BELOW LEFT: Kizil Avlu. **BELOW:** Bergama carpets are typically made only of wool.

Bergama's old town was part Greek-inhabited before the population exchange of Greek and Turkish nationals in 1923.

BELOW: Pergamon's spectacular theatre.

was commissioned by Sultan Beyazit I in 1398–99. The bazaar in the flatlands offers brightly painted shopfronts overloaded with perilously heaped goods – goatskins, cheeses, fruit, honey, yoghurt and pine nuts – as well as some basic, unlicensed restaurants.

The Acropolis

For the energetic, there is a path up to the fabled Acropolis from Bergama, though it's probably best to use it downhill on your return. Most people will arrive by car at the car park and ticket booth at the top. As you pass the scant remains of a monumental gate, you enter one of the greatest centres of Hellenistic civilisation, excavated between 1878 and 1886 by Carl Humann, a railway engineer employed by the Ottoman government. He had been alerted to the existence of the forgotten site by some locals who sold him a piece of mosaic from the **Temple of Zeus**. Its **altar**, of which only the stepped base – underneath two flourishing stone pines – remains, was largely whisked away to Berlin, where its magnificent reliefs, high-

lighting a battle between titans and gods, are now the main attraction in the city's Pergamon Museum.

On the next terrace up lie the equally sparse foundations of the **Temple of Athena Polias Nikephoros**, the oldest temple in Pergamon. Built in the Doric style at the end of the 4th century BC, it was dedicated to the city's patron goddess Athena "who brings victory". The north stoa of the temple abutted the famous library, once filled with over 200,000 volumes collected by Eumenes II and Attalos II. It was later presented to Cleopatra by Mark Antony as a wedding gift and remained in Alexandria until destroyed around AD 641 by raiding Arabs, whose chieftain Amr ibn al-As declared that all books other than the Koran were superfluous.

Still further uphill looms the massive, much-photographed **Temple of Trajan**, dedicated to the deified Roman emperor Trajan, and completed during the reign of Hadrian. German archaeologists have re-erected many of its Corinthian columns, plus most of the stoa which surrounds it on three sides.

Over the precipice from the two temples plunge 80 rows of seats for the incomparably set **theatre**. The most steeply inclined in the ancient world, it still managed to hold 10,000 spectators (and is still used during the annual Bergama Festival). At the very bottom, a long terrace gave access from the upper agora, leading past the orchestra to a small Temple of Dionysus, god of drama, to one side. Pacing the orchestra area, perhaps imagining long-vanished performances, one can make out the holes for stakes supporting temporary scenery – because of the topography and presence of the temple, there was no permanent stage. Standing here, you can confirm the superb acoustics of the theatre: an actor (or tourist) speaking in a normal voice can be heard clearly even at the 80th row of seating.

From the agora, where Carl Humann's grave lies, an ancient street paved in andesite cobbles descends to the **Temple of Demeter** and the remains of a massive **Gymnasium**. This was divided into three sections for different age groups: the lowest level for small boys, the middle terrace for adolescents, and the highest, most elaborate complex for young men. This was flanked by two **baths** – whose marble washbasins are still discernible – and contained an *ephebeion* hall, where training and initiaion ceremonies would be held. By Hellenistic times, the ancient Athenian notion of a two-year course of study aimed at forming "sound bodies and sound minds" through military drills and studies in tactics had evolved into a well-rounded curriculum. This in turn formed the basis of modern secondary and university education from the medieval era to the early 20th century.

Below the gymnasium and lower agora is the **South Gate**, erected by Eumenes II, the main (and very well defended) entrance to the city in ancient times. The perimeter walls nearby show clear evidence of Ottoman restorations, when rubble and bricks held together by mortar were used instead of the mortarless tight fit of Hellenistic masonry.

Çandarlı and Foça

From Bergama a short journey leads southwest to **Çandarlı**, 35km (23 miles) away on the coast. The most direct route is south along the main highway before turning right at the village of Zeytindağ and re-crossing the Bakır Çayı. This (usually) sleepy place occupies a small peninsula jutting into the bay, dominated by a multi-towered 14th-century **Genoese fortress** (closed to the public) in excellent condition owing to recent restoration.

Çandarlı is built on the site of ancient Pitane, but there is precious little to see of that ancient Aeolian city other than old masonry copiously recycled into the castle. The little port-resort is blessed with two sandy beaches: a south-facing one east of the peninsula with its handful of surviving old Ottoman houses, and the more popular one looking west to the Karaburun peninsula and Foça.

Bergama carpets, prominently displayed in the town, are woven, as they have been for centuries, in dozens of surrounding villages. They are all-wool, with motifs reflecting the cosmology and lifestyle of the settled Yörüks who make them, though sadly dyeing and knotting quality in modern specimens are not always what they might be.

BELOW: the Temple of Trajan, on the Acropolis.

BELOW LEFT: Eski Foça manages to retain some elements of its traditional character.
BELOW RIGHT: shining shoes in Çandarli.

Each summer – or warm weekend – Çandarlı comes alive with Turkish families on holiday.

Returning to the main highway, continue around Çandarlı Bay (Çandarlı Körfezi) past **Aliağa**, remarkable only for its industrial port and obsolete, polluting petrochemical complex – among the first set up in Turkey. A few kilometres beyond Aliağa, a turn-off west leads to the contrasting resorts of Yeni Foça and Eski Foça, with startling seascapes en route. First encountered is **Yeni Foça**, with its core of old Greek houses, an exposed beach, and a dominant ethos of second homes pitched at people from Manisa and İzmir. An intriguing target in the hills above, 8km (5 miles) away, is the relatively unspoilt village of **Kozbeyli**, with a much-esteemed spring (potable water is a problem locally), a characterful café noted for its *dibek kahvesi* (coffee ground in a giant mortar and pestle) and more old houses.

Most guidebooks, if they mention Foça at all, refer to **Eski Foça ❽**, the site of ancient Phocaea on the western end of the peninsula, founded by Ionian colonists early in the first millennium BC. Herodotus lauded the Phokaeans as "the pioneer navigators of the Greeks... who showed their countrymen the way to the Adriatic, Tyrrhenia and the Spanish peninsula as far as Tartessus." To achieve these naval feats, the Phokaeans solved the problem of sailing heavily laden boats in shallow waters by designing a new flat-bottomed vessel. They were the founders of many colonies in the Sea of Marmara, the Black Sea and the Mediterranean, including the French city of Marseilles.

The fortress of **Beşkapılar** (originally Byzantine-Genoese; part open as private art gallery), and two historic mosques, sit on a promontory dividing the two bays; ruins of the ancient town are sparse and difficult to find. Along the busier, more attractive north harbour, called **Küçükdeniz** stands a line of charming Ottoman Greek houses, many now restored as accommodation and fish restaurants. Beaches, many of which charge an entrance fee, are found on the 25km

5-mile) stretch of road between ⸱ere and Yenifoça.

"Phokaea" is related to the ancient ⸱reek for "seal", a name perhaps elic⸱ed from the ancients by the suggestive ⸱ontours of the islets seen just offshore ⸱s at Ayvalık, daily boat excursions ⸱sit them) – or perhaps the animal ⸱self, which features on the (pardon ⸱e pun) municipal seal. There are still ⸱id to be a few dozen Mediterranean ⸱onk seals resident locally; a local ⸱search foundation monitors and ⸱pposedly protects them.

⸱eşme and Alaçatı

⸱ess than an hour's drive west of ⸱mir on the motorway, or 80km (50 ⸱iles) along the more leisurely old ⸱ad, Çeşme ❾ is an inevitably pop⸱lar but still attractive family resort ⸱ the tip of the second westernmost ⸱eninsula in Turkey. Besides land ⸱nks to İzmir, there are year-round ⸱rries to the Greek island of Híos ⸱d summer services to Ancona and ⸱rindisi in Italy.

The pace of life has quickened here ⸱nce the turn of the millennium, but you can still enjoy its well-preserved Ottoman domestic architecture, a hamam, and a crumbling 14th-century Genoese **castle**, which contains a small museum of finds from nearby Erythrae. A little theatre hosts events throughout the local late June/early July festival. Remoter attractions include the thermal spas at the busier resort of **Ilıca**, 6km (3½ miles) east, and the superb sandy coves at **Altınkum**, 9km (5½ miles) south.

A similar distance southeast is **Alaçatı**, contrastingly upmarket and trendy with the chattering classes of İzmir. Before about 2002 the homogeneous old, stone-built Greek town of Alátsata offered no tourist facilities to speak of. Most activity centred on the market conducted in the porch of the former church. However, a trickle of restored boutique hotels and nouvelle bistros has become a wave, with prices at – or over – Greek levels. Alaçatı has its own beach 4km (2½ miles) south, though it can't compare to Altınkum unless you're windsurfing or kite-surfing, for which conditions are perfect.   ❑

The Agamemnon thermal baths near Çeşme.

BELOW LEFT:
Çesme statue of
Kaplan Giray,
who was Khan of
Kirim three times.
BELOW RIGHT:
windsurfing at
Alaçati.

İZMIR, MANISA AND SARDIS

İzmir enjoys a stunning position at the head of a long gulf; Manisa's setting is also its salient point, while modern times have left ancient Sardis untouched

urkey's second-largest port and third-largest city, **İzmir ⑩** (ancient Smyrna) is also one of the country's major industrial and commercial centres. For overseas travellers, it has traditionally been a base for excursions to the renowned archaeological sites to the north (Pergamon), east (Sardis) and south (Ephesus), though this role is waning.

Ancient Smyrna

Things have not always been rosy, as İzmir experienced centuries of attack by successive occupying armies – all lured by her crucial geographical location and mild winters. The tiny Neolithic settlement at Tepekule (today Bayraklı, northeast of the centre), grew in size and importance after Ionian colonists arrived during the 9th century BC and turned it into a prosperous settlement. After a period of decline, Alexander the Great moved the acropolis late in the 4th century BC to Mount Pagos; it was soon named Smyrna, possibly after the Amazon queen Samornia.

Roman rule from the 1st century BC oversaw an era of peace and prosperity and the addition of many grand civic buildings, of which little now remains. The city, with a population of 100,000, thrived as the harbour of its rival Ephesus silted up. Smyrna was one of the Seven Churches of the Apocalypse,

and its octogenarian bishop, Polycarp, was martyred in AD 156 for refusing to deny his faith.

Arab seaborne raids of the 7th century AD were the start of many vicissitudes. Seljuk Turks briefly captured the city in 1077, soon to be ousted in turn by the Byzantines, the Genoese, the crusading Knights of Rhodes, Timur's Mongol hordes and minor Turkish emirs before falling finally to the Ottomans in 1415. Under Ottoman administration, the city – now called İzmir – became predominantly

Main attractions
ETNOGRAFYA MÜZESI, İZMIR
SULTAN CAMII, MANISA
MARBLE COURT, SARDIS
ÇAKIRAĞA KONAĞI, BIRGI

LEFT: classical beauty.
RIGHT: the clock tower in İzmir.

TIP

The easiest – and safest – way to get to the Kadifekale is by bus No. 33 from the Konak bus terminal (buy tickets first from the small booth at the bus stop). Walking down from Kadifekale after dark, through a rough neighbourhood, is not recommended.

Christian, the majority being Greek Orthodox, with some Armenian and Levantine Catholics. There were also sizeable Jewish and Muslim minorities. A wealthy terminus on the Silk Road with a cosmopolitan lifestyle, it was dubbed, disparagingly, *gavur* (infidel) İzmir.

The Great Fire of Smyrna

After World War I, Greek troops were authorised by the Allies to land at Smyrna, doing so on 15 May 1919. In their eyes this was a prelude to carving out an expanded Greece straddling two continents, but within three years their imperialist venture had collapsed ignominiously. The routed Greek army poured into Smyrna early in September 1922, to be evacuated by their own fleet on 8 September. The victorious Turkish forces entered the city the next day (a date widely commemorated here), and after pillaging and massacres of Christians in revenge for similar Greek actions, set fires in the Armenian quarter on 13 September, apparently waiting for favourable winds to blow the flames away from the Muslim quarter. Within two days 70 percent of th' city had burnt to the ground, wit' thousands incinerated alive; the onl' non-Muslim district which escape' destruction was Pounda (today calle' Alsancak). *Gavur İzmir*, as probabl' intended, was no more. A quarte' of a million desperate refugees hu' dled at the quayside, trying to avoi' the blaze, while anchored America' French, British and Italian vesse' refused to let them on board unt' the third day of the inferno. This sc' nario, disputed by republican Turkis' apologists (though not terribly stre' uously), is supported by numerou' eyewitness accounts, most notably ' American consul George Horton an' various missionary educators.

İzmir today

In contrast to its past, İzmir no' attracts less privileged Turks from a' over Anatolia searching for work t' support their families. The city thu' presents familiar modern Turkis' problems – an oversubscribed infr' structure (being partly relieved by ne'

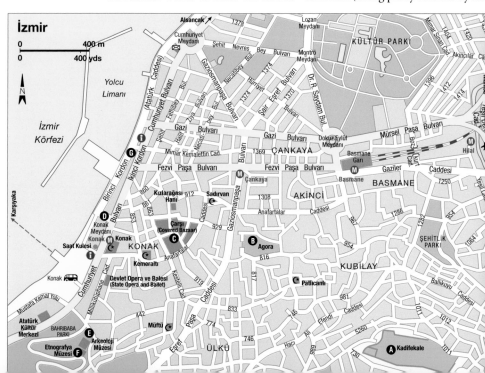

motorways and a small metro system) and sprawling, illegally built shanty-town suburbs to the east. Still, the centre feels cosmopolitan and lively, and locals (aside from a few street hustlers) are laid-back.

The imposing fortress of **Kadifekale** ❶ on flat-topped Mount Pagos rises majestically behind the city and offers unparalleled vistas in all directions. The grounds of the "Velvet Castle" contain a wonderful mixture of people: picnickers, well-dressed citizens out for a stroll, and young romantics gazing into each other's eyes over tea in one of the gently shaded outdoor cafés. Just inside the main gate, climb up the steps leading to the top of the wall for views encompassing the Çeşme peninsula to the west, Karşıyaka across the bay, and the mountains shielding Manisa on the northeast side.

Shopping then and now

Smyrna's ancient marketplace lies just a short distance east of the modern bazaar, via a network of narrow streets. The **Agora** ❷ (daily 8.30am–noon, 1–5.30pm; charge) dates back to late Hellenistic times, but today the relatively small clearing contains colonnades around a central esplanade, built during the reign of Marcus Aurelius late in the 2nd century AD.

On leaving the Agora, turn right along Gaziosmanpaşa Bulvarı; after about 100 metres/yards, take one of the small streets on the left into the **Çarşı** (Covered Bazaar) ❸. Although it cannot compare to the one in İstanbul in terms of variety and interest of stock (except for leather goods and hubble-bubble pipes), it does possess character and atmosphere – and often a few pickpockets. The only explicitly touristy part is the **Kızlarağası Hanı**, a reconstructed Ottoman market, now housing craft workshops, souvenir stalls and courtyard cafés.

You finally emerge from the crowded maze of bazaar lanes onto waterfront **Konak Meydanı** ❹, with its distinctive clock tower, donated by Sultan Abdül Hamit II in 1901, and a charming **mosque** of 1748, ornately decorated with Kütahya tiles. Now pedestrianised except for its bus ranks, Konak also serves as a ferry terminal

Tile detail on the Konak mosque, İzmir.

BELOW: *nargiles* (waterpipes) and spices for sale in Izmir.

İzmir has a sizeable black population – the descendants of Sudanese slaves used as domestic servants and especially wet-nurses throughout the 16th to 19th centuries. Many remained with their master's families after the abolition of slavery.

for commuters to Karşıyaka suburb across the bay.

İzmir's best museums lie just south of Konak in the Bahribab Parkı (sometimes called the Turgutreis Parkı), a few minutes' walk away. The **Arkeoloji Müzesi** (Archaeological Museum) has a varied and interesting collection of Roman monumental art downstairs, while the other floors are devoted to Greek art from Archaic to Hellenistic times. The neighbouring **Etnografya Müzesi** (Ethnographic Museum) **F** has a wider appeal with its reconstructed Ottoman pharmacy, a bridal chamber and circumcision room. The museum also covers the manufacture of the blue beads that serve as an antidote to the evil eye, and features exhibits on camel-wrestling and rope-making (both museums notionally Tue–Sun 8am–5pm; charge).

Around sunset, take a leisurely stroll along the palm tree-lined **Birinci Kordon G**, joining hundreds of locals for a bayside promenade either side of Cumhuriyet Meydanı. On summer evenings the *imbat*, the cooling offshore breeze of İzmir, is best enjoyed seated at one of the many cafés lining the *kordon*.

BELOW: Muradiye Camii, Manisa.

Manisa

From İzmir, the scenic but high-speed Highway 565 winds over forested mountains to the Gediz valley, famous for its sultana grapes. One of these mountains was the ancient Mt Sypilos, which influenced Manisa's earlier name, Magnesia ad Sypilum. Arrayed impressively at the foot of **Sipildağı**, as the sculpted crags are now called, modern **Manisa** ⑪ is an unexpectedly interesting city, held by every power in the area since its legendary founding by warriors returning from the Trojan War.

Alexander the Great liberated the place from the Persians in 334 BC, while a Roman and Pergamene force routed Syrian armies here in 190 BC, setting the stage for Roman and Byzantine prosperity. Manisa finally fell to the Turkish emir Saruhan in 1313. Under the Ottomans it was a favourite training ground for crown princes, sent here to serve as local governors. Most of what you see today was rebuilt after Manisa was destroyed by Greek forces during their retreat in 1922; supposedly only a few hundred buildings were left standing. Although relatively few tourists come here, there is enough to see to spend half a day or longer here.

A handful of well-signposted Ottoman monuments in the centre constitute most of the interest. The **Sultan Camii** with its calligraphy-daubed portico is the oldest (1522), the focus of a *külliye* whose buildings still survive. Just uphill stands the **Muradiye Camii**, one of the last (1583–5) works of master architect Sinan, commissioned by Sultan Murat II. Built to a by then old-fashioned T-plan, it contains a fine carved *mimber* (pulpit) and İznik tiles. The *medrese* next door now houses the **Archaeological Museum** (Tue–Sun 9am–6pm; charge), which has a fountain and mosaics from the synagogue at ancient Sart (Sardis).

In a park near the Muradiye Camii a statue of a bearded, water-pouring figure honours "**Tarzanı**", real name

hmet Bedevi. A celebrated 20th-century local eccentric who lived as a half-clad dervish in the nearby mountains, he planted trees and exhorted others to follow his environmentalist example.

Walking downhill to the west, at the base of the originally Byzantine **andıkkale** citadel, you will reach the named **Crying Rock** (Ağlayan Kaya in Turkish) **of Niobe**, part of **Sipildağı Milli Parkı** (Sipildagi national park). This is allegedly the petrified remains of Niobe, the arrogant daughter of local king Tantalos (from whom we get the word "tantalise"), who derided the nymph Leto for her mere two offspring while boasting of her own 14 beautiful children. These were slain forthwith by Leto's children, Artemis and Apollo, after which the unfortunate Niobe begged Zeus to petrify her and end her pain. Alas, the bereaved mother continued to weep perpetually, the very stone wet from her tears. Unhappily, the tale is more evocative than the site itself, merely a weather-worn outcrop which indeed exudes rivulets for some time after a rain.

Sart (Sardis)

Ancient **Sardis**  (daily 8am–6pm; charge) 100km (60 miles) east of İzmir, and 65km (40 miles) from Manisa, was occupied from at least 1300 BC onwards, growing into a major Roman and Byzantine city. Along the way, it was capital of the Lydians who, according to Herodotus, had the curious customs of permitting women to choose their husbands, and condoning the prostitution of young girls to make them earn their dowries. The Lydians also claimed to have invented all of the pastimes that were common to them and the Greeks, including dice and knucklebones.

An 8th century BC king, Kandaules, allowed one of his bodyguards to glimpse his beautiful wife naked; discovering this, the queen gave Gyges, the bodyguard, the option of death or of murdering Kandaules and becoming king in his stead – which Gyges did. Gyges was the ancestor of Kroïsos (aka Croesus, who ruled 560–546 BC), last of the Lydian kings, who interpreted an ambiguous Delphic oracle to mean that he would be victorious

Attracted by the catch of the day on the Aegean coast.

BELOW: the reconstructed Marble Court at Sardis.

in battle against Persian King Cyrus – which Kroïsos wasn't, causing the end of his empire.

The expression "rich as Croesus" comes from the fact that the Paktolos stream, which still flows by Sardis, washed down gold flecks from Mt Tmolos (today **Bozdağ**), to be caught in sheep fleece. The presence of this wealth was attributed by Ovid to Midas's "golden touch"; eager to be rid of what had become a curse, Midas bathed in the Paktolos on the instructions of the gods, the gold passing from his body into the stream.

The ruins

Bozdağ still looms above the fertile plain of the Gediz Cayı (ancient Hermos River). At its feet lies the **Temple of Artemis** (daily, summer 8am–7pm, winter 8am–5pm; charge), whose massive scale – about 45 x 100 metres (150 x 320ft) – rivals the other three great Ionian temples at Ephesus, Samos and Didyma. Construction began around 550 BC, but it was destroyed in the Ionian revolt; Alexander the Great paid for reconstruction. Today only 15 columns remain erect, just two at full height, but the setting against a backdrop of wooded hills is magnificent. The altar was built at the west end of the temple, perhaps to avoid it being overshadowed by the slopes above.

Much further up these slopes is the **Acropolis**, considered impregnable. Apocryphally, one of the soldiers of Persian Emperor Cyrus saw a defender drop his helmet over the walls and climb down to retrieve it. Using this route, Persian commandos were able to break through, defeating the Lydians in about 546 BC.

The ascent to the Acropolis takes 45 minutes and requires sturdy walking shoes, but the fantastic view from the peak justifies the effort. Some 10km (6 miles) across the Gediz plain is the Lydian **Royal Cemetery**, now called Bin Tepe or "Thousand Mounds" after its tumuli. Just beyond Bin Tepe lie **Marmara Gölü**, Lake Gygaea of antiquity, which attracted early Bronze Age settlement. All these local landmarks appear in Greek and Latin literature. In the *Iliad*, Homer sang of the Gygaean lake, "snowy" Mount Tmolos and the

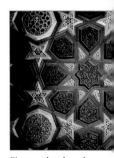

"eddying" Hermos. In Ovid's *Metamorphoses*, a personified Tmolos judged the musical competition between Apollo and Pan.

Downhill from the Temple of Artemis, across the highway, stands another fascinating complex of buildings (daily summer 8am–6pm, winter 8am–5pm; included in temple charge). The **Marble Court** is a grandiose entrance to a Roman gymnasium and baths complex, dating to the early 3rd century AD and carefully reconstructed. Its column capitals are decorated with carved heads of gods and satyrs, including the memorable "Laughing Faun", a masterpiece whose mischievous smile and features show Greek influences. The remains of the largest ancient **synagogue** lie southeast of the Marble Court. A marble table with eagles on the legs occupied the altar end, apparently in defiance of Judaism's ban on human and animal representation in temples. The wall-mounted mosaics are replicas of those in Manisa's Archaeological Museum, but extensive floor mosaics were left *in situ*.

On Bozdağ

The nearest accommodation and food for visitors with transport lies south, up the forested mountain. First stop could be **Bozdağ village**, with famous spring water, a few rustic *pansiyons*, outdoor restaurants and, surprisingly, a ski resort overhead at 2,150 metres (7,050ft). A little further is the reedy lake of **Gölcük**, a favourite beauty spot when the lowlands bake in summer heat, with two proper hotels and restaurants which sometimes serve catfish (*yayın*).

The local surprise, on the southern flanks of Bozdağ, is **Birgi** village, its surviving half-timbered houses culminating in the delightful **Çakırağa Konağı** (Tue–Sun 9am–noon, 1–5pm; charge), the restored 18th-century mansion of a local worthy, with carved wood panelling and extensive murals. Across the ravine stands the 14th-century **Ulu Cami** (Great Mosque), a building with ancient columns upholding a pitched wooden roof and bits of ancient Pyrgion worked into the walls. ❏

Fine woodwork, such as this on the pulpit of İzmir's Aydinoglu Mehmed Bey mosque, can be seen in Çakirağa Konaği.

BELOW: vineyards pattern the landscape around Sardis.

TURKISH FESTIVALS

Turkey offers a vibrant spectrum of cultural festivals: of music, the arts, film, folklore and some quirky rural observances

The Turkish festival year is packed with interest for the visitor. Events organised by the İstanbul Foundation for Culture and the Arts are the best known overseas. April kicks off with the International Film Festival, followed by the Classical Music Festival (June–July), where top international soloists perform in historical venues like Agia Irene church; it overlaps with the July Jazz Festival, encompassing rock as well as jazz groups. Odd-numbered years see the International İstanbul Biennial (Sept–Nov), with art installations scattered at historic venues across the city. Acts are profiled on www.iksv.org, but tickets are bought through other sources.

Coastal resorts and archaeological sites get their fair share of entertainment – ancient theatres and medieval castles make supremely atmospheric venues for catching a spot of Turkish or Western music, ballet, dance or opera, most notably at Ephesus (May–June), Aspendos (June–July) and Bodrum (September). The Altın Portakal (Golden Orange) International Film Festival in Antalya (October) inevitably uses more prosaic facilities, but features some of the best in new local and overseas cinema.

Among religious festivals of most interest to visitors, the Hacıbektaş commemoration (late August) in the namesake village, attended by Bektaşis and Alevîs, is a more genuine manifestation than Konya's overexposed Mevlâna festival (mid-Dec).

Squelchy combat is the theme of the Kırkpınar Oil-Wrestling competition at Edirne (late June/early July). Beastly rather than human antagonists meet, somewhat bizarrely, at Aydın province's camel-wrestling contests (Dec–Jan), and at Artvin's Kafkasör bullfights (late June).

• *For a calendar of festivals and public holidays, see pages 404–5.*

TOP LEFT: the Coolbone jazz band from New Orleans during the Jazz Festival. **LEFT:** camel wrestling involves two males wrestling after an in-heat female is led past them.

ABOVE: henna tattoos feature at traditional festivals. **LEFT:** a fire eater performs during the Islam holy month of Ramadan. Ramao involves fasting, but is also a tir for celebration and feasting.

THE GYPSY SPRING FESTIVAL

The Roma of Thrace have for centuries observed the spring-to-summer transition festival, called Kakava locally but Hıdırellez – or Ederlezi, as in the song made famous by Goran Bregović – everywhere in the Balkans. Hıdırellez is a corruption of Hizir and Ilyas, two prophets in the Shi'ite/Bektaşi tradition, conveniently syncretised with the major Balkan Orthodox saint George (6 May in the old calendar). Accordingly celebrations are held from the evening of 5 May into the next day. The main events are at Kırklareli and especially Edirne's Sarayiçi district, where a bonfire is lit at dusk on 5 May, with crowds singing all around it and a communal meal served. When the pyre attains sufficient size, young Roma men leap over it, a practice thought to bring luck and health for the coming year. At dawn the next day, young girls proceed down to the Tunca in their mother's bridal gowns, accompanied by *zurnas* (shawms) and *davuls* (deep-toned drums), and bathe in the river, sometimes leaving the gowns in the water to be retrieved by others, again for good fortune.

ABOVE: young women wear traditional dress and dance during Youth Day (Commemoration of Atatürk Day), an annual national holiday in May. **LEFT:** Trojan war sand sculpture at the Antalya Sand Sculpture Festival.

TOP: girls don traditional clothing. **LEFT:** Turkish oil wrestlers rely on strength and endurance more than clever moves in this national sport. Tournaments take place throughout the country, with Edirne hosting the annual championships in summer.

THE SOUTHERN AEGEAN

It's not hard to see why the Southern Aegean
region is at the forefront of Turkey's booming
tourist industry: some of the country's best
beaches, with virtually guaranteed sunshine, are
complemented by dramatic ancient ruins

uşadası **⓱**, "Bird Island", faces a
superb gulf partly closed off by
the Greek island of Samos. Until
he 1970s, it was a sleepy place, consist-
ng of little more than a hillside quar-
er with old, tile-roofed houses and the
artly walled medieval Kale district in
he flatlands. Since then Kuşadası and
atellite municipalities have grown
nto a fairly unpleasant conurbation
f almost 100,000; it's the major gate-
ay to Ephesus (Efes) for cruise-ship
atrons, who disembark here much
o the delight of carpet, leather and
nick-knack shop proprietors. For their
enefit tour guides ensure maximum
me for their charges inside the tatty
azaar here, and minimum time at the
uins themselves. If you come alone,
xpect to be hassled and hussled. The
lace's only real virtues are serviceable
eaches, well-developed nightlife, a
arge stock of accommodation and
ood connections for those relying on
ublic transport.

Diminutive **Güvercin Adası** (Pigeon
sland) is connected to the mainland by
causeway. Fortified by the Genoese,
ell-kept gardens and teahouses now
t around its walls. Beaches near town
et fairly crowded in summer; the best,
mptiest and most remote is broad,
ometimes surf-pummelled **Pamucak**,
5km (9½ miles) to the north.

Dilek Yarımadası Milli Park

For a complete antithesis to the
Kuşadası scene, head for the **Dilek
Yarımadası Milli Park** **⓮** (Dilek
Peninsula National Park; daily summer 8am–6.30pm, last exit 7pm, earlier closure spring/autumn; charge),
28km (17 miles) south of Kuşadası.
Although much loved by Turks on
summer weekends, it remains one of
the most pristine environments on
the Turkish Aegean, partly thanks to
the fact that the tip of the peninsula
– its twin summits comprising the

Main attractions

EPHESUS RUINS
EPHESUS MUSEUM, SELÇUK
ANCIENT PRIENE
APOLLO TEMPLE, DIDYMA
FRESCOED MONASTERIES,
    MT LATMOS
PAMUKKALE TRAVERTINES
GÜMÜŞKESEN TOMB, MILAS
ZEUS SANCTUARY, LABRANDA
ZEUS TEMPLE, EUROMOS

EFT: shimmering pools at sunset,
amukkale. **RIGHT:** a corner of the unspoilt
ilek Peninsula National Park.

BELOW: the Library
of Celsus, part of
the Ephesus ruins.

ancient Mt Mykale – is an off-limits
military zone.

Beyond the ticket gate, a paved
road extends 10km (6 miles) past
four beaches: **İçmeler**, **Aydınlık**,
Kavaklı Burnu and the prettiest, fine-
pebble **Karasu**. They all have (expensive) snack bars – locals bring their
own picnics. Between Aydınlık and
Kavaklı Burnu, a walkers-only track
signposted as "**Kanyon**" forges 15km
(9½ miles) south and inland, over the
summit ridge, to Eski Doğanbey village. It takes about four to five hours
to hike. A trailhead placard details the
lush flora and fauna on the mountain.
The forest cover includes wild chest-
nut, arbutus and *Pinus brutia*, as well
as eighteen plant species endemic to
Turkey. The local fauna extends to the
rare white-tailed eagle, jackals, badg-
ers and wild boar, who often appear
at the beach parking lots to raid the
rubbish bins.

Eski Doğanbey, the Ottoman Greek
village of Domatça, has been restored
beautifully by urban trendies but has
no short-term facilities other than a
seasonal park-information centre.

Ephesus (Efes)

Unmatched by any other Mediterranea
archaeological site aside from Pompe
Ephesus ⓑ (Efes in Turkish) appeals t
visitors ranging from serious scholars t
those with a more casual interest.

Strabo, Pausanias and Athenaios a
relate the same colourful foundatio
legend for Ephesus. Androklos, so
of Kodros, king of Athens, had bee
advised by an oracle to establish a ci
at the spot indicated by a fish and
boar. Arriving here late in the 11t
century BC, Androklos and compan
found some locals frying fish by th
seaside; one fish jumped out of th
frying pan, scattering live coals an
setting alight a thicket in which a bo
was hiding. The boar rushed out an
was killed by Androklos, thus fulfil
ing the prophesy. The new city wa
founded at the northern foot of Mou
Pion, with worship of the Athenian
goddess Artemis syncretised easily wit
the indigenous Anatolian Kybele.

By the 6th century BC, Ephesus ha
prospered despite lacking any militar
or political power, thus attracting th
attentions of Lydian King Croesus i

560 BC. The Ephesians stretched a rope around the nearby Temple of Artemis and retreated behind it, believing the goddess would protect them. Croesus and his army, perhaps amused by the townspeoples' naïveté, treated the captured city leniently. The **Archaic Artemis temple** was still under construction, so to please the Ephesians and the goddess, Croesus presented the temple with a set of carved column capitals, one of which had his name inscribed on it. These relics are now in London's British Museum.

In 356 BC – tradition states it was the night of Alexander the Great's birth – the temple was set on fire by one Herostratos, who wanted to be remembered for posterity, a goal he achieved – his act has inspired a Sartre short story and a 2001 Armenian film.

Wonder of the world

The Ephesians at once began building an even finer structure which, when completed, ranked as one of the Seven Wonders of the World. Work was still in progress when Alexander arrived in 334 BC. He was so impressed that

he offered to fund completion, but the offer was politely refused on the grounds that one god should not make a dedication to another. Today, a lone Ionian column looms amid a few foundation blocks, often submerged in a small marsh beside the Selçuk–Ephesus road – a pitiful reminder of what was once a glorious structure.

Ephesus reached its zenith during the Roman imperial era, when Augustus declared it the capital of Asia Minor in place of Pergamon. An inscription from Ephesus at this time calls itself "the first and greatest metropolis of Asia", and indeed it was. The permanent residence of the Roman governor, it had a maximum population of 250,000, and acted as the commercial hub of the Aegean; the only threat to its prosperity was the constant silting up of the harbour by the Kaistros River, today the Küçük Menderes. Despite many inspired or misguided attempts to deepen the channel or divert the river, Ephesus now lies 5km (3 miles) from the sea.

St Paul arrived in AD 51, and within two years gained enough followers to

Turkey has a long bee-keeping tradition, and remains a significant producer today. Local honey is usually included in a Turkish breakfast.

BELOW: sarcophagus at Ephesus, most of whose ruins date from the Roman imperial period.

Ephesus

0 — 500 m
0 — 500 yds

↖ Kuşadası

N

Former Harbour

Church of the Virgin Mary
Olympieion
Acropolis
Gymnasium of Vedius

Koressian Gate

Baths
Stadium

Harbour Gymnasium
Byzantine Palace

Harbour Street (Arcadian Way)

Palaestra of Verulanus
Theatre Gymnasium

Selçuk & Cave of the Seven Sleepers

Byzantine City Wall

Theatre

Temple of Serapis
Lower Agora

Library of Celsus
Brothel

Monumental Archway
Baths of Scholastica

Byzantine Fountain
Temple of Hadrian

Terrace Houses

Marble Avenue
Curetes Street

Memmius Monument

Hercules Gate
Prytaneion
Basilica

Domitian Temple and Inscription Gallery
Odeon

Upper Agora
Varius Baths

Hellenistic City Wall

East Gymnasium

Selçuk

Bülbül Dağı

Circuit Wall

Meryemana ▼
Magnesian Gate

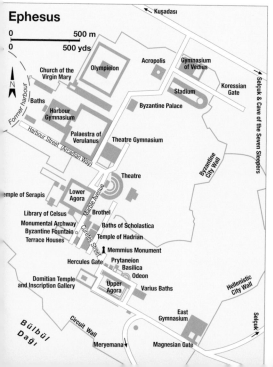

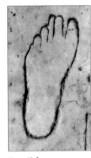

Detail from a supposed brothel advertisement on a wall at Ephesus.

establish a church here. A backlash against the new religion, described in Acts 19:23–19:40, was spurred by secular rather than sacred interests. Demetrius, head of the union of silversmiths who had a lucrative business selling statuettes of Diana (the Roman version of Artemis), was incensed by Paul's proselytising, and arranged a rally of thousands in the theatre shouting, "Great is Diana of the Ephesians!" St Paul wanted to face down the crowd but was restrained from doing so by his companions Gaios and Aristarhos, departing shortly thereafter for Macedonia. Yet Christianity spread quickly in Ephesus and eventually supplanted the pagan goddess's cult.

The ruins

Most of the surviving ruins of Ephesus belong to the Roman imperial period. An exception is the **Circuit Wall**, built by Lysimakhos and an outstanding example of Hellenistic fortification. It has largely disappeared at lower elevations, but stands nearly intact along the crest of **Bülbül Dağı** (Nightingale

Mountain, the ancient Mt Koressos) to the south of the city. Anyone energetic enough to climb up will find gates and towers of high-quality workmanship.

The northerly access road passes the **Gymnasium of Vedius**, a 2nd-century gift to the city from that wealthy citizen. In typical Roman fashion, the building combined a gymnasium and baths. The adjacent horseshoe-shaped Hellenistic **Stadium** was restored during Nero's reign (AD 54–68). Across the road stands the **Church of the Virgin Mary**, built in the 2nd century as a warehouse and converted to a basilica in the 4th century AD – the first known church dedicated to the Virgin.

The city's most impressive thoroughfare, the **Harbour Street** (or Arcadian Way) linking the old port and the theatre, is named after Byzantine Emperor Arcadius, who remodelled it in AD 395–408. About 500 metres (1,600ft) long and 11 metres (36ft) wide, both sides of the streets were covered with porticoes giving onto shops. Excavations unearthed an inscription indicating that the colonnaded street was lit at night by 50 lamps, at a time when only Rome and Antioch shared this distinction.

Beside this street, the imposing 2nd century **Harbour Baths** form one of the largest structures in Ephesus, with a 30-metre (100ft)-long elliptical pool and 11-metre (36ft)-high marble columns supporting a vaulted brick roof. Next door, the **Harbour Gymnasium** has a colonnaded courtyard, paved with mosaic.

The **Theatre**, originally constructed during the reign of Lysimakhos into the slopes of Mount Pion (today Panayır Dağı), was large enough to hold 24,000 people and is still used for the annual May festival. Unfortunately it has been refurbished rather insensitively by the Austrian excavators, but from the top seats there is still a splendid view. Its excellent acoustics were further enhanced in ancient times by the judicious placing of clay or bronze sounding vessels. Below the theatre stands the more sympathetically restored **Library of Celsus**, its façade effectively the logo of the city, like a grandiose film set left behind after the shooting of a Roman spectacular. It was actually built in AD 110–17 by Gaius Julius Aquila for his father Gaius Julius Celsus, still entombed under the west wall. Behind it, and the lower agora, lies the **Temple of Serapis**, which had eight massive columns with Corinthian capitals that individually weighed 57 tons, although apparently the structure was never completed.

At the library, the road bends and becomes **Curetes Street**, which extends up to the **Hercules Gate**. At the beginning of the street on the left stand the **Baths of Scholastica**, built in the 1st century AD and reconstructed early in the 5th century by the lady whose headless statue can be seen in the entrance hall. The originally three-storeyed building was very popular, as both rich and poor could use the complex of heated rooms and pools free of charge, although only the rich could afford the time to linger for hours, gossiping while being massaged by their servants.

Next door, a peristyle house identified as the **Brothel** because of an inscription found in the adjacent latrines, has some delightful mosaics and traces of frescoes. An overly endowed clay Priapus found in the well is now in the Ephesus Museum.

The fascinating **Temple of Hadrian**, begun in AD 118, has four Corinthian columns supporting an arch with a bust of Tyche, the patron goddess of the city, in the centre. The plaster cast on the site of the original frieze (now in the Museum) has three 3rd-century panels depicting gods and goddesses, including Artemis Ephesia, and a 4th-century addition of the Byzantine emperor Theodosios and his family – remarkable when one considers Theodosios's vehement opposition to paganism. On the opposite side of Curetes, the seven **Terrace Houses** (daily 8am–5/6pm; separate charge) offer a compelling portrait of everyday life with their mosaics, murals and under-floor heating systems.

In his will, Gaius Julius Aquila left 25,000 denarii to help maintain the library and buy new works. At its finest, the library contained 12,000 scrolls, which were kept in an inner chamber, surrounded by an outer wall and air cushion to stabilise temperature and humidity. The library was destroyed by invading Goths in AD 262.

BELOW: the Temple of Hadrian.

Selçuk

About 1.5km (1 mile) east of the lower Ephesus access road is the Cave of the Seven Sleepers, a network of catacombs where seven early Christians hid from persecution in the 2nd century, and were walled in by the Imperial Guard. Legend has it that they fell asleep and awoke 200 years later once Christianity had become the state religion.

The small town of **Selçuk** , some 23km (14 miles) northeast of Kuşadası, owes its importance to its proximity to Ephesus, and to its Ephesus Museum. From the tourist office, near the central junction and minibus station, allow a 30-minute walk to Ephesus, though during summer even this short journey can be exhausting. Taxis and minibuses, however, are plentiful. There are also various decent restaurants in Selçuk, any of them preferable to those immediately outside the entrance to Ephesus itself. Given that the town also has attractive accommodation to suit most budgets, plus a few lively bars, it makes a viable overnight base, especially for backpackers and independent travellers. Parking rental cars is also much easier than in Kuşadası.

The **Ephesus Museum** (daily 8.30am–5pm, until 6.30pm in summer; charge) has an exceptional, well-displayed collection, though labelling could be more elaborate. Floor mosaics and a fresco of Socrates from one of the Ephesian terrace houses, cult statuettes, coins and other relics all create a vivid impression of ancient life. Other famous exhibits include a bronze statuette of Eros on a dolphin, a marble one of him embracing Psyche, and two complete marble statues of Artemis, flanked by beasts and adorned with enigmatic bulbous protruberances. A marble, headless statue of Priapus, balancing a tray of fruit (symbolising fertility) on his pride and joy, a smaller, intact figurine of the analogous Egyptian god Bes, intact in all respects, plus the Roman imperial cult hall, with its fine reliefs including one of the deities Selene and Apollo, also feature.

The **Basilica of St John** (8am–5pm closes 6.30pm summer; charge) lies just south of the Byzantine fortress (reopens after repairs in 2012) on the hill of Ayasoluk. St John supposedly lived the last years of his life locally, after his death in about AD 100, a shrine arose over his grave. Emperor Justinian erected a monumental basilica here in the 6th century, which endured until destroyed by Tamerlane's Mongols in around 1402. During the 1960s, what was once one of the largest Byzantine churches was partly restored by a Christian foundation based in Ohio. The presumed tomb of the evangelist lies at the altar end of the central nave, under a simple slab. The now-vanished dome was supported by partly re-erected marble and brick pillars, between which stand blue-veined marble columns bearing the monograms of Emperor Justinian and his wife, Theodora. The baptistry just to the north, with its cruciform plunge-pool, dates from the 5th century.

At the foot of the hill stands the elegant, late 14th-century **İsa Bey Camii** (usually open, except at prayer times), built in a transition between Selçuk and Ottoman styles. There are recycled Roman columns in the vast courtyard, with more inside upholding the gabled roof and dome with its original tilework in the squinches.

BELOW: the İsa Bey Camii, Selçuk.

Meryemana and Şirince

According to one tradition, the Virgin Mary came to Ephesus with St John and lived here from AD 37 until her death in AD 48. Her purported house, **Meryemana** (8km/5 miles south of Selçuk; dawn–dusk; charge), was discovered in 1891 by Lazarist priests from Smyrna acting on a dream of Catherine Emmerich, a simple German nun who never left her convent. It is now a papally endorsed focus of pilgrimage, and merits a visit if only for the wooded paths and mountain streams. The Byzantine building, just possibly with 1st-century AD foundations, has been converted to a chapel and is also a popular outing for Muslims, who venerate Mary by tying votive rags onto a specially provided trellis. Christian Masses are conducted here daily.

Şirince, a formerly Greek village only 8km (5 miles) east of Selçuk, makes a delightful destination after visiting Ephesus, though it too is well established on the tour-bus circuit. It's therefore best to go late in the day, or even stay the night. There is nothing ancient here, just fresh air, traditional houses, two churches (one restored) and a relaxing atmosphere. Known as Kirkince to its Ottoman Greek founders, the village was resettled by Muslims from Macedonia after 1923, who brought their Islamically dubious habit of wine-making with them – though sadly, idiosyncratic basement brews have been replaced by the uniformly dull product of the local cooperative.

Priene

The ancient Ionian city of **Priene** ⑰ (daily 8am–5.30pm, until 6.30pm in summer; charge) is easily reached by a short, scenic drive from either Kuşadası or Selçuk, via the cotton-processing town of Söke; en route pines and olive groves alternate with occasional fields of ripening cotton bolls.

Priene has a spectacular location, on a natural terrace partway up Mount Mykale, its outriders presiding majestically over the ruins. Once an active port established at about the same time as Ephesus, the town had to be moved during the 4th century BC to outpace silt deposition by the River Maeander (today the Büyük Menderes,

Embroidered slippers fit for a sultan.

BELOW: students at a local school visit Priene.

The agricultural land around Lake Bafa was prone to severe drought until the recent introduction of a new modern irrigation system.

BELOW: five of Priene's original Ionic columns have been re-erected.

whose oxbows, lagoons and delta sprawl below the site). Hellenistic Priene was laid out in a grid pattern devised by city planner Hippodamos of Miletus in about 450 BC, and never much tampered with by the Romans, who favoured nearby Miletus.

Entry today is via the southeast gate (the more complete **northwest gate** is used to exit). One of the first structures encountered is the exquisitely preserved, three-sided **Bouleuterion** (Council Hall). Immediately uphill is the horseshoe-shaped **Theatre**, with front-row thrones for city dignitaries and a Roman stage building.

But Priene's most striking monument is the **Temple of Athena Polias**, designed by Pytheos, who also planned the Mausoleum of Halikarnassos, and wrote an architectural manual still consulted in Roman times. During the 1960s, five of the original 30 Ionic columns were re-erected; the rest still lie about like so many sausage-slices.

Miletus (Milet)

There was a Bronze Age settlement here long before the semi-mythical 10th-century BC foundation of the city Miletus by Neleos, another son of King Kodros. However, the present ruins of **Miletus** ⑱ (daily 8.30am–5.30pm, until 7pm in summer; charge) date from after its second foundation, since the original city was destroyed by the Persians in 494 BC. Like Priene, the new town was planned according to Hippodamian principles. Ephesus may enjoy greater fame today, but Miletus was the most important city of the Ionian League. Its enterprising spirit and favourable position on a promontory jutting out into the Gulf of Latmos made it not only the wealthiest emporium of its time but also an intellectual centre.

The finest surviving building here is the 2nd-century AD **Theatre**, seating 15,000 people and surmounted by a Byzantine **castle**. There is some fine relief work on the stage building – including angelic beings duelling with beasts – and huge vaulted passages underneath the seating tiers.

Most of the city buildings to the east are badly ruined. The most interesting, though standing to barely half its original height, is a 2nd-century AD **Nymphaeum**, fed by a vanished aqueduct which distributed water to the entire city. Another recipient of the water was the **Baths of Faustina**, built in about AD 150 in honour of the extravagant wife of Marcus Aurelius. Inside are two interesting spouts which fed the cold plunge pool – one in the shape of the personified rivergod Maeander, the other in the form of a lion.

A short distance away stands the beautiful **İlyas Bey Camii**, built in 1404 by one of the Menteşe emirs, who ruled this part of Anatolia before the Ottomans consolidated their power, to celebrate his return after being held hostage in the Mongol court. The minaret collapsed in a 1958 earthquake, but the great banded-brick dome, delicate carved stone filigree at the entrance and finely worked *mihrab* make it a masterpiece. It was once part of a complex comprising a baths and *medrese*, both of which have been partly restored and fitted with wooden canopies. Just past the mosque on the road to Didyma, a new museum of local finds should open in 2011.

Didyma

The most impressive single monument in the south Aegean is the **Temple of Apollo at Didyma** ⑲ (daily 8am–5.30pm in winter, 9am–7.30pm in summer; charge). There has been an oracle-shrine – but never a town – on this site since the Bronze Age; Ionian settlers merely imposed their cult of Apollo in the 8th century BC. This early phase in Didyma's history ended with the sacking of the Archaic temple by the Persians in 494 BC. When Alexander the Great arrived, the oracle proclaimed him the son of Zeus, which pleased him so much that he retrieved the cult statue of Apollo from Persia and ordered the building of a new super-temple. Work continued for five

centuries, and while it was never actually finished, with only three of the 72 completed Ionic columns still standing, the remains rarely fail to impress, especially towards sunset when you are likely to arrive after a day's touring. Mascots of the site are the two Medusa heads, one with furrowed brow and tight ringlets, mounted just below the ticket booth.

Didyma today stands marooned amidst the mushrooming development of **Altınkum** (officially Didim), Turkey's answer to England's Blackpool, with its curious combination of both Turkish and foreign working-class patronage. The "Golden Sand" of the name is barely findable amongst all the concrete apartment blocks; if you fancy a swim, better to do it just north of Didyma at Mavişehir cove, the ancient Panormos, where seagoing supplicants disembarked to approach the oracle along a sacred way.

Lake Bafa and Herakleia ad Latmos

Certainly one of the oddest places in the Aegean region, **Bafa Gölü** (Lake

Bursting cotton buds drift like snow across the arid summer landscape.

BELOW: village women in Kapikiri.

A spicy harvest of red-hot chilli peppers.

BELOW: Aphrodisias won a reputation as a centre of sculpture.

Bafa) was once an inlet of the Aegean but became cut off by the capricious River Maeander (Büyük Menderes). Its warm, often weedy waters vary from almost fresh to brackish depending on recent rainfall and incursions of seawater up the convoluted channel system of the Menderes. On the northeast shore, **Herakleia ad Latmos ⓴**, one of the most romantic sites in Anatolia (unenclosed; charge during daylight hours), falls within ancient Caria (Karya in Turkish) and more specifically the modern village of **Kapıkırı**. This is easiest approached by a well-marked 10km (6-mile) -long side road from the main Söke–Milas highway.

The serrated volcanic crest of **Mount Latmos**, some 1,500 metres (4,921 ft) high, led to its Turkish name Beşparmak (Five Fingers). A bastion of this wild, formidable mountain curves down to **Kapıkırı**, while the walls of ancient Herakleia with their gates, towers and parapets run up the ridge. The city ruins are scattered

engagingly across the village, and include the square **Athena temple**, the absidal **Sanctuary of Endymion**, a Byzantine **island-castle**, and **tombs**, some with their lids ajar as they were left by early grave-robbers. To really capture the spirit of the place it's best – preferably in spring or autumn when temperatures are more moderate – to either take boat trips on the lake or hike up the mountain. Numerous islets in the lake were a popular refuge in Byzantine times. Kapıkırı *pansiyon* staff are happy to oblige with arrangements or guiding.

West of the village, **İkizadalar** sports another castle and a church, while further beyond, **Menet Adası** is similarly endowed, and faces a white-sand beach where boat trips make a swimming stop. Inland, the most popular targets are the **Yediler monastery** and the **Stylos hermit-cave**, both adorned with fine frescoes from the 11th to the 13th centuries. Deeper into the mountain are more paintings, in this case prehistoric pictographs; several days are needed to explore properly the area.

Aphrodisias (Afrodisias)

Named after the goddess Aphrodite, successor to the more ancient fertility deities Nin and Ishtar, ancient **Aphrodisias ㉑** (Afrodisias in Turkish), whose site was occupied since about 2,800 BC, had grown from a cult centre to a proper city by late Hellenistic times. However, devastated by earthquakes during late antiquity and abandoned by the survivors after Arab raids, the once-splendid city was largely forgotten until, in 1961, the late Professor Kenan Erim of New York University began excavations, funded by *National Geographic* magazine. These revealed an unparalleled cache of sculpture carved from locally quarried marble. Statuary produced here met the needs for effigies across most of the Roman world, from Spain to the Danube, and despite this far-flung dispersal the local museum is still crammed full of examples (daily 8am–6.30pm, until 5.30pm winter, one charge for site and museum).

A loop-trail from the museum forecourt tours the city's highlights, all from the Roman imperial era. The well-preserved **Theatre** had its orchestra and stage converted into an arena for bloody spectacles during the 2nd century. East, beyond the colonnades of the agora, the **Baths of Hadrian** retain their floor tiles, but ironically little is left of the Temple of Aphrodite, the city's patroness, owing to Byzantine interventions. A short detour north from the loop leads to the 30,000-seat **Stadium**, one of the finest in the world, and the venue for quadrennial festivals of sport, music and drama. Finally, the most striking structure is the restored **Tetrapylon**, a monumental columned gateway whose pediments feature elaborate reliefs.

Pamukkale, Hierapolis and Laodiceia

Magical **Pamukkale ㉒** (24 hrs; charge during daylight hours), the "Cotton Castle", lies 19km (12 miles) north of Denizli, off the main highway from Aydin. It's actually a solidified cascade of travertine, formed by calcium bicarbonate-laden hot springs just uphill that have left stalactite-festooned terraces and scallop-shaped

TIP

Aphrodisias' site and museum are 40km (24 miles) southeast of Nazilli, reached by turning south off the main Aydin–Denizli highway. If you lack your own transport, take a tour from Pamukkale, which should allow 2.5 hours at the site. Public transport connections are sparse and likely to leave you stranded. The nearest accommodation and restaurant (suitable for lunch) are in Geyre village, adjacent to the ruins.

BELOW LEFT:
Herakleia tombs by Lake Bafa.
BELOW: the Temple of Aphrodite at Aphrodisias.

TIP

Pamukkale village (Pamukkale Köyü) is directly below the travertine terraces and has a good range of accommodation – best away from the main road. Direct coaches operate from most of the coastal resorts at least once a day.

pools as they drain over the escarpment here and cool. Over the years considerable damage was done by bluff-top hotels (now demolished) siphoning off the flow of water, and too many tourists walking on the travertines, but now – in keeping with Pamukkale's status as a Unesco World Heritage Site – access to the terraces is highly restricted. The only bathing now allowed is in the **Thermal Baths** (daily 8am–7pm; charge), formerly an ancient sacred pool, next to the Hierapolis Museum. It's exhilarating to paddle through what feels like 35°C (95°F) soda water while gazing at submerged ancient column fragments.

On the plateau above the terraces lie the splendid ruins of ancient **Hierapolis** (same admission policy as travertines), founded by Eumenes II of Pergamon as a spa town. Levelled by earthquakes in AD 17 and 60, it was rapidly rebuilt under Roman patronage, attaining its zenith during the 2nd and 3rd centuries. The **Theatre** is vast, and the stage building with its intricate friezes has been reconsolidated by Italian excavators. Below

the theatre yawns the **Plutonium**, small grotto sacred to the god of th underworld, where you can hear gush ing water and the hissing of poison ous gas. A grill guards the cave-mout now, but in antiquity the eunuc priests of Kybele could apparentl enter without ill effect. Nearby, a pr mary **Roman avenue** bisects the cit from the south to north gates, exi ing the latter to a **triple arch** bui by Domitian. Beyond this is the va **necropolis**, its most elaborate tom that of Flavius Zeuxis.

If staying at Pamukkale, don't mi the opportunity to visit **Laodice** (signposted as "Laodikya"), 3km (miles) south. Founded by the Sele cids, it prospered in Roman time before disappearing from histor upon the Seljuk conquest. The site h long suffered from masonry-pilferin but excavations since the millenniu by the local university promise t make it the up-and-coming site the region. A huge stadium, two the tres, a paved street and a gymnasiun baths complex are all benefiting fro archaeologists' attentions.

BELOW: Pamukkale has been created by bicarbonate-rich hot springs.

Milas, Labranda and Euromos

Milas ㉓ is a satisfying county town with a noted Tuesday market; the region famous for its fine fabrics, coarse goat-hair shoulderbags, and earth-toned carpets with geometric patterns.

Milas also has fine examples of Ottoman domestic architecture, often with ornate chimneys, and several interesting mosques including the **Ulu Cami,** built by the Menteşe emirs c.1370. Some 400metres/yds north of this stands the Roman **Baltalı Kapı** (Gate-with-Axe), so called after the double-headed axe carved into the north-facing keystone. The town's most spectacular monument, though, is the **Gümüşkesen**, a Roman tomb 90metres/yds west of the centre; with its Corinthian colonnade supporting a pyramidal roof, it's thought to be a mini replica of the Halikarnassos Mausoleum *(see page 223)*.

Some 15km (9 miles) north of Milas by paved road (albeit one progressively narrowing and abused by lorries from an open-cast mine), the Zeus sanctuary of **Labranda** (unlocked; charge when warden present) has the loveliest setting of any ruin in Caria, on spring-fed terraces at 600-m (2,000 ft) elevation, with sweeping views over the Milas plain. The god was venerated here at least from the 7th century BC, though most of the ruins one can see now were erected 300 years later. Around the **Zeus temple** on the highest terrace are two partly intact **androns** (banqueting halls), a **priestly residence** and a **fountain-house**. **Monumental steps** link these with two **propylaea** (porticoes) and a **Byzantine church** converted from a Roman baths. Despite the salubrious climate and secure water supply, there was never much of a town at this isolated spot, finally abandoned when the Seljuks swept across Anatolia.

Some 13km (8 miles) outside Milas on the road to Lake Bafa, the magnificent **Temple of Zeus** at ancient **Euromos** (free access; charge if warden present) is one of the three best-preserved in Asia Minor. Endowed by Roman emperor Hadrian but never finished, its 16 Corinthian columns are visible from the highway but more dramatic up close. ❏

Ildiz carpet farm at Milas, where kilims and wool and silk carpets are produced.

BELOW: the thermal waters of Pamukkale's Antique Pool are said to relieve many ailments.

BODRUM AND MARMARIS

Either resort is a good starting point for a journey along the Carian coast, with its venerable history and spectacular scenery, varying from sandy beaches to fjord-like inlets

Situated on a peninsula opposite the Greek island of Kos, **Bodrum** ㉔ is one of the most popular resorts in Turkey. As Halikarnassos, this was the birthplace of Herodotus (c.485–425 BC), known to some as the "Father of History" but to others as the "Father of Lies" because of his fanciful travel accounts.

Boats and parties

Until the 1960s, Bodrum was just a pretty Aegean port earning a living from sponge-diving. Today it is one of Turkey's principal yachting centres and also a linchpin in the booming "Blue Voyage" trade. The marina (west) quay is lined with excursion boats and their touts; one-day outings all follow similar itineraries. These typically involve stops at grotto hot-springs at the margin of Kara Ada, visible from Bodrum; the "Akvaryum" at Ada Boğazı, a snorkelling venue now, alas, quite devoid of fish; and a final stop to swim, perhaps at Kargı beach where camels may be ridden.

Bodrum's striking, whitewashed, Cubist-style houses, now protected by preservation orders, crowd narrow central lanes, and are draped with cascades of bougainvillea and other subtropical vegetation. They form a sharp contrast to the main local hedonistic scene of fine dining, shopping and some of the liveliest nighlife in Turkey. Despite the town's assiduously cultivated reputation for offering all things to all visitors, and some hotels staying open year-round, the tourist season remains stuck in the usual Aegean June-to-September groove.

Bodrum Castle

The towers and battlements of the **Castle of St Peter** (Tue–Sun 8.30am– 5.30pm, summer until 6.30pm; charge) dominate the town from its strategic promontory dividing the harbour in two. It was built by the crusading

Main attractions

CASTLE OF ST PETER
BODRUM NIGHTLIFE
GÜMÜŞLÜK, BODRUM PENINSULA
KUMLUBÜKÜ BAY, NEAR MARMARIS
SERÇE INLET, NEAR MARMARIS
MILLENNIAL ÇINAR TREE, BAYIR
ESKI DATÇA
MESUDIYE, OVA BÜKÜ BEACH
MUĞLA, OTTOMAN HOUSES
SULTANIYE HOT SPRINGS,
  KÖYCEĞIZ LAKE
KAUNOS RUINS

LEFT: tourists peruse Bodrum's shops.
RIGHT: Cumhuriet Caddesi in Bodrum.

TIP

Always check before visiting Bodrum Castle (tel: 0252-316 2516). The opening days and times for each individual section vary seasonally and between each other, though at a minimum you can assume they are open Tue–Fri 10am–noon and 2–4pm. There are separate charges for each hall.

BELOW: Bodrum's Museum of Underwater Archaeology.

Knights of St John, who plundered the Mausoleum (*see page 223*) for ready-cut masonry, still visible in the castle walls. The knights arrived in 1402 and continued to work on their castle throughout the 15th century, finally completing it in 1522, but were forced to abandon the fortress shortly afterwards, when Ottoman sultan Süleyman the Magnificent captured Rhodes.

Today, the castle is entered from the west; stairs and gates embellished with coats of arms lead to the lower and upper courtyards with their various towers and special exhibits. Coloured arrows indicate suggested routes, and you can get onto the ramparts for fine views of town and harbour. The **Museum of Underwater Archaeology** (included in castle admission), distributed over several buildings, opened in 1986. The chapel houses a brilliantly reconstructed 7th-century Byzantine wreck, discovered nearby at Yassıada; elsewhere, Mycenaean, Roman and early Islamic glassware is displayed. There's more of the same in the **Glass Wreck Hall**, perhaps the most interesting gallery,

featuring a flat-bottomed Fatimid Byzantine freighter sunk in 1025 at Serçe Limanı near Marmaris, and meticulously restored by archaeologists. Besides its cargo of coloured glass fragments, the crew's personal effects are exhibited.

The **Uluburun Wreck Hall** in the upper courtyard contains a rich trove of Bronze Age objects, including the world's oldest-known shipwreck which sank in the 14th century BC off Kaş. Treasures recovered from the cargo include gold jewellery, daggers, ivory, and a two-panel "book" formerly containing wax and the scarab-seal of Egyptian queen Nefertiti.

The **Carian Princess Hall** beside the French Tower contains the remains and effects of a local 4th-century BC noblewoman, found in a miraculously unlooted local tomb in 1989. The richness of the finds – a golden diadem, drinking cup, and jewellery – lends some credence to the possible identification of the lady as Ada, last queen of Caria, brought back from exile by Alexander the Great in 334 BC. A team of British

Bohemian Bodrum

Long before it became a conventional resort, Bodrum welcomed the bohemian and the eccentric. The earliest such habitué was Cevat Şakir Kabaağaçli (1893–1973), the "Fisherman of Halikarnassos", exiled here in 1925 on a three-year term for sedition. He remained in Bodrum voluntarily for the rest of his life, penning short stories and novels, while pioneering the concept of the "Blue Voyage" by disappearing for weeks at a time on a primitive sponge-diver's boat, as related in a 1994 biopic, *Blue Exile*.

Ahmet and Nesui Ertegün were the sons of the 1935–46 Turkish ambassador to the US, caught the jazz bug there, and stayed. They established Atlantic Records, the label that signed (among others) Charles Mingus, Otis Redding, Aretha Franklin, Led Zeppelin, Ray Charles, John Coltrane and the MJQ – thus largely explaining the popularity of jazz, soul, rock and blues amongst Turkey's chattering classes. Both Ertegüns have passed away now, but for years Ahmet's villa in Bodrum was a hub of summer social life.

Perhaps the most outrageous resident, from 1970 until his death in 1996, was Zeki Müren, among the most accomplished Turkish *sanat* singers and a flamboyant gay transvestite – though he mostly appeared out of drag at his favourite local bar. Zeki's villa, number 19 of the street named after him, contains a small museum of career memorabilia.

forensic specialists has reconstructed her facial profile from the skull.

Children may enjoy a visit to the **English Tower**, packed with armour and with trophies of war adorning the medieval-themed cafeteria. Another potential kids' hit is the Knights' dungeons below the **Gatineau Tower**, where taped groans and mannequins attempt to evoke the horrors which transpired here. The inscription above the door declares *Unde Deus Abest* ("Where God does not exist") – even more chilling when you realise that it was put there by monks.

Mausoleum of Halikarnassos

To the northwest of the castle lies the Mausoleum of Halikarnassos (Tue–Sun 9am–5pm; charge). It was one of the ancient Seven Wonders of the World, consecrated to the memory of ambitious Mausolos, Persian-appointed satrap (king) of Halikarnassos during the mid-4th century BC. The mausoleum was commissioned by his sister/widow, Artemesia the Younger, resulting in a monument topped with a pyramidal roof and a chariot with effigies of Mausolos and herself in triumph. Precious little remains above ground today, after pilferage by the Knights of St John, and removal of the chariot and friezes to the British Museum between 1846 and 1857.

Bodrum peninsula

Bodrum town itself, despite its easterly bay named Kumbahçe ("Sand Garden"), does not offer prime swimming – for better beaches, and sometimes for a more tranquil stay, head out onto the peninsula. Its villages are all easily accessible by bus or (sometimes) boat services, but be warned that, while the town has some zoning controls, the peninsula has relatively few.

Gümbet, 3km (2 miles) west, is effectively a suburb of Bodrum, with a long, if gritty, beach and a youthful, hard-drinking, largely British clientele. **Bitez**, the next bay west some 10km

(6 miles) from town, attracts an older crowd. It offers a windsurfing school and mooring for yachts, but a less good beach.

Ortakent, straddling the main highway west of Bodrum, has an old tower-house dating from 1601 and access, through mandarin orchards, to the longest beach in the area, **Yahşi Sahil**. This is popular with Turkish families and central European package tourists, though the sand can be difficult to access.

At Gürece, leave the main road to follow the narrower one looping around the far southwest shore of the peninsula. The first cove, **Kargı**, alias "Camel Beach" after the beasts ridden here, is a popular target for boat trips, but Bağla cove further on is monopolised by a holiday village. There's better public access for the excellent beach at **Karaincir**, while **Akyarlar** just beyond has a real village feel, with a mosque and mostly Turkish patronage at the various fish tavernas overlooking the picturesque fishing port.

Rounding the lighthouse cape of **Hüseyin Burnu**, you'll find a few

Many Turks wear blue beads to ward off the evil eye.

BELOW: the resort of Gümüşlük is located on the site of ancient Myndos.

Clubbers get foamed at Bodrum's Halikarnossos nightclub.

BELOW: peacocks wander the courtyards of Bodrum's Castle of St Peter.

undeveloped but gently sloping sandy beaches facing the Greek islet of Psérimos, prior to arrival in **Turgutreis** with its ribbon development. This is an unashamedly downmarket resort, mostly of all-inclusive complexes, though the Saturday market is well attended. By contrast, **Gümüşlük** presents an intriguing combination of the posh and the Turkish-bohemian, partly because the ubiquity of ancient Myndos (upon which Gümüşlük is sited) means that villa development is strictly controlled and the shore is vehicle-free. Yachts anchor and swimmers snorkel above submerged archaeological remains, while above ground you can spot ancient walls and towers. The southerly beach is only average, but the little port on the north is an enchanting (if expensive) venue for dining literally on the water.

In the northwest corner of the peninsula, **Yalıkavak** was one of the last working sponge-fishing villages, but now middle-of-the-road tourism predominates. The beach is unspectacular, though the hillside scenery – dotted with 300-year-old windmills

– is appealing when not blanketed i housing projects. Further east on th road circling back to Bodrum, **Farily** (official Gündoğan) is a burgeonin resort aimed at middle-class Turk while **Türkbükü** fancies itself the S Tropez of Turkey. Decidedly upmark hotels, pitched to well-heeled Turk line the approach road and ostenta tious motor-cruisers anchor in th sheltered bay here.

The Blue Voyage

Bodrum is one of the acknowledge termini for the classic **Mavi Yolculu** (Blue Voyage) between here and Ma maris, via the unspoilt, pine-fringe **Gökova Körfezi** ㉕ and other inle between the Datça and Hisarönü peni sulas. The Gökova Gulf is a strictl protected natural area, and coasta settlements are scarce. On the nort shore your boat might call at the littl bays of Mazıköy, Çökertme with its fis tavernas and sheltered beach, or Akbü where wetlands and excellent moo ing sandwich a coarse-pebble beac On the south shore, popular overnigh anchorages include İngilizlimar

(English Harbour), so named after a British naval vessel that sheltered here from pursuing German craft during World War II; Karacasöğüt; and Sedir Adası (alias Cleopatra Island), allegedly a trysting place of Mark Antony and his Egyptian bride.

Many agencies in both Bodrum and Marmaris act as representatives for crewed and skippered *gulets*, the traditional Blue Voyage wooden schooner. Spring and autumn are the most pleasant, and reasonably priced, seasons.

If you'd rather arrange it all before departure, especially as a yacht flotilla, two reputable, unusual booking agencies in Britain are SCIC (tel: 020-8510 9292; www.tussockcruising.com), three Bodrum-based *gulets* which actually travel under sail power rather than (as is usual on such craft) with merely decorative rigging, and Day Dreams (tel: 01884-849 200; www.turkishcruises.co.uk), a larger fleet of *gulets* or schooners welcoming singles and couples.

Marmaris and its peninsula

Marmaris ㉖ is reached along a 32km (20-mile) road off the main highway between Muğla and Fethiye, formerly an old eucalyptus-flanked avenue, but long since superseded by a four-lane divided expressway. An apocryphal tale relates that the town's name derives from an episode when Süleyman the Magnificent disparaged the state of the fortress here by exclaiming "*Mimarı as*" (Hang the architect). Lord Nelson was more impressed by the area's potential when he used the large bay to prepare his fleet before attacking (and defeating) Napoleon's navy at Aboukir in 1798.

The near-perfect natural harbour and splendid setting ringed by pine-clad hills elicit admiration, and Marmaris – with its Netsel marina, the largest in Turkey – unsurprisingly vies with Bodrum as a starting point for cruising. But the town itself, excepting a tiny ex-Greek old quarter around the unloved little castle (now a rather listless museum), has little of interest. Marmaris is principally a downmarket resort for both Turks and foreigners, with an abundance of English comfort food, beer-swilling bars and raucous clubs. Development creeps

Legend has it that the fine-grained sand on Cleopatra Island – found nowhere else along the Turkish coast – was imported from Egypt to make the Queen of the Nile feel more at home.

BELOW: panoramic view of Marmaris and its harbour.

TIP

There are dozens of boat trips available from Marmaris for day-trips around Marmaris Bay, with most departing between 9 and 10.30am and returning around 5pm. Lunch is usually included in the price. Charters on *gulets* or smaller yachts are also a possibility.

down the west flank of the bay to successively calmer satellite resorts – each with a decent sandy beach and water sports on offer – at **İçmeler** (9km/5½ miles away) and **Turunç**, 6km (3½ miles) further along a steep, winding road. By far the best beach, and least developed setting (thanks in part to the walls of ancient **Amos** just above on the headland) is at the next cove, **Kumlubükü**, the end of the line for the east-coast road.

Beyond here, the road – notionally paved but steep, narrow and potholed – forges into the interior of the convoluted, forested **Hisarönü** (or Loryma) peninsula. Here, overland travel is excruciatingly slow, the only really top-standard highways being one from near Turunç to Söğüt, and another from Hisarönü, off the Marmaris-Datça route, to Bozburun. This is truly boat (or walking) country, with marinas or decent anchorages – and shipyards where wooden *gulets* are still built in the traditional manner – at west-coast, beachless **Orhaniye**, **Selimiye** and **Bozburun**. Bozburun, well used now to yacht flotillas and their denizens,

might seem like the end of the world, but persevere to arrive at **Söğüt**. This is an unspoilt village with an inland quarter and a delightful shore *mahalle* (quarter) looking to Greek island Sými, with fishing boats pulled up on the pebble beach.

Once past Söğüt and the poorer nearby village of Taşlıca, the onward dirt track winds through the mysterious remains of ancient Keresse to end at **Serçe Bükü**, a magnificently protected inlet with two simple tavernas and lots of yachts. Pleasure boats also drop anchor at the deep fjord of ancient Loryma, near the tip of the peninsula, where pines have long since yielded to Mediterranean scrub.

Inland attractions are limited to a small **waterfall** near Orhaniye, and the village of **Bayır**, whose glories are a huge *çınar* (plane tree), said to be 2,000 years old, in the main square, and a nearby souvenir stall whose tightly juxtaposed displays recall a Salvador Dalí installation: mannequins in beekeepers' suits, tubular beehives made of mud, dangling gourds, soft-toy donkeys and sheep, plus towels imprinted with the visages of Princess Diana, Atatürk or assorted Shi'ite, Alevî or Bektaşi martyrs and bards.

The Reşadiye Peninsula

A different highway, similar to a roller coaster but of decent width, leads west from Marmaris 69km (43 miles) to **Datça**, a humdrum market-and real-estate town. It's approached through a fertile agricultural landscape whose resort function is owed largely to decent yacht anchorage. The shoreline *mahalle*, draped over promontories separating two rather scrappy beaches, has some appeal, but there's more 3km (2 miles) inland at **Eski Datça**. A stone-built village tastefully restored by urban artists, the local geezers still feel comfortable holding forth in the central *çay bahcesi*.

Beyond Datça lies truly the last frontier of Aegean tourism (and real estate), albeit one that is steadily being

BELOW: Marmaris market.

med since the onward highway was aved. The scenery becomes ever more ramatic, with defiles and forested ags, prior to the turning down to **Iesudiye** and its idyllic **Ova Bükü** each, amply supplied with food and dging. A paved coastal corniche oad continues to bigger and busier **alamut Bükü**, which since the 1990s as grown to be a major resort for urks – and has prepared a small port o attract yachts or excursion boats om Datça. You return to the main ighway through what must be one f the largest almond groves in the orld; everywhere here the almond is ng, and given the nuts' high global rice, the orchards are probably safe om developers.

Ancient **Knidos** ㉗ (daily 8am– pm; charge) occupies Tekir Burun the end of the peninsula. With its vo harbours astride one of the main egean shipping lanes – at least one ways suitable for mooring in this ermanently windy place – you can e why the city was moved here dur- ng the mid-4th century BC, from its rior location near modern Datça.

The site, covering both a mainland district and an island (now joined to the mainland but off-limits), has been sporadically excavated, but there is little to see other than a fine Hellen-stic **theatre** and a Byzantine **basilica** with extensive floor mosaics. All but vanished is the Temple of Aphrodite, which housed a famous **cult statue** of the goddess created by the Greek sculptor Praxiteles (390–330 BC), who supposedly used the famously beau-tiful Athenian courtesan Phyrne as a model. Through sacred prostitution, the love-cult brought Knidos almost as much income as harbour fees. Byz-antine zealots predictably destroyed the Aphrodite, but copies and frag-ments still exist. The statue base and temple site was located in July 1969 by the splendidly appropriately named American heiress and amateur archae-ologist, Iris Cornelia Love.

Muğla

Some 54km (34 miles) north of Marmaris, the provincial capital of **Muğla** ㉘ stands out for several reasons. Its centre is exceedingly well

The sandy beaches and watersports on offer at Marmaris and its peninsula increase the area's appeal to families.

BELOW: the harbour at Datça.

TIP

Don't take an expensive tour to Kaunos – use the rowboat ferry from Dalyan's Kral Bahçesi to the far bank, from where it's a pleasant 15-minute walk to the site.

run, orderly and leafy, with (almost uniquely for Turkey) attractive modern architecture offsetting its famous old hillside quarter of hundreds of strictly protected **Ottoman houses**. Some of these are Greek-built, dating from the 18th and 19th centuries. Two well-preserved medieval *kervansarays* have found a new lease of life: the **Konakaltı Hanı** is now an art gallery, while the **Yağcılar Hanı** contains souvenir shops and tea stalls.

Köyceğiz and Dalyan

Continuing eastwards 40km (25 miles) from the Marmaris junction on Highway 400, the first place of any consequence is **Köyceğiz**, a sleepy, pleasant market town on the eponymous lake, once an arm of the sea, like Bafa Gölü (Lake Gölü). Relatively few foreigners stay, but there are decent hotels (at Turkish, not overseas, prices) and restaurants along the lakefront promenade. Boat tours are offered from here to Kaunos and the local hot springs *(see right)*.

BELOW: view of the Kaunos cliff tombs from the Dalyan river.

A short way south is the riverside resort town of **Dalyan** ㉙. The name means "fish weir", after the system of barriers among the reeds which catch sea bass, caught as they head for the sea after breeding in Köyceğiz Lake. Upstream towards the lake are the open-air **Ilıca mud-baths**, whose gloriously messy contents (which reach 40°C/104°F) are said to address a host of ailments; on the lake's south shore at **Sultaniye**, stands a more conventional round **hot springs** pool under an Ottoman dome (24 hr; charge if warden present). The resort itself, totally given over to foreign tastes, does have a unique riverside setting, with little boats constantly putt-putting up and down past reed-beds.

Daily boat tours, or a road 15km (9½ miles) long, both head for remote **İztuzu Beach** (charge), 3.5km (2.2 miles) of hard-packed, gently shelving sand where giant loggerhead turtles come to lay their eggs during summer. Development of the beach is accordingly limited, and access forbidden at night.

Kaunos

For over a millennium, under Persians, Greeks, Romans and Byzantines, ancient **Kaunos** (daily dawn to dusk; charge) was one of the leading towns of Caria, despite always being considered an unhealthy place due to malarial mosquitoes. It was probably abandoned, however, due to silting up of its harbour – the ancient port is now a bird-haunted, reedy lake.

Parts of the site, on the west bank of the Dalyan Çayı, are clearly visible from the resort in the form of clustered Lycian-style cliff tombs, one incomplete one showing clearly the method of construction – from the top down. Ongoing excavations are exposing progressively more of the hillside city; revealed thus far are a Hellenistic theatre with a nymphaeum outside, Roman baths, a Byzantine basilica, a Doric temple with a colonnade, and below this a fountain-house.

The Impact of Tourism

Internal population movement, water shortages, a decline in traditional crafts, and rapid coastline development – the negative face of Turkey's tourist industry

Bodrum and its peninsula make a useful case study on the effects of tourism in coastal Turkey. Officially about 28,000 live in the town, but during July and August the population of the entire peninsula can swell almost tenfold on any given day, packed into an area of roughly 120 sq km (46 sq miles). The nearby Bodrum-Milas International Airport receives up to 5 million annual arrivals. Unlike at Marmaris or Antalya, the majority of these are Turkish, not foreign, many of whom are residential tourists occupying second homes in the phalanxes of villas which carpet every seaview hillside and greatly outnumber hotel accommodation. There's never been much of a public access ethic in Turkey, and many formerly deserted beaches have had the way to them blocked by private developments.

The world economic crisis has only slowed, not stopped, construction projects, and both short-term tourism and real-estate development have accelerated the demise of traditional local livelihoods. Sponge-diving ceased in the 1960s, while more recently mandarin and olive groves are either cut down or neglected. Mandarins in particular

need ample water, which has never been abundant locally as the numerous surviving *gümbets* (domed Ottoman cisterns) testify. Existing and proposed golf courses will only increase pressure on water resources. Unless water is piped in from the mountains of the interior, or desalinisation plants set up, the sea will eventually invade local aquifers which are limited to the few small coastal plains.

The needs of residential tourists have also warped local commerce: the main roads across the peninsula – continually disrupted by widening works to relieve perennial congestion, or chewed up by construction lorries – are lined by huge shopping malls comprising supermarkets, plant nurseries, builders' merchants, indoor or garden furniture retailers, and bath/kitchen outfitters. Traditional crafts and workshops are gone, or their products – like reed matting – imported from elsewhere in Turkey.

Job opportunities at Bodrum's seaside resorts, as everywhere on the Aegean and Mediterranean coasts, have acted as powerful magnets for internal migration from eastern Turkey, either seasonal (those staffing hotels, shops and restaurants) or permanent, as entire families relocate to set up businesses. This has resulted in momentous social changes in what were historically closed communities, little changed since the 1923 population exchanges deposited Greek-speaking Muslims, expelled from Crete, here.

One also sees plenty of the stereotypical encounters between Turks (usually men) and foreigners (usually women), and the resulting mixed marriages, visible in the tourist trade as restaurant or shop partnerships. ❏

ABOVE: tourists mimic a tin of sardines on the beach at Bodrum's easterly Kumbahçe bay.

THE MEDITERRANEAN COAST

Precipitous gorges, ancient cities, Crusader castles
and gentle turquoise seas make this area a
holiday paradise

The Turks call their patch of the Mediterranean the *Akdeniz* (White Sea); others, familiar with the hue of its translucent waters, prefer the tag "Turquoise Coast", at least for the western portion.

Since the mid-1980s, this area has become a major sun-and-sea destination, via international airports at Dalaman and Antalya, with mega-resorts either side of Antalya. Former fishing villages have metamorphosed into villa-laced boomtowns, and archaeological sites like Side have discos around the temple walls. The only potential brake on seemingly inexorable development is the world economic crisis – certainly not the few and sporadically enforced planning rules. You can still find enchantment away from the mass-market resorts, though for how much longer is a moot point.

We have divided this coast into four sections, based roughly on ancient regions. Lycia, in the west, is the most beautiful, with mountains plunging steeply to a shore of cave-riddled cliffs and secluded coves. Resorts here range from the backpacker haven at Olympos to upmarket, ex-Greek Kalkan and Kaş, via mass-market Ölüdeniz.

Pamphylia is bracketed by the sophisticated city of Antalya on the west and castellated Alanya on the east. Much in between is fertile, scenically humdrum plain, with long, golden beaches and fabulous archaeological sites like Perge, Aspendos and Side to compensate.

Western Cilicia (essentially Alanya to Adana) features rugged coast up to Silifke, with some of the most hotly contested real estate lying beyond, now humming with industrial and agricultural enterprise. The coast bends south into the Hatay, around biblical Antioch (Antakya), the last province to be joined to the republic. The Hatay spent nearly two centuries as a Crusader principality, while today it has more cultural (and linguistic) affinities with Syria. ❑

PRECEDING PAGES: the remains of the aqueduct at the Lycian site of Phaselis.
LEFT: the Lycian legacy is a scatter of elaborate rock-carved tombs. **TOP:** the coast near Adana. **ABOVE LEFT:** dolls made out of pumpkins make typical gifts from Alanya. **ABOVE RIGHT:** Adana's old town.

LYCIA

Enchanting Lycia – largely cut off from the interior of Anatolia until the 1980s – has always been home to proud, independent people. The Lycians have traditionally looked to the sea for trade and cultural cues

The independent-minded Lycians, probably an indigenous, pre-Hittite people (and not settlers from Crete, as Herodotus claimed), occupied the "bulge" between present-day Fethiye and Antalya from around 1400 BC. They had their own language, still to be seen on inscriptions, but are best known for their spectacular tombs.

From the 6th century BC onwards, at least 20 cities in this region banded together in a loose federation, in which each city voted according to its importance. Between 547 and 540 BC, however, Cyrus II conquered western Anatolia; Persian rule was briefly interrupted when Kimon's Athenians

appeared in 454 BC and enrolled th Lycians in the Delian League. Th Hellenistic era began when Alexande the Great re-expelled the Persians i 333 BC, as the cities of Lycia surren dered one by one, some with positiv glee. Shortly afterwards, under Ptole maic rule, the Lycian Federation wa reformed, although the native Lycian language died out over the next cen tury, to be replaced by Greek.

In 197 BC Antiokhos III of Syri ejected the Ptolemies; he in turn wa defeated by Rome in 189 BC. Awarde to Rhodes, the Lycians rebelled and within 20 years, the Roman Sen ate granted the troublesome citie

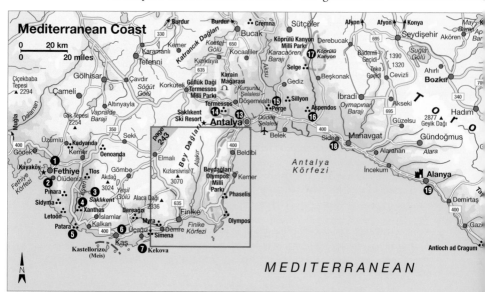

itonomy under a renewed federation. fter the Battle of Philippi in 42 BC, ctor Mark Antony awarded the ter- tory its freedom, leaving it the only art of Asia Minor not under Roman omination. A century later, Emperor espasian (AD 69–79) brought the int province of Lycia and Pamphylia ack under direct Roman control.

Though Lycia became immensely ealthy during the 1st to 3rd centuries, disastrous earthquake in 241 signalled ecline, and after the Arab raids of the h and 8th centuries it remained a mote, backward area. Under Ottoman le the highlands became the realm of rük nomads, whilst the few coastal ttlements were inhabited by Greek rthodox colonists from the islands pposite. Only in the early 1980s was ycia's spectacular shoreline connected the rest of the country by proper ads. Now, even the tiny villages have en discovered by outsiders.

ethiye and Kadyanda

t the western edge of Lycia, **Fethiye** is a growing port and market town cked between a broad, islet-speckled ay and the foothills of Baba Dağı (the cient Mount Antikragos). There has en settlement here since the Lycians founded Telmessos, about 2,500 years ago. Byzantine Makri was renamed in 1934 to honour Fethi Bey, a pioneer- ing World War I Ottoman pilot who crashed to his death in Syria. Most of Fethiye – flattened by earthquakes in 1856 and 1957 – is modern, while the Knights of St John extensively quarried antiquities to reinforce the Byzantine castle overhead (open access), so lit- tle remains of the ancient city except for some temple-type tombs in the cliff looming above. Best of these is the grandiose **Tomb of Amyntas** (up the steps from Kaya Caddesi; daily 8.30am–sunset; charge), so identified from a 4th-century BC inscription. The **Theatre** behind the **tourist office** (İskele Meydanı 1, opposite the main harbour; tel: 0252-614 1527) has been partially excavated, while the small local **museum** (off Atatürk Caddesi; closed for renovations) contains finds from local archaeological sites.

Despite much of the old bazaar hav- ing been converted into attractive shops, restaurants and clubs, and a pedestrian- ised promenade along the working har- bour, Fethiye is now a bit past its sell-by date as a tourist destination. Except for backpackers waiting to board a budget "Blue Cruise", relatively few visitors stay

Choosing henna tattoo designs at Fethiye.

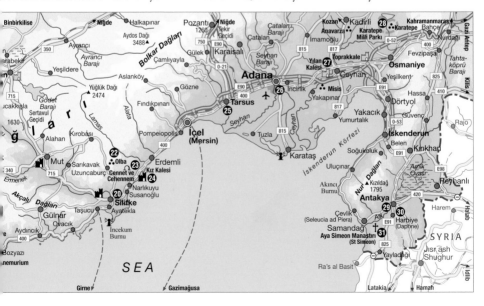

BELOW: Ölüdeniz beach.

overnight, and the town is increasingly a focus of the area's burgeoning second-home trade.

For more cultural stimulation, head north 21km (13 miles) into the hills, beyond sleepy Üzümlü village, to ancient **Kadyanda** (open access but charge if guard present). Of a similar age to Telmessos, the ruins – which include a **necropolis**, fortifications, a long narrow **stadium** with seats, and a **theatre** – nestle in dense conifer forest, with a self-guiding loop path to take you around the highlights. You can either drive here or trek the old, marked path between the village and the site (90 minutes).

Ölüdeniz and Kayaköy

Fethiye itself has no beaches; the nearest is at **Çalış**, 4km (2½ miles), a mosquito-y, declassé resort slowly being converted to holiday homes. The area's premier beach, featuring on every second tourist-office poster of Turkey, lies across the peninsula at **Ölüdeniz ❷**, the "Dead Sea", 25km (15 miles) away.

Until the late 1980s, this was one of the Mediterranean's most beautiful hideways, a cobalt lagoon encircled by platinum sand, with Aleppo pines leaning over the water. But the ove landers' obligatory halt of yore h since become a standard mass-mark resort. The entire valley behind le scenic, adjacent **Belceğiz** beach crammed to capacity with restauran and hotels, most of the latter dom nated by package companies. Th environs of the lagoon – where th last backpackers' campsites just ho on – are a national reserve (dawn dusk; charge for pedestrians and veh cles), though the narrow spit of lar between the lagoon and the open se is host to either parked cars or su loungers. Although Belceğiz prom nade is attractively pedestrianised, th crowds may drive one to the undeve oped forest-service beach of **Kıdra** or the hippie stronghold of "**Butte fly Valley**" with its waterfall, serve by water-buses.

The eerie ghost town of **Kayak** (formerly Levissi) makes a fascinati excursion, easily reached off the ma road between Fethiye and Ölüden or directly up from Fethiye, starti from the street at the foot of the ro tombs. Kaya was home to about 3,5 Greek Orthodox until the populatic exchange of 1923. The Macedonia Muslims who arrived to take the place considered the land poor in cor parison to what they had left behin and soon drifted away; thus most the nearly 600 houses (and three lar; churches) here – the largest such aba doned town in Asia Minor – stan empty and ruined. Plans to conve them to a holiday village have bee thwarted by a strict preservation orde and descendants of the original Gree deportees still return on pilgrimage significant numbers.

Minor Lycian cities – and Saklıkent

Heading east from Fethiye along Higl way 400, turn off briefly along Higl way 350 towards Korkuteli after 22k (13 miles), and follow signs to ancie **Tlos** (open access; charge). The pla was already known to the Hittite

uring the 14th century BC, and the astle here was inhabited until the 800s. A tomb at Tlos was found intact vith its treasure in late 2005. System-tic excavations are finally beginning, nd have revealed an early Christian emetery on the grounds of the evoca-ve **Yedi Kapı baths** with its seven-vindowed apse overlooking the valley. 'he Roman **theatre**, with 34 rows f seats backed against the flanks of kdağ, has some wonderful stone eliefs amongst the tumbled masonry f the stage building.

Nearby **Saklıkent ❸** (dawn–dusk; harge), 44km (26 miles) southeast f Fethiye, is a popular retreat from corching coastal temperatures. This ool, dark gorge emerging from the oothills of Akdağ, about 300 metres ,000ft) high and 18km (11 miles) ng, is impassable to all but the tech-ically equipped after about 2km (1 ile) in (and that's heading downhill, oseiling the many sheer drops). For e rest of us, a boardwalk leads about 50 metres/yds into the gorge to where e Ulupınar springs boil up.

Besides Tlos, other Lycian cities, ostly unexcavated, are tucked away up de valleys off the main, fertile flood-ain of the Esen Çay. **Pınara** (open cess; charge when guard present), km (32 miles) southeast of Fethiye, as a 4th-century BC colony of Xan-os which then became a prominent ember of the Lycian Federation in its vn right. Upon leaving Highway 400, rk left after 3km (2 miles), before aching Minare village, for the final rt-track approach to the site. The rliest town is built at the top of a eer cliff honeycombed with Lycian mbs, of which the most interesting the "**Royal Tomb**" near the ticket oth, with clear reliefs of urban scenes its porch. The heart of the city, st above, is today jumbled masonry ongst pines, though the **theatre** ross the valley is well preserved.

About 12km (7 miles) southwest the Pınara turning, the scattered mains of **Sidyma** (open access)

co-exist with the modern village of Dodurga, much of which has been built with ancient masonry. The main points of interest lie just east, where many free-standing **tombs** of the necropolis, square and gabled rather than rotundly "Gothic" as elsewhere, sport marvellous reliefs.

The Letoön

Coming from Sidyma on the old highway, watch for a sign reading "Kumluova, Karadere, Letoön 10" pointing down the correct side road to the compact but more rewarding ruins of the **Letoön** sanctuary (daily May–Sept 8am–7.30pm, Oct–Apr 8.30am–5pm; charge). Here are three adjacent **temples** dedicated to Leto (a titaness loved by Zeus) and her chil-dren, Apollo and Artemis, together the presiding deities of Lycia. French archaeologists have partially recon-structed **Leto's shrine** with stone from the original quarry, though further restoration is currently sus-pended by official obstruction. Beyond the temples lies a **nym-phaeum**, permanently submerged by the high local water-table, and home to frogs, terrapins and ducks. A well-

In 1984, French archaeologists found inscriptions spelling out the dress code for visitors to the Letoön. Anyone entering the sanctuary had to wear plain garments and simple shoes. Jewellery, elaborate hairstyles and broad-brimmed hats were banned, as were all weapons.

BELOW: exploring the gorge at Saklikent.

Silk worms at a carpet factory.

preserved Hellenistic **theatre** has 16 relief masks above the northeast face of the vaulted entrance passage.

Xanthos

Xanthos ❹, located 1km (¾ mile) from Highway 400, above the town of Kınık (daily May–Oct 8am–7.30pm, Nov–Apr 8.30am–5pm; charge), was the leading town of Lycia, known for pride so fierce that twice its inhabitants preferred mass suicide rather than surrender to a numerically superior foe. The first time was in 540 BC, when the Persian general Harpagos besieged the acropolis; rather than submit, the men of Xanthos made a funeral pyre with their women, children, slaves and belongings and set it alight. "Then, having sworn to do or die, they marched out to meet the enemy and were killed to a man" said Herodotus – except for eight who were away at the time.

In 42 BC, two years after the murder of Julius Caesar, Brutus besieged Xanthos, but again its citizens chose self-immolation, so that he gained control of an empty city, aside from 150 prisoners taken alive. Following Mark Antony's victory over Brutus, he rebuilt Xanthos, which became the capital of Roman Lycia.

The site was virtually intact when British explorer Sir Charles Fellows arrived here in 1838. He returned four years later in HMS *Beacon*, whose sailors spent two months carting away the monuments for exhibition in the Lycian Room at the British Museum.

Today, two tombs in front of the theatre, and an inscribed "obelisk" (in fact also a tomb) have become the trademarks of the site. The so-called **Harpy Tomb** takes its name from an early attribution of the reliefs around the top chamber (a plaster cast of the original in London) depicting winged women. They are now thought to be sirens, carrying away the souls of the dead to the Isles of the Blessed. The other is a regular sarcophagus of the 3rd century BC; a relief on the side, now removed, was three centuries older and had apparently been reused.

The **obelisk** stands at the corner of the Roman agora. Mainly inscribed in Lycian, with a few lines of Greek which have allowed tentative decipher-

Leto and Lycia

According to legend, when Leto became pregnant by Zeus, she fled to escape the wrath of jealous Hera, searching for a land in which to safely give birth to her divine twins. Having done so (most versions say at Aegean Delos), she arrived in Lycia – then called Tremilis – where local shepherds drove her away when she attempted to drink at a spring. However, some wolves guided her and the babies to the Xanthos River; in gratitude, she renamed the region Lycia (*lykos* is the Greek word for wolf), while the goddess had her revenge on the unhelpful shepherds by turning them into frogs. Leto is cognate with *lada* (Lycian for woman), and there is evidence of a previous mother-goddess temple at the Letoön from the 7th century BC.

ing, it recounts the life and times of an unnamed local 5th-century BC hero, cited as the brother of Prince Keriga. East, beyond the "late" (Byzantine) agora, are the remains of a **Byzantine basilica**, which contains superb mosaics in abstract patterns.

Patara

Patara 5 was another powerful Lycian city. Today it is better known for its 15km (9-mile) white-sand beach, the longest in Turkey, often with a considerable summer surf. This giant sandpit is as popular with breeding turtles as it is with baking tourists, and the swamp behind the dunes is a vast archaeological site – thus it is all strictly protected, with most tourist facilities confined to the village of Gelemiş.

To reach Patara (ruins and beach daily May–Oct 7.30am–7.30pm, Nov–Apr 8am–5.30pm; charge, ticket valid one week), leave Highway 400 9km (5½ miles) west of Kalkan, or a similar distance from Xanthos; the site begins 5km (3½ miles) from the main road. Patara was supposedly the winter home of the sun god, Apollo, and had an oracle as famous as the one in Delhi. The town was also the birthplace of St Nicholas, better known today as Santa Claus (see page 242). Before the harbour silted up in the Middle Ages, Patara was a prosperous port; now, its ruins are scattered over a vast area of field, dunes or swamp, though in recent years some monuments have been cleared of vegetation or sand.

At the official entrance stands a triple **monumental arch** (1st century AD), which doubled as part of an aqueduct. Further in, there is a **baths** complex similar to the one at Tlos, and a large paved area, perhaps an **agora**, with many columns re-erected by the excavators. Towards the beach stand the **bouleterion**, where the Lycian Federation apparently met, and the intact **theatre** (2nd century BC), its stage building being rebuilt. From the top, there is an excellent view of the other monuments and of the coastline. A boardwalk leads from a small car park to the beach, which now has a municipally run snack bar employing local people and keeping prices reasonable.

Former Greek ports

In the decades before the 1923 population exchanges, the base of the Lycian "bulge" was inhabited mainly by Greek traders and fishermen, whose attractive ports still bear traces of those times. Harbourside mosques have been converted from Greek churches by little more than the addition of minarets.

Kalkan has become one of the most sought-after havens in Turkey, its original core of Ottoman-Greek houses overhanging steep, narrow alleys long since swamped by mushrooming suburbs of villas. Nearly half the local population is foreign (and largely British); some Turks say, half-jokingly, that they feel they need a passport to go downtown. Sadly, the bohemian ethos and boutique *pansiyons* of the 1980s are largely gone, as second-home ownership has outstripped short-stay tourism; prices and tastes in boutiques, restaurants and bars are pitched at north European

In 42 BC, Brutus and Cassius visited rich Patara, in search of funds for their war against Mark Antony and Octavian. When the citizens refused to pay up, they took the women hostage, but the men stood firm. Impressed by their resolution, the Romans released the women unharmed, whereupon the men paid up in full, without another murmur.

BELOW: pony trekking through Patara's dunes.

TIP

At Kumluca, leave Highway 400 at signs pointing to "Beykonak, Mavikent" for a detour to a scenic stretch of the Lycian Way, from Karaöz down to the French-built lighthouse at Gelidonya Burnu, with the Beş Adalar (Five Islands) as a backdrop. From the trailhead beyond Karaöz, it's an hour's round-trip walk to the cape.

wallets and prejudices.

Although there's only oversubscribed Kömürlük pebble beach in town, the seas around Kalkan are ideal for diving and spear-fishing. As with many karstic shorelines, submarine freshwater seeps are common, especially around sea-caves, making the surface much colder than deeper waters.

If it all gets too much at sea level, head 8km (5 miles) inland and uphill to İslamlar, which is still known by its Ottoman-Greek name Bodamya (Rivers). Streams, greenery and coolness abound here, as well as a handful of trout-farm restaurants.

A dramatic cliff-hugging route east from Kalkan covers the 27km (17 miles) to Kaş. The main features en route are photogenic, coarse-sand **Kaputaş beach**, 6km (3½ miles) along, and the nearby **Mavi Mağara**, the second largest sea-cave in the Mediterranean, with Blue Grotto effects inside – bargain hard in Kalkan for a boat-trip there.

Kaş ❻ (107km/64 miles southeast of Fethiye; 181km/109 miles southwest of Antalya) is a more broad-spectrum, congenial resort than Kalkan, still partly retaining its old identity as a county town. Most recent development has scaled the steep hillside behind, or out along the trailing Çukurbağ peninsula to the southwest. Kaş has retained some style at just-affordable prices (partly because of a substantial Turkish clientele), with excellent restaurants, cafés, bars, designer clothing outlets and upmarket boutiques. But as at Kalkan, there are no significant in-town beaches – hotels with swimming pools are much in demand.

Ancient **Antiphellos**, the predecessor of Kaş, began to develop in Hellenistic times and by the Roman period was the region's leading port. Surviving structures include a Hellenistic **theatre**, with the Mediterranean as an astounding backdrop, less than 2km (1 mile) west of town on Necip Bey Caddesi; nearby stands a unique, square Doric tomb, the **Kesme Mezar**. More rock-cut **Lycian tombs** can be seen on the cliff-face above, while the double-decker **Lion Tomb** stands uphill from the souvenir shops along Uzun Çarşı.

The island of **Meis** (Kastellorizo)

BELOW LEFT: the rocky coast near Kalkan. **BELOW RIGHT:** part of Kas' old identity is still visible.

immediately opposite Kaş, is the easternmost of the Greek islands, and links between the two places remain strong, as the islanders have always shopped in Kaş whatever the state of relations between Turkey and Greece. Now that both are official ports of entry for their respective countries, crossing or staying overnight is easy – a fast ferry makes the trip twice daily in season. On Meis it becomes evident that traditional Kalkan and Kaş architecture is of a piece with the island's.

Kekova

The most popular domestic boat trip out of Kaş is to **Kekova inlet ❼**. Alternatively, you can hire a boat in **Üçağız**, 38km (24 miles) east of Kaş; to drive there, turn off Highway 400 after 18km (11 miles). Since the 1980s, tiny Üçağız has awoken to tourism, most recently through serving as an important halt on the Lycian Way. A day out on the water, visiting Kekova Island or Kale Simena), provides an idyllic combination of sunshine, swimming and historic ruins (see below).

Along the margins of Kekova Island facing the mainland lie the submerged remains of a **sunken city** (called Batık Şehir), destroyed in Byzantine times by a vicious earthquake. To protect submarine artefacts, it is strictly forbidden to snorkel or even swim here; your best view underwater will be with a sea-kayaking expedition, organised by adventure agencies in Kaş. At the southwest tip of the island, called Tersane, you're allowed ashore near the almost-vanished remains of a Byzantine apse.

At the east edge of Üçağız is the Lycian necropolis of **Teimiussa**, its "Gothic" chest-type tombs spread out along the shore. Further around the coast, accessible by a longish walk or a more pleasant kayak-paddle or tour-boat-ride, is **Kale** village (ancient Simena). It sits below the crenellated ramparts of a Crusader castle, within which is a small Greek theatre, seating 200 people. Kale makes for an idyllic stay, though waterside restaurants – mostly having cut deals with boat tours – are undistinguished. A lone Lycian sarcophagus standing in shallow water nearby lures visitors to pose beside it for photographs, an operation made more delicate by the resident sea urchins.

Demre and Myra

Demre is a resolutely modern town, marooned in an ugly sea of tomato-growing greenhouses – one of the least attractive, and airless, spots in Lycia, but there are some local attractions which justify it as a day-trip destination (but emphatically not an overnight).

In the town centre, the **Noel Baba Kilesi** (Church of St Nicholas; daily May–Oct 9am–7pm, Nov–Apr 8.30am–5.30pm; charge) is a much-modified Byzantine church on the site where St Nicholas was bishop during the 4th century AD. The church was originally built in the 6th century over his tomb, extended by Constantine IX in 1043 and again by the Russians in 1862, prior to being recently covered with a hideous protective canopy by Turkish archaeologists. St Nicholas's

Souvenirs depicting St Nicholas are sold in Demre.

BELOW: inside Noel Baba Kilesi in Demre.

One of the carved masks at the ruins of Myra, presumed to be from the frieze belonging to its theatre.

BELOW: Myra's theatre sits below the cliff containing the carved tombs.

purported sarcophagus is clearly an earlier pagan affair intended for a couple, and in any case his remains have not been here since 1087, when a band of devout pirates carried them off to Bari, Italy, where the Basilica of San Nicola was built to receive them. A commemorative Mass is held in Demre annually on 6 December, the saint's feast day, although the town tends to be swamped by Russian pilgrims throughout the year.

Just over 2km (1½ miles) from central Demre, a marked side road follows a stream down to Çayağzı (ancient Andriake), the local harbour since Lycian times. Of Andriake little remains except for a vast 2nd-century AD Roman granary, built by Hadrian as a central supply depot for the entire empire. **Çayağzı** (or rather its keen boatmen) pitches itself as an alternative departure point for Kekova, but otherwise this aspiring resort has yet to get off the ground. Restaurants are few and both they, and the beach, are much inferior to those at nearby Sülüklü, reached by a separate road starting near Hadrian's granary.

Myra ❽ (daily Apr–Oct 8.30am–7.30pm, Nov–Mar 8.30am–5pm charge), 2km (1¼ miles) north of the town centre, was founded in the 5th century BC. It grew into one of the most important cities in the Lycian League, and later into a Christian bishopric, visited by, among others St Paul. Unlike most Lycian cities, survived in some form until the 1300s.

Myra has some of the finest Lycian cliff-tombs (closed), many with "log cabin" features carved into the rock – presumably reflecting domestic architecture of the period. The carvings are mostly in poor repair, but the overall effect of this stacked architecture of death is dramatic. The Roman-era city below the cliff is dominated by a large theatre, whose seating and access tunnels are intact, but part of its stage building has collapsed. However, many relief carvings and inscriptions are still visible, in particular a macabre set of comedy and tragedy masks, presumably from the frieze. Visit as early as possible in the day to catch the morning sunlight on the cliff – and avoid enormous coached-in crowds.

Santa Claus

St Nicholas was born in Patara in about AD 270, later becoming bishop of Demre, where he died in 346. He was a leading member of the Church and a delegate to the Council of Nicaea in 325, known both for his immense kindness and the miracles he performed in his lifetime. The link with Father Christmas stems perhaps from two legends: that he cast three bags of gold coins into the home of a merchant who had hit hard times, enabling his daughters to marry, and that he restored to life three boys who had been cut up by a local butcher. The first of these stories is also said to be the origin of the three gold balls that are still used today as the sign of a pawnbroker. Eventually, this busy saint became patron of Greece, Russia, prisoners, thieves, students, sailors, travellers, unmarried girls, merchants, pawnbrokers and children.

The Dutch, who corrupted his name to Sinterklaas (from which came Santa Claus), began to celebrate by filling the children's clogs with presents on the eve (5 December) of his feast. In America, this custom was soon attached to Christmas, and the shoe became a stocking. The jolly man in red with a white beard was the 20th-century invention of the Coca-Cola company – one of their most enduring advertising campaigns.

...nto the mountains

...inike (ancient Phoenike) is now a ...omewhat nondescript port, the usual ...erminus for *gulet* cruises east from ...ethiye, but mostly a market town for ...ocal citrus and tomato growers. In ...istory, it figures mainly as the site of ...he "**Battle of the Masts**" in 655, the ...rst major naval victory of the Muslim ...rabs over the Byzantines. Finike also ...arks the start of Highway 635, one of ...he few roads to cross the Toros moun- ...ins into inland Lycia, offering a spec- ...cularly beautiful excursion, taking in ...ncient Limyra and Arykanda en route ...) Elmalı.

After 7km (4 miles) along the 635, ...rn right at Turunçova for **Limyra ❾** ...open access), which is 3km (1½ miles) ...ff the main road. This was the 4th- ...entury BC capital of Pericles, ruler of a ...ection of Lycia. His tomb, the **Heroön**, ...opped the highest point of the most ...xtensive necropolis in Lycia; its ...aborate carvings are now in Antalya ...useum. It is a steep 40-minute climb ...p, but the views are astounding. Less ...nergetic visitors may content them- ...lves with the freestanding 4th-century

BC **Tomb of Xatabara** near the theatre, with reliefs of a funeral banquet and the judgement of the deceased. Regrettably, long after sporadic Austrian excavations, the site is now neglected and poorly labelled.

Return to the main road for a further 28km (18 miles) to the mountain hamlet of Arif and the stunning ruins of **Arykanda ❿** (open access; charge if guard present), whose setting has justifiably been compared to Delphi in Greece, overlooking as it does a deep valley between two high mountain ranges. Despite improved signage and access from the highway, Arykanda remains one of the least visited of Lycia's ancient cities. Just above the tiny car park, a **basilica** has fine mosaic floors, including a medallion with two birds. Nearby is an impressive **baths** complex standing 10 metres (33ft) high at the façade, with windows over two storeys and a plunge-pool still visible inside. Uphill from here, one of several "**monumental tombs**" was adapted as a church early in the Christian era. Heading back west across the ravine which divides the site,

TIP

Those pressed for time can return quickly and pleasantly from Arykanda to the coast by backtracking 4km (2½ miles) to Çatallar, and taking the D751 west, via the impressive castle and huge ruined basilica at Dereağzı, until meeting a broader highway down to Kaş.

BELOW: Finike's marina.

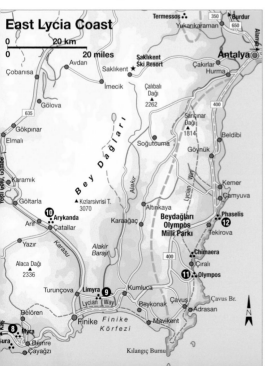

East Lycia Coast

Take the cable car from the resort of Kemer to ascend 2,365 metres (7,757 ft) to Tahtali mountain's summit.

BELOW: Olympos' beach is part of the Beydağlari Olympos National Park.

you'll find the Roman imperial **agora** with its clumsily restored odeon, plus an impressive **theatre** and attractive **stadium** nearby.

The main road continues north, past seasonal **Avlan Gölü**, over fertile agricultural upland devoted to apples, potatoes and sugar beets, to the market town of **Elmalı**, at the foot of 2,269-metre (7,442ft) Elmalı Dağ ("Apple-ish Mountain"). The town has an externally tiled 17th-century mosque and a few dilapidated but once-elegant timber-framed Ottoman mansions, but is mostly the location for a choice in onward itinerary.

Heading southwest towards Kaş also takes you through **Gömbe**, which makes a better lunch-stop (or overnight base) than Elmalı. This is also the turn-off point for expeditions west to scenic, limpid **Yeşil Gölü** (Green Lake), the only such body of water in the Akdağ massif. It's best visited in spring just after snowmelt, for the vivid wild-flower displays. You'll need local directions and preferably a 4WD vehicle to get within a short walk of Yeşil Gölü. You can bag the 3,024-metre (9,921ft) summit of Akdağ in about five hours from there, but an ice axe may be needed until July.

Going west instead from Elmalı towards Fethiye, the minor road northwest, then west, is very scenic and passable to all cars, except in winter when the Göğübeli pass is snowed up. After about an hour's drive, just before meeting Highway 350, you'll pass the side turning to İncealiler, "gateway" village to the extensive remains of ancient **Oenoanda**, one of the last founded (2nd century BC) and highest (1,400 metres/4,600ft) Lycian towns. Although surveyed by a British team in 1996, it has not been excavated in any manner, and the 45-minute path walk up from İncealiler will give you a taste of what visiting Lycian ruins was like 30 years ago. Peeking out amongst the pines on the ridge are necropolis tombs, a massive **aqueduct**, an equally massive Hellenstic **city wall** with towers and windows, and jumbled civic buildings flanking the presumed **agora** inside. You're unlikely to meet another living soul except for the odd hunter, browsing goat or red squirrel.

The Olympic Coast

East from Finike, the first place on the coast (besides Gelidonya Burnu) likely to prompt a stop is **Adrasan**, the beach "suburb" of Çavuş village, where a river lazily meets the sea at a long sand-and-pebble beach overlooked by pyramidal Musa Dağı. It's popular amongst Brits and Turks, with a scuba dive outfitter and boat trips along the rugged coast to otherwise inaccessible Ceneviz Limanı.

From Adrasan, it's an easy drive north 16km (10 miles) along a secondary road to ancient **Olympos** ⓫ (daily Apr–Oct 8am–7pm, Nov–Mar 9am–5.30pm; charge, 1-week ticket available), with the final landward approach through one of the largest backpacker hang-outs in Turkey, a succession of wood-built **"treehouses"** at their busiest before or after Gallipoli's ANZAC Day. Stream and valley exit to the

sea through the ruins, most of them unlabelled and overgrown in tropical profusion, but the determined can find a monumental Roman **portal**, an arcaded **warehouse**, a Byzantine **aqueduct** and various tombs. The far end, guarded by Byzantine-Genoese fortifications, marks the start of an excellent, long sand-and-pebble beach.

Drivers will need to retrace their steps and access this beach by a different road descending from Highway 400 to Çıralı, the burgeoning if still somewhat "alternative" resort. Being part of the **Beydağları Olympos Milli Parkı**, threaded along its entire length by the Lycian Way, and also a sea-turtle hatching ground, means that development here is (theoretically) limited and must be set well back from the beach. The only local cultural diversion is the **Chimaera** (Yanartaş; open access but charge), a 20-minute walk lightly uphill from Çıralı's 60-odd *pansiyons*. The Chimaera is a cluster of unquenchable flames which have burnt since antiquity, when it was the heart of a sanctuary to Hephaestos (Vulcan), god of fire. The flares – fed by a unique mix of gases issuing through tiny fissures – are best seen at dusk.

Phaselis ⑫ (daily, summer 8.30am–7pm, winter 9am–5.30pm; charge) is the most accessible Lycian site, some 33km (21 miles) north of Çıralı, a short distance off Highway 400. Set on a wooded peninsula between three bays, all used as harbours in antiquity and now serving as beaches, it's predictably popular with both bus- and boat-tours. Founded in the 7th century BC by Rhodian colonists, the city had a reputation for unscrupulousness and sycophancy; Emperor Hadrian's visit here in AD 129 prompted the construction of a massive gate at the big-beach end of the main **paved avenue** through the city's heart.

Aside from Phaselis, there is little of interest between Çıralı and Antalya along the increasingly broad and busy Highway 400. The one sizeable port, Kemer, long ago lost any intrinsic charm to overbuilding, and neither will the all-inclusive resorts at Tekirova, Çamyuva, Göynük and Beldibi appeal to casual passers-by. ❏

TIP

Bring a picnic (as well as beach gear) to Phaselis as snack-caravans here are inconveniently placed and expensive.

BELOW LEFT: ruins at Phaselis.
BELOW RIGHT: the Chimaera flame.

PLANTS AND WILDLIFE

Populated by both European and Asian
species, the mountains, plateaux and
coastal regions of Turkey are home to
a rich variety of plant and animal life

Turkey's flora and fauna draws on
two continents – Anatolia lies at
the western limit of many Asian
plant and animal species, while
familiar European species are
much in evidence across the
country. Most of the natural forest
cover disappeared centuries ago, but rich stands of
woodland survive in certain mountain areas:
this varies from the evergreen species
(mostly Aleppo pine) which covers
Mediterranean- and Aegean-facing
foothills to the dense broadleaf forest of
the wetter Black Sea mountains. The barren
appearance of much of the interior is transformed in
May and June when the landscape is carpeted in a
beautiful array of wild flowers.

All the Eurasian land-mammal families are amply
represented, from bats and various rodents on
up to mountain goats, brown bear and grey
wolf. European species such as wild boar
and weasels co-exist with more exotic
wildlife such as jackals, the caracal (Persian lynx),
and even a few leopards in the more remote parts of
the Taurus mountains. The Asiatic lion became
extinct in Turkey in the late 19th century (the only
wild population is now in India).

The Mediterranean and Aegean support rich
marine life, particularly in areas close to nutrient-
bearing river mouths. Dolphins are still often spotted,
while sea turtles lay eggs on less developed
Mediterranean beaches.

Conservation efforts include over 40 national parks
and reserves, and the activities of organisations like
the Doğal Hayatı Koruma Derneği (the local affiliate
of WWF). Forests are strictly protected,
which has kept wildfires far below
the incidence experienced in
Greece, Spain or Portugal.

ABOVE: a fox near Payas Lake, Ka
jackals can also be spotted in this
LEFT: a bee orchid *(Ophrys lutea ssp. ga*
BELOW: a mouflon, a species of mountain
relatively widespread in the east of the co
with a smaller population in the central
mountains in southern

TOP: various reptile species, such as
this Algerian skink, thrive in the dry,
sunny summers. **LEFT:** wild echinops
(globe thistle, a common garden plant
in Europe) on the Anatolian plateau.

BIRD-HAUNTED WETLANDS

Turkey's numerous wetlands act as permanent avian habitats, or vital rest-stops and breeding grounds for birds migrating during spring or autumn between east Africa or the Middle East, and the Balkans. Such environments consist of coastal river deltas, or swamps and lake margins of the interior; many are threatened by illegal construction or reclamation for agricultural use. One locale that seems safe is the Kuş Cenneti (Bird Paradise) at Manyas Gölü near Bursa, where up to 3 million migrators (over 200 species) alight in a good year, including pelicans, storks, herons, spoonbills and spotted eagles. Another, well inland just southeast of Erciyes Dağı, is the Sultansazlığı, a 2,000-hectare (5,000 acre) complex of saline lake and freshwater marsh and reedbed which boasts a similarly broad profile of bird residents. Equal to either is the Aegean-coast bird sanctuary at Çiğli-Sasallı near İzmir, comprising saltpans in the former delta of the Gediz River, which hosts kestrels, plovers, terns, stilts and avocets. On the Mediterranean, the deltas of the Göksu and Tarsus streams are home to black francolin, Smyrna kingfisher and Audouin's gull.

TOP: Dalmatian pelicans in the Gediz estuary.
RIGHT: as in much of Europe, white storks are thought to bring good fortune; their huge nests atop telegraph poles or chimneys are a feature of many Turkish villages.

E: wild poppies, as here at Pergamon, bring a vivid splash of r to the Anatolian countryside in late spring.

PAMPHYLIA

Less proud and more pragmatic than Lycia, Pamphylia was happy to cooperate with Alexander and the Romans, assuring itself a good share of the conquerors' largesse

The broad and fertile Pamphlyian Plain, bound by the blue waters of the Mediterranean to the south and the sculpted limestone peaks of the Toros range to the west and north, possesses a rare natural beauty. This fertile region flourished in the Graeco-Roman period, and the wealthy cities which once blossomed along this coast are now a wonderfully preserved collection of ruins for the visitor to explore. The region is booming today as the sea, sun and sand tourism capital of Turkey, with over 8 million tourists passing through Antalya airport annually. The downside, as ever, is overdevelopment, with much of the shoreline between Antalya and Alanya now lined with lookalike hotels, apartments and golf-courses.

Antalya

The hub of Turkey's Mediterranean coast is **Antalya** ⓱ (ancient Attaleia). Turkey's fastest-growing city, its population has swelled from around 30,000 in the 1950s to over a million today. Although much of the city is now a jumble of high-rise apartment blocks, offices and hotels, its location – overlooking the startlingly blue waters of the Gulf of Antalya to the saw-tooth line of the misty purple Toros Mountains – remains stunning. The central walled old quarter is ranged prettily

around a tiny harbour at the foot of the cliffs, and the city has several lovely park areas, bringing welcome relief in the long, hot summers. It's even possible to swim and sunbathe right in the heart of the city. Despite its rapid development, the places of interest to a visitor are all very central, and it makes a great base to see the surrounding sights, amongst the finest in the country.

Antalya was founded in 158 BC by King Attalus II of Pergamon and bequeathed to Rome in 133 BC.

Main attractions

KALEİÇİ: ANTALYA'S WALLED OLD TOWN
ANTALYA ARCHAEOLOGICAL MUSEUM
TERMESSOS RUINS AND NATIONAL PARK
ANCIENT PERGE
THE ROMAN THEATRE AT ASPENDOS
RAFTING IN THE KÖPRÜLÜ CANYON
TREKKING ON THE ST PAUL TRAIL
THE OLD TOWN OF SIDE

LEFT: the Roman amphitheatre at Aspendos.
RIGHT: Antalya's beach.

The Saat Kulesi (Clock Tower) marks the entrance to Kaleiçi, Antalya's old quarter.

Although badly battered by the Arab invasions of the 7th century, it remained in Byzantine hands until the Seljuks arrived in 1206, and was a regular staging post for Crusaders on their way to the Holy Land. In the 1390s, control was handed to the Ottomans and remained with them until the area was occupied by Italy in 1919. Three years later, it was returned to Turkey.

Kaleiçi, the old town

The heart of Antalya is the beautifully restored walled old quarter known as **Kaleiçi** Ⓐ (inside the castle). The harbour here is filled with wooden leisure craft which ferry tourists out along the foot of the pocked-limestone cliffs on which the city stands, while the alleyways radiating out from the water's edge are lined with alfresco seafood restaurants and cafés along with a veritable swarm of souvenir shops, *pansiyones* and boutique hotels. Walking around the old town on a balmy summer's evening is a delight, with bougainvillea spreading in a riot of purple over the stone and timber fronts of Ottoman-era town houses,

and the scent of jasmine sweet i the air. Be warned, though: everyon wants to sell you something, whethe it's a boat tour or a carpet, a glass o freshly squeezed orange juice or meerschaum pipe, so come prepare with your thickest skin.

Before plunging into the mayhem o the old walled city, pause for a momer beside the equine **Atatürk Heykeli** Ⓑ (Monument) in Cumhuriyet Squar The bronze statue itself is impressiv but, more importantly, it offers the be vantage point in the city. Just to th left, the fortified **Saat Kulesi** (Cloc Tower) at Kalekapısı, built in 1244 a an integral part of the city's defence marks the entrance to the old tow Beside it is the 18th-century **Mehme Paşa Camii**, with its typically Ottoma dome and slender, cylindrical minaret Opposite, to the north across the tra track, is a bustling bazaar, mainly give over to fake designer clothing and foo ball shirts, though part of it is devote more traditionally, to gold.

Just west of the Mehmet Paşa Cam is the **Yivli Minare** Ⓒ (Fluted Minar Antalya's most photographed buildin

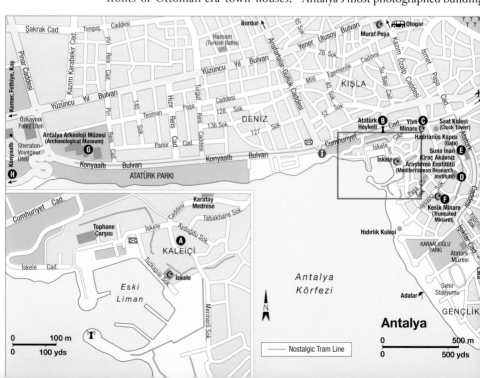

Antalya

provides a magnificent foreground
or the panorama across the bay to
ie mountains, especially at sunset.
's also the symbol of Antalya and its
dest Seljuk monument, dating from
ie reign of Sultan Alâeddin Keykubat
(1219–38). Exquisite turquoise-and-
lue tiles are set into the 8-metre (26ft)-
igh minaret, while the pool in front
of marble. Close by is a simple and
legant 14th-century octagonal *türbe*
omb), made of fine white masonry
i the tradition of Central Asian Turks.
he large whitewashed building to the
de was formerly a dervish convent.
arry on down the hill and you reach
ie elaborately carved entrance of the
aratay Medrese, a religious school
uilt by a Seljuk vizier in 1250.

Within the maze of alleys overhung
y wooden-frame houses, best reached
om Atatürk Caddesi, two Ottoman
ansions and the Greek church of
gios Georgios have been turned into
ie **Mediterranean Research Institute**
) (Suna-İnan Kiraç Akdeniz Araştırma
nstitütü; Kocatepe Sok 25; tel: 0242-
43 4274; Thur–Tue, winter 9am–noon,
–6pm, summer 9am–noon, 2–7.30pm;

charge). The Greek church houses a
permanent exhibition of Çanakkale
pottery, while the building in front of it
is a loving re-creation of a 19th-century
Ottoman house, with a series of rooms
decked out in period style, complete
with lifelike mannequins. Directly
opposite across the narrow street, the
other courtyard house is home to a fine
collection of books and documents
detailing the rich archaeology and
history of the region.

A few blocks further north is **Hadrian's Gate** Ⓔ (known as Üçkapılar to
Turks), a stately triple-arched structure of white marble, built in honour
of the emperor's visit in AD 130. Step
through it to re-enter the modern
world of **Atatürk Caddesi**, a palm-
tree-lined street enlivened by the ringing bell of the passing period tram and
a constantly changing series of clothes-
shops, cafés and pirate DVD outlets.
Head south down Atatürk Caddesi
to **Karaalioğlu Parkı**, atop the cliffs
to the east of the harbour, a peaceful
shady park ideal for sitting out the heat
of the day.

On the clifftops above the harbour

BELOW: the once-
scenic fortified
harbour at Kaleiçı.

The Kesik Minare.

BELOW:
sarcophagus from
the ancient city of
Perge at Antalya's
Archaeological
Museum.

stand the old city walls and ramparts built by the Greeks and restored by the Romans and Seljuks. Here, just outside the park and back in Kaleıçi, is the 13.5-metre (44ft) **Hıdırlık Kulesi**. The sombre lower square section is believed to have been a Hellenic tomb, while the tower itself was built by the Romans in the 2nd century AD, possibly as a lighthouse, and adapted by the Seljuks for defence. From here a marble-clad street leads back into the old town to the **Kesik Minare** ⑥, where a truncated minaret is all that remains of a 13th-century mosque that was struck by lightning in 1851. Originally a 5th-century church dedicated to the Virgin Mary, it was constructed using 2nd- and 3rd-century spoils.

The Archaeological Museum

The **Antalya Arkeoloji Müzesi** ⑥ (Archaeological Museum; Apr–Oct Tue–Sun 9am–7.30pm, Nov–Mar 8.30am–4.30pm; charge) is one of the finest in Turkey. It is located 2km/1 miles west of the town centre, and easily reached from the Old Town by the period tram.

Most of the finds come from the surrounding area, spanning several millennia of prehistory from the Karain Cave, Bronze-Age jewellery and toys from Elmalı, and exquisite classical statuary from Perge and Aspendos, beautifully displayed in the Perge Gallery. The Hall of the Gods displays statues of the Greek gods, Emperors Hadrian and Septimius Severus and their empresses, while the Sarcophagus Gallery even contains the elaborate tomb of a much-loved dog, Stephanos. Other exhibits include parts of a stunning mosaic collection from Xanthos depicting the infant Achilles being dangled by his mother into the River Styx. A display of icons includes the familiar portrait of St Nicholas and a box which once contained his "relics". Facing it is a superb collection of 6th-century church silver, part of which was illegally looted and ended up in Dumbarton Oaks Museum, Washington. There is also a broad-based

hnographic collection with displays
n Turkish lifestyle, dress, musical
struments and carpets.

onyaaltı Beach

) the west of the city is the pebbly
‹m (2-mile) -long **Konyaaltı Beach**
), upgraded in recent years to provide
ntalya with an attractive seafront,
ith several of its finest hotels and a
umber of good restaurants. **Beach
ark**, at the eastern end of the beach,
 a dedicated leisure area with bars,
ightclubs, restaurants and cafés in
undance. On the cliff top above, in
ne grounds of the **AKM Culture Park**,
 a very popular water park, equipped
ith various water slides and rides.
lso here is the **Cam Pyramit** (Glass
yramid), a concert venue, and, next
› it, the **AKM Cultural Centre** which
osts, amongst other events, Antalya's
nnual Altın Portakal (Golden Orange)
ternational film festival.

Many of Antalya's mass-market
otels march in serried ranks along
ne cliff tops of **Lara**. This area, stretch-
ng for nearly 12km (7 miles) east of
ne city, has become an entire suburb of monolithic hotels and holiday
apartments. Many have steep staircases
down the cliff to private swimming
platforms. Beyond the cliffs is Lara
beach, a moderately attractive public
bathing strip which, unlike Konyaaltı,
boasts a beach which is both sandy and
shelves gently into the sea.

North and east of the city

Tucked away in the lofty mountains
northeast of Antalya is a small ski
resort, **Saklıkent** (Hidden City), which
– in a good season – offers reasonable
skiing from early January through to
the end of March. It takes around an
hour and half to drive to 50km (30
miles) from the city centre, more or
less at sea level, to an altitude of 1,800
metres (5,900ft).

The ancients had a taste for inland
vistas, and the plateau behind Antalya,
a separate ancient kingdom known as
Pisidia, is as studded with ruins as the
shores of the Mediterranean. One of
the most remarkable of these inland
sites is **Termessos** ⓮ (daily Apr–Oct
9am–7.30pm, Nov–Mar 8.30am–5pm;
charge), set in the beautiful **Güllük**

Turkish lokum, *also
known as Turkish
Delight, can be found
in flavours other than
the original rosewater,
such as chocolate,
almond, orange,
pistachio and walnut.*

BELOW: inscription
at Termessos, the
ferocious "Eagle's
Nest" of ancient
Pisidia.

Antalya is home to several quarries. These onyx vases and dishes for sale at Perge make typical gifts from the region.

BELOW: Düden Şelalesi (Düden Falls).

Dağı Termessos National Park (same hours as site; separate charge) high in the mountains 37km (22 miles) northeast of Antalya. It is accessed off the N-350 to Korkuteli. The car park is about 9km (5½ miles) along a forest road; there is then a steep 2km (1½-mile) walk to the site. There are no refreshments, so you'll need to bring your own.

The hilltop location and formidable defensive walls of this Pisidian city so daunted Alexander the Great in 333 BC that he abandoned his siege, torched the local olive groves and slunk away.

The origin of Termessos is uncertain, but the founders, who called themselves the Solymians, are identified with the Pisidians who occupied the lake district around Burdur and Eğirdir further north. They called their city the "Eagle's Nest" with good reason. It is perched between summits at about 900 metres (3,000ft), and the views to the coast and across the mountains are magnificent. The ruins are also fasci-

nating. The superb theatre, the mo[st] dramatically situated in Turkey, is th[e] high point of any visit to the site, sta[nd]ing across a narrow canyon to rugge[d] Güllük Dağı (Rose Mountain). Othe[r] remains include an agora, a gymna[sium, an odeon and five enormou[s] water cisterns carved into the roc[k] Dozens of stone sarcophagi climb th[e] hillside to the fire-watch tower above On the way back down to the car par[k] don't miss the tombs, some displayin[g] mock-temple relief-carved façades, cu[t] from the cliff face.

The caves of **Karain Mağarası** (dail[y] 8.30am–5pm; charge) are 27km (1[7] miles) northwest of Antalya, off th[e] N-650 to Burdur, about 6km (4 mile[s] from the main road. Finds from thes[e] remarkable caves go back to the Pala[e]olithic (Old Stone Age), some 30,00[0] years ago. People are thought to hav[e] lived here for nearly 20,000 years, an[d] excavation has yielded tools, axes an[d] other crude implements, the skull o[f] a Neanderthal child, and the bone[s] of an ancient elephant, hippopot[amus and bear. Most are on displa[y] in Antalya and Ankara, but there is [a] small on-site museum.

The limestone country aroun[d] Antalya is riddled with waterfalls, o[f] which the most famous are the **Düde[n] Şelalesi**, two separate cascades o[f] a powerful underground river. Th[e] Upper Falls, which have carved out [a] pretty gorge 14km (9 miles) northeas[t] of town, are a popular local picnic spo[t] Much more spectacular, albeit backe[d] by drab ranks of high-rise blocks, ar[e] the 20-metre (65ft) -high Lower Düde[n] Falls, which crash over the cliff into th[e] sea in the Antalya suburb of Lara. The[y] are best seen from one of the many boa[t] trips leaving from Antalya harbour.

The **Kurşunlu Şelalesi**, about 23k[m] (14 miles) east of Antalya (7km/4[½] miles off the main road), are even mo[re] popular because of their proximit[y] to Perge and Aspendos. The unusua[l] green-coloured water is surrounde[d] by walkways, picnic tables, a children['s] playground and souvenir stalls.

Perge and Sillyon

The most impressive ruins on the Pamphylian coast are at **Perge** ⑮ (daily May–Sept 9am–7.30pm, Oct–Apr 9am–6pm; charge), some 15km (9 miles) east of Antalya along the N-400. Known to the Hittites as far back as 1300 BC, the city was a successful trading centre, which kept itself alive and healthy through pragmatism – it had no defensive walls until fortified by the Seleucids in the 2nd century BC. Alexander the Great was welcomed in, and used the city as a base throughout his Anatolian campaigns. Perge finally declined during the Byzantine era when the river silted up, stranding the port 12km (7 miles) from the sea.

The red **Hellenistic Gate** towers still stand close to their original height, but most of "modern" Perge – the 14,000-seat theatre (closed for restoration for several years), stadium, bathhouses and colonnaded street – belongs to the period of *Pax Romana*. The resplendent **agora** dates from the 4th century AD. The **stadium** (234 metres/775ft long and 34 metres/110ft wide, with seating for 12,000) is one of the best-preserved of the ancient world. Of its 30 outward-facing chambers, 20 were used as shops; several wall inscriptions reveal the names of their proprietors as well as their trade.

The magnificent finds from this ancient city on display in the Antalya Archaeological Museum *(see page 252)* include a 2nd-century sarcophagus depicting the 12 labours of Hercules and numerous colossal statues of gods and emperors. One name that crops up frequently on the bases of statues is that of a woman, Plancia Magna. She was the daughter of the governor and a priestess of Artemis, goddess of the moon and patron of the city, in the 2nd century AD. Her legacy contributed approximately 20 statues to the city; her tomb, or what remains of it, is situated just outside one of the city gates.

To reach **Sillyon** (open access; guide recommended), turn off the N-400 7km (4 miles) beyond Perge, follow the road for 8km (5 miles) to Asar Köyü, then climb up the steep unmarked rocky track to the site. The flat-topped acropolis was once the site of a city

Perge was where St Paul set off on his first proselytising journey in AD 46, heading north from the prosperous city to cross the formidable barrier of the Toros mountains en route to Antioch in Pisidia, high on the Anatolian plateau.

St Paul's Trail

The St Paul's Trail is a superb, way-marked long-distance walking route inspired by the 1st-century AD missionary travels of St Paul. Starting in either Perge or nearby Aspendos, spectacular Graeco-Roman sites set on the rich Pamphylian Plain, twin paths snake their way over the southern spurs of the mighty Toros mountains before joining at the remote, peak-ringed ancient city of Adada. Now a single path, the route forges north through pine forest, along gorges and over high mountain passes to the beautiful blue expanse of Lake Eğirdir, Turkey's largest fresh-water lake. Curling around the mountainous western shore of the lake, the route finally strikes across the rolling Anatolian plateau to Antioch in Pisidia, where St Paul first preached to the gentiles.

BELOW: amongst the ruins at Perge.

TIP

The ancient theatre at
Aspendos hosts an
annual opera and ballet
festival (usually a three-
week period from June
to early July), with a
prestigious mix of
Turkish and foreign
companies. Tickets are
modestly priced,
performances on balmy
evenings spectacular.

as old and rich as Perge (but never
conquered by Alexander). Beware of
tumbling into one of the hidden cisterns when exploring. Sadly, its ruins
were badly damaged during a series
of landslides in 1969, and today it is
usually ignored in favour of its more
spectacular neighbours.

Aspendos

Some 45km (25 miles) east of Antalya
and 5km (3 miles) off the main road,
imposing **Aspendos** ⓰ (daily Apr–Oct
9am–7.30pm, Nov–Mar 8.30am–5pm;
charge) is graced by one of the finest
surviving Roman **theatres** in the world.
Built during the reign of Emperor Marcus Aurelius (AD 161–80) and seating
15,000 people, the elaborate structure
is almost intact, the exception being
part of the upper cornice. It is still used
for concerts today *(see margin, left)*. Its
architect was Xeno, a local lad whose
formula for creating perfect acoustics
remains something of a mystery – a coin
dropped from the orchestra pit can be
heard distinctly from the galleries. The
Seljuks used the theatre as a caravansaray in the 13th century; on Atatürk's

suggestion it was later used for oil wrestling. For 1,800 years it has withstood
earthquakes, the ravages of war, the
weather and the march of time.

Behind the theatre lie the ruins of
the acropolis, agora, nymphaeum, and
what is one of the best surviving examples of an aqueduct from the Roman
world. The annals inform us that the
river was navigable as far as Aspendos
and the city was used as a naval base
improbable though this seems today
as the site is 12km (8 miles) from the
sea. It certainly prospered from trading luxury goods, a tradition kept up
by local shopkeepers today.

The fast-growing, purpose-built
coastal resort of **Belek** is only a
stone's throw from Antalya airport
It has a wonderful white-sand beach
currently shared by a burgeoning line
of seriously upmarket resort hotel
and some rather beleaguered turtles
while inland is a growing sea of cheap
apartment blocks and largely anony
mous "all-inclusive" hotels catering
to their mass-market clientele. There
is also an ever-increasing number of
golf courses.

BELOW LEFT: bars
and shops in Side.
BELOW RIGHT:
Perge's Roman and
Hellenistic gates.

Köprülü Kanyon

A short distance beyond Aspendos, a tarmac road cuts off the main coastal highway and leads up to the beautiful, cool, green **Köprülü Kanyon** ⑰, a high mountain gorge sliced by the tumbling milky turquoise Köprülü Çayı (Eurymedon River). The river has become very popular for white-water rafting, with literally thousands of people a day riding the (by rafting standards fairly tame) bubbling torrent. The journey to **Beşkonak** village, reached after 43km (26 miles), is more life-threatening than the rafting because of the numerous tourist coaches speeding recklessly along the narrow, winding road. The plethora of waterside restaurants at Beşkonak exists largely to feed the white-water rafting hordes. Beyond the town, a dramatic Roman bridge spans the canyon.

A recently paved road leads a further 14km (9 miles) up from the canyon across a high plateau, its soft volcanic rock carved and twisted into columns ("fairy chimneys" redolent of those in Cappadocia) by the wind, to the village of **Altınkaya** (Zerk) and the ruins of ancient **Selge** (open access). Very little remains aside from the magnificent Greek-style theatre with its backdrop of the snowcapped peak of Bozburun. The stadium has been turned into a terraced field for one of the local families. The Roman road, forum, Byzantine basilica and twin temples to Artemis and Zeus are more imagination than fact. Once the swarms of children calm down, they will lead you to the few remains of the ancient town's reliefs and statues, hidden in rock slides and undergrowth.

Side: old crowds and new

Although founded as long ago as the 7th century BC, the atmospheric town of **Side** ⑱ has undergone its most startling transformation over the past 30 years. Until the 1970s it was a sleepy fishing village; most of today's *pansiyon* and restaurant owners were yesterday's fishermen who have lost interest in the humble hook and line. Blessed with good beaches either side of the peninsula on which it stands, evocative Roman and Byzantine ruins and a charming old town, tourism has become big business here. Yet despite the plethora of hotels, restaurants, discos, bars and carpet, designer clothing and jewellery shops, Side retains its charm as a living open-air museum in a spectacular setting.

Side (meaning "pomegranate" in Anatolian) is no stranger to crowds. With a population of some 60,000 in the Hellenistic era, it was the largest, richest port on the south coast, with an unsavoury reputation. Rampant piracy flourished, with prisoners sold as slaves in the town agora then sent to the island of Delos, a notorious depot for human merchandise in antiquity. Alexander the Great's biographer Arrian recorded that when his master captured the city in 333 BC, its people spoke a tongue unknown to the invaders – in fact it remains undeciphered to this day. Ancient Side declined in the 7th century under relentless Arab attacks, and was finally abandoned in 1150 after

The familiar masks of comedy and tragedy grew from Greek theatre.

BELOW: camel rides are available on Side's eastern beaches.

The word Pamphylia means "land of all tribes" in ancient Greek. Historians agree that the fall of Troy in 1184 BC brought about the real settlement of the area as refugees flooded in looking for a new start. Their descendants were unable to find peace, however. Pamphylia has been subjugated at least 10 times in the succeeding millennia.

BELOW: late afternoon shadows at Side's Temples of Apollo and Athena.

earthquakes, too, had taken their toll.

The incoming road follows the line of the original ancient street, and is lined with the ruins of Roman shops. On the left, in front of the massive bulk of the theatre, are the extensive remains of the **agora**; beyond it is a mass of dunes backing an attractive beach. The 20,000-seat theatre is one of the most impressive Roman structures in Turkey, and is now home to an annual music, opera and ballet festival held each September.

Across the road from the agora and theatre, the old **Roman Baths** now house the town **museum** (Tue–Sun, summer 9am–noon, 1.30–7.30pm, winter 9.30am–noon, 1–5.30pm; charge), displaying finds from local excavations, including many fine, albeit headless, statues; St Paul was so convincing as a speaker that the newly converted Christians rushed out and, in a fit of wild overenthusiasm, decapitated their former pagan deities. In fact, Side served as a bishopric in the Byzantine period, and many of the monuments lying in such profusion around the village are relics of the early Christian era.

Running the gauntlet of importuning restaurateurs and souvenir shop salesmen, make your way through the pretty old town to the twin **Temple of Apollo and Athena**. There's little remaining bar a few re-erected columns topped by Corinthian capital and a section of pediment, but its setting (especially at sunset) on the rocky headland is dramatic.

Neighbouring **Manavgat** is a bustling business and farming community. Monday is market day and a good opportunity to buy the local crafts, old coins or rugs found among the fruit, vegetables and squawking chickens. The only other reason to visit the town is for an excursion by boat up the river to the pleasant, if unspectacular, **Manavgat Falls** (Manavgat Şelalesi). Boats leave from Side or – better value and quicker – from the quay beside the main bridge in town. Natural vegetation forms a tropical curtain over the Manavgat River.

A few kilometres on, a yellow sign points up a scenic road to **Alarahan**, a well-preserved and atmospheric Seljuk **caravansaray** on the banks of

the Alara River, constructed in 1231 by Sultan Alâeddin Keykubat I. On a rocky crag above sits **Alara Castle**, its fortress wall running crazily along the summit, a long tunnel leading down through the mountain to the river.

Alanya

Ever-expanding **Alanya** ⓭, 110km (70 miles) east of similarly named Antalya, sprawls along two broad bays as one of Turkey's most popular resorts. The city centre is sliced emphatically in two by a magnificent 250-metre (800ft) -high rocky promontory jutting out into the Mediterranean. On the summit, nearly 7km (4 miles) of ancient curtain walls with 150 bastions wind around three towers, forming the most spectacular and effective fortress on the Turkish coast. There are dizzying views of the sea on three sides, and the orchard-covered foothills of the Taurus Mountains behind. Alanya's winter climate is particularly mild, its setting superb, beaches extensive and location, just a couple of hours' drive from busy Antalya airport, very convenient, so it's no surprise that it has a huge

population of foreign second-homers from northern Europe.

Although the exact foundation date of Alanya is unknown, the city traces its history back to Hellenistic times, when it was named Coracesium, with the Romans, Byzantines, Armenians, Seljuks and Ottomans all taking their turn at power. Pirate chieftain Diototus Tryphon built his fortress on the peak in the 2nd century BC. The Roman general Pompey fought a notable sea battle against the pirates off Alanya in 67 BC. Later, Mark Antony presented the land to Cleopatra, who made good use of its fine timber, both to rebuild her fleet, and for export.

Damlatas Cave, whose weeping rocks are reputed to cure human ills.

As the Byzantine Empire declined, the south coast was poorly defended, and various Armenian dynasties took advantage of the weakness. By the 10th century the town had fallen into obscurity, but remained a difficult place to capture as the Seljuks found

BELOW: the Red Tower's battlements provide a fine view of Alanya's harbour.

The approach to Damlatas Mağarasi, the "Weeping Cave" at Alanya.

BELOW: the fishing fleet in port, Alanya.

out in 1221 when they laid siege to its formidable fortress. Legend has it that Sultan Alâeddin Keykubat I, at his wit's end, gambled on a last desperate bid. He conscripted into his army hundreds of wild goats. Tying a lighted candle to each of their horns, he shepherded his new recruits ahead of his army up the cliffs. The credulous enemy, upon seeing the apparent strength of the invaders, surrendered at once and were exiled to Konya – but not before Keykubat had married the daughter of the ousted leader. Keykubat renamed the city *Alaiye* ("city of Ala") in his own honour. It was captured, in due course, by the Ottomans in 1471.

Today, the markedly different contributions of the Romans, Byzantines and Seljuks to the fortress are clearly discernible. The **İç Kale** (daily, Apr–Oct 9am–7.30pm, Nov–Mar 8.30am–5pm; charge), or inner fortress, was built at the behest of Alâeddin Keykubat I in 1220. Inside is a domed Byzantine church (6th century) dedicated to St George, a flight of red-brick stairs said to have been used by Cleopatra when

she descended to the sea to bathe, sto rooms and numerous cisterns – th largest of which could hold 120,00 tons of water – a hefty advantage du ing protracted sieges. Just outsic the wall, the *bedesten* (inn), restore and operating as a hotel, lies with an attractive tangle of ruinous stor houses, vines and fruit trees.

The road to the castle is a steep 5k (3-mile) climb, and a taxi or *dolmuş* the top is a wise investment. Save you energy for the walk downhill throug carob and fig trees and scented jasmin with stunning views of the harbo below. There are regular teahouses an drinks stands en route.

Just west of the fortress at sea leve next to the tourist office, is the **Dan latas Mağarasi** (daily 6am–10am f patients, 10am–7pm for the publi charge) or "Weeping Cave", an exqu site grotto with curtains of drippir stalactites and stalagmites 15,00C 20,000 years old. Its claimed 80 pe cent success rate in curing respirato ailments, especially asthma, is appa ently due to the atmosphere: 90–1C percent humidity, a constant tempe

ature of 22–23°C (71–73°F), high levels of carbon dioxide and natural ionisation. People come from all over Turkey for this cure, for which a doctor's certificate is required: four hours per day for 21 days. Knots of bescarved women while away the hours as they knit, sew and crochet their way to a clearer respiratory system in this warm, damp enclave. For those interested, doctors in Alanya will examine you and write the necessary report. Note that asthma treatment at Damlataş is not recommended if you suffer from heart problems.

Just round the corner, the compact **Alanya Museum** (Azaklar Sok, south of Atatürk Cad.; Tue–Sun 8.30am–noon, 1–5.30pm; charge) has sections on archaeology and ethnography. The exhibits are carefully chosen and well labelled.

Directly east of the citadel is the city harbour, heavily fortified by Sultan Alâeddin Keykubat I. Chief among the defences was the 35-metre (115ft) octagonal **Kızıl Küle** (Red Tower), designed in 1227 by a Syrian architect, which is now home to a small **Eth-** nographic Museum (Tue–Sun 8am–noon, 1.30–5pm; charge). There are fine views from the battlements. Round the point, at the harbour entrance, is another tower, the **Tophane Küle** (Arsenal Tower), used as a cannon foundry by the Ottomans. Between the two is the **Tersane** (open access; best seen from the water), a series of five huge open workshops which were the centrepiece of the Seljuks' naval dockyard, also built in 1227.

Today, the harbour is humming with activity, lined by pavement cafés, with fishing and tourist boats jostling for space along the quays. Alanya's coast is marked by a series of grottoes, and boat trips can be arranged to any or all – Pirate's Cave, Lovers' Grotto, one where phosphorescent pebbles shine up from the sea bed; or to the "wishing gate", an enormous natural hole in the rocks. It is said that barren women who go through this gate will gain the ability to conceive.

Each side of Alanya boasts good, if somewhat grey, sandy beaches backed by a host of hotels; the eastern part of the town sports a wider selection. ❑

TIP

Most travel agencies in Antalya, Side and Alanya offer day-long rafting trips on the Köprülü river, including transport and meals, as do the hotels along the coast.

BELOW: Alanya beach, with the fortress dominating the hill above.

CILICIA

Turkey's "Pirate Coast" road twists its way
across towering cliffs and down to tiny coves,
a dramatic landscape carpeted with pine forests
and dotted with Hellenistic, Roman and
Byzantine ruins

Main attractions
ANEMURIUM
MAMURE KALESI (ANAMUR
    CASTLE)
ALAHAN MONASTERY
UZUNCABURÇ (ANCIENT
    OLBA)
GÖKSU DELTA
HEAVEN AND HELL CAVES
KIZ KALESI CASTLE
TARSUS (ST PAUL'S WELL)
SABANCI MERKEZ CAMII

BELOW: taking the
oranges to market.

The flat and increasingly built-up
farmland between Alanya and
Gazipaşa does little to prepare
you for the 200km (125 miles) of fabulous coastal scenery ahead. Pine forests
and mud-plastered houses cling precariously to the cliffs, terraced banana
plantations step resolutely down into
the sea, and tiny coves jostle for space.
The views on this beautiful stretch of
the Mediterranean are superb, especially as the terrain is far too rugged
to allow much tourist development.
Beyond Silifke, however, the sum-

mer high-rise retreats of prosperous
Turks begin to dominate the plains
approaching the industrialised port of
Mersin. Diversions inland pierce the
ever-present barrier of the formidable
Toros mountains, home of the semi-
nomadic *Yörük* pastoralists, to give an
insight into timeless rural Turkey.

East to Anamur

Some 20km (12 miles) east of Gazipaşa
it's worth taking a short 2km (1½-mile)
detour to the cliff-edge Hellenistic site
of **Antioch ad Cragum**. It's so difficult
to access that you can easily understand
why the pirates, for which this coast
was notorious in antiquity, were able
to fend off the Romans for so long.

Anamur, 130km (80 miles) east of
Alanya and several kilometres inland
has no particular claim to fame. Its seaside suburb of **İskele**, 5km (3 miles)
south, is a pleasant small resort with
several good basic hotels and fish restaurants along a white-sand beach. The
beach is known for its turtles, and there
is a small **museum** (İskele Cad.; tel
0324-814 3018; Tue–Sun 8am–5pm;
charge) showcasing finds from the Hellenistic, Roman and Byzantine eras as
well as carpets woven by nomads from
the nearby Toros mountains.

About 5km (3 miles) west of town
on the southernmost tip of Asia Minor
slumber the ruins of ancient **Anemurium**, meaning "windy cape" (daily
8am–7.30pm; charge). Founded by
the Hittites in about 1200 BC, the city

ecame a great trading centre and Byzantine bishopric, thriving until a devastating earthquake in AD 580, followed by Arab invasions. The well-preserved ruins of the town, mainly dating from its 3rd-century heyday, are dominated by the cemetery, a vast sprawl of some 50 domed tombs. The setting and the ruins themselves are intensely atmospheric, despite the fact that they adjoin a swimming beach and picnic area.

Five km (3 miles) east of Anamur town, on the N-400, magnificent **Mamure Kalesi** (Anamur Castle; daily 8am–7.30pm; charge) stands romantically with one foot in the sea. The first fortress here was built in the 3rd century AD, but it has had many other incarnations: as a 10th-century pirates' lair, and as the property of 11th- to 12th-century kings of Armenia. The surviving castle was built in 1226 by the great Seljuk Sultan Alâeddin Keykubat I; the mosque and rooms overlooking the sea from the upper battlements were added by Karamanoğlu ruler Mahmut Bey (1300–8). In the late 14th century, it became a mainland toe-hold for the crusading Lusignan kings

of Cyprus, until it was seized by the Ottomans in 1469.

The Göksu delta

Ascending and descending in a series of hairpin turns, passing several more aesthetically pleasing but anonymous castles, the coastal road finally hits the Göksu delta near **Taşucu**, one of the two ferry embarkation points (the other is Mersin) for the Turkish Republic of Northern Cyprus. One hydrofoil service and one car ferry leave from here daily. Taşucu itself is a bustling ferry port with several hotels and *pansiyons* on the waterfront to the east of town.

About 5km (3 miles) further on, at **Ayatekla** (daily, winter 8am–5pm, summer 8am–8pm; charge) just left of the highway, a ruined Byzantine basilica towers above the underground hermitage of St Thecla, one of St Paul's first converts. On hearing Paul preach the virtues of chastity in Iconium (Konya), she promptly renounced her betrothal; on a later visit to the Apostle in prison, she too was arrested and sentenced to be burnt at the stake and tied naked to a pyre in the arena. A

Anemurium's ghostly city of the dead guards the southern point of Anatolia.

BELOW: Anamur's perfect medieval castle.

TIP

Those tackling the coast road east from Alanya to Silifke should set out early in the morning. The road is long and hazardous because of the number of sharp bends and the heavy goods traffic. If travelling by bus, book a seat on the right to make the best of the superlative views.

divinely inspired deluge doused the flames. Wild beasts were brought in to devour her, but "there was about her a cloud, so that neither the beasts did touch her, nor was she seen to be naked", according to Acts of Paul and Thecla, written in the 2nd century by an unknown Asian presbyter.

Silifke

Like all coastal cities in Turkey, **Silifke** ⑳ has ancient roots, but precious little remains of ancient Seleucia ad Calycadnum, which was one of nine sister cities founded by Seleucos Nicator in the 3rd century BC after he had gained control of Syria following the death of Alexander the Great.

The town is dominated by a vast hilltop **castle**, a twenty-minute walk from the centre. Built originally by the Byzantines but heavily altered by the Armenians and Crusaders, it was captured by the Turks in the late 13th century. From the ramparts there is a superb view, with all the town's other monuments laid out like a map at your feet. Directly below are the Roman necropolis, aqueduct and a vast Byzantine cistern carved from the bedrock. The **stone bridge** over the Göksu River also has ancient origins (it was first built by Vespasian in AD 78), while the riverside park surrounds an unexcavated *höyük* or *tel* (archaeological mound), first fortified by the Assyrians in the 8th century BC. On the right of İnönü Bulvarı stands a single column of the 2nd- or 3rd-century AD **Temple of Zeus**; no sign has yet been found of the city's famous oracle of Apollo Sarpedonios. The **Ulu Cami** is of Seljuk origin, and while no trace of decoration remains, the *mihrab* and the entrance are original.

The local tourist office (Gazi Mah, Veli Gürten Bozbey Cad. 6; tel: 0324 714 1151) is enthusiastic and there is a pleasant little **museum** (Tue–Sun 8am–noon, 1–5pm; charge) with a remarkable hoard of Seleucian coins, on Taşucu Caddesi, the main Antalya road.

The road north

Silifke marks the real end of the tourist coast. From here on, the landscape flattens into dreary coastal plains and industrial wastelands, although town

BELOW: white-water rafting is a popular activity in southern Turkey.

such as ancient Tarsus are not lacking in atmosphere. Many choose to take the breathtaking N-715 road north over the mountains to Konya *(see page 298)* and Cappadocia *(see page 305)*, one of the most captivating places in Turkey.

The early stages of this mountain road follow the turbulent path of the Göksu River. The Third Crusade came to an abrupt end some 16km (10 miles) north of Silifke, when Holy Roman Emperor Frederick Barbarossa drowned while bathing on his way to Jerusalem in 1190; a **memorial** marks the spot. He was a long way from home, and in order to preserve his body until he could be taken to Antioch for burial on Christian land, he was stored in a barrel of vinegar. He was later taken back to Germany.

Upstream is the town of **Mut**, worth visiting, with a 14th-century mosque, the Lal Aği Camii, a fortress and two domed tombs. About 20km (12 miles) north of town, the beautiful 5th-century **monastery** at Alahan (daily, winter 8am–5pm, summer 8am–8pm; charge) teeters on the edge of the wild Göksu gorge, with traces of fresco still visible in its baptistery and churches.

The road now rises over the Serta-vul pass, where migrating birds of prey including short-toed eagles, honey buzzards and Levant sparrowhawks congregate in spring and autumn. Another 70km (45 miles) from Alahan, **Karaman** ㉑ was a powerful autonomous emirate from 1277–1467, so famous that early travellers referred to the entire coast as Karamania. Three fine religious schools, the Hatuniye Medresesi, the İbrahim Bey İmareti and the Ak Tekke; a mosque, the Yunus Emre Camii; and a ruined castle are all that remain of a glorious past, while the small museum also contains finds from Canhasan, about 13km (8 miles) northeast of town, a settlement dating back to the 6th millennium BC.

About 30km (19 miles) north, a turning to the left leads to a mountain rising sheer above the plain. On its northern flank is the village of **Maden Şehir** and the once majestic Byzantine **Binbirkilise** ("A Thousand and One Churches"). For two periods, from the 5th–6th and 9th–14th centuries, the area was almost as packed with monasteries and painted churches as Cappadocia. There are some ruins, but most

Adana is famous throughout Turkey for its eponymous kebab, a spicy mincemeat sausage skewered and cooked over charcoal. Locals wash it down with salgam, *a red-coloured and fiery concoction based on beetroot juice.*

BELOW: the Cilician plains are soaked in the blood of successive invading armies.

The Pirate Coast

In antiquity, the rocky, inaccessible coast of Cilicia made the region an ideal hideaway for pirates preying on ships plying the lucrative trade route between Syria and the Aegean. Incredibly powerful and well organised, the pirates were initially tolerated by the Romans, as they provided the slaves needed to work their plantations in Italy. The pirates became too bold for their own good, however, when kidnapping prominent Romans for ransom including, in 75 BC, Julius Caesar himself. Even more seriously, they were seen to be threatening the crucial grain supply from Egypt to Rome. In 67 BC the Roman general, Pompey the Great, was given extraordinary powers to quash the sea-borne menace, and used a mix of threats, diplomacy and pardons to induce their surrender.

Bananas grow in profusion along this stretch of coast, which is also a land of strawberries, thick-skinned oranges and yoghurt.

BELOW: part of the Göksu Delta has been designated a nature reserve.

have sadly been pillaged for building by the local farmers.

There is one other side trip to make before leaving the Silifke area. Tucked high in the Taurus Mountains, near the remote upland village of **Uzuncaburç**, 30km (19 miles) north of town, the ancient city of **Olba** ㉒ (daily, winter 8am–5pm, summer 8am–8pm; charge) suns itself in past glories. Founded by the Hittites, this is a superb conglomeration of Hellenistic, Roman and Byzantine ruins.

The **Temple of Zeus**, built in 295 BC by Seleucos I Nicator (321–280 BC), is one of the oldest such sanctuaries in Asia Minor. During the 2nd century BC, its priests evolved into a powerful dynasty of priest-kings, the Teukrides, who ruled the surrounding town with a rod of iron right through the Roman era. Thirty columns remain standing today, four still with their capitals, the earliest Corinthian capitals in Asia Minor. It was converted to a church in Byzantine times, when the sanctuary was destroyed and walls and new doors were inserted between the columns. Nearby are a five-storey tower (late 3rd

century BC), a monumental gate wi Corinthian capitals and five colum of the **Temple of Tyche** (Fortune each made of a single piece of gran nearly 6 metres (20ft) high, broug from Egypt in the 1st century AD.

The city gate is a massive structu of three richly ornamented arches. distance is the ancient cemetery, a eerie valley of rock-cut tombs.

Wonderful wildlife

South of Silifke is the **Göksu Del** part of which has been designated nature reserve. A wide range of wate birds inhabits the marshes and reec Purple gallinule and black francoli survive the predations of hunters in ve limited numbers, and the beaches a home to gulls and, in the summer eg laying season, turtles. Migrating rapto (*see page 265*) gather here to feed befo resuming their journey across the Med terranean to Africa. Information abou the birds is available from the ÖCK (Environment Ministry) agency, ne the Ayatekla site, tel: 0324-713 0888.

Some 20 kilometres (12 miles) ea of Silifke, **Narlıkuyu**, translated

"Well of the Pomegranate", is a pleasant cove lined with seafood restaurants. It is also home to the remains of a famous **Roman bathhouse** (Tue–Sun 8am–noon, 1–5pm; charge) with a dusty 4th-century AD mosaic floor representing the Three Graces. The spring water was claimed by the ancients to enhance grey matter.

Just south of Narlıkuyu is **Susanoğlu** and the **Mausoleum of Priape the Fearless Satrap**. From this substantial monument juts the sculptured metre-long phallus of the god of fertility. Legend recounts that Priape was the illegitimate son of Zeus and Aphrodite, and that Hera, jealous wife of Zeus, deformed the child, giving him a phallus equal to his height. He was abandoned out of shame by his mother near the Dardanelles, and was brought by shepherds to Lapsacus (Lapseki).

Heaven and hell

Three kilometres (2 miles) north and inland of Narlıkuyu lies the **Corycian Caves** (daily, winter 8am–5pm, summer 8am–8pm). Better known as **Cennet ve Cehennem ㉓** (Heaven and Hell), they were formed by underground chemical erosion. Like all the best natural phenomena, they are considered sacred by pagans, Christians and Muslims alike. Heaven (Cennet Deresi) is larger than Hell, with 452 stairs leading down to a Byzantine chapel, dedicated to the Virgin Mary. This, in turn, blocks the entrance to a cave-gorge with an underground river, thought by some to be the Styx. The cave at the far end was home to an oracle. Just north is the gloomy pit of Hell ("Cehennem"), happily inaccessible without climbing equipment as the sides are concave. It was here that Zeus imprisoned Typhon, the many-headed, fire-breathing monster serpent, father of Cerberus, guard dog of Hell.

A few kilometres east, **Akkaya** has its own Pamukkale in miniature, with smooth white rocks curved like waves, and excellent swimming. On both sides of the highway to Mersin

are regimented rows of oranges and lemons, crops of Roman and Byzantine ruins, the last scattered arches of giant Roman aqueducts and an increasingly cluttered forest of high-rise blocks, corrugated iron and billboards.

Twin castles

Five kilometres (3 miles) east of **Narlıkuyu** stand famous twin medieval castles. On terra firma, 13th-century **Korykos Castle** reuses materials from a city first mentioned by Herodotus in the 5th century BC. On an offshore island, across a 200-metre (650ft) channel, is its sister, **Kız Kalesi ㉔** (the Maiden's Castle), which was a refuge for pirates before it was fortified by Byzantine admiral Eugenius, in 1104, as a link in the empire's border defences during the Crusades. It was later appropriated by the Armenians, Turks and, in 1482, the Ottomans (both castles are open daily 8.30am–5pm; charge). You need to negotiate with a local boatman if you want to get across the water.

Kız Kalesi is a fast-growing resort, mainly frequented by Turkish tourists, and is best appreciated in early summer.

Legend, of course, has its own say with the tired but charming belief that the Maiden's Castle was where King Korykos sequestered his daughter after a dire prediction that she would die from a snake bite. Naturally, a basket of grapes sent to her by a lover contained a viper.

BELOW: gazing into the pit of Hell, one of the Corycian Caves.

This striking statue seems to evoke the confidence of Mersin.

BELOW: traders have descended on Tarsus since the pass through the northern mountains was engineered.

From here until Adana, the coast is lined with holiday apartments, villas and beach-side restaurants, making it hard to see the waves from the busy road.

Mersin and Tarsus

Mersin (İçel) is a pleasant enough city but offers little to detain the visitor. Boats leave daily for Cyprus, and inter-city buses are frequent. A big, largely modern metropolis with a population of around 1.5 million, the best parts are along the waterfront, where there are broad boulevards, shady parks, a decent supply of restaurants and a small **museum** (Atatürk Cad.; Tue–Sun 8am–5pm; charge). The city is also known for its joviality, especially around the permanent market area, perhaps due to the number of sailors who frequent the town.

Sandwiched between the industrial giants, 25km (16 miles) east of Mersin, **Tarsus** ㉕ is frequently overlooked, despite a resplendent history stretching back to at least 3000 BC. Because the site has never been abandoned, the ancient city lies 15–20 metres (50–65ft) below the modern one, while the rav-

ages of war and time have destroyed most vestiges of the past. However, Tarsus is one of the oldest continuously inhabited cities in the world; it was the birthplace of St Paul; and it was certainly here that Cleopatra met and seduced Mark Antony.

When the engineers of ancient Tarsus cut a pass through the northern mountains to the **Cilician Gates**, they created one of the most significant mountain routes of all time; traders and troops have poured through the narrow gorge ever since. Xerxes and Alexander the Great passed here; the latter almost lost his life after bathing in the icy waters of the River Cydnus (Tarsus Suyu). A fearful and haunted pass, it was named the "Gates of Judas" by the Crusaders. On the back of the trade route grew and flourished one of the richest and most powerful cities of the ancient world.

In 41 BC, following his victory at Philippi, Mark Antony sent for the Ptolemite queen of Egypt to punish her for her aid to Cassius. According to Plutarch, Cleopatra arrived "sailing up the River Cydnus in a barge with gilded stern, outspread sails of purple, and silver oars moving in time to the sound of flutes, pipes and harps. Dressed like Aphrodite, the goddess of love, Cleopatra lay beneath an awning bespangled with gold, while the boys like painted cupids stood at each side fanning her." Mark Antony was so entranced that he forgot to scold her and, instead, gave her large chunks of the Anatolian coast.

A few decades later, a local Jewish tentmaker named Saul experienced a blinding revelation on the road to Damascus and was transformed into St Paul. **St Paul's Well**, with its curative water (tested every day for purity) supposedly stands on the site of his family home in the old town. It probably has nothing to do with the Apostle, and was named by the Byzantines or the Crusaders, both of whom had a vested interest in liberally applying biblical names to relics and places of minor

pilgrimage. **Cleopatra's Gate** (also known as the Gate of the Bitch) certainly had nothing to do with the Egyptian queen. On the other hand, both the well and gate are Roman, while parts of a colonnaded **Roman road** have been uncovered in the bazaar, surrounded by narrow alleys and crumbling Ottoman houses. There's a small museum (Tue–Sun 8am–4.45pm) and more modern generations are represented by two mosques, a converted 14th-century Armenian church, the Kilise Camii, and the Makam Camii opposite. Nearby is the Kulat Paşa Medrese, built in 1570. A collection of attractive cafés surrounds the **Şelale**, a wonderfully cooling waterfall/park area on the edge of town.

Adana

A further 40km (25 miles) east, **Adana** ㉖ has grown rich on heavy industry, cotton and citrus. This is the fourth-largest city in Turkey (after İstanbul, Ankara and İzmir), with a population of over 2 million and the only commercial airport in the region. It is an extraordinary enclave of Mercedes cars and designer boutiques, its hotels and restaurants almost entirely dedicated to business travellers.

Few people outside Turkey know of the city's most awe-inspiring sight – the **Sabancı Merkez Camii** (Central Mosque), an enormous, beautiful new mosque whose white marble reflection sparkles in the Şeyhan River next to an impressive Roman bridge. Opened in 1999, it is a shade bigger than the mosque it is modelled on, İstanbul's Sultanahmet (Blue) Mosque. It boasts six minarets, a 51-metre (167ft) dome, is embellished inside with elaborate tiles and gold leaf and can hold 30,000 worshippers. The equally beautiful 16th-century **Ulu Cami**, with its black-and-white stripes and octagonal minaret, has been dwarfed.

There are few sights besides the new mosque. Next to it is the **Archaeological Museum** (Tue–Sun 8am–noon, 1–5pm, summer until 5.30pm; charge), which has some fine exhibits, includ-

ing classical and Hittite statuary, along with some Urartian artefacts. There is a well-designed but tiny **Ethnography Museum** housed in a Byzantine church (Özler Caddesi, on the roundabout opposite the Çetinkaya shopping mall; Tue–Sun 8am–noon, 1–5pm; charge).

One of the city's most eminent sons is novelist Yaşar Kemal, whose pen drips with the ochres and reds of the surrounding Çukurova Plain and the plight of the seasonal cotton-pickers who used to descend on it from the Toros mountains backing the city (now most of them are Kurds from the eastern fringes of Turkey). His most popular work, *Ince Mehmet* (Mehmet My Hawk), has been translated into a dozen languages and, along with Orhan Pamuk, he is Turkey's most celebrated author. The leftist filmmaker Yılmaz Güney also used the city and the surrounding villages as the backdrop for his works on social dislocation and poverty.

About 25km (16 miles) east of Adana, the enormous **US İncirlik Air Base** was used in the 1990 and 2003 Gulf Wars. ❏

Adana is one of the hottest places in Turkey; although temperatures rarely exceed 40°C (104°F), the high humidity makes the heat far more oppressive than in the interior.

BELOW: Adana's old town provides a striking contrast to the city's more brash, modern image.

THE HATAY

Once a backwater, the rapprochement between Turkey and Syria means cross-border trade is booming and the Hatay's role as a gateway to the Middle East is assured. The region also offers some of the best food in Turkey

Main attractions
YILAN KALESI
KARATEPE
ANTAKYA
ANTAKYA ARCHAEOLOGICAL MUSEUM
HARBIYE

BELOW: İskenderun.

Due east of Adana is a tangle of dual carriageways and motorways carrying traffic to and from Europe and the Middle East. South of this motorway lies the isolated province of Hatay, a finger of Turkish territory pushing down into the northern Levant. The topography hereabouts is dominated by the fertile Çukurova Plain, bound to the north by the foothills of the mighty Toros range, guarding the approaches to the central Anatolian plateau beyond, and to the southeast by the equally impressive Amanus mountains. Between the Amanus and the eastern shores of the Mediterranean are the lower Ziyaret and Nur ranges, between which runs the fertile Asi (Orontes) river valley.

In antiquity the region benefited from its strategic location as a Mediterranean terminus of trade routes from Central Asia, Persia and Mesopotamia allowing the development of one of the Graeco-Roman world's wealthiest cities, Antioch (modern Antakya).

Castles on the plain

Today the broad alluvial flats of the well-irrigated Çukurova are devoted to cotton and other cash crops, tended seasonally by thousands of migrant farm workers housed in shabby tent cities. Many castles still dot the region, most built during the Crusades or under Armenian rule.

Yılan Kalesi ㉗ ("Snake Castle", daily 8am–8pm) dominates the plain from its perch above the Ceyhan River. The access road is good, but the climb up to the castle is difficult. Probably built by Armenian king Leo III (ruled 1270–89), the fortress walls and battlements still stand proud, but the buildings inside are wrecked. The origin of its name is obscure; some say the castle had to be abandoned because of snakes, but a more compelling explanation ascribes it to an apocryphal "king of the Snakes", an evil half-man, half-snake who terrorised the region and was eventually overcome and killed in

Tarsus while attempting to kidnap the daughter of the king. A statue of him still stands in the centre of Tarsus.

Just beyond Yılan Kalesi, a road turns north, forking left after 35km (22 miles) to the farming village of **Kozan**, greatly diminished from its former glories as capital of Cilician Armenia. An unmarked road in the middle of town leads steeply upwards and turns through a series of outer walls to the gate of the castle, built by Leo I (1187–1219). The main walls, ringed by 44 towers, form a saddle linking the twin summits of the long, narrow hill. The capture of the castle and King Leo VI, by Egyptian Mamelukes in 1374, marked the end of the southern Armenian kingdom.

Graeco-Roman **Anavarza** (Dilekaya) is hard to reach and is perfect for those with a sense of adventure: turn off the N-400 at Ceyhan, and after 23km (14 miles) turn right towards Ayşehoca; from here it is 4km (2½ miles) to Anavarza. The site has a stadium, theatre, baths, triumphal arch, tombs and mosaics, as well as a heavily fortified Armenian citadel. Anavarza is

entirely unexcavated, and earthquakes have left rubble strewn across the paths like a giant Lego set.

Toprakkale to Karatepe

Osmaniye, 75km (46 miles) east of Adana, is a nondescript town noted for the ultra-Turkish nationalism of its inhabitants. En route you will pass close to the massive black fortress of **Toprakkale** (daily 8.30am–5pm), surrounded on all sides by a motorway junction, demonstrating graphically its crucial position at the crossroads of international trade and invasion routes. Built by the Byzantine emperor Nicophorus II Phocas (AD 963–9), the fortress was used as a base for his successful campaign against the Arabs who had held Antioch since the beginning of the 7th century. Later taken over by the Knights of St John, who remodelled it on Krak des Chevaliers (in Syria), it was eventually abandoned in 1337.

Dating back to the 8th century BC **Karatepe** ㉘ (Tue–Sun 8am–noon, 1–5pm; charge) served both as a castle and summer palace for a neo-Hittite

TIP

To make the most of Karatepe, stock up with supplies in Osmaniye and take a picnic with you to enjoy in a designated area not far from the site's entrance. It's pleasantly cool in the wooded hills and views to the lower Toros are wonderful.

BELOW: fresh produce in the Hatay.

A Taste of the Middle East

The food in the Hatay is distinctively Arab, unsurprisingly given the history of this Turkish province. Look out for hummus, a rarity elsewhere in Turkey, here dripping in melted butter and often topped by creamy pine nuts. Another delicious pulse-based puree is *bakla*, made from broad beans, garlic, olive oil, parsley, cumin and tahini (sesame) paste. Best of the dips, though, is *muhamarra*, a hot, spicy mixture of bread crumbs, ground walnut, tomato paste and hot pepper. Unusual main-courses include *Ispanak Borani*, a stew of spinach, finely-sliced meat, chick peas and yoghurt, and *köfte* (meatballs) stuffed with cheese and walnuts. *Künefe* is a delicious oven-baked dessert of spun wheat, cheese and syrup, and *kabak tatlısı* a mouth-watering candied pumpkin dish best served with a dollop of cream.

Relief sculptures in Karatepe's museum.

BELOW: Roman mosaic in Antakya's Archaeological Museum.

king, Asatiwatas. Today, the ruins stand on a U-shaped rock outcrop in an attractive forest overlooking a reservoir on the upper Ceyhan River. A 1km (²/₃-mile) circular path loops through the woods between the fort's two main gates, which stand *in situ* protected by tin roofs. Karatepe's chief claim to fame is as the place where Hittite hiero-glyphic writing was first deciphered, by comparing it with matching inscriptions in Phoenician script. These hieroglyphs document the building of the city, praising the peace and prosperity of the kingdom, and heaping divine retribution on anyone who dares disturb the gate. Other reliefs consist of wonderfully crude relief carvings, including spear-toting soldiers with hoofed feet, several grinning lions and a superb statue of the Hittite storm god Tarhunzas astride a pair of bulls.

There is a small **museum** at the entrance to Karatepe, with signboards interpreting the site. One of the chief archaeologists involved with the excavation – and its major champion – was Halet Çambel, a formidable Turkish academic. Having fenced for Turkey in the 1936 Olympic Games, she went on to spend some 45 years working on this unique site.

South to Antakya

From Osmaniye, the route south heads across the plains of **Issos**, past a turning to the Sokullu Mehmet Paşa cara-vansaray, *medrese* (religious school) and mosque complex. Directly opposite a seashore Crusader castle, the buildings are superbly lined with coloured marbles and include a marble bathhouse. Local legend claims that it was here that Jonah was cast from the belly of the whale. More certainly, blood soaks the peaceful soil, for this is where Alexander and his army of 35,000 met and defeated Persian emperor Darius and an army of over 100,000 in 333 BC, changing the course of world history.

Alexander's triumph is marked by the town he founded and named after himself immediately after the battle, **İskenderun**. Most of the modern city

was built during the French Mandate, and has a pleasant, Levantine feel with a fine promenade and good fish restaurants. There are also a scattering of still-functioning 19th-century churches which reflect the Hatay's multicultural, multi-faith heritage – Armenian, Greek Orthodox and Catholic. Unfortunately, modern İskenderun is an industrial city and port, and pollution can be a problem.

To the south, en route to Antakya, is a mountain pass known in antiquity as the Syrian Gates, now the **Belen Pass**. The location is much prized by bird-watchers in spring and autumn as it stands astride one of the world's most important migration routes.

To the south, the scenery softens and flows into green rolling hills watered by the Orontes River until the end of the valley pushes against the first outcroppings of the Lesser Lebanon Mountains. Here stands Antakya ㉙, the biblical Antioch, once amongst the most important cities in the ancient world.

Antakya: the past

Following Alexander's death, one of his lesser generals, Seleucos Nicator, established himself as the satrap (governor) of Babylon. During the internecine wars that soon flared between the rival Macedonian generals, Seleucos traded most of his territory in India for 500 war elephants, which won the day against the forces of Antigonus ("the One-Eyed") at the Battle of Ipsus in western Anatolia in 301 BC. The victory established Seleucos as a Mediterranean power. In 300 BC he built his capital across the trade route at Antioch-on-the-Orontes.

Initially conceived of as a *polis*, or city, of some 5,300 male citizens – close enough to the ideal number of Hellenic home-owners advocated by Plato – Antioch soon swelled to a population of nearly half a million, becoming the pre-eminent centre of Hellenic civilisation in the region. The Seleucids lavished attention on

their city, building theatres, baths, gymnasia, a stadium that hosted a revived Olympic Games, and other public buildings, all connected by colonnaded streets.

The Seleucids were, in due course, chased out of Asia Minor by the Romans after several disasters and defeats, starting with the Battle of Magnesia when their famed war elephants stampeded and destroyed their own troops. They next became embroiled in the unsuccessful revolt of the Maccabees in Palestine and a series of destabilising wars in the east with the Parthians, and in the west with Egypt. They were finally conquered in 83 BC by Armenian King Tigranes, son-in-law of the redoubtable scourge of Rome, Mithridates the Great. Within 20 years, Roman legions had taken possession of Antioch, which became the capital of the newly formed province of Syria.

Antioch became a much sought-after prize, changing hands on numerous

Human remains on display in the Archaeological Museum, Antakya.

BELOW: St Peter's Cave, the world's first official Christian church.

occasions over the centuries. During the Byzantine period, it was sacked with cyclical regularity by the Persians. An earthquake in the 5th century killed 250,000 people, and it finally fell to the Muslim Arabs in AD 638. Reconquered by Byzantium in 969, it fell again to the Muslims in 1084, and, after a long siege in 1097, became capital of one of the four Crusader states in the Middle East. When the Mameluke leader Baybars captured the city in 1268, he slaughtered 16,000 soldiers, hustling a further 100,000 off to slave markets in Cairo.

Antakya: the present

Today, the material remains of Antioch's former glory are few and far between. Yet the city has an intense atmosphere that seeps through the narrow alleys of the bazaar and around the minarets, making it one of the most charming and entertaining urban centres in Turkey.

The city is divided neatly in two by the Orontes River; to the west are the wide boulevards and Art Deco of the French colony (1918–38), to the east

BELOW: Antakya bazaar.

the narrow, noisy Arabic old town.

The **Archaeological Museum**, on the roundabout beside the main bridge, is home to a world-class collection of some 50 Roman mosaics (Gündüz Cad. 1; Tue–Sun 8.30am–12.30pm, 1.30–5.30pm; charge), rivalled in Turkey only by that in Gaziantep (see page 354). Most of them, carefully removed from Roman villas in nearby Daphne (see opposite), date from the 2nd and 3rd centuries, and seem to leap off the walls. Here is a life-size "Oceanus and Thetis", with the creatures of the deep clustered around them; there the "Happy Hunchback", dancing in glee with erect penis; here again the "Drunken Dionysos" swaying toward the next winery, aided by a small satyr.

Across the river, the edges of the old town, now one huge bazaar, are marked by minarets. Just across from the concrete **Rana Köprüsü** is the **Ulu Cami** (Great Mosque); up the hill, on Kurtuluş Caddesi, is the **Habib Neccar Camii**, formerly a Byzantine church. Also tucked away in the old quarter are a tiny synagogue much visited by Israeli tourists, and a Catholic church which doubles as a pension for the devout. There's also a fine 19th-century Greek Orthodox church containing some pretty Russian icons and Bibles. The Bibles are in Arabic, the language spoken by the Greek Orthodox here (along with many other Antakya natives).

During the period of Roman rule, Antioch had a large Jewish community and became a crucial staging post in the history of early Christianity. St Peter lived here from AD 47–54, frequently joined by the much travelled Paul of Tarsus and St Barnabas. As a result, the city became the seat of the powerful Patriarchate of Asia, a rival Christian centre to Constantinople – chiefly notorious for its heretic scholars. The tiny cave church of **Sen Piyer Kilisesi** (St Peter's Cave; Tue–Sun 8.30am–12.30pm, 1.30–5.30pm; charge), 2km (1½ miles) off Kurtuluş Caddesi and northeast of the city

centre, is generally regarded as the first Christian church. It was here that the saints gave their new religion a name, "Christianity" (Acts 11:26). The ornate façade was built by the Crusaders. Beyond the church, the mountain road winds 15km (9 miles) to the ruined **Citadel** (3rd century BC–10th century AD).

Daphne (Harbiye)

Some 8km (5 miles) south of Antakya on the road to Syria are the remains of the **Grove of Daphne**, known locally as **Harbiye** ㉚, a favourite place for picnics and recreation for some 3,000 years. Harbiye is, according to Greek mythology, where the nymph Daphne was turned into a laurel bush to escape the unwanted attentions of Apollo. Apollo wove himself a wreath from the leaves, the origin of the laurel of victory.

The Seleucids built a massive temple and oracle complex dedicated to Apollo in the valley, serviced by very real "nymphs" whose duties included delighting the self-deified royal family who claimed descent from the Sun God. Antony and Cleopatra were married here by Egyptian ritual in 40 BC, while the surrounding hills became a wealthy summer resort whose treasure trove of villas produced most of the mosaics now in the Hatay Museum.

In AD 362 the last non-Christian ruler of the Byzantine Empire, Julian the Apostate, visited Antioch. Not realising how out of step with the times he was, he ordered the removal of the bones of a martyred Christian bishop from the oracle of Apollo, thus incurring the wrath of the local Christian populace, who marched in protest against his actions. Despite Julian's apostasy, even in licentious Antioch the pagan age was over.

Today, its ancient buildings vanished, Daphne has been spoilt by suburban sprawl and refreshment stands: tables and chairs are set amid babbling streams of water, and plastic bags clutter the bushes; trout is the major dish.

Pillar dwellars

The early Church attracted many extremists, including a growing number of ascetic monks and other spiritual acrobats who expressed their

TIP

The approach to St Simeon's Monastery is difficult. Leave Antakya on the Samandag road. After 22km (13½ miles), look for a yellow sign and turn left. From here, a rough gravel road loops up the mountain, for about 8km (5 miles).

BELOW: the Poseidon mosaic in Antakya Archaeological Museum.

BELOW LEFT: the wider the better.
BELOW RIGHT: slave-carved sluice at Samandağ.

devotion to God by a complete and utter abnegation of the world.

The most famous of these anchorites was St Simeon the Elder, who devoted his life to sitting atop an increasingly high pillar, while pilgrims flocked to watch him rail against such human frailties as the desire for a good meal and a clean pair of sheets. Local priests even started marketing the saint's waste to the pious for a fee, with the promise that their contributions helped ensure them a place in heaven. "Simonry" was thus launched as a Christian concept.

Following Simeon the Elder's death in AD 459, a younger Simeon was so inspired that he, too, embraced the holy life. In AD 521, at the age of seven, he climbed his own column on a windy promontory of **Samandağ** (Simeon's Mountain). Over the next 25 years, as he fasted, prayed and preached, and the columns grew in height – culminating in a 13-metre (43ft) stone pillar – a thriving monastery grew around his feet. Pilgrims and meditative monks liked nothing more than to see the pious miracle of the young boy sitting atop his pillar in all weathers. An earth-

quake brought the entire complex in its present state of ruins. Today, **Aziz Simeon Manastırı ㉛** (St Simeon Monastery; open access) is remote and little visited, well suited to meditation on the relative freedom of thought of our own time.

Seleucia ad Piera

Back down the mountain, turn left for the coast and **Samandağ**, a supposed resort town which is ugly, sprawling and filthy, its beaches covered in debris and the sea polluted by chemical waste from İskenderun. About 5km (3 miles) north, the village of **Çevlik** ("The Little Cave") is built in and around Antioch's ancient port of **Seleucia ad Piera**. The area is riddled with the tombs and graves of Roman notables, as well as remnants of the harbour walls. The most impressive feat of engineering in the area is the **Titus Tüneli**, a huge canal, up to 30 metres (98ft) deep gouged from the rock during the reign of the Roman emperors Vespasian and Titus (AD 69–81) in a vain attempt to divert mountain streams from silting up the port.

Alexander

Catalyst for the spread of Greek culture, Alexander the Great was one of the most successful military campaigners of all time

Born in 356 BC, Alexander was the son of Philip II of Macedonia and Olympias (daughter of King Neoptolemus of Epirus). Brought up in court, he had the best of tutors, including none other than the great philosopher Aristotle, who taught him science, philosophy and medicine, and filled the young prince's head with the glories of Greek civilisation and a burning desire to liberate ancient Anatolia from the Persians.

Winning his first battle at the tender age of 15, Alexander was a firm favourite of the Macedonian army by the time his father was assassinated in 336 BC. His succession to the throne, at the age of only 20, was assured. Philip had already planned the invasion of Asia; Alexander paused only to tighten his grip on the Greek heartland before heading east, landing in Anatolia in 334 BC, at the head of an army of about 30,000 foot soldiers and over 5,000 cavalry.

It took a little under two years for him to drive the Persians from Anatolian soil, culminating in the decisive Battle of Issos. Unsatisfied, he pressed on, to take Egypt, Palestine and Syria, then Persia itself. He had added Afghanistan, modern Pakistan and northern India before his troops mutinied and forced him to turn back in 327 BC.

Alexander was undoubtedly a superb general, with brilliant strategic insight – and tremendous luck. He was courageous, always to be found in the thick of the action, and enormously charismatic, inspiring total devotion, at least until he pushed them too far and his homesick troops, far from home in the Punjab, refused to go any further. He was also manipulative and pragmatic, using any means at his disposal to win, from military conquest

to marriage. He was adopted by the sister of the satrap in Halikarnassos (Bodrum); while in Egypt, he sacrificed to the god, Apis. In 327 BC, he married Roxana, the daughter of the Bactrian chief Oxyartes (he later took Emperor Darius' daughter, Stateira, as his second wife). He founded some 70 new cities and was the catalyst for the great wave of Hellenisation that swept Central Europe and the Near East.

Yet he was also a Boys' Own adventurer who was far more interested in conquering new lands than ruling the ones he had. In Macedonia, he dreamed of being Greek; once in Anatolia, he coveted Persia. Having conquered Persia, he dressed in Eastern robes and demanded to be treated as a deity (one of the few occasions when his men refused his wishes). He drained Macedonia of money and manpower so thoroughly that it never recovered, and simply left local governors in place as he passed. He hated to be crossed, executing those he felt to have betrayed him, including several of his closest friends and advisers. He destroyed Thebes on a whim and torched the Persian royal palace in a drunken rage.

On 13 June 323, after a short illness, Alexander died, at the age of only 32. He had reigned for 12 years and eight months. Without his force of personality, his empire was doomed, but it is unlikely to have survived much longer, even had he remained alive; it was too big and too unwieldy, and its emperor was a warrior, not a statesman. ❏

ABOVE: Alexander defeats an army of Persians and Hindus at Ephesus. **RIGHT:** Alexander's sarcophagus.

CENTRAL ANATOLIA

The rolling steppes of inland Anatolia are home
to strangely beautiful landscapes and reminders
of long-lost civilisations

It was amid the flat, fertile steppes and gentle rolling hills of the vast central Anatolian landscape that mankind, some 10,000 years ago, is believed to have first abandoned hunting and gathering for agriculture, the momentous development that led on to the domestication of animals and the development of settlements and trade. Some of mankind's earliest settlements are found in the region. Dating back to around 6000 BC, Çatalhöyük, south of Konya, is one of the world's oldest towns. Some way north, Boğazkale was the capital of the Hittite Empire which flourished from about 1800 BC.

It has been a battleground on and off ever since, witness to campaigns by Persians, Greeks, Romans, Arabs, Seljuk Turks and Mongols amongst others. The region served as a granary to both the Roman and Byzantine empires. The capture of the plains by the Turks in the 11th century deprived the Byzantine Empire of its agricultural wealth and helped speed its downfall. Even today, the region produces most of Turkey's wheat, barley and oats: it was the abundance of naturally occurring varieties of these crops which spurred the early development of agriculture here in the first place.

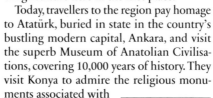

Today, travellers to the region pay homage to Atatürk, buried in state in the country's bustling modern capital, Ankara, and visit the superb Museum of Anatolian Civilisations, covering 10,000 years of history. They visit Konya to admire the religious monuments associated with the world-famous whirling dervishes. They gasp at the remains of the great Hittite settlements. Above all, they flock to Cappadocia, to delight in its extraordinary landscape of conical fairy chimneys, underground cities, anthill-like monasteries and rock-cut churches. ❏

PRECEDING PAGES: the "fairy chimneys" of Cappadocia. **LEFT:** women cooking tomato paste in a street in Tarakli. **TOP:** exhibit in the Museum of Anatolian Civilisations, Ankara. **ABOVE LEFT:** strolling in the hills above Ankara.
ABOVE RIGHT: "evil eye" charms, designed to ward off negative energy.

ANKARA

A vibrant city of more than 4 million people, Ankara is home to the Museum of Anatolian Civilisations, showcasing artefacts from the most important archaeological sites across the country

Main attractions
ULUS MEYDANI
ANKARA KALESI
MUSEUM OF ANATOLIAN
CIVILISATIONS
ALĀEDDIN CAMII
COPPER ALLEY
ATATÜRK MAUSOLEUM

BELOW: old and new buildings juxtaposed in Ankara.

In 1923, Atatürk chose Ankara to be the new capital of Turkey for several reasons; not only was it central geographically, but it was free of associations with the despised Ottomans. A thriving modern metropolis, Ankara also had a distinguished past. It was a flourishing trade and administrative centre in Roman times and is said to have been the place where King Midas, of the golden touch, was born; more certainly, in around AD 400 the city became the summer capital of the Roman emperors, who moved their administration here – at an altitude of 850 metres (2,790 ft) – to escape the baking summer heat of the coast.

Today, hilly Ankara is a residential rather than a touristic city, with its own rather subtle charms. With a population approaching 5 million, it is a place where you can eat out in style, go to a club, visit art galleries or explore an assortment of antiques shops, although it will never be able to match the glamour or interest levels of İstanbul.

Centre of a revolution

Start your sightseeing in **Ulus Meydanı** , where the enormous equestrian statue of Kemal Atatürk forms part of Turkey's history. Its inscription is written in Ottoman (Arabic) script, since the monument predates Turkey's 1928 adoption of the Latin alphabet. Downhill and across the road is the building which housed the first Grand National Assembly from where Atatürk masterminded his three-year war against the Greeks and the Western powers backing them. This is now home to the **Museum of the War of Independence** (Kürtülü Savası Müzesi; Cumhuriyet Bulvar 14, Ulus; Tue–Sun 9am–noon, 1–5pm; charge). Much further downhill, the second **Grand National Assembly** (Büyük Millet Meclisi) is also open to the public (Tue–Sun 9am–noon, 1–5pm; charge), worth a visit to see the original chamber where Atatürk would have addressed delegates.

From the Atatürk statue, head north along Çankırı Caddesi. About 50 metres/yards along, on the right, is the **Vilayet Binası** (Governorate of Ankara), while close by is the **Jülyanüs Sütunu** (Julian's Column), erected in about AD 360, probably in honour of Emperor Julian the Apostate and one of the few surviving Roman columns in Anatolia.

Further along Çankırı Caddesi, on the left, the **Hamamları** ❸ (Roman Baths; daily 8.30am–noon, 1.30–5pm; charge) consist mainly of foundations, although pillars, tombstones and other remnants of the Roman city are also displayed here. The dated Armenian inscriptions on some of the tombstones show that they were reused in the 19th century.

A short detour from Julian's Column will take you to the **Hacı Bayram Camii**, built beside the Temple of Augustus. This is one of the oldest mosques in the city, dating back to the 15th century. Inside is the 15th-century tomb of Hacı Bayram Veli, head of a dervish order that continues to help the poor and needy.

The **Augustus Tapınağı** ❸ (Temple of Augustus) was built by the Phrygians and co-opted for the Roman emperor. His Byzantine descendants later turned it into a Christian church. Near the entrance a long Roman inscription, written in Latin and Greek, relates Augustus' deeds. It remains one of our most important sources of knowledge about the emperor and his times.

Walk up Hisarparkı Caddesi towards the citadel. On the left are the fragmentary foundations of a small **amphitheatre**, discovered in 1984.

The citadel

Between AD 622, when it was taken by the Persians, and AD 838, when it was conquered by the Arabs, Ankara was under constant threat from invaders. Its defenders numbered only a fraction of the population of the earlier city, and rather than quarry new stone, they reused older material to strengthen their walls. Until 1915, the open ground between the inner and outer walls was the Armenian quarter, and several hundred of their number still live in the city.

Julian's Column, home to generations of aristocratic storks.

BELOW LEFT: window-shopping in Ankara.
BELOW: a haircut, shave and update on the gossip.

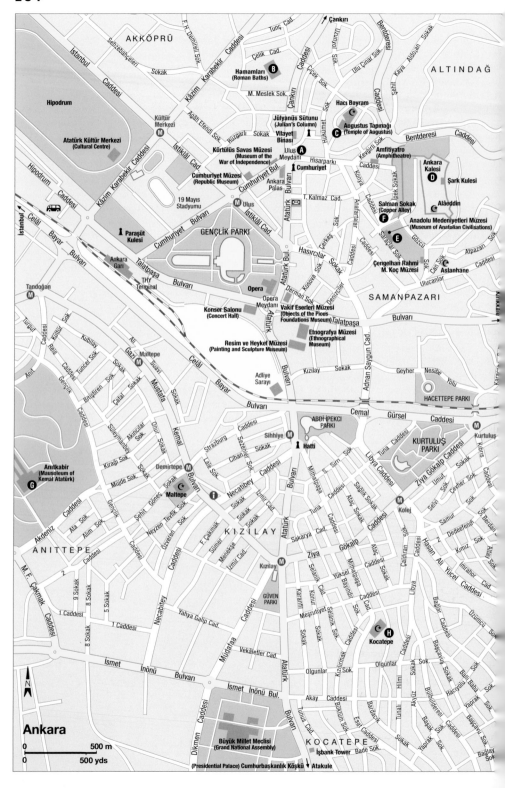

Ankara

0 ────── 500 m

0 ────── 500 yds

The western walls of **Ankara Kalesi**
D (Hısarparkı Caddesi; charge) are
the most spectacular, with a line of
triangular towers jutting out from the
main structure, rather like the prows of
a line of ships. Step through the main
gate and turn left onto a winding path
leading through narrow streets where
the houses have hardly changed in the
last hundred years. This route takes you
to the innermost point of the castle.

The **walls**, built in the mid-7th
century, did not always prove effective.
In AD 838, the Arabs, under Caliph
Mutasim, sacked the city and killed
or took prisoner its entire population. About 10 years later, the Emperor
Michael III restored the walls.

Walk through the winding streets
down to the south gate of the inner
walls and, a few metres above the road,
you will see the remains of a large **tower**
which was probably the residence of
the Byzantine governor. To the right is
the **Alâeddin Camii**, a charming little
mosque adorned with classical columns;
it is one of the earliest Muslim buildings
in the city. Look carefully and you will
also see a number of Byzantine crosses
above the windows. These were intended
as charms against hostile Islamic invaders from the south and east.

In Ottoman times, the Muslim population lived inside the walls and the
non-Muslims, the bulk of the city's
merchants, around the perimeter. Their
houses, with painted plaster walls and
elaborate woodwork, one or two of
them dating back to the 18th century, are
typical of those found in the older cities
all across Turkey. Nowadays they are usually divided up and inhabited by several
families. Many of those in and around
the Ankara citadel have been restored
to their past splendour and turned into
gift shops, coffee houses and restaurants
with stunning views over the city.

Carry on to the south gate in the
outer walls to reach a square in front of
the 19th-century **clock tower**. Across
the road, the **Cengelhan Rahmi M Koç
Museum** (Tue–Fri 10am–5pm, Sat–Sun
10am–7pm; charge), housed in a *kervan-*
saray built in 1522, houses exhibits on
everything from transport to medicine
collected from around the world.

The Museum of Anatolian Civilisations

Turning right from the entrance to the
castle and heading downhill brings
you to Ankara's premier attraction, the
Museum of Anatolian Civilisations
E (Anadolu Medeniyetleri Müzesi;
Kadife Sokak; tel: 312-324 3160; Tue–
Sun 9am–5pm; charge). Housed in
a former *han* (a covered market with
workshops) built by Grand Vizier Mahmut Paşa, this is one of Turkey's finest
museums. Exhibits have the benefit
of English labelling. It focuses on the
pre-classical civilisations of Anatolia,
and contains artefacts from various digs
around the country. The displays begin
with the Palaeolithic, take in Neolithic
Çatalhöyük, the Assyrian trading colony
of Küllepe and pre-Hittite Alacahöyük,
before progressing to Phrygian and
Roman sites. There are also special collections from the Hittite and Urartian
eras. The contents of the Great Tumulus
at Gordion include some fine Phrygian

TIP

If you are staying in
Ankara for a few days
and use the Metro to get
into the centre of town,
buy a block of five
tickets which can be
used on buses as well.

BELOW: Sultanhan
monument with
Luwian hiero-
glyphics at the
Museum of
Anatolian
Civilisations.

Witness the changing of the guard at the Mausoleum of Kemal Atatürk, Ankara.

BELOW RIGHT:
Ankara's famous
Copper Alley.

woodcarvings still in astonishingly good condition after 2,700 years. Particular things to look out for include Neolithic frescoes from Çatalhöyük, vast Hittite stone sculptures, and the emblems of the Bronze Age reindeer gods found in Alacahöyük. Allow two or three hours to do it all justice.

Copper Alley

If you turn left from the castle entrance you will come to a recently restored street which might seem more at home in a small Anatolian town than in the country's capital. Many of the shops here sell wool and goatskins, a reminder that "Angora" – the old form of the city's name – was a world-famous wool centre.

Continue downhill to reach the 12th-century Seljuk **Aslanhane Camii**, whose brick minaret still retains traces of the blue ceramics that once covered it. Inside, the mosque, built upon the foundations of a Roman temple, features an elaborately carved wooden roof, held up by a forest of wooden pillars. At the top of each column is a reused classical capital, some of which

came from the lost temple. To the left, facing downhill, a stone doorway with a lion beside it leads into an old dervish *tekke*, a medieval lodge whose Roman stonework suggests that it was also built onto a Roman structure.

The side streets in this part of town are full of craftsmen's shops, catering to the needs of an agricultural population coming in from the villages. Turn into **Salman Sokak**, to the right of the Aslanhane Mosque, and you are in one of Ankara's most famous shopping attractions. **Copper Alley** 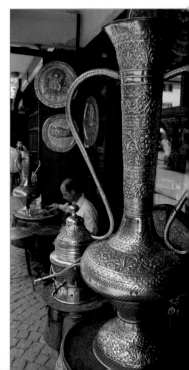 (as Salman Sokak is known among Ankara's foreign residents, even though *salman* means "straw") is exactly what its name suggests. You can find brand-new copper here, but old pewter plates and copper jugs (lined with tin if they are to be used rather than as ornaments), candlesticks, clocks, antiques and curios of all sorts are also on display. In the past, ancient coins and other valuable objects would be in some of these shops, but these days most of the "ancient objects" on sale are fakes. If you want something genuine, try a 19th-century plate with a Greek, Ottoman or Armenian inscription.

Atatürk's last resting place

All travellers to Ankara should visit the **Anıtkabir** Ⓖ, the **Mausoleum of Kemal Atatürk** (Anıt Cad., Tandoğan; tel: 312-231 7975; daily 9am–12.30pm, 1.30–5.30pm). Official visitors never miss this national treasure, as protocol requires that they pay their respects to the founder of modern Turkey here. The first thing that the leader of any new Turkish government does upon taking office is pay a visit to the mausoleum.

The mausoleum is partly designed to imitate Hittite and ancient Anatolian architecture. Each province of Turkey contributed stone to the main hall which contains Atatürk's tomb. His body, however, is not kept in the stone catafalque, but is buried in a chamber beneath it. Within the complex, the **Anıtkabir Museum** (charge) contains books from Atatürk's library, his uniforms and even some of his visiting cards. Vehicles used by the great man are parked outside. On the opposite side of the square is the tomb of Atatürk's deputy and comrade-in-arms, İsmet İnönü, who become Turkey's second president.

Ankara's other attractions

As befits a capital city, Ankara has several museums worth visiting. The newest is the **Objects of the Pious Foundations Museum** (Vakıf Eserleri Müzesi; Tue–Sun 9am–noon, 1–5pm; free), which displays some of the magnificent old carpets from mosques around the country. For Turkish handicrafts and costumes, go to the **Ethnographical Museum** (Etnografya Müzesi; Opera Meydanı; daily 8.30am–12.30pm, 1.30–5.30pm; charge). Next door is the **Painting and Sculpture Museum** (Resim ve Heykel Müzesi; Opera Meydanı; Tue–Sun 9am–noon, 1–5pm; charge), which exhibits the work of most of the best known 19th-and 20th-century Turkish artists.

The **State Concert Hall** (Konser Salonu), near the railway station, stages Presidential Symphony Orchestra concerts every Friday night and Saturday morning in winter. Other theatres include the state opera, two state theatres, and a whole host of smaller private theatres, many of them near the Ankara Sanat Tiyatrosu, just off İzmir Caddesi near the Atatürk Bulvarı at **Kızılay**.

The main shopping areas are around Kızılay, and along Tunalı Hilmi Caddesi in Kavaklıdere. New shopping malls are springing up all over Ankara; one of the most convenient for visitors is the Karum Centre, near the Hilton and Sheraton hotels. Çankaya, the area around Ataküle, and Orhan Mumcu Caddesi have upmarket stores.

Kocatepe Mosque

One of the most impressive sites in the city is the **Kocatepe Camii** ⓗ, on the hill southeast of Kızılay. Ankara's largest mosque, the shrine combines the appearance of 16th-century Islamic architecture and 20th-century technology. A replica of İstanbul's Blue Mosque, with four minarets instead of six, it took 20 years to build and opened to the public in the early 1980s. To enter, take the staircases up to the white marble courtyard. In a modern twist, there is a multistorey car park

and shopping mall underneath it.

Many government ministries are bunched together south of Kızılay, on either side of Atatürk Bulvarı, the main street running north–south through Ankara. Further south, on the right-hand side of the same road, are the buildings of Turkey's parliament – the **Büyük Millet Meclisi** (Grand National Assembly).

Most of the foreign embassies are located along Atatürk Bulvarı and Cinnah Caddesi, which continues uphill to Çankaya and is crowned by the presidential palace, **Cumhurbaşkanlık Köşkü**. In the well-laid-out grounds is a *köşk*, which was **Atatürk's residence** (Sun and holidays 1.30–5.30pm). Also here is **Atakule** (10am–10pm, until 3am if restaurant is open), a 125-metre (413ft) tower with a shopping centre and revolving restaurant on the top floor, one of Ankara's best-known landmarks.

Gençlik Parkı (Youth Park), located between the railway station and Ulus, is one of the city's most popular recreational areas, with many moderately priced bars and outdoor restaurants beside an artificial lake. ❏

Rail enthusiasts should head for the small Railway Museum on Platform 1 of the station, which houses the carriage given to Atatürk by Hitler, and the rusting collection of old steam engines (many German and American) in the Open Air Museum across the tracks.

BELOW: Kocatepe Camii, Ankara's largest mosque.

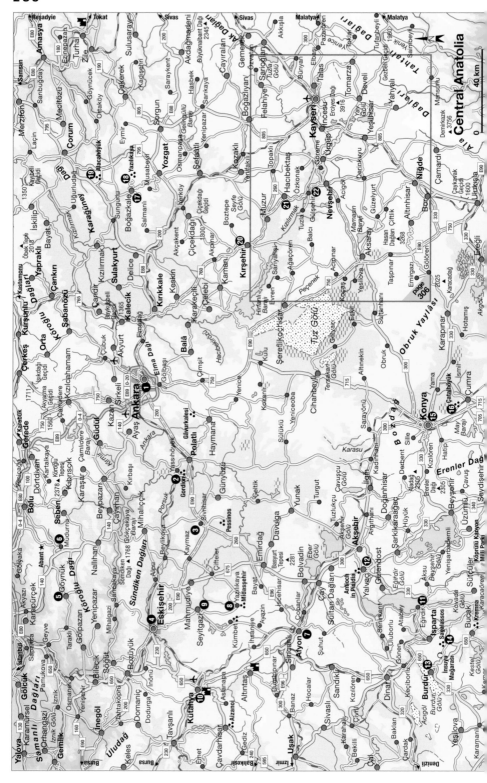

NORTHWEST ANATOLIA

The population may be sparse and much of the landscape may consist of bare hillsides with hardly a tree to be seen, yet this was once the heartland of the formidable kingdom of ancient Phrygia

ree roads head roughly northwest out of Ankara heading for the Sea of Marmara and İstanbul. The first, via Eskişehir, and the second, a remote ramble through the mountains to Beypazarı, Nallıhan and Göynük, connect at Bilecik; the third follows the main highway almost due north into the Black Sea region.

Due west from Ankara

In a famous corruption trial in ancient Rome, the orator Cicero – who was defending a sticky-fingered Roman governor of Phrygia – managed to ridicule the prosecution witnesses by describing them as "ignorant Phrygians who had never seen a tree in their lives". Cicero's other cruel joke comes to mind as you take the E-90 highway out of **Ankara** ① through Polatlı and due west to Eskişehir. This is one of the great roads of history: Alexander the Great, the crusaders and most of the great armies of the Byzantine and Ottoman empires have travelled along it at some time.

About an hour out of Ankara, the town of **Polatlı** is chiefly notable for having been the furthest point reached by the Greek invaders of Anatolia in 1921. The high tidemark of the Greek invasion is, quite literally, marked in concrete on the hill to the north of town. Today, Polatlı is the headquarters of an army tank brigade. It also makes

the perfect base for visiting Gordion.

Myths and legends

About 10km (6 miles) northwest of Polatlı, at Yassıhöyük, lie the ruins of **Gordion** ② (daily 8.30am–5.30pm, Tue–Sun in winter; charge), capital of Phrygia during the reign of the fabled King Gordius and his golden son, Midas, in about 800 BC. It remained a moderately important city into classical times, though it was later eclipsed by Ankara. Gordion is chiefly of interest to true archaeology enthusiasts. There

Main attractions
GORDION
SIVRIHISAR
ESKİŞEHİR
BETPAZARI
KIZILCAHAMAM
MUDURNU

RIGHT: donkeys are still used as working animals in the smaller villages.

The highly intricate Gordian Knot, which tied together the yoke and pole of Gordius' chariot, was kept in the temple for 500 years. Tradition said it could be undone only by the future conqueror of Asia. The puzzle defeated all contenders until Alexander the Great simply sliced the knot in two with his sword.

BELOW: ruined walls at Gordion, ancient Phrygia's capital.

are no romantic classical remains here. There is also a lack of shade, which can pose a problem if you visit in summer.

The most impressive features today are the huge burial tumuli of the Phrygian kings, excavated in the 1950s. The tomb of Gordius is an astonishing 50 metres (164ft) high and 300 metres (985ft) across. When first excavated, what was then believed to be the tomb of Midas was filled with a vast variety of objects, although, disappointingly, nothing golden. A tunnel has been constructed to enable visitors to walk into the centre of the mound, where they can inspect a burial chamber built out of huge cedar trunks which the centuries have turned to stone.

The actual remains of the king and the objects buried with him can now be viewed in Ankara's Museum of Anatolian Civilisations *(see page 285)*. In the museum across the road you can also see the world's earliest mosaic, made out of black-and-white pebbles, while further along the road the walls of the Phrygian capital have been dug out from within the mound that eventually swamped the city.

Sivrihisar ❸ lies about 30km (1 miles) further down the road, whic forks at this point: the northern for runs due west to Eskişehir, while th E-96 branches south for Afyon, an eventually the south and west coast Backed by dramatically craggy rock the town has an interesting 13th century **Ulu Camii** (Great Mosque full of soaring wooden columns cappe with old Roman masonry, a couple c Ottoman mosques, and the ruins of large 19th-century Armenian church Many of the fine old Ottoman house are currently being restored, althoug the town lacks a decent hotel. It's a easy excursion to the village of **Nasre tin Hoca**, the pretty, rural birthplace c Nasreddin Hodja *(see panel, below)*, 13th-century "wise fool" whose imag crops up all over.

About 19km (12 miles) south o Sivrihisar, at **Ballıhisar**, are the Roma ruins of **Pessinos** (open access), one c the three great centres of Roman Gala tia – the region settled by the Cel ("Gauls"; *see pages 33–34)*. Pessinos wa situated in the middle of the Phrygia plain, and historians believe that it wa

Nasreddin Hodja

Aphilosopher and humourist, Nasreddin Hodja (1208–85) lived in northwest Anatolia when the region was under siege by Mongol invaders. He studied in the religious schools at Sivrihisar and Akşehir, a city 200km (130 miles) southwest of Ankara, and later died in Akşehir, where he is buried.

Turkey's most famous folk hero, Nasreddin Hodja figures in jokes throughout the Middle East. His stories, many of which end with a moral twist or clever epigram, are particularly popular among the Turkic peoples. Set in private homes, marketplaces, bazaars, streets, courts and mosques, they describe the minutiae of everyday life, and his subtle jokes and tales exemplify the common sense of the Anatolian people without patronising them.

A typical story goes like this. "One day Hodja brought home a kilo of delicious lamb and asked his wife to prepare it for the evening. Then he set off to the teahouse to while away the rest of the day. Unable to wait, his wife cooked the meat and shared it with her friends. Returning home, the salivating Hodja was told that the cat had eaten the meat. Puzzled, Hodja grabbed the family's mangy cat and put it on the scales. To his surprise, it weighed exactly one kilo, whereupon he barked at his wife, 'If this is the meat, then where is the cat?'"

andoned for the relative safety of ⊽rihisar during the age of invasions ⊓ich began after AD 600.

In recent years, archaeologists have ⊔covered a temple dedicated to Cybele, ⊇ Roman equivalent of the Anatolian ⊃ther goddess, Kubaba. Fragments of ⊐ious Roman buildings are scattered ⊐oss an extensive area around the ⊇am running through the present-day ⊔age of Ballıhisar, although the ruins ⊇ by no means as dramatic as those to ⊔ found elsewhere.

⊔toman heartland

⊔**kişehir** ❹, the Roman and Byzantine ⊃rylaeum, lies about another hour's ⊔ive west of Sivrihisar. Its name means ⊐ld City" in Turkish, and the author-⊇s have been hard at work restoring ⊓me of its old Ottoman houses to ⊇cover some sense of that past. There ⊇ a good provincial **museum** (Hasan ⊔latkan Bulvarı; daily 8.30am–noon, ⊔0–5pm; charge) with mosaics and ⊔tuettes of the Roman period. The ⊇**erschaum Museum** (daily 10am–⊔m; charge), in the Yunus Emre Cul-⊐re Building, contains a collection

of local meerschaum pipes; modern versions are sold nearby. The meer-schaum mines are located at nearby Sepetçi Köyü and Kozlubel.

Today, the city is chiefly a regional industrial powerhouse with factories turning out cement, textiles, clothing and household appliances. Eskişehir also hosts the state railways factory for diesel engine locomotives, a big uni-versity and Turkey's largest air-force base, with F-16 jet fighters constantly flying over the city and countryside on military manoeuvres. Visitors will notice many local people with orien-tal features. They are the descendants of Crimean Tatars who settled in this part of the country after the Turkish-Russian War of 1878.

A little way west is **Inönü**, the scene of two decisive battles in Turkey's War of Independence against the invad-ing Greeks after World War I. Directly north is the Sakarya valley and the roll-ing landscape from which the Ottoman Empire burst onto the world stage. The small town of **Söğüt** has the distinction of being the birthplace of the world-famous Ottoman dynasty which ruled

Turkish Independence War memorial at Inönü.

BELOW: spring in Anatolia.

TIP

Head for Beypazarı on a Saturday to witness the lively market where women sell everything from colourful fabrics to carrot-flavoured *helva*.

Turkey, the Balkans and much of the Middle East until the early 20th century. The first of the great war leaders and father of Sultan Osman I was a frontier warrior named Ertuğrul Gazi who ruled a minor fiefdom in Söğüt in the late 13th century *(see page 44)*. His **tomb** can be visited (daily 9am–5pm). Outside, the area is decorated with the busts of the greatest rulers of all 17 Turkic states.

To the east, across the river and due north of Eskişehir, the village of **Mihalgazi** was home to a Byzantine Greek warrior chief called Mihal Gazi who joined forces with Osman and helped him in his meteoric rise to power. Neglected and forlorn, his grave lies in a grassy meadow to the south of the village. It is a reminder of how the first Ottoman ruler made the transition from village raider to self-styled sultan in a single generation – and how easily his allies were forgotten in the heady rush to power.

Keep heading northwest from Söğüt and you come to **Bilecik**, where Osman's wife and his father-in-law, Edibali, lie buried. A few crumbling fragments of wall mark the site of the Byzantine castle which was captured by one of the very first Ottoman armies.

Northwest from Ankara

This route is definitely the back road from Ankara, leading through remote hills to a succession of small hill and mountain towns – **Beypazarı, Göynük, Taraklı** and **Murdurnu** – so little disturbed by time that they have managed to preserve much of their 19th-century appearance intact.

Under the guidance of a go-ahead local mayor, Beypazarı has carved out a niche for itself as a lovely little Ottoman town with a lively market within easy day-trip reach of Ankara. **Göynük ⑤** deserves to be better known than it is. The approach road is a lonely winding track through the mountains. Once there, you can visit the **Tomb of Akşemsettin**, the first *hodja* to give the call to prayer from Aya Sofya after the fall of Constantinople in 1453. It is lavishly maintained with gifts from the Muslim world. Visit on a Monday morning to witness the colourful local market to which women from surrounding villages bring butter and cheese for sale.

BELOW: the mountain town of Göynük.

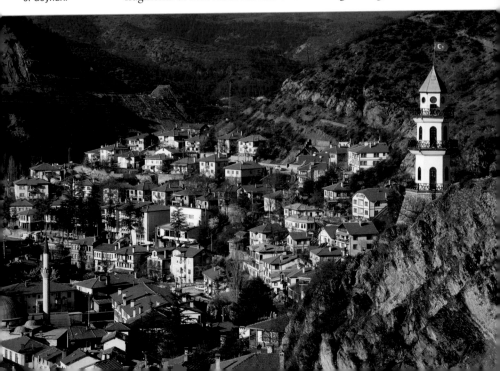

At the far end of the mountain
[ro]ad, just before you reach Bilecik, are
[Ta]raklı and **Gölpazarı**, with a most
[un]usual early Ottoman *kervansaray*,
[li]ke Beypazarı and Göynük, Taraklı is
[fu]ll of wonderful old Ottoman houses
[th]at go largely unseen by foreigners.

[Th]e Ankara–Istanbul
[Hi]ghway

[Th]e main route between Ankara and
[Ist]anbul consists of two parallel highways
[– t]he Trans-European Motorway (TEM)
[an]d the E-89. The TEM is a motorway
[wi]th very few exits; the E-89 is one of the
[m]ost scenic routes in the country, run-
[ni]ng past sometimes gloriously wooded
[an]d mountainous countryside.

Kızılcahamam, with its hills and
[w]oods, is a favourite picnic and resort
[sp]ot, famous for its mineral waters, Turk-
[is]h bath and hot springs. This is also a
[fa]vourite area for wild-boar hunting.

Turn off the main road to reach the
[to]wn of **Çerkeş**. On your way north
[to] the Black Sea region, with its steep,
[wo]oded valleys, you pass the seldom
[vi]sited towns of **Tosya** and **Osmancık**,
[th]e majestic **İlgaz Mountains**, with

their small ski resort, and
Safranbolu, filled with
delightful Ottoman houses
(see page 319).

Alternatively, keep going
along the main road to
Dörtdivan and take the side
road leading to **Kartalkaya**,
a small winter-sports resort
with a dozen ski-lifts and
three hotels. There is little
reason to stop in **Bolu**, a nondescript Anatolian town, but about
32km (20 miles) west, tucked away
in the woods, is the spa-and-hotel
complex of **Abant**, on the shores of
a jade-coloured crater lake. Nearby
Mudurnu ➏ is like a cut-down version of Safranbolu, with a delightful
market, a wonderful old hamam and
many magnificent, if crumbling, Ottoman mansions.

North of the road are the gourmet
centre of **Mengen**, known for the quality of the chefs turned out by its catering colleges, and the **Yedigöller Milli
Parkı** (Seven Lakes National Park),
whose much-photographed lakeside
walks are best visited in autumn. ❑

*Safranbolu gets its
name from the saffron
flower, which grows
locally, and is used as
a dye and in cooking.*

BELOW: bleak
midwinter on the
central plains.

SOUTHWEST ANATOLIA

İstanbul
Ankara

Lakes and mountains, poppies and pottery, the birthplace of Mevlana is a little-visited region rewarding for the adventurous traveller to explore

Main attractions
AFYON
PHRYGIAN VALLEY
KÜTAHYA
EĞIRDIR GÖLÜ
SAGALASSOS
KREMNA
KONYA
MEVLANA TEKKESI (KONYA)
ÇATALHÖYÜK

BELOW: Afyon's legal opium harvest colours the summer landscape purple and white.

Turkey's vast size means that most travellers rarely venture into Southwest Anatolia – a great shame since the Eğirdir region boasts some fabulous lake and mountain scenery. In October when the trees take on autumnal hues this is one of the most beautiful places in Turkey. Ditto the area around Afyon in early summer when the poppies are in bloom. Perhaps the most-visited town here is Konya, birthplace of the revered Mevlana and the whirling dervishes, but Kütahya, further north, also receives a steady stream of visitors keen to admir the produce of its ceramics industry.

Afyon, opium centre

In the lush green area around **Afyo** ❼, southwest of Ankara, the farme grow May-flowering poppies for the opium. The name Afyon even mea "opium" in Turkish, and this is t centre of the country's legal opiu industry, with a state-run factory whi refines opium for the pharmaceutic industry. This is also one of the ma production centres for Turkish marb which is excavated, cut and polishe here, and then used to make floorin gravestones and work surfaces.

The distinctive black crag at the ce tre of Afyon has helped make this o of the best-known towns of provinci Turkey. There is thought to have be a Hittite stronghold here, and the hig rock was also used as a refuge by t Byzantines during their wars again the Arabs. The climb up some 700 ste to **Afyon Castle** (open access) is not f the faint-hearted, but the town belo has many beautiful 19th-century Ott man houses and several fine mosque including the 13th-century Seljuk **U Camii** (Great Mosque) whose roof supported by a sea of wooden colum

Also worth a look are the **Kuyu Mescit** (Mosque of the Well), with tiled minaret, and the 14th-centu **Kubbeli Mescit**. (A *mescit* is a sma simple mosque.) The **Archaeologic Museum** (Kurtuluş Caddesi; Tue–Su

8am–noon, 1–5.30pm; charge) houses relics of the Hittite, Phrygian and Lydian periods found locally.

The Phrygian Valley

A series of villages that once made up the heart of the ancient Phrygian kingdom of King Midas lies north of Afyon in the **Frig Vadisi** (Phrygian Valley). Allow at least two days to explore the valley properly, and don't forget to pack a picnic as the scenery en route is wonderful. **Ayazin** offers rock-cut churches similar to those of Göreme in Cappadocia, while **Kümbet** has a Phrygian tomb from the Roman period with lions carved on it.

Most splendid of all the monuments, however, are those at **Yazılıkaya** ❽ (Midasşehir; daily 9am–5pm), where the flat landscape suddenly gives way to hills and woods, providing the once-great Phrygian city of Metropolis with a hilltop landscape worthy of an Italian Renaissance painting. The most striking sight here is the giant **Midas Monument** (*c.* 6th century BC) with a curious and undeciphered inscription in the Phrygian alphabet. It probably contained a shrine to Cybele (also known as Mida nd, and according to Greek legend, the mother of King Midas). On the north slope the Hittite reliefs show that the site has a history stretching back at least 1,000 years before Midas. On the summit is a stone throne, which, according to the locals, is where King Midas sat with his wives.

About 30km (19 miles) north of Yazılıkaya, a superb Bektaşi *tekke* (convent) crowns the hill to the west of the town of **Seyitgazi** ❾. In some ways, it is even more spectacular – and certainly larger – than the headquarters of the Bektaşi organisation at Hacıbektaş (*see page 303*).

Seyitgazi is named after a legendary Arab warrior who died in the siege of Afyon in AD 740, during the Arab-Byzantine Wars. The story relates how a Byzantine princess fell in love with him, and seeing some soldiers creeping in his direction, dropped a stone

to signal the danger. Alas, it fell on his head and killed him. His tomb, which is about three times the length of a normal man, can be visited. Beside it a smaller one is said to be that of the princess.

Kütahya: ceramic capital

Kütahya ❿ is one of the most picturesque towns in Turkey, with rambling old streets and a **citadel** ringed by a Byzantine fortress. From the 17th century onwards, Kütahya became the home of the best faïence and pottery in the land, its tiles used on countless mosques, its jugs and bowls found in every up-market home. The craft has now been revived and there is an interesting small **Tile Museum** (Gediz Caddesi; Tue–Sun 8am–noon, 1.30–5.30pm; charge) in a former soup kitchen behind the 15th-century **Ulu Camii** (Great Mosque), one of several fine mosques.

Nearby, housed in a theological school, is the small **archaeological museum** (Tue–Sun 8.30am–noon, 1.30–5.30pm; charge). The **Kossuth Evi** (Tue–Sun 8.30am–noon, 1–6pm; charge), a fine Ottoman mansion belonging to

A giant urn at the town entrance advertises Kütahya's main industry.

BELOW: Kütahya's ceramic factories still flourish.

Towering walls still ring the lakeside city of Eğirdir.

BELOW: Lake Eğirdir's reedy shores attract thousands of migrating birds.

a Hungarian revolutionary, which is preserved as it was in the mid-19th century, is also worth a visit.

Some 27km (15 miles) to the southwest is **Çavdarhisar** and the site of ancient **Aizanoi** (9am–noon, 1–5pm; charge), with a fine temple dedicated to Zeus. In antiquity, the city claimed to have been the birthplace of the father of the gods. Seldom visited, this is the best-preserved of Anatolia's Zeus temples and well worth the effort of getting here. There is a huge vaulted chamber beneath.

The Lake District

South of Afyon is a green and attractive region commonly known as Turkey's "Lake District". There are at least seven significant lakes, and the area is well known for its birdlife.

Isparta is chiefly famous for rose oil (attar of roses), an essential ingredient in perfume. The town had a large Greek population until 1924, and a few ruined churches can still be found in the backstreets. A winding hour-long drive brings you to the town of **Eğirdir** ⓫ at the southern tip

of beautiful **Eğirdir Gölü**, the second largest freshwater lake in Turkey. The town was founded by the Hittites and became a regular stop on the King's Way, an important trade route between Ephesus and Babylon in the 5th century BC. Two small islands are joined to the town by a causeway, and the further of them, **Yeşilada**, has several attractive *pansiyons* whose owners can usually arrange boat trips on the lake. The ruins of an old **Seljuk fort** stand on the mainland near the 15th-century **Ulu Camii** (Great Mosque) and the **Dündar** *medrese* (religious school), which has a beautifully decorated portal but is now used as a shopping centre.

The drive up the more attractive eastern side of the lake leads to **Yalvaç** ⓬, the ancient Antioch in Pisidia and much visited by Christian pilgrims because of its associations with St Paul. According to the New Testament, it was here that Paul gave his first recorded sermon. This was so successful that the Gentiles pleaded with him to repeat it the following Saturday and the synagogue was packed. The Jews, out of envy, drove Paul from the city.

Antioch in Pisidia (9am–5pm; large), founded between 301 and 280 BC on the site of a Phrygian settlement by Seleucus Nicator, later became a Roman colony for veteran soldiers. Today the most significant remains on the site are of a temple to Augustus, which was once surrounded by a semicircular colonnaded arcade. Huge baths, a nymphaeum, the aqueduct and an early synagogue (later a church) are also visible. The small **museum** (Tue–Sun 9am–noon, 1.30–5.30pm; charge) in Yalvaç houses relics from the site and the nearby temple to the god Men.

You may wish to continue on from here along the country road which loops back round the top of the lake and heads southwest to **Keçiborlu** via **Senirkent**. Continue west from here, and the road to Denizli and Pamukkale, with its famous travertines, passes **Dinar**, a town levelled by an earthquake in 1995, and **Acıgöl**, a large, sterile salt lake. Alternatively, head south, down the scrubby shore of the vast saline expanse of **Burdur Gölü**, to the town of Burdur.

Burdur ⓑ itself is dull, but it does have a 14th-century **Ulu Camii** (Great Mosque) and a small **museum** (Gazi Caddesi; Tue–Sun 8.30am–noon, 1.30–3.30pm; charge) which contains finds from Kremna and Sagalassos (see below), and Hacılar, a site dating back to 6000 BC.

About 10km (6 miles) south of the town, signposted left off the main road, the well-lit **İnsuyu Mağarası** (daily 8.30am–6pm; charge) is one of the few caves in Turkey that is open to the public, with 600 metres (190ft) of tunnels, seven underground lakes and dramatic displays of stalactites.

Ancient Pisidia

Some 25km (16 miles) east of Burdur, off the N-685 to Isparta, follow signs through the village of Ağlasun to find the ruins of **Sagalassos** ⓓ (daylight hours; charge), which was the second city of Pisidia after Antioch and is currently under excavation and reconstruction. Set 1,500 metres (4,920ft) above sea level on the slopes of craggy Mount Akdağ, it is potentially one of the most complete ancient cities in Asia Minor – its superb 9,000-seat theatre remains just as an earthquake left it. The city centre, including a library, two nymphaea, the upper forum, which includes a *bouleterion* (circular debating chamber) and a monument to Emperor Claudius, and the lower forum with huge baths, is almost completely excavated. Partly reconstructed finds are assembled in a purpose-built workshop in Ağlasun which is slated to become a museum. Superb computer reconstruction drawings illustrate the major vistas and explain the site; the work is a technical masterpiece, and includes investigation of local land-use, road and water systems and plant and animal life in early historical times.

If you keep heading south towards Antalya, you'll reach **Bucak**, the access point for the ruins of **Kremna** (open access), about 13 miles (8 miles) away. The approach road winds attractively along a pine-clad valley to a spectacular clifftop city overlooking the Aksu

Kremna has yielded an account of how the Romans succeeded in retaking the town from a ruthless brigand named Lydius. An inscription tells how Lydius drove out of the city all those too old or too young to be of use. The Romans, however, drove them back, whereupon Lydius hurled them into the ravines around the city. Lydius' downfall came when one of his commanders defected and pointed out to the Romans a gap in the wall.

BELOW: in summer, the salt lake of Tuz Gölü dries to a shimmering pan.

Ceramic plates made in Kütahya can be found for sale throughout the country.

BELOW: Mevlana's tomb, Konya.

Çayı. A massive earthwork used by the Romans to reach the height of the walls when they were besieging the town is still visible today, but many of the buildings have been badly damaged. The walls of the bathhouse, however, stand to their full height and house some fine inscribed statue bases.

Konya

The road south from Ankara to Konya forks off from the Mersin–Adana road (E-90) after about 100km (62 miles) of rather dull scenery. To the west of the road is the vast salt lake known as **Tuz Gölü**, a favourite spot for goose-hunters (note that the lake is more accessible from the road to Aksaray).

Konya ⓯ (Ikonium) was the capital of the Seljuk Empire between 1071 and 1308, and remains a centre of Sufic teaching and a pilgrimage destination for devout Sunni Muslims. Visited by St Paul several times around AD 50, it has become an industrial centre in the last few decades and is now ringed with bleak concrete suburbs which wall in the Seljuk monuments at its heart. The citizens are renowned for their piety

– alcohol is not sold in stores or restaurants, even though one of Turkey's biggest breweries is, ironically, located here. Konya has been a stronghold for Islamic parties since the start of the Republican era.

In the city centre is the **Alâeddin Tepesi** (Aladdin's Hill), which has been built up by successive settlement over the centuries. On the top are the last remaining walls of the **Sultan Sarayı** (Palace of the Seljuk Sultans) and the 12th- and 13th-century **Alâeddin Camii**, once home to some of the oldest carpets in the world (they're mostly in the Museum of Turkish and Islamic Arts in İstanbul now). Of the other major Seljuk monuments in town, the **Karatay Medrese**, an Islamic school built in 1251, is now a **Ceramics and Tile Museum** (Hastane Caddesi; daily 9am–noon, 1–5pm; charge) housing, among other things, tiles depicting distinctly oriental-looking Seljuk princesses. The **Archaeological Museum** (Sahip Ata Caddesi; Tue–Sun 9am–noon, 1–5pm; charge) has some impressive ancient sarcophagi and some of the finds from nearby Çatal

öyük, although the finest have been carted off to Ankara.

Home of the dervishes

Every visitor to Konya wants to see the lovely turquoise-domed **Mevlana Tekkesi** (Kışla Caddesi; daily 9am–5pm, Mon from 10am; charge), the home of the whirling dervishes (*see panel below*). At the heart of the complex is the tomb of Mevlana ("Our Master") Jeladdin Rumi, the founder of the order. Dervish beliefs also appealed to the large Christian population of Anatolia and helped bridge the gap between them and their Seljuk rulers. Mevlana preached tolerance, forgiveness and enlightenment, and his poetry, even in translated versions, is moving and inspirational.

The **Mevlana Festival of the Whirling Dervishes** is held in a specially designed stadium every December, and the piety of most of the audience makes it clear that the *sema* (whirling ceremony) has not lost its religious significance. Performances for tourists are given daily in summer (check locally for details).

Around Konya

About 10km (6 miles) outside Konya is the former Greek village of **Sille**, with the remains of the Church of St Michael and a spring dated to 1732. **Çatalhöyük** ⑯ (daily 8am–5pm; charge), just off the road south to Karaman, is a hugely important archaeological site. From about 6250–5400 BC, this was a prosperous town of some 5,000 people. Rich and poor lived crammed together in houses which ran directly into one another with no streets between them. The only way to gain entry was by climbing through the roofs. It is the first place in the world whose residents are known to have used irrigation and kept domesticated animals. They wove textiles, used simple carpets and traded in luxury goods, notably obsidian, a mineral used for axes, daggers and mirrors. Most striking of all were their shrines, adorned with statuettes and paintings depicting bulls and fertility rites.

The roof of the magnificent **Esrefoglu Camii** at Beyşehir, 77km (48 miles) west of Konya, is supported by wooden columns. Dating from 1299, it is the country's foremost wooden mosque. ❑

A turret of turquoise tiles is the showy high point of Konya's Mevlana Tekkesi.

BELOW: dervishes still whirl, for Allah and the tourists.

The Whirling Dervishes

There was a time when visitors to Turkey could only hope to see the famous whirling dervishes going through their paces in mid-December when they were permitted to perform in Konya. These days, however, it would be hard to visit the country and not come across whirling dervishes of varying degrees of authenticity.

The dervish order was originally founded by Jelaleddin Rumi (1207–73), better known in the West as Mevlana, who was born in what is now Afghanistan but travelled to Konya with his family. Once there, he developed his philosophy of all-enveloping tolerance, at odds in many ways with the modern-day city that houses his shrine. It was Mevlana's vision that gave rise to the idea that, by rotating their bodies over a prolonged period of time, individuals could be brought closer to Allah, and it was during his lifetime that the costume associated with the dervishes, in which white robes represent shrouds and tall conical caps tombstones, evolved. In 1925 Atatürk abolished all the dervish orders as a potential threat to his secular state, and it is only in recent years that they have started to flourish again. While in Konya you should certainly visit the site of Mevlana's tomb, but it's also well worth attending a proper *sema* (dervish ceremony) if you get the opportunity.

EAST OF ANKARA

The journey east of Ankara takes travellers through the Anatolian countryside to spectacular ruins of ancient civilisations and the rock churches of Cappadocia

To the northeast of Ankara is a largely flat area mainly visited by travellers en route to the eastern end of the Black Sea who are keen to explore the World Heritage listed Hittite sites around Boğazkale. The road south to the rock-cut wonders of Cappadocia also kicks off from east of Ankara.

The road east

About 26km (18 miles) east of Ankara, a road known as the "Nato Highway" forks left, leading to the small ski resort of **Elmadağ**.

Kalecik, 80km (50 miles) northeast of Ankara, has a Roman castle with medieval additions and an Ottoman bridge over the Kızılırmak River. Further north along the same road the main sight in **Çankırı** is the **Taş Mescit**, a green-domed 13th-century mental hospital built by the Seljuk Turks, where music therapy helped people adapt to the stress caused by marauding raiders. The town's **Ulu Camii** (Grand Mosque) was built in 1558 by Süleyman the Magnificent, and rebuilt after an earthquake in 1936.

Hittite capital

Anyone staying in Ankara should consider a visit to the ruins of the Hittite capital at **Boğazkale** ⑰ (daily 8am–noon, 1–5.30pm; charge), a drive of two to three hours east of the capital along

the E-88 highway towards Çorum. You can also approach it from the south, climbing a minor road through wild mountains, from Yozgat.

At the height of its prosperity in about 1400 BC, the city (known to the Hittites as **Hattuşa**) was the capital of an empire which stretched south to Cyprus and west to the Aegean. Its massive size and majestic setting are unrivalled. Though the higher slopes are now largely bare, it is not difficult to people them in the mind's eye with homes, warriors, priests, clerks, saddlers,

Main attractions
BOĞAZKALE
ALACAHÖYÜK
KIRŞEHIR
HACIBEKTAŞ
  KARŞI KILISESI
  (CHURCH OF ST JOHN,
  GÜLŞEHIR)

LEFT: Hittite ruins at Boğazkale.
RIGHT: poppies add colour to the landscape.

The Hittites' curious multi-angular stonework is called "cyclopaedean" because the ancient Greeks, living about 500 years later, assumed it could only have been the work of a vanished race of giants.

BELOW: wheat-farming on the plateau.

cobblers and slaves. The sight is made more evocative by the knowledge that, not long after 1200 BC, the city was stormed and burned, and never recovered its former greatness.

The site is best explored by car, as the distances can take their toll under a burning summer sun. Begin on the ramparts, looking down at the **King's Gate** and **Lion Gate**. A section of the stonework is kept clear of rubble and weeds, so that it is possible to see the great stone ramparts more or less as they looked in Hittite times. Further proof of the formidable nature of Hittite architecture is provided by the **Yerkapı**, a 70-metre (229ft) tunnel under the walls.

Lower down, on an outcrop of the hill overlooking the valley, the **Büyükkale** (Citadel) was the site of the Imperial Palace, and it is here that the majority of the 3,350 clay tablets from the emperors' archives were found. Thanks to them, this great, vanished civilisation, virtually unknown 100 years ago, now has a detailed written history. Lower down are the foundations of the **Büyük Mabet** (Great Temple), which,

in its day, may have been the largest building in the world, dedicated to the weather god, Hatti, and the sun goddess, Arinna. In 1986, archaeologists unearthed a bronze tablet engraved with the terms of a treaty here.

Temple to 1,000 gods

The religious heart of the Hittite kingdom lay slightly over 2km (1½ miles) northeast of Boğazkale, in the rock shrine of **Yazılıkaya** ⑱ (daily 9am–5pm; charge). What survives today dates largely from 1275–1220 BC when it was enlarged by the Hittite emperors. There are two main galleries carved from the rock, their walls covered by reliefs of deities wearing tall conical caps. Many of the gods' names are not Hittite at all, but Hurrian or Hatti, showing how the culture and religion of the Hittite warrior aristocracy absorbed the beliefs and traditions of the indigenous people they had conquered. Sungurlu has a museum with reconstructions of the site.

Alacahöyük

A 20-minute drive further along the road will take you to the third great Hittite centre in the area, **Alacahöyük** ⑲ (Tue–Sun 8am–noon, 1.30–5.30pm; charge). Many of the most famous ancient Anatolian emblems, including the deer and the sun disk which have become symbols of modern Turkey, were discovered here during excavations in the 1930s. Alacahöyük is less picturesque than its neighbours, but one can clearly make out the ground plan of the Hittite and pre-Hittite buildings. The **Sphinx Gate** is the most impressive sight; the other reliefs have been removed for safety and are now on display in the Museum of Anatolian Civilisations in Ankara.

Other sights in the area

Although the Hittite cities are undoubtedly the main drawcards, there are other places nearby that are also worth a quick look. Northeast of Alacahöyük, the city of **Çorum** contains a

ne 13th-century **Ulu Camii** which
as built by the Seljuk Sultan Alâed-
n Keykubat.

South of Boğazkale, **Yozgat** was
unded by the Çapanoğlu dynasty,
Turkic clan that was influential in
e region in the 17th century. It is
ominated by the grand **Çapanoğlu
ustafa Paşa Camii**, built in 1779.

Kırşehir ⑳, southwest of Yozgat on
e road to Cappadocia, stands on the
te of the Byzantine city of Justiano-
olis Mokyssos. There are two reasons
break your journey here. The first is
e **shrine of Ahi Evran** (1171–1262),
mystic whose cult has been compared
that of the Masons because of its
sociation with the crafts guilds. Far
ore beautiful is the **Cacabey Camii**
d *medrese*, built in the 13th century
an observatory and later converted
to a mosque. Kırşehir also has a small
useum (daily 9am–noon, 1–5pm)
hich contains some items said to
ave belonged to Ahi Evran as well as
reconstruction of a room from an old
rşehir house.

The road from Kırşehir continues
uth towards Cappadocia, passing
rough **Hacıbektaş** ㉑ which is
amed after **Hacı Bektaş Veli**, the
under of the Bektaşi order of der-
shes who served as chaplains to the
nissaries, the storm-troopers of the
ttoman Empire.

The Bektaşis were a free-thinking, tol-
ant community and it is well worth
siting their shrine (Tue–Sun 8.30am–
2.30pm, 1.30–5.30pm; charge) where
u will usually find local women
aying. The small museum contains
ne examples of calligraphy. Rooms
the lodge tell their own story: the
mmunal eating hall, with its great
uldrons still hanging by the fire-
ace, and the meeting room used by
e "fathers" of the order, rather like a
estern chapterhouse.

On the annual feast day, 16 August,
ektaşis from all over Turkey gather
r three days of celebrations involving
uch singing and dancing.

Further south is **Gülşehir** ㉒, which

sits on the banks of the
Kızılırmak, Turkey's
longest river. The town
centre is dominated
by the huge Karavizer
Cami, paid for by the
"Black Vizier" Seyyit
Mehmetpaşa Silahtar
(1735–81). Gülşehir
is one of the northern
gateways to Cappa-
docia (*see page 305*),
and of more interest is
the stunning rock-cut
Karşı Kilisesi (Church of St John; daily
9am–noon, 1–5pm; charge), on the
southern outskirts, which dates back to
1214. Its remarkable frescoes were only
uncovered in 1995. The one of the Last
Judgement is particularly noteworthy
as this image is not often to be seen in
the Cappadocian churches.

Continuing south to Nevşehir and
Cappadocia you will pass on the right-
hand side of the road what is called
the **Açık Sarayı** (Open Palace; daily
9am–noon, 1–5pm; charge), actually a
monastic centre with at least three separate rock-cut communal buildings. ❑

*A craftsman recreates
an ancient art at
Yazılıkaya.
Reproductions of
ancient figurines and
other artefacts are on
sale at many of the
country's museums.*

BELOW: *Kiss of
Judas* mosaic in
Karşi Kilisesi,
Gülşehir.

CAPPADOCIA

Cappadocia is famed for its eerie lunar landscape, astounding underground cities and spectacular rock-cut churches, their walls decorated with vivid Byzantine frescoes

he French traveller Paul Lucas was the first Western European to leave an account of a visit to Cappadocia in 1706, but the area remained largely unknown to the outside world for two further centuries until Pere Guillaume de Jerphanion stumbled on the rock churches of Cappadocia most by chance during a journey across Anatolia in 1907. Like Lucas, he was stunned by what he saw: "Our eyes were astounded. I remember those valleys in the searingly brilliant light, running through the most fantastic of all landscapes," he wrote. A 10th-century history tells us that local inhabitants were called troglodytes "because they go under the ground in holes, clefts, and labyrinths, like dens and burrows". Paul Lucas himself understood that he was looking at a man-made landscape and thought he saw pyramids being used as houses, and weird statues of monks and the Virgin Mary.

Even now, when the valleys around the town of Ürgüp are relatively easy to reach (the flight from İstanbul to Kayseri takes an hour, with another hour by transfer bus to the hotels), Cappadocia can seem like a lost world to the arriving traveller. It took the 20th century – and perhaps the invention of photography – to make people really appreciate this extraordinary region.

What we call "Cappadocia" today is only a small part of the Hellenistic kingdom and subsequent Roman province which bore the same name. The original province stretched for hundreds of kilometres further east and west. The name is older still. The region is first mentioned in a monument bearing the trilingual epitaph of the Persian King Darius as *Katpatuka* (the "Land of Beautiful Horses"). Several of the fathers of the early Church lived locally, but none of them ever made reference to their unusual surroundings.

Main attractions
ÜÇHISAR
GÖREME
ROCK CHURCHES
HOT-AIR BALLOON RIDES
ZELVE
MUSTAFAPAŞA
KAYMAKLI UNDERGROUND CITY
GÜMÜŞLER
IHLARA VADISI VALLEY

LEFT: the magical landscape of Cappadocia with its otherworldly rock formations.
RIGHT: street scene in Mustafapaşa.

The sight and sound of chickens and other farm animals are never far away in rural Turkey.

Ancient upheavals

The geological explanation for the Cappadocian landscape is relatively straightforward. The whole region is dominated by **Erciyes Dağı ❶** (ancient Mount Argaeus), the third-highest mountain in Anatolia, at 3,916 metres (12,848ft). Millions of years ago, Erciyes erupted, smothering the surrounding area with a torrent of lava extending hundreds of kilometres. This lava then cooled and solidified, before floods, rain and wind did their work, creating deep valleys and fissures in the lava rock, while the slopes were carved into outlandish cones and columns.

Though the white dust from the rocks looks like sand, it is actually much more fertile than the soil of the surrounding central Anatolian steppes. Trees, vines and vegetables grow with ease, a fact which meant that there were always plenty of farmers here. The first of them quickly discovered that the stone of the rock valleys is as magical as it looks, for it is soft until cut into and brought in contact with the air, making it a perfect medium for carving entire buildings out of the rock.

Generations of local people have u[tilised] these unique conditions to hollo[w] out innumerable chambers in the rock over an area of several hundred squa[re] kilometres. Some provided homes f[or] the farmers, others acted as dovecotes [or] stables. Many were used as chapels, cel[ls] and refectories for monks and hermi[ts]. And today, people still live in the cav[e] houses, which are wonderfully cool [in] summer and warm(ish) in winter.

The result is a fairy-tale landscape, [a] child's delight, where it's easy to belie[ve] that dwarves, elves, fairies and oth[er] supernatural beings have just steppe[d] round the corner, or perhaps vanishe[d] through a little doorway in the rock.

Three thousand rock churches

Many visitors only make a brief excu[r]sion to the cones and rock churches [at] Göreme, and spend an hour or two [at] **Zelve** or **Ihlara**. That's a pity, becau[se] Cappadocia is best explored in a le[i]surely fashion on foot, by car or on [a] bicycle. Several local firms also hire o[ut] horses for trekking expeditions. The[re] are an estimated 3,000 rock church[es]

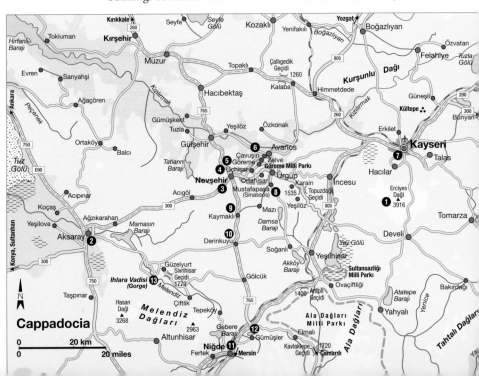

Cappadocia

0   20 km

0   20 miles

in the triangle between Kayseri, Niğde and Aksaray; and new caves, "underground cities" and even churches are still discovered from time to time.

The main roads from Ankara and Konya meet at **Aksaray ②**, which was founded by King Archaelais of Cappadocia. The town contains many Islamic monuments, including the 15th-century **Ulu Camii** (Great Mosque) and the 13th-century **Eğri (Crooked) Minaret**, Turkey's answer to the Leaning Tower of Pisa.

The main transport and business hub for the area is the uninspiring town of **Nevşehir ③**, which has a restored **citadel** and small **museum** (Tue–Sun 9am–noon, 1–5pm; charge), as well as a fine mosque complex paid for by Damat İbrahim Paşa, grand vizier to Sultan Ahmet III and the man responsible for many of the Tulip Era parties in the Topkapı Palace in Istanbul. Otherwise there's nothing to hold the visitor's interest, especially with so much waiting nearby.

Üçhisar ④, 7km (4 miles) east of Nevşehir, is famed for its immense fist-shaped tower of volcanic tufa, honeycombed with chambers. This **citadel** (daily 8am–sunset; charge), the highest point in Cappadocia, offers a spectacular view over what was once a typical Anatolian village below, and also takes in the unworldly rock formations in the Göreme valley. There are several good hotels and restaurants in town.

Many people choose to base themselves in **Ürgüp**, a charming small town known for its boutique hotels, restaurants and locally produced wine. The town is the richest in the Nevşehir region. It is also handily central to the most fascinating area of Cappadocia.

Nearby is **Ortahisar**, with another towering rock apartment block (daily 8am–sunset; charge) and a smattering of small hotels in a village which still retains much of its local atmosphere.

Göreme and its churches

The village of **Göreme ⑤** hunkers down amid the fairy chimneys and, with its excellent facilities and laid-back atmosphere, has become one of the most popular places to stay in Cappadocia. Many townspeople still live in cave-dwellings, and it can be very

TIP

Guided expeditions on horseback are organised by Rainbow Ranch in Göreme, while hot-air balloon tours are available from companies in Göreme, Ürgüp, Uçhisar and Çavuşin. *For more information, see Travel Tips page 427.*

BELOW LEFT: in a Cappadocia cave.
BELOW RIGHT: Göreme village houses.

pleasant to walk among their extraordinary houses, and perhaps meet some modern troglodytes. Many *pansiyons* feature cave rooms or fairy chimneys and prices are very reasonable.

Two km (1½ miles) from Göreme village, on the Ürgüp road, over 30 of the finest churches in Cappadocia are clustered together in the **Göreme Open-Air Museum** (daily 8am–6pm, winter until 5pm; charge, with additional charge for Dark Church – *see below*). Almost all date from the 9th–11th centuries.

The **Church of St Barbara** is decorated with red symbols and figurines, including Christ enthroned, and St Barbara, the patron saint of soldiers. Next door is the main dome of the stunningly restored **Elmalı Kilesi** (Church with the Apple). Also nearby is the **Yılanlı Kilisesi** (Church with the Snake), its walls covered with depictions of St George killing the dragon (or serpent) and other strange creatures (St George was the patron saint of Cappadocia; *see panel, below*). Look also for St Onophrius, a 5th-century Egyptian hermit, a repentant femme fatale who was given a beard to make her unattractive to men and went to live in the desert, where she wore a loincloth and ate only dates. Emperor Constantine and his mother Helena are pictured holding the True Cross which Helena supposedly discovered in Jerusalem.

The **Karanlık Kilesi** (Dark Church), originally part of a larger monastery, has some of the finest Byzantine wall paintings, including a painting showing the betrayal of Christ by Judas. Another shows the Transfiguration with Christ between Moses and Elias on Mount Tabor. Across the road from the main gate, and thus easily missed, the **Tokalı Kilesi** (Church with the Buckle) has a glorious profusion of well-preserved murals on deep-blue backgrounds, including the *Annunciation*, *the Agony in the Garden* and the *Journey to Bethlehem*.

If you arrive to find Göreme's Open Air Museum crowded with coach parties, head instead to the frescoed **El Nazar Kilisesi** (Church of the Evil Eye), signposted off the road to the museum, just past the Tourist Hotel.

The **Kılıçlar Valley** (the Valley of the Swords), running out behind

Saint George

Patron saint of Cappadocia – and, of course, England – Saint George was a Roman Christian soldier in the service of Emperor Diocletian. He is thought to have been born into a noble family in the Levant, while his father (also a Christian) hailed from Cappadocia. He was martyred in AD 303 after Diocletian attempted, unsuccessfully, to force him to renounce his Christianity. The early Christians soon came to venerate him as a saint.

The legend of St George and the dragon is believed to have originated at the time of the Crusades, some eight centuries after his death, and the earliest known account has been traced to Cappadocia. In all likelihood, it is a case of a much earlier pagan legend being appropriated or otherwise mixed up with the story of the Christian martyr.

Tokalı Kilesi, gets its name from the pointed rock formations resembling sabres. The **Kılıçlar Kilesi** (Church of the Swords), about 400 metres (440yds) north of Tokalı, is by far the biggest ecclesiastical complex in the region, but sadly, along with the church of St Eustace and a chapel with a picture of St Daniel in the lion's den, it is closed to visitors.

Çavuşin and Zelve

Çavuşin ❻, 3km (2 miles) to the north of Göreme town, resembles a gigantic caved-in ant hill. Nearby is a ghost town whose inhabitants were moved down the hill after a rockfall in the 1960s. The **Church of Çavuşin**, accessible by a metal ladder, has strip narrative frescoes painted in bright green, pink, orange and dove-blue. Among the vivid portraits are a picture of Melias the Magister, a Byzantine-Armenian general who died as a prisoner of the Arabs in Baghdad in 974, and a Byzantine emperor riding a white horse, identified as John Tzimiskes (968–72) who is thought to have visited the area.

A ghost town, cave-houses and churches (few with frescoes) can also be found in and around **Zelve**, an area made up of three valleys east of Çavuşin. It is a great place for rock climbing and has a vast underground **monastery** (daily 8am–7pm, winter until 5pm; charge), which requires serious physical exertion to explore.

Not everything in Cappadocia is Byzantine. **Avanos**, on the northern bank of the Kızılırmak River, north of Zelve, is famed for its pottery, thanks to the rich red clay found along the river banks. The town has scores of shops selling local ware; some of them will let you try your own hand at throwing a pot.

East to Kayseri

Drive east along the Kayseri road from Ürgüp until you see a sign on the right for the Church of St Theodore, then keep going for about 10km

Chairlift at the Erciyes ski resort near Kayseri.

BELOW: ancient paintings survive in the churches of Göreme, such as at Emalı Kilesi.

TIP

Try to avoid visiting
Cappadocia in July and
August when the heat is
oppressive. May, June
and September are
much nicer.

(6 miles) along a village road through the unspoilt village of **Karain**. Further on, the outstanding **Church of St Theodore** is located in the village of **Yeşilöz**, previously known as Tagar. Ask the keeper (*bekçi*) to unlock the church for you. It has a central dome and unique 11th-century frescoes, plus you can climb up into a gallery to look down on the nave.

Situated on a vast plain facing Mount Erciyes, **Kayseri** ❼ is one of the oldest cities in Anatolia. It served as the capital of the Graeco-Roman province of Cappadocia from 380 BC to AD 17, was conquered by Roman Emperor Tiberius, renamed Caesarea, and remained part of the Roman-Byzantine Empire until 1071, when it came under the control of the Seljuk Turks. Today, it is an industrial city, but does boast numerous 13th-century Islamic monuments, such as the **Hunat Hatun Camii**, the mosque built by the wife of the Selçuk Sultan Alâeddin Keykubat which contains her elaborately carved tomb just inside the main entrance. The tomb's emblem is the Döner Kümbet, which was built in

1276 and contains the tomb of Alâeddin Keykubat's daughter, Şah Ciha[n] Sultan. There is also a small **Archaeological Museum** (Gültepe Ma[h.] Kilşa Caddesi; Tue–Sun 9am–noo[n] 1–5.30pm; charge) and a fascinatin[g] display of upper-class Ottoman li[fe] in the carefully restored 15th-centur[y] **Güpüpoğlu Konaği** (Cumhuriye[t] Mah.; Tue–Sun 8.30am–noon, 1.30[–] 5pm; charge).

Twenty-two kilometres (14 mile[s] northeast of the city near Bünyan a[re] the remains of **Kültepe**, a 19th-centu[ry] BC Assyrian and Hittite trade centre.

Mustafapaşa: town of paintings

Largely Greek towns like **Mustafapaş[a]** ❽ (Sinasos), southwest of Kayser[i] never really recovered from the blo[w] they received with the collapse of th[e] Ottoman Empire and the popula[tion exchange of 1924, which force[d] Muslims living in Greece to move t[o] Turkey and Greek Christians living i[n] Turkey to move to Greece. The hug[e] Church of Sts Constantine and Helen[a] in the town centre is a reminder of ju[st

BELOW: Derinkuyu, underground city.

how prominent the Greek community was at the end of the 19th century.

Every house has its own stone-sculptured balcony and windows. Inside many of them are late 19th-century frescoes, some with the eyes scratched out by the pious Muslim farmers who inherited the houses in the 1920s. Some of these pictures really stand out in terms of how distinctive they are from Islamic art. For example, upstairs in the Old Greek House Restaurant there is a startlingly un-Islamic image of a young woman on a swing. If you walk out into the valley beyond Mustafapaşa you will find a few Göreme-style rock-cut churches, most of them badly defaced with graffiti.

A little further south, the beautiful 25km (16-mile) -long **Soğanlı valley** features numerous 9th- to 13th-century churches, along with several Roman rock tombs. The **Kubeli Kilisesi**, the most unusual of its churches, is built on the top of a pockmarked rock pinnacle and has a rock-cut dome that makes it look like an Armenian church; the **Karabaş Kilisesi**, on the left-hand side

of the valley, has lovely – but poorly protected – medieval frescoes.

Underground cities

No one knows how many underground cities exist in Cappadocia, and more are still being discovered. Some of the tunnels were probably in use as early as the Bronze Age, and Hittite seals show that they took refuge here. Many were used from time to time by Christians from Kayseri and elsewhere as they fled from invading Arab and Turkic hordes. As many as 30,000 people could hide in these deep, catacomb-like structures for perhaps three months at a time.

The underground city of **Kaymaklı** ❾ (daily 8am–5pm, summer until 6pm; charge), located on the road to Niğde, 20km (12½ miles) south of Nevşehir, has eight floors. A further 10km (6 miles) south is the even deeper **Derinkuyu** ❿ ("Deep Well" in Turkish; daily 8am–5pm, summer until 6pm; charge). A complex web of settlements including stables, wine presses, kitchens and wells, Derinkuyu has nine layers, reaching a depth of 55 metres (180ft). Each chamber has been illuminated.

The painted walls of Mustafapaşa are crumbling from neglect.

BELOW: tectonic masterpiece.

Old houses in Niğde.

Southern Cappadocia

The city of **Niğde** ⓫ came to the fore after the 10th-century Arab invasions had destroyed its less easily defended neighbours. It has several 13th- and 14th-century Islamic shrines and monuments, including the **Alâeddin Camii**, built in 1203, with a *bedesten* or covered market below it. The **Akmedrese**, a Seljuk theological school, serves as a museum (Tue–Sun 8am–noon, 1–4.30pm; charge).

One of the finest local churches for Byzantine frescoes is the monastery at **Eski Gümüşler** (daily 9am–6.30pm; charge) in the village of **Gümüşler** ⓬, 8km (5 miles) north of Niğde. Restored by British archaeologists in the 1960s, the monastery church has a completely preserved courtyard (the only one to survive in its entirety). A room upstairs springs a surprise: a smoky wall covered with non-religious pictures of animals and birds. Outside, a winepress and baths have been discovered.

South of Niğde, the uplands of central Anatolia are separated from the southern coast by the magnificent Toros Mountains. After the town of **Ulukışla**, the road climbs until it reaches the famous **Gülek Boğazı** (Cilician Gates), a high pass in the mountains which was, for centuries, the only way between the Anatolian plateau and Çukorova (Cilicia). Commercial caravans and invading armies alike had to scale its treacherous heights to reach Tarsus or Adana and the Mediterranean in the south, or to bring goods to the cities of central and eastern Anatolia. Most travellers today take a modern expressway, the Adana road.

Rock churches of Ihlara Vadisi

To the west of Niğde, over 60 churches have been hewn into the walls of the gorgeous 10km (6-mile) -long, 80-metre (262ft) -wide **Ihlara Vadisi** ⓭. The sheer-sided valley, which encloses the Melendiz River, is excellent for trekking. Most of the churches in this area were built in the 11th century and around a dozen are open to the public. These include the **Ağaçaltı Kilisesi** (Church under the Tree), with 10th- and 13th-century frescoes, one of them showing Daniel in the lion's den; and the **Yılanlı Kilisesi** (Church of the Serpents), whose frescoes depict the entombment of Mary the Egyptian with St Zosimus and a lion. The **Purenli Seki Kilisesi** (Church with the Terraces) contains a chamber tomb, separated by pillared arcades, and frescoes. The **Eğritas Kilisesi** (Church with the Crooked Stone) is one of the valley's most important churches, with several distinguished frescoes, most unfortunately badly damaged.

The **Kırk Damaltı Kilisesi** (the Church of St George) was re-endowed by a Greek nobleman who served the Seljuk Sultan Mesut II at Konya and wore a turban (as the frescoes show) in the last decade of the 13th century. The best approach to Kırk Damaltı Kilisesi is not via the steps at the top of Ihlara valley, but about 3–4km (2–3 miles) downstream near the village of Belisirama. Local children will help you locate it. ❑

Holy Underground

Dig deep and you never know what you may find beneath Cappadocia

I n the early medieval period there were several thousand churches and monasteries in Cappadocia, along with numerous cave-houses and complex underground cities. But who built them all? The history books don't tell us, but there are clues in the fabric of the surviving cave-houses, the remains of tombs and the extraordinary paintings on the walls.

People have inhabited these underground warrens since the Neolithic era, but the soul of the region was forged from the twin powers of religion and repression. From the 3rd century BC, Cappadocia was a series of small, independent states, ruled by priest-kings. Its isolation attracted many early hermits and other holy men, seeking remote corners of the known world where they could serve their god through uninterrupted fasting, prayer and celibacy. Although they became known as monks – literally *monachos* ("solitary ones") – followers inevitably gathered around them and so, in due course, the first Christian monasteries were born. In AD 360, St Basil of Caesarea laid down a set of rules for these emerging communities. These edicts are still in force in the Greek Orthodox Church, and helped form the basis of the Rule of St Benedict in the West.

Far from withdrawing from life, many early monks saw themselves as the spearhead of the Christian movement. Graffiti crosses scrawled on many classical temples date back to the monks' attempts to "disinfect" the great buildings of paganism. At the same time, the monks began to carve an extraordinary series of churches and chapels from the soft Cappadocian rock, basing their architecture on established Byzantine practice, complete with capitals and columns.

Throughout the Roman era (from AD 18) Cappadocia was also a sanctuary for Christians escaping persecution. The Arab invasions of the 7th–9th centuries again saw the area serve as a refuge, with many thousands fleeing for the hills and burrows to escape the relentless march of Islam.

Eventual Arab rule could have spelled the end of the monasteries, but Islam proved more open to religious freedom than Christianity, and Cappadocia flourished in relative safety and stability. Over time, however, the influence of the new religion began to be felt as early "puritans" combined Old Testament prohibitions against idols with the Islamic taboo on human representation. From 726–843, the iconoclasts savagely attacked the frescoes and mosaics; few pre-iconoclast paintings survived the onslaught.

Cappadocia's last great Christian flowering was from the 9th–11th centuries, as the monasteries were redecorated and the land spawned a warrior aristocracy of Byzantine frontiersmen struggling to fend off the Arabs.

The Battle of Manzikert (1071) eventually established Turkish control of this part of Anatolia. The Byzantine landowners were able to survive for another couple of centuries, but by the 14th century the region was firmly under Muslim rule. Only a few small monasteries struggled on in remote corners of the region. Its golden age was over. ❑

ABOVE: the elaborate ceiling of a rock church.
RIGHT: the local rock is perfect for carving buildings.

THE BLACK SEA COAST

Turkey's northern strip is defined by its mountainous isolation, unpredictable weather and a fierce independence

I solated by a chain of high green mountains, the Black Sea region is unlike anywhere else in the country. It is described in ancient Greek accounts – notably the legendary adventures of Jason and his Argonauts – as a terrifying place full of danger; sea-caves leading to Hades, brutal Amazons, and numerous hostile tribes. Medea, the betrayed lover of Jason in Euripides' tragic account, may have been a Laz princess from the far eastern Black Sea, where the kingdom of Colchis and the Golden Fleece were located. Underwater archaeological excavations suggest that the biblical account of the Great Flood could have a factual basis, and remains of human settlements more than 7,000 years old are being studied. The sea itself was once a freshwater lake, until, some time in the sixth millennium BC, rising levels of the Mediterranean breached a rock barrier at the Bosphorus, rapidly enlarging the lake and rendering it salty.

The geography, idiosyncratic music and dance, and linguistic quirks of the region give it a singular identity, one that is enhanced by its inhabitants: the Laz, with their aquiline profiles and fair colouring, are concentrated in the vicinity of Pazar, Ardeşen, Fındıklı, Arhavi and Hopa. In the Hemşin valleys of the Kaçkar range, locals still speak a dialect of Armenian, while near Çaykara and Of people speak a form of Greek, yet boast the highest proportion of mosques and religious schools in Turkey. The Giresun highlands were settled by Alevî Turkic tribes in the 13th century; there are more Alevîs in the Fatsa and Bolaman regions. Georgian is still spoken in a few valleys northeast of Artvin.

With 1,250km (780 miles) of coastline, one may still find small beaches and unspoilt fishing villages west of Sinop, but the four-lane highway between Samsun and Hopa is an eyesore – the traveller anticipating visions of the "shimmering towers of Trebizond" may be in for a shock. Turn inland, however, and winding roads lead to green, wet hillsides, ancient castles and churches, fairy-tale forests and characterful villages. ❏

PRECEDING PAGES: threshing the grain during the autumn harvest in Artvin.
LEFT: fishing boat and its skipper at Ünye. **TOP AND ABOVE LEFT:** Black Sea coast landscapes. **ABOVE RIGHT:** the humid climate and fertile soil suit tea cultivation.

THE BLACK SEA

Much of the Black Sea coast suffers from an overdose of development, but for those with time and transport there is still magic to be found

İstanbul
Ankara

Black Sea beach resorts begin just outside İstanbul, but there are long stretches worth avoiding. Şile is popular with weekending city-dwellers, but horribly crowded, with an often treacherous sea, while Akçakoca was badly hit by the 1999 earthquake, though like Şile it offers a Genoese castle and long, sandy beach. Slightly inland from here lies the Yedigöller Milli Parkı (Seven Lakes National Reserve), a chain of interconnecting semi-natural ponds at their best during vivid displays of autumnal foliage.

Safranbolu and Yörük Köyü

The first unmissable stop is Safranbolu ❶, some 400km (250 miles) east of İstanbul, where some of the grandest Ottoman mansions in Turkey have been beautifully restored, many as affordable pansiyons. Local houses, claimed to number 800, are especially elaborate as Safranbolu prospered as a vital link on a trade route linking İstanbul and Sinop for many years. The town was, and still is, famous for its leather, copper and iron craftsmanship; as its name suggests, Safranbolu is also noted for saffron, some of which finds its way into locally produced lokum and helva.

The old Çarşı quarter (alias Eski Safranbolu) is where interest resides. On arrival, visit the tourist office – off the main square on Arasta Sokak – for a selection of brochures and maps, then head for the nearby Arasta, now a bazaar full of tourist-pitched crafts and antiques. A few alleys east, the courtyarded Cinci Hanı, a 17th-century kervansaray, is worth a look even if you're not staying at the hotel now installed in its premises. Beyond this stands the Kaymakamlar Müzesi Evi (daily 9am–6pm; charge) the best restored and most interesting of three such mansions here. Back on the square, the 17th-century Cinci

LEFT: the Black Sea coast near Sinop.
RIGHT: genteel houses in Safranbolu.

*A day's catch of fresh
brown trout rewards a
patient angler.*

Hamam (daily 10am–6pm) has been beautifully refurbished, with separate male and female sections.

If Safranbolu proves too commercialised for your tastes, there is another "museum village", **Yörük Köyü**, some 18km (11miles) further east, with 150 or so listed houses, one of which, the **Sipahioğlu Konağı** (daily 9am–sunset; charge), is visitable, as is the nearby communal *çamaşırhane* (laundry), now an art gallery. Yörük Köyü was largely inhabited by adherents of the Bektaşi sect, and if you look closely in the laundry you'll see evidence of their doctrines in the 12-sided washing platform (symbolising the 12 imams).

The coastal route

Beyond Safranbolu, there are two possible routes. The first heads north through Bartın to coastal **Amasra ❷** (91km/56 miles), a stunning old town draped over two fortified promontories with surviving Byzantine walls. It seems more north Aegean than Pontic, with sweeping sea views and a maze of cobbled paths through the outer citadel of Boztepe, a Byzantine fortress adapted by the Genoese during the 14th century. Inside are two Byzantine

churches, one converted into a mosqu the other used until 1923.

The winding coast east of Aması rewards the determined, self-propelle traveller with dramatic scenery an occasional timber, shale-roofed dwel ings on the point of collapse. Minibu links are limited and driving cond tions along sheer drops to a crashin sea challenging, though the road su face has been improved. If you hav time, the best way to see this stretc of coast is by bicycle. **Kurucaşile**, sti famed for its boat builders, would b the first conceivable overnight stop fc cyclists; **Cide** has more accommod: tion and a long, pebbly beach. Rive side **İnebolu** is much the liveliest plac en route to Sinop, with a few remair ing Ottoman houses in the centı (mostly unrestored) and good-standaı hotels on the shore.

Sinop ❸, 150km (90 miles) fron Amasra on a jutting peninsula, has th best natural harbour along this coas and accordingly (along with Amasra was settled by colonists from Aegea Miletos during the 7th century BC A competing legend asserts it wa founded by the Amazon queen Sinopᵢ who managed to brush off the eve amorous Zeus by getting him to graı

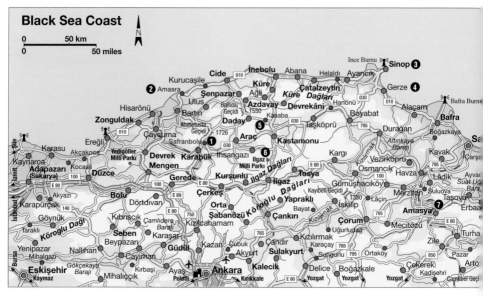

r one wish: eternal virginity. There
e in any case numerous ancient sites
the region (including, apparently,
tediluvian settlements on the Black
a floor). Finds from the more accessi-
e sites are displayed in the **museum**,
hich incorporates foundations of
2nd-century BC Temple of Serapis.
n the same street are a ruined 7th-
ntury church, the **Balat Kilisesi**, and
veral Seljuk and Ottoman monu-
ents, including the 13th-century
âeddin Camii and its accompany-
g **Alaiye Medresesi**, with a carved
arble portal.

Most impressive of all are the enor-
ous **city walls**, parts of which stand to
height of 25 metres (80ft). These were
little help, however, on 30 November
53, when a Russian fleet destroyed a
avily outgunned Turkish squadron
chored here, in one of the opening
gagements of the Crimean War.

The best excursions from Sinop are
Karakum (Black Sand) beach, 3km
miles) east of town, or to the pretty
rbour village of **Gerze ❹**, some
km (24 miles) distant, set back from
e pitiless roar of the motorway. It
tains some old houses, while a few
aterside hotels make it an alterna-
e base to Sinop. The best are those

situated along the point, where from
your balcony you can watch the fishermen unload the day's catch.

A little further on, you'll cross the
delta of the Kızılırmak, a labyrinth
of marsh, reedbed and dune that's an
important (tho ugh as yet unprotected)
haven for birdlife. All this contrasts
markedly with **Samsun**, a grimy city
of nearly one million that's the epicentre of the Turkish tobacco trade. It
does have a worthwhile **Archaeology
and Ethnographic Museum** on Fuar
Caddesi (Tue–Sun 8.30am–noon,
1–5pm; charge), with outstanding
mosaics from a local Roman villa and
elegant 2nd-century BC gold jewellery,
but otherwise it's a place to skip.

The inland route

If you take the inland route eastwards from Safranbolu, your first
stop should be **Kastamonu**, the feudal stronghold of the Komneni clan,
who founded a Byzantine dynasty in
1081 which lasted a century. There are
also a number of Seljuk and Ottoman
monuments, the pick of which is the
Nasrullah Kadi Camii, from 1509.
Some 15km (9 miles) northwest, in
the village of **Kasaba ❺**, stands one
of the finest mosques in Turkey – the

TIP

Predictably, the most
spectacular places in
the region are the
hardest to reach. Public
transport is very limited
both on the inland
village routes and on
the gorgeous coastal
road from Sinop to
Amasra. Plan seriously,
and either hire a sturdy
vehicle, go with a tour
group, or take stout
hiking boots and allow
plenty of time.

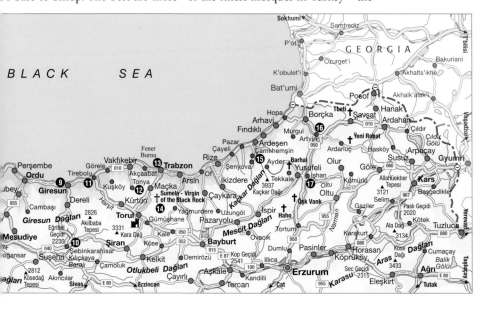

Outside the Sultan Beyazit Camii, Amasya.

BELOW: traditional pre-prayer *abdest* ablutions in Amasya.

carved wooden **Mahmud Bey Camii**, an intricate structure built in 1366 and retaining almost all its original features. Head south from Kastamonu for 63km (39 miles) and you reach the **Ilgaz National Park** ❻ (Ilgaz Milli Parkı), with dense mixed forest and a small but very scenic ski resort popular with Anakarans. You can continue southeast though the pretty Ottoman villages of **Tosya** and **Osmancık** to Amasya, one of the most stunningly set towns in all Turkey.

Amasya ❼ was the first capital of the ancient Pontic kings until they moved to Sinop in 120 BC. Overlooking the Yeşilırmak River, old Ottoman houses cluster around numerous Islamic monuments, while at night floodlights search the cliffs below the citadel for well-preserved cave tombs of the Pontic kings. It was here that the great geographer and historian Strabo was born in 64 BC. Later it became an important Seljuk centre, before being taken by the Ilkhanid Mongols after 1259.

There are two impressive Seljuk mosques – the **Burmalı Minare Camii** (Mosque of the Twisted Mina-

ret) and the **Gök Medrese/Camii**; a 16th-century *bedesten* in the bazaar between Ziya Paşı Bulvari and Atatürk Caddesi – as well as the **Burmahane Medresesi**, built by the Ilkhanids in 1308 as a lunatic asylum. Across from the Sultan Beyazit Camii, on Atatürk Caddesi, the **Amasya Museum** (Amasya Müzesi; Tue–Sun 8.30am–noon, 1–5pm; charge) contains a varied collection of artefacts from the different civilisations that have ruled the city, including carved wooden doors, a Hittite idol, astronomical instruments and Mongol mummies. The riverside **Hazeranlar Konağı** (Tue–Sun 9am–noon, 1.30–5pm; charge) is a restored Ottoman mansion from 1865, carefully refurbished with period furnishings.

Several of the 18 **rock-cut tombs** on the north bank of the river can be visited (daily dawn–dusk; charge); two of them are interconnected by a laboriously hewn tunnel. Variously used by Pontians, Romans, Seljuks and Ottomans, there isn't a great deal left of the structure, nor of the Pontic palace underneath the later accretions, but the view is mind-boggling.

The Hemşinlis

The Hemşinlis are an obscure Caucasian tribe whose language is a dialect of Armenian. Ruy González de Clavijo, Castilian envoy to the court of Timur in Samarkand, characterised them in a 1405 account as nominally Christian brigands who demanded a toll for the right of passage through their mountains. Their conversion to Islam came at some time during the early 1800s, but there was apparently not a single mosque in the region until a century later. The women, in their brightly coloured scarves (worn as turbans) and patterned pullovers, are unmistakable. The Hemşinli diaspora is huge, extending to Europe as well as major Turkish cities, where they are known for their skill as confectioners and pastry chefs. Most make a point of returning here in summer to maintain *yayla* traditions or run *pansiyons*.

East of Samsun

The ghastly four-lane Highway 10 carries heavy lorry traffic east from Samsun towards the border with Georgia, but off the beaten track inland, there are still some lovely, wild places to explore.

Ünye ❽ has a good beach – Uzun-kum – just west, and ample tourist facilities, as well as a pleasant town centre that isn't quite so blighted as others on the Black Sea, retaining traces of its past as Byzantine Oinaion and an important medieval port. The main local site is the Çaleoğlu fortress (open access) just 5km (3 miles) inland, with masonry from the Pontic to Byzantine periods.

Further along the coast some 50km (30 miles), a temple to the Argonauts' leader once stood at the tip of Cape Yason (Cape Jason); a medieval church marks the spot. Ordu, 35km (22 miles) further, is unremarkable other than for a derelict Greek cathedral by the sea and the side road to the beach-encircled crater-lake above Cambaşı Yaylası, 64km (40 miles) south.

Giresun ❾ was the ancient Kera-os, from which is derived "cherry".

The fruit was introduced to the West from here by the Roman gourmet-soldier Lucullus in 69 BC. Today the main attraction is offshore around Giresun Adası, one of the largest islets on the Turkish Black Sea coast, which hosts part of the late-May Aksu Festival. This is based on a far more ancient pagan observance, with fertility and banishing-misfortune rites still persisting amongst the "cultural events".

For those with a historical bent and their own vehicle, the scenic 106km (66-mile) trip over the Eğribel Geçidi to Şebinkarahisar is highly recommended. En route, a right turn at Kümber leads to Tamdere, a friendly place to base yourself if planning a day hike to the glacier lake at Kara-göl, just below the snowy, 3,107-metre (10,193ft) peak of the eponymous mountain range.

Beyond the pass, Şebinkarahisar ❿ sits high on a bluff overlooking the Kelkit valley. This was Pompey's

Highland women dancing in traditional costume at the Kadirga Yayla Festival in the Zigana Mountains near Tonya.

BELOW: Amasya.

BELOW: the modern towers of Trabzon.

Colonia, established after the Mithridatic Wars in 63 BC, although there was a settlement here long before. Byzantine Emperor Justinian's imposing ruined fortress still perches atop a huge basalt rock dominating the town. The area became part of the Ottoman Empire in 1471, when the now-restored **Fatih Camii** was built.

There are also remains of earlier mosques, several Greek churches in nearby villages and – most impressively – the cave-**Monastery of Meryemana**, 7km (4 miles) across the valley in Kayadibi village, which dates from the 5th century AD but was rededicated to St Philip by the Armenians much more recently. It is a stiff climb up the vertiginous cliff, but the site and view are breathtaking. Sadly, the area's strategic value, earthquakes and political turmoil (including a desperate four-week battle between local Armenians and the Ottoman forces who came to deport them in June 1915) have damaged all local monuments.

Tirebolu ⓫ (formerly Tripolis) occupies a crescent-shaped bay bracketed by two headlands, 41km (25 miles) east of Giresun; the eastern promontory is home to a 14th-century Genoese fortress. This has been a substantial port since antiquity, largely on account of the silver mined in the hinterland; these days the main local product is the **hazelnut** (*fındık* in Turkish), of which Turkey is the world's biggest producer. During summer you'll see broad expanses of them everywhere, still unhusked, spread out to dry.

Görele marks the turn-off to **Kuşköy** (Bird Village), 28km (17 miles) inland, so named because its inhabitants are famed for long-distance communication by means of an archaic "whistle language"; an annual July festival, and currently a Unesco-funded film project celebrate it. From Vakfıkebir, it's 20km (12 miles) inland to **Tonya ⓬**, inhabited by Greek-speaking Muslims possibly descended from the most fiercely independent of Pontic tribes. Until the 1980s junta put a lid on matters by severely controlling civilian access to firearms, Tonya was notorious for its bloody vendettas. In the local graveyard, bullets are carved on headstones to represent the number of people the deceased had killed before catching a bullet of his own.

More positively, Tonya is one of several villages to participate in the annual **Kadırga Yayla Festival** (third weekend in July), held at the common boundary point of Tonya, Torul, Görele and Maçka territories and thought to have begun as a peace negotiation after centuries of conflict over grazing lands.

Tall tales of Trebizond

Trebizond – today **Trabzon ⓭** – has had a bewitching reputation for close to two millennia, famed for its wealth, its gold-plated palace and cathedral domes, and its sporadic independence. Founded as a Greek colony during the 8th century BC, Trebizond was to reach its cultural zenith when Alexios I Komnenos and his Georgian supporters took control here in 1204 after the Fourth Crusade's invasion of Constantinople. Their local mini-empire lasted

57 years, in part because Mongol raids forced the Silk Road to divert through the city, encouraging a flourishing trade with the Genoese and Venetians, who were surprised to find this outpost of civilisation in such outlandish territory.

Native son and distinguished church scholar Basilios Bessarion (later turned Catholic churchman) carried memories of its magnificence to Italian exile, not long before Trebizond became the last Byzantine outpost seized by the Ottomans. He described just part of the Komneni's "golden palace" as "a long building of great beauty, its foundation being all of white stone, and its roof decorated with gold and other colours, painted flowers and stars, emitting beams of light as if it were heaven itself". Rose Macaulay's famed 1956 *The Towers of Trebizond* perpetuated this image of a fairy-tale city of sybaritic splendour, its towers "shimmering on a far horizon in luminous enchantment" – although the novel was mainly a penetrating satire on both Turkish and English mores.

In reality, the days of Trabzon's seaborne glory all but disappeared in the late 1800s with the completion of the Ankara–Erzurum railway, and onward roads into Iran. Russia occupied the city from April 1916 to early 1918, after which an attempt by local Greeks to base their "Republic of Pontus" here ended in defeat and the 1923 exchange of populations. The **Atatürk Köşkü** (daily 8am–5pm; charge) is the confiscated mansion of the republic's would-be president.

Trabzon's harbour area and city centre are not glamorous any more; no shimmering towers define the horizon, and Byzantine remains are largely unheralded, with the only hint of past exoticism being a large community of resident Russians. Indeed, trade with Georgia and the Russian Federation supports much of the population of nearly half a million. Tourism is not assiduously promoted, and salubrious lodging is scarce, overpriced and often full of tour groups.

Little remains of the grandiose **city walls** or central citadel (**Ortahisar**) around the site of the Byzantine palace,

Trabzon is the closest large Turkish city to Georgia and Russia, and there are hints of Russian influence in the local architecture.

BELOW: much of the Black Sea coast is steep and rocky.

Quirks of the Black Sea

The Black Sea displays certain peculiarities, a consequence of its uninterrupted connection with the Mediterranean via the Bosphorus, Sea of Marmara and the Dardanelles since the last ice ages ended. Relatively fresh water (18 parts salinity per thousand as against 30–40 parts for proper oceans) occupies its first few fathoms, constantly replenished by the many rivers feeding the Black Sea. The surplus exits via the Bosphorus as a surface current, while a deeper countercurrent of much saltier, denser water from the Aegean heads up into the Black Sea. The result is that layers of less dense, less salty, usually cooler water occupy the top 100 metres (330ft) or so, above the bulk of the sea which forms a sludge of warmer, heavier brine. Since the lighter top layers, supporting abundant marine life, are unable to penetrate the lower depths for mixing and oxygenation, almost 90 percent of the Black Sea's volume is an anoxic, sulphurous wasteland. Dead organisms drift towards the bottom; bacteria oxidizing this organic detritus consume what little oxygen is available, while other bacteria have evolved to use sulphate for metabolising this debris, generating highly toxic hydrogen sulphide. For archaeologists, a major bonanza has resulted, since ancient ships and other artefacts which lie in the deep zone are found exceptionally well preserved owing to the absence of oxidation.

Trekking in the Kaçkar

The wild Kaçkar mountains offer some of the best hiking in Turkey, with magnificent scenery, challenging climbs and *yayla* communities

The glaciated Kaçkar mountains are the highest (3,932m/12,190ft) and most spectacular of the various massifs in Turkey's eastern Black Sea region. The name is derived from the Armenian *khatchkar* (votive relief cross), perhaps suggested by the sculpted nature of the range. Its non-porous granite has resulted in hundreds of midnight-blue lakes and burbling streams. Wildflower displays, especially above the 1,800-metre (5,580ft) contour, are second to none. Best of all is the opportunity to sample life at the various *yaylas* (pastoral communities), inhabited to varying degrees from late June to early September.

As a barrier range rising steeply from the damp Black Sea coast, the Kaçkar's northwest slopes attract mist and rain – lots of it. This is the main trekkers' bugbear, and means that critical pedestrian passes must be conquered before midday, when cloud typically boils up to obscure everything. The southeast-facing flanks, draining towards the

Çoruh River, have more reliable, clearer weather.

The most popular trekking season is summer, but these are the mistiest and most crowded months – popular wilderness campsites, particularly Dilberdüzü in the heart of the range, overflow at this time. May and June have the most spectacular floral displays (and long days), but most passes are still snowed up (requiring ice axe and crampons), and most *yaylas* are yet to be inhabited for the year. September and early October are also fine, with the least mist, though many *yaylas* will be empty.

There are several classic trailhead villages or *yaylas* on either side of the Kaçkar, all with rustic if indoor accommodation and varying levels of supplies, mule hire and guiding services available. On the Çoruh flank, provisions can be purchased in Yusufeli, from where minibuses ply southwest to Tekkale or north to Barhal, Hevek (officially Yaylalar) and Meretet (Olgunlar). Most local place names are of Hemşinli or Georgian derivation, often disguised by clumsy Turkification. On the north side, the highest market town is Çamlıhemşin, departure point for public transport further up to the *yaylas* of Çat and Elevit, or the full-blown resort of Ayder.

Given the complex local topography, with many subsidiary ridges off the main watershed, there are numerous possible itineraries, either as a circuit (allowing storage of extra gear) or as a point-to-point trek. One of the less frequented routes is the northerly trail, which extends from Barhal up towards the Altparmak ridge via the Satibe meadows, before angling over to the Önbolat valley and tackling the Kırmızı pass; the pass leads to Avusor *yayla*, linked by dirt road to Ayder (allow 2 days). In contrast, the classic traverse from Meretet to Dilberdüzü (the main base camp for Kaçkar summit), and then on via ice-filled Deniz Gölü and the Kavron pass, is heavily subscribed. From this pass, there's a choice of looping back to Meretet via Yukarı Kavron *yayla*, the Çaymakçur pass and flower-spangled Düpeduz, or carrying on west to Elevit and the end of a dirt road up from Çat (both 2 to 3 days). For the less committed, low-altitude, 1-day walks link Çamlıhemşin and Ayder via Pokut and Hazındak *yaylas*, or Ayder with Hazındak, Samistal and the lower Kavron *yayla* – where minibuses whisk you the 13km (8 miles) back to Ayder.

Indispensable for any independent hiking is Kate Clow and Terry Richardson's *The Kaçkar* guide and map (www.trekkinginturkey.com). ❏

LEFT: hiking in the Kaçkar mountains near Yukari Kavron.

erched at the west edge of the table-
nd (*trapezous* in ancient Greek) which
as the original point of settlement.
he **Ortahisar Camii** was originally
e 13th- to 14th-century cathedral
f Panagia Khrysokephalos (Golden-
eaded, perhaps after its then-plated
ome); today its glorious frescoes and
oor mosaics have been whitewashed
nd cemented over in accord with
lamic sensibilities – Trabzon is gener-
lly a very conservative, devout place.
he nearby church of **St Eugenios**
he Yeni Cuma Camii since 1461) is
milarly plain; the city's oldest church,
nconverted 9th-century **St Ann** (alias
üçük Ayvasil), is permanently locked.
  Slightly further east, along or just off
edestrianised Uzun Sokak, stand occa-
onal surviving Greek-built mansions;
ne of the most sumptuous, on Zeytin-
k Caddesi, has become the **Trabzon
luseum** (Trabzon Müzesi; Tue–Sun
.30am–noon, 1–5pm; charge). Inside
nis Italian-designed pile the local Belle
poque lifestyle has been re-created;
car exhibit of the basement archaeo-
gical collection is a life-sized bronze
catue of Hermes.

The monastic church of **Hagia
Sophia** (Aya Sofya; daily, Apr–Oct
9am–6pm, Nov–Mar 8am–4pm;
charge) sits romantically 3km (2 miles)
west of the city centre on a bluff overlooking the sea. Erected on the orders
of local emperor Manuel I Komnenos
between 1238 and 1263, it has miraculously retained its vivid and expressive
contemporary frescoes, restored by
David Talbot Rice in 1957–64, depicting scenes from the life of Christ and
the Old Testament.

The only other local "must" is
the Armenian monastic church of
Kaymaklı, 6km (4 miles) southeast on
Boztepe hill; now on the grounds of a
farm, the resident family will happily
show you surprisingly sophisticated
17th-century frescoes of the Last Judgement which survived the 20th century
through the church's use as a barn.

A monastery to remember

The **Monastery of Sumela**, or the **Virgin of the Black Rock ⓮**, in the depths
of the densely forested Altındere,
perches dramatically on a ledge 44km
(27 miles) south of Trabzon, halfway

TIP

Enormous amounts of
money change hands
daily in Trabzon, lending
it a lively "gold rush"
atmosphere – complete
with numerous
prostitutes from the
Russian federation.
Things have calmed
down considerably since
the mid-1990s, but lone
female tourists may still
find themselves
mistaken for
streetwalkers.

BELOW: the cloud-
shrouded
Monastery of
Sumela.

TIP

Some Kaçkar "mountain men" are serious drinkers, and in the past this has led to a number of sexual assaults on tourists. The problem has been resolved in Ayder by banning alcohol sales (except in shops) in the village centre. Restaurants that still offer drinks are outside the village and cater strictly for tourists and guides.

BELOW: layers of frescoes cover the interior of the Monastery of Sumela.

up a sheer palisade above the stream. Legend relates how it was built by two monks from Athens in AD 385, guided by a vision of the Virgin, but it was more likely to have been commissioned by early Byzantine emperors to help convert the pagan natives to Christianity, like several other local monasteries which have essentially vanished. Sumela's heyday, like that of Trebizond, came through patronage by the local Komneni dynasty, which promulgated an edict exempting it from all taxes. Selim the Grim upheld these rights, and other Ottoman sultans even made pilgrimages – such was the place's prestige – but this all ended when the monks departed, together with other local Orthodox, in 1923.

The present buildings probably date from the 12th century and contain many subsequent layers of frescoes, the best being from the 14th and 15th centuries; most have been well restored since 1996, and cover improbable surfaces of the cave-church. Sumela ranks as one of the Black Sea's biggest attractions, with several bus tours daily, and the former stiff hike up the cliff

from the valley bottom will soon be replaced by essentially drive-up access with a car park near the ruins (daily Oct–Apr 9am–5pm, May–Sept 9am– 6pm; charge).

Beyond Trabzon

Beyond the turning for Sumela at Maçka, travel up-valley on the E97 towards the **Zigana pass**, straddling the old caravan route towards Erzurum and Persia; it was here that Xenophon's Ten Thousand first glimpsed the sea in 399 BC, on their way back from Mesopotamia. Today only the twisty old road goes over the pass (2,025 metres/ 6,643ft); a new road just west uses a tunnel. Just south, a castle at **Torul** guards the approaches, while **Gümüşhane** further down the Harşit valley once prospered from its silver mines; the modern town is drab, the abandoned Ottoman settlement 7km (4 miles) away is the thing to see. Some 190km (118 miles) out of Trabzon, the provincial capital of **Bayburt** is home to the remains of Justinian's castle, claimed the largest in Turkey, and an appealing setting on the young Çoruh River.

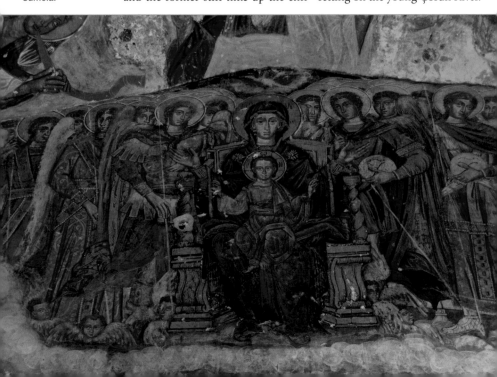

East of Trabzon along the coast, there is little specific to see at Of (pronounced "oaf") or Çaykara just inland, both bastions of Islamic piety. Çaykara, however, is the gateway to the alpine landscape around **Uzungöl** (Long Lake); with plenty of quality accommodation it makes a feasible alternative to Trabzon, and there are more glacial lakes beyond at the base of Halizden peak – though it's a full day's walk there and back.

East of the concreted-over "tea capitals" of **Rize** and **Çayeli**, **Pazar** marks the beginning of the traditional **Laz homeland**. Watch out for men carrying hawks on their wrists; hawking is a traditional Laz sport, and there are even teahouses where fanatics bring their "pets" to squawk in competition with the conversation.

Shortly past Pazar lies the turning inland to the **Hemşin valleys**, the usual northern gateway to the Kaçkar mountains (*see page 326*). **Çamlıhemşin ⓯**, built beside the roaring Fırtına (Storm) River, is the region's main market town and minibus connection point; central Türkü Tourism (www.turkutour.com) is a highly recommended trekking outfitter. Both upstream and downstream you'll notice many magnificent stone-arch bridges, some dating from the 17th century. Probably the best example is the **Taş Kemer**, which spans the Fırtına at **Şenyuva**, where some impressive traditional farmsteads nestle at the end of motorised pulleys transferring supplies across the stream.

On the steadily worsening road up from Şenyuva, single-towered **Zilkale** has a mysterious history. Some claim it dates from the 6th century, but it was more likely built by the Trapezuntine Komneni or a local warlord – for who knows what purpose, given the obscure location. It is, unsurprisingly, reputed to be haunted after dark by its former garrison and their horses. The so-called pavement ends at **Çat**, which has the last conventional accommodation before more primitive *yaylas* – and then true wilderness – take over.

A different, wider road from Çamlıhemşin leads 17km (11 miles) up to the (very) hot-springs resort of **Ayder**, another popular jump-off point for the Kaçkar mountains, with comfortable accommodation.

Nearly every Black Sea native returns for the yearly trip to the mountain pastures. The festival season begins on 6 May (the traditional first day of summer) and from then on, almost every region has a festival marked by partying, ecstatic dancing to the kemençe (three-stringed fiddle) and tulum (bagpipes), drinking, and the practice of ancient (and often very odd) customs.

BELOW: bloodless bullfight at the Kafkasör Festival, Artvin.

Yusufeli lies on the bank of the turbulent Çoruh river, between Ishan and Tekkale.

BELOW: every area has a festival to celebrate the start of summer.

Artvin: "Little Georgia"

The Artvin region is still quintessentially Caucasian and offers some of the most impressive 9th- to 11th-century church architecture in the world, legacy of a flourishing of Georgian medieval culture between Tortum, Artvin and Ardahan. Georgians have inhabited southern Caucasia, including these valleys, since antiquity. The king of Georgia adopted Christianity shortly after his Armenian counterpart, but unlike the Armenians the Georgians never broke with the Eastern Orthodox Church, and managed to maintain de facto independence in the face of Roman, Byzantine and Arab incursions.

Early in the 9th century, a branch of the Armeno-Georgian Bagratid dynasty gained footholds as far south as Ani, and ultimately unified various Georgian principalities into a kingdom in 1008, under Bagrat III. At its peak, under Queen Tamar (r. 1184–1213), Georgia extended almost as far west as Bayburt, ruled from Tbilisi by the world's longest-lasting sovereign dynasty until Russian occupation in 1811. From the late 800s, the valleys south of Artvin were home to some of the finest fresco-painters, stonemasons and architects of the age, resulting in a vast number of fortresses and monastic churches, many of which still survive in village centres or isolated valleys. This golden age came to an end with Persian and Mongol raids of the mid-13th century.

The churches

Artvin ⑯ itself has nothing to recommend it except its annual Kafkasör Festival *(see page 404)* – which lately has also featured wrestlers, musicians and vendors from both Turkey and Georgia – plus (relative) proximity to many Georgian churches. Nonetheless, the surroundings are beautiful, with the fertile land clothed in verdant forests and fruit orchards.

Getting around the nearby valleys with their marvellous Georgian churches is virtually impossible without your own transport. There are no tour agents, car-rental outlets or (usually) *dolmuşes* to the villages by the churches: the only other option is to hire a taxi at an outrageous daily rate from Artvin.

The five most impressive churches e south of Artvin, in the valleys of ne Çoruh and Tortum rivers. **Işhan** (Ishkhani in Georgian) ⑰ is the first, nvolving a 6km (4-mile) climb from the main road to the village, with its huge, nind-blowing church. Work was begun uring the 8th century and only completed 300 years later; the dome rests in four massive columns, while delicate cone carvings adorn the outer walls.

A nearby turning west off the main oad leads to Yusufeli, and thence to ither Tekkale or Barhal; outside of hese villages, close to the southern anks of the Kaçkar are almost identical, gabled domeless churches, erected uring the late 10th-century tenure of David Magistros, Prince of Oltu. **Dört-kilise (Otkhta Eklesia) church**, 6km (4 miles) outside Tekkale village, has ight columns supporting the barrel-ed ceiling and a choir occupying the vest end; the arcaded, derelict building ust northeast was the refectory of this ormer monastic complex.

The church at **Barhal** (Parkhali), 0 minutes' walk outside the village, ssentially Dörtkilise's twin except omewhat smaller, is in better condiion owing to the fact that it has long unctioned as a mosque; admission is asiest at Friday prayers, or try asking t the school for the keys.

Back on the main highway south, just ast Tortum Lake, a turning west leads km (4½ miles) west to Camlıyamaç illage with its massive **Öşk Vank (Oshki)** church, another endowment f David Magistros, which again owes good state of preservation to its long se as a mosque; inside is a very Gothic olonnade, with no two columns like, and surviving fresco fragments. ome 9km (5½ miles) past the lake's outhern end, David's first project, the hurch of **Haho** (Khakhuli) in Bağbaşı, vas once the most celebrated of Georian monasteries, and is still among he best preserved, having served as he local mosque since the 17th cenury. The dome is topped with a coni-al roof of varicoloured tiles; inside the

gallery flanking the church on the south are high-quality reliefs (including the whale devouring Jonah) and frescoes of Apostles and angels in the apse.

Due east of Artvin, more fine churches in the valley of the Berta River are reached from the road to Şavşat. First up is 10th-century **Dolishane** in Hamamlı village, with fine reliefs on the south façade; next, half-ruined **Porta** (Khantza) monastery, in Pırnallı village, is a scenic 45-minute walk up a path from the main highway. **Tbeti**, 11km (7 miles) north of Şavşat at Cevizli village, much battered by treasure-hunters, was originally a monastery where the great medieval Georgian epic poet, Shota Rustaveli (1172–1216) supposedly studied for a period.

Although much searched by post-1920 treasure-hunters who were convinced the departing Georgian Christians had hidden gold on the premises against their eventual return, Tbeti still retains extensive relief work on its apse and south transept. ❑

Children in Yusufeli. Georgians have inhabited the Artvin region's valleys since ancient times.

BELOW: Tortum Lake.

THE GREAT OUTDOORS

There's an abundance of exciting outdoor activities on offer in Turkey, both along the coasts and in the mountains of the interior

With its often dramatic topography, relatively reliable weather conditions and temperate seas, it's hardly surprising that Turkey is becoming an adventure and outdoor sports mecca. Along the Mediterranean and Aegean coasts, **Windsurfing** is a big draw wherever sea breezes and onshore landforms combine to produce ideal conditions, particularly around Bodrum, at Alaçatı near Çeşme, and Aydıncık beach on Gökçeada. All the major southwest coast resorts have well-equipped **yacht marinas**, with the convoluted shoreline between Bodrum and Finike especially rewarding. **Scuba diving** is pitched at most Mediterranean and south Aegean centres, but is most worthwhile out of Bodrum, Kalkan, Kaş and Adrasan; expect to see corals, rock formations and submerged wrecks rather than huge shoals of fish. The cooler northern Aegean, perhaps surprisingly, has good diving at Ayvalık and the Saroz gulf.

Inland, **canyoning** – in the toes of lofty Akdağ – is a refreshing way to spend a summer's day, as is **white-water rafting** along the Dalaman Çayı near Dalyan, the Köprülü Canyon near Antalya, and the Göksu above Silifke. The grandaddy of Turkish rivers is the Çoruh in the northeast, its rapids attracting rafters from far and wide.

You can get airborne on a **paraglider** above Ölüdeniz and Kaş, or more passively (and expensively) in a **hot-air balloon** over Cappadocia – champagne breakfast usually included. The harsh winters in the Anatolian mountains bring reliable snowfall, although the many **ski resorts** are little-known to foreigners.

ABOVE: paragliding over Ölüd[e]
LEFT: the best skiing conditions a[re]
remote Palandöken, above Erzu[rum;]
Uludağ, above Bursa, and Kartalkaya, [above]
Bolu, are more accessible – and crow[ded]

RIGHT: Alaçati, near Çeşme, often has perfect conditions for windsurfing. **BELOW:** mountain biking in Cappadocia.

MOUNTAINEERING AND HIKING

Turkey's rugged interior offers excellent mountain trekking – though you must be resourceful and self-sufficient, as topographic maps are scarce and there's no refuge network as in Europe. The most popular mountains are the glaciated Kaçkar (summit 3,972 metres/13,031ft; *see page 326)*, inland from the Black Sea between Rize and Erzurum. A radically different experience is provided by the limestone Aladağlar (3,756 metres/12,322ft) and Bolkar Toros (3,585 metres/11,761ft), near Niğde. With the PKK rebellion waning, the spectacular Cilo-Sat range of Hakkâri, culminating in 4,136-metre (13,569ft) Mount Reşko, is an up-and-coming area, though it's still best to go with an organised expedition.

But you needn't necessarily head for the alpine zone. Southwestern coastal Turkey has two marked, regularly maintained, long-distance trails: the Lycian Way between Ölüdeniz and Antalya, and the St Paul Trail – purporting to follow in the proselytising footsteps of the Apostle – linking Perge with the Eğirdir region. Both have accompanying guide booklets with GPS-compatible maps (see www. trekkinginturkey.com), and – best of all for those averse to heavy backpacks – a network of village lodging and meal provision is developing along both routes.

TOP: outdoor adventure companies lead treks along the long-distance trails as well as into the mountains. **BELOW:** hiking between Göreme and Çavuşin in Cappadocia's Rose Valley.

E: hot-air ballooning is a great way to see the Cappadocian ﾐape. The best flying conditions are between April to October. **W:** white-water rafting down the Çoruh river. The completion of ﾐir Dam will, however, affect the river's flow.

THE EAST

Few tourists visit the beautiful but troubled plains of the "Fertile Crescent" and the remote plateaux and mountains of the Far East

Eastern Turkey's vast expanse is made up of two distinct regions, the Near East and the Far East. The former is dominated by the River Euphrates, home to a series of giant hydroelectric dams and irrigation canals that have turned the barren flatlands into an agricultural powerhouse. Its crowning historic glory is the 2,000-year-old funerary sanctuary of King Antiochus atop the 2,150-metre (7,050ft) Nemrut Dağı. Gaziantep, dominated by an imposing citadel, is a booming regional hub famed for pistachio nuts – and its archaeological museum houses an incredible collection of Roman mosaics. Further east, ancient Şanlıurfa, the city of prophets, claims to be the birthplace of Abraham and boasts one of the country's most colourful bazaars.

Heading into the far eastern region is Turkey's most overtly Kurdish city, Diyarbakır, famous for its 6km (3½-mile) -long medieval walls. Mardin, overlooking the Syrian border and the Mesopotamian plain, boasts a remarkable collection of honey-hued stone houses, mosques and Syrian Orthodox churches.

Further east and north the altitude increases, and sheep and cattle are grazed by nomadic tribesmen in the shadow of lofty mountains, snow-streaked even in summer. Here the average elevation rises above 2,000 metres (6,560ft), culminating in the 5,137-metre (16,853ft) Mount Ararat in the northeast. Pick of the sights in this remote area is the romantically ruined city of Ani, blessed with a stunning collection of Armenian churches and monasteries, and beautiful Lake Van where the church of the Holy Cross is set on a tiny offshore islet.

Eastern Turkey is an immensely rewarding place to travel despite the long distances and, outside of the major centres, lack of creature comforts. Turkish clashes with the PKK continue, so take advice before travelling, particularly in the Tunceli and Hakkâri regions. ❑

PRECEDING PAGES: the fortified palace Işak Paşa Sarayr, near Mount Ararat on Turkey's eastern border. **LEFT:** the massive head belonging to a statue of an ancient god at Nemrut Dağı's summit. **ABOVE RIGHT:** snow-capped Mount Ararat dominates the northeastern plateau. **ABOVE LEFT:** Ovacik inhabitant.

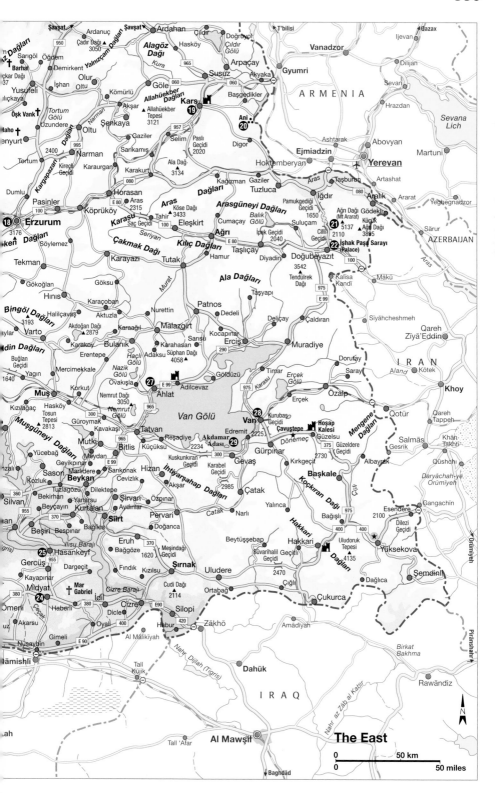

The East

0   50 km
0   50 miles

THE NEAR EAST

This vast, little-known tract of southeast Turkey has some fabulous scenery, from burning plains to towering mountains, and traces of some of the world's oldest civilisations

BELOW: Çifte
Minareli Medrese in
Sivas – poetry set
in stone.

The central Anatolian plateau extends for many bleak and lonely kilometres east of Ankara. Patchy wheatfields alternate with bald hills that centuries of soil erosion have fashioned into eerie sculptures. Brown and ochre predominate, except when the brief glory of May covers the land with grass and wild flowers. This austere landscape is enlivened in patches by plunging gorges and snow-streaked mountain tops. To the south, plateau and mountain give way to the scorched plains of Mesopotamia, newly brought to life by the waters of the massiv Atatürk dam.

Regional capital and sights en route

Erzincan ❶, some 690km/430 miles or 9 hours by bus, east of Ankara, is th largest centre in the region, a modern looking city which was entirely rebuil after the devastating earthquakes o 1939 and 1992. Beyond it, to the north the road leads over remote mountai passes to the Black Sea coast. To th south, the wild canyon of the Uppe Euphrates gradually emerges into th high plateau of the northeast – th Roman province of Armenia Major.

En route between Ankara (or Kay seri) and Erzincan, **Sivas** ❷ (know as Sebastia to Rome and Byzantium deserves a stop for its thriving craft bazaar and its magnificent clutch o Seljuk architecture: the 12th-century **Ulu Cami** and the four theologica and medical colleges of **Gök**, **Çift Minareli**, **Şifahiye** and **Büruciy Medrese**. These all have elaborately decorative 13th-century foundation built by the Seljuk and Mongol gover nors. Look for the decorative animals including pigs, an artistic adaptatio from Armenian design that woul have been anathema to most icono clastic Muslims.

Some 15km (10 miles) east of Kan gal, famed for a gigantic breed of sheep dog named after the town, is **Balıkl Kaplıca** (hot springs), renowned fo

its varieties of skin-eating fish, said to relieve psoriasis. The sleepy iron-mining town of **Divriği ❸** to the east houses perhaps the most significant work of pre-Ottoman Turkish architecture in Turkey, and certainly calls for a detour. The mosque and hospital complex of the **Ulu Cami** was founded in 1228–9 by the Mengücük dynasty, which ruled the area as vassals to the Seljuks. The main portal is outrageously ornate, a riot of highly un-Islamic relief-carved birds and animals. The complex is perhaps the least well known of Turkey's Unesco World Heritage Sites.

Iliç and Kemaliye

From Divriği the railway line heads east to **İliç ❹**. The closest thing Turkey has to a classic one-horse town, İliç was founded solely to service the freight and passenger trains that run through it, with a combined teahouse and flophouse. The town can only be reached with great contrivance by road – it's far better reached by rail (there are several trains each day for the one-hour ride to Divriği). İliç has begun to attract canoe and raft enthusiasts, who shoot the rapids of the Upper Euphrates here before gliding downstream towards the Keban Dam.

From either İliç or Divriği, it's possible to head down to **Kemaliye ❺**, a quaint little town on the west bank of the Euphrates at the spot where the river starts to fill the valley behind the Keban Dam. Formerly known by its Armenian name of Egin, the town was renamed **Kemaliye** (after Mustafa Kemal Atatürk) in 1922 to commemorate its role in the Turkish War of Independence.

Kemaliye provides an abrupt architectural change from the surrounding traditional Muslim settlements. It is clear that the Anatolian Christians of the 19th century not only enjoyed a much higher standard of living than most of their contemporaries, but that an eye for outward appearance and private ease was a primary concern. Some of their fine houses are now listed buildings and are being restored. Many have delicately carved shutters and balconies overlooking attractive gardens. The town is becoming something of a centre for Turkish outtdoor enthusiasts

Detail on the north door of Divriği's Ulu Cami, a UNESCO World Heritage Site.

BELOW: Keban Dam: the power of the future.

Catch a ferry from Elazığ on the south shore of Lake Keban to visit Ovacik and Tunceli on the north shore.

BELOW: crossing the Munzur mountains in winter.

with rafting, hiking up to the surrounding *yaylas* (summer pastures) and mountain-biking possibilities.

This central area, formerly dependent on snowfall and rain for dryland farming, has become a major source of grain for Turkey since the construction of the gargantuan **Keban Barajı**, a dam at the confluence of the Euphrates and Murat rivers as they churn deep and white out of the mountains of the central Anatolian plateau. Completed in 1975, it was the largest dam in the region until the initiation of the even larger and vastly more ambitious Atatürk Dam project downstream near Şanlıurfa.

Tunceli province: a troubled past

Due east, Tunceli province, along the north shore of **Keban Barajı** (Keban Dam), is one of the least developed, most problematic yet indisputably beautiful areas of Turkey. The towering Munzur mountain range, with an average height of over 2,500 metres (8,000ft), is the source of many small white-water streams that eventually merge with either the Euphrates or its major tributary, the Murat. The majority of the region's inhabitants are Kurdish by ethnicity and Alevi by religion and, as a result, they fit uneasily into the Sunni-majority, Turkish nationalist orientated state.

Formerly known as Dersim, Tunceli was the site of a dramatic uprising in 1937, when local inhabitants, under the leadership of Kurdish Alevi tribal leader Seyyid Riza, revolted against the central government, in protest at the region's economic poverty and high government taxes. They blew up bridges, blocked passes into the Alpine valleys and slaughtered soldiers stationed there. Reinforcements were shuttled down the newly constructed railway to the east and the Turkish air force dive-bombed those rebel strongholds beyond the reach of the ground forces.

The general carnage and violence on both sides, as well as the mass forced migration of the survivors to different areas of the country, were such that the entire period has, until recently, been effectively erased from official history only to live on in local memory. It was, in effect, Turkey's Wounded Knee, and only the span of some 60 years has allowed the younger generations to start exploring the roots and consequences of the entire tragic affair.

Tunceli today

The Tunceli region remains underdeveloped, and its remote, jagged mountains, honeycombed with caves provide cover for separatist groups who clash sporadically with the Turkish security forces. If you wish to explore the region, expect the occasional road block, where your papers will be examined by security forces, and you may be quizzed about why you are here.

Elazığ *(see opposite)*, on the south shore of Lake Keban, is a natural jumping-off point. A ferry station some 16km (10 miles) north of town provides transport across the lake, past **Pertek Kalesi**, which once dominated

the valley floor of the Murat River from a high knoll. These days the castle, built by the Mengücük dynasty but much restored in Ottoman times, barely keeps its head above water on an island halfway across the reservoir. Small craft service the route for a nominal fee.

Once on the north bank, the road disintegrates into a gravel path leading up to the mountain town of **Hozat**, once the Ottoman garrison town for the region.

Ovacık and the Munzur Valley National Park

Ovacık ("the little valley") is a pretty mountain town of some 5,000 souls, and makes a good base for exploring the natural wonders of the beautiful **Munzur Valley National Park**. The park is dominated by high mountains, snow-streaked well into summer, and the clear, bubbling waters of the Munzur Çayı. The security situation hereabouts is far more stable than it was, and it should be possible to explore the surrounding high pastures, natural springs, valleys and caves – but make sure you take local advice before setting out.

Tunceli town

The clear, white waters of the Munzur Çayı slowly darken as the silt of scores of mountain streams flush into it, creating a frothing brown river as one proceeds down the mountain towards **Tunceli**. The town, however, has precious little to recommend it – although there are several cheap hotels and an array of rooftop restaurants, enlivened by the relaxed attitude of the local Alevi population towards alcohol. Continue east, either by way of the Pülümür pass to Erzincan and Erzurum, or through Bingöl and Muş to the waters of Lake Van.

The Euphrates region

Back on the southern shore of Lake Keban, **Elazığ** was established in the mid-19th century by, and named after, Sultan Abdulaziz. The distortion in the original name occurred by design in the early years of the republic when many of Turkey's place names were changed to fit better with Atatürk's new nationalism.

Like many of the towns and cities of central and eastern Anatolia, Elazığ

Local resident, Ovacik.

BELOW LEFT: Ovacik street.
BELOW RIGHT: Munzur Çayi (river) in the Munzur Valley National Park.

Malatya is famous for its apricots.

– although pleasant enough – is primarily a military barracks and there is little here to detain the average tourist. On the university grounds, the local **Archaeological Museum** (Tue–Sat 8am–5pm; charge) has a rather ragtag collection of pots and pans, but some good coins, jewellery and carpets, and a number of Urartian items rescued from digs ahead of the flooding of the valley.

The history of **Harput ❼**, a few kilometres up the road on the lakeshore, neatly sums up the whole complex, contradictory and often violent history of east-central Anatolia. The **citadel**, founded by the Hurrians in the 2nd millennium BC, was conquered successively by every army that passed from east to west or north to south, including the Urartians, Hittites, Egyptians, Achaemenids, Macedonians, Parthians, Armenians, Romans, Sassanians, Byzantines, Arabs, Seljuk, Artuk and Akkoyunlu and various other sundry Turks. Until the upheavals of World War I, its population was largely Armenian and the town boasted a huge American missionary college, depicted in a black-and-white period photograph in Harput's tiny museum.

Today, the most significant buildings in the town are the **Ulu Cami** (Great Mosque), with its wildly off-balance brick minaret clinging on for grim death, the austere **Tomb of Arab Baba**, a local holy man, and the paltry remains of the churches abandoned by the Armenians during World War I. On the edge of the site is the wreck of a Byzantine-era castle captured by the Mongol warlord Tamerlane.

South of Elazığ, the Upper Euphrates region is dominated by Nemrut Dağı (*see opposite*) – on a clear day, the strange, man-made nipple of Antiochus' tumulus can be seen from nearly 150km (100 miles) in every direction. It is by no means the only point of interest in this oft-neglected area, but one must often search for charm in the towns and cities.

Malatya

Malatya ❽ is a prosperous town famed throughout Turkey for its apricots, which are grown and dried (often on the flat roofs of the area's tradi

tional houses) and brought in from the surrounding villages for shipment throughout the country and abroad. Malatya's other major claim to fame is as the home town of Atatürk's chief lieutenant, İsmet İnönü. The figure of Turkey's second president surveys the town square from a bronze horse, one of the few places where this honour has been bestowed on someone other than Atatürk. Malatya's **Archaeology Museum** (Tue–Sun 8am–5pm; charge), on Fuzili Caddesi, has a small but significant Hittite collection, mainly finds from the nearby settlement mound of Aslantepe.

Aslantepe itself (Tue–Sun 8am–5pm; charge) lies about 4km (2½ miles) north of town, a substantial mound attractively set amongst stands of apricot trees. Work has been ongoing to turn the site into an open-air museum – and there are plans to bring back the pair of Hittite stone lions which once graced the town (literally "Lion Hill" in Turkish) from the Archaeological Museum in Ankara. Thorough excavations in recent years have uncovered a vast mudbrick palace complex dating back to 4000 BC, with wall paintings from 3200 BC. In late Roman times, the settlement moved 8km (5 miles) north to **Eski Malatya**, which still has a smattering of Byzantine and Seljuk remains, including 6th-century city walls, a 17th-century caravansaray and the **Silahtar Mustafa Paşa Hanı.** Pick of the remains, though, is the 13th-century Seljuk **Ulu Cami**, noted for its beautiful blue-glazed tilework.

The major reason visitors come to Malatya, however, is because it makes a pleasant base for the trip up Mt Nemrut Dağı (*see below*).

Nemrut Dağı

Commagene, a tiny buffer state on the Upper Euphrates, pinched between the fleet cavalry of ancient Parthia and the inexorable legions of Rome, was a historical aberration. It flourished for the briefest instant during the Roman civil wars which pitted the tyrannicides, Brutus and Cassius, against the fragile coalition of Mark Antony and Octavian, only to be crushed and absorbed into the Roman Empire, disappearing from history as Christianity took hold.

Malatya is ideal as a base for those wishing to ascend Nemrut Dağı – and for those with a sweet tooth, as the area's farmers produce huge harvests of cherries and apricots.

BELOW: trekking up Nemrut Daği.

Visiting Nemrut Dağı

The spectacular mountain-top funerary sanctuary of Antiochus I is, for most people, the literal and metaphorical high of a visit to southeast Turkey. Its very remoteness, however, means that an overnight stay somewhere in the vicinity of the site is obligatory. The usual approach to Nemrut is from the south, from either Gaziantep or Şanlıurfa (both 3- to 4-hour drives). There is comfortable accommodation to be found in either hot, nondescript Kahta or, better, up in the mountains at the village of Karadut. From either of these bases you can drive to the summit area yourself (around an hour), or join one of the locally arranged minibus excursions.

Approaching Nemrut from the north, the best base is Malatya. Minibus excursions are organised from the central tourist office. The 3-hour drive into the mountains is lovely and the trips are organised to reach the summit in time for sunset. Accommodation and meals are provided at a simple pension on the mountain, and you have the chance to visit the sanctuary again for sunrise before departing to Malatya.

The major disadvantage of the Malatya approach is that you do not get to see the lesser, but still worthwhile, sites of Karakuş, the Cendere Roman bridge and Arsameia. Also bear in mind that the road, and the statues, are often snow-bound from early November until late March.

The headless eagle flanks one end of the line of ancient god statues at the funerary sanctuary, Nemrut Daği.

BELOW: decapitated but still awesome, giant stone gods haunt the terraces of Nemrut Daği.

Unlike other forgotten states of late antiquity, though, Commagene sealed its place in history thanks to the incredible stone carvings created by its uniquely self-obsessed ruler, Antiochus I, as his own final resting place. Thousands of visitors make the trek to see these fabulous remains atop towering Nemrut Daği.

The genealogy of the house of Commagene is obscure, but it is thought to have started out as a lesser line of the Seleucids of Antioch, who established themselves in the foothills of the Upper Euphrates following the rout of the Seleucids at the Battle of Magnesia in 190 BC. They styled themselves as the twin of the Achaemenians of old Iran on the male side, and the descendants of Alexander the Great on the other – the perfect cultural synthesis of East and West, as sought by Alexander himself.

With the decline of the Seleucids and the rise of Rome during the late Republican era, Commagene seems to have been involved with periodic anti-Roman uprisings along the eastern marches, usually associated with the nascent power of Parthia in Iran. Following the Roman defeat of the Pontic king Mithridates the Great in 63 BC, Antiochus I of Commagene was confirmed in power by Pompey, either as a token of trust for Commagenean support against Mithridates, or, more probably, as a gesture of realpolitik to help secure the distant marches on the Parthian frontier. Whatever the motive, the arrangement did not have the desired effect, and a mere eight years later, in 53 BC, the Romans suffered their most humiliating defeat when Crassus and his legions were destroyed at Carrhae, literally on the doorstep of Commagene. When Mark Antony arrived to re-secure the frontier, Antiochus was obliged to pay a stiff indemnity for neglecting to aid his Roman ally (none dared call it treason).

After a long struggle to maintain its precarious independence between the Rock of Rome and the Hard Place of Parthia, Commagene was finally absorbed into the newly established Roman province of Syria during the reign of Nero. Little remained to mark the position of the country's capital, Samosata (Samsat; about 50km/30 miles south of Kâhta), and what there was has now been drowned by the Atatürk Dam. Commagene might have disappeared altogether from history, but for the massive tumulus on Nemrut Daği. Built by Antiochus for his own glory and honour, it is a fabulous pile of stones and statuary to rival the greatest efforts of the self-deifying pyramid-building Egyptian pharaohs.

The summit

The centrepiece of any tour of Anatolia is a climb to the summit of the 2,150-metre (7,053ft) **Nemrut Daği** ❾ (Mount Nemrut; daily dawn–dusk charge) where the statues of the gods of antiquity lie scattered. The route from the south (*see page 345*) passes a variety of other ruins, including a beautifully

preserved Roman bridge and the citadel of Eski Kâhta (Old Kâhta). Allow at least a day for the excursion. Visitors usually either arrive for sunrise, when the statues on the east terrace are lit by the first red rays of dawn, or for sunset, when the matching statuary on the west terrace is illuminated, equally dramatically, by the setting sun.

A paved road leads up to a car park/café area, from where it's a stiff 20-minute walk up to the summit sanctuary itself. The altitude catches your breath here, and some prefer to let a donkey do the hard work for them. Although quite steep, there is now a well-paved path leading up around the tumulus and down to the car park by a different route.

The first glimpse of the east terrace is truly astounding. For here, atop the highest peak in the region and backed by the mighty tumulus mound (made up of hundreds of thousands of fragments of rock produced when the statues were being carved), is a row of massive headless statues. In front of them, lined up by archaeologists to match the correct body, are the heads

themselves, each around 2 metres (6½ft) high. From left to right they are Antiochus I, Tyche (Goddess of Fortune), Zeus, Apollo and Hercules. Behind the heads is the stepped platform of a great altar, now used by weary visitors to rest after their climb. In ancient times this was a place where ritual sacrifices were carried out at certain important times of the year in honour of the deified Antiochus and his "fellow" gods – witnessed by adoring subjects who had walked many kilometres to get here. The gods were flanked at either end by monumental statues of a lion and an eagle, the heads of which have also toppled.

Round on the west terrace was a near identical row of deified-ruler, gods and noble beasts. Whether due to vagaries in the amount of exposure or the rock they were hewed from, the fallen heads on the west terrace are much less weathered than those on the east, but they have not been lined up with their bodies.

A path loops back down to the car park/café area from the west terrace, affording stunning views of the

BELOW: the view from atop Mt Nemrut.

A stone lion sits next to a headless eagle at the summit of Nemrut Daği. Both creatures were viewed as noble.

BELOW: the Mameluke castle of Yeni Kale.

mountains to the north and, looking back, to the remarkable tumulus of one of history's most enigmatic rulers.

Eski Kâhta

Provided you made a sufficiently early ascent of Nemrut Daği, the first stop on the way back to Kâhta and the plains is usually **Eski Kâhta** (daily 8am–7pm; charge), known in antiquity as Arsameia, the summer capital of Commagene.

There's a fine relief stele of Apollo/Mithridates pointing the way to the ridge-top sanctuary, which once boasted the funerary-sanctuary of Antiochus' father, Mithridates I. En route to the ridge, which is well-marked, are two tunnels leading to an underground cave clearly used in Mithraic rites, when novices would enter the underworld to worship the goddess Cybele, fasting and praying for several days before re-emerging, enlightened, to the rising sun. Both tunnels are blocked by iron grilles for safety reasons, but above the second is a remarkable relief-carved slab, the equal of anything atop Mount Nem-

rut itself. Incredibly well preserved, t[h] stele shows a deified Antiochus sha[k]ing hands with a club-carrying H[er]cules. Just above the tunnel entran[ce] is a Greek inscription said to be t[he] longest in Anatolia.

Also close at hand is the **Yeni Ka**[le] (New Citadel), whose crenellated pa[ra]pets were built by Mamelukes duri[ng] the time of the Crusades. Further alo[ng] the road to Kâhta is the 90-metre (300[ft]) single-span **Cendere Bridge** over t[he] Kâhta Çayı – once known as the Ny[m]phaium River and one of the maj[or] tributaries of the Euphrates – a Rom[an] structure built during the period [of] Septimius Severus (AD 193–211), wi[th] three of its four original columns st[ill] standing. Nearer still to Kâhta is t[he] **Karakuş** (Blackbird in Turkish) tum[u]lus, surrounded by three sets of carve[d] pillars originally topped with relief ca[rv]ings and statues, said to be the buri[al] site of the Commagene royal women[.]

Midway between Nemrut Daği a[nd] Şanlıurfa is the massive Atatürk Bar[aj] (see panel, page 351), well-worth t[he] 20-minute detour from the main ro[ad] to view.

anlıurfa

bout 75km (50 miles) south of the
ant reservoir lies the venerable old
wn of **Şanlıurfa** ⑩. According to
cal tradition, allegedly based on the
oran, it is the birthplace of Abraham,
e father of Judaism, before his migra-
on to Canaan (now Palestine).

But the city's true history is far
ore complex than mere legend. It
as known to the ancient Greeks as
rrhoe or Osrhoe; Seleucus Nica-
r, of Antioch fame, first established
e capital of his eastern Hellenistic
alm here, populating it with Mac-
donian veterans who preferred to
ll it Edessa, after their native prov-
ce. Şanlıurfa remained an important
rrison town into Roman times, and
as one of the first centres of the early
hurch (although it was given over to
e monophysite heresy). It was also in
dessa that the great scientific works
late antiquity were translated, with
mmentaries, into Syriac/Aramaic,
hence they made their way into Ara-
c after the Muslim conquest, only
find their way back to the West fol-
wing the reconquest of the city by
e Byzantines and then the Crusad-
s. Under Baldwin I, the city was the
rst of several Crusader states in the
iddle East.

Edessa was sacked by the Zengi
ynasty during the Muslim "Recon-
uest" of the Holy Land in 114; all
s men were put to the sword and all
e women were sold into slavery. In
e 13th century, following the stand-
d Mongol rape of the Middle East,
ncient Edessa disappeared from his-
ry, re-emerging only after World
ar I. Thanks for its survival as part of
urkey should go to the local popula-
on, who resisted French attempts to
clude it in Greater Syria. In recogni-
on of this feat, the honorific Şanlı was
dded to the old name, Urfa.

Today, Şanlıurfa is a surprising mix
the old and new, with Arab, Kurd-
h and Turkish peasants in for a day's
opping from the countryside hag-
ing in the traditional bazaar, while

young technocrats and engineers
bustle between offices and shops
lining the modern downtown area. A
city of some 200,000, it is earmarked to
become one of Turkey's largest metro-
politan areas in the wake of the building of the Atatürk Dam.

The sights

According to Muslim legend, King
Nimrod had Abraham launched from
a catapult in the city's citadel, to fall
into a pile of burning wood. Happily, God intervened and turned the
fire to water and the faggots to fish.
The **Pools of Abraham** (Balıklı Göl
in Turkish), as they are known today,
are the jewel in Urfa's tourist crown.
Ringed by a couple of Ottoman-era
mosque complexes, they are an oasis
of cool in the pleasantly landscaped
park that unfurls in a swathe of unexpected greenery at the foot of the city's
impressive **citadel** (daily 8am–7pm;
charge), topped by a couple of massive Corinthian columns (according
to local lore the "arms" of Nimrod's
catapult) as well as fortifications.

At the foot of the citadel is the

Şanlıufa traffic lights.

BELOW: the old
part of Şanlıurfa
mixes restored
medieval houses
with warren-like
alleyways.

TIP

To visit Göbekli Tepe, head out of Şanlıurfa on the Mardin road. After 10km (6 miles) there is a sign on the left to Örencik village and Göbekli Tepe. When you reach Örencik (after 9km/5½ miles), turn right and follow a track for 2km (1¼ miles) to the gate. There is no admission charge. A taxi from Şanlıurfa should be around €25.

mosque complex surrounding the **İbrahim Halilullah Dergâhı** (daily 8am–5.30pm), centred around the so-called "Cave of Abraham". Muslim pilgrims line up to enter the cool depths of the cave and, once inside, throw coins into a small pool, and make a wish (usually they are women hoping to become pregnant).

The streets of old Şanlıurfa, with their overhanging medieval houses and warren-like bazaars, are a great attraction. Many have been restored in recent years and turned into boutique hotels and venues for the city's famous "Sira Geceleri" (traditional music evenings, invariably accompanied by food).

Urfa's central **bazaar**, the *kapalı çarşısı*, is perhaps the very best in Turkey, selling everything from local tobacco to hot-pepper flakes and gold jewellery to Arab-style chequered-headscarves. The bazaar's Ottoman-period **Gümrük Han** (Customs House) boasts rows of tiny workshops looking onto a shady central courtyard packed with tea-sipping locals. The **Ulu Cami** is more Arabic than Turkish in style, its rectangular ground plan and pitched roof giving it a quite different appearance from the standard "dome on a square" Ottoman-style mosque. The Ulu Cami is thought to have been built on the site of the Byzantine-era Church of St Stephen. Twenty minutes' walk away is the excellent **Archaeological Museum** (on S. Nusret Cad.; Tue–Sun 8am–noon, 1.30–5.30pm; charge). As well as the usual Greek and Roman finds, there's a remarkable statue of a man, found near the Pools of Abraham. Dating back at least 11,000 years, it has some claim to be the world's oldest statue. Several animal figures were also discovered at the nearby Neolithic site of Göbekli Tepe.

Göbekli Tepe

Antiochus I of Nemrut fame was not the first person to build a cult monument on a mountain top in this part of the world. In fact, he was beaten to it by some 9,000 years by the hunter-gatherers who roamed the hills and valleys north of Şanlıurfa just after the last ice age. The significance of **Göbekli Tepe ⑪** is potentially huge, for here appears to be proof that mankind was

BELOW: Şanlıurfa, city of the prophets.

ble to produce great works of art and monumental structures before settling down into sedentary farming communities. The hilltop here, itself well over 00 metres (2,600ft) above sea level, is surmounted by an artificial mound some 15 metres (50ft) high. Within his mound a German archaeological am have uncovered a series of chambers, complete with stone benches. ocal point of the chambers, though, re beautifully crafted, T-shaped monoliths, several metres high and early intended to represent people. lost are decorated with relief-carved bars, snakes, lions, and other, largely redatory, wild creatures. It seems that his hilltop site had great religious gnificance to the hunter-gatherers who made it, as no evidence of human ccupation has, as yet, been unearthed. s age dwarfs that of, say, Stonehenge, nd ongoing excavations may well roduce more surprises.

larran

outh of Şanlıurfa towards the Syrn border, the landscape once more attens into the Mesopotamian plain.

Thanks to the waters of the GAP project, the barren landscape is now green with cotton and other crops, and the once dirt-poor villagers are gleefully investing in such "luxury" objects as refrigerators and televisions. The many humps punctuating the horizon are ancient settlement mounds, proof indeed that Mesopotamia was once the cradle of mankind.

Further down the dirt road lies ruined **Sümürtar**, a large mound with a labyrinth of passages and underground chambers used by the Sabians, worshippers of the sun, moon and planets, whose culture and religion managed to survive the onslaught of Christianity and Islam until the 11th century. Today, some poorer villagers have been using the chambers as donkey stables. Note the statue of Sin, with a crescent moon on his head, if you can get the donkeys to step aside. The grottoes were clearly used for ceremonial purposes; some seem to have been later converted into subterranean mosques replete with *mihrab* facing in the direction of Mecca.

The creation of the Atatürk dam, as part of the Southeastern Anatolia Irrigation Project, has transformed agriculture around Şanlıurfa.

BELOW: irrigation construction on the plains around Şanlıurfa.

The GAP: an ambitious plan

The **Southeastern Anatolia Project** (or GAP) is Turkey's most ambitious economic undertaking, consisting of a network of 22 dams, 19 hydroelectric plants and hundreds of kilometres of irrigation tunnels and canals in the Euphrates-Tigris basin. It began in 1974 with the aim of transforming this neglected southeastern region into a breadbasket for the Middle East. The centrepiece is the 84 million cubic-metre (3,000 million cubic ft) rock- and earth-filled **Atatürk Barajı**, the fourth-largest dam in the world, at 80 metres (250ft) high, 800 metres (2,500ft) wide at the base and 20 metres (65ft) wide at the top. It was completed in 1992.

The twin 26km (16-mile), 1.8km (1-mile) wide **Şanlıurfa Tunnels** and distribution canals which feed off the giant reservoir now irrigate over 1.7 million hectares (4.2 million acres) of plains and the massive investment appears to have paid off, with cotton now grown in abundance in the region, and pistachios and olives a major cashcrop. The impressive scale of the engineering is well worth a look and has become a popular tourist sight among Turks – indeed, coach tours of the region aimed at the middle classes of Ankara, İstanbul, İzmir and other western Turkish cities are now generally known as GAP tours. Meanwhile, Syria and Iraq, downstream, are less than impressed at the thought that their water could be "turned off" at any time, and have complained bitterly about reduced flow.

The number of bald ibis, a protected species for which Birecik is famous, is starting to grow.

BELOW: the exotic southeast: camels and the distinctive mud dwellings of Harran.

Back towards the main road is the village of **Harran** ⑫ itself, built in and around the ruins of a mighty walled city whose origins date back to the 4th millennium. The Assyrians were here, and worshipped the moon-god Sin. Next came the planet-worshipping Sabians, who only gave up their faith at the point of the sword of Islam. This was also where the Roman statesman Crassus was defeated by the Parthians, with the legion standards captured and brought back in triumph to Ctesiphon to the undying shame of the Romans; Crassus himself reportedly died by having liquid gold poured into his mouth. Later, Julian the Apostate worshipped the moon here on the way to his fateful encounter with Shapur I further east. And Harran was the last stronghold of the Sabians, their tradition finally killed by the arrival of the fanatic Crusaders.

Harran today is famous for its strange beehive-style, mud-rendered dwellings, which until quite recently were inhabited. Now most are used for storage or animal shelter, though a couple of complexes have been done up as cafés (very welcoming, Harran literally bakes

in the summer months). So thorough a job did the invading Mongols do in the 13th century that there's little left of old Harran except rubble, though it's worth exploring the massive inner citadel in the southeast of the site (a possible location of the Sin temple) and the massive Ulu Cami to the north, easily recognised by its distinctive square minaret.

West to Gaziantep

Returning to Şanlıurfa, the oil tanker-filled road heads west to **Birecik**. Now little more than a truck-stop on the Euphrates, the town's main claim to fame, as indicated by a kitsch statue visible from the road, is the endangered bald ibis. A breeding station has been set up here in an attempt to save these exotic birds.

Viewed from the west bank of the river in the late afternoon, Birecik is most photogenic, with the lazy waters of the Tigris rolling past in the foreground, and the white limestone cliff around which the town is built glowing enticingly in the soft light.

A few kilometres beyond Birecik is ancient **Zeugma** ⑬. Founded at

rategic crossing point of the Euphrates
y one of Alexander the Great's generals,
was traditionally an important jump-
g-off point for Roman adventures in
e East, including Mark Antony's dis-
trous campaign against the Parthians
36 BC. Part of the GAP project, the
recik hydroelectric dam made inter-
ational news in summer 2000, when
e remains of several rich Roman
ansion houses were discovered here
st as the dam was about to be filled.
ecorated with elegant mosaics and
escoes, an international rescue effort
ved as much as possible from the
ell-appointed merchants' houses in a
ere 10 days. The Gaziantep Archaeo-
gical Museum *(see page 354)* now
ouses the majority of these remarka-
le finds. Some parts of the ancient city
ere situated above the current water
vel, and there are plans to turn the site
to an open-air museum.

To the west, the area's rolling hills,
overed with ripening wheat in early
ummer, are cut by the tributaries of
e Euphrates, flowing southward to
e desert flats of Syria and Iraq. It
as a subtle but memorable beauty. In
any ways the river marks the point
which Asia really starts – ancient
Mesopotamia, the Land between the
wo Rivers, where civilisation as we
now it began.

arkamış

ome 25km (15 miles) south of Nizip,
the Turkish/Syrian frontier, is one
the most important sites in the area,
arkamış **14**. This once powerful and
ealthy Hittite city was excavated by
eonard Woolley (ably assisted by a
rtain T.E. Lawrence) between 1912
d 1915. As well as uncovering some
perb remains, the best of which are
ow in the Museum of Anatolian
ivilisations in Ankara, Woolley and
awrence became involved in assorted
sputes with the Germans, who were
pervising construction of a section of
e grandiose Berlin–Baghdad railway
hich runs at the foot of the mound
ousing the ancient city. Due to its

strategic position astride the frontier,
the site has been essentially off-limits
for several years. However, relations
between the two countries are currently improving, and work is under
way to clear the minefields around the
site with the eventual aim of reopening
it to visitors.

Gaziantep

Gaziantep **15**, with a fast growing
population of around 1 million, has
been transformed in recent years,
largely as a result of spin-offs from the
GAP project. Traditionally it was a city
associated with copper-beating and
mother-of-pearl inlay work; now it is a
city of factories spinning and weaving
the raw cotton brought in from fields
irrigated by GAP, and processing the
industrial quantities of pistachio nuts
harvested in the surrounding area.

As well as being the region's business
capital, Gaziantep is busily transforming itself into its cultural and tourism
centre. It is well placed to do this, with
a history stretching back several millennia and a central old quarter blessed
with legions of traditional honey-hued

*Mythical King
Gilgamesh, one-third
man, two-thirds god,
was supposedly based
on a Sumerian king
who ruled in 2850
BC. He and his
faithful companion,
Enkidu, lived with
the wild animals
before setting out on
an epic adventure,
vanquishing
everything from
famine to giants.
When Enkidu died,
Gilgamesh chose to
join him in Irkalla,
the place of no return.*

BELOW: local
children at Harran
castle.

The Euphrates harbours river catfish of such size that the stories seem too outrageous to be true. But local fishermen regularly pull out whiskered monsters, weighing up to 200kg (440lb), usually using the net-and-shotgun method.

houses (many now turned into boutique hotels), an impressive castle, bustling bazaar and many old mosques. Despite its modernity, the city has a distinctive Middle-Eastern atmosphere, and boasts some of Turkey's most distinctive and delicious food – notably *baklava*.

Like its sister city Kahramanmaraş, Antep (as most continue to call it) enjoys the honorific "Gazi" ("Fighter for the Faith") bestowed upon it by Atatürk in recognition of the Alamo-like stand the inhabitants put up against French and Senegalese forces at the end of World War I.

Prior to the rescue excavations at Zeugma (*see page 352*), the city's **Archaeological Museum** (İstasyon Cad.; Tue–Sun 8am–noon, 1–6pm; charge) was just another run-of-the-mill provincial museum. Today it is arguably the very best in Turkey, boasting a collection of mosaics as impressive as any found anywhere in the Roman world. Some are displayed wall-mounted, others as they would have been *in situ*, surrounded by pillars and backed by frescoes saved at ther death from the waters of the Bire-

cik dam. The museum, which is well lit and labelled, houses a wealth of other artefacts as well, from the prehistoric period onwards, and deserves a couple of hours of anyone's time.

The partially man-made mound on which the city's massive **kale** (castle) stands has provided finds dating back to the 4th millennium, though the castle itself is largely Mameluke. The views over the town from the castle, especially of the old bazaar quarter at its feet, are wonderful, and within the walls are the remains of an Ottoman-era hamam (bathhouse) and a couple of 19th-century Russian-made cannon. The castle itself has been much restored recently and so have many of the great trading halls and workshops (*hans*) and Syrian-style mosques in the bazaar quarter.

Separated from the bazaar area by the modern city centre is another old quarter, which prior to the Turkish War of Independence was home to the city's sizeable Christian and Jewish minorities. Again, much restoration work has taken place here (too late to save many of the fine old buildings, unfortunately), but there is still enough of the

BELOW LEFT: one of the mosaics in Gaziantep's Archaeological Museum.
BELOW RIGHT: metalware for sale by Gaziantep castle.

old quarter left to get a flavour of what life was once like in a traditional oriental city. Beat-up wooden doors facing neglected streets open onto beautiful courtyard gardens, replete with orange, plum and pomegranate trees, and tinkling fountains. One of the finest 19th-century mansions now houses the excellent **Hasan Süzer Ethnography Museum** (Hanifioglu Sok.; Tue–Sun 8am–12.30pm, 1–6pm; charge). On the hill above the museum is a fine black-and-white domed building. Now the Kurutluş Camii, it was once the Armenian **Church of the Virgin Mary**, dated to 1892.

Kahramanmaraş

The E-90 slices west from Gaziantep to Adana and the Mediterranean coast, while the smaller Highway 835 leads northwest through Arcadian scenery of small neat farms and babbling brooks to **Kahramanmaraş** ⑯.

Formerly known as Maraş, the city acquired the honorific "Kahraman" ("heroic") due to the large number of casualties it suffered during the Turkish War of Independence. Historically

an important outpost guarding the second major pass over the Taurus Mountains, it has been sacked by passing invaders, which may account for the singular dearth of antique buildings in and around the town. The exceptions are the 15th-century **Ulu Cami** (Great Mosque), the **Taş Medrese** and the inevitable **citadel**, within which is the municipal **museum** (Tue–Sun 8am–noon, 1–5pm; charge), with its collection of Hittite reliefs.

The most important personality to emerge from Maraş was the Byzantine emperor Leo the Isaurian, who managed to repel the last great Arab siege of Constantinople in AD 717. It was during his reign that we first hear of the iron chain which closed off the Golden Horn to enemy warships. Today, aside from the pretty mountain scenery in the region, Kahramanmaraş is known primarily for the best ice cream in Turkey – a combination of cold sugar and cream with a peculiar elasticity and longevity; vendors throughout the country are obliged to wear traditional Maraş costumes in accordance with some unwritten law. ❏

Local heroes guard the entrance to Gaziantep kale (castle).

BELOW: some of the incredible mosaics discovered prior to the completion of the Birecik hydroelectric dam are now on show in Gaziantep's Archaeological Museum.

PROPHETS AND PREACHERS

From Noah's perch on Mount Ararat to Abraham's birthplace, Anatolia is steeped in the legends and history of the Bible and early Christianity

Many sites mentioned in the Old Testament are located in eastern or central Anatolia. Indeed, many scholars believe that the Garden of Eden was between the Tigris and Euphrates (ancient Mesopotamia) in southeast Turkey, though all efforts to find it have failed.

The permanently snowcapped Mount Ararat (Büyük Ağrı Dağı), the biblical resting ground of Noah's Ark, is on Turkey's border with Armenia. Muslim tradition believes that the Ark came to rest on the slopes of the vast Mount Cudi, in Siirt province, about 350km (220 miles) further southwest, near the Iraqi border.

According to Genesis, Abraham and his family lived in Harran, about 50km (30 miles) south of Şanlıurfa. This is also where Abraham took Sarah, where Jacob hid when Esau threatened to kill him, where Rebecca drew water for Abraham's servant, and where Jacob rolled off the stone lid to water Laban's sheep.

Turkey's many New Testament sites tend to be in the western portion of Roman Anatolia. Among them are Antioch (Antakya), Seleucia ad Pieria (Çevlik), Iconium (Konya), Tarsus – the birthplace of St Paul – and Myra (Demre), where St Nicholas (Santa Claus) served as a bishop in the 4th century. The so-called Seven Churches of Revelation were actually sites of early Christian communities. They are Smyrna (İzmir), Pergamon (Bergama), Thyatira (Akhisar), Sardis, Philadelphia (Alaşehir), Laodicea, near the city of Denizli, and, of course, the great city of Ephesus.

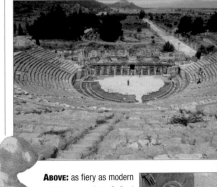

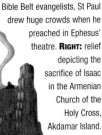

ABOVE: as fiery as modern Bible Belt evangelists, St Paul drew huge crowds when he preached in Ephesus' theatre. **RIGHT:** relief depicting the sacrifice of Isaac in the Armenian Church of the Holy Cross, Akdamar Island.

BELOW: Noah's Ark is believed to have come to rest on Mount Ararat as the flood waters receded.

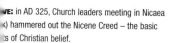

...E: in AD 325, Church leaders meeting in Nicaea ...k) hammered out the Nicene Creed – the basic ...s of Christian belief.

THE ROAD TO DAMASCUS

St Paul was probably the greatest of the early Christian missionaries and theologians. Born in Tarsus around AD 10, he was a Jew with Roman citizenship, a tentmaker by profession and a zealot by nature. He spent his early years as a rabbi and Pharisee, promoting the persecution of Christians.

After a revelation (some say a blinding vision of Jesus) while on the road to Damascus, all his zeal went into proselytising and converting both Jews and Gentiles to Christianity. He never actually met Jesus.

He then crisscrossed Anatolia and the Eastern Mediterranean. His many writings (letters to the Romans, Corinthians, Galatians, Philippians, Thessalonians, Philemon, and possibly also to the Ephesians and Colossians) are the earliest extant Christian texts.

The concept originated with Christ, but it was Paul who laid down the rules of the Church. In AD 58, he was arrested, and sent to Rome, imprisoned and eventually martyred.

LEFT: a 16th-century Ottoman miniature showing the sacrifice of Abraham. **BELOW:** St Paul's Church in Tarsus, one of the oldest continuously inhabited cities in the world, and the birthplace of St Paul.

...VE: St Peter lived in Antioch (Antakya) for many years. It was ...that followers of Jesus first gathered secretly in a cave church.

...E: Abraham, father of the Jewish nation, spent his childhood in ...rfa. His tomb lies in Birket Ibrahim Mosque *(detail pictured)*.

THE FAR EAST

There is no trace of Europe left in this vast, distant swathe of land, bordered by Syria, Iraq, Iran, Armenia and Georgia. Turkey's Far East is foreign even to many of its countrymen

urkey's Far East feels quite different to the rest of the country, which is hardly surprising given that the bulk of the population here is ethnically Kurdish, a people with their own distinctive language and culture. In the Ottoman era, Kurdish chieftains pursued a fiercely independent existence in Anatolia's highest and most remote region, and even today many Kurds resist assimilation into mainstream Turkish society.

The region is best accessed by road either via Trabzon and Gümüşhane in the Black Sea region, or via Şanlıurfa close to the Syrian border. This chapter is split into two – the Northeast and the Southeast – to reflect both routes; they meet at Lake Van. Alternatively, there are good air links from İstanbul and Ankara to Erzurum, Van and Diyarbakır.

THE NORTHEAST

Somewhere between the old Silk Road cities of **Gümüşhane** and **Bayburt** the traveller crosses the geographical boundary between the Black Sea and the plateau, as well as the ancient historical boundary between the Pontic-Greek and Armenian cultural zones. Today the region is almost exclusively Muslim, sometimes fiercely so; places selling alcohol in conservative cities such as Erzurum are few and far between,

and women draped in all-enveloping chadors are not an unusual sight. The Christian Armenians, deported during World War I, have left behind little but their beautiful churches, and today's population is a mix of Turks and Kurds.

The main route into the high plateau climbs steeply from Trabzon through fertile farmland, lush deciduous forest and then pine-carpeted mountains to **Gümüşhane** (*see page 328*) and **Bayburt ⓱**. The provincial capital is dominated by a stupendous fortress, first built by Justinian, rebuilt by the

LEFT: the Church of St Gregory in the ruined city of Ami. **RIGHT:** detail on the Yakutiye Medrese, Erzurum.

BELOW LEFT: native to eastern Turkish hot springs, skin-eating fish are used to treat psoriasis.
BELOW RIGHT: Erzurum's Lala Mustafa Paşa Camii.

Bagratids, fortified by a Turkish lord in the 13th century, and destroyed by the Russian army in 1828. After Bayburt, the road climbs to the bleak grandeur of the **Kop Geçidi**, a pass which commands a stunning panorama, before dropping down to the most important city on Turkey's northeastern plateau, Erzurum

The high plateau

Higher than the central Anatolian basin by about 1,000 metres (3,000ft), the northeastern plateau is broken up by a series of mountain ranges, culminating finally in the single, overwhelming peak of Mount Ararat. Snow buries all for a good half of the year, cutting off many villages from the rest of the world. In spring, these high pastures are an orgy of grass and wild flowers grazed on by huge herds of sheep and cattle.

Historically, the plateau provided a natural route between Asia Minor and the Orient. It was here that the ancient east–west trade route crossed into the Roman-Byzantine world; caravans carrying silk and other oriental riches made their way from China across Central Asia and Persia into Anatolia. From Erzurum, they continued westward to Sebastea and Caesarea, or crossed the Zigana pass to Trebizond (Trabzon).

This accessibility proved to be a mixed blessing, as wave after wave of invaders also broke into Anatolia through the northeast, leaving ruin and desolation in their wake. Between 1828 and 1918, the region was the scene of four wars between the Ottoman Empire and Russia, in each of which the Tsarist armies succeeded in breaching Turkish defences as far as Erzurum. In the war of 1878, Russia occupied – and held until 1919 – the provinces of Artvin and Kars as far as Sarıkamış.

Erzurum

Ancient Theodosiopolis, named after Emperor Theodosius I ("the Great") who fortified it in the 4th century, **Erzurum** is a sombre, austere city, whose outward aura is somehow reflected in the faces of its inhabitants. One of the coldest places in Turkey, visit in winter and it's possible to ski at the country's best resort, which in a good season boasts 3 metres (10ft) plus of crisp

owder snow from December through
o March. In summer the resort, at the
oot of the **Palandöken Dağları** range
which reaches 3,176 metres (10,420
t) and dominates the city to the south
offers alternative accommodation and
mbience to conservative Erzurum.

The city itself offers an array of histor-
cal monuments, which have managed
o survive a history of constant warfare
nd destruction, not to mention serious
arthquakes in 1939 and 1983. All exist-
ng works are of Islamic origin, as any
f the Armenian Christian monuments
hat survived the depredations of World
Var I – including the cathedral – were
ubsequently razed.

There are three *kümbets* (domed
ombs), of which one is the oldest
istorical building in town, ascribed
o Emir Saltuk, the feudal lord whose
dynasty dominated the area for a cenury after the Turkish conquest. The
Ulu Cami (Great Mosque) was built
n 1179 by his grandson. The town's
rchitectural masterpiece, the **Çifte
Minareli Medrese** (Twin Minaret
eminary), was built, like its coun-
erpart in Sivas, under Seljuk sultan

Alâeddin Keykubat II. The Mongols, in
their turn, built the **Yakutiye Medrese**
(seminary or Koranic school) in 1310,
naming it after the local governor of
Ogeday, a grandson of Genghis Khan
who held court in Tabriz. The Ottomans then rebuilt and resettled the
city, contributing the graceful **Lala
Mustafa Paşa Camii** in 1563.

Beyond Horasan, some 60km (37
miles) east of Erzurum, the road forks,
the left branch heading northeast to
Sarıkamış and Kars, eventually linking up with Artvin, in the Black Sea
region. The other heads due east to
Doğubeyazıt and Ararat, with a turn-
off running south to Van.

The road to Kars

About 150km (90 miles) northeast of
Erzurum, **Sarıkamış**, huddled into the
surrounding cold, dark taiga of giant
pines home to wolves and bears and the
endless rows of old Russian barracks,
reminds the visitor that he or she has
entered what used to be an outpost of the
Tsarist Empire. There's a ski resort here to
rival that at Erzurum, though the runs are
generally easier, curving down through

Kars is known throughout Turkey for its dairy products, and particularly its cheese.

BELOW: troglodyte houses near Kars.

gentle pine forest rather than the bleak, treeless mountains of Palandöken.

Kars ⑲ has a 19th-century grid layout, unique in Turkey, that, along with the dusty, once-graceful buildings of the city centre, owes its existence to the Russians during their final, 41-year-long occupation after 1877. Following decades of neglect, Kars is beginning to tidy itself up, and a few of the graceful Russian town houses are being converted into boutique hotels and trendy cafés.

The old city, which served as capital to the Bagratids (*see page 45*) in the 10th century, is now a slum clinging to the hillside across the Kars stream. It is dominated by a **fortress** of the usual Urartian-Byzantine-Armenian-Turkish-Mongolian-Russian pedigree, worth a visit mainly for its panoramic views of the town and the plateau beyond.

The town's other major historical sight is the Armenian **Cathedral of the Holy Apostles** at its foot, built in AD 937. Today a (little-used) mosque, its relatively crude form serves as a taster for much greater glories at nearby Ani. There's also a small **museum** on the eastern edge of town (daily 8am–5pm;

charge), with an interesting ethnography section and some artefacts from Kars' Armenian and Russian past.

Ani: abandoned city

The ruined city of **Ani** ⑳ (daily 8.30am–6.30pm; charge) lies around 45km (28 miles) southeast of Kar. With a spectacular setting on an exposed bluff separated from neighbouring Armenia by a dramatic gorge, it is one of Turkey's most impressive sites.

A town existed in the pre-Christian era, before the Gamsaragan dynasty of Armenian lords held it for several hundred years. In AD 961, it became capital of the powerful Bagratids and from then until the mid-11th century was one of the most important cities in the Near East, with a population in excess of 100,000. Well defended by mighty circuit walls, the city blossomed, and dozens of beautifully decorated churches were built. Ani subsequently fell to the Byzantines in 1045 and the Seljuk Turks in 1064. It was later re-occupied by the Armenians, until it finally fell to the Mongols in the 13th century. Shaken by the depradations of Tamerlane, it was terminally abandoned following an earthquake in the 14th century.

Allow at least half a day to make the most of Ani, plus an hour each way for the drive from/to Kars. Entry to the city is through impressive **Aslan Kapısı** (Lion Gate), from where a signed path meanders its way from church to church. Most obvious is the **Church of the Redeemer**, striking because only half of its bulk survives, the rest having fallen victim to a lightning bolt. Clinging to a cliff face above the Arpa Çayı is the exquisite **Church of St Gregory** and its lovely frescoes. Back on the bluff is the monumental but austere **Ani Cathedral**. There are several more worthwhile churches to see, all built from the local red sandstone as well as the **Menüçer Cami**, the sole mosque. Note that the border is sensitive and you should not point your camera towards Armenia – it upsets the *jandarma* (rural police force).

East to Ararat

The main road to Iran from Erzurum follows the line of the ancient caravan route and carries regular convoys of intercontinental trucks heading for Iran, Afghanistan and beyond.

Approaching **Doğubeyazıt**, the towering 5,137-metre (16,853ft) volcanic peak of **Ağrı Dağı ㉑** (Mount Ararat) hoves into view. Its relative elevation over the surrounding plain – over 4,000 metres (13,000ft) in the north – makes it one of the sheerest profiles in the world. This is further enhanced by the incomparable impact of its single, symmetrical, conical mass. On a typical hazy day, the base of the mountain blends into the blue sky, leaving the enormous white cap of snow hovering eerily in space. The search for the remains of Noah's Ark has been underway ever since the French nobleman Pitton de Tournefort first scaled the mountain in 1707 *(see margin, right)*.

şak Paşa Sarayı

Nearby, a few kilometres above the scruffy town of Doğubeyazit, the exotic **şak Paşa Sarayı ㉒** (Tue–Sun 8am–pm) was built in the 18th century. A delightful architectural mishmash of Georgian, Armenian and Seljuk styles, its lavishly relief-carved walls, domes and minarets make it an orientalist's dream. Although surprisingly built with Mount Ararat hidden by a ridge, its situation is spectacular, with grand views down across the plain this Kurdish chieftain's fortified-palace complex once controlled.

THE SOUTHEAST

The southeastern corner of Turkey is a fascinating and physically very diverse region in which Turks, Kurds and Arabs co-exist, sometimes uneasily. With a few isolated exceptions, such as the vineyard-covered hills of the Tor Abdin plateau, the landscape is austere. The biblical Euphrates and Tigris rivers cut their way through bare, rocky mountains and desert-like plain, and temperatures in the lowlands soar to well over 40°C (104°F) for weeks on end in summer. By way of contrast, the high plateaux and valleys of the mountain ranges around Lake Van are snow-bound six months of the year, and the transhumant

In 2010 evangelical archaeologists from China and Turkey claimed to have found a 20-metre (65ft) wooden structure, made of planks fastened by tenon-joints, embedded in glacier ice high on the slopes of Mount Ararat. Sceptics claim an elaborate hoax by local Kurdish guides, who make a good living from ark-hunters.

BELOW: Mount Ararat towers above the plateau.

TIP

To hear a church service in a language closely related to that used by Christ, visit Mardin's Church of the Forty Martyrs (Kirklar Kilise) on a Sunday morning.

pastoralists who are the back bone of the local economy are confined to their winter villages.

Access can be difficult to this troubled part of the country. Heading due east across the plain from **Şanlıurfa** *(see page 349)*, below Mardin and Midyat close to the Syrian border, the long and dangerous E-90 highway is much used by tankers en route to and from Iraq. Meanwhile, the road north and east from Diyarbakır to Iran becomes increasingly hazardous as it enters the high mountains around Lake Van.

Mardin

Perched majestically on a bluff above the chequerboard expanse of the Mesopotamian plain, **Mardin ㉓** is the most beautiful and visitor-friendly town in southeast Turkey. It is just a few kilometres north of the Syrian border, with the land hereabouts the closest Turkey gets to a true desert: be prepared for summer temperatures in excess of 40°C (104°F).

Sometimes known as the "White City" because of the pale stone its beautiful old houses are made from, once-scruffy Mardin has been rejuvenated in recent years and is now the focal point of tourism in the region. Its mixed Kurdish, Turkish, Arab and Syrian Orthodox (Suriyani in Turkish) population bears testament to its chequered past. A centre for the Syrian Orthodox Christians since the 5th century, its much depleted Christian population still worships at some of the town's remaining churches, notably the 6th-century **Church of the Forty Martyrs** (Kırklar Kilise). The most important building in Mardin, though, is Islamic. The **Sultan Isa Medese** (daily 9am–6pm; free) is a religious seminary of great beauty, with a magnificently carved portal and elegant twin fluted domes. There are dozens of other Islamic buildings of significance dotted throughout the narrow backstreets, many of them renovated with EU grants. The Arabs conquered Mardin in the 7th century, and it became "capital" of a local fiefdom, that of the Artukids, between the 12th and 14th centuries. The **Mardin Museum** (Tue–Sun 9am–6pm) boasts a selection of finds dating back to the Assyrian era, and is housed in a delightful 19th-century mansion.

Deyrul Zarafan and the Tör Abdin

The **Deyrul Zarafan Monastery** (daily 8.30am–noon, 1–4.30pm; charge), 6km (4 miles) southeast of the town, was founded in AD 495 on the remains of a temple to the sun. Once the seat of the Syrian Orthodox Patriarchate the monastery includes a church with beautiful relief frieze-work, a wooden throne and litters once used to carry Church dignitaries.

Deyrul Zarafan is the showpiece of the Syrian Orthodox Church in the region, but its spiritual centre is the isolated monastery of **Mar Gabriel** (daily 9am–11.30am, 1–4.30pm; free guided tour), a large, walled monastery complex set amidst the rolling hills of the Tör Abdin ("Mountain of the Servants of God") some 20km (12 miles) south of the town of Midyat. There are several more Syrian Orthodox churches

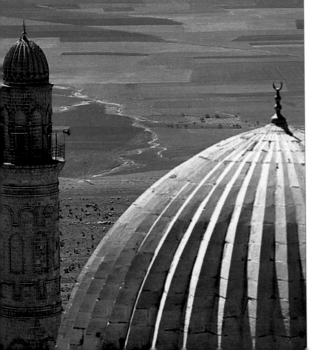

BELOW: chequered plains stretch out below a Mardin mosque.

in old **Midyat** ㉔ (60km/37 miles east of Mardin), their bell towers clearly visible from the main road in the centre of the town. The old town, built on the slopes of a low hill, is crowned by a gorgeous mansion house, former home of a prosperous Syrian Orthodox merchant family.

The once-sizeable Syrian Orthodox community of Mardin and the Tör Abdin was drastically reduced in the upheavals of World War I, and again in the war between the Turkish security forces and the separatist PKK (Kurdish Workers' Party) in the 1980s and 90s. Now only a few thousand remain.

Hasankeyf

The old town of **Hasankeyf** ㉕, a one-hour drive north of Midyat, has for years been threatened by the massive İlisu dam project. The Turkish government seems intent on pushing the project through, despite the fact that Hasankeyf has been placed on the list of 100 most threatened heritage sites in the world. Atop a dramatic cliff frowning down on a lazy curve of the green Tigris below, are the scattered remnants of a once-great **medieval city** (daily dawn–dusk; charge), with a mosque, palace, houses and cisterns. Spanning the river are the piers of an Artukid bridge, once the largest in Anatolia, and across on the north bank is the exquisite tomb of Zeynel el-Abdin, complete with an onion-shaped dome gleaming with turquoise tiles.

Diyarbakır

Diyarbakır ㉖, some 90km (56 miles) north of Mardin and set on the Tigris, is one of the most vibrant, if troubled, cities in Turkey. It is famed for its massive black basalt walls, second only to the Great Wall of China in size, and gigantic watermelons fed on a mixture of water from the Tigris and fertiliser made from pigeon guano. It is also notorious elsewhere in Turkey for the sometimes militant Kurdish nationalism of its inhabitants, and violent demonstrations break out here periodically. Beware of these, and also pickpockets

and stone-throwing kids in the back alleys and on the walls.

The city was annexed by Rome in AD 297, and became a vital part of the line of defence between the Roman and Parthian/Sassanian empires of Persia. Ceded to the Persians after Julian the Apostate's ill-fated campaign down the Euphrates in AD 362, Diyarbakır was conquered once again by the Byzantines and held until the walls were breached by Muslim armies in AD 639. It was later taken by the Ummayad and Abbasid Arabs, Marwani Kurds, Seljuks, White Sheep Turcomans and Safavid Persians, before finally falling to the Ottomans in 1515. Most of the mosques, *medreses* and houses of interest date from the Ottoman period.

A quarter Christian Armenian until 1915, Diyarbakır is now Turkey's preeminently Kurdish city. Save for the military, civil servants, a few Arabs, and the last surviving Syrian Orthodox families, the population of the city is overwhelmingly Kurdish.

The most distinctive of the town's 22 older mosques is the **Ulu Cami** (Grand Mosque), about halfway down

Inside the Syrian Orthodox Church of the Virgin Mary, Diyarbakır.

BELOW: the majority of Diyarbakir's inhabitants are Kurdish.

İzzet Paşa Caddesi, Diyarbakır's main drag, between the Harput and Mardin gates. The oldest place of Muslim worship in Anatolia, this was originally the Church of St Thomas. Similar in design to the much grander Umayyad Mosque in Damascus (a city which Diyarbakır closely resembles), the Ulu Cami is built, like its counterpart in Şanlıurfa, on the courtyard plan of Arabian mosques. Nearby is the **Nebi Cami**, built in 1530. It, like many of Diyarbakır's mosques, mansions and *kervansarays*, is attractively built from alternating bands of white limestone and black basalt.

At the end of the street is the entrance to the **İç Kale** (citadel), complete with the early Byzantine **Church of St George**, now undergoing restoration along with the rest of the interior, which until 2008 was a Turkish military base. Just outside the citadel is the Artukid Hazreti Süleyman Cami, built in 1155.

The **Kasım Padişah Cami**, better known as the Four-Legged Minaret Mosque, one of many 16th-century structures in town, has a peculiar minaret, standing in the middle of a crowded thoroughfare, and local legend has it that wishes come true to those who pass under it seven times. Down a winding and child-clogged street from here is the crumbling, roofless 19th-century Armenian church of **Surp Giargos** (St George). Just before it is an older church, the **Keldani Kilisesi**, still used by the handful of Chaldean Christians left in Diyarbakır. Most vibrant of the city's remaining churches, though, is that of the **Virgin Mary**, a beautiful Syrian Orthodox church dating back to the 3rd century AD. It has been lovingly restored by the Süriyani diaspora, and is used by the remaining Syrian Orthodox population of just five families.

The city walls

Stretching for some 5km (3 miles) around the old city, and once possessing 82 defensive towers, the great basalt walls of Diyarbakır were first built during the reign of Constantine but have been restored repeatedly since. They are still in remarkably good shape in spite of repeated battering by sundry armies throughout history and feature inscriptions and geometric and animal designs.

The main north entrance to the old town is the **Harput Gate**, once known as the **Bab-al-Arman** (Gate of the Armenians). Upon entering, a road leads west along the walls to the **Urfa Gate** and beyond that, the **Ulu Beden**, from where there is access to the top of the walls through passages which, unhappily, double as public toilets. The ramparts have been restored recently, but still lack a guard rail so take care. It's now possible to walk as far as the southern **Mardin Gate**, with great views of the Tigris River meandering below. The slums which once clung like limpets to the inside of the walls have now been cleared and replaced by green parkland.

From Diyarbakır, the main road northeast towards Van heads through Silvan to **Bitlis**, famous for its tobacco. It's a chaotic town, ranged along a river gorge and dominated by a mighty **castle** built on an imposing outcrop by one of Alexander's generals.

BELOW: a baker in Bitlis.

Lake Van

Turkey's largest inland body of water, Van Gölü (Lake Van) stands some 1,650 metres (5,500ft) above sea level. Flushed with the run-off from innumerable small streams in the surrounding mountains, it has no visible outlet save for evaporation, which accounts for the lake's high salinity.

At the western head of the lake is Tatvan, a dull town but a useful base for excursions along the north shore. The most interesting of these is **Ahlat** ㉗, a half-hour drive away. Here is a cemetery to die for, where hundreds of beautifully inscribed Seljuk tombstones stand sentinel on a forlorn plain above the lake. Dotted around them are some superb *kümbets*, polygonal tombs with conical roofs built to house deceased Seljuk, Turkoman and Mongol chieftains. Between Tatvan and Ahlat a summer-only road leads north towards the lesser **Nemrut Dağı**, a volcanic mountain sporting a spectacular triple crater lake.

Also north of Lake Van is **Süphan Dağı**, a mountain popular with climbers. Beyond that, the attractive village of **Adilcevaz** is tucked away in a green valley spilling down to the lake shore. Above it are the remains of an Armenian church and the Urartian citadel of Kefkalesi.

Van: an ancient city

On the lake's eastern shore, **Van** ㉘ is essentially a modern city, laid out on a grid plan between a towering volcanic peak and the lake. It has a long history, however, and was the capital of the Urartian empire in the 8th century BC. The Urartians' major foe, the Assyrians, attacked Van many times between the 9th and 7th centuries BC. In 590 BC it was conquered by the Medes, and later became a part of the Seleucid Empire.

The town and its environs developed a distinctively Armenian character over the following centuries despite succumbing successively to the Persians, Romans, Arabs, Byzantines and, following the battle of Manzikert in 1071, the Muslim Turks. What happened to the old town during World War I remains highly controversial. Armenians claim the Turks butchered the innocent

The Urartian castle at Lake Van, one of the world's oldest-surviving fortresses.

BELOW: Lake Van.

TIP

Much of eastern Turkey
is under snow and
freezing conditions from
November through to
April, and access to
some of the sites during
this period is impossible.
Try to visit in spring,
summer or early
autumn.

Christian inhabitants of the town, the Turks counter that Van was destroyed by the invading Russians, aided and abetted by treacherous Armenians. Whatever the truth, the town was totally levelled and the new city built a couple of kilometres away.

The city centre is pleasant, with comfortable hotels and reasonable eating places, but has little to hold one's attention bar its fine **museum** (Tue–Sun 8.30am–12.30pm, 1.30–5.30pm; charge). The garden is full of interesting Urartian statuary, including a relief-carved stele of a god, and several slabs embellished with Urartian cuneiform inscriptions.

Old Van is to be found between the new Van and the lake, in a melancholic but beautiful expanse of meadow and swamp. Today, all that remains are the minaret of the **Ulu Cami**, scattered fragments of the town wall, a couple of badly damaged Armenian churches and, by the south wall, a pair of attractive and recently restored Ottoman-era mosques. Of more interest is the famous Rock of Van, **Van Kalesi** (daily 8.30am–7.30pm; charge), overlooking the ruins of Old Van, topped by crumbling mud-

brick battlements and riddled with the tombs of Urartian notables. Of most interest is the **King Argishti** (786–762 BC) **tomb**, hollowed out of the southern cliff face and accessed via a set of well-worn steps. Also carved into this cliff, and only visible from the old town below, is a massive trilingual inscription dedicated to King Xerxes of Persia. Take care when exploring, as drops are sheer and there are no safety rails.

Akdamar Island

The primary reason for any visit to Van is a trip to the superbly restored 10th-century **Armenian Church of the Holy Cross** (daily 8.30am–6.30pm; charge) on **Akdamar Adası** **㉙**, an island reached by a 5km (3-mile) boat ride from a point along the lake shore just past the town of **Gevaş**, some 40km (24 miles) southwest of Van.

With the entire edifice of the Byzantine state about to collapse before the Turkish onslaught, and with only his kingdom standing between the warrior hordes and the soft underbelly of central Anatolia, the Armenian king, Gagik Atsruni, had the church and its palace

BELOW: the
Armenian Church of
the Holy Cross,
Akdamar island.

A new image for an ancient trade route.

mplex built as a retreat. The church in the standard Armenian style, with conical dome atop four axes, with ne most impressive feature being the rnate relief-work on the façade, depicting the Old Testament: a veritable zoo f animals and birds rings the roof, oor and walls. A major restoration roject has recently been completed.

The island setting is a delight, its cliffs nging with the cries of Armenian gulls, lmond trees a sea of blossom in spring, nd the towering peaks south of the ke reflected in azure waters. There are few swimming places where you can ke a dip in the sodium-rich waters.

Hakkari province

ust south of Van, a turn-off leads south o Hakkâri, Turkey's remotest corner. is also, along with Tunceli *(see page 42)*, the country's most problematic rovince, squeezed between Iraqi and ranian Kurdistan, with considerable eparatist sentiments of its own. Travel n the area is safe on major highways, ut potentially dangerous on country oads and in the mountains. The secu-ty forces check papers at roadblocks in the mountains here, and view visitors leaving the main roads and sights with suspicion. Clashes between the Turkish military and Kurdish separatists still occur, so avoid venturing too far off the beaten track.

The first site of interest, 28km (17 miles) south of Van, is **Çavuştepe** (daily 8.30am–7.30pm; charge), a Urartian citadel perched dramatically on a mountain spur. The quality of the stonework here is breathtaking, as is the remarkable inscription carved into the temple doorway. Next up is the dramatic **Hoşap Kalesi**, built by the Kurdish despot Sarı Süleyman ("the Blond") in 1643.

The road south leads to **Hakkari**, through the spectacular gorge of the Zab River. The 4-hour journey from Van here is a scenic joy, but Hakkari is itself both dull and problematic. Anti-state feelings run high in this economically deprived mountain town, and the Iraq border to the south is regularly infiltrated by Kurdish separatists. The mountains, though, are glorious, and, if you can access them, the Nestorian patriarchal church of **Koçhanes**, 20km (12½ miles) to the north, is worth visiting. ❑

BELOW: workers heading home from the fields.

PKK and Kurdish Separatism

Despite several government initiatives, the dirty war continues between Turkish security forces and the separatist Kurdish Workers' Party (PKK), a Marxist group aiming to form an independent Kurdish state in southeast Turkey. More than 40,000 civilians, soldiers and PKK guerrillas have been killed since hostilities began in 1984, and nearly 3,000 villages have been depopulated. Four million people – mainly Kurds – are refugees. Although OHAL (State of Emergency Rule) was lifted in 2009, restrictions on movement continue to affect local Kurds, who in many regions cannot access the high pastures to graze their animals. Turkish soldiers, most of them conscripts, continue to die in PKK attacks (usually by mines), and this has led to a rise in anti-Kurdish, nationalist Turkish feeling in much of the country. Northern Iraq provides a relatively safe haven for the PKK, who still cross the border from the Iraqi Kurdish enclave to carry out their attacks – despite massive Turkish reprisals.

There are signs of hope, however. The PKK leader Abdullah Ocalan, captured in 1999 and in solitary confinement on an island prison near İstanbul, now says he is prepared to accept something less than an independent Kurdish state. The AKP government has committed itself to a solution to the Kurdish "problem", and a once-taboo subject is now routinely discussed at all levels of society.

371

TRANSPORT
ACCOMMODATION
EATING OUT
ACTIVITIES
A – Z
LANGUAGE

⁂INSIGHT GUIDES | TRAVEL TIPS

TURKEY

TRANSPORT

GETTING THERE
AND GETTING AROUND

By Air

Flight time to İstanbul from London is around 3½ hours, from New York about 9 hours.

Many international airlines have regular direct or connecting flights from major European cities to İstanbul's Atatürk International or Sabiha Gökçen airports, plus İzmir and – very rarely – Ankara; from North America, the only direct flights are from New York (Delta and Turkish Airlines, THY) and Chicago (THY). From the UK, the scheduled direct carriers to İstanbul only are THY, Cyprus Turkish Airlines and British Airways (BA).

Among no-frills airlines, Pegasus and EasyJet link the UK with İstanbul's Sabiha Gökçen Airport, located on the Asian side. Various international carriers, either no-frills or charter, also fly direct from the UK to the international airports at İzmir, Bodrum, Antalya and Dalaman.

Reaching any other Turkish city, in particular Adana, Kars, Kayseri, Trabzon or Van, will involve a connection through İstanbul – often somewhat easier (and possibly cheaper) done with THY. For domestic flights, see opposite.

Travel to and from the airport

Whichever airport you fly in to, the easiest option to get from the airport into the nearest town is by taxi, of which there is never a shortage. Specimen fares to popular destinations are often posted at taxi ranks, though in practice taxi meter readings can end up slightly higher. The fare

will be registered on the meter and should come to under US$30. Although cab drivers may not be that good at finding their way around, if you know the name of your hotel, and the area it is in, you will get there.

Hotels can arrange transfers, but this can be much more expensive. It can sometimes be the only option on the coast, however, where some hotels are a couple of hours' drive from the nearest airport.

Major cities also have airport buses, often timed to coincide with the arrival or departure of scheduled flights.

İstanbul The easiest and cheapest way of getting into İstanbul is on a combination of the metro and tramway (change at Zeytinburnu or Aksaray) which will take you to the heart of Sultanahmet in approximately 50 minutes.

There is also an efficient bus service from **Atatürk Airport** (located in Yeşilköy to the west of the city) to the centre, operating every 30 minutes between 5am and 11pm. This makes one stop at Aksaray (where you should alight for connections to the old-city districts of Sultanahmet and Eminönü) before terminating in the centre of the new city at Taksim Square. For queries, tel: 0212-465 4700.

From **Sabiha Gökçen Airport**, situated out in the Asian suburbs near Pendik, there is an hourly shuttle bus, on the hour, into Taksim; depending on traffic the transfer can take between 1 and 2 hours. Alternatively take the E10 bus to Kadiköy, which connects with Turyol ferries across the Bosphorus to Eminönü or Karaköy – although this is not recommended for people with heavy baggage.

When leaving Turkey, allow plenty of time for checking in, especially in the high season. Long queues can build up both for the security checks and for check-in and passport formalities.

By Sea

Between May and October there are car-ferry crossings from Ancona and Brindisi on the Italian Adriatic coast, taking 30–60 hours to arrive at the Aegean resort-cum-port of Çeşme. These routes are much used by Turkish migrant workers, returning home for their summer holidays. Timetables vary from year to year. Currently two companies operate: **Marmara Lines**, www.marmaralines.com **Mesline MedEuropean Seaways** Italian agent at www.cemar.com

Car and passenger ferries sail between the Turkish ports of Ayvalık, Çeşme (near İzmir), Kuşadası, Bodrum, Marmaris and Kaş, and the respective Greek islands of Lésvos, Híos, Sámos, Kos, Rhodes and Kastellórizo. Services, provided by both Turkish and Greek boats, run at least once daily between April and October, and sporadically (typically once or twice weekly) in winter. One useful information source is www.feribot.net.

By Rail

Arriving in Turkey by train from Western Europe is an enjoyable experience if you have sufficient time to make the trip. It's a minimum three-day, three-night journey from Britain, with a typical itinerary being London–Paris–Munich/Vienna–Budapest–Bucharest–İstanbul.

Airlines

Airlines flying between Turkey, Britain and North America

British Airways: www.ba.com
Delta Airlines: www.delta.com
EasyJet: www.easyjet.com
Jet2: www.jet2.com
Cyprus Turkish Airlines: www.kthy.net
Pegasus Airlines: www.flypgs.com
Thomas Cook: www.flythomascook.com
Thomson: www.thomsonfly.com
Turkish Airlines (THY): www.thy.com

Domestic airlines in Turkey

Turkish Airlines (THY): www.thy.com, national call centre 444 0849, or 0212-225 0566
Anadolujet: www.anadolujet.com, national call centre 444 2538
Onur Air: www.onurair.com.tr, national call centre 0212-663 2300
Pegasus Airlines: www.flypgs.com, national call centre 444 0737
Sun Express: www.sunexpress.com, national call centre 444 0797

Dalaman, Denizli, Diyarbakır, Erzurum, Gaziantep, İzmir, Kayseri, Konya, Malatya, Nevşehir, Samsun, Sivas, Trabzon and Van. Note that this list tends to expand or contract annually, as new routes are added and unprofitable destinations are dropped. Security is strict and you will be asked to point out your baggage from a pile on the runway before it is transferred to the plane.

By Bus

Turkey has excellent bus services, both inter- and intra-city. Although this is still the preferred method of long-distance travel for many locals, since it is cheap, reliable and generally comfortable, an increasing number of visitors opt to fly between the main centres to avoid the long overnight journey. If you prefer to stick with buses, however, you can leave Ankara at 10pm and be at the south coast by 8am the following morning. Likewise you can reach Cappadocia from İstanbul on an overnight bus.

Competition between companies is intense; the best – Ulusoy, Varan and Metro – are more expensive and have comfortable, modern buses with proper air conditioning and free refreshments, as well as the traditional libations of lemon cologne. Increasingly, onboard videos are being replaced with television programmes regardless of the fact that the satellite systems come and go, rendering transmission unreliable.

Tickets are easy to obtain; when you approach the ticket offices (which are often next door to one another), touts may pressure you to travel with their company, so choose with care. Places are reserved, and unaccompanied women will not be seated next to a man they do not know. Smoking is never allowed on board.

Inter-rail and Eurail passes are valid in Turkey, but are unlikely to save you much money.

An excellent source of information is the website www.seat61.com, which has every possible routing to Turkey, and links for ticket purchases for the various legs of the journey (it's not possible to buy a single return ticket from the UK, which anyway will cost around £600 for second-class standard travel).

Trains from Europe arrive at Sirkeci Station in Eminönü, in the heart of old Constantinople. A new high-speed train tunnel under the Bosphorus, the Marmaray, is due to link the European side with Haydarpaşa Station on the Asian side of İstanbul, but work has been delayed by the discovery of the original Byzantine docks; it is expected to open in 2012.

For rail information in İstanbul: tel: 0212-527 0050 (European lines); tel: 0216-336 4470 (Asian lines).

By Bus/Coach

Long-distance coach services operate from major European cities, especially in Germany and Austria, as well as from the Middle East, Russian and central Asian states. Coaches arrive at the Esenler Coach Station, Bayrampaşa, northwest of İstanbul; tel: 0212-658 0505/1010. There are buses and a metro from there to the centre of the city. For details, see *City Transport, page 374.*

By Car

It is possible to drive to Turkey via Bulgaria or Greece, or via Italy, with a ferry to Turkey *(see above).* EU money has seen the completion of the Via Egnatia expressway across northern Greece, and also vastly improved motorways across Bulgaria to the border town of Svilengrad.

At the point of entry you will need to show the car's registration documents and your driving licence. Your car details will be stamped into your passport, allowing you to drive it for six months in Turkey duty-free. You will also be issued with a certificate which you should keep with you at all times. You must leave the country with the vehicle; should you write your car off during your stay, you will need special papers to certify that it has not been sold in Turkey.

Documents

In addition to a valid driving licence, you will need the vehicle's log book and proof of ownership (and a power of attorney as proof of permission if you are driving someone else's vehicle), a Green Card (from your insurance company) and insurance (check you are covered for the Asian side of the country and for breakdown). Drivers may use their national licence with a Turkish translation for up to three months, but are advised to take an international licence.

GETTING AROUND

Domestic Air Travel

There is a good network of reasonably priced domestic flights serviced by Turkish Airlines (THY; *see above for details*), Pegasus, Onurair and Atlasjet. You need to be flexible about timing if booking at short notice on a popular connection in a busy season (for example, to the Aegean and Mediterranean airports over a public holiday). Early-morning and evening flights between Ankara and İstanbul also fill up quickly. Though you can, of course, still book and pay at a walk-in travel agent, all airlines (and the best fares) are increasingly web-based.

You can fly direct to the following cities from İstanbul Atatürk Airport: Adana, Ankara, Antalya, Bodrum,

BELOW: Sultanahmet tram, İstanbul

Major Inter-city Bus Companies

Hidayet Turizm
www.hidayet.com.tr
National call centre: 0212-444
0002
Kamil Koç (İstanbul, western and
southern destinations, and Ankara)
www.kamilkoc.com.tr
National call centre: 0212-444
0562
Metro
www.metroturizm.com.tr
National call centre: 0212-444
3455
Pamukkale (İstanbul, western and
southern destinations)
www.pamukkaleturizm.com.tr

National call centre: 0212-444
3535
Ulusoy (İstanbul, Ankara,
Black Sea region, İzmir and
the Aegean, Antalya and the
Mediterranean, plus international
destinations)
www.ulusoy.com.tr
National call centre: 0212-444
1888
Varan (İstanbul, Ankara, western
and southern destinations,
international)
www.varan.com.tr
National call centre: 0212-444
8999

There is no comprehensive
national or local timetable, so you
have to work out the best route and
departure time for yourself. Most
routes are operated by several
different companies.

Long-distance bus stations

Most long-distance buses depart
from the main bus station *(otogar)*
in each town, nowadays often on
the outskirts, and there will be ticket
offices there and in the city/town
centre. There will usually be a minibus
service *(servis)* to take you from out-
of-town bus terminals to the centre,
or (more likely) vice versa. Most long-
haul journeys take place at night.

İstanbul has two main bus
stations: at **Esenler** (Bayrampaşa,
10km/6 miles northwest of the city),
and **Harem** (on the Asian side). The
former geographical separation of
destinations from each has more
or less dissolved, with most buses
stopping at both. Coming from central
Anatolia, alight at Harem and take
a ferry to your likely destination on
the European side – far quicker than
continuing to Esenler.

By Train

The three largest cities (İstanbul,
Ankara and İzmir), and many places
between and beyond, are connected
by Turkish State Railways (TCDD), but
the network is limited to the interior
– there is no coastal railway on either
the Aegean or Mediterranean shores.
Therefore, for travel in much of the
country, the bus is the only option.

Rail fares are, however, cheaper
than buses – a second-class ticket
from Ankara to İstanbul on the
new high-speed train costs about
€21, with 20 percent discount for
return journeys – and comfortable,

especially in first class, though non-
express services will be noticeably
slower.

The best connections are between
İstanbul, Ankara and İzmir. The *Mavi
Tren* (Blue Train) or *Ekspres* (Express)
services reach their destinations in
times comparable to going with one of
the more up-market bus companies.
The high-speed *Mavi Tren* between
İstanbul and Ankara leaves İstanbul's
Haydarpaşa Station at 11.50pm,
and reaches Ankara at 8am the
following morning; it has a dining car,
couchettes and sleepers. This is an
entertaining way to travel if you have
the time.

Purchase tickets and reserve
seats or sleepers up to two weeks in
advance, preferably from the station
at which your journey will begin. You
should in theory be able to book
a ticket to and from anywhere in
Turkey in İstanbul, Ankara or İzmir,
but it can sometimes prove difficult.
Sleepers get booked up, especially
over public holidays. Choose between
a *küşetli* (pull-down couchette-style
compartment with six sharing, pillows
provided but no bedding); *ortülü*
küşetli (four bunks, bedding provided);
or *yataklı* (first class, with two or three
beds, linen included).

The following trips may also be of
interest:

BELOW: İstanbul was the original
destination for the world's most
famous train.

• **The Doğu Express** to Kars, which
departs from Ankara twice daily,
taking some 27 hours to wind its
way across Anatolia via Kayseri and
Erzurum to the far eastern border
region.
• Three weekly trains from Tatvan on
Lake Van to Ankara (and optionally
beyond to İstanbul – total journey
time 38 hours). For train buffs only.

Reservations and Enquiries

In theory, the **Turkish State
Railways'** website (www.tcdd.gov.tr) has
an English-language booking option,
but we defy you to make it work. If you
insist, the rail buff's site www.seat61.com
has a guide to attempting this. Most
people just go to the station in person,
scan placards and confirm schedules
with staff. Phones are rarely
answered, and if so by monolingual
staff. It can be well worth paying any
small commission asked and having
train tickets issued by major Turkish
travel agents, especially those in and
around Sultanahmet in İstanbul.

City Transport

For all information on public transport
in İstanbul, tel: 0212-333 3763.

İstanbul buses

City buses are largely run by İstanbul
municipality and have the letters IETT
on the side. Most journeys cost about
1.50TL.

Although you can still pay at the
front of some buses, most are now
geared to electronic ticketing and
locals pay using an *akbil* swipe card.
You pay around 7TL for an *akbil* and
then load as much money as you want
onto it, and it can be used on all forms
of local transport. When boarding a
bus, press it against the meter at the
front. More than one person can use
the same *akbil* (press it against the
meter for each traveller). If you board
a second mode of transport within
1½ hours, the second journey is
discounted. If you need to top-up your
credit, look for the *Akbil* sign at ticket
booths. Fixed price daily and weekly
akbil are also available.

Bus fares are cheap but journeys
can be slow, and it is advisable
not to travel during rush hours as,
predictably, it gets extremely crowded.

There are also private *dolmuş*
(minibuses), usually yellow, which
tend to be faster. On these you
pay your fare to the driver or his
assistant, it being dependent on
your destination. A *dolmuş* driver
will often let passengers off between
stops, although this is rapidly being

phased out for safety reasons.
All buses have a board in the front
window and at the side listing the
main destinations on the route. There
are maps of the network at bus-stop
shelters.

Metro and Tram

Ankara, İstanbul and İzmir all have
efficient, if limited, metro systems.
İstanbul's, as much overground light
railway as underground metro, has a
southern line running from Aksaray
out to Atatürk airport, plus a northern
line running from Şişhane via Taksim
to Levent. There is an overground tram
beginning at Zeytinburnu, passing
close to the Aksaray metro station
and then the main tourist centres of
Sultanahmet and Eminönü before
crossing the Galata Bridge to Kabataş.
Buy tokens from adjacent booths.
A "nostalgic" tram runs up İstiklâl
Caddesi between Tünel and Taksim
every 20 minutes, while the tiny Tünel
funicular – one of the oldest in the
world – saves commuters the steep
walk up from the Karaköy ferry docks.

Dolmuş

An economical method of
travelling around a city or to a
neighbouring town is by dolmuş
(literally "full", sharing the same
root as the Turkish word for the
country's stuffed vegetables).
A kind of shared taxi, usually a
minibus, the dolmuş travels along
a fixed route for a fixed fare, paid
to the driver. At the start of the
route, it may not set off until it
is full, which can entail a wait,
although this is increasingly rare.

Taxis

Taxis (taksi) are bright yellow,
reasonably priced and plentiful. In
the cities and big towns it is often
unnecessary to look for one; they will
find you, signalling by slowing to a
crawl alongside you or hooting. You
should check the meter is switched
on; it almost invariably will be, but it is
still worth checking.
İstanbul now has one flat rate,
with a 2.5TL minimum fare and 1.4TL
per kilometre; elsewhere the tariff
doubles between midnight and 6am.
There are inevitably a few drivers
who do their best to multiply the fare
by driving round in circles or simply
saying that the meter is broken; try
and check roughly how much it should
be before getting in. Most, however,
will try their hardest to help you, even
if they speak little or no English.

ABOVE: İstiklal Caddesi, İstanbul.

It helps to have your destination
written down in case of difficulties in
comprehension, and also because
your driver may also be new to
the area – there is no equivalent
requirement to London's "the
knowledge". State the area location
first, eg, Sultanahmet, and go into
detail later. When your driver gets
close to his destination, he will ask for
directions. If crossing the Bosphorus
in İstanbul, the bridge toll will be
added to your fare.
Most taxis operate independently
around a local base, which may be
no more than a phone nailed to a
telegraph pole. There are few radio-
controlled networks. Hotels and
restaurants will always be able to find
you a taxi.
Fixed prices can be negotiated for
long distances or sightseeing tours
with waiting time built in.

Water Transport

Ferries

Car and passenger ferries sail
between the Turkish ports of İzmir,
Çeşme (near İzmir), Kuşadası,
Bodrum, Ayvalık and Marmaris (with
links to the Greek Islands). The
timetables and companies operating
on these routes vary considerably
each year. For details and ticket
reservations, contact travel agencies.

Private Cruise Boats

The following companies offer luxury
cruises for small groups:
Iliada Tourism
Tel: 0212-243 2164/7/9
www.iliadatourism.com
With a number of smaller luxury
yachts, Iliada also run M/S Halas, a
luxurious yacht sleeping 28. Often
used by the British Royal Family, it
operates in the Bay of Fethiye from
the end of June until the end of
October, and can be chartered for
the rest of the year.
Hatsail Tourism & Yachting Inc.

Sea of Marmara ferries

Around the Sea of Marmara, car
ferries and sea-buses cross between
Pendik on the northern shore,
east of İstanbul, and Yalova on the
southeastern shore, and between
Yenikapı (near Aksaray) to Mudanya,
Yalova and Bandırma, the latter
convenient for İzmir and the Aegean.
There are also more informal services,
usually April–October only, from
Tekirdağ to Erdek or Bandırma on the
southern shore of the Sea of Marmara
Short-hop ferry links operate between
Eceabat on the Gallipoli peninsula
and Çanakkale, and between Gelibolu
and Lapseki.
Timetables for İstanbul-based
services can be found at any of the
seabus or ferry terminals in İstanbul,
or online at www.ido.com.tr.

İstanbul boat services

Divided by the Bosphorus and the
Golden Horn, İstanbul has a busy
network of large steamers, small water
buses that operate like dolmuşes,
catamarans, hydrofoils, seabuses and
water taxis. Crossing the water is an
essential part of a visit to the city.
From the main jetties at Eminönü,
Karaköy, Kabataş and Beşiktaş on the
European side, you can catch ferries
to Kadıköy or Üsküdar on the Asian
side; buy a jeton at the gişe and drop
it in the slot at the entrance to the
jetty (iskele), or use your akbil pass
(see page 374). Each jetty serves
one destination which is prominently
displayed.
The privately operated dolmuş
water buses, called "motors", cross
at certain points, notably between
Üsküdar and Beşkitas, mopping up
commuter traffic at rush hour, and
running until 1am when the state
ferries have closed. Again, you pay by
jeton or use your akbil. A ferry service
also leaves from near the northern
end of the Galata Bridge to go up the
Golden Horn to Eyüp.

Tel: 0212-241 6250
www.hatsail.com
Bosphorus cruises for groups or
executive meetings with lunch/
dinner and cocktails; also yacht
cruises on the Aegean and
Mediterranean seas.
Blue Guide
Marmaris
Tel: 0252-417 1128
www.blueguide.com
Gulet sailing holidays around the
Bodrum Peninsula and along the
south coast.

Frequent ferries leave Kabataş for the Princes' Islands or Adalar, off the Asian shore in the Sea of Marmara. The journey takes an hour and stops at all the islands before terminating at Büyükada, the largest island. The **hydrofoils** serving the outer suburbs are more expensive; the timetable is arranged to suit commuters, so most trips are in the morning and evening, but they can whisk you to the Princes' Islands in 30 minutes. Fast **catamaran seabuses** offer services from Kabataş and Bostancı to Bakırköy, Yenikapı and Kadıköy but are mainly aimed at commuters. For information, tel: 0212-444 4436.

Free timetables covering the İstanbul water-transport system are available at the ticket offices; the timetables alter in mid-June and again in mid-September.

A new **water taxi** service allows groups of people to summon water transport in exactly the same way as a normal taxi although prices are not cheap (tel: 0212-444 4436).

Bosphorus cruises

A **Bosphorus cruise**, tel: 0212-522 0045, can be a lovely way to view the elegant waterside mansions or *yalıs* lining the banks of this strait separating Europe from Asia. **Public ferries** leave three times daily in summer and twice daily in winter from the Eminönü jetty and go all the way to Anadolu Kavağı, where you can stop for lunch before the return journey. If you want a shorter trip, try one of the more frequent **TurYol private boats** (around 1½ hrs), from the same docks: tel: 0212-251 4421; www.turyol. com.tr.

Driving in Turkey

Driving in Turkey can be alarming for newcomers. However, if you keep calm and drive cautiously you will be perfectly safe. The condition of main roads is usually reasonable (and improving all the time), although on secondary roads you should avoid driving at night if at all possible.

Road conditions

The road network is extensive, with new toll motorways in the western half of the country either completed or under construction. Otherwise, there are numerous dual carriageways, and many three-lane roads where the central lane is used for overtaking.

Smaller roads are not well lit, nor well enough signposted, and hazards include trucks and tractors with no (or maybe one) light illuminated, horses and carts, disabled vehicles with no warning triangles (look for piles of rocks instead), more piles of rocks from landslides, flocks of sheep or goats, ambling cattle and near-invisible cyclists or pedestrians. Few of the mountain roads have crash barriers or other protection and most have narrow hard shoulders. On these secondary roads, always allow ample time for road journeys – at an average speed of no more than 60kmph (37mph).

Surfaces are reasonable, but the overall engineering of the road can be poor, making them excessively dangerous in wet weather and leading to unexpected potholes. Roadworks are a constant problem, especially in the east – and traffic can go from four to two lanes with little or no warning.

Many vehicles on the road are buses and trucks, and many of the

ABOVE: an İstanbul ferry boat.

lorries (referred to in Turkish as *tır* after their international acronym) are elderly, overloaded and underpowered (and often barrelling down the middle of the road). When empty, they can barrel along at surprising speeds. There are more on the road at night – another reason not to drive after dark.

Road marking and signposting is reasonable on the new motorways, but elsewhere lane-lines are faded and junction signposting can be deficient when not downright perverse. Archaeological sites and other points of interest (some decidedly specialist) are assiduously marked by brown signs with white lettering, or yellow placards with black lettering.

Rules of the road

Drive on the right and, unless it is signed otherwise, give way to traffic joining from your right, even on a roundabout or multiple junction where you might think you had right of way.

At motorway junctions, be prepared for traffic coming from unexpected directions, and do not expect to be able to get back on to the motorway easily if you make a mistake. Some dual carriageways have very broad hard shoulders, alarmingly used by locals in the wrong direction, to avoid long drives to the nearest junction.

Traffic lights A flashing yellow arrow means you may turn right with care even if the main light is red.

Safety Everyone is supposed to wear a seat belt, and to carry a warning triangle and a first-aid kit. Almost no one does. You will usually see a small cairn of rocks, or similar, in the road to warn of a breakdown, but only at the last minute as they are usually placed very close to the vehicle in question.

Drink driving Blood-alcohol limits are in line with European countries – 50mg alcohol per 100ml of blood – so just two beers will put you over the limit.

Blue Cruises by *Gulet*

A "Blue Cruise" (*Mavi Yolculuk*) is a delightful way to visit the coastal sights of the southwestern shores of Turkey – sailing on a traditional wooden schooner, or *gulet*, at a leisurely place, stopping to swim or sightsee at places of interest on the way. This can be the best way to visit ancient sites, many of which were originally only accessible by sea.

The boats are fully crewed, and usually very comfortable, with every need catered for. You can either book as a group, taking over a whole boat (they vary in size and number of berths); or individually, in which case you will not be able to choose your travelling companions. Some tour companies offer holiday tours with

knowledgeable guides on board.

Cruises start from many different ports, large and small, on the south Aegean and Lycian coasts; you can more or less choose where you would like to begin, depending on your arrival point.

July and August are the most expensive months and very popular, but it can be too hot, especially for ruin-tramping on shore. Spring is quieter, but the sea can be cold. Aficionados enjoy September or even October, when the crowds have gone but the sea is still warm.

"Blue Cruises" are bookable locally, or through specialist overseas adventure travel agents. *See also pages 426–8.*

Traffic police operate control points on the access roads to many cities. You should always carry your driving licence, passport, the car's log book, insurance certificate, pollution compliance and roadworthiness certificates, and vehicle registration, as you may be asked for any or all of them. Make sure rental cars have all of these in the glove box before setting out. They may also run seat-belt checks, breath tests and speed traps and check for faulty vehicles.

Traffic offences are punishable by stiff fines of 200–400TL (with a "discount" for payment within 10 days); take the ticket to a designated bank to pay – the days of the cop trousering the fine and supposedly issuing a receipt appear to be over.

Driving etiquette

Although Turkey has much the same highway code as other countries, the population does not always obey it. As a result, the country suffers a much higher rate of road-traffic accidents per number of vehicles than the UK. Things are gradually improving as the roads get better and more people take proper driving tests, but the golden rule must always be to drive defensively.

Expect the unexpected: sudden stops, reversing, heedless pulling out. Some driver signals mean the exact opposite of their UK or USA equivalent. Flashed headlights by an oncoming vehicle on a narrow road or bridge means "I am coming through", not "please go first"; however, on a broader road, it usually means "beware, police checkpoint ahead".

There is a lot of hooting, mostly to warn that you are being passed, or (from behind) to hurry you up. A loud hoot means keep out of the way; two short pips on the hooter sometimes means "thanks".

Do not expect traffic to stop to let you out of a side turning; you have to push in. Do not expect people to use their indicators, or their handbrakes on a hill. Cars in front of you on a steep hill will almost always roll back, so leave room. Do expect overtaking on all sides, last-minute lane changes on motorways, cutting in, and people driving very close to you.

Breakdowns

If you break down in your own car, your insurance documents should tell you what to do. British motoring associations have reciprocal agreements with the Turkish Touring and Automobile Association, TTOK (www.turing.org.tr); the American AAA

does not; other nationalities should check the position before travelling. For hire cars, always check the spare tire and tool kit beforehand, and get instructions as to what to do in event of a breakdown; "unauthorised" repairs may not be reimbursed.

Petrol

Fuel is generally the most expensive in the world after Japan. The western two-thirds of Turkey are well supplied with petrol stations, many open 24 hours, some of which are good places to stop for a meal and a rest as they are well equipped and have clean toilet facilities. The further east you go, the more infrequent the stations become, and you would be wise not to let your tank run low.

Petrol (benzin) is available in three grades. Lead-free petrol (kurşunsuz) is sold at most petrol stations in the more developed parts of the country, but can be hard to come by in the more remote rural areas. Diesel (mazot) is available everywhere, but beware of bargain-priced diesel, which is likely to be exceptionally dirty.

In most of the country it is possible to pay by credit card.

Parking

Take heed of no-parking signs, especially those with a pictograph of a tow truck in action. Although the fines for parking illegally are relatively small, retrieving a car that has been towed away is extremely time-consuming – the pound is often on the far side of town.

On-street parking areas (look for an otopark sign) are manned by watchmen who will approach as you park, and either give you a receipt or place a ticket on your windscreen. Charges vary, but are not exorbitant – around 2TL for two hours in central İstanbul. In some places on the southwest coast it's a flat-rate 3–4TL. There are also some multistorey car parks, a few on-street meters and ticket machines, and valet parking at the smartest hotels and restaurants.

Car hire

To hire a car you must be over 21, and need to have held a licence for a year. You will also need a credit card for the damages deposit. Outlets exist in most cities and tourist areas, or you can book in advance through multinational chains or consolidator/aggregator websites.

Car hire in Turkey varies wildly in price depending on how and where you hire. Walk-in rack rates for the smallest, entry-level cars

are typically €45–50 equivalent per day, though you'd be foolish to hire on spec when online pre-booking rates will be no more than half that, especially for longer periods (see below for a list of useful companies). Only at the very beginning and tail end of the season are locally quoted rates likely to be advantageous. Antalya, Dalaman, Bodrum and (sometimes) İzmir airport are the least expensive places to rent from; İstanbul, Marmaris, Kuşadası and just about anywhere in the east are the most expensive.

VAT (sales tax), basic insurance and collision-damage waiver (CDW) should be included in the price, but the waiver excess (the amount you are liable for before the excess takes effect) is not. If you rent for more than 2 weeks a year, then it's well worth taking out insurance for this rather than buying it (expensively) from the rental company; www.insurance4carhire.com is a recommended company selling such an annual policy to US- and UK-based drivers.

Hiring through an international company or a nationwide local chain like Almira should allow you to return the car to a different point for no extra charge.

If you pre-book through a consolidator, it is vital to ring the local affiliate company a day beforehand to check that all rental details have registered correctly. Tales abound of the wrong-category car being set aside, or the car allocated to the wrong location, or specified extras (like child seats) not being provided, unless this is corrected in advance.

Motorcycles, scooters and bicycles can all be hired in coastal resorts.

Car Hire Consolidator/Aggregator Websites

In the UK:
www.comparecarrentals.co.uk
www.auto-europe.co.uk
www.carehire3000.com
www.rentalcargroup.com
www.holidayautos.co.uk

A CCOMMODATION

HOTELS, YOUTH HOSTELS, BED & BREAKFAST

Until the mid-1980s, most visitors to Turkey were independent travellers, and outside İstanbul or Ankara accommodation was usually simple, even spartan. Today, however, the country offers all conceivable varieties of accommodation: from basic forestry-department campsites to the most luxurious hotels.

It is still true that there is the broadest choice in the most developed resorts and cities of the western two-thirds of the country, but more out-of-the-way destinations can offer unique places to stay. On the Aegean and Mediterranean coasts, huge international resorts (in the main indistinguishable from each other) are interspersed with even more anonymous small concrete blocks for those on a tighter budget.

But since the 1990s there has been a backlash against both, and boutique hotels aimed both at discerning Turks and more demanding foreigners are proliferating, either new-built or restorations of traditional buildings, in Mardin, Gaziantep, Safranbolu, Antalya, İstanbul, Foça, Eski Datça, Şirince and Edirne, to name just a few of many places. But beware – the Turkish term *butik* is much (ab)used to justify charging over the odds at any establishment with a bit of stone cladding outside and cast-iron bedframes inside.

Recent changes in the law have opened the floodgates for second-home ownership by foreigners within municipalities, and sometimes outside of them, along the resort coasts. The resulting building boom, combined with the global financial crisis, has left huge ranks of unsold, identikit *costa*-style villas and apartments, especially at Kalkan and around Bodrum or Dalyan, and many of these are for rent.

TYPES OF LODGINGS

Hotels

Choosing a hotel

Obviously, your choice will be affected by the kind of holiday you wish to have, how much money you wish to spend and the amenities you are looking for.

In busy resorts and cities noise may be a factor: if you are choosing your hotel on the spot, ask to see the room first – this is quite normal and expected. If choosing a hotel during the day, think about the proximity of after-dark activity; somewhere that is peaceful at 10am may be throbbing with music from the club behind all through the night.

Hotel categories

The Ministry of Tourism classifies all hotels from one to five stars, with the majority between two and four. Boutique hotels are often categorised separately as *ösel* (special) accommodation.

At one-star level you will get an en-suite room that is basic but modern and reasonably comfortable. A three-star hotel will usually have a bar-restaurant, air conditioning and better furniture in the rooms, fairly reliable hot water, and probably a swimming pool.

Four- and five-star hotels include local franchises of major international hotel chains like Accor, Iberostar, Hilton, Best Western and Swissotel, and Turkish chains like Dedeman, Majesty or Merit. Although their rack rates are astronomical, competition is intense, so that at quieter times these hotels offer extremely attractive packages, either through their own websites or consolidator sites like www.booking.com.

All-inclusive mega-complexes are proliferating, especially around Kuşadası, Marmaris and parts of the Mediterranean coast. While in theory good value, they have generated complaints about poor food standards and swarms of hidden charges.

Apart-hotels

These offer some of the independence of being in your own flat, but with the services associated with a comfortable hotel. In İstanbul they have succeeded in renovating and adapting attractive older apartment buildings without substantially changing their character. Some multi-star hotels also offer apartments within the hotel.

BELOW: Buyuk Londra hotel, İstanbul.

İstanbul: New City or Old City?

Most of the best-kept and most famous Byzantine and Ottoman sites are in what is known as the "old city", the area encompassed by the Marmara Sea and Golden Horn. As a consequence, this is where most visitors stay, and the area is home to hundreds of small *pansiyons* and hotels (which means there is plenty of choice), – as well as carpet shops, hawkers, overpriced and uninspired eateries, and virtually no sign of real Turkish life outside the tourism industry. There is little nightlife – a boon to some and a disappointment to others.

In recent years there has been a boom in good mid-size, mid-range hotels in the Taksim area. It

is only a 15-minute taxi ride to the Sultanahmet/Bazaar Quarter, you will be spoilt for choice in terms of restaurants, cafés and clubs, and there is a better chance to witness authentic Turkish life instead of dodging carpet dealers and con artists. On the other hand there will not be the same opportunity to whip back to your room for a quick break mid-sightseeing. A good alternative is the Beyoğlu district, just across the Galata Bridge, with a growing (but still limited) range of small hotels. There are a cluster of apartments for rent (2 or 3 nights minimum) in the picturesque streets around the Galata Tower, many of which have superb views.

in historic buildings such as old Ottoman mansions or *kervansarays*. Many are in the oldest and most interesting parts of towns. These offer the amenities of three-, four- or five-star hotels (and at the same prices), but with some limitations (such as no lift, due to the age of the buildings). Many are very atmospheric, and are decorated in old Turkish style. However, be aware that many were refitted during the 1980s and are now once again ripe for an overhaul in every respect – converted *kervansarays* in particular were beset by rising damp, reverberating nightclubs and prostitution mafias.

The concept was introduced during the mid-1980s by the long-time director of the Turkish Touring and Automobile Club, Çelik Gülersoy (1930–2003), a tireless conservationist and campaigner for the protection of Turkey's historical and cultural heritage. His conversions of old Ottoman terrace houses in Sultanahmet's Soğukçeşme Sokağı, though controversial for their loud colour schemes (claimed to be faithful to the original paint-jobs), became Turkey's first real boutique inns.

Pansiyons

A Turkish *pansiyon* or guesthouse falls somewhere between a simple hotel and a bed and breakfast. They can be lovely places to stay, as good as or better than a one-star hotel, especially if run by a family. At some seaside resorts you will find that the more basic ones are often used by Turkish families on their summer holidays, and are pitched at their needs with self-catering kitchens and multi-bedded rooms. The more expensive examples will have en-suite facilities in every room. In some, hot water is heated only by solar panels on the roof – and may run out, though this is often true of many hotels in season as well.

Hostels, Treehouses, Trekkers' Lodges

Accommodation is so reasonably priced in Turkey that hostels per se are restricted to big backpackers' meccas such as İstanbul, Kuşadası, Fethiye, Çanakkale and Köyceğiz. Along the Lycian coast, an interesting adaptation of these – which has arisen to get around a ban on permanent buildings in protected areas – is the so-called "treehouse" lodges, particularly at Olympos and Faralya, near Ölüdeniz. Along the Lycian Way and St Paul trails, as well as in the Kaçkar mountains, growing numbers of trekkers' lodges have essentially a hostel format with multi-bedded rooms and shared toilet facilities.

Self-catering

There are many comfortable villas and apartments with pools available, with

more springing up all the time. Rapid development does mean, though, that you should be careful to ensure that your location is not in the middle of a building site – Google Maps and web-based feedback sites may prove useful. Some UK package agents (*see page 427*) specialise in providing quiet, rural, "genuine" locations, but these may not have pools. Apartments are also available in İstanbul, with the best situated in Beyoğlu.

Camping

Some *pansiyons* with gardens may allow pitching a tent. Otherwise, more elaborate campsites *(kamping)* are situated close to the principal seaside resorts, and have all the necessary facilities, including showers, shops, restaurants and children's activities. They generally cost around as much as staying in a cheap hotel, especially when per-vehicle fees are figured in. More basic, but often far nicer and cheaper, are the score or so of forestry department sites along the Aegean and Mediterranean coasts – often with their own beach, and an excellent choice if travelling with a combi-van or caravan.

You can actually camp almost anywhere in Turkey except designated historic or natural sites, provided you don't damage farmland or light fires in forests. However, it's not an option for those who value their privacy, except in parts of the higher mountains where camping out is essential.

Historic Hotels

Special licences are granted by the tourism authorities to hotels housed

Hotel Listings

The accommodation listings on the following pages describe the pick of hotels, boutique hotels and *pansiyons* for each region of the country. Within each category, hotels are in order of luxury (with the most de-luxe and expensive first).

İstanbul and Ankara hotels are more expensive, and we have given them a different set of price categories. Because of past fluctuations of the (currently fairly stable) lira, price brackets are based on euro equivalents and are an indication only. Bargaining is sometimes possible, especially out of high season. Many inexpensive hotels will not accept credit cards, so check on booking.

The Season

Outside İstanbul, Cappadocia, the ski resorts and the coast near Antalya, many hotels close between October and April. Of those that remain open through the winter, many will have only solar hot water systems and no central heating; check carefully before booking.

ACCOMMODATION LISTINGS

Hotels in İstanbul and Ankara have different price categories to hotels in the rest of Turkey.

İSTANBUL

İstanbul's five-star accommodation is in line with that in New York or any major European city in both quality and price. Prices for *pansiyon* accommodation can be very reasonable.

Hotels

Ceylan Inter-Continental
Taksim
Tel: 0212-368 4444
www.istanbul.intercontinental.com.tr
In the city centre, this luxurious hotel commands superb views of the Bosphorus and city skylines. It has 390 rooms and suites, including four suites for the disabled. Restaurants include Turkish, French and Californian, and there are bars and de-luxe banqueting and convention rooms, sports facilities and so on. €€€€

Conrad Istanbul
Yıldız Caddesi, Beşiktaş
Tel: 0212-310 2525
www.conradistanbul.com
A huge hotel with 625 rooms and 32 suites. Excellent Italian and Turkish restaurants, French patisserie, and live jazz in the bar every night. Health club with indoor and outdoor swimming pools, and 24-hour business centre. Convenient if not especially beautiful location with wonderful views of the Bosphorus and Yıldız Imperial Gardens. €€€€

Four Seasons Sutanahmet
Tevkifhane Sokak 1, Sultanahmet
Tel: 0212-402 3000
www.fourseasons.com/Istanbul/
There are views of Aya Sofya and the Blue Mosque from this neoclassical building, with 54 rooms and 11 suites, as well as top-notch service, splendid decor (complete with Ottoman antiques) and all modern conveniences. The restaurant offers top-quality Turkish and Continental

cuisine. Hard to remember that it was once a prison. €€€€

Grand Hyatt
Taşkışla Caddesi 80090, Taksim
Tel: 0212-368 1234
http://istanbul.grand.hyatt.com
In a low-rise and relatively restrained building, this deceptively large (332 rooms and 11 suites) classic is right in the centre of İstanbul's "Conference Valley". Features include Italian, Ottoman and Japanese restaurants, a bar, lounge, business centre, conference facilities, Turkish bath, floodlit outdoor pool and tennis courts. €€€€

Mövenpick Hotel Istanbul
Büyükdere Caddesi, 4 Levent
Tel: 0212-319 2929
www.movenpick-hotels.com
Chic hotel in the business district with 249 rooms with desks and Internet connections, state-of-the-art meeting facilities, health club, pool, an excellent restaurant, and Mövenpick ice cream. €€€€

Polat Renaissance
Sahilyolu Caddesi, Yeşilköy
Tel: 0212-414 1800
www.polatrenaissance.com
This thoroughly modern business hotel, one of İstanbul's best near the airport and the World Trade Centre, has the added advantage of a location in a quiet residential neighbourhood overlooking the Sea of Marmara. It has the largest in-house conference facility in the city, 354 rooms, 20 suites, two non-smoking floors, numerous bars and restaurants, a pool, Turkish bath, and fitness and beauty centres. €€€€

Swissôtel The Bosphorus
Bayıldım Caddesi 2, Maçka
Tel: 0212-326 1100
www.swissotel.com
480 rooms and 23 suites. Excellent sports and health facilities (including outdoor

and indoor pools, jacuzzi, sauna, tennis and so on), six restaurants, and banqueting facilities. Superb views from a hilltop location close to Yıldız Park. €€€€

Historic hotels and *pansiyons*

Anemon Galata
Büyükhendek Caddesi 11, Kuledibi, Beyoğlu
Tel: 0212-293 2343
www.anemonhotels.com
Delightfully restored old house-hotel with 23 rooms and seven suites, in a perfect position right beside the Galata Tower. The rooftop bar and restaurant have one of the finest views in the city, over the Bosphorus and Golden Horn. A rare hotel in the new part of town that is furnished in antique style. €€€

Armada
Ahırkapı Sokak, Ahırkapı
Tel: 0212-455 4455
www.armadahotel.com.tr
Right beside the Byzantine city walls, this 110-room hotel is new but built in the style of 16th-century row housing. Quiet location near the Marmara coast but within walking distance of all main sites. An ecologically aware hotel that uses only olive-oil soaps – no detergents. Authentic Turkish food in acclaimed Ahırkapı restaurant; also offers Greek music nights as well as Turkish classical music *(fasıl)*. €€€

Ayasofya Konakları
Soğukçeşme Sokak, Sultanahmet
Tel: 0212-513 3660
www.ayasofyapensions.com
A charming cobbled lane full of restored wooden houses furnished with period furniture, located directly behind Aya Sofya. 57 rooms, four suites, three restaurants (one in a Byzantine cistern), café,

bars, Turkish bath and even a research library on old İstanbul. €€€

Hotel Celal Sultan
Salkımsöğüt Sokak 16, Sultanahmet
Tel: 0212-520 9323
www.celalsultan.com
Classically restored, cosy town house (53 rooms, two suites) with Ottoman-style decor and double-glazed windows. International cable TV and great view of Aya Sofya from the roof terrace. €€€

Çırağan Palace Hotel Kempinski
Çırağan Caddesi, Beşiktaş
Tel: 0212-326 4646
www.kempinski.com
One of İstanbul's most prestigious (and expensive) hotels, the hotel is partly a replica of a lost Ottoman palace. Superb Bosphorus setting and proximity to the city centre also pluses. Two gourmet restaurants, one Ottoman (Tuğra), one more general (Laledan). There are 295 rooms and 27 suites, 12 in a rebuilt Ottoman palace. Outdoor swimming pool and outdoor jazz club. €€€€

Empress Zoë
Akbıyık Cad, Adliya Sokak 10, Sultanahmet
Tel: 0212-518 2504
www.emzoe.com
The American owner has turned this small, supremely popular hotel (25 rooms and 12 suites) near Topkapı Palace into something unique, complete with Byzantine wall paintings and a garden which incorporates

the ruins of a 15th-century Turkish bath. €€

Four Seasons Istanbul at the Bosphorus
Çırağan Caddesi No. 80, Beşiktaş
Tel: 0212-381-4000
www.fourseasons.com
Superb new 166-room hotel right on the Bosphorus and partially housed inside a restored 19th-century palace. Every luxury imaginable is available here although the omnipresence of the water will be the main drawcard, especially as the hotel is a little way away from the main attractions. €€€€

Hotel Kariye
Edirnekapı (beside Chora Church/Kariye Museum)
Tel: 0212-534 8414
www.kariyeotel.com
Unique, peaceful location for lovers of Byzantium. This elegant hotel in a restored Ottoman mansion is right next to one of İstanbul's most exceptionally preserved churches. Superb Asitane Restaurant specialising in historic Ottoman dishes and traditional court music, 22 rooms, five suites and a garden pavilion. €€€

Hotel Kybele
Yerebatan Caddesi 35, Sultanahmet
Tel: 0212-511 7766/67
www.kybelehotel.com
A colourful treasure house of Ottoman antiques with a lobby lit by over 1,000 historic lamps. 16 rooms, two suites, restaurant and delightful courtyard. English, Japanese and other languages spoken. €€

Hotel Nomade
Divanyolu, Ticarethane Sokak 15, Sultanahmet
Tel: 0212-513 8172
www.hotelnomade.com
Run by French-educated twin sisters, this homely 16-room hotel with a rooftop terrace will appeal to well-travelled internationalists, intellectuals and solo females. €

Park Hyatt
Bronz Sokak No. 35, Teşvikiye
Tel: 0212-315 12 34
http://istanbul.park.hyatt.com
Housed in a 19th-century mansion block that has

been completely made over, this 90-room hotel has a Presidential Suite that takes up two floors and has its own private entrance. Lavish bathrooms are called "wet rooms"; the bar boasts a matchless array of international wines; and it goes without saying that there are several restaurants on site. €€€€

Pera Palace Hotel
Meşrutiyet Caddesi 52, Tepebaşı
Tel: 0212-222 8090
www.perapalace.com
Historic "museum-hotel" overlooking the Golden Horn with a string of famous guests including Agatha Christie and Mustafa Kemal Atatürk. Completely restored and modernised between 2008 and 2010. Expect the standards of a five-star hotel but with added ambience. €€€€

Sirkeci Konak
Taya Hatun Caddesi 5, Gülhane
Tel: 0212-528 4344
www.sirkecikonak.com
Marvellous 52-room hotel attached to walls of historic Gülhane Park and very close to sights and tram line. Rooms come with every comfort down to heated bathroom floors. Small basement swimming pool and on-site restaurant focusing on Turkish cuisine. Tip-top service. €€€

Sarı Konak
Mimar Mehmet Ağa Caddesi 42-46, Sultanahmet
Tel: 0212-638 6258
www.istanbulhotelsarikonak.com
Elegant, family-run hotel in a restored house with 20 rooms and five suites very close to main attractions. Lovely rooftop terrace with view of Sea of Marmara. €€€

Hotel Splendid Palace
Nisan Caddesi 23, Büyükada, Prince's Islands
Tel: 0216-382 6950
www.splendidhotel.net
Lovely historic building with spectacular sea views on an island with more horses and traps than cars. Amenities include a garden restaurant and pool. Great for those in search of perfect peace and quiet. €€€

ABOVE: the Four Seasons İstanbul at the Bosphorus.

Vardar Palace Hotel
Sıraselviler Caddesi 54-56, Taksim
Tel: 0212-252 2888
www.vardarhotel.com
Great central location for those in town for the lively nightlife of İstiklal Caddesi. Built 100 years ago in First National Architecture style, it has been thoroughly restored with 40 en-suite rooms, TV, minibars and so on. €

Yeşil Ev
Kabasakal Caddesi 5, Sultanahmet
Tel: 0212-517 6785
www.istanbulyesilev.com
A rebuilt wooden mansion, previously the home of an Ottoman pasha, located between Aya Sofya and the Blue Mosque. 18 rooms and one suite with period decor, intimate walled garden with conservatory and good restaurant. Book well in advance. €€€

Apart-hotels and apartments

Galata Residence Hotel
Bankalar Caddesi, Felek Sokak 2, Galata/Karaköy
Tel: 0212-292 4841
www.galataresidence.com
This huge 19th-century Jewish mansion is uniquely located near Galata Tower – the old "international" neighbourhood – and has been elegantly restored to provide 22 one- and two-bed apartments with fully equipped kitchens and bathrooms, air-conditioning and TV. The rooftop restaurant has spectacular view over the Golden Horn to the old city; atmospheric bar

in the basement. €€–€€€

Istanbul Holiday Apartments
Tel: 0212-251 8530
www.istanbulholidayapartments.com
A range of 22 well-appointed apartments available for short-term stays (2 nights minimum). The best are in the 1920s mansion blocks close to the Galata Tower; as well as a great location, those on the upper floors (no elevator) have magnificent views across the Golden Horn and Bosphorus to Sultanahmet. Other apartments are located around Taksim Square, Kabataş (south of Taksim) and also in the Sultanahmet-Çemberlitaş area. €€–€€€

Mega Residence
Eytam Caddesi 33, Maçka
Tel: 0212-296 7920
www.megaresidence.com
The Residence is superbly placed between "Conference Valley" (Taksim) and its concert halls, and the heart of the city's best shops, restaurants and art/antiques galleries. 30 rooms, 15 with kitchenette in a classic, bay-windowed apartment building. Boardroom, private parking and all business facilities. €€

PRICE CATEGORIES

Price categories for İstanbul are per night for a double room during the high season, including breakfast:
€ below €75
€€ €75–120
€€€ €120–200
€€€€ over €200

THRACE AND MARMARA

Bursa

Artıç Hotel
Atatürk Cad, Ulu Cami Karşısı 95
Tel: 0224-223 5505
www.artichotel.com
Set back a bit from the boulevard, this business hotel has slightly bland, carpeted rooms with all the usual amenities (junior or full suites are worth the extra charge), and bird's-eye views of the mosque domes from its breakfast salon. Rooms €€, suites €€€.

Kitap Evi
Burç Üstü 21, Saltanat Kapısı, Hisar (Tophane)
Tel: 0224-225 4160
www.kitapevi.com.tr
Bursa's only *butik otel* offers six themed rooms and suites (some old-fashioned, some cutting-edge in design) with dark-wood floors and sometimes open-plan baths. Front units have glorious views but some traffic noise; quieter ones face the rear-garden café/restaurant. Limited street parking. Rooms €€, suites €€€.

Safran Hotel
Ortapazar Caddesi, Arka Sok 4, inside Saltanat Kapısı, Hisar (Tophane)
Tel: 0224-224 7216
Converted wooden-house hotel with limited parking nearby. Unlike the common areas, the rooms themselves are blandly modern; a very decent in-house restaurant, good breakfasts and friendly, helpful staff make up for this. €€

Çanakkale

Anzac Hotel
Saat Kulesi Meydanı 8, opposite clocktower
Tel: 0286-217 7777
www.anzachotel.com
Well-run, three-star affair whose 2007-redone rooms with flat-screen TVs and big bathrooms belie a grim exterior. Onsite restaurant and separate mezzanine café screening Gallipoli documentaries; a roof bar

is planned. Private parking. €€€

Cumalıkızık
Mavi Boncuk
Tel: 0224-373 0955
www.cumalikizik-maviboncuk.com
The slightly higher standard one of two restoration inns in the village centre, recognisable by its half-timbered upper storey; just six rooms, so booking usually necessary, especially at weekends. €

Kervansaray
Fetvane Sok 13
Tel: 0286-217 8192
www.anzachotel.com/kervansaray.htm
Justifiably popular hotel, co-managed with the *Anzac*, installed in a 1903-vintage judge's mansion and a rear annexe. Best of the mansion rooms with their mock Belle Epoque furnishings are no. 206 or 207, overlooking the garden with its single suite. Less distinguished are the annexe rooms, above the breakfast area serving above-average starts to the day. €€

Tusan Hotel
Güzelyalı, Intepe
Tel: 0286-232 8746
www.tusanhotel.com
Popular, simple country hotel surrounded by gardens and pine groves, 14km (9 miles) south of Çannakale just above a beach. Indoor and outdoor restaurants, a pool and water sports. Book well ahead. €€€

Edirne

Antik
Maarif Cad 6
Tel: 0284-225 1555
www.edirnehotelantik.com
Eight large if slightly chintz-decor rooms over three floors in this sympathetically converted Belle Epoque mansion with an afffiliated garden restaurant. Dedicated parking. €€

Rüstempaşa Kervansarayı
İki Kapılı Han Cad. 57
Tel: 0284-212 6119
www.edirnekervansarayhotel.com

This 16th-century *kervansaray* designed by Sinan is now a hotel, with cool, cell-like rooms (freezing in winter!) wrapped around a pleasant courtyard. Street noise is kept down by thick walls (and tiny windows); bathrooms were recently revamped, but room furnishings are painfully spartan. €€€

Taşodalar
Hamam Sok 3, behind Selimiye Camii
Tel: 0284-213 1404
www.tasodalar.com.tr
Edirne's quietest boutique hotel, this stone-built structure dating from the 15th century is ideal for families and drivers (with its private, secure car park by the rear tea-garden/restaurant). The nine rooms have dark-wood floors and trim, though other decor mixes genuine antiques with kitsch; upstairs rooms look towards the mosque. €€€€

Gallipoli Peninsula

Gallipoli Houses
Kocadere village, 7km (4 miles) north of Kabatepe road
Tel: 0286-814 2650
www.gallipoli.com.tr
A restored main house and newer garden units offer genuinely boutique comfort. Breakfasts are hearty, while suppers are gourmet standard, with a full wine cellar. Advance booking essential, especially in April–May and autumn. Half-board only. €€€€

Gökçeada (İmroz)

Gökçeada Windsurf Club
Aydıncık beach,
Tel: 0286-898 1016
Stone-clad bungalow complex with contemporary earth-tone decor and big bathrooms, intended largely for students at the in-house windsurf school. But provided space is available, casual trade won't be declined.

Zeytinli (Agii Theodori)
Zeytindali Hotel
Tel: 0286-887 3707
www.zeytindalihotel.com
An old Greek shop has become a superbly refurbished, stone-clad inn. The decent ground-floor restaurant is the only full-service eatery in the village. €€

İznik

Cem
Göl Sahili Yolu 34
Tel: 0224-757 1687
www.cemotel.com
Well-run, renovated lakeside hotel, set quietly in a gap of the city walls. Cheery earth-tone decor in rooms and suites, bathrooms with small tubs and a competent ground-floor restaurant. €€

Kıyıköy

Endorfina
Near Aya Nikola monastery
Tel: 0288-388 6364
www.hotelendorfina.com
In a resort dominated by basic Turkish family-style *pansiyons*, the only comfortable, well-managed spot is this designer hotel with a wood-decked pool and seafood restaurant. €€€

Termal (Yalova)

Çınar/Çamlık
Resort centre
Tel: 0226-675 7400
www.yalovatermal.com
Two co-managed luxury hotels, with a third stablemate under construction. The *Çınar* is originally nineteenth-century, the smaller of the existing pair, with more Belle Epoque charm. €€€

THE AEGEAN COAST

Adatepe

Hünnap Han
Upper mahalle
Tel: 0286-752 6581
www.hunnaphan.com
Named for the jujube tree in the serene walled garden, this inn comprises a rambling, 1750-vintage main *konak*, with pointed-stone and wood-trim rooms, and two remote annexes nearly as old, one a house suitable for groups or families. Half-board only €€€€

Alaçatı

Taş Otel
Kemalpaşa Caddesi
Tel: 0232-716 7772
www.tasotel.com
This former Greek village near Çeşme must now have at least a dozen restoration inns of boutique calibre; this, installed in an 1890s mansion, was the first and still about the best. Breakfast is served on a terrace overlooking the lawn-set pool; just 7 rooms, so bookings – especially at weekends – are mandatory. Open all year. €€€€

Assos/Behramkale

Both Assos harbour (İskele) and the adjacent hill village of Behramkale are established retreats for

BELOW: picturesque alleyway in the old part of Marmaris.

İstanbul's young and trendy, with the overspill heading to Kadırga beach. Owing to preservation edicts, both Behramkale and İskele lodgings are in the main converted from traditional stone houses. Booking is essential during summer or over national holiday periods.

Assosyal
East end of Behramkale
Tel: 0286-721 7046
2009-opened boutique inn, its designer interiors contrasting sharply with the stone masonry of the 3 wings. Breakfast is taken on the north-facing conservatory-terrace, well sheltered from the prevailing wind; by night it works as a restaurant. €€€

Biber Evi
Behramkale square
Tel: 0286-721 7410
www.biberevi.com
Peppers *(biberler)* are the theme here – 20 types in the garden, and pepper-portraying tiles in the 6 units. The fireplace-lounge-bar is the big winter hit, though the upper terrace is the *pièce de résistance*. Host Lütfi is a fount of local lore. €€€ B&B, €€€€ half-board (obligatory in season).

Tekin
Behramkale village entrance
Tel: 0286-721 7099
One of the very few budget/backpackers' options in the area: simple but serviceable en-suite room, with on-site restaurant and a communal balcony upstairs. €

Yıldız Saray
Tel: 0286-721 7025
www.assosyildizsarayotel.com
Two affiliated hotels: one, just about the first building you encounter in İskele, its eight upstairs rooms with modernised baths, (sometimes) fireplaces, sea views, and a good seafood restaurant downstairs, and a 2008-built bungalow complex behind the middle of Kadırga beach, with a large pool. €€ İskele, €€€ half-board only at Kadırga.

Ayvalık

Drivers will find parking especially problematic in the old quarter here; they may prefer to stay on Cunda island, though we have noted town establishments with parking possibilities.

Annette's House
Neşe Sokak 12
Tel: 0542-663 3193
www.annetteshouse.com
Occupying two joined old houses by the Thursday market plaza, these tasteful, white-trimmed rooms are not all en suite but at least have a fair number of bathrooms down the hall. Top-floor family quad. Breakfasts are served by the helpful German owner in the plant-filled garden. €€

Albayrak Taş Konak
Cunda (Alibey) Adası, Şafak Sok 15
just below windmill and chapel
Tel: 0266-327 3031
www.otelalbayrak.com
About the most comfortable of a dozen or so lodgings in the old Greek town, newly built in mock-tradition, stone-clad style, with bay views from the front rooms and the breakfast terrace. €€€

Sızma Han
Gümrük Caddesi, İkinci Sok 49
Tel: 0266-312 7700
www.butiksizmahan.com
Beautifully redone olive-oil press from 1908; rooms are low-key modern with veneer floors and furniture, but preserved stone pointing. Common areas include a competent, seafood-strong seaside terrace restaurant and a fireplace lounge; limited street parking. Booking essential at peak times. €€€

Taksiyarhis
Mareşal Fevzi Çakmak Cad. 71
Tel: 0266-312 1494
www.taksiyarhispension.com
One of the most idiosyncratic Aegean *pansiyons*, inside two knocked-together Greek houses, immediately behind the eponymous church. Each room is eclectically but

tastefully decorated, plus there are two view terraces (breakfast served on the higher one) and a kitchen for guests' use. All rooms are air conditioned, but baths are down the hall. €€

Bafa Gölü

Agora Butik Otel
Kapıkırı village
10km (6 miles) north of Bafa village on the Söke-Milas highway
Tel: 0252-543 5445
www.herakleia.com
The most comfortable and ambitious of the handful of lodgings in this lakeside village built amidst the ruins of ancient Herakleia ad Latmos. Besides conventional rooms, they have 3 detached restored houses. Lodging is only on a weekly basis – if that doesn't suit the nearby Kaya Restaurant has a more modest *pansiyon* let by the night. Full board only. €€€

Birgi

Birgiçınaraltı Pansiyon
Tel: 0232-531 5358
Email: aytacpoyraz@hotmail.com
The only place to stay in this historic, idyllic village, but fortunately it's a goodie, with simple but wood-floored rooms, and home cooking on offer from the proprietor's wife. €€

PRICE CATEGORIES

Price categories are per night for a double room during the high season, including breakfast:
€ below €35
€€ €35–75
€€€ €75–120
€€€€ over €120

Bodrum Peninsula

Gümüşluk

Gümüşluk Otel
Inland from south beach
Tel: 0252-394 4828
www.otelgumusluk.com
Small hotel built around a pool, with pleasant lawn gardens adjacent. Inland position, but the somewhat bland if spacious rooms offer the highest standard at this resort. €€€

Sysyphos Pansiyon
Beach, south end
Tel: 0252-394 3016
Email: info@sysyphos.net
Classic, long-running Turkish "alternative" *pansiyon* spread over three buildings arrayed around a garden bar. Room amenities are basic for the price, but the compound – and the sunset from the front rooms – has considerable charm. €€

Karaincir

Sunny Garden Nilüfer Hotel
Main road, east edge of settlement
Tel: 0252-393 8110
www.sunnygardenhotels.com
Middle-of-the-road resort hotel, but with large, reasonably furnished rooms, friendly, fluent English-speaking management, sea views and a large pool. Breakfast is okay, but best eat supper at nearby Akyarlar. €€

Yalıkavak

Lavanda Hotel
Hillside at outskirts
Tel: 0252-385 2167
www.lavanta.com
Small (8-unit), quiet hillside hotel with some self-catering apartments and panoramic sea/mountain views. Large swimming pool, extensive lush gardens. Food prepared with vegetables grown on the premises, accompanied by a well-stocked wine cellar. Open May–Oct. €€€€

Bodrum Town

Antique Theatre Hotel
Kıbrıs Şehitleri Cad 243
Tel: 0252-316 6053

www.antiquetheatrehotel.com
Small (20 rooms, several suites) luxury hillside hotel arrayed around a pool, with great views towards the castle and the bay. The on-site gourmet restaurant is affiliated to the prestigious Chaîne des Rôtisseurs Association. €€€€

Karia Princess
Myndos Cad. 8, Eskiçeşme Mahallesi
Tel: 0252-316 8971
www.kariaprincess.com
Probably the best town-centre accommodation. Although within walking distance of the busy waterfront, it feels quiet and secluded. A classy place capable of hosting weddings; its Turkish bath is one of the best you'll see along the Aegean coast. Open all year. €€€€

Manastir Hotel
Barış Mevkii, Kumbahçe
Tel: 0252-316 2854
www.manastirbodrum.com
Pleasant, whitewashed hotel on the site of a former monastery, a rather steep climb up from the flatlands. All rooms have balconies and the hotel has a pool, fitness centre, sauna and two restaurants. €€€

Su Hotel
1201 Sok 15, Tepecik Mahallesi
Tel: 0252-316 6906
www.suhotel.net
A fair-sized, oasis-like complex arrayed around one of the largest pools in the town. Individual balconied rooms are still in cheery pastel shades, the exterior done up in Aegean blue and white. The owner is helpful and knowledgeable. €€€

Bozcaada (Tenedos)

Armagrandi
Dolaplı Sok 4–6, off road to beaches
Tel: 0286-697 8424
www.armagrandi.com
Old wine warehouse sympathetically converted to a stunning boutique hotel, with exposed ceiling beams, stone pointing and some skylights to make up for scarce windows.

ABOVE: Bodrum has no shortage of comfortable resort hotels.

Breakfast area, and some parking, out back. Open year-round. €€€

Katina
Yirmi Eylül Caddesi, Kısa Sokağı, near church
Tel: 0286-697 0242
www.katinaas.com
Designer hotel occupying two former Greek houses, with every room different save for grey-wood lattice ceilings throughout. Breakfast at tables in the lane under the vines, or at the cosy café opposite. Open April–Oct. €€€

Çeşme

Altın Yunus Tatilköyü
Kalemburnu Boyalık Meydanı, Ilıca
Tel: 0232-723 1250
Attractive, large, family-friendly low-rise resort built around a sandy bay, with luxurious fittings and all possible mod cons and entertainments. €€€

Çeşme Kervansarayı
Next to the castle
Tel: 0232-712 7177
www.cesmekervansaray.com
This 16th-century *kervansaray* built, as ever, around a fountain courtyard was set to emerge in late 2010 from a comprehensive overhaul as one of the area's most luxurious boltholes – the deluxe suite will reportedly cost 800 euros per night. €€€€

Herakles Butik Hotel
Ildır, 22km (14 miles) northeast of Çeşme
Tel: 0232-725 1025
www.heraklesbutikotel.com
In a converted Greek waterside mansion, at the edge of a village kept relatively undeveloped by its proximity to the ruins of ancient Erythrae and the

resulting preservation order. Open all year. €€

Dalyan

All these listings are riverside outfits along quiet, sought-after Kaunos Sokağı.

Dalyan Resort
Tel: 0252-284 5499
www.dalyanresort.com
Self-contained riverside complex that's the town's most comfortable digs, with four grades of tasteful, travertine-tiled units, an airy domed restaurant, rental canoes and hamam with mud therapy offered. It's popular with package operators. Standard rooms €€, suites €€€.

Kilim Hotel
Tel: 0252-284 2253
www.kilimhotel.com
Attractive small hotel with good-sized rooms (some air-conditioned), proper stall-showers, a palm-shaded pool and plenty of the kilims that give the place its name. €€

Lindos Pansiyon
Tel: 0252-284 2005
www.lindospension.com
Well-appointed rooms with double beds and proper stall showers, including three upstairs balconied units. Pleasant library-lounge facing the river for cool weather, and genial English-speaking management. İztuzu-bound boats can be flagged down here, otherwise free canoes available. Open late March–end Oct. €€

Foça

Foça Konak
Reha Midilli 140, corner 149 Sok, Küçükdeniz Bay

Tel: 0532-617 2035 or 0232-812 3809
The newest of a few local boutique hotels occupies a former Orthodox priest's mansion, with two upstairs units preserving high ceilings and original wood cabinetry. Three more rooms occupy stone utility buildings in the back garden with its lawn-bar. €€€€.

Iyon
198 Sok 8, Ismetpaşa Mahallesi
Tel: 0232-812 1415
www.iyonpansiyon.com
Welcoming *pansiyon* with a choice between fairly basic rooms in a restored Greek house or more spacious, comfortable ones in a rear garden annexe. Breakfast (or drinks) served on the raised front deck, which glimpses the sea. €–€€

İzmir

Antik Han Hotel
Anafartalar Caddesi 600
Tel: 0232-489 2750
www.otelantikhan.com
Charming small city-centre hotel in a restored Ottoman mansion enclosing a courtyard, with on-site restaurant. Can be noisy, during the day at least. €€

Hilton
Gaziosmanpaşa Bulvarı 7
Tel: 0232-441 6060
www.izmir.hilton.com
The 34-storey Hilton, apparently the tallest building in this earthquake-prone region, has large (37 sq m) rooms, indoor pool, fitness centre, sauna and a 31st-floor bar. €€€€

Kuşadası

Bakkhos
5km (3 miles) southeast of town on the Kirazlı road
Tel: 0256-622 0337
www.bakkhos.com
Ten-unit guesthouse in one of the most beautiful agricultural valleys inland from Kuşadası. There's a pool, vast gardens, pleasant Turkish-Dutch management, roofed-over common patios, and half-board available (except Nov–March when B&B only), with supper

served in a wonderful barn-style diner. Otherwise, nearby Kirzalı village has simple eateries. €€

Club Caravanserail
Inside the Öküz Mehmet Paşa Kervansaray, Atatürk Bulvarı 1
Tel: 0256-614 4115
www.kusadasihotels.com/caravanserail
The Hollywood-fantasy version of Turkey, in a restored early 17th-century *kervansaray* replete with palm trees and belly-dance shows in the courtyard restaurant. The parquet-floored rooms are elegantly furnished in a retro way. €€€

Kismet
Gazi Beğendi Bulvarı, Türkmen Mahallesi, north of town centre on the Selçuk road
Tel: 0256-618 1290
www.kismet.com.tr
Originally built in 1966 by Princess Hümeyra Özbaş, a grand-daughter of the last sultan, this venerable hotel set on its own peninsula is essentially a self-contained resort, still run by her descendants. Royalty and leadership of many states, and various domestic celebrities, have stopped in, but it's not hopelessly snooty; the 100 rooms are airy and unpretentious, plus there's a large pool. Open all year. €€€

Villa Konak
Yıldırım Cad. 55
Tel: 0256-614 6318
www.villakonakhotel.com
Attractively restored old-town, hill-quarter mansion whose tasteful rooms are set around several small courtyards filled with fruit trees and magnolias. Bar, restaurant, garden and pool. Mid-April to mid-Nov. €€€

Marmaris and around

Aqua
İçmeler
Tel: 0252-455 3636
www.hotelaqua.com
Five-star, self-contained, all-inclusive complex that's rated the best of several such in the region. Facilities include indoor/outdoor pool, hamam, fitness

centre, watersports, tennis court and kids' club. €€€

Dionysos
Kumlubükü
Tel: 0252-476 7957
www.dionysoshotel.net
Upscale, olive-grove-estate hotel. The 27 units are arrayed for privacy, so that you see see mainly the walls and tile roofs of the other cottages; some have private pools – complementing the giant, communal infinity pool. The à la carte restaurant is excellent. Most units available only through Exclusive Escapes (see page 428). €€€€

Royal Maris
Atatürk Cad. 34
Tel: 0252-412 8383
www.royalmarishotel.com
Right opposite the town beach, this three-star hotel has contemporary if somewhat bland rooms – the best with bay views – somewhat small rooftop and indoor pools, hamam and fitness centre. €€€

Sardunya Bungalows
Selimiye
Tel: 0252-446 4003
Twelve distinctly designed rooms in stone-built bungalows set slightly back from the bay; an ideal place to end a Blue Voyage, though that said the accommodation is mostly an appendage to the busy, expensive restaurant up front where yachts can tie up right at the table. Good value on half-board at €€€.

Pamukkale

Colossae Thermal Hotel
Karahayıt
Tel: 0258-271 4156
www.colossaehotel.com
This village on the plateau behind Pamukkale has been completely overrun by large spa hotels since those actually atop travertines were demolished. This is one of the best, with pretty rooms and gardens, two pools, several restaurants and a full health and beauty thermal centre. €€€€

Kervansaray
İnönü Caddesi, Pamukkale Köyü
Tel: 0258-272 2209

www.kervansaraypension.com
Long-established *pansiyon* run by the welcoming Kaya family. En suite rooms are in warm pastel tones, with many overlooking attractive riverside greenery. Competent rooftop restaurant. Free pickup from Denizli. Open all year. €€

Selçuk

Barim
1045 Sok 34
Tel: 0232-892 6923
www.barimpension.com
Restored old-stone-house *pansiyon* in a traffic-free location, with courtyard garden and contemporarily appointed rooms. If full, there are several other similar establishments in the nearby alleys. €€

Kalehan
North end of main through road (Highway 550)
Tel: 0232-892 6154
Highest-standard hotel in Selçuk, with antique and mock-Ottoman decor wedded to modern units, and a competent restaurant. Extensive garden and pool, with views up to the castle. East parking, but set back enough from the highway to minimise noise. Open all year. €€€

Şirince

Nişanyan Hotel
Top of south slope of village
Tel: 0232-898 3208
www.nisanyan.com
Superbly atmospheric outfit comprising a five-room central hotel building with sweeping views, several restored village houses suitable for families, and the idyllic cottages on the hillside above. Hotel €€€, houses/cottages €€€€.

PRICE CATEGORIES

Price categories are per night for a double room during the high season, including breakfast:
€ below €35
€€ €35–75
€€€ €75–120
€€€€ over €120

THE MEDITERRANEAN COAST

Many of the giant resort hotels along this coast, between Phaselis and Alanya, cater to an almost exlusively German, central European or Russian clientele and offer all-inclusive packages designed for people who never move from the premises except when escorted. Casual arrivals may not be accommodated, and you need to check the position of hotels if you want the freedom to move around; some are 20km (12½ miles) from the nearest town.

Adana

Mercan Hotel
Girmez Çarşısı
Tel: 0322-351 2603
www.otelmercan.com
Spotless accommodation right in the heart of Adana. Few frills but all the necessities (eg air-conditioning). Great value. €€

Seyhan
Turhan Cemal Beriker Bulvarı 18
Tel: 0322-455 3030
www.otelseyhan.com.tr
Stylish tower block overlooking the river in the town centre, with several restaurants and bars, a swimming pool, health club and nightclub. €€€€

Adrasan

Aybars
North bank of river, near beach
Tel: 0242-883 1133 or
0532-314 1887
www.aybarshotel.com
Small, personable hotel whose large balconied rooms overlook lush grounds and a decent restaurant with seating on platforms in the river. Open April–Nov. Half-board. €€€

Anamur

Eser Pansiyon
İnönü Caddesi 6, İskele
Tel: 0324-814 2322
www.eserpansiyon.com
Well-shaded, long-

established and friendly family pension a block back from the beach front. Rooms are simple but air-conditioned. €

Hotel Hermes
İskele Mevkii 33006
Tel: 0324-814 3950
Friendly, simple seaside hotel. All rooms have central heating, air conditioning and balconies. The hotel also has a pool and sauna. Prices are half-board. €€

Antakya

Antik Beyazit Hotel
Hükümet Caddesi 4
Tel: 0326-216 2900
www.antikbeyazitnoteli.com
Beautifully restored French-colonial mansion run by a local journalist. Popular with the Turkish intelligentsia. €€€

Dedeman Hotel
Atatürk Bulvarı 114
Tel: 0326-221 8080
www.dedeman.com
Swish five-star international standard addition to the reliable Dedeman chain, with pool, fitness centre and Middle Eastern cuisine on offer in the dining room. €€€

Savon Hotel
Kurtuluş Caddesi 192
Tel: 0326-214 6355
www.savonhotel.com.tr
Once an Ottoman olive oil and soap factory, this mellow building has been lovingly converted into a charming small hotel. Good Turkish-Italian restaurant. €€€

Antalya

There are numerous small hotels and *pansiyons*, most of them crafted-from delightful old Ottoman-era houses, in the old town (Kaleici). Konyaalti Beach to the west of the city has recently been developed for tourism, with a line of new hotels backing the splendid esplanade. Many of the city's larger hotels and package-tour properties are in Lara, a modern suburb

along the seafront about 12km (7½ miles) east of the city.

Alp Paşa Hotel
Barbaros Mahallesi, Hesapcı Sokak 30
Tel: 0242-247 5676/243 0045
www.alppasa.com
Atmospheric Ottoman-style old-town hotel, with 60 rooms, Turkish bath, garden bar and excellent restaurant. It's a nice hotel but much-used by upmarket groups and not as individual as it once was. €€€

Bagana Horseclub
Yukara Karaman Koyu
Tel: 0242-425 2270/2044
www.baganahorseclub.net
A horse ranch with several excellent chalet rooms around a swimming pool, and an excellent bar and restaurant. Very handy for the ruins of Termessos and walks in the national park, as well as riding. €€€

Hillside Su
Konyaaltı
Tel: 0242-249 0700
www.hillside.com
A study in minimalism, everything from the sheets and towels to the doors, tables and light-fittings are white. It's a concept that works, especially given its great location next to Konyaaltı beach and its Olympic-sized pool.
€€€€

Otel Tuvana
Karanlık Sokak 18
Tel: 0242-247 6015
Secluded and quiet hotel in the old town, beautifully restored, with a relaxed atmosphere and garden with pool. €€€€

Sabah Pansiyon
Hespaçi Sok 60
Tel: 0242-247 5345
www.sabahpansiyon.8m.com
Long-established and deservedly popular budget choice in Antalya's old town. Spotless, cheap, cheerful and offering some of the best-value home-cooked meals in the old town. €

Sheraton Voyager
100 Yıl Bulvarı, Konyaaltı
Tel: 0242-249 4949
www.sheraton.com

Situated on the cliff-top in the northeastern corner of Antalya's massive Kültür Parkı, this swish hotel is one of the best-value of its class in the city. It has several excellent restaurants and bars, attractive gardens, a jogging track, pool and fitness centre – and the museum is a couple of minutes' walk away. €€€

Villa Perla
Kaleiçi
Tel: 0242-248 9793
www.villaperla.com
Atmospheric family-run hotel in a very tastefully converted Ottoman house, with 11 rooms, private courtyard garden for outdoor eating and small pool. €€€

Çıralı

Emin Pansiyon
On the beach road
Tel: 0242-825 7155
www.eminpansiyon.com
A good budget option with its mostly wood-built chalets, with plenty of landscaped space between them. Superior breakfasts include omelettes, quince jam and carob syrup. Friendly family management, ample private parking. €€

Myland Nature Pansiyon
North end of beach strip
Tel: 0242-825 7044
www.mylandnature.com
Superior wooden chalets, redone in 2007, are set in six hectares (15 acres) of orchard with free-range chickens on patrol. Free morning yoga sessions with Pınar, one of your English-speaking hosts, in the activities hall; dedicated sunbeds on beach 70m/

yds distant. The restaurant features organically grown food. Open late March to early Nov. Credit cards accepted. €€€

Odile Hotel
Just past mid-beach
Tel: 0242-825 7163
www.hotelodile.com
The best-value top-end affair, and the only solid-built one, comprises 36 large, decently equipped rooms and suites completely overhauled in 2008, set in lush gardens around a large pool. On-site restaurant, mixed clientele and yoga/massage teaching area. Closed Nov–Feb. €€€

Fethiye

Ece Saray
Marina quay, Birinci Karagözler Mahallesi
Tel: 0252-612 5005
www.ecesaray.net
Beyond doubt the top lodging in central Fethiye, this low-rise hotel occupies impeccably landscaped grounds in a quiet corner of the shore esplanade. The plush rooms all have sea views, and common facilities include a spa, fitness centre, infinity pool and two bar/restaurants. Good value. €€

Villa Daffodil
Fevzi Çakmak Caddesi 115, İkinci Karagözler Mahallesi
Tel: 0252-614 9595
www.villadaffodil.com
Mock-Ottoman mid-range hotel on a quiet shoreline spot out of the centre. A pool, on-site restaurant, hamam and landscaped grounds, plus fair-sized pine-and-tile-decor rooms, make it popular, with booking recommended. €€

Iskenderun

Hotel Cabir
Ulucami Caddesi 16
Tel: 0326-612 3391
www.cabirhotel.com
Iskenderun's best hotel – all 35 rooms are clean and comfortable and there is a bar and disco. €€

Kalkan

Owlsland
Bezirgan Yaylası, west mahalle,
15km (9 miles) above Kalkan via İslamlar
Tel: 0242-837 5214 or 0535-940 1715
www.owlsland.com
Scottish-Turkish-run B&B installed in a 150-year-old rural house, named after the Scops and little owls resident in the nearby almond trees. The cooking is excellent, the location remote, so take half-board. At 720m elevation, you'll

ABOVE: colourful shopfronts in Kaş.

need the woodstoves in the minimally restored but en-suite rooms to stay warm during spring or autumn. Closed Dec–Feb; B&B €€€, half-board €€€€.

Türk Evi (Eski Ev)
Lane up from Süleyman Yılmaz Caddesi, Yalıboyu Mahallesi
Tel: 0242-844 3129
www.kalkanturkevi.com
One of the last survivors amongst Kalkan's 1980s "alternative" *pansiyons*, this well-restored old house has welcoming common areas, wood-floored rooms upstairs and tiled-floor units downstairs, all with mosquito nets and kilims, some with fireplaces (there's no other heating – or air con). Open in winter also by arrangement. €€

Villa Mahal
1.5km (1 mile) east of town, easterly bay shore
Tel: 0242-844 3268
www.villamahal.com
At Kalkan's most exclusive

lodging, a segmented veranda snakes around the ten irregularly shaped standard rooms, while steps continue down past an infinity pool to the sea and lido – with jaw-dropping views all the way. A pool suite and two detached cottages are furnished in the same designer-minimalist decor; the tiered setting among olive trees guarantees privacy. Open May–Oct. €€€€

Kaş

Aquarius
Çukurbağ Yarımadası, South-shore loop road, about 3.5km (2 miles) out
Tel: 0242-836 1896
www.aquariusotel.com
Discreet establishment in lush landscaping, with two wings of small but cheerful rooms with veneer floors bracketing a large kidney-shaped pool. But the main selling point is the best swimming lido on the peninsula, right opposite Meis (Kastellorizo) island. €€€

Arpia
Çukurbağ Yarımadası, North-shore loop road, 7km (4 miles) out of town
Tel: 0242-836 2642
Email: arpia@bougainville-turkey.com
Rooms in two grades were overhauled in 2006, but the place, accordingly upgraded from *pansiyon* to hotel, really scores for its sunset views, private lido and decent breakfasts. Open Easter to mid-Nov. €€

Gardenia
Küçükçakıl shore road
Tel: 0242-836 1618
www.gardeniahotel-kas.com
The most ambitious boutique hotel in Kaş has just 11 varied rooms and suites distributed over four floors, their Philippe Starck decor and marble floors juxtaposed with somewhat garish art in the common areas. The proprietors speak American English. Buffet breakfast to 11am; no children under 12. Prices vary by position in the building, but mostly €€€

Hideaway Hotel
Eski Kilise Arkası 7
Tel: 0242-836 1887
www.hotelhideaway.com
Thoroughly refurbished in recent years – especially the baths – this is the most attractive mid-range option in town, with especially airy third-floor rooms and a pricier luxe jacuzzi suite. Common areas include a small plunge pool, a TV-lounge-cum-library, and a stunning rooftop restaurant with homestyle cooking. Very outgoing, multilingual hosts; credit cards accepted. Open all year. €€

Kız Kalesi

Club Hotel Barbarossa
Çetin Özyaran Caddesi
Tel: 0324-523 2364
www.barbarossahotel.com
Comfortable, pleasantly designed hotel with 103 rooms on a private beach, with views across to Kız Kalesi. There's a good swimming pool, water sports, disco and indoor and outdoor restaurants. Prices are half-board. €€€

Hotel Hantur
Ahmet Erol Caddesi
Tel: 0324-523 2367
www.hotelhantur.com
Pleasant four-storey hotel set right on the beachfront with great views across to the offshore castle. Rooms are spacious and bright, with air-conditioning and satellite TV standard. €€

Mersin

Hilton
Adnan Menderes Bulvarı 3310
Tel: 0324-326 5000
City-centre tower block with all the usual efficiency and conveniences of the Hilton chain. €€€

PRICE CATEGORIES

Price categories are per night for a double room during the high season, including breakfast:
€ below €35
€€ €35–75
€€€ €75–120
€€€€ over €120

TRANSPORT · ACCOMMODATION · EATING OUT · ACTIVITIES · A – Z · LANGUAGE

Ölü Deniz

Oyster Residences
Middle of Belceğiz promenade
Tel: 0252-616 0765
www.oysterresidences.com
The area's first boutique hotel, with 26 large, wooden-floored rooms arranged around a fair-sized pool. Also has direct beach access. €€€€

Seyir Beach Hotel
Far east end Belceğiz promenade
Tel: 0252-617 0058
www.seyirhotel.com
Extremely good value for terracotta floored and wood-trim units, some galleried, sleeping two to four; package-free, fairly easy parking nearby, a pool (though you hardly need it unless the sea is rough) and a recommended attached restaurant (Kumsal). €€

Olympos

Kadir's Top Treehouses
Furthest inland establishment
Tel: 0242-892 1250
www.kadirstreehouses.com
This was the place that started the treehouse trend on this coast back in the early 1990s, and it (plus its several rivals) have become obligatory stops for backpackers. Not many creature comforts, but the bungalows-on-stilts are veritable works of art. The bar is probably the liveliest in the valley. €

Patara

All accommodation is actually in Gelemiş village, just inland from the ruins; almost all establishments lay on a daily shuttle to Patara site and beach.

Golden Pansiyon
Village central junction
Tel: 0242-843 5162
www.pataragoldenpension.com
Caters to budget travellers with sizeable rooms, some balconied, all double-glazed and air-conditioned, at the village's first pansiyon (established 1983). Its restaurant sometimes has trout or ocean fish on the menu. Uniquely here, open all year. €

Patara Delfin
Halfway up easterly ridge
Tel: 0242-843 5120
www.pataradelfinhotel.com
Variable-sized rooms with a large pool and half-board available at the co-managed St Nicholas restaurant. €€

Patara View Point Hotel
Top of east ridge
Tel: 0242-843 5184 or 0533-350 0347
www.pataraviewpoint.com
Well-established hotel with an unbeatable setting, American-style wall showers in the bathrooms, a pool-bar where breakfast is served, and a cushioned, Turkish-style night-time terrace with fireplace. Mar–Nov. €€

Side

Beach House
Barabraos Caddesi
Tel: 0242-753 1607
www.beachhouse-hotel.com
Small, friendly family-run hotel with bright, airy-rooms with balconies overlooking the eastern beach. One of Side's first hotels, it has plenty of character and is extremely well-run. €

Lale Park
Lale Sokak 5
Tel: 0242-753 1131
www.hotellalepark.com
Within the town's old walls, this spotless stone-built establishment is set in a shady garden which boasts a small pool. The rooms are not overly spacious but are beautifully appointed. €€

Tarsus

Şelale
Tel: 0324-614 0600
Large, spacious modern hotel on the edge of the city with outdoor pool, near the waterfall. €€€

Taşucu

Lades Motel
Atatürk Caddesi
Tel: 0324-741 4008
www.ladesmotel.com
Best placed base for the crossing to Northern Cyprus, the Lades is cheerful and boasts cool, spacious rooms, sea views and a decent pool. €€

CENTRAL ANATOLIA

Ankara

As capital, Ankara's hotels are particularly geared to business travellers. Prices often match the convenience, however.

Angora House Hotel
Kalekapısı Sokak 16–18, Hisar
Tel: 0312-309 8380
Ankara's most charming small hotel with six individually decorated rooms in a restored

Ottoman house in the citadel. Within walking distance of many attractions. Booking essential. €€

Ankara Hilton S.A
Tahran Caddesi 12, Kavaklıdere
Tel: 0312-455 0000
www.hilton.com
One of the city's biggest hotels, geared up for foreign business executives, the Ankara Hilton has 324 rooms and 24 suites, plus full facilities. €€€€

Crowne Plaza
Mevlana Bulvarı 2, Ankamall Yanı, Akköprü
Tel: 0312-303 0000
www.cpankara.com.tr
Right beside a huge shopping mall, this 263-room hotel has some of the most attractive rooms in the city, conveniently located right beside a metro stop. It has three restaurants, a bar, conference rooms, and a

health club. €€€€

Gordion Hotel
Büklüm Sokak 59, Kavaklıdere
Tel: 0312-427 8080
www.gordionhotel.com
Supremely smart hotel just off popular Tunal Hilmi shopping street with 42 rooms and three suites decorated with lush Ottoman-style fabrics. Indoor pool and sauna plus rooftop restaurant. €€€€

Grand Hotel Ankara
Atatürk Bulvarı 183, Kavaklıdere
Tel: 0312-425 6655
Located across from the National Assembly, the Grand Hotel Ankara is the city's oldest de-luxe hotel, with 192 rooms and 14 suites. The hotel also has two restaurants, two bars, casino, meeting room, a conference hall and banquet facilities, a nightclub, pool and health centre. €€€€

Houston Hotel
Güniz Sokak 26, Kavaklıdere
Tel: 0312-466 1680
www.hotelhouston.com
Comfortable, efficient and friendly 59-room modern hotel in an excellent city-centre location. 50 rooms with private bathroom, telephone, satellite TV and air conditioning. €€

Sheraton Ankara Hotel and Towers
Noktalı Sokak, 06700 Kavaklıdere
Tel: 0312-457 6000
www.sheratonankara.com
One of the best hotels in

the city, the Sheraton is connected to the Karun Shopping Centre, which has dozens of gift shops, jewellers, and carpet and copperware sellers. The hotel has 304 rooms, 16 suites, a bar, three restaurants, casino, meeting room, beauty centre, pool, sauna and jacuzzi. €€€€

Bolu

Hotel Dorukkaya
Kartalkaya Mevkii
Tel: 0374-234 5026
www.kartalkaya.org/dorukkaya.html
Located in Kartalkaya, a popular ski resort in the Bolu Mountains. It has a swimming pool, fitness centre, sauna, restaurant, several bars and seven ski lifts. Open December to April only. €€€

Çankırı

Ilgaz Doruk Hotel
Ilgaz Doruk Mevkii, Kayak Merkezi, Ilgaz
Tel: 0376-417 2010
www.ilgazdorukotel.com
Located in the Ilgaz Mountains ski resort, the

hotel has 52 rooms, 4 suites, a restaurant, bar, discotheque, sauna and nightclub. €€

Cappadocia

Anatolian Houses
Gaferli Mahallesi, Göreme
Tel: 0384-271 2463
www.anatolianhouses.com
Fantasy writ large in this splendid boutique hotel hunkered down amid the fairy chimneys. Pick from circular beds, cowhide covers and many other decorative quirks in the spacious bedrooms. Indoor pool and Turkish bath. €€€€

Esbelli Evi
Ürgüp
Tel: 0384-341 3395
www.esbelli.com.tr
The cave hotel that kick-started the restoration and conversion movement in Cappadocia is still one of its very finest, with 12 enormous suites, a lounge perfect for making new friends, and a set of pretty gardens and courtyards. The owner prides himself on offering a home-from-home service for all his guests. €€€

Kelebek Hotel and Pension
Aydınlı Mahallesi, Göreme
Tel: 0384-271 2531
www.kelebekhotel.com
Magnificent views, a small outdoor pool, a cute Turkish bath and a wide range of rooms to suit all budgets are just some of the features of this wonderful hotel. €€

Les Maisons de Cappadoce
Belediye Meydani 6, Üchisar
Tel: 0384-219 2813
www.cappadoce.com
Thirteen cave houses of varying sizes (sleeping 2–6), with kitchens, views, gardens and delightfully chic decor. €€€

Sacred House
Barbaros Sokak, Ürgüp
Tel: 0384-341 7102
www.sacred-house.com
A love-it-or-loathe-it phantasmagoria of a hotel whose bathrooms must be some of the most original and splendid in the whole country. Small on-site restaurant. Within easy walking distance of town centre. €€€€

Sofa Hotel
Orta Mahallesi, Avanos
Tel: 0384-511 5186

www.sofahotel.com
The 34-room Sofa Hotel is in an artily restored pair of old Cappadocian houses. There's an outdoor restaurant, café and bar. €

Traveller's Cave Hotel
Aydınlı Mahallesi, Göreme
Tel: 0384-271 2780
www.travellerscave.com
In a splendidly quiet location at the top of old Göreme, this delightful hotel consists of a set of cavé rooms wrapped around layers of garden. €€

Kayseri

Hotel Almer
Osman Kavuncu Caddesi, Kayseri
Tel: 0352-320 7970
www.almer.com.tr
Catering primarily to business travellers, this smart, modern, 75-room city-centre hotel is convenient for all Kayseri's main attractions. €€

Hotel Selçuk
Babalık Sokak 4
Tel: 0322-353 2525
www.otelselcuk.com.tr
Located near the main tourist attractions of the city, Hotel Selçuk has 82 rooms and a restaurant. €€

THE BLACK SEA COAST

Amasra

Amastris
Büyük Liman beach, south end
Tel: 0378-315 2465
Recently renovated to luxury standards, this offers both standard doubles and bungalows, buffet breakfast and a large pool if the sea doesn't appeal. Closed in winter. €€€

Timur
Çekiciler Çarşısı 57
Tel: 0378-315 2589
www.timurotel.com
One block north of Büyük Liman, this small hotel (18 rooms, 3 suites) is popular for the sake of its comfortable rooms with new baths, English-speaking management, pleasant, loft-style breakfast salon and quiet position. €€

Amasya

Emin Efendi Mansions
Hatuniye Mahallesi,
Hazeranlar Sokak 66
Tel: 0358-213 0852
Fine 200-year-old Ottoman house jutting out over the Yeşilırmak River, below the royal tombs. The *pansiyon* wing is basic, with non-en-suite rooms, though the hotel area is much plusher. The *pansiyon* has a vine-shaded courtyard with laundry and self-catering kitchen; the hotel a restaurant and common room containing a piano and an open fire. *Pansiyon* €€, hotel €€€

İlk Pansiyon
Gümüşlü Mahallesi, Hitit Sokak 1
Tel: 0358-218 1689
Email: ilkpansiyon@hotmail.com

This old Armenian mansion is one of the most beautifully restored houses in Amasya, refurbished by the owner, an architect committed to urban renewal. The six rooms are all of different sizes and individually furnished with antiques; bathrooms are recessed in cabinets. Everything surrounds a vegetated courtyard. €€

Artvin

Hotel Karahan
İnönü Caddesi 16
Tel: 0466-212 1800
The only (relatively) comfortable, reliably prostitute-free, hotel in town. Although unprepossessing from the outside, this 48-room hotel

offers superb views from many of its balconied rooms and its good restaurant. The owners speak good English and can help if necessary with touring arrangements to the nearby Georgian churches. €€

Gerze

Körfez Turistik Tesisleri
End of harbour point
Tel: 0368-718 2476
A gem for lovers of simplicity and solitude, all the rooms in this small, basic motel have balconies overlooking the sea; from those on the right you can watch the fishermen trawling by night. Good restaurant. €€

Kaçkar Mountains

Ayder
Kuşpuni Otel
South slope
Tel: 0464-657 2052
www.kuspuni.com
The most comfortable establishment of many in the village, popular with Turkish yuppies and expats. Rooms vary in size but are all en suite and heated. The regional food comes in copious helpings. Half-board €€€.
Fora Pansiyon
North hillside
Tel: 0464-657 2153.
www.turkutour.com
Bohemian, trekker-friendly atmosphere, with a *teleferik* to hoist up your backpack, 7 chestnut-wood-built, balconied (if shared-bath) rooms, a sauna, a lovely terrace where supper is served, and welcoming, hosts. Half-board €€.

Barhal
Karahan Pension
1.2km (¾ mile) out on the Altıparmak road
Tel: 0466-826 2071
This attractive pension has a covered roof-terrace dorm sleeping up to 15, or "treehouse"-style double chalets. Summer only. €

Çat
Cancık
Village centre
Tel: 0464-654 4120
The highest comfortable facility in the Fırtına valley

that you'll find prior to heading off into the eastern Kaçkar, or coming down from the mountains: just 6 wood-trim rooms upstairs, and a combination general store/grill restaurant downstairs. Half-board €€.

Meretet (Olgunlar)
Kaçkar Pansiyon
Tel: 0466-824 4432
www.kackar.net
The most luxurious, and largest, of the south-slope trailhead *pansiyons*, with large en suite rooms and a self-catering kitchen. You can rent trekking gear here if needed. The proprietor also acts as a guide. €€

Safranbolu

The Çarşı quarter of this small museum town is renowned for its beautiful old mansions, many of which have been converted into hotels and *pansiyons*. From about a dozen options, some of the best follow.

Bastoncu Pansiyon
Hıdırlık Sokağı 4, next to Kaymaklamlar Evi
Tel: 0372-712 3411
www.bastoncupension.com
Good-value backpackers' institution that also attracts older travellers for the sake of well-renovated rooms, with en-suite baths and carved ceilings, in this 300-year-old building. A mix of dorms and inexpensive doubles; economic evening meals. €
Gül Evi
Hükümet Sok 46
Tel: 0372-725 4645
www.canbulat.com.tr
The town's top standard is offered at this architect-refurbished boutique hotel, where modern comforts (like unusually large bathrooms) balance the Olde Worlde feel found in almost all such mansions. Attached café-bar, but no restaurant. Rooms €€€, palatial suite €€€€.
Havuzlu Asmazlar Konağı
Çelik Gülersoy Cad 18
Tel: 0372-725 2883
www.safranbolukonak.com

One of the first and still among the best of the mansion conversions, the older of the two linked buildings is famous for its enormous indoor pool and fountain, which provided water for the original 18th-century owners and is now surrounded by café tables. Rooms, with tiny bathrooms, all have brass beds and kilims. Either the indoor or garden restaurant is worth dining at even if you don't stay here. €€€

Şavşat

Laşet Motel
Off main road towards Ardahan, 8km (5 miles) east of Şavşat
Tel: 0466-571 2136
www.laset.com.tr
The only serious tourist facility in the eastern Georgian valleys, this rustic wood-trimmed inn with standard rooms, detached bungalows and licensed restaurant occupies an idyllic setting on part-forested mountainside. €€

Sinop

Zinos Country Hotel
Ada Mahallesi, Shore Road
Tel: 0368-260 5600
www.zinoshotel.com.tr
Not quite in the open country, but large, tasteful, wood-trim-and-white rooms in a mock-Ottoman compound with sweeping sea views offers the best standards in the Sinop area. On-site restaurant and private swimming platform, though Karakum beach is not far away. €€€

Trabzon

Horon Hotel
Sıramağazalar Cad. 125
Tel: 0462-326 6455
www.hotelhoron.com
Best of the very few mid-range hotels in town, on a fairly quiet street off the main square. Some rear rooms have sea views (no balconies though), all have renewed baths, and the rooftop restaurant is a big plus. €€€

Zorlu Grand Hotel
Kahraman Maraş Caddesi 9
Tel: 0462-326 8400
www.zorlugrand.com
The city's only 5-star hotel, pitched squarely at business travellers, with gym, indoor pool, two bars and restaurants, plus a garishly over-the-top lobby. The 160 units, all with marble-clad bathrooms, include a dozen suites. Overpriced; web bookings or bargaining in person may produce discounts. €€€€

Ünye

Kumsal Hotel
3km (2 miles) west of town centre, Uzunkum beach
Tel: 0452-323 4490
www.kumsal.com.tr
Just 27 wood-trimmed, simply but tastefully furnished rooms, with a choice of garden, mountain, or sea views (the latter the quietest). Restaurant, but no pool – no need really as you're beside one of the best Black Sea beaches. €€

Uzungöl

İnan Kardeşler Tesisleri
60km (37 miles) inland from Of
Tel: 0462-656 6021
www.inankardeslerotel.com
This all-wood combination bungalow-inn, restaurant and trout farm is a favourite last-night stop on the way back to Trabzon, or as a base for rambles in the mountains. The restaurant is good; as everywhere around the lake, there is no alcohol. €€€

BELOW: Trabzon streetscape.

THE EAST

Diyarbakır

Balkar Hotel
Kibris Caddesi 38
Tel: 0412-228 7133
www.balkarhotel.com
Situated right by the walls of the old city and aimed at business customers, it is surprisingly quiet, tastefully furnished. €€
Dedeman Diyarbakır Hotel
Elazığ Caddesi, Yeni Belediye Sarayı Yanı
Tel: 0412-229 0000
Outside the city walls in the new part of town, this chain-hotel is the city's safest bet, with 98 rooms and two suites, a restaurant/ bar, fitness centre and pool. €€€
Otel Büyük Kervansaray
Gazi Caddesi
Tel: 0412-228 9606
A lovely black and white stone-built 16th-century *kervansaray*, refurbished into atmospheric glory. Courtyard garden, restaurant and pool, but rooms are on the small side. €€€

Doğubeyazıt

Sim-Er Hotel
Iran Transit Yolu 3km, PK 13
Doğubeyazıt, Ağrı
Tel: 0472-312 4842
Hotel with 125 rooms on the edge of Doğubeyazıt, much frequented by overlanders and Ararat trekking groups. It boasts excellent views of Mount Ararat. €€

Erzurum

Dedeman Palandöken Ski Centre
Palandöken Dağı PK 115
Tel: 0442-234 6400
Email: hotels@Dedeman.com.tr
Set in a ski resort but open all year. The ski season is usually from mid-November to May. €€€
Kral Hotel
Erzincankapı 18
Tel: 0442-218 1624
A concrete block, but the most comfortable of Erzurum's central hotels, with ornate bathrooms and

views to the mountains from some rooms. €€

Gaziantep

A Butik Hotel
Baymahli Sokak 1
Tel: 0342-230 1013
www.butikaotel.com
Good-value boutique hotel fashioned from a late-19th-century Armenian dwelling, the classy rooms are located around a shady central courtyard. €€
Anadolu Evleri
Koroğlu Sok 6
Tel: 0342-220 9525
www.anadoluevleri.com
Perhaps the most tastefully restored and converted of Gaziantep's old town houses, it's ideally located to explore the castle and surrounding bazaars. €€€
Katan
İstasiyon Caddesi
Tel: 0342-230 6969
Well situated for the city's wonderful archaeological museum, it has comfortable air-conditioned rooms and views over the castle. €€

Kahramanmaras

Ramada
Mahçiçek Bulvarı
Tel: 0344-233 211010
A shiny white tower block giving what you'd expect from a Ramada, but good value for a central location in this fast-growing city. €€

Kâhta

Zeus Hotel
M. Kemal Paşa Caddesi
Tel: 0416-725 5694
www.zeushotel.com.tr
Uninspiring position on the western edge of dusty, scruffy Kahta, but this place is an oasis of green, with comfortable rooms overlooking a well-tended garden and good-sized pool. €€€€

Karadut

Karadut Motel Pansiyon
Karadut village
Tel: 0416-737 2169

www.karadutpansiyon.net
Basic place on the edge of the traditional village of Karadut (Black Mulberry), it has simple en-suite rooms and home-cooked meals. Views over the mountains are a delight, and the owner arranges tours to Nemrut. €

Kars

Kars Hotel
Halitpaşa Caddesi
Tel: 0474-212 1616
www.karsotel.com
This 8-room boutique hotel has been lovingly converted from a splendid Russian occupation-era town house. It's a much-needed addition to Kars' previously dire range of hotels, and is situated in the heart of the town. €€€€

Malataya

Altın Kayısı
İstasiyon Caddesi
Tel: 0422-211 4444
www.altinkayisi.com
Smart business hotel with pool and garden, situated on the edge of town. €€€

Şanlıurfa

Hotel Arte
Atatürk Bulvarı
Tel: 0414-314 7060
www.otel-arte.com
Designer-style hotel right in the business centre of the city, but only a short walk to the tourist sites. Spotless and well run, it's a real addition to the city's traditional hotel scene. €€
Cavahir Konak Evi
Selahattin Eyub Camii Karşısı
Tel: 0414-215 9377
Exquisite sandstone mansion converted into an exquisite small hotel. Rooms are beautifully furnished and decorated, and regular musical/feast evenings are held here in the summer months. Well located within walking distance of Urfa's famous sites. €€€
Hotel Harran
Sarayönü Caddesi, Ataturk Bulvarı
Tel: 0414-313 2860

www.hotelharran.com
Located in the city centre, the long-established Harran Hotel now boasts a new block. The large pool out back is a god-send in Şanlıurfa's sizzling summers, and there's a bar, Turkish bath, sauna, jacuzzi and fitness centre. €€
Manici Hotel
Şurkavı Alışveriş Merkezi 68
Tel: 0414-215 9911
www.maniciurfa.com
A modern hotel built in the style of the traditional architecture of the old city, each air-conditioned room is individually furnished with hand-painted furniture and exotic soft furnishings. €€€

Van

Büyük Urartu
Cumhuriyet Caddesi
Tel: 0432-212 0660
www.buyukurartuotel.com
Van's longest-established quality hotel, it is looking a little careworn but its central location and customer service compensate. €€
Tamara Otel
Yuzbaşıoğlu Sokak 1
Tel: 0432-214 3296
www.tamaraotel.com
In a moderately quiet sidestreet off the main drag, the Tamara is Van's best hotel. Part-boutique, part-designer, it has a decent bar and restaurant. €€€

PRICE CATEGORIES

Price categories are per night for a double room during the high season, including breakfast:
€ below €35
€€ €35–75
€€€ €75–120
€€€€ over €120

TRANSPORT

ACCOMMODATION

EATING OUT

ACTIVITIES

A – Z

LANGUAGE

E ATING OUT

RECOMMENDED RESTAURANTS, CAFÉS & BARS

Choosing a Restaurant

It is difficult to go hungry in Turkey, and the food is often excellent. From the sesame-sprinkled bread rings (simit) sold in city streets to the most elaborate Ottoman palace cuisine, there is something here for all appetites. There also plenty of Western-cuisine restaurants in resort areas and the largest cities: many affluent Turks have acquired more sophisticated tastes, so you can find numerous fashionable restaurants offering anything from sushi to Argentine grills.

Some hotels have excellent restaurants offering ethnic cuisine, plus lavish buffets available in their breakfast salons, especially for Sunday brunch. However, don't assume that fancy decor and well-dressed waiters necessarily mean a good meal; often, you will find the simpler restaurants offer better food.

Credit cards

Most establishments in the larger cities and resorts accept all major credit cards (but rarely American Express). Elsewhere the cheaper restaurants will only accept cash.

Types of Restaurant

Although the word restoran is applied to almost anywhere where food is served, Turkish restaurants fall into several different categories:
• **Balık lokantası:** fish restaurants serving hot and cold meze (a mixed selection of starters, which can make up a whole meal, see Order As You Go, opposite), freshly caught fish and shellfish. You will be welcome to look at the fish available in order to

choose. Fish is more expensive than other meals in Turkey, and is normally priced by weight. Less touristed, out-of-the-way coastal spots will be cheaper. All will be licensed.
• **Et lokantası:** restaurants specialising in meat dishes. May or may not be licensed.
• **Kebapçı:** a kebab house. Usually no alcohol served.
• **Kendin pişin kendin ye:** Literally, cook and eat your own. Meat by the kilo is sold to diners, who grill it themselves at a tableside mangal (barbecue); a limited range of meze and salad is usually also offered. Not usually licensed.
• **Köfteci:** a meatball specialist. Usually no alcohol served.
• **Lokanta:** the basic neighbourhood restaurant, feeding local businessmen as well as visitors at lunch time. These are reliable places to eat, and it is easy to choose as the food is displayed in hot cabinets. A waiter will bring your choice to your table. No alcohol served.
• **Mantı/Gözleme Evi:** serves Turkish ravioli and filled pancakes.
• **Meyhane:** translated somewhat

inadequately as "tavern". Some of these places are smoky drinking dives, dedicated to rakı, wine (and sometimes song) over food, but the best are also famous for their delicious cooking. Meze are often especially good here.
• **Muhallebici:** Turkish pudding shop – for milk-based puddings and muhallebi.
• **Ocakbaşı:** tables are arrayed around a central charcoal grill so that diners can watch meat dishes being prepared. Usually licensed.
• **Pastane:** at a Turkish pastane – the word "pasta" means pastry or gâteau in Turkish – you can buy all the sticky oriental sweets like baklava, more elaborate western gateaux and sometimes milk-based desserts. It's usually possible to eat in, but they may not serve coffee and tea.
• **Pideci/Lahmacun:** specialises in the Turkish equivalent of pizza.

Teahouses, Cafés and Bars

For more about the çayhane/kahvehane (tea or coffee houses) see the feature on page 96. Some

Bill-Padding Scams

In many Turkish restaurants there is no printed menu, and even where one exists, it is a good idea to confirm prices of especially unusual mezes or fancy mains, and of alcohol. In the more popular foreigner-patronised resorts, there is a whole range of often hidden charges which can bump up even printed-menu prices by as much as 30 percent if deployed together: küver (cover), servis üçreti (service

charge), garsoniye (waiter's "commission"). If things appear on your table which you have not specifically ordered – typically pickles, garlic bread, çiğ börek (puff bread), mini-meze, bottled water – you will certainly end up paying for them unless accompanied by the magic words ikramızdır (with our compliments). You should also review bills carefully at the end, and request itemisation if in doubt.

Turkish men seem to spend their lives in these places, smoking and playing backgammon, but they are not used to tourists (especially women).

Plenty of elegant European-style cafés are springing up, offering Turks the experience of French-style baguette sandwiches, Italian cappuccinos and American cheesecake. Many smart cafés turn into bars at night, and some will have live music.

Expensive hotel bars often have a view, for which you pay in the inflated price of the drinks. Some offer a "British pub" or other theme to bring in custom. In most you can find snacks; in some a full meal will be available.

Order as You Go

In fish restaurants and *meyhanes*, large trays with assorted plates of cold meze will be brought round: simply point to the ones that take your fancy. Later, you will be asked for your choice of hot meze (*sıcak mezeler*), and later still for what you'd like as a main course. You can order as you go, and it is quite all right to stop after the meze if you have had enough. Bread and bottled drinking water will be brought automatically but usually attract a modest cover charge.

RESTAURANT LISTINGS

İSTANBUL

Fish restaurants

Balıkçı Sabahattin
Seyit Hasan Koyu Sok. 1, Sultanahmet
Tel: 0212-458 1824
Popular old-town seafood restaurant serving a variety of regional specialities. €€

İskele
Yahya Kemal Caddesi 1, Rumelihisarı
Tel: 0212-263 2997
Housed inside a pretty little decommissioned ferry terminal near the Ottoman castle on the Bosphorus shore, this popular fish restaurant has a romantic waterside setting. Sea bass is recommended. €€€

Kıyı
Kefeliköy Caddesi 126 Tarabya
Tel: 0212-262 0002
www.kiyi.com.tr
Swish fish restaurant featuring original Turkish art and photography by contemporary masters. Open noon–midnight. €€€

The outdoor fish restaurants by the fish market off the northern end of Galata Bridge are also a good bet.

Traditional Turkish

Karaköy Lokantası
Kemankeş Caddesi 133, Karaköy
Tel: 0212-292 4455
Housed in the pretty tiled building that used to house the Estonian Consulate close to the port, this restaurant is popular with real İstanbul workers as well as visitors and offers good, cheap food with a regularly

changing menu. Open 7am–11pm. €

Hacı Abdullah
Sakızağacı Caddesi 17, Beyoğlu
Tel: 0212-293 8561
www.haciabdullah.com.tr
Long-established Turkish restaurant serving authentic home-style Ottoman Turkish cuisine. Menu changes daily. Try the *hünkar beğendi kebab* (beef stew served on a bed of aubergine purée) or the *kuzu tandır* (roast lamb). No alcohol. Open noon–11pm. €

Hacı Baba
İstiklâl Caddesi 49, Taksim
Tel: 0212-244 1886
www.hacibabarest.com
This classic Turkish restaurant offers a superb selection of *şiş kebab* and a generally varied menu. In summer the balcony overlooking the garden of a Greek church makes it especially appealing. Open noon–midnight. €€

Havuzlu
Gani Çelebi Sokak 3, PTT Yani
Tel: 0212-527 3346
www.havuzlurestaurant.com
Best of the restaurants inside the Covered Bazaar, specialising in kebabs and delicious meze. Open noon–5pm. €

Kallavi Taverna
İstiklâl Caddesi, Kallavi Sokak 20, Beyoğlu
Tel: 0212-251 1010
Aytor Caddesi 1, Levent
Tel: 0212-282 7070
Sefik Bey Sokak 9, Kadıköy
Tel: 0216-414 4468
Three small, upmarket but lively Turkish *meyhane* each offering a reasonable

all-in price for the night, including excellent food, drinks and live music. Extremely popular with local yuppies and office parties; reservations essential. Closed Sunday. €€

Refik
Sofyalı Sokak 6-8, Tünel
Tel: 0212-243 2834
A popular spot in a hyper-trendy part of town with Turkish and foreign intellectuals, embassy sorts and the occasional celebrity. Part of the charm is the complete lack of concern for decor. Specialises in Black Sea dishes, especially fish. Open noon–11pm. €€

Yakup 2
Asmalımescit Sokak 35/37
Tel: 0212-249 2925
www.yakuprestaurant.com
When Refik's (around the corner) gets crowded and service is slow this is an excellent alternative. Owned by a relative of the avuncular Refik, it's similar in atmosphere but open later. €€

Oriental

Çin Büfe
Turnacıbaşı Sokak 6, Galatasaray
Tel: 0212-251 8702
Pleasingly authentic small Chinese restaurant with very affordable prices. Contemporary Asian decor. Open noon–10pm. €€

Çok Çok Thai
Meşrutiyet Caddesi 51, Tepebaşı
Tel: 0212-292 6496
www.cokcok.com.tr
Thai restaurant with chic decor that blends both

Turkish and Thai influences. Offers a mouth-watering menu with a great selection of cocktails. Open noon–midnight. €€€

Dubb Indian Restaurant
İncili Çavuş Sokak 10, Sultanahmet
Tel: 0212-513 7308
One of Turkey's rare Indian restaurants, Dubb serves a tasty if fairly standard menu for prices higher than you'd pay in the UK. Open noon–3pm, 6–11pm. €€–€€€

French/ Mediterranean

Café du Levant
Rahmi M. Koç Museum, Hasköy Caddesi 27, Hasköy, Golden Horn
Tel: 0212-369 6607
French-style bistro in the grounds of the city's industrial museum, with excellent food prepared by French chefs. Open noon–10pm. Closed Monday. €€€

Ulus 29
Adnan Saygun Caddesi, Ulus Park
Tel: 0212-265 6181
Stunning Bosphorus view and gourmet French cuisine, with imported wines and champagne. Open noon–4pm, 8pm–1am. Brunch on Sunday. €€€

PRICE CATEGORIES

Prices per person for a single meze platter and/or soup, a main course, and one drink, in Euros (Turkish lira – at 2 lira to €1)

€ under €10 (under 20TL)
€€ €10–18 (20–36TL)
€€€ €18–25 (36–50TL)
€€€€ over €25 (over 50TL)

International

360
Mısır Apartmanı,
İstiklal Caddesi 311
Tel: 0212-251 1042
www.360istanbul.com
One of the city's most talked about venues and the winner of various restaurant awards, 360 offers, as its name suggests, superb panoramic views of the city as well as an international menu that includes pastas, grills, sushi and curries with the occasional Turkish ingredient thrown in. There is also a bar with DJ and live music at the weekends. Reservations essential. Open 1–3pm, 7.30pm–3am. Closed Mondays. €€€

Laledan
Çırağan Palace Hotel Kempinski
Tel: 0212-326 4646
Highest-quality international cuisine in a fabulous setting – a palace hotel on the shore of the Bosphorus. Terrace open in summer, live music, seafood specials on Monday and Tuesday. Open daily 7–11am, 7–11pm. €€€

Leb-i derya
Kumbaracı Yokuşu,
Kumbaracı İş Hanı 57/7, Tünel
Tel: 0212-293 4989
www.lebiderya.com
Chic restaurant-bar in a rooftop location with stunning views of the mosques that has proved very popular with a well-heeled, youngish clientele. Open 4pm–2am; 10am–3am at weekends. €€€

Rejans
Emir Nevruz Sokak 17, Galatasaray
Tel: 0212-244 1610
www.rejansrestaurant.com
Faded grandeur in this nostalgic favourite, founded in the 1920s by White Russian refugee aristocrats. Glowing write-ups in French guidebooks, however, should tell you something about the quality of the food – try the *piroshki*, *borscht*, beef stroganoff and stewed duck washed down with lemon vodka. Reservations recommended for dinner. Open noon–3pm, 7–11pm. Closed Sunday. €€

Sunset Grill & Bar
Ahmet Adnan Saygun Caddesi,
Yol Sokak 2, Ulus Parkı
Tel: 0212-287 0357
A Californian-style restaurant set on a hill with an exquisite view of the Bosphorus. Very trendy, it serves mainly grill dishes. Enjoy the bar after sunset. Open 7pm–midnight. €€€

Cafés and patisseries

Andon
Sıraselviler Caddesi 51, Taksim
Tel: 0212-251 0222
www.andon.com.tr

ABOVE: sesame seed bread.

Street Cuisine in İstanbul

Recognised by the swanky, high-domed opera-set interior built at the turn of the century, Çiçek Pasajı (Flower Seller's Alley) – off the main pedestrian thoroughfare of Istiklal Caddesi – is a raucous, touristy, covered lane full of *meyhanes* (taverns) and the sound of gypsy music. A short distance to the west (and again just off İstiklal Caddesi), the narrow lanes of

Different floors offer different specialities. The bar upstairs serves deli pastries and coffees.

Cadde-i-Kebir
İstkilal Caddesi,
Imam Adnan Sokak 7
Tel: 0212-244 4364
A café/bar owned by one of Turkey's more controversial film directors, Reis Çelik. Imported German beer and light meals.

Cafeist
Takkeciler Sokak 41–45,
Grand Bazaar
Tel: 0212-527 9853
One of a row of petite but popular cafés in the Grand Bazaar. Serving typical bistro fare and beverages, it's worth tracking down.

Dulcinea
İstiklal Caddesi, Meşelik Sokak 20
Tel: 0212-245 1071
www.dulcinea.org
Creative modern decor and very trendy. Offers a wide selection of imported drinks and light meals. Live jazz at

Asmalimescit are jammed with tables in summer. Down by the water's edge below the Galata Tower, the Fish Market also has a parade of good (if basic) restaurants.

The former fishermen's quarter of Kumkapı, located off the coast road to the immediate west of Sultanahmet, boasts numerous restaurants all bunched together along a few narrow streets.

weekends. A bit pricey.

Kaktüs
İstiklal Caddesi,
Imam Adnan Sokak 4
Tel: 0212-249 5979
This tiny Parisian-style bistro and bar with live music attracts an arty clientele.

KV Cafe
Tünel Geçidi
Tel: 0212-251 4338
Delightfully atmospheric café in a passage facing the Tünel funicular. Best at night.

Paul
Valikonağı Caddesi 36, Nişantaşı
A sleek, Parisian-style pastry house. Expensive but very French. Branches also in Ortaköy and Yeniköy.

Urban
İstiklal Caddesi, Kartal Sokak 6A
Tel: 0212-252 1325
Hidden down a back alley, this relaxed café/bar is in a restored historic building which originally opened in the 1920s. A good selection of imported drinks, coffee and light meals.

THRACE AND MARMARA

On the whole, restaurants in these regions don't have the

pretensions or sophistication of those found in İstanbul, Ankara and the coastal resorts. But you certainly won't go hungry, and meals will usually be a good deal cheaper.

Bursa

The fish restaurants along Sakarya Caddesi in the city centre, near the former

Jewish quarter, serve alcohol and have something of the lively atmosphere of İstanbul's *meyhanes*. The restaurants in the Kültürpark are overpriced and not recommended.

Arap Şükrü
Sakarya Cad 27 & 6
Tel: 0224-221 1453
Going for well on seven decades now, these competing establishments

with near-identical offerings of seafood, meze and booze. €€€

Cumurcul
Çekirge Caddesi 18
Tel: 0224-235 3707
Attractively converted old house in Çekirge, with the usual range of meze, kebabs and grills. Book ahead at weekends. €€€

Kebapçı İskender
Ünlü Caddesi 7, Heykel

Tel: 0224-221 4615
The owners claim to be descended from the inventor of the famed *Iskender kebab*. Open all year. €

Safran
Inside eponymous hotel, Ortapazar Caddesi, Arka Sokak 4, Hisar district
Nouvelle à la carte restaurant purveying cold and hot mezes, meat and mushroom stews. Licensed. €€€

Çanakkale

Cafeka
Cumhuriyet Meydanı 28/B
Tel: (0286) 217 4900
Attractively priced, generic-Mediterranean fare in elegant (for Çankakkale) surroundings, though coffees (as implied by the name) are centre stage. Licensed, with a decent wine list. €€

Sardunya
Fetvane Sokak 11
Tel: 0286-213 9899
Most established of several similar youth-orientated *ev yemekleri* lunch spots (this one closes at 8.30pm) on what's also the main street for student nightlife. Housed partly in an old Belle Epoque house, this also has back-garden seating for downing savoury set-price, self-served stews and salads; unlicensed. €

Yalova
Eski Balıkhane Sokak 31
Tel: 0286-217 1045
Unusual mezes and what's claimed to be the town's widest range of seafood,

at tables upstairs or in the ground-level conservatory of this historic building, but fish prices are also Çanakkale's highest. €€€€

Edirne

Balkan Piliç Restaurant
Saraçlar Caddesi 14
Tel: 0284-225 2155
Not just roast chicken (*piliç*) but other meats, and vegetable stews. Unlicensed. €

Melek Anne
Maarif Cad. 18
Tel: 0284-213 3263
Café serving from an old house in a shady, secluded courtyard; the snack menu includes *mantı, menemen* (egg fry-up with tomatoes and peppers), *gözleme, katmer* (sweet crêpe). Opens 9am, so suitable for breakfast. €

Niyazi Usta
Ortakapı Caddesi 9
Tel: 0284-213 3372
Edirne's local speciality is *ciğer tava* (deep-fried calf liver with tomato-onion-and-chilli garnish), and the premier *ciğerci* is reckoned this tasteful two-storey affair. Unlicensed. Closes at 9.30pm. €

Villa
On River Meriç, 1.5km (1 mile) south of town on the Karağaç road
Tel: 0284-223 4077
Meat and meze, plus sometimes *yayın*, are the stock-in-trade at this lone surviving riverside restaurant. Open all year, but busiest in summer for the outdoor terrace with views of the elegant bridge. €€

Gelibolu (Gallipoli)

Yelkençi
Outer corner of the harbour pool
Tel: 0286-566 4600
A reliable venue for good portions of seasonal fish such as *mezgit, kanat* (baby lüfer) and *istavrit*, with good mezes and alcohol – and no bill-fiddling, as may occur at flashier neighbours. €€

Gökçeada

Barba Yorgo
Tepeköy (Agrídia)
Tel: 0286-887 4247
Island-born Yorgo returned from İstanbul upon retirement to open this enduringly popular Greek-island-style taverna with keenly priced mains and meze, accompanied by his own wine (and during the summer season, very likely live music and dancing). €€

Çelik Pansiyon Diner
Aydıncık beach
Tel: 0286-898 1011
Doesn't look like much from the outside, but serves up very competent home-style dishes at budget prices; your best option at this popular beach. €

Panayot Usta
Zeytinli (Ágii Theodóri) centre
No phone
Arguably the best of several small, mostly Greek-run cafés, specialising in *muhallebi* sweet topped with thick vanilla *dondurma*. Panayot is also very proud of his giant *dibek kahvesi* pestle-and-mortar. €

Son Vapur
Kale (Kástro) seafront

Tel: 0286-887 2874
Zeytinli (Ágii Theodóri) village approaches
Tel: 0286-555 395 5152
The Kale branch is a trendy *meyhane* with some unusual mezes, seafood mains and restrained prices for the location; the Zeytinli annexe is more mainstream in menu and works a shorter season. €€

Gölyazı (Apollyon Gölü)

Pehlivan Balık Restaurant
Tel: 0532-717 2929
Unassuming-looking wooden-box affair overhanging the water, with lake fish like *turna* (pike) on offer as well as tasty mixed-meze platters. Licensed. €€

İznik

Köfteci Yusuf
Atatürk Caddesi 75
Tel: 0224-757 3597
Main branch of a small local chain (other outlets on the Yalova and Mudanya roads) that's a quick-serving, friendly, salubrious carnivore heaven. Unlicensed. €

Tekirdağ

Opposite the Eski İskele, main taxi rank and bus stops are a row of 24-hour eateries specialising in the local signature dish, the savoury, onion-laced rissoles called *tekirdağ köfteleri*. The Ali Baba is as good as any and does generous portions. All are unlicensed. €

THE AEGEAN COAST

There's no shortage of mediocre places, especially overlooking picturesque fishing harbours. Following, however, are some of the more distinctive, long-established and/or good-value places.

Akyarlar

The coastal village on

the Bodrum peninsula is crammed with seafood restaurants, mostly patronised by Turks.

Kaptanin Yeri
7 Sok 5, Alley off of Yalı Caddesi
Tel: 0252-393 7358
An exception to the fishy ethos locally – unpretentious and quick-serving under a giant ficus. The menu comprises

homestyle meat-based dishes, a few meze platters and puddings. Licensed. €

Sofra (Yalovalı Balıçı)
Yalı Cad 6
Tel: 0252-393 6985
Friendly service, good mezes, and unbeatable views over the port from the terrace; beware that apparently cheap fish prices are partly offset

by a mandatory "cooking charge". €€

Ayvalık

Balıkçı
Balıkhane Sokak 7, beside Kaptan Otel
Tel: 0266-312 9099
Affordable quality seafood, with live Turkish music on some weekend nights. €€

Deniz Kestanesi

Karantina Sokağı 9
Tel: 0266-312 3662
The most elegant (and expensive) seafood restaurant in town, with a designer interior to match. €€€€

Babakale

Bayır

Beyond Marmaris, Hisarönü Peninsula, Mehmet'in Yeri, Main square
Tel: 0252-485 7109
Not the obvious, overpriced restaurant under the famous plane tree here, but the one beyond, with a view and a brief but excellent menu of pide, meze, salad, beer, ayran. An ideal lunch stop if touring the countryside here. €

Uran Hotel Restaurant

Tel: 0286-747 0218
The rooms here may be exceedingly basic, but the downstairs restaurant has some of the freshest and cheapest fish for some ways around, plus salads; not much else on the menu. €

Bergama

Bergama Ticaret Odası Sosyal Tesisleri

In the restored Greek school, 150m/yds uphill from the Ulu Cami
Tel: 0232-632 9641
The only licensed outfit in the town centre, with municipally subsidised – and thus low – prices for grills and mezes. Pleasant indoor environment with big windows overlooking the valley. €€

Bodrum

La Jolla Bistro

Neyzen Tevfik Caddesi 174
Tel: 0252-313 7660
www.lajollabodrum.com
Small, chic bistro near the marina whose menu fuses Mediterranean starters, steak-house standards and sushi. Bodrum's largest selection of wines and coffees. Open 9am–11pm, but sushi bar 6–10.30pm. Open all year. €€€

Nazik Ana

Eski Hükümet Sok 7
Tel: 0252-313 1891
Something of a miracle in often glitzy Bodrum: ultra-cheap, fill-your-plate specials comprising 3 home-style dishes, plus salad. Sweets and beer also on offer. The stonewall, canopied courtyard with wood-bench seating is a cool refuge on a summer day. €

Sünger Pizza

Neyzen Tevfik Caddesi 218
Tel: 0252-316 0854
Popular pizza and pasta restaurant with lovely views from its rooftop terrace. Packed most evenings, so arrive early. Open 10am–11pm. €

Yağhane

Neyzen Tevfik Caddesi
Tel: 0252-316 3705
www.yaghanebodrum.com
Combination art gallery and upscale restaurant installed in a former olive mill, with a menu best described as

ABOVE: fresh fish in Bodrum.

nouvelle Ottoman, featuring lots of carpaccios and rocket with everything. Wide range of rakı, not just the usual Yeni label, and a mix of imported and Turkish wines. €€€€

Bozburun

Möwe Martı Meyhane

Atatürk Statue plaza
Does what it says on the tin – meze and seafood platters – at relatively restrained seaside prices without the aggressive

touting found on the yacht quay around the corner. €€

Orfoz

East flank of main bay, next to Sabrina's Haus Hotel
Tel: 0252-456 2337
www.orfoz.com
Accessible on foot or by shuttle boat only, this is about the most exclusive restaurant in the region. Only about 8 to 10 gourmet dishes (including smoked eel) are offered per day, for a similar number of tables; the chef-owner cooks and serves himself. Justifies its cult status. €€€€

Bozcaada (Tenedos)

Salkım

Çinarçarsi Caddesi 20
Tel: 0286-697 0540
Cozy, 10-table bistro with more creative cooking than the port restaurants, featuring local dishes like sardines wrapped in grape leaves. €€€

Şehir Restaurant

Fishing harbour
Tel: 0286-697 8017
One of the very few waterside restaurants with consistently good cooking for meat or fish, and straightforward billing policies. Open most of the year. €€

Çeşme

İmren

İnkilap Cad 6/A
Tel: 0232-712 7620
The town's oldest surviving restaurant, founded in 1953 by immigrants from Yugoslavia, has atrium seating and a traditional lokanta-style menu with a Balkan touch; their signature dish is papaz yahnisi (whole baked carp stuffed with rice). Open all year. €

Dalyan

Çağrı Pide Salonu

Gülpınar Çarsi İçi
Tel: 0252-284 3427
Despite the name a very decent, licensed all-rounder, with grills and a few well-executed mezes, tucked

away near the entrance to the local minibus terminal. €

Eylül Restaurant

Davran Pasajı 9/D
Tel: 0252-284 5305
Best of a cluster of similar places in the tiny central bazaar for ev yemekleri (home-style food), including the local variant of köfte. Unlicensed; open 24 hr. €

Ley-Ley

Okçular, 6km (3½ miles) north
Tel: 0252-284 4669
Much attended by wealthier Turks for the sake of its authentic Turkish mezes (albeit in small portions). An efficient army of uniformed staff is in attendance. €€€

Saki

Riverbank, by Kral Bahçesi and rowboat ferry to Kaunos
Tel: 0252-284 5212
The only genuine meyhane in town, with abundant vegetarian mezes as well as meat platters. Open April–Oct. €€

Datça

Fevzi'nin Yeri

Behind Kumluk Beach
Tel: 0252-712 9746
Excellent meyhane-cum-fish-taverna, with old-fashioned meze platters, cheeful nautical decor and strictly seafood mains. A cult hangout among locals and visiting Turks. €€

Eski Datça

Datça Sofrası

Village centre
Tel: 0252-712 4188
The only full-service restaurant in the old village, with imaginative dishes like yoğurtlu bakla (beans in yoghurt sauce) and sarımsaklı bademli köfte (meatballs with garlic chips and the local almonds). The portions could be bigger but the quality is decent. Licensed; open most of the year. €€

Eski Doğanbey

Karina anchorage

Tel: 0532-744 2134
After visiting ancient Priene and/or Miletos,

skip the touristy tavernas adjacent and head instead a few kilometres west to this road's-end seafood specialist, housed in an old Ottoman customs warehouse. The menu's limited to keenly priced wild fish like bass, sole and *lida*, calamari rings and a few cheap (if small) meze platters; your waterside dining companions may include large mama-and-babies flotillas of ducks. €€

Eski Foça

Fokai
121 Sokak No. 8, behind the castle
Tel: 0232-812 2186
The place for quality fish here, with farmed and fresh items clearly separated, good garnishes or mezes, and a mostly Turkish clientele. Open all year. €€€

Gölcük

Gölcük Otel Restaurant
Tel: 0232-558 1333
Reasonably priced, licensed grill-restaurant in a travellers' interval (Birgi to Sardis) rather short on such. Seating on the lawn or in a gazebo over the water. In summer catfish (*yayın*) may be on the menu. Closed winter. €

Güzelçamlı

Calender
National park gate
Tel: 0256-646 3738
The best value of three fish restaurants in a row here, the last place for a proper meal before entering the Dilek Yarımadası Milli Park. But it's perhaps a better venue to watch the sunset over Samos island across the way. The fish is good, accessibly priced and mostly wild; shame about the exceptionally small meze plates. Summer seating by the water; in winter by a fireplace upstairs. €€

İzmir

Altınkapı
1444 Sok 14/A, Alsancak

Tel: 0232-422 5687
Founded in 1978 but with resolutely modern decor, this makes a pleasant change from the all-pervading seafood, and the trendy-bar ethos of this district; meat specialists, with favourite dishes döner, roast chicken, lamb chops and every kind of *pide*. Full pudding menu, and licensed (though dipping into the wine list adds a € to the category). €€
Balık Pişircisi Veli Usta
Birinci Kordon 212/A
Tel: 0232-464 2705
Eternally popular fish-grill restaurant, with booking (or early evening arrival) needed to ensure a table. €€
Deniz
Inside İzmir Palace Otel,
Atatürk Caddesi 188/B
Tel: 0232-422 0601
Very highly regarded by the citizens of İzmir, who return here regularly for speciality seafood dishes like whole fish baked in salt. Good-value set menus; reservations often necessary. Open all year. €€€

Kozbeyli (near Yenifoça)

Selluka Yemek Evi
Central meydan
Tel: 0232-826 1062
Limited but very tasty menu of home-style food such as *mantı*, rice with mushrooms and pistachios, and *sütlaç*. Unlicensed. €

Kumlubükü Bay

Near Marmaris
Kumlubükü Yacht Club
(Hollandali Ahmet)
Tel: 0252-476 7242
www.kumlubukuyachtclub.com
A local institution since 1981, making it one of the first restaurants on the Hisarönü Peninsula, this is a firm favourite with yachties who can sail right up and berth. The seafood-strong menu comprises Turkish and Chinese specialities, served at a romantic wood deck. €€€€

Kuşadası

Avlu
Cephane Sok 15, Kaleiçi
Dishing up traditional hearty steam-tray fare at indoor or outdoor tables, this place is frequented by tourists and locals alike. Grilled lamb a speciality; has a beer licence. 8pm–midnight. €
Holiday Inn Restaurant
Kahramanlar Caddesi, near corner İsmet İnönü Bulvarı
No relation to the eponymous hotel chain, this is actually one of central Kuşadası's best-value spots, with tasty kebabs and spicy starters. Licensed for beer. €
Manisa
For the likely duration of a day-visit, several unlicensed courtyard restaurants in the restored Ottoman Yenihan – signposted everywhere in the centre – will be more than adequate for requirements.

Marmaris

Mazgal
Barbaros Cad. 147, Old Town
Tel: 0252-413 6898
Deceptively basic looking, but good, cheap, fresh seafood, served outdoors at pavement tables in the heart of the old town. €
Ney
26 Sok 24, Old Town
Tel: 0252-412 0217
Just a few steps uphill from the preceding listing, housed in an old Greek house with marina views, and rather more polished. Just a few tables as it's very much a one-person, owner-chef affair, so booking in season advisable. €€

Ören

Mercan Balık Evi
Yalı Mahallesi, pedestrianised shore promenade
Tel: 0541-591 4848
The middle of three seafood restaurants on the "strip" here, its motto – and menu – "whatever is caught fresh that day". Plain presentation but honest, friendly and reasonably priced. €€

ABOVE: chef at the ready.

Selçuk

Ejder
Cengiz Topel Cad 9
Tel: 0232-892 3296
A prime location in the pedestrian zone opposite the stork-stooked aqueduct, plus a well-balanced menu of meat with an east-Anatolian flair, vegetarian platters (the wife's domain) and fresh mezes, combine to make a winner. €
Selçuk Köftecisi
Şehabettin Dede Cad 8
Tel: 0232-892 6696
The house speciality is the local variant of *köfte*, a bit dearer than expected, but unusually this place has a beer licence. Also a few veggie starters and salad on offer; quick serving and pleasant outdoor seating under a canopy. €

Söğüt

Denizkızı/Mermaid
Marmaris region, end of the Hisarönü Peninsula, Cumhuriyet (shore) Mahallesi
Tel: 0252-496 5032
www.sogutdenizkizi.com
The last building, at the end of the *mahalle*

PRICE CATEGORIES

Prices per person for a single meze platter and/or soup, a main course, and one drink, in Euros (Turkish lira – at 2 lira to €1)
€ under €10 (under 20TL)
€€ €10–18 (20–36TL)
€€€ €18–25 (36–50TL)
€€€€ over €25 (over 50TL)

TRANSPORT · ACCOMMODATION · EATING OUT · ACTIVITIES · A – Z · LANGUAGE

(neighbourhood)
overlooking a small pebble
beach, is the setting for
some excellent seafood and
unusual meze like diced
pazı (chard) spiked with
chillis. A real find in an area
generally sown with steeply
priced establishments;
yachts can't tie up here,
and that makes all the
difference. There's a
pansiyon upstairs if you
can't tear yourself away.
Open in winter. €€€

Şirince

Ocakbaşı
Aabove marketplace, on the
western slope
Tel: 0232-898 3094
Very friendly, simple,
family-run place with stews,
unexpected meze like *deniz
börülce, gözleme*, and a
taste of the wine allowed
before ordering a whole
bottle. There are great views
over the village from the
terrace. €

Yaylaköy

Yılmaz'ın Yeri
Top of the pass, 9km (5½ miles)
south of Kuşadası on the Söke
highway
Tel: 0256-668 1023
The best of a cluster of
meat-strong restaurants
here, always crowded with
locals for traditional meze
in decent portions, an
infinity of kebabs, and a
very reasonable wine list.
During the day there are
views over Davutlar towards

the Dilek Peninsula. €€

Yeşilyurt, near Assos

Han
Across from mosque
No phone
Slightly pricey but very
pleasant, the only
independent restaurant
in this trendy village near
Adatepe, doing unusual
dishes like *otlu börek*
(pastry stuffed with wild
greens). €€

THE MEDITERRANEAN COAST

Adana

Onur Kebap
Cevat Yurdakil Caddesi
Tel: 0322-454 6630
One of Adana's best-
regarded kebab and grill
joints, this is the place to
come for the eponymous
Adana kebab, lamb-chops,
chicken or *lahmacun*. Wash
it down with *salgam*, the
fiery local beetroot juice. €

Alanya

**Köyüm Gaziantep
Başpınar**
Hükümet Caddesi
Tel: 0242-513 5664
Cheap and cheerful kebab
and *lahmacun* place right in
the heart of Alanya. Popular
with locals and visitors. €
Mahperi
Alanya Harbour
Tel: 0242-512 5419
There's a fast turnover
of restaurants in Alanya
but the Mahperi has been
going for a number of years
because of its reliable fish
and steaks, good service
and moderate pricing.
Great location right by the
harbour, too. €€€
Ottoman House
Damlataş Caddesi 23
Tel: 0242-511 1421
Close to the harbour and
set in the gardens of an
old Ottoman mansion is
this restaurant offering
traditional Turkish and
fish dishes. A play-garden
keeps the children happy

and there's live music every
night. €€

Anamur

Kap Anamur
Iskele Meydani
Tel: 0324-814 2374
Located in the central
square, Kap Anamur serves
excellent fish within small,
cosy rooms. Considered the
best restaurant in town. €€

Antakya

Antakya Evi Restoran
Silahlı Kuvvetler Caddesi 3
Tel: 0326-214 1350
A traditional Antakya
mansion with a choice of
rooms for dining on hot and
spicy Turkish food, in the
tradition of the Middle East.
Open for lunch and dinner
all year round. €€
Antakya Sofrası
İstiklal Caddesi 6
For a full range of Antakya's
distinctive (for Turkey)
Middle East style cuisine
this simple eatery is
unbeatable, best at lunch
times when local artisans
tuck into the home-made
fare. The bargain prices are
a bonus. €
Samlioğlu Künefe Salonu
Next to Ulu Cami
Serving only *kunefe*, the
local delicacy made of spun
wheat, cream cheese and
honey, and served hot. €
Sultan Sofrası
İstiklâl Caddesi 20/A
Tel: 0326-213 8759

This local restaurant serves
an incredible range of
Syrian/Turkish specialities.
Often packed as the locals
appreciate the reasonable
prices and snappy service.
Best at lunch times as it's
unlicensed. €€

Antalya

Fish, unless it is locally
farmed (sea bass and sea
bream) is very expensive,
but tasty. Most of the best-
regarded fish restaurants
are now in suburbs such as
Lara rather than around the
old town harbour.
  Just outside the old
town's walls, near the
corner of Atatürk and
Cumhuriyet Caddesi, is an
alley of cheap and cheerful
outdoor restaurants serving
a variety of Turkish dishes.

7 Mehmet
Atatürk Kültür Parkı 333
Tel: 0242-238 5200
www.7mehmet.com
Slick marble and pine
decor, and excellent-quality
Turkish food. This is where
Antalya's politicians and
businesspeople cut their
deals. €€–€€€
China Garden
Konyaaltı Caddesi
Tel: 0242-248 7835
Situated on the cliffs just
west of the town centre and
easily reached by the period
tram, the China Garden
is the city's only Chinese
restaurant. The food is

ABOVE: Turkish tea *(çay)*.

very good, if pricey, and the
views over the bay superb,
especially at sunset. €€
Hasan Ağa
Mescit Sokak 15, Kaleiçi
Tel: 0242-247 1313
Long-established and very
popular, with a characterful
indoor dining area in an
old Ottoman house, plus
a delightful walled garden
shaded by citrus trees.
There's a serve-yourself
buffet meze table, with
fish and grills to follow.
Live Turkish music most
evenings. Good value. €€

PRICE CATEGORIES

Prices per person for a
single meze platter and/or
soup, a main course, and
one drink, in Euros (Turkish
lira – at 2 lira to €1)
€ under €10 (under 20TL)
€€ €10–18 (20–36TL)
€€€ €18–25 (36–50TL)
€€€€ over €25 (over 50TL)

Urcan Balık Lokantası
İstiklal Caddesi 2
Tel: 0242-244 5768
www.urcanantalya.com
Very plush fish restaurant on the cliff-top just east of the city centre, and reachable by tram from the old town. Excellent food and service, you'll be dining with Antalya's well-heeled. It's expensive, but quality. €€€

Vanilla
Hesapi Sokak 33, Kaleiçi
Tel: 0242-247 6013
www.vanillaantalya.com
Prominently situated to catch the well-heeled clientele from the Alp Paşa Hotel, this chic establishment serves up Turkish and international cuisine at reasonable prices. €€-€€€

Çıralı
Eat at the row of upscale beachside restaurants if you must – once – but you'll get far better value inland at the diners of these *pansiyons*.

Cemil Pansiyon
Shopping "strip", hamlet centre
Tel: 0242-825 7063
More home-style cooking with good vegetable-based mezes. €€

Jasmin Pansiyon
Beach road, about 200m/yds behind independent restaurants
Tel: 0242-825 7247
Unusually for Çıralı, *mantı* and *pide* on offer, plus grills. €

Fethiye

Göcek
Café Bunka
Far west end of bay promenade
Tel: 0252-645 1411
An annexe of the Japanese Cultural Centre in İstanbul, and probably the only genuine sushi bar on the Turkish coast. €€€€

Meğri Lokantası
Çarşı Caddesi 30
Tel: 0252-614 4046, 614 4040
Decent *ev yemekleri* and puddings, supposedly open 24hr. Cash only; €€. There is a more blatantly touristy annexe further into the old bazaar at Likya Sokak 8–9. €€€

Finike

Deniz 2
Kordon Caddesi
Tel: 0242-855 2282
A cheerful local restaurant frequented by Turkish lorry drivers and locals alike. Good plain Turkish cooking. Open all year. €€

İskenderun

Saray
Atatürk Bulvarı 57
Licensed place with traditional Hatay starters such as hummus, with quality kebabs and grills to follow. €€

İslamlar

Çiftlik
Village centre
Tel: 0242-838 6055
Least expensive and most homely of a half-dozen trout farm/restaurants here, run by a friendly family; scoff very good trout with simple vegetable garnish and flat *yufka* bread while perched above the fish ponds – and a great view. €

Kalkan

Eateries here are dominated by the Brit expats' home-from-home environment; you'll have a daunting task finding normal Turkish cooking at normal prices, at least in the town centre or along the gentrified waterfront.

Bar BQ
Menteşe Mahallesi, start of road to Kalamar district
Tel: 0242-844 2844
Reasonably priced (for Kalkan) licensed all-rounder, with emphasis on meat dishes. Open all year. €€

Caretta Caretta Pansiyon Diner
1.5km (1 mile) out of town, west bayshore
Tel: 0242-844 3435
One of the last surviving "alternative" *pansiyons* from the 1980s, with owner-chef Gönül Kocabaş doing her famous *gül böreği* and home-style mains to a loyal repeat clientele on

the seaview terrace. Open May–Oct. €€

Korsan Meze
Harbour front
Tel: 0242-844 3622
As implied by the name, some very creative mezes precede mains, but as with all restaurants in town, clarify any hidden charges in advance. Open May–Oct. €€€

Kuru'nin Yeri
3.5km (2 miles) east of Kalkan, en route to Kaputaş beach
Tel: 0242-844 3848
Best of a trio of roadside restaurants clustered here, doling out inexpensive dishes like *mantı, nohutlu et* (chickpeas with meat chunks), *şakşuka* and corn bread. Open all year. €

Kaş

As you'd expect for a market town of over 7,000, there are restaurants for every taste and wallet here, from 24-hour *işkembe* (tripe soup) kitchens near the main mosque to fish-and-meze outfits as exclusive as any in the country.

Bahçe/Bahçe Fish
Top of Uzun Çarşı, behind the Lion Tomb
Tel: 0242-836 2370
The best cold or hot mezes in town, for some years now, served in the *bahçe* (garden); mains are less exciting, though there may be candied quince for dessert. Their seafood annexe just opposite (book separately on 836 2779) is also excellent, with unusual mezes like marinated sea bass fillet. Both open May to early November. €€-€€€

Chez Evy
Terzi Sokak 2
Tel: 0242-836 1253
A unique blend of French country cooking and Turkish staples makes this small backstreet restaurant one of the most popular in town; book ahead. €€€

Natur-el
Gürsoy Sokağı, off Uzun Çarşı, Çukurbağlı Caddesi
Tel: 0242-836 2834
Enjoy mains like *hunkâr beğendi* and *cevizli nar*

tavuk (chicken in walnut and pomegranate sauce) at this upscale indoor-outdoor restaurant. Plenty of choice for vegetarians. Open April–Nov. €€

Sultan Garden
Hükümet Caddesi, Opposite Sahil Güvenlik (Coast Guard station)
Tel: 0242-836 3762
The place for a romantic tête-à-tête, featuring unusual mezes like *paçanga böreği*, good lamb-based mains. Outdoor open May–Oct, small conservatory may work in winter. €€€€

Kaya Köyü

Cin Bal
Rural locale, eastern approach
Tel: 0252-618 0066
Locals' favourite and vegetarians' nightmare, where whole hung sheep figure prominently as decor. This is a *kendin pişin kendin ye* place, where you buy superb lamb by the kilo and then cook it yourself at tableside (there's also *tandır kebap* for the lazy). Open all year. €€

Sarnıç
Edge of ruins
Tel: 0252-618 0153
Most successful of several nouvelle restaurants in the area, with quality live music some evenings and service on a lovely courtyard. The kitchen occupies part of one of the few restored houses here, downstairs from an informal museum of local ethnographic finds. Open most of year. €€€

Village Garden
Kınalı Mahallesi
Tel: 0252-618 0259
Family-run, mostly outdoor place whose own-grown vegetables jostle on the menu with meat and seafood platters. April–Nov. €€

Kemer

Köyceğiz
Alila, Lakefront near town centre
Tel: 0252-262 1150
The kitchen staff of this hotel produce unheard-of mezes like stewed artichokes, yoghurt with

coriander greens, and caper shoot marinated in sour pomegranate syrup, while main portions are generous; it's understandably popular, so book ahead. €€

La Paz
Liman Caddesi, 119 Sokak 17
Tel: 0242-814 4420
www.la-paz-restaurant.com
Wide-ranging menu with fish, large selection of steaks, pizzas and traditional Turkish casseroles too. €€

Mersin

Haci Baba Et Lokantası
Tel: 0324-238 0023
www.hacibabarestaurant.com
A Mersin institution which blurs the boundaries between the various categories of Turkish eateries with its fresh seafood, grills and delicious array of desserts. Licensed. €€

Ölü Deniz

Kumsal Pide
Belceğiz esplanade, southeast end
Tel: 0252-617 0058
Fabulous pide in large portions and equally big meze platters at low prices. Substantial local clientele, so it's open most of the year. Licensed.€

Patara

All listings are in Gelemiş village centre and work an April to November season.
Golden Restaurant
Tel: 0242-843 5162
The original (founded in 1982) and still one of the best of the village restaurants, specialising in trout and grills. €€
St Nicholas
Tel: 0242-843 5154
The restaurant attached to the eponymous pansiyon

is more sophisticated (and expensive) than the village norm, but dishes are well presented. €€€€
Tlos Restaurant
Tel: 0242-843 5135
Big portions of traditional ev yemekleri, done by a chef from Bolu. Good value. €

Saklıkent

Hüseyin Güseli'in Yeri
On the approach road to Saklikent Gorge
Tel: 0252-636 8113
Turkish pancakes and grills cooked over an open fire are the highlights of this basic family-run restaurant. Closed in winter. €

Side

Liman
29 Liman Caddesi (towards the temple)
Tel: 0242-753 1168

One of the best of the many fish restaurants lining the waterfront. Open all year. €€
Soundwaves
Liman Caddesi, Selimiye Köyü, Küçük Plaj
Tel: 0242-753 1607
Attractive restaurant overlooking the east beach, serving surprsingly classy food despite the pirate-ship theme. A mix of Turkish and international fare, with a good choice of alcoholic beverages. €€

Tarsus

Şelale
Tel: 0324-624 8010
The poshest of several restaurants and cafés clustered around the waterfall where Alexander the Great supposedly swam. It is by far the nicest place to eat in the hot, dusty city. Open all year. €€

CENTRAL ANATOLIA

Afyon

Ikbal Restoran
Uzunçarşı Caddesi 21
Tel: 0272-215 1205
Doner kebab specialist. Also, try its kaymaklı ekmek, a sweet and thick Anatolian cream made by boiling the milk of water buffaloes. €

Ankara

Boyacızade Konağı Kale Restaurant
Berrak Sokak 9, (by the Museum of Anatolian Civilizations), Kaleiçi
Tel: 0312-310 1515
Turkish cuisine, including manti, a ravioli-like dish served with a spicy tomato sauce. Outdoors there is a fountain and splendid city views. €
Café des Cafes
Tunalı Hilmi Caddesi 83, Kavaklıdere
Tel: 0312-428 0176
Bistro-style café with eclectic decor serving French-style crêpes, salads and desserts. €€
Gusto
Mega Residence, Tahran Caddesi 5,

Kavaklıdere
Tel: 0312-468 5400
Intimate Italian restaurant, a happy-hour bar and delicious food. Live music at weekends. €€
Kale Washington
Doyran Sokak 5/7, Kaleiçi
Tel: 0312-311 4344
Delightful restaurant with excellent Turkish food and fine views in a restored Ottoman mansion inside the castle area. Terrace in summer. Open noon–midnight. €€€
Köşk
İnkilap Sokak 2, Kızılay
Tel: 0312-432 1300
Great place to eat İskender kebab or İnegöl köfte (rissole-like meatballs) in an area very popular with students. €
Merkez Lokantası
Çiftlik Caddesi, 72/A, Atatürk Orman Çiftliği
Tel: 0312-211 0220
Set in a farm 15km (10 miles) from central Ankara in a relaxed outdoor atmosphere. Excellent grilled meat and vegetable dishes. €€

Zenger Paşa Konağı
Doyran Sokak 13, Kaleiçi
Tel: 0312-311 7070
www.zengerpasa.com
Perched up in Ankara's citadel in a restored 19th-century Turkish mansion, Zenger Paşa serves delicious grilled meats with pilav (specially cooked Turkish rice) and pides (Turkish pizza), with a bird's-eye view of the city. €€

Eskişehir

Şomine Et Lokantası
Köprübaşı Caddesi
Tel: 0222-220 8585
In a town that is unusually low on eating places, this is a good choice serving a wide range of Turkish staples. €

Göreme

Alaturca
Müze Caddesi
Tel: 0384-271 2882
Big, centrally located, attractively decorated restaurant offering everything from light

lunches and bar snacks to Turkish cuisine for dinner. €€

Kayseri

Elmacıoğlu İskender Et Lokantası
Tel: 0352-222 6965
Long-lived and deservedly popular family restaurant specialising in İskender kebab (döner kebab served on a bed of pide with a serving of yoghurt, and butter and tomato sauce) but with a wide range of other familiar dishes too. €

Konya

Köşk Konya Mutfağı
Mengüç Caddesi 66
Tel: 0322-352 8547
Partially housed in an old Konya mansion and partly in its garden, this inconspicuous restaurant is a good place to try out some unusual dishes such as höşmerim, a warm dessert. €€
Şifa Lokantası
Mevlana Caddesi 29

Tel: 0322-352 0519
This is one of the best places to sample Konya's very own *tandır* kebab, which is baked in a pit until the meat falls off the bones. It's served on *pide* bread and is finger-lickingly gorgeous. €

Üçhisar

Elai
Eski Göreme Yolu
Tel: 0384-219 3181
Elegant restaurant with an international menu and decent choice of wines. €€€

Ürgüp

Ziggy's
Tevfik Fikret Caddesi 24
Tel: 0384-341 7107
İstanbul comes to Cappadocia in terms of decor and pasta-heavy menu but with wonderful

views and ambience. €€
Şömine
Cumhuriyet Meydanı
Tel: 0384-341 8442
Traditional Turkish fare, with *testi kebab* (spicy lamb with tomatoes, onions and peppers baked in a clay pot) a house special. €

THE BLACK SEA COAST

See also the hotel listings *(pages 389–90)* for more restaurant ideas, but here are some independents.

Amasra

Çeşmi Cihan
Büyük Liman Caddesi 21
Tel: 0378-315 1062
Currently the most popular, good-value local seafood place, overlooking the eastern bay. €€

Canlıbalık
Küçük Liman Caddesi 8
Tel: 0378-315 2606
Coastal restaurant serving fresh, unusual fish dishes. Lively atmosphere and sea views. €

Safranbolu

Kadıoğlu Şehzade Sofrası
Çeşme Mahallesi, Arasta Sokak 8
Tel: 0372-712 5657
Normally priced grills,

fancier meat dishes like *kuyu kebab* (lamb roasted in a clay pit) and *pide*. €

Sinop

Saray
İskele Caddesi
Tel: 0368-261 1729
The most renowned of several seafront places, doing Black Sea mackerel and other fish along with mezes. Licensed. €€

Trabzon

Murat Balık
No phone
Atatürk Meydanı, north side
Little place doing Black Sea fish with salad. Unlicensed. €€
Üstad Lokantası
Atatürk Meydanı 18
Tel: 0462-326 5406
Lunchtime favourite with all the usual steam-tray dishes and some meat grills. €

THE EAST

Diyarbakır

Aslan Yemek Salonu
Kibris Caddesi
Standard kebabs with a delightful leavening of more regional dishes. Also specialises in a traditional honey and clotted cream breakfast. €
Selim Amca
Ali Emiri Caddesi 22
Tel: 0412-224 4447
The speciality here is *kaburga*, tender rack of lamb stuffed with fragrant rice, but the *içli köfte* (a spicy mince-meat dumpling) is equally good. Unlicensed. €€

Erzurum

Güzelyurt Restoran
Cumhuriyet Caddesi 54
Tel: 0442-235 5001
Famed for its kebabs, this traditional white-tablecloth establishment is the place businessmen come to enjoy a meal with alcohol in this most conservative of cities. €€

Gaziantep

İmam Cağdaş Restoran
Uzunçarşı 49
Tel: 0342-231 2678
www.imamcagdas.com
Established in 1887, this is the best restaurant in a city noted for its food. The kebabs and *lahmacun* are done to perfection, as is the *baklava*. Unlicensed. €
Kırkayak
Kemal Köker Caddesi
Tel: 0342-232 1500
Palatial place in a leafy park, it serves up a number of Ottoman-style and local speciality dishes. Unlicensed. €€

Mardin

Cercis Murat Konak
Birinci Caddesi
Tel: 0216-410 9222
www.cercismurat.com
Dine on delicious local south-eastern Turkish dishes in the intricately carved dining room or gaze down and out over the Mesopotamian plain from

the cool of the terrace. There's even local wine available. €€

Midyat

Cihan Lokantası
Cizre Yolu Uzeri
Tel: 0482-464 1566
If you're visiting Midyat or Mar Gabriel monastery, this is the place to lunch, with local specialities like lamb ribs and crusted pilaf rice. €

Şanlıurfa

Cavahir Konak Evi
Selahhattin Eyub Camii Karşısı
Tel: 0414-215 9377
A set meal in the delightfully atmospheric surroundings of Urfa's best-preserved mansion house, accompanied by a traditional band, makes for a perfect night out. €€
Gülhan
Atatürk Bulvarı
Tel: 0414-312 2273
Appetising grills served amid spotless surroundings. Unlicensed. €

Urfa Sofrası
Şehirmerkezi
Tel: 0414-315 6130
The usual range of kebabs, plus *pide* and pizza for vegetarians. Unlicensed. €

Van

Bak Hele Bak Yusuf Konak
Van Belediye Sarayı
Tel: 0432-214 2938
Herb cheese, butter, honey butter, clotted cream and a lot more besides. €
Halil İbrahim Sofrası
Cumhüriyet Caddesi
Tel: 0432-210 0070
A vast place dishing up everything from grilled trout to *pide* and kebabs. €

PRICE CATEGORIES

Prices per person for a single meze platter and/or soup, a main course, and one drink, in Euros (Turkish lira – at 2 lira to €1)
€ under €10 (under 20TL)
€€ €10–20 (20–36TL)
€€€ €18–25 (36–50TL)
€€€€ over €25 (over 50TL)

A CTIVITIES

THE ARTS, CULTURAL FESTIVALS, NIGHTLIFE, SHOPPING AND SPECTATOR SPORTS

THE ARTS

Developing the Turkish people's interest in Western arts and culture was an important part of Atatürk's raft of reforms in the early years of the republic. This included the introduction of Western art forms such as classical music, ballet and opera, as well as encouraging painting and sculpture – mediums restricted or forbidden under Islam.

Music and Dance

Classical

Ballet, classical music and opera are well established in Turkey, though opportunities for seeing performances vary from city to city; İstanbul, Ankara and İzmir have large venues and their own symphony orchestras, ballet and opera companies, which tour elsewhere. The standard is variable, especially for opera and ballet.

It is not easy to find out about programmes much in advance, and tickets can be difficult to get hold of. Sometimes seats are sold out, or given to sponsors before the public can buy them.

The annual cultural highlight in Turkey is the repertory of İstanbul-based festivals (April–October), comprising classical music, theatre, blues, jazz, and art installations. At any of these you will get the opportunity to hear world-renowned soloists, orchestras and conductors, plus the cream of home-grown talent.

Traditional Turkish

Music has an exceptionally rich tradition in Turkey. Traditional Turkish folk music (*halk müziği*) is a living art, and immensely popular – you will hear some form of it everywhere you go. It has blended inextricably with Western pop and rock, to give Turkish pop a distinctive flavour. For more in-depth coverage of local music, *see the feature article on pages 106–107*.

Although some of the shows put on for tourists at resorts, complete with dinner, can be shoddily done, some of the most expensive hotel restaurants in İstanbul have folk music and dancing performed to the highest standards to accompany your Turkish dinner. A "village" music and dance performance will often include a belly dancer – popular even with the most sophisticated.

Types of music

Sanat and *fasıl* music (both traditional Turkish styles) are best heard live, and are played in numerous bars and *meyhanes*.

Arabesk, melancholic and sentimental Oriental pop ballads will probably be the first thing you hear in Turkey, blaring out from every taxi and minibus.

Classical Ottoman and religious music is played by distinguished groups such as that of the İstanbul Municipal Conservatory, and can be heard in concert halls, and on radio and television, often broadcast live.

Especially in the western third of the country, where large numbers of refugees from the Balkans have settled over the past century-plus, recognisably Balkan melodies with lyrics in Turkish, Macedonian or even Romany have become popular since the 1990s.

At some dervish *tekkes* or lodges, visitors are permitted to watch the remarkable devotional music, including (in the case of the Mevlevis) the famous "whirling" dance. Performances can be long – some visitors will prefer the abbreviated versions on offer in tea gardens around Sultanahmet in İstanbul.

Jazz, rock and pop

İstanbul is now firmly established on the touring rock and jazz circuit. Home-grown bands thrive and you can hear live jazz in bars and nightclubs, and more formally in a concert hall.

İstanbul

Performing arts venues
Atatürk Cultural Centre (AKM)
Taksim Square
Tel: 0212-251 5600
Venue shared by the State Opera and Ballet, Symphony Orchestra and State Theatre Company. Currently closed while its future is decided.
Cemal Reşit Rey Concert Hall
Harbiye
Tel: 0212-232 9830
www.crrks.org
Large hall with varied programme.
Lütfi Kırdar Convention and Exhibition Centre
Next to the Hilton Hotel and CRR Concert Hall, Harbiye
Tel: 0212-373 1100
www.icec.org
One large hall (capacity 2,000); four smaller halls (capacity 500 each), plus meeting rooms, a large restaurant and terrace.
Turkish Cultural Dance Theatre
Firat Culture Centre, Yeniçeriler Caddesi, Çemberlitaş
Tel: 0554-797 2646
Excellent programme of Turkish dance

Listings Information

Programmes are not published very far in advance, even for the state opera and ballet. *Hürriyet Turkish Daily News* and *Today's Zaman* carry the cinema listings for İstanbul, İzmir and Ankara. *Time Out İstanbul* has weekly listings for İstanbul in its English-language edition. Ordinary Turkish newspapers carry arts listings – in Turkish only, but it is fairly easy to work out what is being listed.

Festival-ticket booking is always centralised, which makes things easier. However, the festival organisers try out new systems and locations every year in an attempt to improve both service and sales, so things can change from season to season.

İstanbul

Atatürk Cultural Centre (AKM)
Taksim
Tel: 0212-251 5600 (but ticket office currently closed).
İstanbul Foundation for Culture and Arts (for information on and tickets to the İstanbul festivals and Biennial)
Sadi Konualp Caddesi 5, Şişhane
Tel: 0212-334 0700
www.iksv.org
Organises world-class events such as the International Film, Theatre,

Classical Music and Jazz festivals, as well as the İstanbul Biennial (in odd-numbered years); links to ticketing outlets.
Biletix
Tel: 0216-556 9800
www.biletix.com.tr
Offers telephone, walk-in and internet booking for all major arts and sporting events. Open Mon–Fri 8.30am–10pm, Sat–Sun 10am–10pm. Sales outlets across the city (*satış noktaları*), as well as in Ankara, İzmir, Bursa, Antalya, Trabzon and Konya.

Ankara
Opera and ballet tickets can be purchased from **Atatürk Bulvarı Opera Meydanı**, Ulus.
Tel: 0312-324 2210.
For musical events, contact the **SCA Music Foundation**, Tunalı Hilmi Caddesi 114/43.
Tel: 0312-427 0855.

İzmir
İzmir Culture Foundation
Mithatpaşa Cad 138, Karataş.
Tel: 0232-482 0090.
www.iksev.org
All you need to know about the International Festival and the European Jazz Festival.

from 10 different regions of the country, performed every Thurs night, including whirling dervishes and belly dancing.

Cultural centres
Many foreign cultural centres maintain libraries, offer language classes and sponsor concerts, cultural activities and films.
Aksanat Cultural Centre
İstiklal Caddesi 8, Akbank Building, Beyoğlu
Tel: 0212-252 3500
www.akbanksanat.com
Interesting programmes of recorded jazz and classical music via a large laser-disc screen. Also painting and sculpture exhibitions and drama.
French Cultural Centre
French Consulate, İstiklal Caddesi 4, Beyoğlu
Tel: 0212-334 8740
www.infist.org
Short film festivals and other cultural events in French.
Goethe Institute (German Cultural Centre)
Yeni Çarşı Caddesi 32, Beyoğlu
Tel: 0212-249 2009
www.goethe.de/istanbul

Good reference library and regular events.
Süleymaniye Library
Ayşekadın Hamam Sokak 35, Beyazıt
Tel: 0212-520 6460
Thorough reference collection on Ottoman culture and history.
The Women's Library
Facing Fener Jetty on Golden Horn
Tel: 0212-534 9550
Diverse works for and about women, with regular cultural events. Open Mon–Fri 10.30am–6.30pm.

Art
Turkish painting and sculpture have a short history, with Turkish artists now experimenting with conceptual art. The huge Biennial Exhibition brings together a heady mix of international contemporary artists, with the emphasis on showcasing Turkish artists.

Commercial art galleries
Every financial institution seems to have decided to sponsor modern art, so you will find many small art galleries tucked into the ground or

reception floor of office headquarters in the big cities. The art exhibited is not always for sale. There are many other small commercial galleries, some of which double up as bars or cafés. Current exhibitions will be featured in city-guide magazines such as *Time Out İstanbul*.

İstanbul
İstanbul is richly endowed with galleries large and small.
Borusan Kültür ve Sanat Merkez
İstiklal Caddesi 213, Beyoğlu
Tel: 0212-336 3280
www.borusansanat.com
Exciting contemporary art, as well as concerts and recitals.
Contemporary Art Marketing (CAM)
Abdi İpekçi Caddesi, Altın Sokak 2/3, Nişantaşı
Tel: 0212-248 8149
Trendy gallery with corporate flair.
Dulcinea
Meşelik Sokak 20, Beyoğlu
Tel: 0212-245 1071
www.dulcinea.org
One of İstanbul's newest and most stylish galleries, below the popular restaurant of the same name.
Galeri Baraz
Kurtuluş Caddesi 141, Kurtuluş
Tel: 0212-225 4702
www.galeribaraz.com
Off the beaten track, but worth seeking out for those with an interest in Turkish abstract art. Huge collection dating from the 1950s.
Galeri Nev
Maçka Caddesi 33, Maçka
Tel: 0212-231 6763
www.galerinev.com
Perhaps the best gallery for Turkish contemporary art. Young English-speaking owners.
Milli Reasürans Gallery
Maçka Caddesi 35, Maçka
Tel: 0212-230 1976
www.millireasuranssanatgalerisi.com
One of İstanbul's posher galleries featuring popular Turkish artists.
Tem
Vali Konağı Caddesi, Prof. Dr. Orhan Ersek Sokak 14/2, Nişantaşı
Tel: 0212-247 0899
www.temartgallery.com
One of İstanbul's best galleries, with an excellent collection of Turkish contemporary art. Also holds international exhibitions. The owner speaks good English.

Ankara
Akpınar Sanat Galerisi
Güneş Sokak 31, Kavaklıdere
Tel: 0312-468 7960
Galeri Nev
Gezegen Sokak 5, Gaziosmanpaşa

Tel: 0312-437 9390
Same owners as Galeri Nev in
İstanbul.
Hobi Café Sanat Galerisi
7 Caddesi 3, Bahçelievler
Tel: 0312-215 0113

Antalya
Antalya Güzel Sanatlar Galerisi
Cumhuriyet Caddesi 55
Falez Hotel Gallery
Konyaaltı Falez Mevkii
Tel: 0242-248 5000

Cinema

Cinema is very popular, and there has
been a boom in contemporary Turkish
film in recent years. Antalya, Ankara
and İstanbul host film festivals.
Increasingly cinemas show
Turkish-made films instead of
Hollywood movies. International films
are usually shown in the original
language with Turkish subtitles
(alt yazılı) – though the title will be
translated into Turkish. If the film has
been dubbed, Türkçe (Turkish) will
appear on the programme listing or
poster outside the cinema – this will
usually be the case with cartoons and
films suitable for children. At any one
time there will usually be a choice
of half a dozen or so foreign films in
İstanbul, Ankara, İzmir and Antalya.
Across the rest of Anatolia, most
places of any size have a cinemaplex,
often in edge-of-town shopping
malls. Films always have a 15-minute
interval.
If you want to see the latest
Turkish films with English subtitles,
you'll have to visit during one of the
major international film festivals,
such as the Golden Orange in Antalya
(autumn) or the İstanbul Film Festival
(spring).
The free weekly sheet, Sinema,
which you can pick up at any cinema,
lists the current week's programme.
The website www.gencsinema.com, while
only in Turkish, also has a useful,
easily decipherable list of all cinemas
and screenings (use pull-down menu
seanslar for the latter). Some of the
more popular ones are:

CULTURAL FESTIVALS

January

Ağrı – Aşık (Bards) Festival
Selçuk (İzmir) – Camel Wrestling
Festival, 3rd Sunday; camel wrestling
also takes place in Denizli and Aydın.

February

İzmir – Camel Wrestling.

March

Çanakkale – 1915 Sea Victory
Celebration.
İzmir – European Jazz Days.
Manisa – Mesir (traditional medicine)
Festival.
Ankara – International Film Festival.

April

Ankara – International Music Festival.
Aydın – Sultanhisar-Nyssa Culture
and Arts Festival.
Bursa – International Tulip Festival.
Çanakkale / Gallipoli – Anzac Day.
İstanbul – International Film Festival;
Tulip Festival.

May

Alanya – International Rafting
Triathlon.
Ankara – International Film Festival
and International Caricature Festival.
Antalya Sand Festival – sand
sculpting on the beach.
Aydın – Erik Culture and Arts Festival.
Bartın – Strawberry Festival.
Bergama – Festival of Pergamum
(with drama in the amphitheatre).
Birecik (Şanlıurfa) – Kelaynak Festival
(dedicated to the bald ibis which is
virtually extinct).
Ciğli (İzmir) – Bird Sanctuary
Celebration.
Edirne – Hıdırellez Gypsy Festival.
Ephesus (Selçuk) – Festival of Art and
Culture.
Eskişehir – Yunus Emre Arts and
Culture and Art Week (Yunus Emre
was a 13th-century humanitarian
poet and mystic).
Giresun – International Aksu Festival.
İstanbul – International Theatre
Festival.
Karacasu (Aydın) – Afrodisias Culture
and Arts Festival.
Konya – Javelin and Jousting
Competition.
Kırklareli – Kakava Festival.
Marmaris – International Yachting
Week.
Silifke – International Music and
Folklore Festival.

June

Adıyaman – Commagene Tourism and
Cultural Festival.
Alanya – International Beach
Volleyball Tournament.
Artvin – Kafkasör Festival, with
bullfights, bazaars and music.

Aspendos – Opera and Ballet Festival.
Bandırma – "Bird Paradise" Culture
and Tourism Festival.
Bergama – International Pergamon
Festival.
Bursa – International Bursa Festival
(continues into July).
Edirne – traditional Kırkpınar Oil-
wrestling Competitions (late June or
early July).
Foça (İzmir) – Music, Folklore and
Water Sports Festival.
İstanbul – International (Classical)
Music Festival; into July too.
İzmir – International Music
Festival.
Kemer (Antalya) – International
Golden Pomegranate Festival.
Rize – Tea and Tourism Festival.

July

Abana (Kastamonu) – Sea Festival.
Akşehir (Konya) – Nasreddin Hoca
Festival.
Antakya (Hatay) – Tourism and
Culture Festival.
Çeşme – Sea Festival and
International Song Contest.
Çorum – Hittite Festival.
Datça – Arts and Culture Festival.
Gerze (Sinop) – Cultural Festival.
Ihlara (Aksaray) – Tourism and
Culture Festival.
İskenderun – Culture and Tourism
Festival.
İstanbul – International Jazz Festival;
continues into August.
Kabaoğuz (Amasya) – Yayla Festival.
Kadırga (Giresun) – Yayla Festival.
Kargı-Tosya-Taşköprü – Yayla Festival.
Kuşadası – Music Festival.
Kütahya – Traditional Ceramics
Festival.
Malatya – Apricot Festival.
Mesudiye (Ordu) – Yayla Festival.
Samsun – International Folk
Festival.

August

Ankara – Bilkent International
Anatolian Music Festival.
Antalya – 30 August, Zafer Bayrami
(Victory Day). A national holiday.
Ardeşen (Rize) – Laz Atmaca (Hawk)
Festival.
Avanos (Nevşehir) – Tourism and
Handicrafts Festival.
Bursa – International Folklore Festival.
Çanakkale – Troy Festival.
Hacıbektaş - Hacı Bektaş Veli
commemoration (Bektaşi and Alevi
ritual singing and dancing).
Keçiborlu (Isparta) – Türkmen Nomad
Festival.
Mengen (Bolu) – Traditional Turkish
Cooking and Chef's Festival.

September

Aksaray – Yunus Emre Culture and Art Week.
Bodrum – Opera and Ballet Festival.
Diyarbakır – Watermelon Competitions.
Eskişehir – Meerschaum *(Lületaşı)* Festival.
İstanbul – Arts Fair, Electronical Music Festival, Biennial (latter odd-numbered years).
Konya – Javelin and Jousting Competition.
Safranbolu – Architectural Treasures and Folklore Week.

October

Alanya – Culture and Festival; Triathlon Competition.
Antalya –Altın Portakal (Golden Orange) International Film Festival.
Bodrum – International Sailboat Race.
Bozburun (Marmaris) – International Gulet Festival.
İstanbul – International Arts Biennial continues.
İstanbul– Akbank Jazz Festival, Efes Pilsen Blues Festival.
Ürgüp – Wine and Grape Harvest Festival.
29th – Cumhuriyet Bayrami (Republic Day). Everywhere. A national holiday.

November

Bursa – International Karagöz and Shadow-theatre Festival.
Marmaris – International Yacht Races.
Nationwide – Anniversary of Atatürk's death (10th).
Nationwide – Teacher's Day (24th).

December

Aydin province –Camel Wrestling.
Bursa – International Karagöz (Shadow-Theatre) Festival.
Konya – Mevlâna Festival (10–17); whirling-dervish performances.

NIGHTLIFE

Turkish nightlife has traditionally revolved around *meyhanes* (taverns), bars, restaurants and *gazinos* (music-halls offering Turkish cabaret or dancing). In the major cities and resorts, however, Western-style nightclubs exert a powerful pull on the young and more affluent.

You'll find a range of bars from the simple to exotic and elegant; some have live music, others a theme (Mexican, British pub...).

The best clubs and dance-bars are as good, with as up-to-date sounds, as you'd find anywhere – nearly as expensive, and as vulnerable to fashion as clubs in New York or London. Along the coast, many of the larger hotels have their own clubs, most of which are open to non-residents.

Venues

İstanbul

Babylon
Seyhbender Sok. 3, Asmalımescit, Tünel
Tel:0212-292 7368
www.babylon.com.tr
İstanbul's best and most famous live-music club serving up an inspirational mix of world music, jazz and electronica, with some world-famous names in the line-up from time to time. Book ahead.

Balans
Balo Sokak 22, Istiklal Caddesi
Tel: 0212-251 7020
www.balansmusichall.com
Live rock music venue with concerts and DJ-led parties in the heart of Beyoğlu. Check out their website for forthcoming events.

Hayal Kahvesi
Büyükparmakkapı Sokak 19, Beyoğlu
Tel: 0212-244 2558
By day a cosy café, by night a live-music venue featuring jazz and rock, with a young clientele. Open every day 11am–2am. No credit cards.

Hayal Kahvesi Çubuklu
Burunbahçe, Beykoz
Tel: 0216-413 6880
Elegant, isolated summer spot for the well-heeled, right on the water's edge, but still in the city. In summer a private boat runs every half-hour from Istinye on the European side of the Bosphorus. Restaurant and café open noon–midnight, bar until 2am; live music after 11pm and a large dance floor. Sunday brunch 10.30am–3.30pm. All major cards accepted.

Pano
Hamalbaşı Caddesi 26, Tepebaşı
Tel: 0212-292 6664
An old Greek wine house dating from 1898 renovated with sensitivity to its original layout, complete with old wooden vats and rough but drinkable wine on tap at low prices. Cultivates an Old İstanbul atmosphere.

James Joyce – The Irish Pub
Istiklal Caddesi, Balo Sokak 26
Tel: 0212-224 2013
The oldest and best-established

ABOVE: Halikarnas club, Bodrum.

Irish pub in İstanbul offers ceilidh dancing and live Irish music, as well as blues and African rhythms most nights. Imported Guinness and classic Irish pub grub. Very popular with foreigners.

Jukebox
Nizamiye Caddesi 14, Taksim
Tel: 0212-292 3656
With a spacious dance floor, this immensely popular club is a requisite stop for the best local and guest DJs. Usually packed at weekends.

Nardis Jazz Club
Kuledibi Sokak 14, Galata
Tel: 0212-244 6327
Atmospheric and cosy jazz venue in the shadow of Galata Tower.

Nuteras/Nupera
Meşrutiyet Caddesi 149, Beyoğlu
Tel: 0212-245 6070
Located next to the famous Pera Palace Hotel is this rooftop club with great views. There are dance parties with local and guest DJs. Pricey drinks and a dress code rules. Open 6pm–2am.

Reina
Muallim Naci Caddesi 44, Ortaköy
Tel: 0212-259 5919
www.reina.com.tr
One of the hottest clubs in Turkey and more on the swanky side (be prepared for the high-flying prices), Reina is a vast complex dedicated to nightlife and filled with bars, restaurants and dance floors accommodating up to 2,500 people.

Roxy
Aslanyatağı Sokak, Sıraselviler, Taksim
Tel: 0212-249 1283
Trendy, expensive youth venue with great live international bands. Open 6pm–3.30am. No credit cards.

XLarge
Meşrutiyet Caddesi, Kallavi Sokak 12, Beyoğlu
Tel: 0506-788 7372
www.xlargeclub.com
Gay and lesbian venue.

Thrace and Marmara

Apart from a few local discos, there is little or no nightlife – as Westerners understand the term – in this part of Turkey. Notices of occasional concerts and events appear on posters and in shop windows. For a city of its size, Bursa is particularly bereft of venues owing to an Islamicist municipality, which has pretty well succeeded in killing off formerly lively Sakarya Caddesi.

Bursa
Biramania
Sakarya Caddesi 63
Beer specialists, as the name implies – and about the only place left on this lane where you can drink without eating.

Edirne
Getto
Saraçlar Caddesi 143
Uncomplicated booze-and-music bar – the only midtown one – whose name recalls the former Jewish population in this neighbourhood.

Aegean Coast

Bodrum
Halikarnas
Cumhuriyet Caddesi
Tel: 0252-316 8000
www.halikarnas.com.tr
The most famous (and expensive) open-air club on the Turkish Aegean coast. It starts moving after the midnight laser-and-light show.
Hadigari
Dr Alim Bey Caddesi 37
Tel: 316 0048
www.hadigari.com.tr
Live concerts by name Turkish performers interspersed with DJ party nights.
Küba
Neyzen Tevfik Caddesi 62
Tel: 0252-313 4450
www.kubabar.com

Cabaret

This form of entertainment, which can include expertly performed traditional music and belly dancing, should not be dismissed since it is not always designed to empty the hapless tourist's wallet. Cabaret is a genuine, popular Turkish celebration, often laid on as part of lavish family events, and at its best it can be very, very good.

Dinner and show together will come to US$70–100 (£40–60) a head, more if you find yourself lavishly tipping the belly dancer.

Open-air bar with a Latin theme in terms of the music and atmosphere, popular with the high-society set. Also a restaurant at the rear. Open 9pm–4am.
Ora
Dr Alim Bey Caddesi 19/21
Tel: 0252-316 3903
Cramped, noisy but fun, and claims to be open 24 hours a day.

Çeşme
Nyks Club
İnkılap Cad, Garanti Bankası Yanı
Tel: 0232-712 0998
Special events and local DJ nights.

İzmir
Alsancak, in particular the old houses along or just off Gazi Kadınlar Sokağı and Kıbrıs Şehitleri Caddesi, has emerged in recent years as the trendy nightlife district. Venues change regularly; below are a few likely survivors.
Boombox
Gazi Kadınlar Sokağı
Tel: 0232-464 6849
Opus
1453 Sok 9
Tel: 0232-464 9092
Punta
Kıbrıs Şehitleri Cad107
Tel: 0536-304 6646
Rain
1649 Sok 79, Bayraklı
Tel: 0532-755 4445
Where many end up after starting the evening in Alsancak: a large outdoor restaurant club on the north side of the bay.

Kuşadası
Ecstasy
Sakarya Sokak 2, Kaleici district
Tel: 0256-613 1391
Spread out over two floors, this popular club attracts crowds of up to 1,000. The more down-market, British-and-Irish-style nightlife is centred on Barlar Sokak.

Marmaris
Crazy Daisy Bar
Bar Street 121
Tel: 0252-412 4856
www.crazydaisybar.com
Ear-shattering music (sometimes live) and piles of heaving bodies make this one of the best venues on Bar Street, the centre of all Marmaris nightlife.

Mediterranean Coast

Alanya
Auditorium Open Air Disco
Dimçayi Mevkii
Noisy, lively open-air disco. Summer only.

Janus Restaurant and Café-Bar
Rıhtım Girişi
Tel: 0242-513 2694
Large, lurid-pink harbour-front café/restaurant/bar through the day, with late-night dancing. Open round the clock.

Antalya
Club Ally
Sur Sokak 4, Kaleiçi
Tel: 0242-244 7704
www.ally.com.tr
Big, open-air dance venue in the old town, for cashed-up locals and visitors.
Club Arma
Kaleiçi Yatlimanı 42, Antalya Marina
Tel: 0242-244 9710
www.clubarma.com.tr
One of Antalya's most popular bars, built into a cliff and entered via the harbour road. A smart restaurant by day, at night it turns into an open-air disco.
King Bar
Yat Limanı
Kaleiçi
Tel: 0242-268 4048
www.thekingbar.com
Eclectic, long-established venue for jazz, rock and other music for late-night revellers.

Fethiye
Deep Blue
Hamam Sokağı
www.deepbluefethiye.com
Convivial drinks bar with taped music, open 11am–3am.
Ottoman Café
Karagözler Caddesi 3/B
Tel: 0252-612 1148
Ottoman-style, with carpets, cushions and nargiles (hookahs) aplenty, on two levels. Plays a mix of Turkish and modern dance-floor hits, equally popular with locals and tourists. Visit early in the evening to ensure admission; open daily 9pm–3am.

Kalkan
Kleo Bar
Next to Korsan
Tel: 0242-844 3330
Lovely tranquil spot at the water's edge featuring live modern Turkish music. Closed in winter.

Kaş
Hideaway
Cumhuriyet Cad 16/A, Lane off old market square
A local institution, this secluded garden bar/café has 1960s–70s rock-and-blues soundtrack and perennially popular Sunday breakfast.

Cover Charges

İstanbul's nightclubs often have extremely high cover charges (on the grounds that Turkish females don't usually drink much) which may not be well displayed and yet appear infuriatingly on your bill at the end of the evening, especially if there is live music. The charge usually includes a few drinks, however. Check before you enter.

Mavi/Blue
Cumhuriyet Meydanı
The oldest car-café here, packed with trendy youth from late afternoon until the small hours.
Red Point Club
Süleyman Topçu Sokağı
An old barn has been converted into the town's premier after-hours dance club, with a packed dance floor after midnight and rock/soul soundtrack.

Side
Oxyd
Denizbükü Mevkii
About 3km (2 miles) from Side on the harbour road to Kumköy
Tel: 0242-753 4949
www.oxyd-disco.com
Side's most popular disco, located on the west beach, has some interesting architecture to its name: from the outside it resembles a Moroccan mud building, but step inside and the decor is futuristic. An open-air pool adds to the appeal.

Ankara
Cabare
Atakule, Çankaya
Tel: 0312-440 2374
Elegant club with glorious views, on the second floor of Atakule tower. Live pop music at weekends. Closed Sun.
North Shield
Guvenlik Caddesi 111, Çankaya
Tel: 0312-466 1266
Turkish-style English pub with English beer, whisky, pub grub and international food. Pleasant and popular. Open daily noon–1am.
Seğmen Bar
Gazi Mustafa Kemal Bulvarı 151, Tandoğan
Tel: 0312-231 7760
Playing Western music, this is a good place to socialise with Turks.
Manhattan
Çevre Sokak 7, Çankaya
Tel: 0312-427 6263
www.manhattan.gen.tr
Live jazz, rock and blues bands play in this intimate setting.

Murphy's Dance Bar
Ankara Hilton, Tahran Caddesi 12, Kavaklıdere
Tel: 0312-466 0054
www.murphysdancebar.com
Different dance and disco programme on offer every night. The evening kicks off early with lessons in Latin and Tango before moving on to the evening's theme – which can range from a nostalgic delve into old musical favourites, to singles' nights. Check the website for the weekly programme.
Pampero Café
Aşkabad Caddesi 45/1, Bahçelievler
Tel: 0312-222 8844
Café and restaurant with live Turkish music at the weekends.

SHOPPING

Shopping in Turkey can be a delight, and with a willing, honest, multilingual shopkeeper, can be highly educational – though as elsewhere, quality goods are not cheap, and increasingly uncommon.

In the more frequented bazaars, you have to burrow hard to find anything of value, and some spots (like Kuşadası) are more or less a complete waste of time. Like much of the rest of the Mediterranean (and the world), Turkey is being overwhelmed by an avalanche of cheap tat produced in the Far East, as well as mass-produced "orientalia" (Syrian backgammon sets, Egyptian/Moroccan lanterns).

It is not necessarily true that you will get a better bargain in out-of-the-way areas; "buying at source" generally does not work as a strategy in Turkey, especially for carpets, as wholesalers have descended on such places long before you.

Where to Shop

Turkey offers many different shopping experiences, from the glitzy to the gritty. Labyrinthine bazaars *(çarşılar)* are older versions of the same idea, culminating in İstanbul's amazing Kapalı Çarşı (Grand Bazaar), whose stalls and workshops sell every imaginable product. There are also excellent local weekly street markets, great for Turkey's wonderful fresh produce if you are self-catering, and occasional flea markets *(bit pazarı)*.

You can also find more sophisticated, individual and independent shops offering fashion, interior design and gifts. At the

outskirts of most sizeable towns in the western two-thirds of the country there will be a vast shopping mall, complete with parking, supermarket, cinemas, fast-food courts and cut-price designer-label factory outlets.

What to Buy

Textiles, clothing, carpets, pottery and tiles, metalwork, semiprecious and precious stones and jewellery, leather and glass all fall into various categories of quality and price. You can easily go home with a bag full of shoddily made souvenirs with a Turkish-kitsch flavour. Or you could spend some serious money and kit out a small museum with the finest craft work.

Antiques
Rummaging in junk shops and flea markets is very entertaining, and although you are not supposed to take antiques out of Turkey, anything of more recent vintage than the mid-1800s is unlikely to cause trouble at customs.

Old Turkish things used to be dirt cheap because newly wealthy Turks wanted everything modern, Western and glitzy. But since the early 1990s, trendy Turks have become very keen on old Ottoman pieces for interior decorating, so prices have skyrocketed.

For items of European origin, it is possible to get export permission, and good shopkeepers will know the procedure and be able to tell you if you may legally export any particular item. Antiquities and antique Turkish things are another matter, and there are severe penalties for anyone caught trying to take these out of the country without a special export licence.

Books
There's a thriving second-hand and antiquarian book trade, and some

BELOW: İstanbul's Grand Bazaar.

very good dealers who run shops in İstanbul and elsewhere and stalls at flea markets. However, the appetite for foreign-language books is great and prices are inflated. You'll also find maps and prints, but anything with a Turkish subject has become fashionable and will again be very expensive.

Carpets and kilims

A carpet is a handmade rug with a raised pile, while a kilim is flat woven. They can be made from cotton, wool, silk or a mixture. Designs and techniques are regional.

You do not have to be an expert to buy a good carpet, but it helps. It is worth remembering that London and New York are world-class carpet markets in their own right, and that department stores and chains all over the world buy new and antique Turkish carpets and repetition kilims and offer them at competitive prices, so there is no special reason why your find should be a bargain.

On the other hand, if you let yourself be guided by what you like and, most importantly, do some research before making a commitment, you can go home with something you really love.

Within Turkey, certain places are carpet-trading centres. The Grand Bazaar in İstanbul is one, but Cappadocia in Central Anatolia (especially Kayseri) is another, as dealers travel there to sell.

Buying a carpet can rarely be done in a hurry, and can take half a day of tea drinking and discussion, enjoyed by both customer and dealer. If you are serious, it would be worth doing a little background reading beforehand. *See also pages 110–11.*

Copper and brassware

You will find many wonderful things made of hand-beaten copper or brass: samovars, ewers, milking pails, circular trays, lunch box sets, pots and pans, cauldrons and so on. Craftsmanship is excellent; the heavier the gauge, the more expensive. The same applies to hand-applied as opposed to machine-pressed patterns. Today, the main centre for manufacture of such items is in Gaziantep, and to a lesser extent the old town of Ankara, where the Samanpazarı is the recognised (and rather gentrified) focus of the trade. If you intend to actually use a vessel, it needs to be lined with tin inside.

China, glass and pottery

Turkey has a thriving industry churning out household glass and china at extremely good prices – if your luggage allowance can take it. At a more rarefied level, some factories make beautiful replicas of traditional and museum pieces.

The Yıldız factory, by the Yıldız Palace and Park in İstanbul, makes delicate pretty porcelain in royal Ottoman style. Paşabahçe, with shops all over Turkey and its products in every store, makes not only the household stuff but also the pretty blue-and-white swirled *çeşmibülbül* glass vases and ornaments.

At Avanos, in Cappadocia, you can watch potters working the local red clay into shapes that haven't changed since classical times. Prices are very reasonable, though many items are not exactly portable. Artist potters are beginning to use traditional decorative motifs in a freer, inspirational way, and their work is on sale at the better-quality shops.

Jewellery, gold and silver

Some highly skilled craftsmen are based in the jewellery workshops of the Grand Bazaar in İstanbul. You can find silversmiths, too, working to the highest standards. It is also possible to order something to be made specially. The choice can be overwhelming.

Gold and silver are sold by weight, with something added on for the work involved; you can only haggle for the value of the labour. Precious and semiprecious stones are usually well priced, but you do need to know what you are doing.

Amber and turquoise are common, but real gems are also there if you want them.

Leather

Turkey is a major producer of leather goods and there will undoubtedly be leather-goods shops wherever you go. Jackets, bags, briefcases and small leather items such as wallets, key-holders and card cases can all be good buys, but look hard at the styling and finish and not just the price tag. Shoes, however, tend to be of poor quality, and anything likely to catch your eye may well be imported.

Turks are charmed by international labels, so you will see these in expensive shops at astronomical prices. However, markets may well have convincing copies of this season's Prada or Gucci style.

Music and musical instruments

CDs of Western music, pressed locally under licence, can be very cheap. Bootleg copies are even cheaper, but

---

Opening Times

Shops are generally open Mon–Sat 9am–6/8pm (later in summer, especially in resorts). A selection of local shops in any busy neighbourhood, and more so in the cities, will be open late into the evening. Large shops open later, and town-outskirts shopping malls are open seven days a week, approximately 10am–10pm (to midnight for some supermarkets).

Shops do not close for lunch, but small shops may shut briefly for prayers, especially at midday on Fridays.

Street markets begin around 8am, and may start packing up in the mid-afternoon. The Grand Bazaar and Spice Bazaar in İstanbul are open 8.30am–7pm (closed Sun).

BELOW: the Old Book Bazaar in İstanbul's Beyazit neighbourhood.

if you are caught importing them on return home, they will be confiscated and you may face a fine. CDs of Turkish music are inexpensive by Western standards – typically 8–22TL – but in these days of cheap (or free) MP3 downloads, CD shops are becoming an endangered species in Turkey.

Traditional Turkish instruments – wind, percussion, stringed – can be a good buy, and are available in specialist shops typically grouped together in larger towns. Avoid buying them in touristy places since they will be overpriced and of poor quality.

Tiles and ceramics

Vast numbers of decorated plates, bowls, ewers and tiles are manufactured and peddled in supposed "Kütahya" or "İznik" style; these will be cheaper and in a wider range of styles if you can get to Kütahya or İznik proper. Some are mass produced, others are handmade, and prices will reflect this. The cheapest items are made with a serifgraf (appliqué) technique, not hand-painted, something fairly obvious on close examination of the surface. Innovative, and sometimes successful, designs are emerging alongside ever-popular tradtional motifs like flowers and the kadırga (the Ottoman naval galley). For a discussion of what goes into a quality İznik tile, see "İznik Tile Manufacture" on page 171.

Fashion

Turkey has its own established and sought-after fashion labels. Limon Company, Yargıcı and Mudo are among the top young(ish) and trendy designer names; Vakko and Beymen are equivalent to Harvey Nichols or Saks; while "diffusion" ranges, such as Vakkorama and Beymen Club, offer more youthful, cheaper styles. Local fashion houses, however, do tend to be overwhelmed with one idea each season, which can make for a cloned effect both inside the shop and out in the fashionable streets.

Prices are more reasonable than in London, although it is harder to find pure natural fabrics. Turkish leather jackets, wallets and bags are usually better value than shoes. In Kaş, several local designers will custom-make clothes from handwoven fabrics over the course of your holiday, for prices that needn't necessarily break the bank.

Turkey is also a manufacturing base for many foreign companies, so you can find very cheap jeans, T-shirts, sweatshirts and other casual gear. Be wary, however, of prices too good to be

Gifts and Souvenirs

The range of presents you can go home with from Turkey is huge:
• Bowls, vases and ornaments carved in green or gold onyx from Cappadocia.
• Embroidered or brocade leather-soled slippers, fezes, embroidered and beaded hats, and for the fancy-dress cupboard any number of gaudy costumes including belly-dancing outfits for all ages and sizes. Check out the bazaars.
• A nargile, or hubble-bubble pipe (very much back in fashion). Some countries may, however, consider these to be narcotics paraphernalia – check in advance.
• Meerschaum, a soft white stone intricately carved to make pipes. Although quarried in the Eskişehir region, the pipes are sold everywhere. Look carefully at the quality of the stone and the carving, and shop around to make sure you pay the right price.

• Backgammon sets (tavla). These are plentiful and not too heavy (though universally made in Damascus).
• The mavi boncuk, or blue glass beads used to warn off the evil eye (nazar), come attached to key rings and dog collars, as large ornaments, bracelets and tiny earring pendants.
• Karagöz shadow puppets. Made of painted leather, they originally came from Bursa but can be found elsewhere.
• Consumables, such as a bag of pistachios; pine nuts; spices, such as vanilla pods, sumac or saffron; boxes of cezeriye (carrot Turkish delight); baklava pastries; dried fruit; Black Sea tea; or a jar of thyme (kekik) honey from the Aegean.
• The Doşem shops attached to the country's museums offer wonderful reproductions of ancient pottery, glass and figurines at keen prices.

true – there is a brisk trade in designer fakes, extending to watches and footwear as well as clothes. Sometimes this is done with some panache and humour – as in signs reading "Genuine Fakes Sold Here" – but far more typically in goods with legitimate labels applied to overpriced knockoffs which fall apart within two weeks. Down several alleys off İstiklâl Caddesi in İstanbul, you will find massive outlets of overstock or "seconds" (defolv), some in designer brands. There is a particularly big collection near Odakule (Galatasaray) in the alley adjoining the Paşabahçe glass shop.

Textiles

Bursa is famous both for producing silk and for its excellent cotton towels and bathrobes, but you can also find reasonably priced pure-cotton sheets and pillowcases. Women's scarves are available everywhere, from lavishly decorated silk to simple rustic cotton. Soft-cotton 1970s-style cheesecloth is made at Şile on the Black Sea and other places; you'll find tablecloths, lace-edged scarves and embroidered cotton blouses.

Everyday items that might be useful include cotton peştemels (sarong-style wraps worn in the hamam), which are good for the beach, and attractive cottons that can be bought by the metre.

Specialist dealers in the Grand Bazaar in İstanbul and elsewhere may be able to offer you ravishing old textiles: costumes from some forgotten harem, brocade coats and waistcoats, or delicately edged handkerchiefs. However, these things are getting rarer (and dearer) every day.

Shop Listings

İstanbul

Antiques and Curios
Antikarnas
Faik Paşa Yokuşu 15, Çukurcuma
Tel: 0212-251 5928
Ottoman and European antiques, as well as religious and decorative objects.
Antik Palas
Süleyman Seba Caddesi, Talimyeri Sokak 2, Maçka
Tel: 0212-236 2460
www.antikas.com
Superb collection of Ottoman and European paintings and antiques; monthly auctions.
Atlas Pasajı
Istiklal Caddesi 209, Beyoğlu
Enter this unique arcade past a historic cinema complex. Everything from antiques to costumes to central Asian jewellery and alternative music.
Beyazıt Sahaflar Çarşısı
Textbooks and a few antiquarian books in this atmospheric old market

on the Beyazıt side of the Grand/ Covered Bazaar.

Cendereci
Eytam Caddesi 27/1, Maçka
Tel: 0212-231 0942/231 7286
Beautifully hand-crafted silver.

Çukurcuma
A cluster of streets in central Beyoğlu containing at least 50 shops selling basic second-hand furniture and junk to top-price antiques.

Döşem
Topkapı Palace Complex
Gift-shop chain that offers some of the best bargains and unquestionably the best collection of Ottoman and ancient reproduction jewellery, textiles, ceramics, silks and glassware.

Eren
Sofyalı Sokak 34, Tünel
Tel: 0212-251 2858
Old and new art and history books, maps and miniatures.

Horhor Bit Pazarı (flea market)
Horhor Caddesi, Kırık Tulumba Sokak 13/22, Aksaray
A five-storey, upscale antiques market with marvellous selection.

İstanbul Handicrafts Centre
Sultanahmet, beside Yeşil Ev Hotel
Tel: 0212-517 6785
A series of crafts workshops in a restored religious school *(medrese)*. Visitors can watch the artisans at work as well as purchase wares.

Kapalı Çarşı (The Grand Bazaar)
İstanbul's legendary bazaar is a labyrinth of over 4,000 tiny shops offering everything from tourist trash to gold to icons, textiles and antiques. Competition keeps prices keen but beware of touts. Open Mon–Sat 9am–7pm.

Librairie de Pera
Galip Dede Caddesi 8, Tünel
Tel: 0212-243 7447
One of the oldest and best antiquarian bookshops in İstanbul. Turkish, Greek, Armenian, Arabic and European books, maps of the Ottoman Empire, Old İstanbul etchings and prints, photographs and original watercolours.

Paşabahce
İstiklal Caddesi 314, Beyoğlu
Tel: 0212-244 0544
www.pasabahce.com
Turkey's main manufacturer of glass, with some of their jugs, glasses and vases in a distinctive blue-and-white striped design.

Urart
Abdi İpekçi Caddesi 18/1, Nişantaşı
Tel: 0212-246 7194
www.urart.com.tr
Distinctive silver and gold jewellery as well as metalwork, painting and sculpture often based on designs of great antiquity but with modern flair. Branch at the Swissôtel.

Books
Galeri Kayseri
Divanyolu Caddesi 11, Sultanahmet
Tel: 0212-516 3366
Large selection of English-language books on Turkey and related themes.

Homer
Yeni Çarşı Caddesi 12/A, Galatasaray
Tel: 0212-249 5902
www.homerbooks.com
Great stock of books (many academic titles) in English.

Librairie de Pera
Galip Dede Sokak 22, Tünel
Tel: 0212-245 4998
One of the oldest and best antiquarian book shops in İstanbul, but very expensive of late. Turkish, Greek, Armenian, Arabic and European books, maps of the Ottoman Empire, Old İstanbul etchings and prints, photographs and original watercolours.

Pandora
Büyükparmakkapı Sokak 3, Beyoğlu
Tel: 0212-243 3503
www.pandora.com.tr
Large selection of foreign books including many academic and regional titles at fair prices.

Robinson Crusoe
İstiklal Caddesi 389, Tünel-Beyoğlu
Tel: 0212-289 6968
Great selection of English-language books, many of local interest.
There are also numerous small news-

stands around Taksim Square and the Sultanahmet district in İstanbul which sell a selection of foreign newspapers and magazines.

Music
Galip Dede Sokak
The neighbourhood around the tram stop at Tünel, at the bottom of İstiklal Caddesi, is İstanbul's music district, with the best selection of Turkish CDs, traditional instruments and rock'n'roll gear. Zühal is an international distributor with four branches here and one in Antalya.

Lale Plak
Galip Dede Sok 1
Tel: 0212-293 7739
Compact but well-organised and well-priced stock of the quality Turkish music of interest to foreigners; the shop has been going since the days of 78s.

Carpets
Gördes Halı
Nurosmaniye Caddesi Bab-ı Ali Sokak 15/17, Cağaloğlu
Tel: 0212-514 2304
www.gordes.org

Güneş Öztarakçı
Mim Kemal Öke Caddesi 5, Nişantası
Tel: 0212-225 1954
www.gunescarpet.com

Fashion and Leather
Punto
Sahilyolu Beşkardesler, 4, Sokak 16, Zeytinburnu
Tel: 0212-546 8750
www.puntoleather.com
Factory-outlet shop for one of Turkey's biggest and best leather designers. This is only one of a number of excellent leather shops in this small shopping district halfway between the old city and the airport.

Thrace and Marmara

Bursa
Karagöz Antique Shop
Eski Aynalı Çarşı 12
Tel: 0224-222 8727
www.karagozshop.com
Karagöz (Bursa shadow puppets) and other traditional articles.

Koza Han
The centre of the Bursa silk trade for several hundred years, with masses of tiny shops selling material, shirts, ties, scarves and fashion at knockdown prices.

Aegean Coast

Bergama
Şadırvan Halı
Kadriye district, Corner of Küçükkaya Köyü Yolu
Tel: 0232-633 2719

Haggling

Haggling is on its way out except in tourist traps like the Grand Bazaar in İstanbul and some places on the coast. Elsewhere, you may be able to wangle a discount if you are buying in bulk.

Tradesmen in tourist areas start their prices high, especially for tourist goods, so you can usually begin bargaining at around half the initial stated price. After a bout of intensive haggling, and several glasses of tea, the shopkeeper will respect you all the more when you finally reach an agreed price.

You can cease haggling and leave once it's evident that prices will remain unreasonable, but once you have agreed a price it is very bad form to walk away.

Signs announcing that prices are fixed usually mean what they say.

TRANSPORT

ACCOMMODATION

EATING OUT

ACTIVITIES

A – Z

LANGUAGE

ABOVE: trinket boxes made out of bone on sale at İstanbul's Grand Bazaar.

Carpet warehouse and weaving centre where you can see how they are made before choosing your own.

Bodrum
Vivaldi
Çarşi Mahallesı, Dr Alim Ekinci Cad 27
Tel: 0252-316 7179
www.marmaracini.com
Quality tile and ceramics shop, linked to its own kiln in Kütahya; proprietor Okan speaks perfect Australian English and, if you contact him in advance, will alert the kiln to your needs.

Marmaris
All recommended shops are in Tepe Mahallesi, essentially the covered bazaar just west of the castle hill.
Nomads Turkish Art
45 Sok 16
Tel: 0252-413 3813
www.marmarisnomads.com
High-quality Kütahya ceramic ware (including some tiles); if you contact in advance, they can also obtain İznik ware.
Nur-Bal
Yeniyol Caddesi, İlgün İş Merkezi 17/4
Tel: 0252-412 3731
www.marmarisnurbal.com
The Marmaris area is famous for its honey and this small shop has a good selection.
Paradise Carpet and Kilim
42 Sokak 15
Tel: 0252-412 0338
Old established shop with a huge selection of carpets and kilims, but haggle as usual.
Vogue Jewellery and Diamond Centre
Mustafa Kemal Paşa Cad B1 Blok,

Kumtaş Gökçe Plaza 32, Cami Avlu Mahallesi, Armutalan/Marmaris
Tel: 252-417 8383
www.voguediamond.co.uk
Up-market emporium with stunningly displayed jewellery and precious stones. Free shuttle service from town centre.

Mediterranean Coast

Antalya
Almost the entire old town has become a tourist bazaar, with every second shop selling carpets, jewellery, ceramics and fake designer fashion. Some shopkeepers are persistent importuners, but easily fobbed-off if you ignore them. Most locals and many visitors now do their buying in one of the new shopping centres – biggest are 5 Migros and Özdilek.
Ardıc Kitabevi
Selekler Çarşısı 67
Tel: 0242-247 0356
Foreign-language books, magazines and newspapers.
Taki & Sanat
Paşa Camii Sokak 18, Kaleiçi
Tel: 0242-248 1177
Trustworthy silversmith who makes traditional and contemporary pieces at reasonable prices.
Yörük Halı
Mescit Sokak, Kaleiçi
Tel: 0242-241 2063
Friendly, reliable English-speaking stockist of carpets and kilims.

Fethiye
There is a colourful daily market, between Çarşı Caddesi and Tütün Sokak, selling food, souvenirs and high-quality fakes. It grows hugely

when villagers swarm in by the busload on Tuesday mornings.
Telmessos Gold Galerie
Atatürk Caddesi 4
Tel: 0252-612 2809
www.telmessosgold.com
Fine selection of gold and precious stones. European and Turkish designs.
Tunç Leather
Paspatur Mevkii, Hamam Sok 1
Tel: 0252-612 3743
Good selection of leather jackets and bags.

Kaş
This pretty little town is crammed with boutiques guaranteed to make even the reluctant shopper salivate. It is one of the more upscale and certainly most convenient shopping centres along the coast, specialising in carpets, jewellery, bathware and designer fashion.

Antiques
Old Curiosity Shop
Lise Sokak, Muhtar Alışveriş Merkezi Yanı
Tel: 0242-836 1663
A museum's worth of well-selected Ottoman items, ranging from barely portable ones intended to adorn a second home to small objects.

Carpets
Magic Orient
Hükümet Caddesi, corner Cumhuriyet

Sales Tax/VAT

VAT (KDV), at rates between 8 and 23 percent, is included in the price of most goods (you will see a sign saying KDV *dahildir*), though it may be itemised separately on some restaurant and shop receipts.
You can obtain a tax refund only on goods bought from shops authorised for VAT-exempt transactions, which will have to be sales in Turkish lira (rather than in hard currency) to holders of foreign, non-EU passports. There are not many of these shops around, but it is worth asking or looking for tell-tale window signs.
There is a laborious procedure to go through – only worthwhile for larger purchases – whereby you obtain a special VAT-free invoice from the shop and submit it to customs on departure. Eventually, the shop is supposed to send you your refund in your own currency (a very few will offer on-the-spot cash or cheque refunds).

Meydanı
Behind Effendi Café-Bar
Tel: 0242-836 3775

Fashion
All three boutiques have resident designers who make up clothes using local hand-loomed fabrics.
Butik Sera
Bahçe Sokak
Tel: 0242-836 1501
Papilio Butik
Uzunçarşı 16/B
Tel: 0242-836 2895
Tufan Designer
İbrahim Serin Cad 24
Tel: 0242-836 2917

Jewellery
Argentum
Uzun Çarşı
Tel: 0242-836 1673
Silver specialists, with antiques, modern and traditional designs.

Music
Dem Müzik Evi
Bahçe Sok 5–6
Tel: 0242-836 4420

Ankara
ABC Kitabevi
Selanik Caddesi 1/A, Kızılay
Tel: 0312-431 2114
Dost Book Shop
Karanfil Sokak 11, Kızılay
Tel: 0312-425 2464
The above bookshops stock some English-language titles.

Carpets
The Flying Carpet Shop
Filistin Sokak, 3/A, Gaziosmanpaşa
Tel: 0312-426 3334

Copperware!!!!
Güzel İş Bakır
Salman Sok 31, Samanpazarı
Tel: 0312-324 1436
İhsan Geredeli
Salman Sok 38/G, Samanpazarı
Tel: 0312-324 3487
Going since the 1970s; both antiques and own-made, high-quality ware.

Gifts
Zeki-İsmet Candan
Ataturk Boulevard 67/18, Kizilay
Tel: 0312-433 7726

Avanos
Cave Pottery (Chez Galip)
Tel: 384-511 5758
www.chez-galip.com
The most famous of several pottery workshops in this Cappadocian village.

SPORT AND LEISURE

Spectator Sports

Soccer/football is the national obsession; the fortunes of favourite teams are closely followed, with much celebration after a victory. Galatasaray, Beşiktaş and Fenerbahçe are the three İstanbul-based teams with a national following. Small boys wear the strip, and you'll see coloured scarves and flags flying and hear car horns blaring on the night of a match. A Turkish match is a thrilling event, and the atmosphere inside the ground dramatic and emotional. Trouble is always anticipated, so you can expect to see armoured vehicles and water cannon in readiness outside the ground.

Basketball is also a popular spectator sport, and is played by youths all over the country.

Ice hockey The national team is surprisingly successful considering the country has only one proper rink, in Ankara.

Camel wrestling is a popular spectacle in the southwest Aegean from December to February – especially in Aydın and İzmir provinces – involving two bull camels in rut. An annual festival takes place at Selçuk in January.

Local sports

Oil wrestling
This ritualised form of wrestling, *yağlı güreş*, in which contestants wear nothing but leather shorts and are coated with olive oil, is described on page 161. The year's highlight is the (late June or early July) Kırkpınar Festival near Edirne, when up to 1,000 people compete. For tickets, try the Edirne tourist office, tel: 0284-213 9208.

Cirit (jirit)
A wild, ruthless game vaguely akin to polo. *Cirit* ponies are trained to gallop from a standing start and turn on the spot. It is exciting but cruel, as ther animals are sometimes treated roughly.

Birdwatching

An increasingly popular outdoor activity. Several places in Turkey are designated as "bird paradises" *(kuş cenneti)*, a flamboyant name for sanctuaries, which come in varying standards.

One of the best places for serious birders is the complex of freshwater marsh, salt lakes and mudflats in

the area known as Sultan Sazlığı, southeast of Cappadocia. At the crossroads of two important migrating routes, 250 species have been recorded as visiting, and 69 have settled to breed. Autumn is the best time to visit. Most exciting for the lay person are the vast flocks of flamingoes and other interesting birds such as pelicans and storks. You can spend the night on the edge of the marshy area and be taken out onto the water at dawn.

Golf

In a bid to draw more wealthy tourists to Turkey, the country has rapidly developed golf and new courses are opening all the time.

The Klassis Golf and Country Club, the Kemer Golf and Country Club in İstanbul and the National Golf Club in Belek have all been settings for senior European Professional Golf Association (PGA) tournaments. Most accept day visitors and many top hotels have arrangements for their guests. In spite of this activity, only about 1,000 people, of whom 300 are expatriate foreigners, actually play the game in Turkey.
Alternative Travel & Holidays
146 Kingsland High Street, London
E8 2NS
Tel: 020-7923 3230
www.turkishgolf.com
UK tour operator specialising in golfing holidays in Turkey.

Ankara
Ankara Golf Club
Ahlatlibel Golf Tesisleri
Tel: 0312-489 8182
Ankara's only golf club; the 9-hole course is open Apr–Nov.

Belek
A purpose-built golf resort, developed to the highest standard, with four excellent golf courses (so far) and around 23 four- or five-star hotels, all with players' privileges. This is golfing heaven. The Turkish tourist office publishes a brochure on golf-based holidays in Belek.
National Golf Course
Tel: 0242-725 4620
Tat Golf Belek International Golf Course
Tel: 0242-725 4080
Gloria Hotel Golf Resort
Tel: 0242-710 0600

İstanbul
İstanbul Golf Club
4 Levent
Tel: 0212-324 0742
Turkey's oldest course, established

ABOVE: skiing is increasingly popular.

in the late 19th century by British businessmen living in the city. Members and guests only.

Kemer Golf and Country Club
Tel: 0212-239 7010
Golf and tennis.

Klassis Golf and Country Club
Silivri
Tel: 0212-727 4050
by Tony Jacklin, 100km (60 miles) outside İstanbul. Also tennis, swimming, riding and a health farm.

Horse Riding

Facilities vary enormously, but horse riding can be a wonderful way to explore the Anatolian landscape. Short treks, from two hours to a full day, can be arranged at centres in Cappadocia and from the southern coastal resorts. There are also riding stables in the vicinity of İstanbul, but on the whole these are open to club members only.
Be upfront about your experience or lack of it, and you will have to use your judgement on the safety of the horses and the establishment. There are almost no ponies in Turkey, and the high level of Arab blood in the horses makes them pretty but skittish.

Ankara

Ankara Atlı Spor Kulübü
Çiftlik Caddesi, 22; Gazi Mahallesi
Tel: 0312-213 2192
www.aask.org.tr

Antalya

Bagana Ranch
On the road to Termessos
Tel: 0242-425 2270
www.baganahorseclub.net
Ride up into the mountains on a day trail with picnic lunch.

Cappadocia

A number of companies offer horse-riding tours – often the best way to see individual churches.

Akhal-Teke
Avanos
Tel: 0384-511 5171
www.akhal-horsecenter.com
Kirkit Voyage
Avanos
Tel: 0384-511 3148
www.kirkit.com

İstanbul

İstanbul Atlı Spor Club
Maslak
Tel: 0212-276 2056
www.istanbulatlisporkulubu.com
Samandıra Atlıspor Club
Samandıra
Tel: 0216-311 4333

Ice Skating

Ankara

GSIM Buz Pateni Sarayi
Adnan Ötüken Park, Bahçelievler
Tel: 0312-223 5776
Year-round ice-skating at Turkey's only Olympic-sized ice rink. Open usually 9am–11pm. Amateur hockey matches at weekends.
Atatürk Buz Pateni Lokantasi
Kurtulus Parki İçi
Tel: 0312-433 0422
Ice-skating is also possible at this outdoor rink, set in a pleasant park in the city centre. Open Oct–Apr. The restaurant is open year-round.

İstanbul

Galleria Shopping Mall
Ataköy
Tel: 0212-560 8550
Cheerful shopping-centre ice rink for fun rather than serious sport. Open daily 9am–10pm.

Skiing

Around 60 percent of Turkey lies at an elevation of 1,000 metres (3,300ft) or more, and the rugged mountainous areas of the east are three times the size of the Alps. Snow blankets these sparsely populated provinces for around seven months of the year.
Skiing was first introduced in Turkey at the end of World War I. The Russian army, retreating from the mountains of occupied eastern Turkey, left behind hundreds of skis that Turkish troops began to use.
Today, thousands of people ski in Turkey, and the country is beginning to attract winter tourists. Skiing is considered chic, but is generally overpriced by Turkish standards – and under-equipped, though lift networks are being improved. Little of the skiing is particularly challenging for the experienced.

Ski resorts

There are over a dozen ski resorts, of which only overrated Uludağ, near Bursa in northwest Anatolia, has much name recognition overseas, or much choice of accommodation. The best snow conditions and piste network are in the east, at remote Palandöken, near Erzurum (several hotels), and Tekir Yaylası on Mt Erciyes (Cappadocia), both with seasons extending from November to April. Up-and-coming resorts between İstanbul and Ankara are Kartalkaya, in Bolu province, and Ilgaz Dağı. Also of interest are Sarıkamış, in Kars province, and Davraz near İsparta, which has more reliable snow than much-touted Saklıkent ("ski in the morning, swim in the afternoon") above Antalya.

Tennis

Tennis is popular among the members of swanky private clubs. Visitors can sometimes book courts by the hour. Holiday villages and complexes and five-star hotels will usually feature tennis courts.

Ankara

Ankara Tennis Club
19 Mayıs Stadyum İçi
Tel: 0312-311 5658
www.atk.org.tr

Antalya

Antalya Tenis Ihtisas ve Spor Kulübü
100 Yıl Bulvarı, Konyaaltı (next to the Sheraton Hotel)
Tel: 0242-238 5400
www.atik.org.tr

İstanbul

ENKA Sports Centre
Istinye Yolu
Tel: 0212-276 5084
Indoor and outdoor tennis, as well as swimming, basketball and volleyball.
Levent Tennis Club
Akasyalı Sokak 3, Levent
Tel: 0212-279 2710
TED Tennis Club
Tarabya Caddesi, Tarabya
Tel: 0212-262 9080
www.tedclub.org.tr

Walking and Mountaineering

Turks are just beginning to become interested in recreational walking, but the emphasis tends to be on organised group walks (there are some popular local rambling clubs). Independent walkers are severely hampered by the lack of good large-scale maps, although there are now two proper signed long-distance hiking routes: the Lycian Way and the St Paul's Trail. Tour companies can take you to good areas for hill and mountain walks, but you can also get a great deal of pleasure in striking out for a short distance on your own.

Mount Ararat has opened up to mountaineering again but you must go with a guide. There are specialist agencies that can take you to climb the extinct volcanoes of the Central Anatolian Plain and there is a growing interest in the Kaçkar Mountains along the Black Sea coast *(see page 326).* The Taurus Mountains along the south coast are generally less formidable, and several national parks, such as Olympos and Ter-messos, offer good day treks for the reasonably fit. Cappadocia offers a huge variety of walking, from easy day trips to more vigorous climbs on Mount Erciyes.

Watersports

Turkish resorts now offer sailing, surfing, windsurfing, kite-surfing, scuba diving and snorkelling, paragliding and water-skiing to a much higher and safer standard than was previously the case.

Swimming

Swimming in the sea is generally uncomplicated, but there are some areas, especially along the Black Sea coast, where seemingly inviting beaches conceal dangerous currents. On the more frequented south and west coasts, there may be lifeguard thrones (variably staffed) and internationally compliant systems of signal flags for water conditions.

Some areas are also home to sea urchins and the occasional jellyfish, so use of a pair of goggles to spot them in advance is advisable, as well as waterproof flip-flops. Turkish beach hygiene can leave a lot to be desired, too, and busy beaches will be marred by litter.

Many hotels have pools, often more than one at multi-star outfits. In winter, indoor hotel pools can be fun, though expensive on a day-use basis.

Scuba diving

Along the entire coast between the north Aegean and Alanya, accredited scuba schools offer properly supervised instruction leading to internationally recognised certificates, usually over a five-day course of instruction. Since all these waters have been heavily overexploited commercially, fish tend to be scarce, but in some places submarine attractions include caves and other formations, archaeological remains or submerged wrecks of variable vintage (mostly 20th century). Ancient shipwrecks, even if already excavated, are generally off-limits. Already qualified divers should bring their certification along – PADI, BSAC and CMAS are all recognised. The best Aegean/Mediterranean dive venues are (going from northwest to southeast) near Gallipoli, Ayvalık, Bodrum, Kalkan and Kaş. At present it is strictly forbidden for amateurs to dive anywhere in the Black Sea, or east of Alanya.

Adrasan
Diving Center Adrasan
Mid-beach
Tel: 0242-883 1353
www.diving-adrasan.com

Ayvalık
Körfez Diving
Central quay
Tel: 0266-312 4996
www.korfezdiving.com

300 Bar
Central quay
Tel: 0532-405 3168
www.300bar.com.tr

Alanya
Active Divers Club
Iskele Caddesi 2
Tel: 0242-512 8811
www.activedivers.com
Diving tours, underwater photography and PADI courses, from the Pasha Bay Hotel.
Dolphin Dive
Tel: 0242-512 3030
www.dolphin-dive.com

Antalya
Jasmin Diving Centre
Tel: 0242-316 3020
www.jasmindiving.net

Bodrum
Askin Dive Centre
Tel: 0252-316 4247
www.askindiving.com
Erman Diving
Tel: 0532-213 5989
www.ermandive.com

Fethiye
Dolphin Diving
Quay, behind post office
Tel: 0535-717 3130
www.dolphindiving.com.tr
Diver's Delight
Opposite the tax office

ABOVE: tackling a white-water river.

Cumhuriyet Mahallesi
Tel: 0252-612 1099
www.diversdelight.com
İbrice Limanı (Saros Gulf)
Yalçıin Dive Centre
Tel: 0532-737 2333
www.yalcindalis.com

Kalkan
Kalkan Diving
Kalamar Beach Club
Tel: 0532-553 2006
www.kalkandiving.com

Kaş
Anemone
Yacht marina
Tel: 0533-342 2533
www.anemonedc-kas.com
BT Diving
Çukurbağlı Cad 10
Tel: 0242-836 3737
www.bt-turkey.com/diving.php
Marmaris
Diver's Delight
Kaybal Cad 63, İçmeler
Tel: 0252-455 3885
www.diversdelight.com.tr

White-Water Rafting

Turkey's rivers are rapidly growing in popularity, with rafting done on the Çoruh, running parallel to the Kaçkar Mountains; the Dalaman Çayı, near Dalyan; and the Köprülü Çayı and Göksu, exiting the Toros ranges near Antalya and Silifke respectively. More gentle canoeing is offered on the Esen Çayı near Patara.

Except for the Çoruh whose Grade-5 rapids make it a world-class river (albeit one threatened by a dam), none of these rivers is especially dangerous, so you can even consider rafting for an exciting family day out. All the same, always wear the helmets provided and distrust any company that does not insist on their use. Rafting is easiest organised on the spot, either direct with outfitters or through your package company's rep.

Windsurfing and Kite-surfing

Although equipment and instruction for board-sailing in particular is a fixture of most prominent resorts, the really serious activity takes place where near-constant winds blow over helpfully shaped promontories jutting into the Aegean near Bodrum and Çeşme, as well as on the island of İmroz (Gökçeada).

Alaçatı and Urla (near Çeşme)
Kite Turkey
Dominic Whiting
Tel: 0538-381 5686
UK office: 020-7193 5159
www.kite-turkey.com

Bitez
Rush Windsurfing
www.rushwindsurf.itgo.com

İmroz (Gökçeada)
Gökçeada Windsurf Club
Aydınlık beach
Tel: 0286-898 1016
www.surfgokceada.com

Turkish Baths (Hamams)

For a relaxing experience, visit an old-fashioned Turkish bath *(see pages 148–9)*.

İstanbul (old city)
Cağaloğlu Hamam
Yerebatan Caddesi 34, Cağaloğlu
Tel: 0212-522 2924
www.cagalogluhamami.com.tr
Priced for tourists (up to US$60/£35 for the works), but superb care is offered in this 400-year-old bathhouse. Fabulous bar around the old courtyard, full of antiquities and almost Moorish in feel. Men: 7am–10pm; women: 8am–8pm. Group bookings taken.

Çemberlitaş Hamam
Vezirhan Caddesi 8, Çemberlitaş
Tel: 0212-522 7974
www.cemberlitashamami.com.tr
Another bath of great antiquity, built by the great Ottoman architect Sinan. Traditional bathing with separate sections for the different sexes. Open 6am–midnight.

Aegean Coast
Bodrum
Bodrum Hamamı
Cevat Şakir Caddesi
Fabrika Sok 42, opposite otogar
Tel: 0252-313 4129
www.bodrumhamami.com.tr
Surprisingly traditional for touristy Bodrum, with marble facing and separate areas for men and women. Open daily 6am–midnight. Shuttle service from many hotels.
Bardakçı Hamamı
Dere Sok 22, Kumbahçe Mahallesi
Tel: 0252-313 8114
Dating from 1749, with a marble-clad interior; mixed bathing. Open 7am–midnight.

Marmaris
Datça Caddesi, 136 Sok 1
Armutalan, 2km (1½ miles) from the centre
Tel: 0252-417 5374
www.hamamcilarltd.com
A huge, modern tourist-oriented bath. Shuttle bus from the Tansas Shopping Centre. Open daily 9am–10pm.

Mediterranean Coast
Alanya
Mimoza Turkish Bath
Kültür Caddesi 19
Tel: 0242-513 9193
All-in-one experience for the body, mind and social life; with a café.

Antalya
Nazir Hamam
Saat Külesi Arkası 4
Kaleiçi
Tel: 0242-243 9776

Ottoman-era mosque and the most atmospheric in the city.
Sefa
Kocatepe Sokak 32, Kaleiçi
Tel: 0242-241 2321
www.sefahamam.com
A safe bet right in the old town, well-patronised by visitors.

Fethiye
Old Turkish Bath
Hamam Sok 2, Paspatur Bazaar
Tel: 0252-614 9318
www.oldturkishbath.com
Mixed bathing at Fethiye's 16th-century bathhouse, in the middle of the bazaar, and now mostly geared to tourists. Open daily 7am–midnight.

SIGHTSEEING TOURS

Local travel agents, hotels and pensions offer, or help you find, a wide choice of worthwhile tours. English-speaking guides can always be provided. Tours vary from half a day for part of a city, to a couple of weeks to cover extensive areas of interest. You can tailor your tour to your needs, and engage a private guide, car or minibus and driver by the day. Be warned that many guides on the mass-market tours will take you to particular shops or restaurants where they get commission; there is generally no way to avoid this other than putting together your own small-group tour.

İstanbul

Most tours take visitors to a standard repertoire of the main sites. For tours of off-the-beaten-track sites see the listings in *Time Out İstanbul*. There are plenty of full- and half-day trips, as well as cruises along the Bosphorus or to the nearby Princes' Islands.

Elsewhere

Tours of the Aegean region include visits to Ephesus, Sardis, Pergamon, Aphrodisias and Pamukkale, plus to special-interest sites like carpet "farms", Turkish baths and Şirince village. Attractions inaccessible to coaches/buses are not generally offered, or if so only in small minibuses. On the Mediterranean, typical big-coach destinations include the ancient ruins of Myra, Phaselis, Termessos, Perge, Aspendos and Side.

Faith tourism, which highlights the Seven Churches of the Apocalypse or historic Jewish sites, is becoming increasingly popular.

Istanbul Parks and Playgrounds

There are several good parks in İstanbul: at Emirgan and Yıldız, for example. Park Orman at Maslak has a swimming pool among other family facilities. Increasingly smaller parks around town also come with good free play equipment.

Tatilya, 18km (11 miles) west of the airport on the E5 motorway out of the city, is İstanbul's only theme park. It is fairly small, but clean and well run, with safe rides for various

age groups, plus cafés and shops.
Darica Bird Paradise and Botanical Garden, Darica, is 45km (28 miles) from İstanbul off the E5 going east. It has 70 hectares (170 acres) of gardens and a zoo with a surprising range of species including zebras, kangaroos, penguins and exotic birds. The zoo is acceptably well kept, and there is also an excellent play area with good equipment, and several cafés.

A – Z

A HANDY SUMMARY OF PRACTICAL INFORMATION, ARRANGED ALPHABETICALLY

A dmission Charges

Almost all museums and archaeological sites in Turkey have admission charges, which vary from 4TL for minor attractions to a whopping 20TL for premier sites like Topkapı Palace or Ephesus. Unfortunately no discount schemes apply for foreigners – student cards included. Some remote sites have a single warden who may (in broken English) give a private tour of the site, for which an additional tip is expected.

Addresses

Addresses can seem idiosyncratic to Western eyes; in rural areas, there will be no street names, but the district (*mahalle*) of a particular village is important. Five-digit postcodes are assigned to distinguish the hundreds of identically named villages in different regions.
   Street names precede the number; if the address is on a minor alley, this will usually be included after the main thoroughfare it adjoins. When two

numbers are separated by a right-hand slash, the first is the building number, the second the flat or office number. Standard abbreviations include "Cad" for *Cadde(si)* (avenue or main street), "Bul" for *Bulvarı* (boulevard), "Meyd" for *Meydan(ı)* (square), "Sok" for *Sokak/Sokağı* (alley) and "PK" for *Posta Kutu* (Post Box). Other useful terms are *kat* (floor), *zemin* (ground floor), *asma* (mezzanine), *han(ı)* (office block), *mahalle* (district or neighbourhood) and *çıkmaz(ı)* (blind alley). *Karşısı* means "opposite to", as in *PTT karşısı*. So if you're given an address as follows – Atatürk Caddesi, Zindan Çıkmazı, Aydın Apartmanı 28/2, Ulupınar, 44582 Mazıköy – this means Flat 2 of a named apartment block at no. 28 of the Zindan cul-de-sac, off Atatürk Caddesi, in the Ulupınar *mahalle* of the larger Mazıköy postal district.

B udgeting for Your Trip

Turkey is no longer the bargain-basement destination it was in the 1970s and 1980s – rates in the south

and west coastal resorts, or İstanbul, are comparable to anywhere in the European Mediterranean, though costs in the far east are significantly lower. If you insist on trying to replicate the Hippie Trail experience, staying in Lycian "treehouses" or the few remaining hostels, travelling only by bus and train (especially overnight to save on accommodtion), eating in the simplest *lokantas* and avoiding wine or *rakı*, you could just get by on £25/$40 equivalent per day. Staying in modest hotels, having the occasional fish meal and signing on for local excursions or adventure activities will see the daily average budget rise to £60/$100 per person. For a really comfortable existence, encompassing a share of car rental (and the horrendous fuel costs that entails) while booking into multi-star hotels, count on at least £100/$160 per day per head.

Business Travellers

Visitors on business will often be guests of a Turkish company, and the visit will be governed by the rules of hospitality. You can expect to be whisked from place to place by chauffeured car and thoroughly entertained after hours. Although your hosts may speak good English or German, you may prefer to engage an interpreter.

The top hotels in the main cities are geared to business travellers and will be able to provide meeting rooms, office and conference facilities, and be relied on to receive and pass on telephone messages in English.

C hildren

Aside from waterparks in or near many coastal resorts, Turkey has few obvious facilities for children, but Turks adore babies and children, and will be delighted you have brought yours along, making a huge fuss over them. City streets, most especially in İstanbul, are far from buggy-friendly, however; high kerbstones and steep and uneven surfaces make them almost impossible to push. Buses are often crowded and their entrances are high and awkward. Bring a rucksack-style baby carrier or papoose; you will quickly realise why most Turkish babies are simply carried in their parents' arms.

Discounts

Normally you pay for children over seven years old on public transport, but you may not pay at all for under 12s at museums. It often seems to be at the whim of the attendant. Hotels offer anything from a third to 50 percent off both room rates and set-meal charges.

Accommodation

Hotels will almost always put up extra beds if there is space in your room. Most places have family rooms, sometimes for as many as six, and even *pansiyons* may have small apartments/suites with a mini kitchen included at no extra cost. You'll need to ask in advance if you need a cot.

Food

There are plenty of Turkish dishes that Western children will find acceptable without having to resort to fast food, although pizzas, burgers and chips can be found easily enough.

Restaurants rarely offer meals specifically for children, but they will do their best to find something for them to eat, even if you can't see anything obvious on the menu. If you would like something plain, ask for *çok sade*, very plain, or *acısız*, not

peppery hot. *Çocuklar için* means "for the children".

Dishes children may like include grilled *köfte* (meatballs) and any grilled meat, lamb or chicken *şiş kebabs*; grilled steak or chicken *(tavuk* or *piliç ızgara)*; all kinds of Turkish bread; *sade pilav* (rice); and *pide* (Turkish pizza) – except perhaps for the spicy *sucuklu* kind. Chips are *patates tava*, or in resorts – *çips*!

For dessert, Turkish rice pudding *(sütlaç)* is excellent, or you can always ask for a plate of sliced fresh fruit (fruit should always be peeled, to be on the safe side), or *dondurma*, as good as Italian gelato and just as adored by kids.

Babies

Breast-feeding mothers need not feel shy, but as Turks are modest in public, you should be discreet. Wear something loose, or use a large scarf or beach wrap to screen yourself and your baby – this is what rural Turkish women do, and it will come in useful to protect you from hot sun.

Ready-made babyfood can only be found in Western-style supermarkets, which are thin on the ground, and formula is expensive, so you may prefer to bring your own supplies. Restaurants will be happy to heat milk for you.

What to bring

You will need plenty of good sunblock (minimum 30 SPF), hats, and loose, light clothes for children in summer. July and August are uncomfortably hot in southern resorts for children unused to such heat and it can be difficult to get them to sleep.

In case of tummy upsets, bring prepacked sachets of rehydration salts such as Dioralyte; babies can take this from a bottle. Disposable nappies and other baby gear such as Johnson's toiletries are easily found in supermarkets, if expensive for imported brands.

Sightseeing

Very little in Turkey is specifically devised with children in mind, but there are one or two purpose-built attractions. Holiday villages notionally geared to families may still have only minimal play equipment. Foreign travel companies, such as Mark Warner and Club Mediterranée, tend to have good facilities as part of their all-inclusive packages, with childcare for younger children and entertainment for older ones.

Depending on their age and interests, children should enjoy some

sightseeing. Palaces can be difficult, as you may have to join a guided tour (even if your children like that sort of thing, the guide's English is often difficult to understand), but scrambling around ancient ruins is usually good fun. In the cities, if you get desperate, you can always head for one of the shopping malls where you will find a children's play area, clean lavatories and fast food.

İstanbul

Take a ferry: one of the best things to do with children in İstanbul is to travel anywhere in the city by water, since there is so much to see. **Topkapı Palace** is usually a hit with children. There is plenty of space for them to run around; the Harem can be claustrophobic, although older children might be fascinated. The carriages, costumes, miniature paintings and fabulous treasury are all of interest to children. **The Archaeological Museum** has a children's section (although captions are in Turkish), and a mock-up of the Trojan Horse to climb on. **The Rahmi Koç Industrial Museum, Hasköy**, is a museum of transport and industrial technology, brilliantly converted from an anchor-and-chain factory. There are a number of working models of steam locomotives, engines and mechanical toys with buttons to press to make them work. **Yerebatan Cistern, Sultanahmet**. Fantastic, enormous, atmospheric underground water tank from the Byzantine era. Children can run around on the wooden walkways among the gigantic marble pillars. There are also fish to spot swimming in the water. **Askeri Müzesi (Military Museum), Harbiye**. Children may like the sultans' campaign tents on display here, and the ferocious and beautifully decorated curved daggers. The museum is also the venue for performances by the Mehter, the re-created janissary band (summer daily around 3pm). **Rumeli Hisarı**. The castle at Rumeli Hisar, a little way up the Bosphorus, is a good place for a scramble around, although caution is advised as there are steep drops and no safety rails.

Cappadocia

With its incredible lunar landscape, underground cities to explore, and hundreds of caves and rock-cut churches, plus the possibility of pony trekking and seeing pottery made in Avanos, Cappadocia is packed with interest for children.

The coast

Sand, swimming pools, sea and water sports are all obvious attractions for kids of all ages. Ancient cities are usually good value as there are plenty of things to climb on, space to run around and, if the parents have done some homework, some cracking stories about what went on there.

Bodrum

The castle of St Peter, home to the Museum of Underwater Archaeology in Bodrum, is a terrific place for kids. It is full of the mysteries of pirates, Crusaders, naval battles and shipwrecks, and even a restored torture chamber.

Climate

Three main climatic zones exist:
• **The Aegean and Mediterranean regions**. These have a typically Mediterranean climate with hot summers and mild winters, with temperatures rising the further south you go.
• **The Black Sea region and the Marmara zone** (which includes İstanbul), which has warm summers, mild winters and relatively high rainfall year-round; İstanbul is drier than points further east.
• **The central and eastern Anatolian regions** (including Ankara), which have hot, dry summers – furnace-like in the southeast, but less hot at higher altitudes. Winters are very cold on the high plateaus.

When to Visit, What to Wear and What to Bring

Clothes Your needs will vary greatly according to the part of Turkey you will be visiting and the time of year. In the height of summer, light, cotton clothing for the Marmara, Aegean and Mediterranean areas is essential, including a long loose cotton shirt to cover your arms and shoulders against the sun, a hat and a high-factor sunscreen, especially if you intend to visit archaeological sites where there can be little or no shade.

For the Black Sea region you may need a light sweater in the evening, a light waterproof mac and water-resistant footwear. Humidity is high. At altitude in central and eastern Anatolia, summer evenings can also be cool.

Footwear Comfortable, sturdy shoes are essential for tramping over historical and archaeological sites. Even the pavements on city streets can be uneven or cobbled. Repairs (at a *kunduracı*) are cheap, locally produced orthopaedic sandals

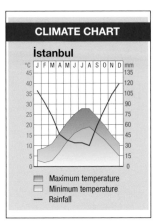

CLIMATE CHART
İstanbul

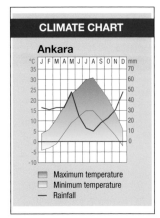

CLIMATE CHART
Ankara

somewhat less so (from 30TL for those made from synthetic materials, suitable for the beach, up to 70TL for all- or mostly-leather versions).
Wet-weather gear Although Turkey is often regarded as hot all year round, winter travellers will soon discover that it has as much rain, snow and ice as many areas of Europe; parts of the country are at high altitude and experience very severe winters. Especially in the Black Sea region, tough water-resistant footwear and a raincoat or jacket will prove invaluable.
Insect repellent Mosquitoes (non-malarial except in the far southeast) can be a severe annoyance especially along the coast in summer, so bring a good repellent. Burning coils, or plug-in electric antibug devices that you use with a tablet, are available locally.
Tampons can be difficult to track down, though you will normally find Western brands of sanitary towels. It makes sense to bring your own.

Crime and Safety

Turkey has an enviably low crime record. This reflects Turkish society: restricted access to guns, low incidence of drug use, respect for law and order, and, most important of all, close-knit communities and enduring family ties. Foreigners and tourists are regarded as guests, so are very well treated; in normal circumstances you can expect the police to be polite and helpful.

Tourist areas are regularly patrolled by special *Turizm* or Foreigners' Police, who should do their best to help you and should speak some French, English, German or Arabic. For telephone numbers, *see box on page 420*.

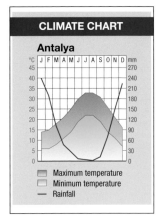

CLIMATE CHART
Antalya

Inevitably, there is still some crime, especially in urban areas blighted by poverty and unemployment. In tourist resorts, other foreigners are not above suspicion – never leave money or cameras in your room. Car crimes and break-ins are possible and purse-snatching and pickpocketing are on the increase in crowded places such as the Grand Bazaar and Istiklal Caddesi in İstanbul. There are also instances of tourists being drugged and robbed.

So take the same precautions as you would at home – don't leave valuables or your bag visible in a car, use a handbag with a long strap slung diagonally over the shoulder and don't walk down dark streets on your own at night.

Make sure that your travel insurance covers you for both the European and Asian sides of Turkey.

Drugs

The film *Midnight Express* is always brought up in this context, much to the annoyance of the Turks. But although the script may have been exaggerated, anyone found in possession of drugs can expect long-term imprisonment.

Military zones

These are normally clearly marked in several languages, often also by a sign with a picture of an armed soldier. You should keep clear (especially in a parked car which could be considered a car bomb), and also avoid photographing anything with a military content.

Political security

There have been small-scale attacks in southeastern Turkey and İstanbul, related to Kurdish separatists. In addition, there is some anti-Western (and considerable anti-Israeli) sentiment: al Qaeda proxies have targeted Western interests in the country and there have been violent demonstrations in the major cities. Take current local advice before travelling to the far southeast.

Tourist crime

Not all the many millions of Westerners who flood into Turkey each year are well behaved. The Turks take a very dim view of drunken tourists scaling statues of Atatürk, or being anything other than respectful to their national icons, religion, women or football teams.

Customs Regulations

You are allowed to bring into the country up to 200 cigarettes (400 if bought in a Turkish duty-free shop), 50 cigars, 200g pipe tobacco (500g if bought in Turkey), 75cl alcohol, 5 litres wine or spirits, 1kg chocolate and 1.5kg coffee.

Exiting into the EU, into Greece in particular, the duty-free limit for souvenirs is currently €430 – the value of purchases must be backed up by receipts. Within this allowance are one 750ml bottle of wine, one carton of cigarettes and one litre of spirits (ie rakı). Carpets and leather jackets are especially likely to provoke Greek suspicions.

Exporting antiques

It is strictly forbidden to take antiques, including rugs and carpets, out of the country. Should you buy anything old or old-looking, be sure to have it validated by the seller, who should get a clearance certificate from the Department of Antiquities – often something handled by the directorate of the nearest museum. Respectable carpet dealers should be familiar with

the procedure. Fossils, by the way, are considered antiquities.

D isabled Travellers

Turkey has very few facilities of any kind for the disabled. Even manoeuvring a wheelchair in İstanbul, for instance, is a strenuous challenge. There are next to no toilet facilities for disabled people, and mosques will usually not allow wheelchairs in. However, as with everything in Turkey, people are friendly, kind and helpful, and will do their best to assist you in getting into a museum or building.

The powers that be are aware that they have to do something about this situation, so things are slowly improving. There are now a very few low-level telephone booths, and buses with wheelchair access. The Turkish Tourist Office in London issues a guide to facilities for the disabled in Turkey, and there is a Turkish Association for the Disabled in İstanbul; tel: 0212-521 4912.

For more detailed information, it is worth contacting your country's own disabled association before you travel:

UK
RADAR (Royal Association for Disability and Rehabilitation)
12 City Forum, 250 City Road, London
EC1V 8AF
Tel: 020-7250 3222
Fax: 0870-141 0337
www.radar.org.uk

US
SATH (Society for Accessible Travel and Hospitality)
347 Fifth Avenue, Suite 605
New York NY 10016
Tel: 212-447 7284
Fax: 212-447 1928
www.sath.org

E lectricity

Voltage is 220–240 volts, 50Hz, out of two standard, continental-European round-pin sockets. Supply in rural areas (including many resorts) is highly variable (ie prone to blackouts) and unbuffered. Do not leave laptops, mobile phones are other portable devices charging in your room in your absence, as sudden, violent electrical storms are quite likely to zap them.

Embassies and Consulates

Turkish consulates abroad

UK
Rutland Lodge, Rutland Gardens,
Knightsbridge, London SW7 1BW

Tel: 020-7591 6900
www.turkishconsulate.org.uk
USA
5th Flr, 821 United Nations Plaza,
New York, NY 10017
Tel: 212-949 0159/62/63. 2525
Massachusetts Avenue NW,
Washington DC 20008
Tel: 202-612 6700
www.washington.emb.mfa.gov.tr

Foreign embassies and consulates in Turkey

Although all embassies are in Ankara, consulates in İstanbul may be able to handle visa and passport matters, eg if you require a visa for travelling to somewhere else. In popular tourist areas, you may find an honorary consul, a local person appointed to take on consular responsibilities.
Australia
MNG Building, Uğur Mumcu Cad 88, 7th Floor, Gaziosmanpaşa, Ankara
Tel: 0312-459 9521
Asker Ocağı Cad 15, Elmadağ, Şişli, İstanbul
Tel: 0212-243 1333
Canada
I Cinnah Caddesi 58, Çankaya, Ankara
Tel: 0312-409 2712
İstiklâl Caddesi 373/5, Beyoğlu
Tel: 0212-251-9838
Ireland
Honorary Consul: Ali Riza Gurcan Caddesi, Merter Iş Merkezi, 2/13
Tel: 0212-482 1862
New Zealand
Iran Cad. 13/4, Kavaklıdere, Ankara
Tel: 0312-467 9054
Yeşilçimen Sok 75, Ihlamur, İstanbul
Tel: 0212-327 2211
South Africa
Filistin Sok. 27, Gaziosmanpaşa, Ankara
Tel: 0312-446 4056
UK
Şehit Ersan Caddesi 46/A, Çankaya, Ankara
Tel: 0312-455 3344
Meşrutiyet Caddesi 34, Tepebaşı/ Beyoğlu
Tel: 0212-334 6400
USA
Atatürk Boulevard 110, Kavaklıdere, Ankara
Tel: 0312-455 5555
Kaplıcalar Mevkii 2, İstinye
Tel: 0212-335 9000

Etiquette

Compared with Western Europe, Turkish society is traditional, particularly in rural areas. It is therefore important to remember a few ground rules to avoid causing offence. Your visit is governed by the rules of hospitality that form a substantial part of the infrastructure of Turkish society, and which mean that you are truly regarded as a guest and (mostly) to be accorded the utmost help. This will show itself in the extent to which people will offer endless cups of tea, personal hospitality, invite you to their home, all of which can be gracefully and tactfully refused if you wish, without giving offence.

Feet are regarded as unclean – so don't put them where someone might sit, or point them towards anyone. Should you be invited into a Turkish home, remove your shoes.

On the beach

Beachwear is worn only on the beach, and heading inland bare-chested is considered extremely offensive. Topless sunbathing is frowned upon, although all too many tourists strip off at the first patch of sand. At some family resorts you will still see women entering the water fully clothed.

In mosques

Non-Muslims should not enter a mosque during prayer time, and not at all on Friday, the holy day. The call to prayer from the minaret comes five times a day between dawn and nightfall.

Both men and women should be modestly dressed. For women this means a longish skirt or trousers, and covered shoulders. For men, shorts are not acceptable. Before entering, remove your shoes. You can leave them outside or carry them. Women should cover their heads, so you should always carry a scarf or hat. Off the beaten tourist track there may not be an attendant to supervise you, but do follow these guidelines to avoid giving offence.

Take care not to disturb, touch or walk in front of anyone who may be at prayer. The larger, more famous mosques are open throughout the day from the first prayer to the last one at night. Smaller ones may only open at prayer times; you may have

Emergency Numbers

Ambulance (public)	112
(see below for İstanbul services)	
Police	155
Fire	110
Forest fires	177

Turizm (Foreigners') Police
İstanbul, tel: 0212-528 5369
Ankara, tel: 0312-384 0606
Antalya, tel: 0242-243 1061
İzmir, tel: 0232-417 3785

to find a caretaker (bekçi) or wait for prayer time, and enter as the worshippers leave.

In Turkish Baths

The traditional Turkish bath (hamam) has its own etiquette. The sexes are segregated, either in different parts of the bath or by different times or days. Some tourist hamams allow mixed bathing, but you will pay more.

Contrary to popular belief, the vast majority of hamams offer a relaxing and invigorating experience which is nothing to be afraid of. Modesty is the order of the day; both men and women should keep their underpants on and cover themselves with a wrap (peştamal).

The easiest way to enjoy a Turkish bath is to go with someone who has been before and knows the ropes; otherwise just watch your neighbours and copy them.

You don't need to have anything with you, but you can of course take along your own wrap, towels, loofa mitt and toiletries, as buying the latter two on the spot can be expensive. See also pages 148–9 for more about hamams.

Privacy is sacrosanct

Family life in Turkey is very private, so public displays of affection, even hand-holding between husband and wife, are rarely seen in the streets outside the main cities. To avoid causing offence, it is wise to honour these traditions.

G ay and Lesbian Travellers

Turkish attitudes to gays, or to overtly gay behaviour, are contradictory. On the one hand, they adulate their own amazingly exhuberant transvestite or transsexual singers; on the other, they can be publicly intolerant of gay couples.

Homosexual acts between adults over 18 are legal, and in İstanbul and coastal resorts such as Alanya, you'll find greater tolerance and even some gay bars and discos. Be circumspect in public and you shouldn't have any problems.

H ealth and Medical Care

Turkey is a pretty safe country as long as you are sensible. If you do fall ill, the standard of health care in private facilities in the big cities is getting better all the time, but you should still have medical insurance to cover the costs (see opposite). Most drugs are available without prescription from

ABOVE: in a Turkish bath.

pharmacies (eczane). For details of these and medical treatment within the country, see opposite.

Health advice

In the UK, detailed health advice, tailored to individual needs, is available from MASTA (Medical Advice for Travellers Abroad). They have a web-based system and travel clinics throughout the UK. www.masta-travel-health.com.

Alternatively, you could try the Fleet Street Travel Clinic, tel: 020-7353 5678; www.fleetstreetclinic.com.

Health hazards

Traveller's diarrhoea is the main hazard, best avoided by paying attention to food and water hygiene. Drink only bottled water or water from a spring marked as potable, wash and/or peel all fruit and vegetables, and ensure cooked food is piping hot. It's safest to eat freshly prepared local produce. Refrigeration – especially of cold mezes – can be poor, even in tourist resorts, so only eat fresh batches of these. Grilled meat or fish is usually safe if properly cooked through. Do not buy midye dolması (stuffed mussels) from street-sellers in summer.

Some form of diarrhoea treatment and pre-packaged sachets are a useful addition to your first-aid kit. But should you succumb, it's advisable to resort to drugs only if you absolutely have to. The best treatment is to maintain fluid levels with plenty of non-alcoholic drinks or rehydration salts, eat very plain food and avoid dairy products. Even if fluids are repeatedly vomited, rehydration therapy will eventually work. If the diarrhoea lasts more than 48 hours, seek medical advice.

Sun and heat The other major hazards in summer are heatstroke and sunburn. The answer is pure common sense. Wear a hat and sunglasses, put on a wrap on the beach, use high-factor sunblock and aftersun cream, drink plenty of water and soft drinks, and cut down on alcohol intake. If you or your companions get an overwhelming headache, are dizzy or disoriented and cannot bring your body temperature down, put the patient in a cool bath and get someone to ring for a doctor. True heatstroke is a serious medical condition. **Stings and bites** If you stand on a sea urchin, ray, weever fish or similar sea creature, or are bitten by any animal, it is vitally important to seek medical attention as soon as possible. Stings can produce a severe allergic reaction, while a bite may require vaccination against rabies. While waiting for the doctor, the best first aid is to encourage limited bleeding, wash the bite-wound thoroughly for several minutes, then bandage it (but do not suture). You should expect to undergo five injections of human diploid cell vaccine (HDCV), to be started within 24 hours, together with a single human rabies immunoglobulin (HRIG) jab.

Inoculations

As a rule, inoculations are not necessary, but it is always wise to be up to date with polio, tetanus and tuberculosis when travelling. Should you plan to visit eastern Anatolia, consider immunisation against typhoid.

Antimalarial tablets are recommended in summer in the Tigris and Euphrates basins, along the border with Syria and Iraq.

You may wish to consider immunisation against hepatitis A (spread through contaminated food and water). As everywhere else, Aids and hepatitis B are prevalant and precautions should be taken.

Medical insurance

An insurance policy, including cover for medical evacuation, is essential, as medical costs in Turkey are high and EU reciprocal agreements do not apply.

If you already have a general annual travel policy, check that it will cover you on the Asian side of the country (not all companies consider Turkey "Europe").

Medical treatment

Pharmacies

These should be your first port of call for treating minor ailments. There is a rota system whereby one pharmacist in every district – the *nöbetçi* – stays

open 24 hours for emergencies, and the address will be noted in pharmacists' windows.

Most standard drugs are available in Turkey without a prescription. Although self-treatment is not recommended, it is easy to replace routine medication at any pharmacy *(eczane)* should it be necessary. It is a good idea to show the pharmacist the empty container, to be sure that you are being given the right drug. Remember that generic drugs can be marketed under different names.

Doctors and dentists

Though some doctors and dentists in the cities do speak English or German, and many have been trained abroad to a high standard, unless it is an emergency, it is better to wait until you return home for treatment. Most four- and five-star hotels have a doctor on call with some English and/or German in case of emergency.

Hospitals

Although there are a number of excellent private hospitals in the major cities, health care does not generally meet Western expectations of nursing and aftercare, though some hospitals are better than others, and are fine in an emergency. The further you go from the major cities, the more limited medical facilities become.

It is also vital to note that hospitals work on a pay-as-you-go basis, requiring payment on the spot in advance of any required treatment, including scans and X-rays. This has been known to happen even in extreme emergencies. It is one very good reason to keep some cash and a credit card on you at all times.

Ambulances

Certain services operate independently; others are attached to particular hospitals. The average Turkish ambulance is little better than a taxi, and in a minor emergency a taxi can be the best and quickest way to get to hospital.

İstanbul, for example, is relatively well provided with ambulances, but so bad is the traffic during the morning and evening rush hours that many drivers stubbornly refuse to give way to the emergency services. The following are worth ringing, however: **Medline** is a private company that serves hospitals in İstanbul (tel: 444 1212). Their ambulances have emergency equipment, and a doctor and paramedic on board. www.medline. com.tr.

The International Hospital has well-

equipped ambulances, including a boat that can navigate the Bosphorus (and beat the traffic) and a helicopter during daylight hours only. Tel: 444 0663.

Emergency Hospitals

Ankara
Bayındır Hospital, Kavaklıdere
Tel: 0312-428 0808
Çankaya Hospital, Çankaya
Tel: 0312-426 1450
Güven Hospital, Aşağı Ayrancı
Tel: 0312-468 7220
Antalya
Akdeniz University Hospital
Tel: 0242-227 4343
InterHospital
Tel: 0242-311 1500
Bodrum
Özel Hastanesi
Mars Mabedi Caddesi, Çesmebasi
Mevkii 22-43
Tel: 0252-313 6566
İstanbul
American Hospital, Güzelbahçe
Sokak, Nisantaşı
Tel: 0212-311 2000
Çağlayan Florence Nightingale
Hospital, Abide-i Hürriyet Caddesi
290, Şişli
Tel: 0212-230 2021
German Hospital, Sıraselviler Caddesi
119, Taksim
Tel: 0212-293 2150
International Hospital, Yeşilköy
Tel: 0212-663 3000
Taksim İlk Yardım (Emergency
Hospital), Sıraselviler Caddesi, Taksim
Tel: 0212-252 4300
İzmir
Başkent Hospital, Bostanlı, Karşıyaka
Tel: 0232-330 5230
American Hospital, 1375 Sokak,
Alsancak
Tel: 0232-484 5360
Sağlık Hospital, 1399 Sokak 25,
Alsancak
Tel: 0232-463 7700

Internet

Turks have a passion for new technology, and are very keen on the internet – it is probably one of the most wired-up (or rather, wire-less) societies in the world. Government offices, media, universities and even modest businesses have websites, and late at night the youth of Turkey log on and chat. Every large town is plastered with internet cafés, as disposable income is not yet sufficient to permit universal private computer ownership. Wi-fi zones are common, and even surprisingly modest *pansiyons* will have them in common areas, if not every room. Most internet cafés will let you log on with your own laptop, cheaply or for free, but with so many bars and restaurants advertising wireless zones this isn't really necessary.

The Turkish keyboard has certain characters located differently to those on English-language keyboards. The @ is produced by simultaneously pressing "ALT" and "q". The Turkish dotless ı is where you'd expect the western "i" to be.

M aps

Decent maps are notoriously difficult to come by for Turkey. Except for those packaged together with commercial trekking guides to the Kaçkar mountains and St Paul Trail (see www.trekkinginturkey.com), there are no publicly available large-scale topographic maps, as these are seen as a threat to national security. Currently the best touring maps are the seven 1:500,000 sheets published jointly by Kartographischer Verlag Reinhard Ryborsch in Frankfurt; these may be officially out of stock but can still be found from online dealers. Once in Turkey, the 1:400,000 atlas produced by *Atlas* travel magazine is very accurate, but poorly printed and thus difficult to read. The best regional touring maps are Sabri Aydal's 1:250,000 products for Cappadocia, Lycia, Pamphylia and Pisidia, available from bookshops and museums in those regions. Insight Fleximaps (Turkey 1:2,400,000) and İstanbul (1:12,500) are durable, laminated maps. Otherwise, the best source of Turkey maps online is US-based www.omnimap.com.

Media

Turkey has been enjoying a media explosion. Quantity does not necessarily mean quality, however. The radio waves are so crowded with channels that stations have to take turns; there are dozens of regular TV channels, while apartment buildings bristle with aerials and dishes as people tune in to the world's cable and satellite networks.

Television

From a single state-run TV channel at the beginning of the 1980s, Turkey now has over 12 main channels, the majority of which are privately owned. You will find additional regional channels depending on where you are. Although entertainment programmes, soap operas, game shows and pop videos dominate the

small screen, some channels also show foreign films (sometimes with subtitles) and international sports.

Through satellite and cable, dozens of foreign channels including BBC Entertainment, BBC World, MTV and CNN can be viewed. Visitors will usually find satellite or cable in the major hotels, although you should check before booking if this is important to you.

• **TRT Channel 2** broadcasts the news in English, French and German at 7pm and 10pm.

Radio

Until the early 1990s, only state-run stations were on air, and broadcasts were inclined to be more soporific than stimulating. Today, İstanbul alone has so many private stations playing Western pop and rock, with news broadcasts thrown in, that they jostle for frequency space, and it can be difficult to get a clear signal on the station you want.

• **Açık Radyo** (FM 94.9) and Metro FM (97.2MHz) broadcast rock, jazz and soul.

• **TRT3** (FM 88.2, 94 or 99MHz) State-run Radyo Üç appeals to more sophisticated listeners, playing jazz, Latin and classical music. TRT3 also broadcasts news in English, French and German following the Turkish bulletin at 9am, noon, 2pm, 5pm, 7pm and 10pm.

• **BBC World Service** can be received if you have a shortwave radio with a good aerial, but reception is not very clear.

Newspapers and magazines

In Turkish There are over a score of major Turkish newspapers, chasing a relatively small reading public and competing with radio, TV and the internet.

Sabah and *Hürriyet* are Turkey's bestselling national mainstream newspapers and leading public-opinion makers, though not

necessarily espousing the highest-quality journalism. The secularist *Cumhuriyet* upholds Atatürk's vision, while *Zaman* is mildly Islamicist. *Radikal* and *Taraf* offer the boldest alternative and/or investigative journalism.

You will see Turkish editions of many international magazines, plus countless popular Turkish weeklies and monthlies. *Atlas* is a quality monthly travel title with English text summaries.

In English International newspapers and magazines can be found at news-stands and bookshops in tourist areas and hotels. Newspapers are usually a day or two late, and sold at many times the UK cover price.

A local English-language daily paper, the *Hürriyet Daily News* (www.hurriyetdailynews.com), provides coverage of local and international events. As well as listing cinemas showing English-language films, and the main satellite and TV channel programmes, it is useful for its classifieds, should you be looking for an apartment, local travel agent or Turkish lessons. Another, rather good daily paper in English is *Today's Zaman* (www.todayszaman.com), its Islamic affiliation not very obvious, with a wide range of good columnists.

Cornucopia is a glossy, bimonthly English-language magazine featuring Turkish arts, history and culture from a rather elitist perspective. It is stocked at better Turkish bookshops selling foreign-language publications, or you can subscribe at www.cornucopia.net, which also has an excellent online bookshop and reviews archive.

Tourist guides

The Guide is a useful English-language city-guide magazine, published bimonthly in İstanbul, annually for Ankara and Bodrum. It offers visitors practical information, arts news, and restaurant and shopping listings.

Time Out publishes a weekly listings magazine in İstanbul and a monthly English-language edition, also online at www.timeoutistanbul.com/english.

Books

It can be hard to find foreign-language books outside İstanbul and Ankara, although many large hotel shops have a few, often uninspired, titles, usually in English, French or German. They can cost anything up to double their original price.

See *Further Reading* on page 434 for a list of books on Turkey.

Money

Currency

The currency is the Turkish lira (TL), subdivided into 100 kuruş. At the time of writing, 1 TL was equivalent in value to 0.51 euros (US$0.66/£0.43). Coins come in denominations of 5, 10, 25 and 50 kuruş, plus 1TL; bills are denominated as 5, 10, 20, 50, 100 and 200 TL. Unlimited foreign currency and up to US$5,000 of TL can be brought in, but you will always get a better exchange rate within Turkey.

Obtaining cash

Banks are plentiful in Turkey, but they are slow, and with the increasing number of ATMs (see below) you can easily get through your whole stay without entering one. Travellers' cheques are a lot of hassle and not recommended. Given that the risk of theft is low, it is easier to use foreign currency, whether US dollars, sterling or euros, which can be used directly for larger souvenir purchases. Most traders are happy to haggle in all three.

Credit and debit cards

Major credit cards are accepted by more and more shops, restaurants, hotels and petrol stations. Fewer outlets accept Amex, which can only be used with certain bank-linked countertop machines (particularly Garanti Bankası). Chip-and-PIN routine is now the norm (you may be asked to sign slips as well).

ATMs

There are 24-hour cash dispensers accepting credit cards and bank cards using your PIN, on every street corner; there are also many stand-alone machines in remoter resorts or on ferry docks, inside bus stations, etc.

The machines usually offer you a choice of six languages in which to conduct your transaction, but they issue only Turkish lira. If a machine starts being exceptionally slow or uncooperative, cancel the transaction, if possible, and find another machine; eaten cards or double-billed transactions because of mysterious "timing out" issues are not unknown.

Foreign-exchange offices

Foreign currency is in great demand in Turkey so you won't have to look very hard for a place to change foreign-currency notes. Sterling and euros can attract a better rate than less frequently traded currencies. Foreign-exchange offices (döviz büroları) are usually much more efficient than banks, though they generally offer poorer rates. They are plentiful and open Mon–Sat 8.30/9am–7pm. No commission is charged for cash. Allow 15 minutes minimum for a bank transaction, including waiting in line; take a number from the dispensing machine and wait for your teller window (gişe) to come free.

Tipping

It is customary to tip a small amount to anyone who does you a small service: the hotel cleaner, porter, doorman who gets you a taxi and so on. Even in cinemas you give something to the person who shows you to your seat.

The only potential difficulty is arming yourself with plenty of small change (bozuk para) in advance. At the time of writing, anything between 50–100 kuruş would be in order. In restaurants, round the bill up by 10 percent, unless service has been included.

Taxis are the exception: you don't tip taxi drivers and they do not expect it, though you can round the fare up to the nearest suitable figure as change can be a problem.

Credit Card Hotlines

The numbers to ring if your card is lost or stolen during your stay in Turkey are:
American Express
Tel: 0312-935 3601.
Diners, Mastercard and Visa
Tel: 00 800 13 887 0903.

O pening Hours

Offices Generally Mon–Fri 9am–6pm.
Government offices 8am–4.30pm in winter; 8.30am–5pm in summer.
Shops Most close on Sunday, but major stores open all week. The large shopping centres and smart clothes shops open later, at 10am, closing between 8pm and 10pm. Some supermarkets stay open until midnight. Small neighbourhood stores are generally open 8am–8.30/9pm; some only shut up for the night at around 10pm.
Banks Mon–Fri 8.30am–5pm, with some closing between noon and 1.30pm; a few main branches also open Saturday morning. Most private banks remain open over lunch. Several banks at İstanbul airport are open 24 hours a day.
Petrol stations Larger ones remain open 24 hours a day; others will close between 9 and 11pm.

Public Holidays

1 January New Year's Day
23 April Independence and Children's Day
19 May Atatürk's Birthday, and Youth and Sports Day
30 August Victory Day
29 October Republic Day
10 November Atatürk's Death Anniversary, observed at 9.05am

P hotography

Taking photographs is perfectly acceptable in almost any context; Turks are generally pleased to be included in photographs, and of course if on holiday themselves will be snapping away. It is polite, however, to ask first and to respect their wishes if they say no. Veiled women often prefer not to be photographed. Some people may ask for a copy; if you take their address or email, do send the pictures.

Museums sometimes charge for the use of cameras or videos; flash photography may not be allowed as it can damage paints and textiles.

Mosques usually allow discreet flash-free photography – be tactful.

If you are still using **film**, quality developing is readily available at prices comparable to Europe, and most photo shops will also transfer or print from all common digital cards. Film is expensive, but prices are lower in photographic shops than at tourist shops (which usually have only a limited supply).

Postal Services

A post office (postane) is marked by the letters **PTT**, and is usually open Mon–Sat 9am–12.30pm and 1.30–5pm. Sirkeci Post Office in İstanbul is open daily 24 hours. Services at the larger PTTs include poste restante and metered phones (the latter often available a bit later than postal services, especially in tourist areas where they can be attended until midnight). There are also small PTT kiosks in tourist areas where you can get stamps, post letters and buy phonecards. Stamps are available only from PTT outlets.

PTT postboxes are yellow, marked PTT and şehiriçi (local), yurtiçi (domestic) and yurtdışı (international).

Airmail takes a week or so to reach the UK/US. Express post costs more, but is supposed to take no more than three days to arrive. If you are sending a parcel, the contents will be inspected, so don't seal it

TRANSPORT ACCOMMODATION EATING OUT ACTIVITIES A – Z LANGUAGE beforehand. Rates within Turkey are very reasonable – a couple of TL to send a book or a small packet, for example.

R eligious Festivals

Turkish religious holidays are linked to the Islamic lunar calendar and move back 11 or 12 days each year. Secular festivals may also move to coincide with weekends, and precise dates can change annually. Plenty of Islamic websites can inform you as to when the major festivals will fall in the Western calendar.

During these major holidays, shops and businesses are closed, though local shops will usually reopen on the second or third day.

Ramazan Anyone will tell you that the worst time to travel in Turkey is during the holy month of Ramazan (Ramadan), when a majority of the population (even non-devout Muslims) pride themselves on fasting from dawn to dusk. This includes the intake of water and cigarettes, with the result that taxi drivers may put you out as the sunset approaches so they can stop to eat, many restaurants close all day or have very limited offerings, and many people are extremely irritable.

Until 2014, Ramazan will fall in August, the summer heat accentuating the ordeal. The holiest point of Ramazan is Kadir Gecesi or The Night of Power, between the 27th and 28th day, when the Koran was said to have been revealed to Mohammed; mosques are full as it is believed that prayer is especially efficacious on this night.

Şeker Bayram The fast of Ramazan ends with a three-day celebration, Sugar Holiday, when everyone, especially childen, is offered sweets wherever they go.

Kurban Bayram The Feast of the Sacrifice is a four-day holiday celebrating the substituting of a sacrificial ram for Abraham's son Ishmael. It involves the ritual throat-slitting of beasts, though no longer in public.

New Year Most Turks observe New Year's Eve and New Year's Day with family and friends, or take a holiday skiing or on the balmy south coast.

Miraç Kandili, currently occurring in June, celebrates the Prophet Mohammed's nocturnal journey to Jerusalem and ascension to heaven on a winged horse. Though not an official holiday, mosques are especially illuminated, as they are all during Ramazan.

Nevruz (Persian New Year) is celebrated thoughout eastern Turkey and elsewhere. Originally thought to be a Zoroastrian fire festival, it is now associated with Kurdish and Alevî traditions in Turkey.

Religious Services

Turkey is officially a secular state, although 99 percent of the population are Muslim. There are significant Jewish, Armenian and Greek Orthodox minorities, but these remain concentrated in İstanbul and İzmir.

However, due to its long history of mixed races and cultures, Turkey has hundreds of non-Muslim places of worship. Most are now places of historical interest but İstanbul, Ankara and İzmir still have some functioning churches and synagogues.

Attending a service can be a way of meeting people who live and work in the place you are visiting, and of experiencing the building in its intended setting.

S moking

Smoking has long been banned on public transport, airports and terminals, while as of mid-2009, it was also prohibited inside all public buildings, bars, clubs and restaurants, on pain of a 67TL fine. The rule is mostly obeyed, with nicotine addicts retiring outside to the pavement. Outside terraces constitute a grey area – in the Aegean regions and İstanbul you may still see people puffing away on hubble-bubbles there.

T ax

Taxes, chiefly VAT (KDV) at varying rates, are included in the prices of some goods and services, but you may see them itemised separately as a component of the price on a bill or receipt.

Some stores offer VAT-free shopping for tourists living outside the European Union (look out for signs in the window). If you wish to take advantage of this, you need to get an official VAT-free invoice or you will not be able to reclaim the tax at the airport on your way out. (This is already said somewhere else...)

Telephones

Public phones

Most public phones use phonecards (*telefon kartları*) and can be found in the streets or grouped in busy areas such as bus and railway stations and

airports. Some post offices (PTTs) also have metered phones for which you pay after your call.

Phonecards can be bought from PTTs, newsstands and vendors near groups of phone booths. They come in different denominations from 50 to 350 units. For cheap international calls, buy an Alocard from any PTT branch; scratch clear the 12-digit PIN and then dial the access number from any public phone.

There are also credit-card phones at airports and in the lobbies of some five-star hotels in major cities. Never phone from your hotel room, other than the briefest of local calls to land lines, unless you want to be landed with a horrendous bill.

Useful national and international codes and operator services are posted in phone boxes. Instructions in card-phone boxes are in English, French and German as well as Turkish, and these days the phones may well ask you which language you would prefer when you pick up the receiver.

Mobiles

Almost all Turks have mobile phones. Most European mobiles will log on to one of the local networks, but you shouldn't use it for anything other than text messaging. Making or receiving calls is extortionately expensive, as Turkish networks are not subject to EU price caps for roaming – bills of £120 on return home are not uncommon. Do yourself a favour and purchase a local SIM card on a pay-as-you-go package; they start from about 20TL and will save you a lot of money. You are supposed to register the phone upon purchase to prevent the number being disconnected within 2 or 3 weeks. If your phone cannot be unblocked for "alien" SIMs or the Turkish SIM rejects it (with a "phone unregistered" message), buy a used local phone for 60TL. Visitors from north America will be unable to access any Turkish network unless they have a quad-band phone.

Dialling codes

Country code
If dialling Turkey from abroad: 90

Common regional codes
You don't dial the area code if calling the area you are in. If calling from abroad, drop the initial 0.

Adana	0322
Ankara	0312
Alanya/Antalya	0242
Bodrum/Marmaris	0252
Bursa	0224
Çanakkale	0226

Cappadocia	0384
Çeşme	0232
Diyarbakır	0412
Edirne	0284
Erzurum	0442
İstanbul Asian side	0216
İstanbul European side	0212

(use these codes if calling from one side of the city to the other)

İzmir	0232
Kars	0474
Kayseri	0352
Konya	0332
Kuşadası	0256
Kütahya	0274
Pamukkale	0258
Samsun	0362
Selçuk	0232
Sinop	0368
Trabzon	0462
Van	0432

International codes

Australia	61
Canada	1
Ireland	353
New Zealand	64
UK	44
USA	1

Dial 00 and then the country code, followed by the number.

Useful Numbers

Directory enquiries (İstanbul) **118**
International operator **115**
International directory enquiries **115**

Toilets

You will probably find traditional Turkish squat toilet facilities disconcerting. There may well be a choice of Western-style and squat toilets. Arm yourself with a supply of paper (which goes in the bin, not the hole, as the drains can't cope with it).

You will find clean Western-style facilities in the more up-market hotels and restaurants, shopping malls and at all museums and archaeological sites. Public toilets in cities can be revolting; in rural places sometimes sparkling clean; those at motorway and road-side service stations, acceptable. Special baby-changing rooms are starting to put in an appearance.

You will usually be charged 50 kuruş to 1TL per visit in public facilities, so keep a supply of small change available.

Tourist Information

Local tourist information offices

Government-run tourist information offices, *Turizm Danışma Burosu*, are marked with a white oval sign featuring

a coloured "i". They are usually open Mon–Sat 9am–5pm, though the one at İstanbul Airport is open 24 hours a day, and in summer those in busy resorts may stay open into the evening.

Don't expect that much from them, however; there are a few outstanding ones (like the Sultanahmet office in İstanbul), but in many, especially in less-visited areas, staff may not speak even rudimentary English. Some have useful lists of accommodation but may have no facilities to make bookings. In some cities local associations have set up their own rival facilities which can be a great improvement. For instance, the Alanya Hotels Association (ALTID) has regulated prices and standards, organised beach lifeguards and extra security, and staffs its office with English-speakers.

Main tourist offices:

İstanbul – Sultanahmet Square
Tel: 0212-518 8754
Also at the airport, station, Sirkeci train station, Karaköy ferry port and Hilton Hotel.
Alanya – Damlataş Caddesi 1
Tel: 0242-513 1240
Ankara – Gazi Mustafa Kemal Bulvarı 121A
Tel: 0312-231 5572
Antalya – Cumhuriyet Caddesi, Ozel İdare Altı 2
Tel: 0242-241 1747
Bodrum – Barış Meydanı
Tel: 0252-316 1091
İzmir – Akdeniz Mahallesi, 1344 Sokak 2, Pasaport
Tel: 0232-483 5117
Also at the airport.

Tourist offices

UK
4th Floor, 29–30 St James's Street, London SW1A 1HB
Tel: 020-7839 7778
www.gototurkey.co.uk
USA
821 United Nations Plaza, New York, NY 10017
Tel: 212-687 2194
www.tourismturkey.org

Websites

Turkey hotels:
www.smallhotels.com.tr
Charming small hotels across the country.
İstanbul hotels:
www.istanbulhotels.com
Useful accommodation website.
Travel advisories:
www.fco.gov.uk
www.travel.state.gov
Regularly updated travel and general

health advice from the UK Foreign and Commonwealth Office and US State Department.
Health for travellers:
www.cdc.gov/travel
Advice on health from a US government site.
General tourist information:
www.goturkey.com
Official tourist-office site includes extensive information on tourism within the country.
www.allaboutturkey.com
Incredibly informative site maintained by tourist guide Burak Sansal.
www.turkeytravelplanner.com
Excellent US-run website on travel in Turkey, including an active discussion forum.
www.trekkinginturkey.com
Everything about major trekking areas and long-distance routes, including printed guides and maps.

Tour Operators and Travel Agents in Turkey

İstanbul

Arnika
Istiklâl Caddesi, Mis Sokak 6/5, Beyoğlu
Tel: 0212-245 1593
Daily and weekend tours to the countryside around İstanbul.
Art Tours
Valikonağı Caddesi 77/3, Nişantası
Tel: 0212-231 0487
Fax: 0212-240 4945
Flight reservations, city tours, car rental, incentive and congress organisation.
Fest
Barbaros Bulvarı, Barbaros Apt 74 D.20, Balmumcu
Tel: 0212-216 1036/7
Expert guides arrange tours to lesser-known corners of the city and off-the-beaten-track regions of the country, including the Black Sea.
Fotograf Evi
Istiklâl Caddesi, Tütüncü Çıkmazı 4, Galatasaray
Tel: 0212-249 0202
Photography and travel club geared towards young people. Organises weekend nature walks and slide shows.
Gençtur
Istiklâl Caddesi 212, Galatasaray
Tel: 0212-244 6230
Fax: 0212-244 6233
Student travel agency offering discount cards, as well as nature tours near İstanbul.
Grup Günbatmadan
Istiklâl Caddesi, Zambak Sokak 15, 4th floor, Beyoğlu
Tel: 0212-245 5954

Fax: 0212-245 6035
Organises trekking at all levels around the country.
Meptur
Büyükdere Caddesi 26/3, Mecidiyeköy
Tel: 0212-275 0250
Fax: 0212-275 4009
Tailor-made group tours, reservations, city packages, corporate travel.
Plan Tours
Cumhuriyet Caddesi 83/1, Elmadağ
Tel: 0212-234 7777
Fax: 0212-231 8965
www.plantours.com
City sightseeing tours, seminars and congresses, ticketing, hotel reservations, car and yacht rentals, hunting trips, Jewish heritage tours.
Setur
Cumhuriyet Caddesi 69, Elmadağ
Tel: 0212-230 0336
Fax: 0212-241 0240
www.setur.com.tr
Car rental, aeroplane tickets, tours and conference organisation.
Sunday Holiday
Abdülhakhamit Caddesi 82/2, Taksim
Tel: 0212-256 4156
Fax: 0212-256 8808
www.sundayholiday.com.tr
Tailor-made group tours, hotel reservations, city packages, conventions and corporate meetings.
Türk Ekspres
Cumhuriyet Caddesi 47/1, Taksim
Tel: 0212-235 9500
Fax: 0212-235 2313
www.turkekspres.com.tr
Long-running full-service travel agency with offices also in the Conrad and Hilton hotels, offering air tickets, car rental and a wide range of city tours. Local Amex representative.
Yesil Bisiklet
Lalezar Sokak 6/A, Selamiçeşme, Kadıköy
Tel: 0216-363 5836
www.yesilbisiklet.com
Cycling club/shop with cycling gear and maintenance. Organises trips.
Viking Turizm
Mete Caddesi 18, Taksim
Tel: 0212-334 2600
www.vikingturizm.com.tr
A Rosenbluth Network company and general sales agent of Seaburn Cruise Lines, offering airline ticketing, corporate and leisure travel, conferences and incentives.

Thrace and Marmara

Bursa
Karagöz Tourism & Travel Agency
Kapalı Çarşı, Eski Aynalı Çarşı 12
Tel: 0224-221 8727
www.karagoztravel.com
Guided tours of Bursa and northwest

Turkey, by a shadow-puppet master.

Çanakkale
Kenan Çelik
Tel: 0532-738 6675
www.kcelik.com
This professor at the local university offers by far the best custom tours of the Gallipoli battlefields, taking you to little-known sites; you must have your own car though.

Eceabat
Crowded House Tours
Tel: 0286-814 1565
www.crowdedhousegallipoli.com
Operating out of the eponymous hostel; the best mainstream group tours of the Gallipoli battlefields.

Aegean Coast

Bodrum
Arya Yachting
Caferpaşa Caddesi 21/1
Tel: 0252-316 1580
www.arya.com.tr
Yachting or *gulet* excursions and inland tours.
Askin Dive Centre
Tel: 0252-316 4247
www.askindiving.com

İzmir
Rainbow Tours
Esen 1 Sokak 6/G, Narlıdere, İzmir
Tel: 0232-239 5196
www.rainbowtourturkey.com
Pilgrimage tours of Christian and Pauline sites in Turkey.

Dalyan
Kaunos Tours
Central junction
Tel: 0252-284 2816
www.kaunostours.com
Outfitters for scuba, white-water rafting, horse riding and mountain biking; also car hire.

Marmaris
Alternatif Turizm

Çamlik Sok 10/1
Tel: 0252-417 2720
www.alternatifraft.com
Main local outfitters for sea-kayaking, river-rafting, canyoning, trekking; many other storefront agencies subcontract to them.

Mediterranean Coast

Adana
Adalı Turizm
Stadyum Caddesi 37/C
Tel: 0322-453 7440
Full-service travel agency handling flights, packages, accommodation, car hire and local excursions.

Alanya
Alraft Rafting and Riding Club
Biçakçı Köyü Mevkii
Tel: 0242-513 9155
Tantur
Yunus Emre Caddesi 16
Tel: 0242-513 3362
www.tantur.com.tr
One of Turkey's largest tour operators offering yacht charters, destination tourism and special-interest holidays.

Antalya
Medraft
Yeşilbahçe Mahallesi, Portakal Çiçeği Bulvarı, Hüseyin Kuzu Ap. 14/3
Tel: 0242-312 5770
www.medraft.com
Mithra Travel
Hesapçi Sok 70, Kaleiçi
Tel: 0242-248 7747
wwwmithratravel.com
Sightseeing tours, walking tours, mountain bike and car hire.
Pamfilya
Işiklar Caddesi 57/B
Tel: 0242-243 1500
Fax: 0242-242 1400
Sightseeing tours, yacht charters, rafting and trekking.
Skorpion Turizm
Fevzi Çakmak Caddesi 12/5
Tel: 0242-243 0890

Sightseeing tours and a host of outdoor activities, including mountaineering, jeep safaris, trekking and village tours.

Fethiye
Be There Yachting and Travel Agency
Fevzi Çakmak Caddesi 12/1, Yacht Marina, Fethiye
Tel: 0252-614 7711
Daily excursions, travel reservations, yachting and *gulet* cruises.
BeforeLunch Cruises
Quayside
Tel: 0535-636 0076
www.beforelunch.com
Specialists in high-quality, 3-night/4-day cruises in the Gulf of Fethiye.
Explora
Ölüdeniz, Fethiye
Tel: 0252-616 6890
www.exploraturkey.com
SkySports
Ölüdeniz-Fethiye
Tel: 0252-617 0511
www.skysports-turkey.com
The most established of several outfitters here taking clients on tandem paraglides off nearby Baba Dağı.

Kaş
Amber Travel
Halk Konutlari, Petrol Ofisi Yani
Tel: 0242-836 1630
Good for tailor-made, country-wide cultural itineraries.
BT Adventure & Diving
Çukurbağlı Cad 10
Tel: 0242-836 3737
www.bt-turkey.com
Respected, long-standing outfitter for sea-kayaking, scuba and canyoning in particular.
Dragoman
Uzun Çarşı 15
Tel: 0242-836 3614
Similar, and similar-quality, offerings as BT but also hiking and cultural tours.

Central Anatolia
Ankara
Aloha
Cinnah Caddesi, 39/B, Çankaya
Tel: 0312-440 9855
Travel agent for flights and tours worldwide; local car hire.
T&T
Abdullah Cevdet Sokak 22/9, Çankaya
Tel: 0312-440 9234
Tours throughout Anatolia.
Tanzer
Abdullah Cevdet Sok. 24/2, Çankaya
Tel: 0312-441 4181

Cappadocia
Kapadokya Balloons Göreme
Nevşehir Yolu 14/A, Nevsehir
Tel: 0384-271 2442
www.kapadokyaballoons.com
Idyllic hot-air-balloon rides over Cappadocia's landscape.
Heritage Travel
Yavuz Sokak 31
Tel: 0384-271 2687
Can organise your travel arrangements for Cappadocia and throughout the country.
Middle Earth Travel
Gaferli Mah. Cevizler Sokak 20, Göreme
Tel: 0384-271 2559
www.middleearthtravel.com
Hiking in Cappadocia and along the Lycian and St Paul's Trails, plus climbing on Mount Ararat. Local tours and sightseeing, too.
Red Valley
Cumhuriyet Meydanı, Ürgüp
Tel: 0384-341 5061
Walking and sightseeing tours and cave exploration through the magical Cappadocian landscape.

Black Sea Coast
Ordu
Enis Ayar
Tel: 0452-223 1337
Trekking and mountaineering guide, who has recently had a film made about his tireless conservation efforts. Operates all year, but specialises in winter trips to the peak of Karagöl, one of the highest of the Black Sea region. Experienced climbers only for winter climbs.
Agencies in İstanbul that specialise in Black Sea Tours include **Abelya Tourism**, **Fest** and **Fotograf Evi** *(see İstanbul page 425)*.

The East
Diyarbakır
Bat-Air
İnönü Caddesi 9
Tel: 0412-223 5373
www.batairturizm.com
Gaziantep
Kantara Turizm
Atatürk Bulvarı, Şaban Sokak 2/3
Tel: 0342-220 6300
Fax: 0342-220 6302
www.kantara.com.tr
Special tours of the dam and irrigation

Time Zone

Turkish Standard Time is 2 hours ahead of Greenwich Mean Time. In common with Europe, it advances by one hour in summer (end March to end Oct).

projects of the massive southeastern Anatolia Project.
Zöhre Turizm
Ataturk Bulvarı, Ari Sinemasi Karşisi
Tel: 0342-220 5857
Fax: 0342-231 4238
www.zohreturizm.com
Regional tours to archaeological sites such as Nemrut Dağı.

Şanlıurfa
Harran Nemrut Tur
Özel Dünya Hastanesi Arkası
Tel: 0414-313 1928

Van
Ayanis Turizm
Cumhüriyet Caddesi
Tel: 0432-214 2020
www.ayanis.com
Sightseeing tours of the Van area and other parts of the east.
Çarpanak Turizm
Maraş Caddesi 23, Van
Tel: 0432-214 4464
Fax: 0432-214 3087
www.carpanakturizm.com
Day tours to the local sites and airline ticketing.

Package Tours

Unless you are planning to move around a lot, packages are usually much more reasonable than booking independently, particularly if you want to stay in top hotels. The choice of packages is enormous, whether you are looking for a villa holiday, adventurous mountaineering, cultural tours, wildlife spotting, or a simple flight/accommodation deal.

United Kingdom
Adrift
Tel: 01488-71152
www.adrift.co.uk
Currently the sole UK outfitter for rafting trips on the mighty Çoruh, Turkey's best whitewater river.
Anatolian Sky
Tel: 0121-764 3550
www.anatolian-sky.co.uk
Offers two-centre holidays, golfing, *gulets*, wedding packages and city breaks in İstanbul plus a selection of southwest coastal resorts.
Andante Travel
Tel: 01722-713 800
www.andantetravels.co.uk
Up-market tours to major (and many minor) archaeological and historical sites, led by distinguished professors or other experts in their fields.
Cachet Travel
Tel: 020-8847 8700
www.cachet-travel.co.uk
Selected villas and hotels along the

Turquoise Coast, plus İstanbul and Cappadocia; guided, low-season special-interest tours.

Exclusive Escapes
Tel: 020-8605 3500
www.exclusiveescapes.co.uk
The best portfolio of boutique hotels and villas in Lycia, as well as in the Loryma Peninsula, Datça, Cappadocia and İstanbul. Noted for a high level of customer service, and thus repeat business.

Exodus Travel
Tel: 020-8675 5550
www.exodus.co.uk
Emphasis on mountain biking and hiking along the Lycian coast; also more conventional expeditions staying in village inns.

Gölköy Centre
Tel: 020-8699 1900
www.yogaturkey.co.uk
Week-long yoga courses at a retreat on the north shore of the Bodrum peninsula.

Greentours
Tel: 01298-83563
www.greentours.co.uk
Three annual, 1- or 2-week natural history tours, usually inland from the Mediterranean coast. Enthusiastic and knowledgeable guides.

The Imaginative Traveller
Tel: 01473-667 337
www.imaginative-traveller.com
A wide variety of escorted overland tours, many suitable for families, covering the whole country and touching on some lesser-known spots as well as the name attractions.

Metak Holidays
Tel: 020-8290 9292
www.metakholidays.co.uk
Hotel-based packages in a range of southern coastal resorts.

United States

ATC Anadolu Travel & Tours
Tel: 1-800-ANADOLU or 212-486 4012
www.atc-anadolu.com
Luxury hotel bookings, *gulet* cruises and customised itineraries. Specialises in first-time visits.

Blue Voyage Turkish Tours & Travel
Tel: 1-800-818 8753 or 415-392 0146
www.bluevoyage.com
Tailor-made tours, set itineraries and comfortable hotels.

Cultural Folk Tours
Tel: 1-800-935 8875
http://culturalfolktours.com
Led (and musically accompanied) by Bora Özkök, these tours are several notches above the usual bus-tour dross, giving real insight into seldom-visited parts of Turkey.

Wilderness Travel
Tel: 1-800-368 2794, (510) 558 2488

www.wildernesstravel.com
Offers 3 annual, 2-week group tours to western Turkey, mixing sea cruising with on-land activities.

V isas and Passports

Visa requirements and costs for entering Turkey vary substantially according to your nationality. All travellers need a passport valid for at least six months.

Citizens of the following countries require visas, which can be obtained at the point of entry into Turkey: UK (£10/€15), Canada ($60/€45), Australia ($20/€15), USA (US$20/€15), Belgium (€10), the Netherlands (€10) and Ireland (€10). You must pay in hard currency at the booth before passport control. Photographs are not required. You will be issued with a multiple-entry tourist visa valid for three months. Holders of British National Overseas passports must apply at the consulate in advance of travel.

Provided that they have a valid passport, nationals of many countries (including France, Germany and New Zealand) do not need a visa for visits of up to three months. The tourist visa will be stamped into the passport free of charge. Nationals of South Africa are now able to obtain visas upon entry, but are only granted one month.

Not surprisingly, visa requirements are subject to change, and it is highly advisable to check the Turkish Ministry of Foreign Affair's website (www.mfa.gov.tr) before departure.

If you overstay the length of your tourist visa, fines on exit are stiff – starting from 140TL per day of overstay. Some people reckon it better to accept voluntary deportation with the proviso of being banned from re-entry for 6 months.

Extending your stay

Anyone wishing to stay in Turkey beyond three months can extend their tourist visa just once, at the nearest foreigners' division at the Security Department of any provincial capital. However, this usually proves such a hassle that most travellers leave the country before the end of the three-month period, staying outside Turkey (in Greece or Bulgaria, typically) for 24 hours, then re-entering with a fresh tourist visa.

W eights and Measures

Metric, although land is still sold by the *dönüm* (1000 sq m).

Women Travellers

Turkish attitudes towards women are liberal in cosmopolitan cities and tourist areas, but more restrictive in provincial towns. Women in rural regions cover their heads with scarves as much as a means of protecting their hair from dust and dirt as for reasons of religious conservatism, although Islamic fundamentalism has gained ground among some groups in recent years.

Travelling alone

The major cities in Turkey and tourist areas are liberal and Westernised, and are very safe compared with many other countries. Leering and suggestive comments may be irritatingly common, but physical attacks are rare. Women visitors should not be afraid to travel alone, or to go out in the evening, although provocative dress may create problems, and at night you might feel more relaxed with a companion.

In some situations, however, Turks do still segregate the sexes. On buses you are not expected to sit next to a male stranger. Restaurants often have a designated *aile salonu* (family room), and sometimes prefer a lone woman to sit there.

No Turkish woman, whether on her own or with a male partner, is welcome at a traditional coffee shop or tearoom (*kahvehane* or *çayhane*) – they are strictly male preserves, although foreign females are usually treated as honorary men if they want to go in.

Harassment

You should expect Turkish men to chat you up, often in an outrageously flamboyant fashion, but you can reduce harassment to a minimum by dressing respectably and looking as if you know where you are going. Turkish women get some degree of harassment too, but they cope by sticking together and mastering the brush-off. Unfortunately touts tend to be very good at manipulating foreign females.

If you are groped by a stranger, speak up loudly; the shame will usually be enough to scare him off and everyone nearby will make it a point of honour to rush to your defence.

What to wear

In the big cities you will see young Turkish girls wearing whatever is the current fashion, be it shorts, miniskirts or Lycra. Foreigners are advised to dress fairly conservatively though. Cover up your swimming costume or bikini when you leave the beach.

LANGUAGE

UNDERSTANDING THE LANGUAGE

Atatürk's great language reform took place in 1928–29, when the Arabic script was replaced by a modified Roman alphabet, and the vocabulary saw many Persian and Arabic words yield to those of Turkish or French origin, with the intentions of simplifying the language, boosting literacy – and creating a barrier to enquiry into the Ottoman past. One legacy of the flowery elaborations of Ottoman speech is the way Turkish people exchange formal greetings: these pleasantries and politenesses follow a set routine in which both sides of the exchange follow formulaic patterns of questions with set answers.

Turkish is undoubtedly a difficult language for Europeans to learn. Although the grammar is consistent and logical, with few irregularities, and pronunciation follows phonetic spelling, both the vocabulary and grammatical structure are very different from any language that English-speakers may have tackled before. The vocabulary in particular is difficult to remember, especially over a short visit, though you may recognise a few words of French or English origin once you have deciphered the Turkish spelling.

It is probably most useful to try to master basic pronunciation, so you can say addresses and place names correctly, and read and use some set phrases. In most places it's rare that you won't be able to find someone speaking either English or another Western European language.

Pronunciation

As spelling is phonetic, pronunciation is the easiest part of learning the language, once you have mastered the few different Turkish vowel and consonant sounds.

Letters are always pronounced in the same way. One tricky consonant is the "c", which is always pronounced "j" as in "jump", so the Turkish word "cami" (mosque) is pronounced "jah-mi", and "cadde" (road, street) is pronounced "jah-des-i". The soft "g" (ğ) is never voiced, but lengthens the preceding vowel. Also, look out for the dotless i, "I (ı)", which sounds like the vestigial vowel between the "b" and the "l" in "stable"; it is quite different from the dotted "İ (i)". Compare "ızgara" (grill, pronounced uh-zgara) with "incir" (fig, pronounced in-jeer). Double consonants are both pronounced – there are no diphthongs. Each syllable in a word carries (approximately) equal stress, as do words in a phrase.

The basic rules of pronunciation are as follows:

c "j" as in jump
ç "ch" as in chill
s "s" as in sleep
ş "sh" as in sharp
g "g" as in good
ğ is silent, lengthens the previous vowel, and never begins a word
a "ah" as in father
e "e" as in let
i with a dot as in sit
ı without a dot is an "uh" sound, like the second "e" in ever
o is pronounced "o" as in toad
ö with diaeresis is similar to "ur" as in spurt, or German "oe" as in Goethe
u is pronounced like "oo" as in room
ü is like the "ew" in pew, or u-sound in French "tu" (impossible without pursing your lips).

Useful Words and Phrases

Days of the Week
Monday Pazartesi
Tuesday Salı
Wednesday Çarşamba
Thursday Perşembe
Friday Cuma
Saturday Cumartesi
Sunday Pazar

Months
January Ocak
February Şubat
March Mart
April Nisan
May Mayıs
June Haziran
July Temmuz
August Ağustos
September Eylül
October Ekim
November Kasım
December Aralık

Emergencies

Help! İmdat!
Fire Yangın!
Please call the police Polis çağırın
Please call an ambulance Ambulans çağırın
Please call the fire brigade İtfaiye çağırın
This is an emergency Bu acıldır
There has been an accident Kaza vardı
I'd like an interpreter Tercüman istiyorum
I want to speak to someone from the British Consulate İngiltere konsoloslugundan biri ile görüşmek istiyorum

Numbers

1	bir
2	iki
3	üç
4	dört
5	beş
6	altı
7	yedi
8	sekiz
9	dokuz
10	on
11	on bir
12	on iki
20	yirmi
21	yirmi bir
22	yirmi iki
30	otuz
40	kırk
50	elli
60	altmış
70	yetmiş
80	seksen
90	doksan
100	yüz
200	iki yüz
1,000	bin
2,000	iki bin
1,000,000	bir milyon

To make a complex number, add the components one by one eg, 5,650,000 = beş milyon altı yüz elli bin (in Turkish spelling these would normally be run together).

Greetings

Hello Merhaba
Good morning (early) Günaydın
Good day İyi günler
Good evening İyi aksamlar
Goodnight İyi geceler
Welcome! Hoş geldiniz!
Reply: It is well we have found you! (ie, **Happy to be here!**) Hoş bulduk!
Please, with pleasure, allow me,

BELOW: bureau de change.

please go first (multi-purpose, polite expression) Buyurun
Don't mention it Rica ederim
Pleased to meet you Çok memnun oldum
How are you? Nasılsınız?
Thanks, I/we am/are fine Tesekkürler, iyiyim/iyiyiz
My name is... Adım...
I am English/Scottish/American/ Australian Ben İngilizim/İskoçyalım/ Amerikalım/Avustralyalım
We are sightseeing Geziyoruz
We'll see each other again ("see you") Görüşürüz
God willing İnşallah
Goodbye Hoşça kalın or Allaha ısmarladık
Reply: **"Go happily"** Güle güle (only said by the person staying behind)
Leave me alone Beni rahat bırakin
Get lost Çekil git
I don't want any İstemiyorum

Essentials

Yes Evet
No Hayır/yok
OK Tamam
Please Lütfen
Thank you Teşekkür ederim/sağol/mersi
You're welcome Bir şey değil
Excuse me/I beg your pardon (in a crowd) Affedersiniz
Excuse me Pardon
I don't speak Turkish Türkçe bilmiyorum
Do you speak English? İngilizce biliyor musunuz?
I don't understand/I haven't understood Anlamıyorum/Anlamadım
I don't know Bilmiyorum
Please write it down Onu benim için heceleyebilir misiniz?
Wait a moment! Bir dakika!
Slowly Yavaş
Enough Yeter
Where is it? Nerede?
Where is the...? ... Nerede?
Where is the toilet? Tuvalet nerede?
What time is it? Saatiniz var mı?
At what time? Saat kaçta?
Today Bugün
Tomorrow Yarın
Yesterday Dün
The day after tomorrow Öbür gün
Now Şimdi
Later Sonra
When? Ne zaman
Morning/in the morning Sabah
Afternoon/in the afternoon Öğleden sonra
Evening/in the evening Akşam
This evening Bu akşam
Here Burada
There Şurada

Money

Bank Banka
Credit card Kredi kartı
Exchange office Döviz bürosu
Exchange rate Dövis kuru
Traveller's cheque Seyahat çeki
ATM Banka makinesi

Over there Orada
Is there a foreign-language newspaper? Yabancı gazete var mı?
Is there a minibus? Minibüs var mı?
Is there a telephone? Telefon var mı?
Yes, there is Evet, var
No, there isn't Hayır, yok
There is no ticket Bilet yok
There is no time Zaman yok

Sightseeing

Directions

How do I get to Bodrum? Bodrum'a nasıl giderim?
How far is it to...? ...'a/'e ne kadar uzakdır?
Near Yakın
Far Uzak
Left Sol
On the left/to the left Solda/sola
Right Sağ
On the right/to the right Sağda/sağa
Straight on Doğru
North Kuzey
South Güney
East Doğu
West Batı

Sights/Places

City Şehir
Village Köy
Forest Orman
Sea Deniz
Lake Göl
Farm Çiftlik
Church Kilise
Mosque Cami(i)
Ruins Harabeler, örenyeri
Post office Postane
What time will it open/close? Kaçta açılıcak/kapanacak?

Travelling

Car Araba
Petrol/gas station Benzin istasyonu
Petrol/gas Benzin (super/normal)
Diesel Mazot
Fill it up, please Dolu, lütfen
Flat tyre/puncture Patlak lastik
My car has broken down Arabam arızalandı
Bus station Otogar
Bus stop Durak
Bus Otobüs
Train station Gar/İstasyon

Train *Tren*
Taxi *Taksi*
Airport *Havalimanı/Havaalanı*
Aeroplane *Uçak*
Port/harbour *Liman*
Boat *Gemi*
Ferry *Feribot/Vapur*
Quay *İskele*
Ticket *Bilet*
Ticket office *Gişe*
Left luggage *Emanet*
Return ticket *Gidişdönüs bileti*
Can I reserve a seat? *Reservasyon yapabilir miyim?*
What time does it leave? *Kaçta kalkıyor?*
Where does it leave from? *Nereden kalkıyor?*
How long does it take? *Ne kadar sürüyor?*
Which bus is it? *Hangi otobüsdir?*

Health

Remember that in an emergency it can be quicker to get to hospital by taxi.
Clinic *Klinik/Sağlık Ocağı*
Dentist *Dişçi*
Doctor *Doktor*
Emergency service/room *Acil servis*
First aid *İlk yardım*
Hospital *Hastane*
Pharmacist *Eczacı*
Pharmacy *Eczane*
I am ill *Hastayım*
I have a fever *Ateşim var*
I have diarrhoea *İshallim*
I am diabetic *Şeker hastasıyım*
I'm allergic to... *Karşı ... alerjim var.*
I have asthma *Astim hastasıyım*
I have a heart condition *Kalp hastasıyım*
I am pregnant *Gebeyim/Hamileyim*
It hurts here *Burası acıyor*
I have lost a filling *Dolgu düştü*
I need a prescription for... *İçin ... bir reçete istiyorum.*

Accommodation

Hotel *Otel*
Pension/guesthouse *Pansiyon*
Single/double/triple *Tek/çift/üç kişilik*
Full board *Tam pansiyon*
Half-board *Yarım pansiyon*
With a shower *Duşlu*
With a bathroom *Banyolu*
With a balcony *Balkonlu*
With a sea view *Deniz manzaralı*
With air conditioning *Klimalı*
Centrally heated *Kaloriferli*
Lift/elevator *Asansör*
Room service *Oda servisi*
Key *Anahtar*
Bed *Yatak*
Blanket *Battaniye*

Road Signs

Dikkat *Beware/Caution*
Çekme bölgesi *Tow-away zone*
Yavaş *Slow*
Dur *Stop*
Araç giremez *No entry with vehicle*
Tek yön *One way*
Çıkmaz sokak *Dead-end road*
Bozuk satıh *Poor road surface*
Düşük banket *Abrupt verge/shoulder*
Yol yapımı *Roadworks*
Yol kapalı *Road closed*
Yaya geçidi *Pedestrian crossing*
Şehir merkezi/Centrum *City centre*
Otopark ücretlidir *Fee-paying carpark*
Park yapmayınız *Do not park here*

Pillow *Yastık*
Shower *Duş*
Soap *Sabun*
Plug *Tıkaç*
Towel *Havlu*
Basin *Lavabo*
Toilet *Tuvalet*
Toilet paper *Tuvalet kağıdı*
Hot water *Sıcak su*
Cold water *Soğuk su*
Dining room *Yemek salonu*
I need/...is necessary *lazım/... gerek*
I have a reservation *Reservasyonım var*
Do you have a room available? *Boş odanız var mı?*
I'd like a room for one/three nights *Bir/üç gece için bir oda istiyorum*
I'm sorry, we are full *Maalesef doluyuz*
Is there wireless internet? *Kablosuz varmı?*
What's the password? *Şifre nedir?*

Shopping

Price *Fiyat*
Cheap *Ucuz*
Expensive *Pahalı*
No bargaining (sign) *Pazarlık edilmez*
Old *Eski*
New *Yeni*
Big *Büyük*
Bigger *Daha büyük*
Small *Küçük*
Smaller *Daha küçük*
Very nice/beautiful *Çok güzel*
This *Bu*
These *Bunlar*
That *Şu*
I would like... *İsterim...*
I don't want *İstemem*

There isn't any *Yok*
How much is it? *Ne kadar?*
How many? *Kaç tane?*
Do you take credit cards? *Kredi kartleri geçerlimi?*

Eating Out

Table *Masa*
Cup *Fincan*
Glass *Bardak*
Wine glass *Kadeh*
Bottle *Şişe*
Plate *Tabak*
Fork *Çatal*
Knife *Bıçak*
Spoon *Kaşık*
Napkin *Peçete*
Salt *Tuz*
Black pepper *Kara biber*
Starters *Mezeler*
Soup *Çorba*
Fish *Balık*
Meat dishes *Et yemekleri*
Grills *Izgara*
Eggs *Yumurta*
Vegetarian dishes *Etsiz yemekleri*
Salads *Salatalar*
Fruit *Meyve*
Bread *Ekmek*
Peppery hot *Acı*
Non-spicy *Acısız*
Water *Su*
Mineral water *Maden suyu*
Fizzy water *Soda*
Beer *Bira*
Red/white wine *Kırmızı/beyaz sarap*
Fresh orange juice *Sıkma portakal suyu*
Coffee *Kahve*
Tea *Çay*
A table for two/four, please *İki/dört kisilik bir masa, lütfen*
Can we eat outside? *Dışarıda yiyebilir miyiz?*
Excuse me (to get service or attention) *Bakar mısınız?*
Menu *Menü*
I didn't order this *Ben bunu ısmarlamadım*
Some more water/bread/wine, please *Biraz daha su/ekmek/sarap, rica ediyoruz*
I can eat... *Yiyorum...*
I cannot eat... *Yiyemiyorum...*
Can you bring the bill? *Hesabımız verirmisiniz?*
Service included/excluded *Servis dahil/hariç*

For Vegetarians

I eat only fruit and vegetables Yalnız meyve ve sebze yiyorum
I cannot eat any meat at all Hiç et yemiyorum
I can eat fish Balık yiyorum

Menu Decoder

Kahvaltı/Breakfast

Beyaz peynir White cheese
Kaşar peyniri Yellow cheese
Domates Tomatoes
Zeytin Olives
Salatalık Cucumber
Reçel Jam
Bal Honey
Tereyağ Butter
Extra dishes which you may order
for a more substantial breakfast:
Haşlanmış yumurta Hard-boiled
eggs
Rafadan yumurta Soft-boiled eggs
Menemen Scrambled-egg omelette
with tomatoes, peppers, onion and
cheese
Sahanda yumurta Fried eggs
Sucuklu yumurta Eggs fried with
cured dry sausage
Sade/peynirli/mantarlı omlet
Plain/cheese/mushroom omelette

Çorbalar/Soups

Haşlama Mutton broth
Tavuk çorbası/tavuk suyu Chicken
soup
Düğün çorbası Wedding soup
(thickened with eggs and lemon)
Ezogelin çorbası Lentil soup with
rice
Mercimek çorbası Lentil soup
Domates çorbası Tomato soup
İşkembe çorbası Tripe soup
Paça çorbası Lamb's feet soup
Şehriye çorbası Fine noodle soup
Yayla çorbası Yoghurt soup
Tarhana çorbası Soup made from a
dried sourdough base

Soğuk mezeler/Cold starters

These are usually offered from a large
tray of assorted dishes, or you can
choose from a cold cabinet; there are
dozens of variations.
Beyaz peynir White cheese
Zeytin Olives
Turşu Pickles – Turkish pickles are
sour and salty, sometimes spicy but
never sweet
Beyin salatası Raw lamb brains

Patlıcan ezmesi Aubergine purée
Piyaz White-bean salad with olive oil
and lemon
Barbunya pilaki Marinated red
kidney beans
Antep esmesi Spicy hot red paste or
salad of chopped peppers and tomato
Çerkez tavuğu Shredded chicken in
walnut sauce
Haydari Dip of chopped dill and
garlic in thick yoghurt
Cacık Yoghurt, cucumber and herb
dip
Semizotu Purslane in yoghurt
Fava Purée of beans
Dolmalar Any vegetable stuffed with
rice mixed with dill, pine nuts and
currants
Yalancı yaprak dolması Stuffed vine
leaves without meat
Mücver Cougette/zucchini frittata
Midye dolması Stuffed mussels
Biber dolması Stuffed peppers
Lakerda Sliced salt-cured, then
marinated, bonito
Hamsi Fresh anchovies preserved
in oil
Zeytinyağlı Vegetables cooked with
olive oil, served cold
Deniz börülcesi Marsh samphire
İmam bayıldı Aubergine stuffed
with tomato and onion, cooked with
olive oil

Sıcak mezeler/Hot starters

Sigara böreği Crisp fried rolls of
pastry with cheese or meat filling (can
also be triangular: muska)
Arnavut ciğeri Albanian-style fried
diced lamb's liver
Kalamar tava Deep-fried squid
rings
Midye tava Deep-fried mussels
Tarator Nut and garlic sauce served
with above, or with fried vegetables
Paçanga böreği Turnovers stuffed
with pastırma (cured beef)

Salata/Salads

Karışık Mixed
Çoban salatası "Shepherd's salad"
(chopped mixed tomato, cucumber,
pepper, onion and parsley)

Yeşil salata Green salad
Mevsim salatası Seasonal salad
Roka Rocket/arugula
Salatalık Cucumber
Domates Tomatoes
Marul Lettuce
Semizotu Purslane
Söğus Sliced salad vegetables with
no dressing
Roka Rocket

Types of pide (Turkish pizza)

Kıymalı topped with minced meat
Sucuklu topped with dry sausage
Yumurtalı topped with chopped egg
Kuşbaşılı topped with small meat
chunks

Et yemekleri/Meat dishes

Kebap Kebab
Döner Sliced, layered lamb grilled on
revolving spit
Tavuk döner As above, made with
chicken
Şiş kebap Cubed meat grilled on
skewer eg, **kuzu şiş** (lamb), **tavuk şiş**
(chicken)
Adana kebap Minced lamb grilled on
skewer; spicy
Urfa kebap As above; not spicy
Bursa/İskender/yoğurtlu kebap
Dish of döner slices laid on pieces
of bread with tomato sauce, melted
butter and yoghurt with garlic
Piliç Roast chicken
Pirzola Cutlets
Izgara Grill/grilled – usually over
charcoal
Köfte Meatballs
Köfte ızgara Grilled meatballs
İnegöl köftesi Mince rissoles laced
with cheese
Kiremitte kebap Meat grilled on a
ceramic plate
Bıldırcın ızgara Grilled quail
Kuzu tandır/fırın Lamb baked on
the bone
Hünkâr beğendili köfte Meatballs
with aubergine purée
Kadınbudu köfte "Ladies' thighs":
meat and rice croquettes in gravy
Karnıyarık Aubergines split in half
and filled with minced lamb mixed
with pine nuts and currants
Kavurma Meat stir-fried or braised,
cooked in its own fat and juices
Çoban kavurma Lamb fried with
peppers, tomatoes and onions
Dil Tongue (beef)
Saç kavurma Wok-fried meat,
vegetables and spices
Etli kabak dolması Courgettes
(zucchini) stuffed with meat
Etli nohut Chickpea and lamb stew
Etli kuru fasuliye Haricot bean and
lamb stew
Kağıt kebabı Lamb and vegetables
cooked in paper
Güveç Casserole

Common Signs

Giriş/Çıkış Entrance/Exit
Tehlike çıkışı Emergency exit
Giriş ücretsiz/ücretli Free/paid
admission
Açık Open
Kapalı Closed
Varış Arrivals
Kalkış Departures
Askeri bölge Military zone
Sigara icilmez No smoking
Girmek yasaktır No entry

Fotoğraf çekmayınz No
photographs
**Lütfen ayakkabılarınızı
çıkartınız** Please take off your
shoes
Bay Men
Bayan Women
Tuvalet/Umumi Toilet
Arızalı Out of order
İçme su, içibilir Drinking water,
potable

ABOVE: taxi rank on Istiklal Caddesi, İstanbul.

Balık yemekleri/Fish dishes

Most fish is eaten plainly grilled or fried, and priced by weight. It will be less expensive if it is local and in season. Always ask the price – whether by weight *(kilosu)* or portion *(porsyon)* – before ordering.

Balık ızgara *Grilled fish*
Balık tavada *Fried fish*
Balık şiş *Cubed fish grilled on skewer*
Alabalık *Trout*
Levrek *Sea bass*
Lüfer *Bluefish*
Hamsi *Anchovies*
Sardalye *Sardines*
Karagöz *Two-banded bream*
Mercan *Pandora, red bream*
Çipura *Gilt-head bream*
Uskumru *Atlantic mackerel*
İstavrit *Horse mackerel*
Palamut *Small bonito*
Kalkan *Turbot*
Gümüş *Silverfish (like whitebait)*
Barbunya *Small red mullet*
Tekir *Large red mullet*
Kefal *Grey mullet*
Kılıç balığı *Swordfish*
Dil balığı *Sole*
İskaroz *Parrot fish*
Karides *Shrimp, prawns*
Karides güveç *Prawn casserole with peppers, tomato and melted cheese*
Hamsi pilav *Rice baked with anchovies*

Sebze/Vegetables

Ispanak *Spinach*
Bamya *Okra, lady's fingers*
Soğan *Onion*
Kusru fasulye *White haricots*
Mantar *Mushrooms*
Bezelye *Peas*

Tatlı/Desserts

Baklava *Layers of filo pastry with nuts and syrup*

Ekmek kadayıf *Bread pudding soaked in syrup*
Güllaç *Dessert made with layers of rice wafer, sugar and milk flavoured with rose water*
Tavuk göğsü *Milk pudding made with pounded chicken breast*
Kazandibi *Caramelised version of tavuk göğsü*
Dondurma *Turkish gelato*
Muhallebi *Rice flour, milk and rose-water blancmange*
Sütlaç *Rice pudding*
Aşure *"Noah's pudding" made with dried fruits, nuts, seeds and pulses*
Kabak tatlısı *Candied pumpkin*
Ayva tatlısı *Candied quince*
Kaymaklı *with clotted cream*
Komposto *Poached fruit*
Krem caramel *Caramel custard, French crème caramel*
Pasta *Gâteau-style cake, patisserie*

Meyve/Fruits

Kavun *Honeydew melon*
Nar *Pomegranate*
Muz *Banana*
Kiraz *Sweet cherry*
Vişne *Sour cherry*
Şeftali *Peach*
Elma *Apple*
Armut *Pear*
Üzüm *Grape*

Soft or cold drinks

Su *Water*
Maden suyu *Mineral water*
Soda/gazoz *Sparkling water*
Ayran *Yoghurt whisked with cold water and salt*
Meyve suyu *Fruit juice*
Vişne suyu *Sour cherry juice*
Nar suyu *Pomegranate juice*
Karadut *Black mulberry juice*
Sıkma portakal suyu *Orange juice*
Şerbet *Sweetened, iced fruit juice drink*

Limonata *Lemon drink*
Şıra *Grape must*
Boza *Millet-based drink*
Buz *Ice*
Taze sıkılmış *Fresh squeezed*

Hot drinks

Çay *Tea*
Açık *Weak*
Demli *Dark, brewed*
Bir bardak çay *Glass of tea*
Bir fincan kahve *Cup of coffee*
Ada çayı *"Island tea" made with dried wild sage*
Elma çayı *"Apple" tea made with chemical flavouring*
Kahve *Coffee*
Neskafe *Any instant coffee*
Sutlu *With milk*
Şeker *Sugar*
Türk kahvesi *Turkish coffee*
Az şekerli *With little sugar*
Orta şekerli *Medium sweet*
Çok şekerli *Sweet*
Sade *Without sugar*
Süzme kahve *Filter coffee*
Salep *Hot, thick sweet winter drink made of powdered salep root, milk and cinnamon*

Alcoholic drinks

Bira *Beer*
Siyah *Dark (beer)*
Cintonik *Gin and tonic*
Votka *Vodka*
Yerli *Local, Turkish*
Şarap *Wine*
Şarap listesi *Wine list*
Kırmızı şarap *Red wine*
Beyaz şarap *White wine*
Roze şarap *Rosé*
Sek *Dry*
Antik *Aged*
Özel *Special*
Tatlı *Sweet*
Şişe *Bottle*
Yarım şişe *Half bottle*
Rakı *Turkish national alcoholic drink, strongly aniseed-flavoured*

Alcohol

Turkish vintners include: Doluca and Kavaklıdere (the two biggest, with vineyards and cellars nationwide), Turasan (Cappadocian), and Sevilen and Feyzi Kutman (Aegean regions).
Turkish beers: Efes Pilsen, Efes Dark, Efes Lite (low alcohol), Efes Xtra (high alcohol), Gusta (a wheat beer), Tuborg, Carlsberg
Spirits, especially rakı, are made in Turkey by a half-dozen private companies.

FURTHER READING

There are plenty of books in English about all aspects of Turkey: such a complex country with so many layers of history and culture couldn't fail to generate a wealth of histories, memoirs, poetry, fiction, biographies and travel writing. Not much Turkish writing has been translated into English, however. Some good books in English have been written and issued by Turkish publishers, but are difficult to obtain outside Turkey.

Ancient History and Archaeology

The Hittites, by O.R. Gurney. Classic history of the earliest Anatolian civilisation for non-specialists. Gurney practically invented Hittite studies single-handedly.
Troy and the Trojans, by Carl Blegen.
Çatal Höyük, by James Mellaart. Mellaart *(see page 31)* was a tricky character, but also the first excavator of this site.
On the Surface: Çatalhöyük 1993–1995, by Ian Hodder. The resumption of excavations, predicted to last another three decades.
Hattusa, The Capital of the Hittites, by Kurt Bittel.
Schliemann of Troy: Treasure and Deceit, by David Traill. Schliemann's reputation as an archaeologist crumbles here, along with the walls of Troy, though the latter fare better in the end.

Byzantine, Ottoman and Republican History

Byzantium, three volumes: *The Early Centuries*, *The Apogee* and *The Decline and Fall*, by John Julius Norwich. Thorough, accessible, readable and entertaining account of the history of the empire up to the Ottoman conquest of 1453.
The Decline of Medieval Hellenism in Asia Minor and the Process of Islamization from the Eleventh through the Fifteenth Century, by Speros Vryonis: Or, how the Byzantine Empire culturally became the Ottoman Empire.
Constantinople, City of the World's Desire, 1453–1924, by Philip

Mansel. Outstandingly researched portrait of the imperial city. Scholarly and gripping, with a mass of information, anecdote and analysis.
The Fall of Constantinople, 1453, by Steven Runciman. Still the definitive account of the event, by the late great British medieval historian.
The Ottomans, Dissolving Images, by Andrew Wheatcroft. Analysis of trends in Ottoman social life, and its perception by the West – amply demonstrated by period art, cartoons and photos.
The Ottoman Centuries, by Lord Kinross. Highly readable, one-stop history.
Osman's Dream, by Caroline Finkel. Meticulously researched history of the Ottoman Empire, broader in scope than Kinross's volume – and with more modern scholarship.
The Ottoman Empire: The Classical Age, 1300–1600, by Halil Inalcik.
On Secret Service East of Constantinople, by Peter Hopkirk. Brilliant account of Turkish and German conspiracies against Britain and Russia after 1914, by the author of *The Great Game*.
Gallipoli, by Les Carlyon. The best of several extant studies of the campaign, so clearly written you don't even need a map to follow the narrative.
The Making of Modern Turkey, by Feroz Ahmad. Lively and unorthodox, full of wonderful anecdotes. His *Turkey: The Quest for Identity* updates matters to 2003.
Turkey, A Modern History, by Erik J. Zürcher. The best single title for the post-1800 period (up to 2004) – a revisionist demolition of sacred (republican) cows. Includes partisan, annotated bibliography.

Minorities and Ethnic Issues

The Armenians, by Sirapie der Nersessian.
From Empire to Republic: Turkish Nationalism and the Armenian Genocide, and **A Shameful Act: The Armenian Genocide and the Question of Turkish Responsibility**, by Taner Akçam. One of a growing

contingent of Turkish academics confronting the events of 1895 and 1915 unflinchingly, Akçam shows how CUP ideology made them almost inevitable, and that the cover-up of the massacres – which only began in earnest during the 1930s – was both essential to Turkish republicanism and remains at the heart of Turkey's current problems.
A Modern History of the Kurds, by David McDowall. About one-third of this book is devoted to Turkey's Kurds; current only to 2003.
The Lost Messiah: In Search of the Mystical Rabbi Sabbatai Sevi, by John Freely. Sevi's millennial, Kabbalistic, 17th-century movement in İzmir and Salonica produced the Dönme, a crypto-Judaic sect disproportionately prominent in modern Turkish history.
Twice a Stranger: The Mass Expulsions That Forged Modern Greece and Turkey, by Bruce Clark. Compassionate study, with interviews of survivors, of the 1923 population exchanges, which both countries are still digesting three generations on.

Current Views and Analyses

Sons of the Conquerors: The Rise of the Turkic World, by Hugh Pope. A readable collection of essays on the Turkic peoples and cultures.
The New Turkey: The Quiet Revolution on the Edge of Europe, by Chris Morris. Long-serving BBC correspondent writes accessibly on political Islam, Greeks and Armenians, the Kurdish question, and Turkey's EU accession quest.
Crescent and Star: Turkey Between Two Worlds, by Stephen Kinzer. Another journalist's account, this time a former *New York Times* correspondent, whose down-to-earth, hands-on approach brings the contemporary country to life.
Turkey Unveiled, by Nicole and Hugh Pope. Interlinked essays by two foreign correspondents who spent most of the 1980s and 1990s in the country. Sound assessment of most issues, despite their evident affection for the country, but a bit too much in

thrall to Özal, whom they got to know pretty well.

Lives and Letters

Atatürk: The Biography of the Founder of Modern Turkey, by Andrew Mango. More focused on military events than Kinross's volume (see below), but authoritative.
Atatürk: The Rebirth of a Nation, by Lord Kinross. Still probably the best overview of the man and his times.
An English Consul in Turkey, Paul Rycaut at Smyrna 1667–78, by Sonia Anderson. Rycaut spent 17 years in Turkey, 11 as consul in Smyrna, whose contemporary English community is vividly described in this biographical study.
Beyond the Orchard, by Azize Ethem. Account of life in contemporary Turkey by a British woman who married a Turk and settled on the south coast. She now lives near İznik and writes of life there for Cornucopia magazine.
Everyday Life in Ottoman Turkey, by Raphaela Lewis.
Istanbul: Memories of a City, by Orhan Pamuk. A literary journey through the city interwoven with a highly personal account of the childhood and family life of Turkey's Nobel laureate.
Portrait of a Turkish Family, by Irfan Orga. Vividly and movingly describes the author's family life and his growing up first as a child in Ottoman Turkey before World War I, then through the war and the years of Atatürk's reforms.
The Imperial Harem of the Sultans, The Memoirs of Leyla Hanımefendi (Peva Publications, 1995, available in İstanbul). The only contemporary account of daily life at Çırağan Palace during the 19th century, originally published in French in 1925, which gives a vivid portrait of this hidden world.
The Turkish Embassy Letters, by Lady Mary Wortley Montagu. Collection of lively and intelligent letters, written in 1716 when the writer's husband had just been appointed ambassador. One of the most fascinating of early travel writers.
Under a Crescent Moon, by Daniel de Souza. Turkish society viewed through the prism of a foreigner's incarceration during the early 1980s; often blackly funny, and in its empathy the antithesis of Midnight Express.

Art and Architecture

A History of Ottoman Architecture, by Godfrey Goodwin. Comprehensive

and definitive, covering every kind of building all over Turkey. Goodwin's other great book is a monograph on Sinan, the greatest of the Ottoman architects.
Byzantine Architecture, by Cyril Mango. Analysis of the most important churches, about a quarter of these falling within modern Turkey.
Early Christian and Byzantine Architecture, by Richard Krautheimer.
Ancient Civilizations and Ruins of Turkey, by Ekrem Akurgal. Published in Turkey, sometimes sold (for inflated prices) at archaeological sites; comprehensive but beware dated scholarship.
The Church of Hagia Sophia in Trebizond, by David Talbot Rice. The full story from the head of the team which restored its brilliant frescoes.
Imperial Istanbul, by Jane Taylor. Includes all the Ottoman monuments of Bursa and Edirne as well.
Eastern Turkey: An Archaeological and Architectural Survey, by T.A. Sinclair. Four massive, prohibitively priced volumes (consult a university library), but it has absolutely everything east of Cappadocia, with useful maps.
Turkish Art and Architecture, by Oktay Aslanapa.

Carpets

Kilim: The Complete Guide: History – Pattern – Technique – Identification, by Alastair Hull and José Luczyc-Wykowska. Comprehensive illustrated survey of Turkish kilims.
Kilims: Masterpieces from Turkey, by Yanni Petsopoulos and Belkis Balpınar. Less rigorous but more available than Petsopoulos' rare but definitive Kilims: Flat-Woven Tapestry Rugs (o/p).
Oriental Rugs: Turkish. Volume 4 of this series, by Kurt Zipper and Claudia Fritzsche. Weaving techniques, symbols and rug categories, plus regional surveys of distinctive patterns.

Modern Travel Writing

Black Sea, The Birthplace of Civilisation and Barbarism, by Neal Ascherson. History, ethnology and ecology around this great inland sea, from Herodotus to the fall of Communism, with a 2007 update. Although only two chapters are devoted to the Pontus and the Bosphorus, still highly recommended.
The Bridge, by Geert Mak. The Galata Bridge and its often louche

social milieu is the starting point for a brilliant, alternative summary of the city around it. Mak uses life around the Galata Bridge in İstanbul as a metaphor for the wider country.
A Fez of the Heart, by Jeremy Seal. The author travels around Turkey in search of a real fez, the red felt hat banned in 1925, and offers a perceptive alternative view of modern Turkey.
From the Holy Mountain, A Journey in the Shadow of Byzantium, by William Dalrymple. Starting from Mount Athos in Greece, the author follows the trail of Eastern Christianity into the Middle East. Although only one section is devoted to eastern Turkey, Dalrymple's view of the status of living Christians and their monuments is deservedly pessimistic (though there has been improvement since the early-1990s vintage of the account).
In Turkey I Am Beautiful, by Brendan Shanahan. This 2008 travelogue combines a story of goings-on behind the scenes in an İstanbul carpet shop with a quick whip round the east of the country.
South from Ephesus: An Escape from the Tyranny of Western Art, by Brian Sewell. Contrarian art critic's view of pre-mass-tourism coastal Turkey of the 1970s and early 1980s. Both curmudgeonly and very funny in spots.

Anthologies

Istanbul, A Traveller's Companion, selected and introduced by Laurence Kelly. A wonderful collection of extracts from 14 centuries of writing, arranged around landmark buildings to act as a background guide, which brings to life sites that visitors can still see.
Istanbul, Tales of the City, selected by John Miller. Pocket-sized eclectic collection of prose and poetry, including pieces by Simone de Beauvoir, Disraeli and Gore Vidal.
Turkish Verse, by Nermin Menemencioğlu. Living Poets of Turkey, by Talat S. Halman. Although published in Turkey, may be easier to find than the preceding title.

Fiction

The Aviary Gate, by Katie Hickman. Gripping historical romance set in the Topkapı Palace harem at the end of the 16th century.
Birds Without Wings, by Louis de Bernières. Set in and around a fictionalised version of Kaya, near

Fethiye, and the World War I Gallipoli battlefields, this humane historical novel chronicles contemporary events that were to rip mixed Muslim and Christian communities apart.
The Forty Rules of Love, by Elif Shafak. Wonderful, lyrical relating of the story of the relationship beween Celaleddin Rumi (Mevlana) and Shams of Tabriz.
Gardens of Water, by Alan Drew. Tragic romance set against a backdrop of the terrible 199 earthquakes that devasted north-eastern Turkey.
Mehmet My Hawk, by Yasar Kemal. Until the advent of Orhan Pamuk, the best-known Turkish novelist in translation. This is just one, the most famous, of many novels, some set in and around İstanbul, some epics set in rural Anatolia.
The Rage of the Vulture, by Barry Unsworth. Historical novel by the best-selling author, set in the twilight years of the Ottoman Empire and focusing on Sultan Abdülhamid II.
Rebel Land, by Christopher de Bellaigue. Central republican authority confronts rural Kurdish society, Alevî and Sunni, after the Armenian deportations, in a remote east-Anatolian county town. An even-handed exploration reading like a thriller, from the days of Sultan Abdülhamid II to the second AK victory in 2007, by a former Kemalist partisan.
Tales from the Expat Harem: Foreign Women in Modern Turkey, edited by Anastasia M. Ashman and Jennifer Eaton Gökmen. Mixed bag of accounts of local life by foreign women who have settled in Turkey.
The White Castle, The Black Book, The New Life, Snow, The Museum of Innocence. Novels by Orhan Pamuk, translated by Güneli Gün. Introspective, perceptive, sometimes over-complex but much-lauded contemporary Turkish writer who won the Nobel Prize for Literature in 2006.
The Flea Palace, The Bastard of Istanbul, by Elif Shafak. The first is a sort of Turkish equivalent to Cairo-set *The Yacoubian Building*; the second raised hackles amongst nationalists with its tale of an Armenian-American girl in search of her roots sheltering with a Turkish family.

Food and Cooking

Classic Turkish Cookery, by Ghillie and Jonathan Basan, introduced by Josceline Dimbleby. A beautifully illustrated book which places Turkish cooking in its geographical and cultural context; the recipes are a practical and authentic introduction to the best of Turkish dishes, gleaned from sources all over the country.
Timeless Tastes, Turkish Culinary Culture, project director Semahat Arsel. Published to celebrate the 40th anniversary (in 1996) of the Divan Hotel, long renowned for its kitchen and its patisserie. The book has several authors: experts on culinary art and history, and professional chefs who give their recipes. This history of Turkish cooking at the most elevated level is illustrated with Ottoman miniatures and engravings.
The Art of Turkish Cooking, by Neşet Eren. First issued in 1969, the excellence of this book lies in its simple instructions, and the use of ingredients that are readily available (a characteristic of Turkish cooking anyway). The style is a little dated, but the recipes are authentic. A less lavish choice than the above two books.

Guides

Aegean Turkey, Lycian Turkey, Turkey's Southern Shore, Turkey Beyond the Maeanders, by George E. Bean. Scholarly specialist guides to the archaeological sites of Turkey, compiled from Professor Bean's research. Mostly out of print, but the 1960s-vintage scholarship has aged relatively well.
A Handbook for Living in Turkey, by Pat Yale. Information on all aspects of life in Turkey for those considering move to the country.
Istanbul, An Archaeological Guide, by Christa Beck and Christiane Forsting. Neatly designed, tiny pocket-sized book with black-and-white photographs. The only guide to include some of İstanbul's most interesting recently built, renovated or redesigned buildings and structures.
Strolling through Istanbul, A Guide to the City, by Hilary Sumner-Boyd and John Freely. First written and published in the early 1970s and one of the first proper guides to the

Send Us Your Thoughts

We do our best to ensure the information in our books is as accurate and up to date as possible. The books are updated on a regular basis using local contacts, who painstakingly add, amend and correct as required. However, some details (such as telephone numbers and opening times) are liable to change, and we are ultimately reliant on our readers to put us in the picture.

We welcome your feedback, especially your experience of using the book "on the road". Maybe we recommended a hotel that you liked (or another that you didn't), or you came across a great bar or new attraction we missed.

We will acknowledge all contributions, and we'll offer an Insight Guide to the best letters received.

Please write to us at:
Insight Guides
PO Box 7910
London SE1 1WE
Or email us at:
insight@apaguide.co.uk

city, this book is still valuable, though it has outlived one of its authors. The other, John Freely, still lives and works in İstanbul, and few are more knowledgeable than he.
The Heritage of Eastern Turkey, by Antonio Sagona. Illustrated guide to the archeology and history of eastern Turkey, from the Neolithic to the Selçuk periods.

Other Insight Guides

There are a number of other Insight Guides which highlight destinations in this region.

Insight Step by Step: Istanbul offers a series of walking tours exploring various facets of the city. *Insight Smart Guide: Istanbul* features detailed listings in a unique A–Z format. *Insight Select Guide: Istanbul* offers a collection of over 100 inspiring ideas to help you make the most of your stay in the city. Insight Fleximaps *Istanbul* and *Turkey* are hard-wearing laminated maps with recommended sights and practical information.

ART AND PHOTO CREDITS

AKG Images 26TL, 36
Alamy Images 7CL, 23, 89, 106, 152, 153T, 155, 158, 161, 168T, 168B, 169B, 170T, 185T, 191BL, 229, 243, 250, 277B, 280, 290B, 291T, 292, 298T, 299B, 303B, 305, 312B, 312T, 323T, 326, 330B, 341T, 342B
Anadolu Ajansi 66
Axiom Photographic 70/71
Bodo Bondzio 118, 206
Bridgeman Art Library 127
Emre Cagatay 262, 302
Nevzat Cakir 125, 291
Isa Celik 260B
Christie's Images 32, 50
Ed Clayton 95
Corbis 22B, 31, 77, 79, 81
Rebecca Erol 6C, 84, 107, 128B, 251
Rebecca Erol/Apa 9BR, 12/13, 14/15, 35, 77B, 80, 85, 93L, 93R, 98, 103, 105TL, 108, 109B, 122, 123all, 124, 129, 130BR, 132, 133B, 135T, 135B, 136B, 137, 139T, 140B, 141, 141T, 142, 144BL, 144BR, 145T, 146B, 159B, 372, 374, 375, 376, 378, 379, 392, 402, 407, 408, 409, 410, 422, 426, 429, 430, 433
Sitki Firat 364
Getty Images 62, 67, 69, 75, 76, 78, 86
Thomas Goltz 276R, 369B
Albano Guatti 33, 83, 170B, 264, 311, 340, 361B, 367T
Semsi Guner 43, 52, 74, 100, 133T, 143B, 254B, 275, 276L, 295B, 295T, 298, 309B, 329, 352T
iStockphoto.com 7BL, 7TR, 9CL, 10B, 10T, 11T, 21, 22, 116/117, 136T, 138, 150/151, 153B, 154, 159T, 163B, 166, 171B, 195BR, 203T, 304, 307L, 309T, 313B, 313T, 317B, 349B, 373, 382, 384, 385, 413, 414, 416, 420
Mehmet Kismet 296
Lyle Lawson 24/25, 164, 196, 210
Mary Evans Picture Library 26BR, 27TR, 34, 44L, 177B, 177T, 277T

Frank Noon/Apa 1, 3BL, 4BL, 5BR, 6/7T, 6BL, 6BR, 7BR, 7C, 7CBR, 8B, 8T, 9C, 9TR, 11/12, 11B, 11C, 19B, 19T, 20, 26BL, 28, 30L, 82, 87L, 87R, 88, 90, 91, 92L, 92R, 94, 105R, 112/113, 114/115, 119BL, 119TR, 131B, 140T, 162, 163T, 173, 175, 176, 178/179, 181B, 181T, 182, 183B, 183T, 186B, 186T, 187, 189, 190, 191BR, 192B, 192T, 193, 194L, 194R, 195BL, 195T, 197, 199L, 199R, 200, 201B, 202L, 202R, 203B, 207, 208, 209B, 209T, 210B, 213B, 214B, 214T, 215B, 216B, 217L, 217R, 218, 219B, 219T, 220, 221, 222, 223B, 224B, 224T, 225, 226, 227B, 227T, 228, 230/231, 233all, 235, 236, 237, 238B, 239T, 239, 240L, 240R, 241B, 241T, 242B, 242T, 244B, 244T, 245L, 245R, 248, 249, 252B, 253T, 254T, 255, 256L, 256R, 257B, 258, 259B, 259T, 260T, 261, 263, 266B, 267, 268B, 269B, 269T, 271, 272B, 272T, 273T, 274, 281all, 282, 283BL, 283T, 285, 286all, 287, 293T, 300, 301, 303T, 317C, 317T, 318, 319, 322B, 322B, 323B, 325, 327, 328B, 328T, 330T, 331B, 331T, 334/335, 336, 337B, 337T, 342, 343all, 344all, 345B, 345T, 346B, 346T, 347B, 348T, 349T, 351B, 351T, 352, 353, 354L, 354R, 355B, 355T, 358, 359, 360R, 361T, 362, 363B, 365B, 365T, 366, 367B, 368, 383, 386, 387, 388, 390, 394, 396, 397, 398, 401, 405
Richard Nowitz 4T, 18, 180, 232
Refik Ongan 68
Christine Osborne 72
Scala Archives 308
Topfoto 38, 42, 44L, 45, 46, 47, 49, 51, 63, 73
Werner Forman Archive 27CL, 29, 30R, 39, 41, 99
Marcus Wilson-Smith/Apa 37, 101, 104, 157B, 157T, 160, 167T, 169T, 171T, 172, 174, 174T, 185B, 188B, 188T, 191T, 199T, 201T, 211, 212, 213T, 215T, 223T, 257T, 289, 370

Phil Wood/Apa 2/3T, 40, 44R, 102, 128T, 130T, 130BL, 143T, 216T, 252T, 253B, 263T, 266T, 268T, 270, 273B, 283BR, 296T, 297, 299T, 306, 307R, 310, 311T, 314/315, 316, 320, 324, 348B, 369T
Ibrahim Zahan 350

54-55 AKG Images 54TL, 54BL, 54BR, 54/55T, 55TR, 55BR; iStockphoto.com 54CR; Werner Forman Archive 55BL, 55BC, 55CR
96-97 Rebecca Erol/Apa 96B, 96BR, 96C, 96/97T, 97TR; Rebecca Erol 96CR, 97B; Frank Noon/Apa 97CL
110-111 Frank Noon/Apa 110BL, 110BR, 110/111T, 111BR; iStockphoto.com 111BL, 111TR
148-149 iStockphoto.com 148B, 148CR, Rebecca Erol/Apa 148C, 149BL, 149BR; Tips Images 148/149T; Alamy Images 149TR
204-205 Alamy 204BR, 204C, 204TL, 205B, 205CL; iStockphoto. com 204BL, 204/205T, Tips Images 205TR
246-247 Frank Noon/Apa 246BL, 247BL; Alamy 246BR, 246C, 246TL, 246/247T, 247BR, 247TR
332-333 All images iStockphoto. com
356-357 AKG Images 356B, 356T, 356BCR, 356/357T, 357TR; Frank Noon/Apa 356CR, 357BR, Phil Wood/Apa 357BL, Alamy 357C, Mary Evans Picture Library 357CL

Map Production:
original cartography Lovell Johns, updated by Apa Cartography Department
© 2011 Apa Publications GmbH & Co. Verlag KG (Singapore branch)

Production: Linton Donaldson and Rebeka Ellam

INDEX

Numbers in bold refer to principal entries